PRESIDENTS
AT WAR

ALSO BY STEVEN M. GILLON

Len Lomell: D-Day Hero

America's Reluctant Prince: The Life of John F. Kennedy Jr.

Separate and Unequal: The Kerner Commission and the Unraveling of American Liberalism

The Pact: Bill Clinton, Newt Gingrich, and the Rivalry That Defined a Generation

Pearl Harbor: FDR Leads the Nation into War

The Kennedy Assassination—24 Hours After: Lyndon B. Johnson's Pivotal First Day as President

Lee Harvey Oswald: 48 Hours to Live

The American Paradox: A History of the United States Since 1945

"That's Not What We Meant to Do": Reform and Its Unintended Consequences in Twentieth-Century America

The American Experiment: A History of the United States

Boomer Nation: The Largest and Richest Generation Ever, and How It Changed America

The Democrats' Dilemma: Walter F. Mondale and the Liberal Legacy

Politics and Vision: The ADA and American Liberalism, 1947–1985

PRESIDENTS
AT WAR

*How World War II Shaped a Generation of
Presidents, from Eisenhower and JFK
Through Reagan and Bush*

STEVEN M. GILLON

DUTTON

DUTTON

An imprint of Penguin Random House LLC
1745 Broadway, New York, NY 10019
penguinrandomhouse.com

Copyright © 2025 by Steven M. Gillon
Penguin Random House values and supports copyright. Copyright fuels creativity,
encourages diverse voices, promotes free speech, and creates a vibrant culture. Thank you
for buying an authorized edition of this book and for complying with copyright laws by not
reproducing, scanning, or distributing any part of it in any form without permission. You
are supporting writers and allowing Penguin Random House to continue to publish books
for every reader. Please note that no part of this book may be used or reproduced in any
manner for the purpose of training artificial intelligence technologies or systems.

DUTTON and the D colophon are registered trademarks of Penguin Random House LLC.

Book design by Daniel Brount

LIBRARY OF CONGRESS CATALOGING-IN-PUBLICATION DATA
has been applied for.

ISBN 9780593183137 (hardcover)
ISBN 9780593183144 (ebook)

Printed in the United States of America

1   3   5   7   9   10   8   6   4   2

The authorized representative in the EU for product safety and compliance is
Penguin Random House Ireland, Morrison Chambers, 32 Nassau Street,
Dublin D02 YH68, Ireland, https://eu-contact.penguin.ie.

To my mom, June C. Gillon

CONTENTS

PRESIDENTS
AT WAR

Preface

I t was a cold, blustery day in Washington, DC, as John F. Kennedy, a two-term Democratic senator from Massachusetts, prepared to take the oath of office to become the thirty-fifth president of the United States. JFK sat in the second of four leather chairs arranged in a semicircle around the inaugural platform on the freshly painted East Portico of the White House. To his right sat outgoing president Dwight Eisenhower; on his left were vice president–elect Lyndon Johnson and then the outgoing vice president—and JFK's vanquished 1960 opponent—Richard Nixon.

There was a clear changing of the guard taking place. At forty-three, the tanned and youthful JFK was the youngest man ever elected to the presidency; he was replacing Eisenhower who, at seventy, was the oldest up to that time. The last president born in the nineteenth century was passing on the reins to the first born in the twentieth.

Despite the festive mood and the happy faces, deep resentments burned just beneath the surface. Kennedy respected Eisenhower as a general but not as a person. He often dismissed him as "that old asshole." Throughout the campaign, JFK attacked Eisenhower's policies and the man himself, creating a portrait of a befuddled president who was over his head in the White House, incapable of leading the nation in a dangerous world. But Ike was immensely popular, and Kennedy needed his support, especially on foreign policy issues. For his part, Ike found JFK inexperienced and arrogant, dismissing him as "that young whippersnapper" or "Little Boy Blue."

Although Nixon had faithfully served Eisenhower for eight years as his vice president, Ike never forgave him for refusing to withdraw from the ticket after a campaign funding scandal rocked Ike's 1952 presidential campaign. For his part, Nixon resented how Ike let him twist in the wind. If that were not enough, in 1956 Ike tried to persuade Nixon to step down as vice president and instead serve in his Cabinet. Their relationship turned downright cold during the 1960 campaign when, at a press conference, Ike claimed that he could not recall anything substantive that Nixon had contributed to his administration. Nixon reflected later that "there was little personal feeling between us. I gathered that I was considered a trusted lieutenant to the commander, but with the differences in our age and temperament, I was not a personal friend."

Kennedy and Johnson's relationship was a marriage of convenience. The Kennedy camp was still seething over LBJ's last-minute maneuvers to steal the nomination at the Democratic convention in Los Angeles. "I can't stand to be pushed around by that forty-two-year-old kid," LBJ complained. Unable to add to his delegate count, LBJ tried to force defections from Kennedy by spreading rumors about JFK's health, claiming that he was unfit and unprepared to be president. He told a reporter that Kennedy was a "little scrawny fellow with rickets." Johnson surrogates declared that Kennedy was suffering from Addison's disease, a potentially fatal disorder of the adrenal glands. Although true, Kennedy denied the charge vehemently and went on to win the nomination on the first ballot.

Despite Johnson's clumsy effort to block his nomination, the pragmatic Kennedy shocked the convention when he turned around and asked LBJ to join the ticket. But logically, it made sense. Johnson was one of the party's most prominent and skilled legislative leaders. The Massachusetts Catholic realized he needed a southern Protestant on the ticket. Johnson could help in several of the southern states, especially vote-rich Texas. Kennedy also worried about leaving a disgruntled and temperamental Johnson in the Senate, where he would have the power to block much of his agenda.

Ironically, the two opponents in the 1960 presidential contest probably had the closest relationship. Kennedy and Nixon were each elected to Congress in 1946 and served together on the same Education and Labor Committee. In 1952, when Nixon was selected as Eisenhower's running mate, Kennedy, who had also won a Senate seat, wrote him a two-page handwritten letter, calling him "an ideal selection" that would "bring to the ticket a great deal of strength." At the time, the vice president maintained an office in the Senate, and the two men were directly across the hall from each other. Nixon was always invited to Kennedy's office birthday parties. Just as Kennedy supported him in 1952, Nixon promised Kennedy that he would not campaign against the Massachusetts senator when he ran for reelection in 1958. The election had chilled their friendship, but they shared a begrudging mutual respect.

Despite their personal rivalries and differences in style and politics, the four presidents on the inaugural platform that day, along with the three who followed—Gerald Ford, Ronald Reagan, and George H. W. Bush—were bound not just by the presidential office but also by their experiences in World War II. It would be the defining event of their lives. The war would shape their personalities and help mold their characters more than any other event in their lives. Kennedy spoke for his generation when he said, "The war made us. It was and is our single greatest moment. The memory of the war is a key to our characters. It serves as a break wall between the indolence of our youths and the earnestness of our manhoods. No school or parent could have shaped us the way that fight shaped us. No other experience could have brought forth in us the same fortitude and resilience. We were much shrewder and sadder when that long battle finally finished. The war made us get serious for the first time in our lives. We've been serious ever since, and we show no signs of stopping."

JFK had both an abstract and personal connection with the war. Kennedy was a "rising" senior at Harvard University when he traveled extensively through Europe in 1938, getting a firsthand look at the brutality of Adolf Hitler's army and the futility of the British effort to appease his ambitions. In August 1939, at the end of a seven-month journey through Europe and the Middle East, the twenty-two-year-old Kennedy looked out his hotel window in Berlin and watched as Nazi storm troopers marched past.

His experience allowed him to frame the question that he would grapple with for the rest of his life and that would shape his response to a number of crises during his presidency: How do democracies, with their need to respond to public opinion and a web of competing interests, mobilize to confront totalitarian regimes that can marshal the full power of the state for a cause? JFK's reference point was British prime minister Neville Chamberlain's 1938 trip to Munich to negotiate with Hitler, who was demanding to annex parts of neighboring Czechoslovakia. After he returned to London, Chamberlain had told cheering crowds that he had secured "peace for our time." Instead, Hitler's armies seized the remainder of Czechoslovakia in 1939 and invaded Poland as well later that year. A generation of Western leaders would learn the "lessons of Munich": that aggression needed to be met with force, and compromise with the enemy was futile.

On September 3, 1939, two days after Hitler invaded Poland, Kennedy sat in the visitors' gallery of Britain's House of Commons along with his mother, brother Joe, and sister Kathleen. Kennedy listened as a mournful Chamberlain announced that his policy of appeasement had failed. The speaker who made the biggest impression on Kennedy that day, however, was the incoming prime minister, Winston Churchill. Kennedy sat transfixed as Churchill inspired the nation with a call to arms. "Outside, the storms of war may blow and the lands may be lashed with the fury of its gales, but in our own hearts this Sunday morning there is peace." Kennedy was witness to the beginning of World War II, an event that would transform him and the nation.

═══════

With the exception of Ronald Reagan, who spent the war at home in California, each of the future presidents demonstrated enormous courage, volunteering for duty and insisting on being sent directly to the front lines. They were legitimate members of the celebrated "Greatest Generation" that defended freedom and democracy from the unprecedented threat posed by Nazi aggression in Europe and Japanese imperialism in the Pacific.

The future presidents learned lessons from the war and then tried to implement them when they occupied the Oval Office. Lyndon Johnson could have been speaking for all the future presidents who fought in the war when he said, "From the experience of World War II, I learned that war comes about by two things—by a lust for power on the part of a few evil leaders and by a weakness on the part of the people whose love for peace too often displays a lack of courage that serves as an open invitation to all the aggressors of the world."

For this generation, the Munich analogy served as a conceptual prison that left them blind to the forces of nationalism sweeping through Asia and Latin America, and supremely confident in America's mission to transform the world in its own image. The Munich analogy shaped both how presidents viewed international crises and the way they justified their actions to the public. There was no better example of this blindness than Vietnam, where more than fifty-eight thousand Americans lost their lives in an unnecessary war. The problem is that analogies allow presidents to ignore complicated circumstances and impose a cookie-cutter approach to different parts of the world. It also stymied debate by confusing diplomacy with appeasement. Because Hitler was the one figure that an entire generation associated with evil, presidents have been quick to draw parallels between the Nazi dictator and a host of postwar enemies. In nearly every case, however, the comparison was false. Fortunately, Hitler was a singularly evil leader. "Invocations of the Munich analogy to justify the use of force," observed historian Jeffrey Record, "are almost invariably misleading because security threats to the United States genuinely Hitlerian in scope have not been replicated since 1945."

The same arrogance that shaped the presidents' views of America's role in the world infected their perceptions of American society. The battle against Fascism during the 1930s and Communism after the war convinced them of the superiority of American values and the fundamental soundness of American institutions. They eschewed ideology, refusing to consider there were problems that might require rethinking basic assumptions or questioning established institutions. "Today," JFK declared in a 1962 commencement address at Yale University, "the central domestic problems of our time are more subtle and less simple. They do not relate to basic clashes of philosophy and ideology, but to ways and means of recasting common goals—to research for sophisticated solutions to complex and obstinate issues."

Many members of this generation of leaders believed that prosperity made ideology moot; that economic growth served as a panacea that would solve all social problems. Each of the future presidents witnessed how wartime spending had lifted the nation from the depths of the Great Depression and set the stage for the prosperity that followed. Even liberals, who before the war experimented with various philosophies of redistributing wealth, now embraced the gospel of economic growth, convinced that all groups in society would benefit from a constantly growing economic pie. For inspiration they turned to John Maynard Keynes, the British economist whose 1936 book *The General Theory of Employment, Interest, and Money* challenged the conventional economic wisdom that fluctuations in *supply* created downturns in the business cycle and instead proposed that a lack of *demand* produced the Great Depression. With minor tinkering of fiscal and monetary policies governments could, he argued, end the boom-and-bust cycles that had plagued nations in the past. If demand was low, the government should stimulate growth by running deficits, either by increasing spending, cutting taxes, or both.

This was the message that many liberals wanted to hear: A proactive federal government could practically guarantee a continuing stream of economic growth that would benefit all Americans. There was no need for major change, liberals now believed; American institutions were fundamentally sound, in need of only minor tinkering. "Keynes, not Marx, is the prophet of the new radicalism," gloated the historian Arthur Schlesinger Jr. in his influential 1949 book *The Vital Center: The Politics of Freedom.* JFK summed up this thinking when he declared, "A rising tide lifts all boats."

Not all the future presidents, however, shared the supreme confidence that the nation had the tools to guarantee a constantly expanding eco-

nomic pie. Those men who entered the war as fiscal conservatives—
Eisenhower, Nixon, Ford, and George H. W. Bush—continued after the
war to worry that excessive government spending, whether on domestic
programs or defense, could potentially cripple the economy. Never embracing the liberal faith in Keynesian economics, they viewed the economy as fragile and prosperity as tenuous. (In 1971 Nixon professed his
fidelity to Keynesianism, but his conversion was the result of political
desperation, not economic conviction.) Nixon and Ford, struggling to
adapt to the enormous changes taking place in the international economy, and the nagging problem of stagflation, broke with the Kennedy
and Johnson administrations by stressing the limits of American economic power. Ronald Reagan was an outlier. Like Kennedy and Johnson,
he believed in the unlimited potential of the American economy, but his
embrace of supply-side economics abandoned traditional Republican
faith in fiscal responsibility and turned Keynes on his head by rewarding
the producers of wealth instead of the consumers.

The great irony of World War II is that it produced a generation of
presidents who believed in slow, incremental change, while it aroused the
expectations of a generation of reformers—women, workers, and especially African Americans—who demanded significant structural changes
to address their grievances. "The war changed our whole idea of how we
wanted to live when we came back," explained a veteran. Americans who
fought in the war felt they deserved "a good job, a respectable life." African Americans, who looked for continued improvement in their economic
conditions and opportunities once the war ended, forced every president
to confront the gap between American ideals and social realities.

The oath of office was scheduled to be delivered at noon, but the proceedings ran late because Senate pages needed to fetch additional chairs for
VIPs who'd crashed the event without tickets. Kennedy tried to break the
awkward silence by asking Ike about something they shared: service during World War II. The conversation had started during the ride to the
Capitol in the bubbletop limousine that morning when the young navy

lieutenant asked the supreme commander of Allied forces in Europe if he had read a new best-selling book about D-Day, *The Longest Day*, written by Cornelius Ryan. Eisenhower said he had heard about the book but had not read it, but Kennedy picked up the topic on the inaugural stand. According to Robert Kennedy, his brother "was fascinated that Eisenhower had never read the book."

Cardinal Richard Cushing, the archbishop of Boston and a Kennedy friend, was supposed to deliver a brief invocation but instead droned on for an excruciating eight minutes. As the cardinal approached the podium, he saw smoke coming from the floor of the lectern. Fearing that it might be a bomb timed to detonate while Kennedy was speaking, the cardinal offered up his body in sacrifice until an electrician identified that crossed wires were the source of the smoke. Only then did he stop speaking. Watching the scene in front of him, Eisenhower leaned over and whispered to JFK, "You must have a hot speech."

Kennedy was visibly annoyed. Flipping through the pages of his bound speech, he asked, "Is everything set?"

It was—finally, the event was back on track. Opera star Marian Anderson sang "The Star-Spangled Banner," a Greek Orthodox archbishop read a short speech, and LBJ took the oath of office. After the eighty-six-year-old Robert Frost struggled through a reading of his poem "The Gift Outright," it was JFK's turn. He stood, removed his overcoat, set down his silk hat, and proceeded to take the oath from Chief Justice Earl Warren. Deeply tanned, youthful, and energetic, he stood out against the backdrop of white-haired politicians. He raised his left hand and placed the right on the Bible and took the oath of office.

"We observe today not a victory of party but a celebration of freedom," he declared, his crisp Boston accent cutting through the frigid air.

The shadow of Munich hung over Kennedy's inaugural address. Unlike leaders in the 1930s, he argued that his generation welcomed the challenges that lay ahead. "Let the word go forth from this time and place, to friend and foe alike, that the torch has been passed to a new generation of Americans," he thundered. "In the long history of the world, only a few generations have been granted the role of defending freedom

in its hour of maximum danger. I do not shrink from this responsibility—
I welcome it." Negotiation was necessary, he told those bundled before
him and the sixty million Americans watching on television, but unlike
Chamberlain, he stressed that it must be from a position of strength. "Let
us never negotiate out of fear," he declared. "But let us never fear to negotiate." The message was clear: In contrast to leaders in the 1930s, his generation was up to the task of defending freedom. "Let every nation know,
whether it wishes us well or ill, that we shall pay any price, bear any
burden, meet any hardship, support any friend, oppose any foe to ensure
the survival and success of liberty."

The speech represented a generational call to arms, modeled after
Winston Churchill's efforts to inspire the British to confront the evil of
their time. The most memorable sentence in the speech represented JFK's
answer to how democracies can compete with totalitarian states, whether
they be Germany or the Soviet Union: "Ask not what your country can
do for you—ask what you can do for your country." A president could
not use state power to compel sacrifice, but he could use the power of
persuasion to forge a hyper-nationalism that could unite the nation behind a common cause.

Wanting to tap into the widely shared lessons learned during World
War II, which had ended only sixteen years earlier, Kennedy focused almost exclusively on foreign policy in his inaugural speech. As he spoke,
African Americans in the South were being denied basic political and
civil rights, and the national poverty rate hovered around 20 percent, but
the new president mustered only a brief mention of domestic issues: "If a
free society cannot help the many who are poor, it cannot save the few
who are rich." Convinced that economic growth would eventually mute
class divisions and provide African Americans with the economic power
to challenge the status quo, Kennedy removed most references to domestic challenges from speechwriter Ted Sorensen's earlier drafts of the
speech.

Commentators universally praised the speech. *The New York Times*
called the inaugural "eloquent, superb," while columnist James Reston
declared it "a revolutionary document." JFK's speech gave powerful and

eloquent expression to the "Munich trap" that would confound all the World War II veterans who occupied the White House. Like JFK, they depicted the world divided between the free and the unfree; a zero-sum game where any gain for the Soviets represented a blow to America's national interest. However, the Munich trap led successive American presidents to commit men and resources to prop up a corrupt government in South Vietnam even as they privately acknowledged that the United States could not win a war in the jungles of Southeast Asia. Each of the presidents who expanded America's involvement in the war—Eisenhower, Kennedy, and Johnson—and those who refused to end it—Nixon and Ford—understood the limits of the Munich analogy. But still they expanded America's commitment, not because they believed the US could win but because they feared having to explain to the American public why it lost.

For these men, and millions of others, service in the armed forces constituted a common rite of passage. People who had lived all their lives in small, provincial communities suddenly found themselves in new and unfamiliar places, meeting new and unfamiliar people. The war exposed those like Nixon—who grew up in rural Whittier, California—to people of different backgrounds; for those who were born into wealth and privilege, as were Kennedy and Bush, it became the great equalizer, where their social status, family names, and vast wealth did not matter.

Despite differences in temperament and background, their service in the war forged a common bond. Not only did their time in the White House provide them with unique perspectives, but also they shared the common experience of wartime service. Not surprisingly, they often overlooked partisan differences and personal animosity to rely on one another for advice and encouragement. Both JFK and Johnson sought Eisenhower's advice on foreign policy issues. And the opposite could happen as well: Richard Nixon, who lived long enough to see two Republicans elected to the office he once held, ended up turning against both Reagan and Bush because he believed they were too soft on the Soviets.

For all these men, the crucible of world war solidified their ties to the nation they would someday lead. Now, as the generation that fought in World War II dwindles, it is worthwhile to reflect on this thorny relationship between combat, leadership, and national identity. The war's legacy, and the lessons these seven presidents learned (or perhaps forgot), continue to shape the landscape upon which future presidents stand.

Part 1

THE WAR

CHAPTER 1

═══

"Day of Infamy"

DECEMBER 8, 1941
WASHINGTON, DC

Lyndon Baines Johnson, a thirty-three-year-old congressman from the Hill Country around Austin, Texas, sat in the House chamber on December 8, 1941, waiting for President Franklin D. Roosevelt to deliver one of the most important speeches of his life. The day before, Japanese planes had attacked the American naval base in Pearl Harbor, Hawaii. When the attack ended, 2,400 Americans lay dead. More than 900 were entombed in the USS *Arizona* when it exploded and sank. Japanese pilots disabled or sank eighteen ships—all eight battleships, three light cruisers, three destroyers, four auxiliary craft—and 188 aircraft. The Japanese lost 29 planes and 96 men.

This was not the way Roosevelt had wanted America to enter the war. Since April 1940, Hitler's army had overrun Denmark, Norway, the Netherlands, Luxembourg, and Belgium. In response, FDR started preparing the nation to aid the Allies even as he promised to keep the nation out of the war. Following the fall of France in June 1940, Roosevelt abandoned any pretense of neutrality by committing the United States to a policy of "all aid to the Allies short of war." When Britain lost eleven destroyers in less than two weeks, Churchill asked Roosevelt for help. The president came up with a clever way around the neutrality laws passed in the 1930s that prevented him from directly selling arms to Britain. He responded with a destroyers-for-bases deal, offering the British fifty World War I destroyers in exchange for ninety-nine-year leases on bases in the Caribbean and Newfoundland. Congress also approved Roosevelt's request for additional funds to rearm the nation, and it authorized the first peacetime conscription in American history. In January 1941 FDR proposed a lend-lease program, which allowed the United States to provide Britain with valuable war materiel.

While most Americans focused on the deteriorating situation in Europe, Japan was fulfilling its territorial ambitions in Asia. Since the 1890s, Japanese leaders had coveted the Manchurian region in northern China, which contained abundant natural resources that the import-dependent Japanese needed desperately. In 1931 Japan seized Manchuria, established a puppet government, and confiscated the land. Six years later, the Japanese army murdered hundreds of thousands of people in the Chinese capital of Nanjing, leaving the city in ruins in what has been called the Nanjing Massacre.

The United States criticized Japanese aggression in East Asia but lacked the power to challenge Japan's predominance in the region. Throughout the decade, Roosevelt engaged in a delicate balancing act: He tried to use economic leverage, especially Japan's dependence on foreign oil, to tame Japanese aggression, while avoiding an open conflict that would distract resources from the European theater. "I simply have not got enough navy to go around—and every little episode in the Pacific means fewer ships in the Atlantic," Roosevelt complained.

Despite his worry, the interventionist logic of American policy moved the United States and Japan closer to confrontation. In July 1939 Roosevelt terminated the 1911 Treaty of Commerce and Navigation with Japan. This move effectively threatened the Japanese with an economic embargo, in hopes that they would be shocked into tempering their aggression in the region. However, intimidation did not deter Japan. In September 1940, Japanese forces secured bases in French Indochina, which included Cambodia, Laos, and Vietnam. America immediately imposed a partial embargo on high-quality scrap iron and steel. Japan responded three days later by announcing the Tripartite Pact with Germany and Italy, which pledged its signatories to come to one another's aid in the event of an attack "by a power not already engaged in war."

Then, when Japanese forces overran the rest of Indochina in July 1941, the administration reacted by freezing Japanese assets in the United States and by ending all shipments of oil. Japan now faced a difficult choice: Either it could submit to American demands or conquer new territory to secure oil for its war machine. But since peace with the United States now seemed impossible, Japan prepared for war.

The attack on Pearl Harbor was only the beginning of a plan to cripple the United States fleet so that Japan could dominate the Pacific region. Three hours later, Japan launched attacks against US naval bases in the Gulf of Davao in the Philippines and the island of Guam. They followed on December 8 with still more attacks on Thailand, which surrendered within just five hours. At three o'clock the same day, Japan assaulted Singapore before sending planes to bomb Khota Bharu in British Malaya. Coming one after another, these coordinated strikes left the United States scrambling to decide on the best course of action.

━━━━━━━━

The lanky, six-foot-four-inch Johnson jumped to his feet as the polio-stricken FDR struggled down the center aisle of the ornate House chamber, clinging to the arm of his son James. He sat down once House Speaker Sam Rayburn, a fellow Texan, introduced the president.

Roosevelt scanned the hall before flipping open a black leather notebook containing his speech. "Yesterday," he said in a strong, resonant voice, "December 7th, 1941—a date which will live in infamy—the United States of America was suddenly and deliberately attacked by naval and air forces of the Empire of Japan." He accused the Japanese government of dishonesty for launching attacks even as it pretended to negotiate for peace, before reaching a dramatic conclusion: "I ask that the Congress declare that since the unprovoked and dastardly attack by Japan on Sunday, December 7, a state of war has existed between the United States and the Japanese Empire." With that, LBJ rose once again and gave Roosevelt a standing ovation, along with all but one of the other assembled members. Only Republican congresswoman Jeannette Rankin of Montana, a pacifist, remained seated.

If Japan's goal was to cripple the United States, the attack actually had the opposite effect, stirring a patriotic fervor and calls for revenge. Across the nation, young men flooded into recruiting stations.

Among those rushing to defend the nation were the very men who would later assume the presidency. Some—like Eisenhower, Kennedy, Johnson, and Reagan—were already in uniform. The attack on Pearl Harbor pushed others—Nixon, Ford, and Bush—to join the military. JFK, Nixon, Ford, and Bush all lobbied to get to the front lines. Each could have stayed behind, either in civilian life or with a cushy desk job in the States. Instead, they were part of a generation that used their power and connections to get closer to the battle, not run away from it. Politics also played a role. A few, especially Nixon and Ford, were already thinking of running for elective office and were aware that the road to political power ran through the battlefields of World War II. But the main motivation was simple: patriotism. The nation had been attacked, and they wanted to play a central role in its defense. They felt a moral obligation to protect the nation.

LBJ's motives, however, were a little more complicated.

Three days later, on December 11, after Germany and Italy declared war on the United States, Roosevelt sent a declaration asking Congress to declare war against the two other Axis powers. "The forces endeavoring to enslave the entire world now are moving toward this hemisphere," he warned. The House quickly and unanimously approved war resolutions against Germany and Italy by votes of 393 to 0 and 399 to 0, respectively.

After the vote, Johnson rose to his feet and asked the chair to recognize him: "Mr. Speaker! I ask unanimous consent for an indefinite leave of absence." Speaker Rayburn asked the chamber if there were any objections. The members of Congress remained silent. Rayburn slammed down his gavel. "Is there objection to the request of the gentleman from Texas? . . . So be it."

Lyndon Baines Johnson was born in 1908 in Stonewall, Texas, a depressed rural area of the Texas Hill Country. The eldest of five children born to Sam and Rebekah Johnson, he grew up poor, without either electricity or indoor plumbing. "When I was young," Johnson said, "poverty was so common that we didn't know it had a name." After a few years drifting about aimlessly and getting into scraps, Johnson refocused and completed his education at Southwest Texas State Teachers College in nearby San Marcos. He then taught school for a few years while carrying out unpaid political work in his free time. That side gig fueled his true passion. In 1931 he relocated to Washington after securing a job as a clerk for a Texas congressman.

By 1937, at the age of twenty-eight, Johnson had decided to run for Congress himself. His strategy for winning the election was to tie his fortunes to President Roosevelt. "His campaign," wrote biographer Robert Dallek, "became a celebration of FDR and an appeal to the idea that Lyndon Johnson was the single candidate in the race who would give the president unqualified support." Campaign posters declared confidently, "A vote for Johnson is a vote for Roosevelt's program."

Despite Johnson's strategy, the two men only met for the first time shortly after LBJ's victory. Roosevelt happened to be in the Gulf of Mexico on a fishing trip and sent word that he wanted to see Johnson, who was there to greet the president when his boat docked in Galveston. Roosevelt invited LBJ to accompany him on a campaign trip through Dallas in his specially designed railroad car. They established an instant rapport. FDR telephoned aide Tommy Corcoran after his return and reported, "I've just met the most remarkable young man. Help him with anything you can."

Since coming to Congress in 1937, Johnson had earned a reputation for his fierce political ambition, his genuine desire to help the less fortunate, and his unwavering belief that government had a responsibility to provide opportunity to all Americans. He ran unopposed in 1938 and 1940, winning reelection to the House both times.

In addition to supporting the New Deal, LBJ enthusiastically backed FDR's defense measures. So, in the spring of 1940, when it appeared likely that the United States would enter the war in Europe, Johnson applied for a commission in the US Naval Reserve and was given an appointment as a lieutenant commander. His support for the commander in chief remained unconditional. "America and the world today are blessed that destiny has given us a great and mature man to lead us," he told a joint session of the Texas legislature in April 1941. "President Roosevelt is a leader whose judgment has been found good and fair. We can trust and follow him. He embodies the spirit of love for fellow man in which democracy was born and with which it will carry forward to the future when peace comes, and the trial is past."

When a Senate seat opened in the summer of 1941, LBJ threw his hat in the ring. But despite strong support from the White House, he lost the race. Throughout the campaign, Johnson had pledged to go to the front lines if the United States found itself at war. "If the day ever comes when my vote must be cast to send your boy to the trenches, that day Lyndon Johnson will leave his Senate seat and go with him!" He repeated the pledge at every campaign stop, and it drew the same enthusiastic response from patriotic Texans. At times he made it sound more dramatic, saying that he would never be stuck at a desk job in Washington when war came. Instead, he "would be in the front line, in the trenches, in the mud and blood with your boys, helping to do that fighting." That vow became his campaign theme, printed on flyers and postcards. Though he never made it to the Senate, the pledge stuck.

Over the next few months, the thirty-three-year-old LBJ would engage in a delicate dance of deception, declaring publicly that he was going to the front lines while privately lobbying to stay closer to home. "He wanted something big in Washington, really big," Corcoran reflected. "He had everyone working on it for him."

When he finally got a chance to participate more directly in the war, LBJ did not give up his congressional seat. Instead, he unofficially left his office in the able hands of his smart, shrewd, and politically savvy wife, Claudia Alta Taylor. She had earned the nickname "Lady Bird" as a child when her nurse noted that she was "purty as a lady bird." Born into a prominent and wealthy family, she managed to pay her way through college and planned to become a reporter until she met LBJ, then a congressional aide. "He was excessively thin, but very, very good-looking, with lots of black, wavy hair, and the most outspoken, straightforward, determined manner I had ever encountered."

Initially, Undersecretary of the Navy James V. Forrestal assigned Johnson to inspect shipyards in Texas and California, but he ended up disliking the job. In early March 1942 he wrote FDR's private secretary, Grace Tully, from San Francisco: "Things are very dull here with me. How I yearned for activity and an assignment where I can be reasonably productive. I hope sometime you run across something that you think I can do well 24 hrs. per day."

While Johnson was traveling the West Coast, Japan continued its onslaught against Western interests in the Pacific, overwhelming Wake Island, Guam, Borneo, Singapore, and the Philippines. American forces were humiliated time and again. In Guam, Japanese soldiers forced Americans to strip down to their underwear and watch the Japanese flag replace the Stars and Stripes. In Manila, the invading force destroyed nearly half of the Pacific Air Force. In the Philippines' Bataan Peninsula, more than seventy-five thousand American and Filipino solders were forced to surrender and then march sixty-five miles in oppressive heat without food or water. Australia, New Zealand, and India were now vulnerable to invasion, and Japan approached what Roosevelt called "a dominating position from which it would prove most difficult to eject her."

As the war ground on, some Texas newspapers started questioning what Johnson was up to and how he was spending his time. *The Houston Post* opined that "if Mr. Johnson should be merely getting himself a safe, warm naval berth . . . the voters would be certain to react accordingly." Johnson responded by saying that the job in California was temporary and that he could be sent to a combat zone at any time. "I am under orders from the Secretary of the Navy, and the Commander-in-Chief," he wrote in response to a constituent's question about his service. "I don't give the orders, but I do take them. Today I am here, tomorrow I don't know where I will be, but it will be where they think I can do the most."

The clock was ticking. Johnson had been warned that FDR was soon going to issue an order requiring all members of Congress in the service to either resign their seats or return home. He also had to file to run either for reelection to the House or for the Senate by May 31, and he knew there would be considerable attention focused on his military career. In desperation, he headed back to DC in April for another meeting with Roosevelt.

While pledging to join the battle, he was also lobbying the White House for a high-level position in Washington. White House aide Jonathan Daniels noted in his diary that Johnson "wants for the sake of political future to get into danger zone though realizes talents best suited for handling speakers and public relations." Another aide echoed Daniels's observation: "Lyndon Johnson is anxious to get out some place where the bombs are dropping." He had even suggested being made an admiral.

On April 13 Johnson told the president's appointment secretary that he would stay in Washington for as long as it took to get a meeting with FDR. Johnson finally got to see FDR on Sunday, April 26. Roosevelt was sympathetic to LBJ's plight, and he certainly did not want to cause political problems for one of his most loyal supporters. He proposed sending LBJ to Australia as part of an inspection tour of the Pacific. Roosevelt was still angry that General Douglas MacArthur had left the Philippines unprepared for the Japanese attack on December 8 despite having advance notice of it. He did not trust MacArthur, convinced that he often let his ego cloud his judgment. With the war effort going poorly in the Pacific, FDR could use someone objective to travel there and report back to him. "We were directed to get below the top brass," LBJ remembered, "below General MacArthur's command headquarters in Australia, to the men in combat and see for ourselves what they were facing. President Roosevelt wanted his eyes and ears in the field. I was the navy officer picked to go."

The mission made little sense. Johnson had no military expertise to judge MacArthur's strategy in the Pacific. He was in the navy but would be inspecting the army and army air forces. FDR may have wanted to get a pair of trusted eyes on events in the Pacific, but he was also throwing Johnson a political bone.

So, on May 7, 1942, five months after Pearl Harbor, Johnson boarded a massive PB2Y Coronado flying boat for the long trip to the Pacific. He was finally on his way to the war zone.

John F. Kennedy was enjoying a rough-and-tumble touch football game near the Washington Monument when he learned of the Japanese attack. That moment galvanized him like no other before or since.

Kennedy could have avoided serving altogether. He had been plagued by health problems his whole life, everything from debilitating gastrointestinal ailments to crippling back pain. In the unlikely event that he passed the physical, his rich and well-connected father, former US ambassador to the United Kingdom Joseph P. Kennedy, could have found him a comfortable desk job in Washington. But Jack was determined to serve, and instead of using his family connections to avoid service, he used them to get close to the danger zone.

What motivated him?

Most of all, JFK was driven by a genuine sense of patriotism and personal courage. Having traveled throughout Europe and witnessing firsthand the menace posed by Hitler's armies, Kennedy was convinced that Western values of freedom and democracy were at stake. He had studied and written about that threat for years; now he felt it was necessary for him to play a tangible role in winning the war. In an August 1941 interview with the navy, JFK stated, "As an American citizen, it is my duty to my country to volunteer my services for whatever branch of the service I am equipped. I am interested in coming into the Intelligence Service because I think I can exert my best efforts in it." The evaluation described him as "an exceptionally brilliant student" with "unusual qualities and a definite future in whatever he undertakes."

Sibling rivalry also played a role. In June 1941, following Germany's invasion of the Soviet Union, Jack's older brother Joe, who had been parroting his father's isolationist views and had predicted a German victory, dropped out of his last year at Harvard Law School and volunteered for the Naval Aviation Cadet Program of the US Naval Reserve. A stunned Joe Sr. offered to use his connections to get his younger son a comfortable desk job in Washington, but Jack refused. He knew that the rigorous training would aggravate his many health problems, especially his bad back, but he intended to join any branch of the service that would accept him.

Getting there was not easy. He had volunteered for both the army and navy officers' schools but was denied in both cases because of his poor health. So, Jack did what the Kennedys did when they needed help: He turned to his father. In October 1941, two months before Pearl Harbor, Joe Sr. contacted Captain Alan Kirk, who had been a naval attaché during Kennedy's ambassadorship and was now head of the Office of Naval Intelligence. "I am having Jack see a medical friend of yours in Boston tomorrow for physical examination and then hope he'll become associated with you in Naval Intelligence," he wrote. A few weeks later, the board of examiners miraculously declared Jack "physically qualified for appointment." Biographer Robert Dallek noted, "Reading the report of his exam, one would think he never had a serious physical problem in his life."

Later that month, Kennedy began working as an ensign in the Office of Naval Intelligence in Washington. Since he did not have security clearance, his job consisted of summarizing reports from overseas stations and including them in bulletins. He found the work tedious and uninspiring— certainly less glamorous than that of his brother Joe, who was earning his wings. After Pearl Harbor, the work became more challenging, forcing him to work long hours, but Kennedy dreamed of being out at sea and on the front lines of the battle.

Kennedy's brief stint in the military almost came to an end when he fell in love with a stunning blond, blue-eyed Dane, Inga Arvad, a daily columnist for the *Washington Times-Herald*. Of Jack, Inga wrote fondly, "He had the charm that makes birds come out of their trees." Jack nicknamed her "Inga Binga," and he spent much of his free time with her, much to the consternation of the FBI, which suspected her of being a German spy because she'd managed to get access to Hitler when other Western journalists could not. "One likes him immediately," she wrote of Hitler in 1935. In fact, Hitler had attended Inga's wedding to her now ex-husband. With the direct approval of President Roosevelt, the FBI tapped her phones, intercepted her mail, and kept her under constant surveillance.

In January 1942 the FBI leaked the story of Jack's affair with Inga to gossip columnist Walter Winchell, who published the story in the *New York Daily Mirror*. Within twenty-four hours, Kennedy received new orders to take a desk job at the Charleston Navy Yard in South Carolina. It could have been worse. Captain Howard Kingman, the assistant director of the Office of Naval Intelligence, wanted Kennedy discharged from the navy entirely. Jack told a reporter later, "They shagged my ass down to South Carolina because I was going around with a Scandinavian blonde, and they thought she was a spy!"

Kennedy found the Charleston job just as boring as the one in Washington. He was responsible for instructing defense plant workers on how to protect both themselves and their plants against enemy bombing. "Jack finds his present post rather irksome," Rose Kennedy wrote in a round-robin letter to the family in February, "as he does not seem to have enough to do and I think will be glad to transfer." His friend Lem Billings recalled later that Kennedy "was very frustrated and unhappy."

Adding to his plight, Jack's back problems flared up again that spring. On March 24 he requested a ten-day leave from the navy so that he could travel again to Boston's Lahey Clinic for treatment. On April 9 he requested six months of inactive duty so that he could have surgery to relieve the pain. He would spend part of the next few months in and out of hospitals in Charleston and Boston, his goal of serving in a combat zone appearing increasingly remote.

———

On December 7, Richard Nixon and his wife, Pat, decided to attend a movie matinee in Hollywood, California. On the way, they stopped at Pat's sister's house. When they arrived, Dick's brother-in-law said he'd heard a radio report that the Japanese had bombed Pearl Harbor. Richard was not alarmed. "I was sure that it was just one more of the frequent scare stories we all had been hearing," he reflected. He and Pat continued on their way. But before the movie finished, the theater manager stopped the film and announced that all servicemen needed to report immediately to their stations. As people streamed out of the theater, Nixon spied a newsboy holding a newspaper with the screaming headline "Japs Bomb Pearl Harbor." As he walked over, the newsboy shouted, "We are at war, mister!"

Over the past few years, Nixon had watched events unfolding in Europe and hoped that the United States would not be drawn into the conflict. He was among the millions of Americans who cheered when British prime minister Neville Chamberlain declared that he had achieved "peace for our time." Raised a Quaker and committed to pacifism, he abhorred war. "I was as close to being a pacifist as anybody could be," Nixon remembered. "I thought at this time that Chamberlain was the greatest man alive, and when I read Churchill's all-out criticism of Chamberlain, I thought Churchill was a madman."

A few weeks earlier, the twenty-eight-year-old Nixon had accepted a job at the Office of Price Administration in Washington, DC. President Roosevelt had established the OPA to create and enforce a system of rationing purchases of various consumer goods, including tires, cars, gasoline, and sugar. Nixon, who in 1940 had considered running for the California State Assembly but ended up campaigning for the Republican presidential candidate Wendell Willkie, saw the position as a way of getting to know Washington. It "seemed a good opportunity to go to Washington and observe the working of the government firsthand," he wrote in his memoirs.

It was also a ticket out of Whittier, where he seemed destined to spend his life working in his father's general store and gas station. "He came from humble folk and was born in the turn-of-the-century California equivalent of a log cabin," observed biographer Stephen Ambrose. The Nixon family struggled to make ends meet, and Richard's parents were not particularly nurturing. His father was loud and boisterous, his mother quiet and cold. "Two more temperamentally different people can hardly be imagined," Nixon remembered. "In her whole life, I never heard her say to me, or anyone else, 'I love you.'"

Nixon learned that the best way to win the affection of his parents was to excel at school. And that he did. He graduated near the top of his high school class and won the "Harvard Prize" as the "best all-around student." The award came with a full scholarship to Harvard University, but Nixon was forced to turn it down because he could not afford the living expenses.

Instead, he enrolled in local Whittier College in September 1930. Once again he excelled in his studies, getting elected president of the student body, winning debate competitions, and appearing in plays even while still living at home and helping to run the family's store. He graduated second in his class and earned a scholarship to Duke Law School, which he accepted.

A pattern emerged. Nixon was disciplined, hardworking, and bright. Inept in private conversations, he transformed into a skilled actor and debater onstage in front of large groups. His dark features and slumped shoulders gave people the impression that he was brooding, aloof, and moody, thus earning him the nickname "Gloomy Gus." "He never had any close friends in college," remarked one schoolmate. "He was a loner." His debate coach remembered that "there was something mean in him, mean in the way he put his questions, argued his points."

Although he once again graduated near the top of his law school class, Nixon was unable to get a job at the big New York firms. The FBI also turned him down. So, he went back to Whittier at the age of twenty-four and joined a small law firm. It gnawed at him that classmates with lower grades landed prestigious jobs on Wall Street, while he was forced to return to his hometown. He described feeling "bitterly defeated" by the rejections, which only motivated him to strive to become more than just a small-town lawyer.

In February 1938 he met Patricia Ryan, a recent graduate of the University of Southern California. Although both her parents had died when she was young, Pat managed to put herself through USC. Attractive and outgoing, she taught business education classes at Whittier Union High School and joined the Whittier Little Theater group, where she met Nixon while reading audition lines.

Richard was smitten. "I found I could not take my eyes away from her," he recalled. "For me, it was a case of love at first sight." It was not the same way for Pat, however, who did everything possible to discourage him from pursuing her. Although she initially made clear that she was not looking for a relationship—even trying to set him up with her roommate—he courted her relentlessly, writing notes, poems, and songs. The more often she told him that she was not ready to settle down, the harder he pursued her. On Friday nights, he drove her to Los Angeles so she could go on dates, then picked her up on Sunday nights and drove her back home. When he learned that she loved to ice-skate, he took up the sport, even though one friend described him as "the worst ice-skater in the world."

Eventually Pat relented and agreed to marry him. One week before their wedding day on June 21, 1940, news came that France had fallen to the German army. The country officially surrendered the day after they wed. That pivotal event was an omen for how much the war would shape their marriage, not only during its early years but also throughout Nixon's presidency.

In early January 1942 Dick and Pat loaded up their brown 1935 Chevy for the trip across country to Washington, now the capital of a nation at war. "Our greatest hopes," Pat observed before leaving for Washington, "were to get some job with the government, where we could contribute to the winning of the war."

They arrived in Washington on the afternoon of January 9, Nixon's twenty-ninth birthday. He went straight to the OPA's temporary offices and was sworn in as a government official. In his résumé, he described his job there dryly: "Supervise digest and publication of summaries of all rationing interpretations. Handle administrative duties and set up procedures to be followed by new rationing units and by the regional offices. Act as consultant to members of the various rationing units on procedures, interpretations, and policies." It was tedious work, but this marked Nixon's first real exposure to the inner workings of Washington.

By all accounts, Nixon was competent, conscientious, and energetic. He took pride in the work. "What really made it mean something," he said, "was that we felt that we were part of a bigger cause." By June, he was the acting chief of the entire Rationing Coordination Unit. "Bright, anxious to assume responsibility and with a great capacity for work," was how one supervisor described him. The supervisor admitted to being "greatly impressed by [Nixon's] clear, careful, and analytical mind, as well as by his ever cheerful and pleasant personality."

There remained a part of Richard, however, that never fit in. Part of the reason was sheer culture shock. Washington was a bustling town, full of the type of East Coast elites who had rejected him when he applied for jobs at New York's most prestigious law firms. Furthermore, assigned to the section dealing with rubber rationing, Nixon was once again struck by the fact that many other people with fewer qualifications were ranked higher and earned more pay. That experience only reinforced his deep sense of grievance, reminding him that he grew up on the wrong side of the tracks. He resented the liberal Jews whom Roosevelt appointed to run the agency—a resentment that would fester over time. One of his supervisors said that Nixon seemed "uncomfortable among the liberals, the Eastern law school graduates, the Jews he rubbed shoulders with on the job."

Nixon would work at the Office of Price Administration for only eight months, but the experience shaped many of his later views toward government and bureaucracy. In the years immediately after the war, Nixon complained about the inefficiencies of large bureaucracies while highlighting the necessity of their work. Bureaucracies were "inherently inefficient because they offer no financial incentive to operate efficiently," he told audiences in 1946. But he also praised the people who worked there and underscored the need for government regulations. "The agency did a necessary job during the war," he said. He criticized those who called for dramatically reducing the size of government. "In our complicated modern economy," he scribbled in handwritten notes, "government must of necessity operate" through agencies. He also praised the "thousands of public servants, capable people" who worked in government.

In later years, however, Nixon took a harsher tone when describing his OPA experience. Nixon went back and reimagined his time there to fit his growing anger toward the Washington establishment and those in government whom he blamed for destroying his presidency. "I cannot say that my eight months at OPA were particularly happy ones," he reflected in his memoirs, "but at least they were instructive." He critiqued the OPA for "the terrible paperwork . . . the mediocrity of so many civil servants . . . [the] people angling for something and anxious not to miss the bandwagon . . . some of the remnants of the old, violent New Deal crowd." Nixon liked telling the story of the questionable advice that his boss gave him when he complained: "[B]uild a little staff. Request two or three people to assist you, and then we can raise you to a P-5." Nixon stated, "But I don't need a staff," to which his boss replied, "Then you won't get a promotion."

Though he could have avoided combat by staying at the agency, which was considered essential to the war effort, Nixon wanted to get closer to the battlefield. "Many men in OPA were able to get draft deferments and spent the war in their offices," he stated. "Despite my Quaker background and beliefs, I never considered doing this." Like JFK, he was driven by a sense of patriotism and idealism; a feeling that he should contribute to the war effort. And, like LBJ, Nixon recognized that in order to be politically viable, he would need to prove that he did more than sit behind a desk enforcing regulations that he did not always believe in. Thomas Emerson, who had hired Nixon, reflected that "Nixon must have picked up the DC message very quickly: that any man who wanted to go into politics must have a war record." It was, in Emerson's words, "accepted dogma in Washington."

By the summer of 1942, Nixon was trying to find a way to get into uniform and closer to combat. Since the draft expanded to include men his age without children, Nixon figured it would be better to go in as an officer. "When I heard that young lawyers were being recruited as officers for the Navy, I talked to Pat about it and applied for a commission," he remembered. Pat supported his decision. "I would have felt mighty uncomfortable if Dick hadn't done his part," she recalled.

His interview went well. "This applicant makes a very favorable impression and is considered good officer material," wrote the navy officer who interviewed him. "It is believed his exceptional scholastic record and subsequent experiences in the field of law, together with his executive experience with the Office of Price Administration, will qualify him for Air Intelligence or administrative duties."

With that shining endorsement, in August 1942 Richard Nixon was sent to the Naval Officer Indoctrination School at Quonset Point, Rhode Island.

Seventeen-year-old George H. W. Bush was wrapping up the first semester of his senior year at Phillips Andover Academy, an exclusive prep school in Massachusetts. As he walked across campus that Sunday afternoon, he heard someone shout that Japan had bombed Pearl Harbor. "My God," he recalled thinking, "this changes everything." For months, he had been listening to CBS radio broadcasts with Edward R. Murrow and William L. Shirer, which left him convinced that it was only a matter of time before the United States would be fighting Hitler's armies in Europe. But the Japanese attack caught him off guard. Sometime later that afternoon, as he learned more about the attack, Bush decided that he had to join the war effort. "After Pearl Harbor, it was a different world altogether," he recalled. "It was a red, white, and blue thing. Your country's attacked, you'd better get in there and try to help."

Signing up to fight was a family tradition. He knew that his father had enlisted and fought on the front lines during World War I. Roosevelt's speech the next day only magnified his desire to fight. "The war became his central reality," noted biographer Jon Meacham. As air drills began sounding across campus, the student newspaper chimed in, describing the war as "a desperate life and death struggle" and enthusiastically endorsing Roosevelt's decision for war. "If the government fails, we will fail, and likewise if we fail in our duty at the present time, we jeopardize the steadfastness of the government's cause."

Bush was another future president who could have avoided service. He was raised in a wealthy New England family. His father, Prescott Bush, a successful investment banker, represented Connecticut in the US Senate from 1952 until 1963. Even family friend Henry L. Stimson, the secretary of war, advised young George to go to Yale, earn a degree, and then decide whether he wanted to join the war effort—assuming that the war was still going on after four years.

Bush had an added incentive to stay stateside. A few weeks after Pearl

Harbor, he met Barbara Pierce, a charming seventeen-year-old from Rye, New York, who was attending boarding school in Charleston, South Carolina. That night, Barbara told her mother about the most "heavenly boy" she had met at the Greenwich Country Club's Christmas dance. Bush, too, told his mother about "the niftiest girl at the dance." The two went on an official date the following evening and, over the next few months, exchanged letters and arranged to meet again during spring break. George then invited Barbara to his senior prom.

As their relationship blossomed, Bush successfully wrapped up his final year of high school, where he served as captain of the baseball and soccer teams and won election as senior class president. His father continued to push him to go to Yale. But George's mind was already made up. On the day he turned eighteen, he headed to Boston and was sworn into the navy as a seaman second class, using his family connections to secure a spot in the navy's pilot-training program. "I was a scared, nervous kid," Bush recalled. "[But] I knew what I wanted to do. It was an easy call—no second-guessing, no doubts."

In August 1942 his father saw him off from New York City. That was when Bush observed his father cry for the first time. "So off I went, scared little guy," he reflected. "Got on the train, didn't know anybody."

———

Fifty-one-year-old Brigadier General Dwight D. Eisenhower, known affectionately as Ike, was serving as the chief of staff of the Third Army at Fort Sam Houston, near San Antonio, Texas, on December 7, 1941. He was exhausted, having recently staged a successful military exercise during war games in the swampy Louisiana backwoods that involved about a half million men spread across 3,400 square miles. His careful planning led to a smashing victory for his Third Army in the mock battle and promotion to brigadier general. "Powerful figures in Washington took note," observed biographer William Hitchcock.

After working at the office that morning, he decided to go home and take an afternoon nap. "[I don't want to be] bothered by anyone wanting to play bridge," he instructed his wife, Mamie. As he recalled later, "My dreams were of a two weeks' leave I was going to take, during which my wife and I were going to West Point to spend Christmas with our plebe son, John."

No sooner had his head hit the pillow than his wife awakened him. There was an urgent call from Washington. Japan had attacked Pearl Harbor. "I reacted with an instinctive focus on short-term possibilities— and a fleeting hope that this report simply could not be true," he reflected. At the time, Ike had no "four-year panoramic view of a vast national program that would carry our fighting forces across two oceans from di- saster to victory."

Immediately, his vacation plans evaporated, and Eisenhower found himself once again working long days, responding to a flurry of War Department orders to transfer antiaircraft units and soldiers to the West Coast in anticipation of a Japanese land assault. At the same time, Amer- ican troops also needed to guard industrial plants and ensure the safety of ports along the Gulf of Mexico.

However, on the morning of December 12, the day after Congress declared war on Germany and Italy, Ike received an urgent phone call from Walter Bedell Smith, secretary of the general staff. "The chief says for you to hop on a plane and get up here right away. Tell your boss that formal orders will come through later."

"The chief," Ike knew, referred to Army Chief of Staff General George Marshall, a cold, aloof man with a keen eye for military talent. Although ten years older than Ike, the two men looked and carried themselves in a similar manner. They were both six feet tall with athletic builds, figures of propriety in their neatly tailored uniforms. Both were also chain smokers. (Eisenhower inhaled four packs of Camels a day.) Eisenhower described Marshall as "remote and austere"—an accurate assessment given Marshall's insistence that everyone, including the president, call him "General Marshall."

Although they had met only three brief times, Marshall knew Ike by his sterling reputation. Major General Charles Thompson, who com- manded the Third Infantry Division, summed it up best when he said that Ike was widely known for being "affable, energetic, dynamic, zeal- ous, original, loyal, capable, dependable, and outstanding."

Marshall had sought out Eisenhower to help develop battle plans, but

Ike was disappointed about being on the sidelines. He wanted to be leading troops, but it looked like he would be spending the entirety of the war at a desk in Washington. "Heavy-hearted," he wrote in his memoirs, "I telephoned my wife to pack a bag, and within the hour I was headed to the War Department." When bad weather grounded his plane in Dallas, he boarded a train to DC's Union Station, arriving early on Sunday morning, December 14—exactly one week after the attack.

At this point, Eisenhower was a career soldier who had never led men into combat. Born in Denison, Texas, on October 4, 1890, Eisenhower grew up in Abilene, Kansas, where he did well enough in school to earn admission to West Point. In 1915 he graduated from the military academy in the middle of his class, sixty-first out of 164.

Later that year, while stationed at Fort Sam Houston, Eisenhower met and fell immediately in love with nineteen-year-old Mary Geneva Doud, whom everyone called Mamie. They came from very different backgrounds. She grew up in a wealthy family surrounded by servants; he had always lived a spartan life. But they were both outgoing and enjoyed the company of friends. She described him as "just about the handsomest male I had ever met." He proposed on Valentine's Day 1916, and they married five months later, on July 1, 1916—the same day that Ike was promoted to first lieutenant. She embraced her role as an army wife. "Ike was my career," she said later.

Afterward, Eisenhower bounced around from one disappointing position to another, but along the way, he impressed his superiors, including General George S. Patton, with his understanding of military tactics and superior organizational skills. Perhaps his greatest asset was his calm personality and his ability to placate the delicate egos of powerful men. Ironically, the army found him so valuable that it kept him stateside during World War I so that he could train future infantry troops for combat—even though Ike wanted nothing more than to join the field of action. His soldiers respected him for being fair and consistent, though he was also a strict and demanding disciplinarian, even when it came to playing cards. If he caught a man cheating, he would offer him two options: resignation or court-martial.

Finally, on his twenty-eighth birthday—October 14, 1918—Ike got the gift he most desired: The army gave him orders to assume command of an armored unit in France starting on November 18. "My orders to France have come," he told Mamie in disbelief. But on November 11, 1918, the armistice ending WWI was signed. Disappointed once again, Ike vowed to a colleague that he would stop at nothing to get another opportunity: "By God, from now on I am cutting myself a swath and will make up for this."

It would take quite some time for Ike to make good on that vow. In 1925 he graduated first in his class of 245 officers from the Command and General Staff College at Fort Leavenworth, Kansas. Several important positions soon followed: Panama, Washington, DC, and a challenging four-year tour in the Philippines under the egotistical but brilliant General Douglas MacArthur. The latter experience enabled him to observe the situation in the Pacific firsthand, while continuing to distinguish himself in front of his superiors. After war in Europe broke out in September 1939, Eisenhower eventually ended up as the chief of staff of the Third Army. He spent the next two years mostly in the United States preparing soldiers for war—which is why he was back at Fort Sam Houston when the attack on Pearl Harbor erupted.

AS SOON AS HE ARRIVED IN WASHINGTON, EISENHOWER WENT TO SEE Marshall right away. The chief did not mince his words, offering a grim assessment of the situation. The Pacific Fleet had been crippled and was not prepared to confront Japan. The navy's aircraft carriers had been out to sea during the attack, thankfully, but there were not enough supporting ships. There was genuine fear that Japan would invade Hawaii or even the mainland, so they wanted to use the carriers for defense.

Finishing his report, Marshall asked Ike pointedly, "What should be our general line of action?"

"Eisenhower was startled," wrote biographer Stephen Ambrose. He had just stepped off the train, was not up-to-date on war plans, and had no staff. He hesitated for a second before responding, "Give me a few hours." Three hours later, Ike returned to see Marshall, this time with a three-page, triple-spaced memorandum in his pocket. Marshall liked to be briefed without notes, so Ike summarized his strategy. He knew that the Philippines could not be saved, but he was also aware that the prestige of the US Army was at stake, and they could not simply abandon MacArthur. "General," Ike wrote, "it will be a long time before major reinforcements can go to the Philippines, longer than the garrison can hold out," but he insisted that the United States "do everything for them that is humanly possible. The people of China, of the Philippines, of the Dutch East Indies will be watching us. They may excuse failure, but they will not excuse abandonment." Ike's main conclusion was that the United States "must take great risks and spend any amount of money required. . . . We dare not fail." Marshall nodded. "I agree with you. Do your best to save them."

Marshall then gave Eisenhower a lesson in leadership that he would carry with him during his command and, later, into the presidency. "Eisenhower," he said, "this department is filled with able men who analyze their problems well but feel compelled to always bring them to me for final solution. I must have assistants who will solve their own problems and tell me later what they have done. The Philippines are your responsibility." Eisenhower recalled that he decided at that moment "to do my own work to the best of my ability and report to the general only situations of obvious necessity or when he personally sent for me."

On December 22 Prime Minister Churchill traveled to Washington for a meeting with Roosevelt. The two leaders created a Combined Chiefs of Staff to direct Allied military efforts. Once again Marshall turned to Eisenhower to draft a proposal for the new position. It was Christmas Day, but Ike hammered out a five-page draft before midnight. Both Marshall and President Roosevelt endorsed it. Eisenhower's clear thinking and strategic sense convinced Marshall that he should play a larger role in planning for the war.

In February 1942, when Marshall reorganized the War Department, he named Eisenhower as the chief of the Operations Division (OPD), where he was responsible for planning and directing all military operations. Marshall also promoted him to major general, bypassing 162 more senior men.

By that time, Ike had concluded that the United States did not have enough men or materiel to engage fully in a war against Japan and Germany. He thus needed to establish clear priorities. Although he initially supported rushing supplies to MacArthur, Eisenhower changed his mind, wanting to focus resources on defeating Hitler. "We've got to go to Europe to fight, and we've got to quit wasting resources all over the world—and still worse, wasting time," Eisenhower confided to his diary.

Over the next few months, Ike worked to the point of exhaustion. He started each morning with cigarettes and numerous cups of scalding black coffee. "Every day is the same—7:45 A.M. to 11:45 P.M.," he wrote in his diary. He worked sixteen-hour days, seven days a week, eating quick meals—usually a hot dog and black coffee—while he worked. Occasionally, his frustration boiled over. "Tempers are short! There are lots of amateur strategists on the job—and prima donnas everywhere," he divulged in his diary. "I'd give anything to be back in the field." He disliked his lack of freedom, complaining, "My God, how I hate to work by any method that forces me to depend on someone else."

When his father died in March 1942, Eisenhower remained in Washington. "War is not soft," he wrote. "It has no time to indulge even the deepest and most sacred emotions." On the evening of the funeral, he didn't stop working until seven thirty. "I haven't the heart to go on tonight," he confided in his diary. To make matters worse, Ike missed Mamie. Though she managed to move to Washington to be near her husband, they rarely got to see each other.

The stress and fatigue did not stop Eisenhower from excelling at his job. Marshall realized that he had discovered a natural leader and a consummate professional who met every challenge he confronted. "Eisenhower and Marshall made a dynamic team, among the best general officers the US Army ever produced," observed Hitchcock.

―――――――

On Sunday, December 7, 1941, Gerald Ford, a University of Michigan football standout and a recent graduate of Yale Law School, was working in his law office in Grand Rapids, Michigan. Driving home later that afternoon, he turned on his car radio and learned the horrifying news of Pearl Harbor. Up until that moment, Ford had been a committed isolationist, convinced that the United States should remain out of the conflict that was engulfing the globe. A member of the America First Committee, an isolationist lobby group, he shared the belief common in the Midwest that the two oceans would protect America from hostilities. Now everything flipped instantly. He walked into his home, looked at his parents, and said, "Mother, Dad, I am going to volunteer for the navy tomorrow morning."

The war also scrambled Ford's political ambitions. He had already been active supporting Republican Wendell Willkie's unsuccessful 1940 run against President Franklin D. Roosevelt. Now, as he reflected decades later in his memoirs, "There was no doubt in my mind that the United States would go to war, that the war would be long and that everything would change very quickly for me." Like JFK, Nixon, and Bush, Gerald Ford was driven by a strong sense of patriotism—the nation was at war, and he felt compelled to contribute to the effort.

Initially, Ford applied for a position with the Naval Intelligence Service, the same branch where JFK was serving, but due to the long wait time, he decided to apply as an instructor in the navy's V-5 (aviation cadet) program. In April 1942 he was commissioned as an ensign in the Naval Reserve and, after one month of training in Annapolis, Maryland, was promoted to lieutenant (junior grade) and sent to flight school at Chapel Hill, North Carolina, attended by 15,200 cadets. There he would serve as one of eighty-three instructors working in both the military and athletics departments, teaching basic seamanship, gunnery, and first aid while also coaching in football, baseball, and swimming.

Ford proved to be a natural. A strapping man with broad shoulders, deep-blue eyes, and blond hair, he stood six feet tall and weighed 199 pounds of solid muscle. He was born Leslie Lynch King Jr. in Omaha, Nebraska, on July 14, 1913, but three years later, his mother divorced his father and married Gerald Rudolph Ford, a paint store owner and the man whose name Leslie would adopt as his own. A standout high school football player, Ford gained admission to the University of Michigan in 1931. In his senior year, he became the team's starting center and received offers from two professional football teams, the Detroit Lions and the Green Bay Packers.

In his spare time, he tried to become a pilot, but his age (twenty-nine) and poor eyesight disqualified him. So, Ford was left with his cushy assignment—one that would have kept him far from the combat zone. "But there was a war going on," he recalled. "I wanted desperately to be part of it, so I wrote letters to everyone I knew, pleading for a billet on a ship."

He wrote one of those letters to a Grand Rapids acquaintance, Lieutenant Commander Harold B. Corwin. "Unfortunately, from my point of view I want to go to sea in some capacity and it looks like most of the men in this part of the Navy are going to be ashore for the duration," he confessed. He wanted to be on either a destroyer or a PT boat. It seemed to him that the few men who managed to get to sea duty possessed inside information on how to navigate the bureaucracy, so he asked Corwin to point him in the right direction. "I want to get to sea very badly and will do whatever is legitimate to get there." Corwin responded quickly, laying out the steps that Ford needed to take and promising to "put in a good word" for him.

The common thread running through the experiences of all future presidents was that Pearl Harbor represented an important turning point in their lives. Patriotism, sometimes combined with political calculation, prompted them to join the service and lobby to get closer to the front lines. The one exception was Hollywood actor Ronald Reagan.

"I have no intention of doing a chapter on 'Where Was I on December 7?'" Reagan wrote in his 1965 autobiography *Where's the Rest of Me?* "I was in bed sleeping—how exciting can I make that?" he admitted candidly. His brother's phone call awakened him, but unlike the other future presidents, thirty-year-old Reagan showed no great desire to join the fight after hearing the news. Yet the self-portrait that Reagan painted was of a man who wanted to fight but who was sidelined solely due to his weak eyesight. What Reagan failed to mention was that behind the scenes, his powerful agent and well-connected motion picture studio, Warner Bros., were lobbying to keep him safe in Hollywood.

For Reagan, as with millions of other American men, the call to arms came at an inconvenient time. He grew up in Dixon, Illinois, the son of an alcoholic father and a loving, nurturing mother. After graduating from Eureka College in 1932, Reagan started working as a radio announcer in Davenport, Iowa. Over time, he would become one of the most popular sports announcers in the Midwest, and in 1937 he accompanied the Chicago Cubs on a spring training trip to California. While there, he auditioned for a screen test at Warner Bros. Studios, which subsequently signed him to a $200-per-week contract. He made a series of B-grade movies until 1940, when he played Notre Dame University football star George Gipp—the Gipper—who died tragically at the age of twenty-five from pneumonia, in *Knute Rockne, All American*. When the bombs fell on Pearl Harbor, Reagan was convinced that he had finally achieved his dream of Hollywood stardom.

He and his wife, actress Jane Wyman, had a young child and had just moved into a new two-bedroom, two-bathroom, shingled ranch high above Sunset Boulevard. He had recently finished filming *Kings Row*, and there was already Oscar buzz about his performance. (The movie was nominated for an Academy Award for Best Picture in 1943 but did not win.) Even before the movie was released, the studio wanted to renegotiate his contract and triple his salary, but Reagan was so confident that it would be a success that he wanted to wait. Reagan's agent, Lew Wasserman, warned him that in the event of a war, he could be drafted. "We don't know how much time you have," Wasserman warned. "Let's get what we can while we can."

The previous summer, Reagan had been called to active duty as part of the first peacetime draft in American history. The 1940 law required all men between the ages of twenty-one and thirty-five to register. After Pearl Harbor, however, the age limit expanded to eighteen to sixty-four, though with only those between eighteen and forty-five being drafted. The law did not impact Eisenhower, Kennedy, and Johnson, who were already in uniform. Bush was too young, Ford was still in law school, and Nixon was exempt because of his Quaker faith. Reagan's agent wrote a letter that studio boss Jack Warner copied in his own writing and sent to the assistant secretary of war, requesting a deferment for Reagan on the grounds that his being drafted would create a serious financial loss for the studio and for the actor. In addition, the letter pointed out the advantages of having a Hollywood star wearing the uniform, given that at least one war-related film for Reagan was in the works. "Therefore," Wasserman's letter concluded, "in view of these facts, we respectfully request that said Ronald Reagan be placed in the war department reserve pool. In the event that this cannot be done, we also request that he be placed in a deferred class for so long a reasonable period of time as will be necessary to adjust our production schedules and rearrange our plans." Less than one week later, the War Department gave Reagan a temporary deferment until October 1941. A few more deferments followed until finally, in March 1942, his luck ran out.

That month, Reagan "received a letter that didn't even need opening: on the outside, stamped in red, were the words 'immediate action active duty.'" He was ordered to report for active duty in fourteen days at Fort Mason, in San Francisco, where he would work as a liaison officer loading convoys and troops bound for Australia.

Once he arrived at Fort Mason, Reagan was given a physical exam and failed the vision portion. One of the doctors said his eyesight was so bad that he would probably shoot his own general. Another doctor in the room concurred: "Yes, and you'd miss him." The final report read, "Confined to the continental limits, eligible for core area service command or war department overhead only."

Besides his poor eyesight, Reagan had powerful forces working on his behalf to keep him at home. The whole time he was away, Jack Warner was busy persuading the army to create an Army Air Corps motion picture unit. His efforts were boosted when the director of selective service, Colonel Lewis B. Hershey, issued a ruling in early February 1942 that the film industry was "an activity essential in certain instances to the national health, safety and interest, and in other instances to war production." Hershey therefore instructed California officials to defer "actors, directors, writers, producers, cameramen, sound engineers and other technicians" who could not be replaced or whose drafting "would cause a serious loss of effectiveness."

Thanks to Warner and Hershey, Reagan would spend only five weeks at Fort Mason before being transferred back home to Los Angeles and assigned to the newly created First Motion Picture Unit (FMPU).

As the war raged overseas, Reagan made movies during the day and slept in his own bed at night. Yet the studio went out of its way to project an image of Reagan as a war hero, fearing that if the public perceived him as getting preferential treatment, his image would be damaged. Jack Warner made sure that Reagan appeared on the cover of fan magazines in full uniform, grinning widely, with an American flag in the background.

CHAPTER 2

═══

"Boy! It's Rough up Here, Isn't It!"

JUNE 9, 1942
LAE, NEW GUINEA

The Japanese onslaught only gained momentum in the months after Pearl Harbor. President Roosevelt's speechwriter Robert Sherwood recalled later that the Japanese advance was so swift that the "pins on the walls of map rooms in Washington and London were usually far out of date." Japan planned to isolate Australia from the Allies by seizing the chain of islands that ran from the top of New Guinea through the Solomons and the Fijis to Samoa. Through the winter and early spring, one major city after another fell to the invading army. When Singapore surrendered on February 15, 1942, Winston Churchill described it as "the greatest disaster to British arms which our history records." By mid-March, Japanese forces overran Malaya, Java, and Borneo. They also landed on New Guinea, where American and Filipino troops eventually surrendered on May 6.

The crippled US fleet could do little to deter the Japanese advance. On February 27, 1942, the Allies lost five warships in the seven-hour Battle of the Java Sea. In May opposing American and Japanese carrier groups fought the punishing four-day Battle of the Coral Sea, the first in naval history carried out entirely by aircraft. Tactically, the Japanese gained another victory, sinking the carrier USS *Lexington* and damaging another carrier, the USS *Yorktown*. Strategically, however, the battle represented a victory for the Allies, who, for the first time, stopped a Japanese invasion force.

The mixed results did not deter Japan from trying to seize the Midway Islands in early June. The Japanese assembled a vastly superior fleet, but the Americans held a decisive intelligence edge. Navy code breakers had cracked Japan's codes, allowing them to anticipate the enemy's strategy. The United States mobilized 115 aircraft on Midway and combined that with the firepower of three aircraft carriers. Waves of US bombers dealt a devastating blow to the Japanese navy, sinking all of its heavy carriers and one heavy cruiser. The United States lost the USS *Yorktown* but saved Midway from invasion. The battle marked the first major American victory against Japan and a turning point in the war. With control of Midway, US forces could for the first time take the offensive against Japan.

Lyndon Johnson left Washington on May 2, 1942, two days before the Battle of the Coral Sea, en route to Honolulu before continuing to Auckland, New Zealand. He spent eight days visiting Allied facilities on Palmyra Island, Canton Island, the Fiji Islands, and New Caledonia as part of his inspection tour for FDR. On the last leg of the trip, he met Lieutenant Colonels Francis R. Stevens and Samuel E. Anderson, who were conducting their own inspection tours. The three men decided to travel together and work as a team. They soon formed a close bond, with Stevens and Anderson nicknaming Johnson "Johnnie."

Johnson's travels during this time are well documented, as he kept a diary and carried a movie camera to record his observations. "Like a lot of young men in a hurry to be where the action is," he reflected, "I was saying my goodbyes when my wife thrust a sixteen-millimeter camera into my hand and said, 'Send pictures.' I always followed orders from her." (For years after, dinner guests at the Johnson residence were required to watch the homemade movies, with LBJ providing narration.)

Over the next few weeks, Johnson quizzed everyone he met, from generals to the men who worked in the mess halls. He counted the number of American battleships, destroyers, cruisers, and submarines and realized that the Japanese had more of everything. It was one thing to read a report about shortages of gasoline, ammunition, food, and clothing. It was another to talk directly to the servicemen who were charged with fixing planes, storing ammunition, and trying to maintain some minimum standard of living. The one thing he heard mentioned more than anything else was the paucity of planes. "Give us planes, and we'll be home for Christmas," everyone told him.

Anderson described Johnson as "very quick to learn" and possessing "remarkable efficiency." "Commander Johnson was interested in the overall problem in the Southwest Pacific," Anderson related. "He was out to pinpoint and try to understand the nature of their difficulties. His mission—and this was absolutely clear—was to be able to return to the president with the kind of information he needed to carry through conflicting reports from the SWPA [Southwest Pacific Area], and to carry out his planning with a clearly objective analysis of the situation in the theater."

Johnson was not impressed by what he saw. In Palmyra he highlighted the "inadequate water supply," pointing out that there was "not a man on the island" who "wouldn't leave in a moment. Army food lousy. Army management about as bad. . . . Inadequate defense. No radio detector system." In the Fiji Islands, Johnson reported on the shortage of cigarettes and the incidence of disease: 11 cases of "clap" and "syphilis very prevalent."

On May 25 the three men met with General Douglas MacArthur, who had been pleading with Washington for more men and materiel. General Eisenhower, however, had already committed the United States to a Europe-first strategy, which infuriated MacArthur.

Johnson was awed by MacArthur. "He was always immaculately attired and looking much younger than his years. I can never forget those conferences because for several hours we were treated with an exposition rarely equaled in my experience." MacArthur spent two hours giving them an overview of the situation in the Pacific, and Johnson took four pages of notes.

The outlook certainly looked bleak. The opponent "had the most efficient air force in the world. They were disciplined, well trained, and deadly effective. The Japs have progressed at will and taken what they wanted because of only one thing," Johnson recorded MacArthur as saying. The American side of the ledger was deficient in every way. "Why do we have some of our best carriers in the Atlantic?" MacArthur asked, complaining that he had received fewer than a thousand planes and few replacement parts. According to Johnson's recollection of MacArthur's assessment: "We have been unable to go all out because of the limited equipment available. Therefore, our strategy has necessarily been to continue sniping attacks on the enemy and try to prevent him from consolidating and getting set, and this the planes and pilots have performed wonderfully. American pilots were courageous but inexperienced. Ground forces were in excellent shape but were inexperienced, lacking both training and seasoning."

Over the next few weeks, Johnson assured MacArthur through intermediaries that he would be a strong advocate for him back in Washington. But he wanted something in return: the opportunity to participate in a mission. Johnson was desperate to get a photo op from the front lines so that he could prove to skeptical constituents that he had seen combat. Although MacArthur could use a connection in Washington, especially someone who had the ear of President Roosevelt, he remained reluctant to send Johnson into the danger zone.

But Johnson finally got his chance on June 9, when the Twenty-Second and Nineteenth Bomb Groups planned their first major coordinated airstrike against the Japanese at Lae, an important enemy installation on New Guinea's northern coast, along with another called Salamaua. The Allies were based at Seven Mile Drome on the south shore of New Guinea. For the past few weeks, both sides had been taking turns raiding each other. By all accounts, Johnson faced a dangerous mission. He would likely encounter not only Japanese fighters but also an elaborate antiaircraft system on the ground. Japan's Zeros were faster and more maneuverable than American planes, and their pilots were better trained. During their most recent run on May 24, skilled Japanese pilots shot down five of six American bombers. On any given run, between 15 percent and 25 percent of US planes would not return. The steep mountains and potential for violent storms made for an even more perilous mission.

They would also be flying over shark-infested waters. Sometimes pilots would fly low and see fins poking through the water's surface.

When MacArthur heard that the congressman was planning on joining one of the raids, he instructed his aides to dissuade Johnson from the idea. He did not want Johnson to be the first congressman killed on a mission. LBJ insisted, though, saying that he had come to the Southwest Pacific to "see personally for the president just what conditions were like, and I cannot find out what they *are* like if I don't go along on this mission."

On the morning of June 9, Johnson, wearing khaki pants and a dark-blue navy jacket, was assigned to fly with Lieutenant Willis G. Bench on the Martin B-26 Marauder named *Wabash Cannonball*. Johnson climbed into the narrow cubicle behind the cockpit but stayed only for a minute before exiting the plane to relieve himself. When he climbed back on board, Francis Stevens had taken his seat. "Sorry, Johnnie," the lieutenant colonel said. "I'm staying here because I'm comfortable. Find yourself another plane."

Johnson walked over to another plane, the *Heckling Hare*, and asked the captain if he could fly with them. "Fine. Sure, you can go." Johnson then asked each member of the crew if he minded. Corporal Harry Baren, who manned the tail gun of the B-26, replied in a welcoming tone, "Heck, no. C'mon along if you want." The rest of the men all nodded their agreement.

Sergeant Claude A. McCredie asked Johnson if he wanted to see the bombs as they were being prepared for the mission. "He showed close interest in what we were doing," McCredie remembered. "In fact, I was startled at the questions he asked me." There had been other dignitaries who visited the base, but he found Johnson to be different. "You can tell at once if a man is interested or if he's just acting to put on a show. Most of that type would never dream of going along on a combat mission—not against Lae, especially. Down there at the time, the word *Lae* was almost synonymous with hell, and the odds were about one in four or five that you wouldn't make it back from the mission."

Johnson seemed curious about everything, and as they waited to board, he peppered the crew with questions. Most of all, he wanted to know if there was anything they needed. "Sure there is, Commander. Get us some fighters out here," Baren responded. "It would be a pleasure for those Zeros to have somebody to worry about, instead of our worrying about them. Fighters—that's what we need." Johnson then raised the issue of shortages of parts and supplies. "Listen, Commander, it is probably not as bad as you've heard," Baren replied. "It's at least twice as bad as anything you've heard."

Johnson also got an earful about MacArthur, whom the men were far less enamored of than he was. "I told Johnson," Baren reflected later, "that we couldn't have cared less about what the papers were saying about MacArthur back in the States. Out here, when the chips were down, he was probably the most unpopular man we knew of." Many men shared his view, Baren explained, because "a lot of our people were being killed without any real reason." They would see MacArthur's "fancy press pictures" and read reports that American forces were launching counterattacks against the Japanese, shooting down their Zeros. "Well," Baren said, "if we ever shot down as many planes as his headquarters used to say, we'd have wiped out the Jap air force in two months."

It was not until they were about to board the plane that Baren realized that Johnson really was accompanying them on the mission. He was shocked. "Commander, what are you doing here anyway?" he asked. Johnson laughed and told him he was going on the raid, to which Baren responded by calling Johnson "crazy." "We had pilots and crewmen who had made a few missions and then flat refused to fly over Lae or Rabaul anymore; they couldn't have cared less if they were court-martialed or not. To them, Lae especially was suicide." Baren could not understand why a congressman would want to participate in a mission to "get his head shot off."

Baren tried to convince Johnson to back out while they were still on the ground. "Commander, let me give you some advice," he said. "This ain't no milk run, believe me! You don't need to come along and get shot up to find out about conditions here, or the things we need; we'll tell you that if you're smart, Commander, you'll stay right here on the ground. You can get all the reports you want right from the operations tent—just like all the other people."

Despite Baren's attempts to persuade him, Johnson still insisted on going. "The only way a man could ever know what things were like was to go out and see it with his own eyes, and to experience it for himself," Johnson recalled saying.

"He sure didn't go much for secondhand information," recalled Sergeant McCredie. "He was absolutely determined to get on that mission with us."

According to flight records, the bombers took off at 8:51 A.M. for the two-hour, twenty-minute round trip to Lae, New Guinea. The group consisted of three Boeing B-17 heavy bombers, followed by twelve B-26s, divided into three V-shaped formations. The *Heckling Hare* was in the last formation. As they taxied for takeoff, Johnson sat in a small compartment usually reserved for the navigator and the radio operator. Once in the air, he positioned himself underneath a clear Plexiglas window on the top of the plane. From there, he had an impressive 360-degree view of the skies. He did not have to wait long for action.

Flying at an altitude of fourteen thousand feet, the *Heckling Hare* suddenly lost power. The right generator failed even before they made it to the bombing location. Reluctantly, pilot Walter H. Greer realized that they needed to abandon the mission. The plane was carrying a full crew and was loaded to its maximum weight, so it needed all the power it could muster. Greer jettisoned the bombs to lighten the load. Gradually, the plane fell back and out of formation.

Then someone yelled, "Here he comes!" They were now sitting ducks for the Japanese Zeros that were rapidly swarming around them. Being in a crippled plane surrounded by enemy aircraft was a recipe for disaster. Over the next few minutes, chaos ensued. "All the sudden we were getting hit all over the place," recalled a crew member. "You could feel the bullets banging against and into the plane. And those cannon shells; there wasn't any mistake about them! Captain Greer maneuvered the plane, swerving back and forth to avoid the Zeros that were pursuing him." "It sure was rough up there," waist gunner Lillis Walker remembered. "We were really getting shot up pretty bad. The Zeros stayed with us, working us over, a long-running fight while they kept whacking away at us."

Standing on a stool looking out through the Plexiglas bubble, Johnson had a bird's-eye view of the fight. According to Baren, Johnson was staring straight into the face of death. When Baren asked LBJ to move so that he could get to the radio, the congressman stepped down and exclaimed, "Boy! It's rough up here, isn't it!" Baren nodded but kept his attention focused on the Zeros circling them. Then Johnson asked, "You get kind of scared, don't you?" Baren looked him right in the eyes. "Yeah; I'm always scared up here."

The whole attack lasted between ten and thirteen minutes. By all accounts, Johnson remained unruffled throughout the ordeal, with Walker describing him as "just as calm as if we were on a sightseeing tour . . . just calm, and watching everything." McCredie echoed Walker, saying Johnson looked as "cool as a cucumber" even with bullets flying past and barely missing their target. Even biographer Robert Caro, a tough Johnson critic, described his conduct on the *Heckling Hare* as "bold and courageous, nonchalant in the face of danger."

When the *Heckling Hare* finally landed, officers rushed toward the plane to see if their VIP was safe. Johnson grinned and said simply, "It's been very interesting." The *Wabash Cannonball*, the plane Johnson had boarded originally, was not as lucky. It had been hit by cannon fire and crashed into the ocean, killing Colonel Stevens and the entire crew.

The next day, Johnson began the long journey back home, with a stopover in Melbourne on June 18 to meet again with MacArthur and report his findings. MacArthur was angry that Johnson had gone on such a dangerous mission, but was relieved about his safe return. In his diary, LBJ described MacArthur as "very sad" and saying in a low voice, "Glad to see two fellows here where three were last. It was a mistake of the head to go on combat mission, but it did justice to your heart. It was just what I would have done." After listening to Johnson for almost an hour, the general announced that he was posthumously awarding Stevens the Distinguished Service Cross and LBJ the Silver Star, the nation's third-highest combat decoration.

The Silver Star citation read:

While on a mission of obtaining information in the Southwest Pacific Area, Lieutenant Commander Johnson, in order to obtain personal knowledge of combat conditions, volunteered as an observer on a haz-

ardous aerial combat mission over hostile positions in New Guinea. As our planes neared the target area, they were intercepted by eight hostile fighters. When at this time the plane in which Lieutenant Commander Johnson was an observer developed mechanical trouble and was forced to turn back alone, presenting a favorable target to the enemy fighters, he evidenced marked coolness in spite of the hazard involved. His gallant action enabled him to return with valuable information.

Johnson's brush with death was not over, though. On the first leg of the trip home, he developed a fever. Instead of resting and getting treatment, he dismissed it as a cold and insisted on continuing his journey because the president was waiting for his report. By the time they landed in the Fiji Islands, Johnson's condition had worsened. His fever spiked to 103.6 degrees; he was shaking uncontrollably and grew delirious. A doctor who examined him said he was seriously, perhaps critically, ill with pneumonia and moved him to a hospital, where he was treated, and remained for a few days before traveling to Pearl Harbor. By July 10, he was recovered and back in Washington.

Clearly Johnson did not deserve the Silver Star. If anyone deserved such an award, it was the pilot who successfully navigated the plane in the face of withering Japanese fire. But Johnson was the only man on the *Heckling Hare* to receive the medal—something that the other crew members learned about only in 1964, with the publication of Martin Caidin and Edward Hymoff's account of the events in their book *The Mission*. It is not difficult to speculate about MacArthur's motives. He needed allies in Washington, and he gave LBJ the Silver Star to consummate their agreement that Johnson would be his advocate.

The big winner, however, was LBJ, who could now go back to his constituents and say that he had not only been in combat but also received a medal for his courage. Although Johnson seemed to have pangs of guilt and even drafted a letter saying that he could not accept the award, the benefits were too good to pass up. Even before he left Melbourne, American papers were reporting on his heroism and composure in battle. Texas newspapers echoed Johnson's account that he "was under fire." "Thrilling Experiences Recounted Before Local Friends," shouted the *Brenham Banner-Press* on July 28, 1942. When in December, six months after the event, a reporter questioned Johnson about his combat experience, he responded, "I was out there in May, June, and part of July. We exchanged greetings quite often. They paid us very busy visits every day for a time." The exaggerations only grew as time passed. He claimed that the crewmen nicknamed him "Raider," and that a few had been wounded during the exchange.

Once back home, the newly minted war hero lost no time stumping the campaign trail. MacArthur did not have any Silver Stars to pin on Johnson, so he went to a local Army-Navy store and purchased one that he brought back to Texas for campaign rallies. Caro noted that Johnson had the Silver Star presented to him and pinned on his jacket repeatedly, "as if for the first time." Claiming the nickname "Raider Johnson," LBJ also told audiences that he saw fourteen Zeros shot down in flames. He would wear the small lapel pin for the rest of his career. Journalist Ronnie Dugger wrote that the medal was "one of the least deserved but most often displayed Silver Stars in American military history."

Johnson's mission, and his later efforts to exaggerate it, revealed his obsession with filtering every problem through a political lens and his faith in his ability to bend truth to his will. About his war experience, a friend noted that Johnson "could convince himself of anything, even something that wasn't true." That ability, biographer Caro noted, "proves to be the single most significant implication of his war service." That quality would reemerge when he was in the White House two decades later and would be derisively referred to as the "credibility gap."

ON JULY 16, 1942, JOHNSON REMOVED HIS UNIFORM, WAS RELEASED from active duty, and returned to Congress. As expected, FDR had ordered all members of Congress in uniform to return to work or resign their seats. LBJ's top priority when he got home was to share his findings with the president. American planes in the Pacific, he reported, were infinitely inferior to the Japanese fighters. He made the same case that MacArthur had been making for months. They were so low on parts that many airmen were reluctant to fly the planes. He reserved his harshest criticism for military leaders in the region who were fighting the war "from the ground or from behind a desk."

Yet Roosevelt had grown tired of hearing MacArthur's gripes even when they were coming from his personal emissary to the region. Although Washington spent an enormous amount of money in the Pacific, Roosevelt had settled on prioritizing the fight against Hitler in Europe over the battle with Japan. He showed little interest in Johnson's report and brushed him off.

Unable to convince Roosevelt, LBJ took his complaints to the public. On a July 26 radio broadcast, he demanded that "indecisive, stupid, selfish, and incompetent generals, admirals, and others in high military positions" be removed and that the nation provide its fighting men with better equipment. "We must make it clear that it is no longer a crime to cut red tape. We are going to have to give our men leadership and equipment superior to that of any in the world." The following month, he told another radio audience that the nation needed to purge its "indecisive, unimaginative, nonaggressive" military leaders.

Next, Johnson took his message to the House floor, asserting that his wartime experience had taught him that civilian leadership needed to be skeptical of everything the military told them. He spoke about the imperative of ridding the armed forces of "an incompetence among our generals, admirals, and others in high military positions," then went on to condemn the "deadwood" at home, of "men who have become entrenched in power," men whose "notions" of combat were "dangerously outmoded." In short, LBJ argued that for America to win, it needed to streamline its war machine and provide superior leadership for its fighting men. Unfortunately, it was a lesson that he would forget when he waged his own unwinnable war while president.

On July 27, a few weeks after Lyndon Johnson returned from the Pacific, John F. Kennedy had recovered enough to be transferred to the Naval Reserve Midshipmen's School at Northwestern University outside of Chicago. There he would take classes to learn the basics of seamanship.

On the way there, he stopped in DC to see Inga, who by now had moved on and refused to sleep with him. She was shocked by his appearance. "He is going on active sea duty," she told a friend on a call recorded secretly by the FBI. But he looked "like a limping monkey. . . . He can't walk at all." She found it "ridiculous" that he was still on active duty. At any time, Kennedy could have used his many physical ailments, especially his back and ulcerative colitis, as excuses—but he never did. He was now getting some relief from corticosteroids, which helped in the short run but likely aggravated his back and adrenal problems in the long run. (Two years after the war, doctors diagnosed Jack with Addison's disease, which resulted from a hormonal imbalance of the adrenal glands.)

Kennedy ended up unimpressed with the school. In a letter to his close friend Lem Billings, he complained, "This goddamn place is worse than Choate," the exclusive Connecticut prep school where he and Billings roomed together in the mid-1930s. But he kept his sights on the bigger picture, saying, "[T]his thing is bigger than you or I—it's global—so I'll string along." It was here that Jack became fascinated with PT boats and decided that he wanted to command one. The navy used the fast, heavily armored ships to harass enemy shoreline installations, disrupt supply lines, and attack larger ships. Kennedy was particularly impressed by the exploits of two naval officers, John Harllee and John D. Bulkeley—both PT boat boosters. Bulkeley had already earned a Congressional Medal of Honor for rescuing General MacArthur from the Philippines in early 1942. Thanks to Harllee and Bulkeley, PT boats appeared glamorous and heroic. There was an added benefit for Kennedy: The navy was desperate for sailors to man the boats. The two instructors promised an "early command" and lots of action—exactly what Kennedy was looking for. He understood that PT boats were little more than floating bombs made up of plywood on top of large gas tanks. But the danger only made an assignment on one of the boats even more attractive to him.

Given his back and other health issues, Kennedy's chances of being chosen for PT duty should have been slim. But his father intervened once again. Joe Sr. invited Bulkeley to lunch and asked if he could get his son one of the fifty slots available for PT school (out of one thousand applicants). Bulkeley recalled that Joe "wanted Jack to get into PT boats for the publicity and so forth, to get the veteran's vote after the war." Whatever the reason, Joe Kennedy was thrilled when Bulkeley agreed to get Jack accepted into the service. But he made one final request: that his son not be sent someplace "too deadly."

On October 1, 1942, Kennedy traveled to Melville, Rhode Island, a stone's throw from the family compound in Hyannis Port, for an intensive eight-week class on how to command a boat.

The constant theme in Kennedy's life up until this point was his relentless desire to be on the front lines and the intense pain from which he suffered. "Jack came home," Joe Sr. wrote after Jack had spent some days in Hyannis Port before heading to his assignment, "and between you and me is having terrific trouble with his back. . . . I don't see how he can last a week in that tough grind of torpedo boats." A roommate observed that Jack "was in a lot of pain, he slept on that damn plywood board all the time, and I don't remember when he wasn't in pain."

Despite his agony, Jack performed exceptionally well, so much so that the school wanted him to stay behind as an instructor. Kennedy resented that prospect. "Boy, I got shafted," he complained bitterly to friends. He did not endure all this suffering to be sidelined as an instructor in Rhode Island. He appealed the decision but lost. So, once again he tapped into his family network. He knew that his father would not support him and instead turned to his grandfather John Francis "Honey Fitz" Kennedy, a former mayor of Boston, who set up a meeting with Senator David L. Walsh of Massachusetts, the chairman of the Senate Naval Affairs Committee and a Kennedy family friend. The appeal got Kennedy out of Rhode Island, but instead of being sent to the Pacific, he found himself on patrol duty near the Panama Canal. So, Kennedy turned a second time to Walsh, who wrote a letter on his behalf.

All the string-pulling paid off. On March 6, 1943, Kennedy boarded a troopship in San Francisco. He would eventually find himself in the Solomon Islands, where Japanese and US naval forces were engaged in a ferocious battle for control.

On August 6, 1942, George H. W. Bush began active duty as an aviation cadet. Normally, the navy required at least two years of college to be accepted to aviation school, but the navy needed pilots, and it needed them immediately, so it dropped the college requirement and cut down training to an intensive ten months.

For the next eleven months, Bush crisscrossed the country from air base to air base, learning the skills necessary to fly a plane in combat. His first stop was the quaint university town of Chapel Hill, North Carolina, where the navy established a preflight school to train naval pilots. The first cadets enrolled in May 1942, with about three hundred more men showing up every two weeks. Among those in Bush's class was Ted Williams, the Boston Red Sox star slugger who'd hit .406 in 1941. And although there is no evidence they ever met, there was another future president at Chapel Hill at the same time. Gerald Ford had begun his navy service as an instructor there in May, whipping young recruits into shape and conducting strength and conditioning classes.

We have a good sense of what Bush was experiencing, because he wrote daily letters to his parents, a few friends, and Barbara. (Unfortunately, nearly all of his letters to Barbara have gone missing, but the others survived.) Taken together, the letters reveal a young man driven by patriotic fervor and a sense of duty to defend the nation. He was also still a teenager, and so his letters are filled with the youthful enthusiasm of a boy learning to play with a new toy. He described his feelings of wonderment as he advanced through each stage of the process, from first taking the controls, to flying without instruments during the day and night—"the biggest thrills of my life." When he climbed into the cockpit for the first time, his legs were shivering, but "once in the air I was completely cool much to my surprise" and "completely confident for some reason." At one point during the training, he learned how to strafe ships. "What a thrill to shoot in and then pull out over the deck." He recounted the exhilaration of coming in low, just above the water "at terrific speeds turning and twisting. Nothing like it."

The training was difficult, and he missed his family and friends, but Bush never doubted his decision to join the navy. Despite the challenges, he "wouldn't change positions with any fellow in civilian life. The Navy itself is great," he observed, "but what we are here for is even greater." Like JFK, Bush performed so well that the navy asked if he would stay stateside for a few additional months to train new recruits. He was not interested, though. "I might as well be in college," he wrote. "My heart is set on getting out with the fleet or at least to some combat zone." Offered the choice between carrier- or land-based assignments, Bush chose aircraft carriers and was sent to Fort Lauderdale, Florida. There he was introduced to the TBM Avenger bomber, the navy's largest single-engine bomber, and the one that he would fly in combat. The aircraft required three crew members—a pilot, gunner, and radioman—and it carried a two-thousand-pound payload.

This was not Bush's first time away from home, but at Andover he had been surrounded by privileged students like himself. Not in the navy. He described his class as a "queer one—a pretty tough lot, but some really swell fellows also some pretty cheap characters." He often pointed out the differences between educated men who had morals as opposed to those with little education, money, or principles. The behavior of the less-educated men bothered him. While he found navy propaganda that demeaned the Japanese people and their culture "sickening," he noted that some "fellows swallow it all." They were, he observed, those with "below average intelligence." The intelligent guys knew why they were fighting, Bush believed, and did not need "to be 'brainwashed'" in order to be motivated.

His main complaint, and one that he returned to often, was about the bad behavior among many of the men. Gambling was common, even though it violated the rules. "I can quite frankly say I have not and do not intend to get in on it." He believed that those who gambled were "the ones who really have never had a thing." He was especially judgmental of the promiscuousness that he witnessed. Many of the women living near the base "believe in satisfying any sexual urge." These girls, he concluded, "were not prostitutes, but just girls without any morals at all." He admitted to having the same urges but allegedly knew how to control them because he had been raised and taught differently.

In response to his mother's pointing out that he was too judgmental and some of his opinions "unjust," Bush stood his ground. "We are going through a period of relapse as far as morals go," he wrote to her. He recognized that the emotional distress of the war was partly to blame, but for him that simply was "no excuse." "Married women with husbands over-seas fighting are as great offenders as common playgirls. The whole thing is almost sickening." Even in 1943, Bush was complaining about the breakdown of traditional values. "A society where faithlessness is replac-ing devotion and where immorality is replacing decency surely cannot be a permanent fixture of a civilized community."

And then there was Barbara, who seemed like an ideal contrast to all this perceived indecency. Although their letters to each other went miss-ing, she was a constant topic of conversation in his correspondence with his mother. "I miss her more than she knows, Nance," he confessed to his sister. "I don't know why but she seems so perfect a girl—beautiful, gen-tle, a wonderful sense of humor. . . . I think of her all the time and would love to see her." He even had "BAR" painted on the side of his plane in white.

By the end of the year, Bush had finished his training and was ready for combat. In December 1943 the navy assigned him to the carrier USS *San Jacinto*, and he thereafter made his way to the Pacific.

━━━━━━━

Richard Nixon described his first week in the navy as "the longest I've ever known." He was not physically prepared for the rigors of training, and he missed Pat terribly. It was the first time they had been apart since marriage. He wrote to her every day, professing his love. "I may not say much when I'm with you—*but all of me loves all of you all the time.*"

After two months of training, Nixon listed "ships and stations" as his first choice for duty. But from the beginning, the navy believed that Nixon was best suited for an intelligence or administrative position. On October 9, 1942, he received the order to travel to Iowa's Naval Air Station Ottumwa within five days.

He did little to hide his disappointment. "I expected to be assigned to a battle fleet in the South Pacific or the North Atlantic," he reflected. "When I reported for duty, I found that the station was still under con-struction. Its uncompleted runway stopped abruptly in the middle of a cornfield."

The Nixons made the best of a bad situation. Pat got a job as a bank teller, and Richard served as an aide to the executive officers. In addition, he volunteered to host a radio show and helped other officers with their tax returns. While Nixon would later write that "the warmth and friendliness of our new neighbors" helped them overcome his disappointment over the assignment, these California transplants never truly adjusted to the harsh Midwest winter.

Throughout his entire time in Iowa, Nixon lobbied for an assignment on a ship. One day he happened to see a notice calling for officers under the age of twenty-nine to apply for sea duty. "I was exactly twenty-nine," he recalled, "and I sent the application in immediately." With the recent losses in the Pacific, the navy was desperate for men. He and Pat discussed the situation, and while she worried for his safety, she supported his decision to play a more active role in the war.

On March 30, 1943, Nixon formally requested a new assignment. "It is requested that I be transferred from duty at the US Naval Air Station, Ottumwa, to sea duty," Nixon wrote the head of navy personnel. He listed his "seagoing" experiences as operating "small boats off coast of Southern California" and a "one month cruise" to the Caribbean. The request was granted.

This would be the second time that Nixon left behind a comfortable position far from the battlefield for a spot near the front lines. Like LBJ, Nixon had politics on his mind. He knew that serving in the war, especially in combat, would boost his political career after the war. But unlike LBJ, politics was not central to his reasoning. Like many other future presidents, Nixon was driven by a patriotic desire to contribute to the war effort. Though he would never reach the battlefield, it was not for lack of trying.

In May 1943, he received orders to travel to San Francisco for his overseas assignment. He and Pat packed up their car and drove west to visit family and friends before Richard went off to the Pacific. He described his visit with his parents as "painful." He believed that his Quaker mother and grandmother opposed his decision to fight and would have preferred that he join the Red Cross and participate in the war effort without violating their pacifist principles. He understood their position but felt that he "could not sit back while my country was being attacked." The problem with Quaker pacifism, he reflected, "was that it could work only if one were fighting a civilized, compassionate enemy." Those ideas were not relevant when dealing with the evils posed by Germany and Japan.

On May 31, the entire family went to the train station in Los Angeles to see Richard and Pat off. "As Pat and I stood on the wooden block getting ready to board the train, I turned to take one last look. I think we all realized that we might never see each other again." His stoic mother held in her emotions, but his father sobbed uncontrollably.

After that emotional farewell, Nixon boarded the transport USS *President Monroe* for his trip to the Pacific.

Meanwhile, the situation in Europe had not improved much. The major Allied powers—Britain, Russia, the United States, and China—faced a bleak situation. The Axis powers—Germany, Italy, and Japan—possessed well-trained infantry and war-tested armies. On land, the German panzer divisions, formations of tanks, traveled as far as fifty miles a day and mobilized firepower unequaled by the West. German wolf packs of submarines controlled the oceans. In the first eleven months of 1942, Hitler's dreaded U-boats sank a total of eight million tons of shipping. At one point, the Axis powers controlled one-third of the world's population.

General George Marshall delegated to Dwight Eisenhower the responsibility of translating Roosevelt's "Hitler First" strategy into a concrete battle plan. The situation on the ground in Europe had grown more complicated since June 1941, when Hitler made the fateful decision to turn against Germany's former ally, the Soviet Union. Overnight, the führer transformed a one-front struggle against a weakened Britain and a still-neutral United States into a two-front conflict. He sent 3.3 million men into Russia, and in less than a month, they had advanced more than three hundred miles into Soviet territory.

With the Soviets now fighting more than two hundred German divisions on the Eastern Front, Joseph Stalin desperately pleaded with Churchill and Roosevelt to relieve the pressure by opening a second front: a massive Allied military invasion of western Europe.

Initially, the United States responded favorably to the Russian request, with Eisenhower and Marshall developing a specific plan to achieve that goal. Stage one, code-named Bolero, called for the massive buildup of Allied troops in England. Stage two, code-named Roundup, called for organizing an assault on the French coast—somewhere between Calais and Le Havre—with a target date of April 1, 1943. It would be an enormous operation, requiring 48 divisions, 5,800 combat aircraft, and 7,000 landing craft. After a long discussion, Roosevelt gave final approval to the plan with only a few minor changes.

But Eisenhower soon grew dissatisfied by the slow pace of preparing for the operation. "Our planning for BOLERO is not progressing!" he vented in his diary on May 21, 1942. Marshall was also frustrated, and in June he sent Eisenhower to England to assess the American command structure's ability to carry out such an ambitious plan. Ike recalled that Marshall was concerned because "American officers on duty in London were not familiar with the broader problems and objectives of the War Department." After meeting with senior commanders, Eisenhower agreed that they "were definitely in a back eddy." Ike returned to Washington and informed Marshall that there needed to be a single commanding general who would have absolute authority over all branches of the service. On June 8, the day before LBJ's mission in New Guinea, Eisenhower presented his plan to Marshall.

"Does this directive suit you?" Marshall asked. "Are you satisfied with it?"

"Yes, sir," Ike responded.

"I'm glad it suits you," Marshall said, "because these are the orders you are going to operate under."

"Me?" Eisenhower asked.

"You. You are in command of the European theater."

Ike's appointment was announced on June 11, and three weeks later, he was promoted to lieutenant general, catapulted ahead of sixty-six major generals. He now ranked eighteenth among all officers on active duty.

Almost overnight, Eisenhower was transformed into an international celebrity, his image gracing the front pages of British newspapers. He looked like a US soldier from central casting, standing erect with broad shoulders offset by his relaxed smile, sandy gray hair, and gray-blue eyes.

He cultivated the press, which reciprocated by giving him positive coverage. *The New York Times* noted that Ike "talked informally off the record with British and American correspondents, giving an excellent demonstration of the art of being jovially outspoken without saying much of anything."

Even early in his command, Eisenhower learned the importance of using his warm and outgoing personality to build relationships with the key players. Leadership, he insisted, was about more than strategy and tactics; it was also about building relationships based on trust. That was especially true of his rapport with Churchill. The two men talked nearly every day, and Ike was a frequent visitor at the British prime minister's country home, Chequers, occasionally spending the night. But it was not just Churchill who was swayed by Ike's charisma. He impressed other members of the British high command as well. "I liked him at once," recalled Admiral Sir Andrew B. Cunningham. "He struck me as being completely sincere, straightforward, and very modest."

It was in the early days of his time in London that Eisenhower forged the philosophy of leadership that would carry the Allies to victory and later shape his approach to the presidency. "The one quality that can be developed by studious reflection and practice is the leadership of men," Eisenhower wrote to his son, John. And leadership required optimism because stress and strain could "wear away" at a leader's confidence, he observed. In that case, a commander had to "preserve optimism in himself and his command. Without confidence, enthusiasm, and optimism in the command, victory is scarcely obtainable." Biographer Stephen Ambrose observed that Ike always did his best "from that moment to the end of his life, to conceal with a big grin the ache in his bones and the exhaustion in his mind."

During a meeting on June 25, 1942, Eisenhower laid out his expectations for the staff, ones that reflected the values he lived by. "That an atmosphere of the utmost earnestness coupled with determined enthusiasm and optimism was to characterize every member of this staff and every subordinate command in England; that pessimism and defeatism would not be tolerated, and that any person who could not rise above the recognized obstacles and bitter prospects that lie in store for us, has no recourse but to ask for instant release from this theater." Being positive also encompassed a casual but responsible attitude. He insisted that "all staff work was to be characterized by an absence of formality." He also told officers they did not need to abide by the usual chain of command but were expected "to solve their own problems wherever possible and not to get in the habit of passing the buck up."

The fact that the British press and leadership liked Eisenhower gave him an advantage in dealing with his first—and perhaps most formidable—task: overcoming the enormous cultural, political, and military differences between the American and British armies and fusing them into a single fighting force. He began by organizing his command structure so that US officers reported to a British officer and vice versa. He came down hard on American officers who got out of line. When told of how an inebriated American officer questioned the courage of British soldiers, Eisenhower "went white with rage" and threatened to "make the son of a bitch swim back to America." Respect needed to apply on both sides in order for victory to be achieved.

It did not take long for Eisenhower to sense that Churchill, who was never enthusiastic about an invasion across the English Channel, was beginning to backtrack on his promises. "There seems to be some confusion of thought as to the extent of the British commitment," Eisenhower wrote Marshall. He was right. The enormous battlefield losses during World War I weighed on Churchill. He convinced Roosevelt to delay the second front and proposed instead a joint British-American landing in the "soft underbelly" of the enemy in North Africa and Italy, code-named Operation Torch. Eisenhower strongly opposed the mission, believing that the best way to end the war was to strike at the heart of the German war machine. But not only did Roosevelt overrule him, he placed Eisenhower in charge of the operation. Ike later described the day of the president's decision, July 22, 1942, as "the blackest day in history."

The assault would test Eisenhower's organizational and leadership skills. Convoys headed for England had to be redirected to the Mediterranean, and three American divisions in England would now be reshipped to the new battlefront. Those troops, which had been training for fighting in northern Europe, also had to be retrained for mountain and desert warfare. At the time, Torch was the largest amphibious operation ever attempted, and Eisenhower, who had no combat experience and had been in a leadership position only for a few months, had just two months to pull it all together. Despite his doubts, Eisenhower committed himself to making the mission a success and proving that American and British forces could work together.

The invasion commenced on November 8, 1942, and dragged on for seven months. Eventually the Allied forces overwhelmed Italian and German forces, but it took much longer than expected, with unacceptably high casualties. The British military command blamed Eisenhower for making poor strategic and political decisions, moving too cautiously, and allowing the Germans to fortify their positions. Churchill complained that Ike's army was "all tail and no teeth," and a British general wrote that "Eisenhower as a general is hopeless!" Yet Eisenhower still managed to maintain the support of the two men who mattered most: Roosevelt and Marshall.

Ultimately, the extraordinary capability of the retooled US economy to produce weapons of war provided the key advantage in the campaign. Between 1941 and 1943, America attained more than an 800 percent increase in military production. By then, the United States was responsible for half of all the manufacturing in the world, constructing tanks, airplanes, and ships in record time. At its peak, the nation built a ship a day and an airplane every five minutes. General Lucius Clay, who handled military procurement, observed: "We were never able to build a tank as good as the German tank. But we made so many of them that it didn't really matter."

Having survived the North African campaign, Ike now needed to acquiesce to another British strategic demand and encroach upon Italy. The invasion of Sicily in the summer of 1943 suffered from many of the same problems that plagued the earlier campaign, but once again the Allies emerged victorious. Sicily surrendered on August 16, clearing the path for the Italian campaign, which dragged on into the winter. But by now, Roosevelt had bigger plans for Eisenhower.

In late 1942 the government gave the First Motion Picture Unit (FMPU) at Warner Bros. permission to go back to making commercial movies, as long as it continued to produce films for the military. The studio's first big commercial film was *Casablanca,* starring Humphrey Bogart. The role of Rick Blaine was originally supposed to go to Ronald Reagan, but the military initially insisted that he could not make for-profit movies while still in uniform.

Reagan was bitterly disappointed. He had hoped to follow up the success of *Kings Row* with another major Hollywood hit. *Casablanca* would win the Oscar for Outstanding Motion Picture in 1943 and reignited Bogart's career, transforming him into one of the most popular actors in Hollywood. Reagan experienced a second blow that year when *Kings Row* failed to win any Oscar nominations. As Reagan put it years later, "*Kings Row* was the only picture I was in for which there was ever any talk of getting an Academy Award. But that year, Warner Bros. also made *Yankee Doodle Dandy*, and in those days, the studios usually got behind only one picture in the Oscar race."

Reagan badgered his agent and the studio to get him in a commercial feature. In February 1943 Warners arranged for Reagan to appear in *This Is the Army,* which had been a successful Orson Welles Broadway musical. "It was a thrill for me to get away from the desk and feel once again that I was part of the picture business," Reagan reflected. The movie, loaded with seventeen patriotic songs, including Kate Smith's "God Bless America," was enormously successful, taking in $10 million and putting Reagan back again at the top of the industry popularity polls.

The actor hoped that *This Is the Army* would open the door to other big movies, but when none came his way, he stayed busy doing more US Army propaganda films. His most notable movie was the twenty-six-minute *The Rear Gunner* (1943), which told the story of a friendly Air Corps lieutenant, played by Reagan, charged with training a wayward farm boy to become a gunner. The film ended with the boy becoming a hero and winning the Distinguished Service Cross. "It was twenty-six minutes of pure Hollywood corn," observed the journalist Bob Spitz. But it hit a nerve with young men, who sometimes rushed from the theater to the local recruitment office.

The movie was so successful that Reagan was asked to perform in dozens of short films, either playing himself on-screen or serving as narrator.

In *Recognition of the Japanese Zero Fighter* (1943), the actor played a hot-shot pilot who needed to learn to distinguish between an American P-40 aircraft and a Japanese Zero. The next two years brought *For God and Country* (1943), *Target Tokyo* (1945), and *The Fight for the Sky* (1945). The short films, which were shown in theaters before the main feature, may not have been professionally rewarding, but they increased Reagan's public profile. Only Errol Flynn received more fan mail than Ronald Reagan. (The studio paid Reagan's mother $75 a week to answer the mail.)

Reagan spent much of 1944 narrating the FMPU's Special Film Project 152 series: simulations of what American pilots would see when they started their raids over Japan. Special-effects people built a replica of Tokyo. "Above this they rigged a crane and camera mount and could photograph the miniature," Reagan recalled, "giving the effect on the screen of movies taken from a plane traveling at any prescribed height and speed."

"Gentlemen," his voice intoned, "you are approaching the coast of Honshu on a course of three hundred degrees. You are now twenty miles offshore. To your left, if you are on course, you should be able to see a narrow inlet. To your right . . ." He would then mention some of the landmarks guiding the bombers to their target. Finally: "Bombs away." The films were used to train pilots at American bases in the Pacific.

Although most of the movies were filmed in Culver City, a short commute from the Reagan home in the Hollywood Hills, the studio was eager to create the impression that Reagan was overseas fighting with the troops. It had reason to be concerned. Many actors who avoided service saw their careers suffer as a result. But the studio still worried that if it appeared Reagan was receiving preferential treatment by remaining at home, the response would be the same.

The studio's public relations team worked overtime to feed the fan magazines stories that made it appear that Reagan was overseas. When Reagan was sent back from San Francisco to Los Angeles, the popular fan magazine *Modern Screen* wrote the "inside story" of how the actor had been sent temporarily back to Burbank to make movies. "It's nine months now since Ronald Reagan said, 'so long, button nose,' to his wife and baby and went off to join his regiment," it declared in January 1943. The article went on to describe Jane Wyman's loneliness as she looked around for her husband before realizing that he was gone, with the clear implication that he was off to war along with thousands of other men. The studio orchestrated a scene where Reagan arrived for the premiere of *This Is the Army* as if he were returning from the front lines. Warner Bros. even released publicity shots of Jane writing her husband letters as if he was fighting abroad. Of course, Reagan was home the whole time. But a reader of popular magazines would think he was fighting in the trenches abroad.

The magazines also presented Ronald and Jane as the ideal American couple. Reagan was "the perfect American officer who had gone to war," one fan magazine wrote, "despite the responsibility of a wife and daughter." The studio depicted Wyman as a dutiful wife who spent her time at home tending to her heroic husband and their adopted child, Maureen.

But it was all an illusion. Wyman continued making movies throughout the war and had no desire to be a housewife. The war altered the power relationship between the two, something Reagan had trouble accepting. Almost overnight, Reagan went from being one of the highest-paid actors in Hollywood to living off his $250-per-month military salary. While Reagan's career stagnated, Wyman's took off. Reagan had a hard time accepting that his wife was the primary breadwinner, and Wyman resented that Reagan could not provide for them the way she had expected. "By 1945, the distance between them stretched beyond the professional," wrote Reagan biographer Marc Eliot, "they were barely speaking to each other and technically no longer living under the same roof." (Jane Wyman filed for divorce in 1948.)

Reagan had lots of downtime, along with long periods of mundane paperwork and administrative duties. He filled much of the time by reading. Not only did he comb through a handful of newspapers every day, but also he became a devoted reader of *Reader's Digest*, which would have a profound impact on his thinking. The homespun stories and inspirational pieces provided him with a broad understanding of what was taking place in the world while showing how to appeal to an audience by employing a breezy style filled with heroic tales and clever anecdotes.

In many ways, the war served as a turning point in Reagan's life. It provided him with the opportunity to learn about politics while also giving him experience as a military propagandist. He would read stories and then share them with just about anyone who would listen. Screenwriter Irving Wallace, who was stationed with Reagan, called him "a lovable scatterbrain." He was, Wallace concluded, a "man who parrots things—shallow and affable." Even his wife could not escape his lectures. "All he talks about morning, noon, and night is world affairs," she complained.

Not only did Reagan develop a new interest in politics, but his views were beginning to evolve. Before the war, he had been a staunch liberal and a strong supporter of Franklin Roosevelt, but his encounters with the military bureaucracy made him question his faith in government. In this sense, his experience was similar to that of Richard Nixon, although Nixon had been a Republican before the war.

During the war, Reagan explained in a 1971 letter, his job required him to work closely with the "federal civilian bureaucracy." Like Nixon, he did not like what he witnessed. "I saw empire building and was disgusted by the smug, 'business as usual' attitude of the bureaucrat—the professional government career man at a time when young men were dying all over the world." That experience, combined with his battling Communists in Hollywood—the "most evil force that has ever confronted decent men in the entire history of mankind"—and a brief exposure to the bungling leadership of the British Labour Party while filming a movie in London, convinced the future president that less government is always better. "If government has any real excuse for even existing," he wrote, "it is that government assures us that it will mobilize the full collective power of all the people to defend the rights of even the least-individual among us if that individual's rights are being unjustly denied, *anywhere in the world.*"

To illustrate his growing skepticism about government, Reagan told the story of a captain who came to his office and complained that he needed a new secretary; his current one could not even spell the word *cat*. It seemed simple to solve. Reagan invited the person in charge of civilian personnel to his office and asked the captain to share the story with her. She listened sympathetically, then said, "All right, I'll draw up the papers, and you sign the charges, Captain."

"What do you mean, 'charges'?" Reagan asked.

The woman explained that in order to fire someone, they first had to go through a trial similar to that of a military court-martial. The captain was shocked. "To hell with it. I don't care if we lose the war—I won't do it." In the end, the incompetent secretary received a promotion and higher pay to get her out of the way so that they could hire someone new. "No one in the administrative hierarchy of civil service will ever interfere with this upgrading process because his own pay and rating are based on the number of employees beneath him and the grades of those employees," Reagan observed. "It's a built-in process for empire building."

For many of the veterans who went on to occupy the White House, the war had a leveling impact. It forced them to deal every day with people whom they likely would never have met in civilian life. Not so Reagan: He was working with the same Hollywood actors, producers, and sound people as he had before the war.

While Johnson was back home in Washington, DC, where he felt most comfortable, three other future presidents—Kennedy, Nixon, and Bush—had successfully lobbied not only to join the war effort but also to get as close to the front lines of combat as possible. Their experiences over the next few years would shape their personalities and teach lessons that they would carry with them to the White House.

CHAPTER 3

========

"Sound General Quarters!"

AUGUST 3, 1942
BLACKETT STRAIT

Having blunted the Japanese advance at Midway, the Allies began their bloodied advance across the islands of the South and Central Pacific, pushing closer to the Japanese homeland. The Allies were looking for a place to seize the offensive, and they found it on Guadalcanal, a remote island in the Solomon chain. The Japanese were building an airstrip on the island, which, if completed, would allow them to control the skies over the shipping lanes used to supply Australia and New Zealand. If, however, the Americans gained control of the island, they could launch air assaults against Rabaul, the command center for Japanese operations in the southwestern Pacific.

On August 7, 1942, the United States launched its first offensive amphibious landing of the war on Guadalcanal. The outcome would determine control of the Pacific. Initially US troops faced little resistance, but Japan rushed in reinforcements, precipitating a ferocious struggle marked by deadly battles on the ground, at sea, and in the air. For six months, the two sides fought a brutal war of attrition for control of the island. It would be one of the longest, most complicated, and most consequential battles of the campaign, involving six separate naval battles and three clashes on land.

Japan used destroyer convoys, nicknamed the "Tokyo Express" by the US Marines, to shuttle men and reinforcements to the battle. By September, there were more than six thousand Japanese troops on the island, while bombers from Rabaul conducted regular raids on Henderson Field. After Roosevelt sent word to the Joint Chiefs of Staff to "make sure that every possible weapon gets into that area to hold Guadalcanal," more men and matériel flooded the island, overwhelming the Japanese forces.

While the US Marines and Australian infantry took control of Guadalcanal, the navy failed to prevent Japan from evacuating many of its men who had been trapped on the island. They survived to fight another day. Following the victory at Guadalcanal in February 1943, the Americans went on the offensive, rolling up Japanese-controlled islands as they pushed closer to Rabaul.

For nearly two years, John F. Kennedy had been lobbying to get closer to the action. Now he would have his first exposure to combat. "He was thrilled at going to the Solomons," Joe Sr. wrote to his other children. "It will certainly be a wonderful experience, and I just hope and pray he will come out of it all right."

In April Kennedy took command of the battle-worn PT-109, which had already participated in twenty-two combat patrols between November 1942 and February 1943. Constructed with one-inch mahogany planks, the eighty-foot-long vessel was a weaponized speedboat, boasting three powerful engines, a 20 mm antiaircraft gun, two .50 caliber machine guns, and four torpedo tubes. "It was designed for speed," wrote Captain John Bulkeley, who helped popularize the boats, "and in speed lies its beauty." Despite all the hype, the boats had serious deficiencies. Kennedy's craft was not equipped with radar, and the navy never trained the crew in proper use of torpedoes in combat—evidence, Kennedy said, of the "superhuman ability of the navy to screw up everything they touch."

THE BOAT WAS IN DESPERATE NEED OF REPAIR WHEN KENNEDY TOOK over. Its sluggish engines cried out for an overhaul, the rats and roaches infesting the interior had to be exterminated, and the exterior needed a new paint job. After a few weeks, Kennedy realized that the PT boats were not very effective at firing torpedoes and would be more lethal if they were repurposed as gunboats. In early August he traveled to an army base on the recently recaptured island of Rendova, took a 37 mm antitank gun, and had it installed on the front deck of the ship.

Kennedy's first tasks were to rehabilitate the craft, select a new crew, and prepare them for a fresh offensive planned for the summer. None of the thirteen men was from a wealthy family nor were they graduates from elite universities. Kennedy selected Ensign Leonard Thom, a six-foot-two, 220-pound former Ohio State University football star from Sandusky, Ohio, as the chief executive officer. Gunner's Mate Second Class Charles Harris had been a factory worker in Watertown, Massachusetts, before the war. Similarly, Radioman Second Class John Maguire had been working in a factory before volunteering for service in the South Pacific. He was not impressed when he met JFK for the first time. "Geez," he thought to himself, "I don't know if I want to go out with this guy. He looks fifteen." Patrick "Pappy" McMahon, at thirty-seven the oldest member of the crew, had been a public school teacher in California before volunteering for service after Pearl Harbor. He left behind a wife and son. Torpedoman Second Class Andrew Kirksey also had a wife and two children back home. Torpedoman Second Class Raymond Starkey, married with a son, had transferred to PT-109 because his previous skipper had been an "Ivy League snob." Rounding out the crew were Seaman First Class Raymond Albert, Gerard Zinser, Harold Marney, and former truck driver William Johnston. Edgar Mauer served as quartermaster and cook. And, at the last minute, Ensign George "Barney" Ross asked Kennedy if he could accompany them on a mission.

Kennedy described the conditions in the South Pacific as "rugged," but that did not fully capture the challenging experience. Not only was it unbearably hot and humid but there was also the constant threat of disease-carrying mosquitoes and flies. The men often slept on the boat in sweat-soaked clothes, and their diet consisted of various forms of canned meat, powdered eggs, and baked beans. Although Kennedy had enjoyed a life of privilege with servants and chauffeurs, he never complained about these primitive conditions.

Many of the men knew that Kennedy was the wealthy son of an American ambassador, but he seemed like just another one of the guys.

His crewmates respected him and liked him. He possessed a magnetism that drew men from diverse backgrounds. "There was an aura about him that I've never seen duplicated in anybody else," recalled a fellow officer. "He was an extraordinary fellow." Another reflected, "He was terrific. He was a good man. He took care of us all the time. He would go over to Guadalcanal and bum supplies, particularly ice cream. He was crazy for ice cream." Kennedy not only secured ice cream for himself, but he also bartered with army PX stations for candy bars, real eggs, bread, and cheese for his men.

The hardship of battle disabused Kennedy of his naïve belief that war was heroic. "It's one of those interesting things about the war," he wrote his lover, Inga Arvad, "that everyone in the States . . . want[s] to be out here killing Japs, while everyone out here wants to be back." The men in the war zone did not care about politics, "they just want to get home—morning, noon, and night." He then corrected himself, saying he did not mean to say "they—I meant WE."

All this time spent on the ground prompted Kennedy to develop a healthy skepticism of the military. When his parents told him about Douglas MacArthur's popularity on the home front, Jack answered, "Here he has none" and was, in fact, "very, very unpopular." Jack pointed out that MacArthur had earned the nickname "Dugout Doug" for refusing to come out of his "dugout" in Australia. Local commanders were just as incompetent as the generals. "Just had an inspection by an Adm.," he informed Inga in one witty passage. "He must've weighed over 300—and came bursting through our hut like a bull coming out of chute three."

In mid-July 1942 Kennedy's PT boat joined twenty-five others to support an American effort to seize control of the island of New Georgia. Their mission was to disrupt the Tokyo Express, which was supplying fresh soldiers and equipment aimed at reversing the advance of US forces in the islands farther north.

On a moonless, starless night on August 2, PT-109, with thirteen crew members, was patrolling Blackett Strait, south of the volcano Kolombangara in the mid–Solomon Islands, surrounded by Japanese-controlled islands on all sides. The fifteen PT boats were about forty miles away from their base on Rendova. Their mission was to form a picket line to intercept the Tokyo Express, but the men could not even see their hands held up in front of their faces. "It was as dark as if you were in a closet with the door shut," remembered George Ross.

On this night, the Express consisted of three Japanese destroyers acting as transports, with a fourth serving as an escort. Some of the PT boats had intercepted the Express as it made its way south, but the encounter did not go well. They fired thirty torpedoes, which either missed or failed to detonate. Those boats that had fired their torpedoes were then ordered back to base, leaving Kennedy and two other PT boats in the strait hoping to catch the Express as it returned from dropping off its supplies.

At 2:13 A.M., Kennedy was at the wheel in the cockpit, with radioman John Maguire standing near him. Ensign Thom, Charlie Harris, William Johnston, and Andrew Kirksey were resting on the deck. Ensign Harold Marney stood watch near the forward gun turret, while Ross was stationed as a lookout on the front deck near the 37 mm gun. Raymond Albert stood watch near the machine gun on the port side of the boat, with gunner Raymond Starkey acting as lookout in the rear gun turret. Pappy McMahon was below in the engine room. Only one of their three motors was engaged, with the other two idling to cut down their wake and avoid detection from Japanese planes.

According to the official naval intelligence report, at 2:27 A.M., "a dark shape loomed up on PT-109's starboard bow 200–300 yards in distance."

"Ship at two o'clock!" Marney shouted. At first glance, Kennedy thought that it was one of the other PT boats. "As soon as I decided it was a destroyer, I turned to make a torpedo run," he told a reporter shortly after his rescue. "The destroyer then turned straight for us. It all happened so fast there wasn't a chance to do a thing."

"Sound general quarters!" Kennedy shouted.

It was too late.

The massive hull of the two-thousand-ton Imperial Japanese Navy destroyer *Amagiri,* or "Heavenly Mist," sliced through the tiny PT boat. On board the *Amagiri,* Lieutenant Commander Kohei Hanami had purposefully rammed the vessel. "We crashed right into it," he remembered. As it knifed through the boat, members of Kennedy's crew could hear the excited Japanese voices coming from the deck of the ship. "I saw the enemy ship break in two with a tremendous roar," recalled Hanami. "White gasoline flames shot out. The torpedo boat disappeared in the dark. I knew that at least one half and probably both halves sank."

The impact knocked Kennedy down. "This is how it feels to be killed," he thought to himself. He lay on the deck looking up as the destroyer ripped his boat in half. Kennedy's part of the boat remained afloat because of the undamaged watertight compartments in the front. An eerie silence followed as the *Amagiri* disappeared into the darkness. The only sound and smell came from burning gasoline.

"Who's aboard?" Kennedy shouted in anticipation. Ross, Harris, McMahon, Johnston, Zinser, and Starkey responded. Two men did not answer: Kirksey and Marney. Their bodies were never recovered.

Realizing that the gasoline fire was only ten feet away, Kennedy shouted, "Over the side!" fearing that it would explode the remaining gas tanks.

Fortunately, the destroyer's churning wake pulled the fire away from the boat, and after only a few minutes, the men swam back and clung to what remained of their vessel.

From the darkness, Harris shouted, "Mr. Kennedy! Mr. Kennedy! McMahon is badly hurt." Jack, who had been a member of the Harvard swim team, stripped down and swam out to McMahon and Harris. "How are you, Mac?" the young lieutenant asked.

"I'm all right. I'm kind of burnt." McMahon had been pulled away from the ship by the destroyer's wake but surfaced in a fiery pool of 100-octane fuel that seared his face, chest, and hands.

"How are the others?" Kennedy asked.

Harris responded, "I hurt my leg."

Since McMahon was incapacitated and the tides strong, it took nearly an hour for Kennedy to tow the injured man back to the boat, using his life vest strap. The exhausted Harris followed just behind them. He wanted to give up, but Kennedy would have none of that, yelling, "I will not allow you to die!"

Kennedy ordered Mauer and Maguire to spot their shipmates still in the water. Thom, Zinser, Ross, and Albert swam back to the sinking hull, with Thom pulling Johnston, who had consumed gasoline and was unable to swim on his own. Finally, Starkey also made his way back to the wreckage.

It was now around five in the morning, more than three hours after the collision. The eleven survivors gathered around the remains of PT-109. All were exhausted, several had been sickened by the fuel fumes and salt water, and a few were hurt—although none as badly as McMahon. Their lifejackets helped keep them afloat, but their waterlogged clothes threatened to pull them beneath the surface.

As they trod the dark, shark-infested waters, Kennedy hoped that the two remaining PT boats would come to their rescue. But both vessels had already fled the area, their crews having assumed that everyone aboard Kennedy's boat had been killed. The men of PT-109 started to grow angry that they had been abandoned. "We were waiting for the other PT boats to come back," John Maguire recalled bitterly. "Those sons of bitches ran away from us."

Throughout the night, the tide pulled the men farther out into the vast expanse of the Solomon Sea, making the prospect of a rescue increasingly remote. It was obvious they could not survive by gripping the hull of a sinking ship. "We clung to the unburned bow of the boat for nearly twelve hours," remembered Kennedy, "and we left it only when it was just a foot above water."

At around ten o'clock, the hull turned over and was nearly submerged. Kennedy decided that their best bet would be to head to a piece of land on the horizon.

"I'll take McMahon with me," he instructed. "The rest of you can swim together on this plank. Thom will be in charge."

Around two o'clock, Kennedy grasped the strap of McMahon's life vest in his teeth and began towing him in the direction of the small island, swimming the breaststroke in intervals of fifteen minutes or so, then stopping to rest. He would use the breaks to reassure McMahon and the other men that they would make it.

Around sundown, they finally arrived on Plum Pudding Island, a sandbar in the middle of the Pacific. Kennedy was exhausted, his back throbbed with pain, and he felt nauseous from all the salt water he'd swallowed. Both his and McMahon's limbs were slashed and bruised by sharp coral as they struggled through shallow water and onto the beach. With his feet still in the water, an exhausted Kennedy planted his face on the dry sand and rested. He had been in the ocean for fifteen and a half hours.

Neither he nor the badly burned McMahon could walk, so they crawled on their hands and knees across ten feet of beach to take cover in the trees and bushes. The other nine survivors straggled ashore soon after. They sheltered behind bushes, recovering from the ordeal, breathing hard, and gazing at the massive outline of an enemy-held island across the narrow Ferguson Passage.

Even staying on this tiny sandbar was potential suicide. Kennedy knew that it was only a matter of time before the Japanese discovered them, and it was unlikely that Allied ships would be patrolling in the vicinity. Kennedy decided to rest until evening before swimming out to Ferguson Passage in hopes of flagging down a PT boat. It would be a risky move. He could just as likely be discovered by a Japanese destroyer as an American ship, and even a US vessel—perhaps mistaking him for a downed Japanese pilot—would probably shoot.

Despite the limited chance of success, Kennedy decided this was their last hope. He stripped down to his underwear, put on shoes to protect against the jagged coral, donned a life jacket, attached his .38 revolver to a lanyard around his neck, and then plunged into the dark waters. Having been warned that barracuda would sometimes swim up to a man and rip off his testicles, he decided to swim the backstroke. By ten at night, Kennedy reached the Ferguson Passage and swam out to open water. After treading water for hours, he realized that PT boats were not traveling the Ferguson Passage that night.

Kennedy then tried to make his way back to Plum Pudding Island, but he was too drained to fight the powerful tide that swept him past the island before dumping him on the sandy shore of another unoccupied island. He collapsed on the beach, and when he woke up, he swam the half mile back to Plum Pudding Island. "He was completely exhausted, slightly feverish, and slept most of the day," the navy reported. But then, as well as later, he would never allow pain to prevent him from achieving his goals.

Kennedy now needed to make another life-or-death decision. On August 4, after several unsuccessful efforts to flag down friendly ships, Jack decided the men needed to move again, this time to the slightly larger island of Olasana, which would hopefully have fresh water and coconuts. Once again Kennedy hauled McMahon for the three-hour journey while the other men clung to timber. By the time he reached shore, the cuts on Kennedy's feet had swollen and festered. But he never complained about the pain.

Olasana Island proved a disappointment. Though it had coconuts, some of the men drank the milk too quickly and became sick. It rained that night, so they desperately tried licking the moisture off leaves. But when the sun rose the following morning, they saw that bird droppings covered many of the leaves, so they dubbed the place Bird Island.

By the fourth day, many of the men felt demoralized and discouraged—and for good reason. They were hungry, thirsty, and losing hope that they would ever be rescued. McMahon's condition had worsened considerably, and if his wounds became infected, he would die a miserable death in front of them. They were surviving on rainwater and had only a few rancid coconuts to eat. Yet if Kennedy had doubts about their chances of survival, he never let on. Instead, he stayed constantly upbeat, reassuring his men that they would be rescued. "We're going to get back if I have to tow this island back!" he vowed.

Kennedy asked Ross to swim out with him to Cross Island, which was about four hundred yards wide and closer to the Ferguson Passage, meaning they could spot a rescue boat from there. Once on land, Kennedy and Ross crawled through the thick brush to the other side of the island, where they spied "a small rectangular box with Japanese writing on the side." They grabbed it and pulled it back into the brush. Inside were thirty or forty small bags of crackers and candy. Then, farther up the beach, they came across a one-man canoe and a barrel of potable rainwater. They also spied two islanders standing by a grounded Japanese barge. The natives, assuming that Ross and Kennedy were Japanese, quickly fled in a two-man canoe.

That night, Kennedy took the one-man canoe into Ferguson Passage again but without success. Ross decided to spend the night on Cross, while Kennedy returned to the men with the candy and desperately needed water. When he arrived after midnight, he learned that the two islanders he and Ross had seen on Cross had stopped by Bird Island and shared yams and cigarettes with the sailors. "We're saved," the excited sailors told Kennedy. "Two locals have found us!"

Fortunately for Kennedy, the two men, Biuku Gasa and Eroni Kumana, served as Allied scouts. In an often-told story, Kennedy used a jackknife to scratch words into a green coconut husk: "NAURO ISL . . . COMMANDER . . . NATIVE KNOWS POS'IT . . . HE CAN PILOT . . . II ALIVE . . . NEED SMALL BOAT . . . KENNEDY." He handed the coconut to the islanders, repeating "Rendova, Rendova." One of them seemed to understand, and the two paddled off. The ordeal of PT-109 was about to come to an end.

The ordeal aggravated Kennedy's back problems. According to his medical records, he spent ten days recuperating from the "symptoms of fatigue and many deep abrasions and lacerations of the entire body, especially the feet." Yet he was still humiliated by the sinking of his boat and insisted on getting back into the action.

Despite his eagerness, Kennedy harbored no illusions about the painful costs of war. In his letters home after the incident, he wrote about how the war had changed him. "It certainly brought home how real the war is," he divulged to his parents in September 1943. "When I read that we will fight the Japs for years if necessary and will sacrifice hundreds of thousands if we must—I always like to check from where he is talking— it's seldom out here. People get so used to talking about billions of dollars and millions of soldiers that thousands of dead sounds like drops in the bucket. But if those thousands want to live as much as the men I saw— they should measure their words with great, great care."

On October 1, over his parents' strong objections, JFK took command of a new PT boat and oversaw its conversion from a torpedo launcher into a more lethal gunboat. A week later, he was promoted to full lieutenant. "I won't leave as long as they have a job for us, but once they have us just sitting around, I'll be ready," he wrote to his father. "Please don't do anything till I let you know." He put his parents at ease with his trademark humor, telling the family patriarch, "When I do get out of here, you'll find that you have a new permanent fixture around that Florida pool. I'll just move from it to get into my sack. Don't worry at all about me—I've learned to duck—and have learned the wisdom of the old naval doctrine of keeping your bowels open and your mouth shut—and never volunteering."

Kennedy didn't hesitate to undertake many of the perilous tasks that followed. "He had guts," said one crewman. "No matter how dangerous the mission was, he'd always volunteer." On October 16 Kennedy's squadron of PT boats moved to Vella Lavella, where it engaged with and disrupted Japanese barges carrying materiel to their troops. Again, the intense combat and horrible conditions took a toll on his already fragile health. His weight plunged to 150 pounds, and he was limping around with a cane. His persistent back trouble was intensifying, with an X-ray showing "chronic disc disease of the lower back," according to his medical records. He would be diagnosed with malaria, an ulcer, and colitis, or inflammatory bowel disease. By December, Kennedy had grown fully disillusioned by the war. He wrote Inga that men were dying to defend "just God damn hot stinking corners of small islands and a group of islands and a part of the ocean we all hope never to see again."

In January 1944 Kennedy returned to the States, where he was awarded the Navy and Marine Corps Medal, along with Ensign Leonard Thom. The injuries he suffered during the PT-109 incident also qualified him for the Purple Heart.

But the consequences were more far-reaching than simple decorations for a uniform. Kennedy's time in World War II, and especially on PT-109, would be the defining experience of his too-short life. "He emerged from his war experience hardened, wiser, more mature, and with self-confidence from having performed his duties and earned the esteem of his men," observes biographer Fredrik Logevall. "Thrown together with individuals from vastly different backgrounds and economic circumstances, he developed a greater appreciation for the diversity of the American national experience." The very war that shattered lives also opened Jack up to people and perspectives that he never would have encountered had he stayed home in the safety of the Kennedy bubble.

JFK's experience not only changed him but also transformed the way the public viewed him. If PT-109 had not sunk, there likely would never have been a President Kennedy. Before the war, he had been the precocious son of a wealthy ambassador. Now he was a celebrated war hero.

Word of Kennedy's heroism spread quickly. Two reporters were on the PT boat that came to Kennedy's rescue: Leif Erickson of the Associated Press and Frank Hewlett of the United Press. On August 19, 1943, Erickson's story ran across the top of the front page of *The Boston Globe*, positioned above the masthead with the headline "Kennedy's Son Hero of PT-Boat Saga." The story received extensive coverage and was well received by a public hungry for tales of daring war heroes. Then nearly a year later, on June 17, 1944, a long article about the PT-109 episode appeared in *The New Yorker*, written by John Hersey. Thanks to Jack's powerful father, *Reader's Digest* published a condensed version that August.

Until PT-109, Jack had lived in the shadow of his high-achieving older brother, Joseph Jr., the heir apparent to their father's oversized ambitions for the next generation of Kennedys. Joe Sr. was grooming Joe Jr. for a future in national politics and hoped that he would one day be elected president. But now it was his younger brother who had blossomed into a decorated war hero; author of a well-received book, *Why England Slept*, that examined the consequences of Britain's appeasement policies toward Germany in the late 1930s; and a media sensation. Instead of congratulating Jack, his fiercely competitive brother Joe questioned why he had allowed his ship to get sunk. "What I really want to know," Joe wrote Jack after he read the *New Yorker* article, "is where the hell were you when the destroyer hove into sight, and exactly what were your moves, and where the hell was your radar?"

Joe discovered that he had been displaced as the leader of the next generation of Kennedys on September 6, 1943, when he returned home to Hyannis to celebrate his father's fifty-fifth birthday. A big Boston crowd mingled at the party, including family friend and Boston police commissioner Joseph Timilty. During the dinner, Timilty raised his glass and proposed a toast "to Ambassador Joe Kennedy, father of our hero, our own hero, Lieutenant John F. Kennedy of the United States Navy." Joe, who was on his way overseas, was devastated over not being included in the toast. Timilty, who shared a room with him during that weekend celebration, could hear Joe "crying in the other bed" afterward.

It is likely that jealousy drove Joe to volunteer for a dangerous secret operation on August 12, 1944—some called it a suicide mission—to fly a plane loaded with twelve tons of explosives. The plan was for Joe and his copilot to parachute out of the plane and allow it to be guided via remote control to a complex of German rockets. But something went horribly wrong. The plane exploded eighteen minutes into the flight, instantly killing both men.

With Joe Jr. dead, Joe Sr. transferred his ambitions onto his second child, the esteemed war hero. "It was like being drafted," JFK reflected later. "My father wanted his eldest son in politics. *Wanted* isn't the right word. He demanded it."

Kennedy would emerge from the war with two competing and sometimes contradictory beliefs. On the one hand, his own study of Britain's policy of appeasement, combined with his war experience, convinced him that America needed to remain vigilant and stand firm against aggression. But on the other hand, the death and destruction that he witnessed made him reluctant to use force and deeply skeptical of the military. He would carry these two competing notions with him to the White House, and this contributed to his confusing political style: bold, aggressive rhetoric juxtaposed with behind-the-scenes efforts to avoid conflict and negotiate settlements. As he would soon discover, one of the problems with this approach was that his rhetoric could take on a life of its own and ultimately limit his range of action.

Late in May 1943, after an eighteen-day journey crammed with three thousand other men aboard the *President Monroe,* Richard Nixon arrived on the island of Espiritu Santo in the New Hebrides. This was the southern front of the Allied campaign through the Treasury and Solomon archipelago. While Kennedy's PT-109 patrolled Japanese-held waters farther north in the Solomons, Nixon served as an officer in the South Pacific Combat Air Transport Command (SCAT) under Admiral William "Bull" Halsey. Despite his best efforts to get closer to the action, Nixon would repeatedly find himself to the rear of the shifting battle lines as the Allies pushed closer to the Japanese homeland.

According to Carl J. Fleps, his Marine Corps commander, Nixon was responsible for making sure "the passengers all got aboard the proper airplanes" on outgoing flights. For planes returning from the front lines, his top priority was "to look out for the wounded." The big C-47 cargo planes would land in the afternoon, and Nixon's team would unload their cargo and have the planes ready to take off sometime between two and four in the morning to avoid being detected by Japanese pilots during the day.

Work was slow, and he was bored much of the time. American forces had moved farther north as part of their island-hopping campaign, leaving Nixon far from combat. In August 1943 he complained to Pat that "the damn central office" was preventing him from getting closer to the action. He wanted to be transferred to a "less civilized place, where I would feel I was doing more."

Nixon thought he might have figured a way out, though. "I am working on an angle. . . . Keep your fingers crossed and wish hard!" He lodged a complaint with Fleps, claiming that he was living too comfortably and even had access to milk shakes and ice cream. Nixon insisted that he wanted "to get into something where the smell of combat was closer," to be part of the SCAT team that supported landing parties. "Lieutenant Nixon said he would like very much to be recommended to be in charge of the SCAT detachment to make the next invasion," Fleps recalled.

Nixon finally got his wish in January 1944, when he was sent up the line to Bougainville, the largest of the Solomon Islands. "Our job," recalled Nixon's tentmate Hollis Dole, "was to bring the planes in and to load them with the wounded and to send them out, unload the high-priority materials such as radar equipment . . . ammunition, foodstuffs, medical supplies, and the like."

No sooner had Nixon settled in than the Japanese attacked. The Americans had captured the airfield only a few months earlier, and Japanese bombers from nearby Rabaul struck often. "When it was over," he wrote in his memoirs, "we counted thirty-five shell holes within a hundred feet of the air bunker six of us shared. Our tent had been completely destroyed." Because their tent sat at the end of the runway, hidden in the island vegetation, they were an easy target for bombers trying to destroy the airfield. "On quite a few occasions, both Mr. Nixon and I would have to jump out of our sacks, leap through the door and down into the foxhole," recalled Dole. "We spent many nights there, many hours in this particular area."

Nixon managed to avoid Japanese bombs, but he could not avoid the island's many poisonous critters. One night, they slept in a tent that had screens but no mosquito netting. Nixon woke up to find a "lobster-red" centipede, "about an inch and a half wide and eight or nine inches long," crawling on his body. He flicked the creature away, but unfortunately, it landed on Dole and bit him. "This put me in the hospital for several days and caused intense pain," Dole recalled. In later years, Nixon would introduce Dole as "the man that I put in the hospital from the centipede."

Besides the bugs, Nixon recalled the "oppressive monotony" and lonely days "filled with seemingly interminable periods of waiting while the action unfolded thousands of miles away." He tried to pass the time by playing poker. His strategy was conservative, but he was occasionally willing to play a bluff. One of his fellow players claimed that "Dick never lost" a game, but Nixon downplayed his poker prowess. "My poker playing during this time has been somewhat exaggerated," he pleaded in his memoirs.

When he wasn't playing poker, Nixon wrote Pat, who was in San Francisco working as an analyst for the Office of Price Administration, the same government agency where Richard had worked before joining the navy. She corresponded with him every day and often sent packages filled with books, including *The Communist Manifesto,* published in 1848 by Karl Marx and Friedrich Engels. "I have always wanted to read Karl Marx in order to be familiar with it," he wrote. His most-read book, though, was an "old, illustrated Bible" that he had brought with him from Whittier.

Throughout his time abroad, Nixon lived with men from varied backgrounds, learning to drink, swear, and smoke cigars for the first time. According to biographer Roger Morris, those he worked with side by side "were the classic, almost Hollywood-cast cross section of the navy, young men from New York slums and the Midwest, one from a wealthy family in the South, a Mexican, an Indian, an Italian, and the inevitable Texan."

Some of Nixon's relatives credited his exposure to such an ethnically and racially diverse group of men from different parts of the country with broadening his horizons. "He learned how to get along with people," reflected cousin Lucille Parsons, "boys from all over the country to work with. He said he never knew what it was like to be associated with people brought up in all these different ways. . . . When he came back from that, he was really much more humble; I mean, he saw how the other half lived."

Amid the pressures of war, he developed a meaningful connection with these men and tried his best to improve their quality of life. "Many fighter and bomber pilots came through Bougainville on their way to battle missions," Nixon recalled in his memoirs, "and I felt that they deserved the best we could possibly give them." Describing himself as a "first-rate scrounger," he used his position as a navy supply officer to procure food and drink. He even opened up "Nick's Hamburger Stand," also called "Nick's Snack Shack," where fighter pilots could stop by for burgers, Australian beer, and cold juice. According to one officer, he would trade "everything from captured Japanese rifles to introductions to the army nurses who arrived to take care of the casualties." If Lieutenant Nixon could not trade for something, he would "liberate" it. He also set up a small, informal school teaching the men about the basics of business law.

In turn, Nixon received high praise from his men. "He was an extremely efficient guy, always affable and always cool," recalled Fleps, who said "unflappable" was the best adjective to describe him. "He always had a sense of team play. I think this was in his nature, and he had a very fine sense of organization, not only of accepting responsibility but of delegating it as well."

Nixon had no qualms about taking off his shirt and working side by side with others. On January 24, only a few days after his arrival, the base had to unload thirty C-47 cargo planes and load bombs onto fighters for a bombing mission over Rabaul. Nixon labored next to his men and completed the task in five hours. His assistant, James Stewart, observed how Nixon remained "a calm island in a storm . . . shy, competent, never lost his cool."

Nixon managed to secure not only the loyalty of his men but also praise from his superiors. He received a Letter of Commendation from the Commander of the South Pacific Area and South Pacific Force, applauding him for "meritorious and efficient performance" as well as "sound judgment and initiative."

There were, however, signs of the two Nixons even while he was serving in the Pacific. Dole described him as "very quiet and unassuming until he had to occupy stage center, and at that time he became a completely different person, quite articulate, extremely competent in expressing himself and very outgoing." The future president, Dole observed perceptively, "always seemed to be two people: one, very quiet, very much in background, and actually somewhat morose. But when the chips were down, it was just as if he were electrified. He knew what to say, how to say it, and he became quite animated and smiled."

Like Kennedy, Nixon could have had a comfortable life in the rear, but he continually chose the most dangerous parts of the job. On February 15 he was part of the invasion force that stormed Green Island. Unfortunately for his ambitions, the Japanese had already abandoned the island, and American forces landed on the beach unopposed. Nixon noted in his memoirs, "The only danger came from a few straggling snipers and the ever-present giant centipedes." One of Nixon's friends echoed him: "The only real danger was the possibility of a banyan tree falling on you during a storm." Though Green Island experienced roughly the same number of bombings as Bougainville, Nixon was clearly disappointed. "I think he was really anxious to do something more for his country than land on an unopposed island," Fleps recalled.

Here Nixon was downplaying the challenges that he and the other Seabees faced on the island. They had to build roads, clear trees, erect tents for fifteen thousand men, and construct a runway so that American fighters could launch attacks against Japanese-occupied islands. Nixon and his team worked twelve-hour shifts to get the work done. Since there was no fresh water on the island, the men were forced to labor in the oppressive heat and humidity while being limited to a ration of two gallons per day for washing, drinking, and cooking. "The men swam in the lagoon to get clean," he said in a 1946 speech. "But they found that it was infested with fungus. It seemed that the only alternative was to wait until they returned to the States to get a bath."

But it was here that he would finally see the horrors of war up close. The Seabees were still constructing the airfield when an army B-29 Superfortress that had been damaged flying over Rabaul crash-landed. Nixon and the other men cheered as the bomber seemed to make a successful soft landing but then watched aghast as it burst into flames after hitting a bulldozer that had accidently been left on the strip. "I can still see the wedding ring on the charred hand of one of the crewmen," he would recall of the bodies they pulled from the wreckage.

Nixon would later write that his experience in the war cemented his political ambitions. "The war, I think, was the real catalyst in that it brought me face-to-face with a world of problems and issues of literally earth-shaking importance and thus forced on me a reassessment of the responsibilities of a citizen of the world." It seems more likely, however, that Nixon entered the war already hungry for a political career and discovered for the first time that he could relate to a highly diverse group of men. The war did not push Nixon into politics so much as it gave him the confidence to believe that he could be successful as a politician.

By July 1944, the navy had started winding down operations in the South Pacific and ordered Nixon to return to the States. He moved initially to Alameda, California, where he served as a building and grounds officer. Four months later, the navy sent him to the East Coast to oversee the termination of defense contracts. In October 1945 Nixon was promoted to lieutenant commander, but, by then, he was already eyeing a potential campaign for Congress. He received an honorable discharge on December 31, 1945.

In May 1943, at the same time that Richard Nixon arrived in the Pacific, newly promoted Lieutenant Gerald Ford finally got his wish to join a navy ship in the war zone: the USS *Monterey*, named for the 1846 Battle of Monterey during the Mexican-American War, when General Zachary Taylor, later to become the twelfth president of the United States, led a ragtag group of army regulars and Texas Rangers to victory over the Mexican army.

By this point, the US Navy had discovered the importance of projecting air power, so it began converting Cleveland-class cruisers into Independence-class light aircraft carriers that could be built and sent into battle faster than regular carriers. Initially, Ford was part of the pre-commissioning crew that took the ship out for test runs to make sure it was seaworthy and that all the equipment worked properly. Commissioned in June, the *Monterey* housed 1,500 men and carried thirty-three aircraft, including twenty-four F6F Hellcat fighters and nine TBM Avenger torpedo bombers.

The ship's captain gave Ford three assignments. He would serve as the second division officer, responsible for overseeing a crew of ninety enlisted men and two junior officers whose tasks were to handle lines when docking and anchoring, along with fueling at sea. He was also the gunnery officer, managing the 40 mm rear antiaircraft guns. And, not surprisingly, he was appointed athletic director. As they sailed from Pearl Harbor to the Pacific, Ford led the men in calisthenics and even persuaded the captain to build a basketball court on a lower deck. He found that basketball was "our best conditioning sport, for the officers and men get more exercise in a shorter time."

By the time the *Monterey* arrived in the Gilbert Islands in November, the Americans had a plan for defeating Japan. It involved a thrust into the central Pacific Ocean, assaulting Japan's outer defensive perimeter in the Gilbert and Marshall Islands before penetrating the Carolines and Marianas. At the same time, Douglas MacArthur would drive toward the Philippines and Formosa (now Taiwan). From there, the United States could launch air strikes against the Japanese homeland.

The *Monterey* was part of the Fifth Fleet's Fast Carrier Task Force. Boasting eleven flattops with some seven hundred airplanes, it represented perhaps the largest concentration of aircraft carriers ever assembled. Over the next few months, the task force of carriers, cruisers, and destroyers continued pounding Japanese installations at Truk, Palau, Hollandia, Saipan, Tinian, and Guam. In its first thirteen months at sea, the *Monterey* engaged in constant battle.

The first mission was to support the army's landings on Makin Island on November 19. Later, its fighters and bombers carried out attacks against Japanese camps on the islands of Nauru and New Ireland. These offen-

sives were akin to poking a hornet's nest, as waves of Japanese planes re-
taliated against US ships. Ford was in the thick of the action, standing on
the carrier's fantail to direct fire from the antiaircraft guns. He recalled,
"The Japanese planes came after us with a vengeance. We had many general quarters calls, and it was as much action as I'd ever hoped to see." At
seven o'clock in the evening on Christmas, Ford was on duty when he
spotted an enemy bomber heading straight for the *Monterey*. Fortunately,
the ships managed to shoot it down before it could drop its deadly cargo.

The gunners who reported to Ford offered him high praise. "Nothing
ever seemed to rattle him," said Seaman Second Class Ronald Smith.
"One day we came under attack, and I dived for cover in the hatchway. I
looked up, and there was Lieutenant Ford. He smiled and asked me,
'Why the hell are you in such a hurry?'" Smith agreed: "He was real
popular. We could always approach him without worries. He was the sort
of officer who made sure his men had something to eat before he sat down
himself. And he never had to pull rank or throw his weight around to get
loyalty from any of the men under him."

Ford's superiors praised his performance, giving him the highest
marks possible for leadership and rating him as "outstanding" compared
to officers of his rank. Ford, one report concluded, "has a remarkable personality and an exceptional military character." Captain Stuart Ingersoll
wrote of Ford: "He was one of the finest officers I have ever seen, and I
would be glad to have him anywhere in any job, at any time. He was the
best Officer of the Deck on my carrier, and I shall never forget him."

Ford liked his men, and he got a rush from directing the guns, but he
was dissatisfied with his assignment in the rear of the ship. Feeling "a bit
restless in the gunnery division," he confessed that he "wanted to do
something more challenging." When he learned that the ship's navigator
was being transferred, Ford applied for the job and got it. "I didn't have
any idea how to take a sighting," Ford admitted later, but he learned
quickly. "As a result, I became the officer of the deck during general quarters, which meant I was on the bridge with the captain, the navigator, and
the air officer during combat."

Through the summer and fall, the USS *Monterey* would participate in
just about every major naval engagement in the Pacific. In June 1944 it

joined in the Battle of the Philippine Sea, one of the most lopsided naval battles in history. The American carrier group downed more than three hundred Japanese planes while losing only eighteen fighters and twelve bombers in what was dubbed "The Great Marianas Turkey Shoot." The battle revealed how the balance of power had shifted in the Pacific. In the first year of the war, Japan's fighters reigned supreme in the sky; their equipment was superior and their pilots better trained. But by this stage of the war, many of their most experienced pilots had been killed in action, replaced by young, poorly trained substitutes flying a dwindling number of now-outdated aircraft.

In July the USS *Monterey* joined other carriers to conduct air strikes over Guam. After a twenty-four-day layover in Pearl Harbor, the carrier group continued its advance, attacking the Philippines, Okinawa, and Formosa. The ship and its crew moved from one firefight to another, dodging Japanese bombs, torpedoes, and, as the Japanese grew more desperate, kamikaze pilots. During the assault on Formosa, the ship's gunners had to man their battle stations for twenty-four consecutive hours.

Ford described how the Japanese planes swarmed the ship as it prepared to steam away following a successful strike against Formosa in October 1944. "The noise was deafening," he recalled of the ship's guns. "A torpedo from one of the planes nearly hit us and crashed into the side of the cruiser USS *Canberra* instead. Another torpedo smashed into the USS *Houston,* another cruiser. After a fierce few minutes, the attack was over." The cruisers were so heavily damaged they needed to be towed away, but by the next morning, they were still only eight miles off the coast. They were, he reflected, "a sitting target for the Japanese" who "attacked us all day long. Our guns blasted away and finally drove them off."

While serving as the navigator, Ford would nearly lose his life—not to Japanese fighters but to a typhoon, the worst ever recorded by an American fleet. That disaster left him injured and his ship damaged beyond repair.

═══

On Wednesday, June 9, 1943, in a simple ceremony in Corpus Christi, Texas, George Herbert Walker Bush received his gold ensign's bars. He was now an officer of the US Naval Reserve. At only eighteen years old—three days shy of his nineteenth birthday—he was likely the youngest commissioned pilot in the Naval Air Service.

He was still a long way from being ready for combat, but a few days after graduation, he was shipped to Fort Lauderdale to learn to fly torpedo bombers. It was here that Bush was introduced to the plane that he would soon navigate in combat. At forty feet long and sixteen feet high, with a fifty-two-foot wingspan, the TBM Avenger (torpedo bomber built by Grumman) dwarfed all the other planes. "On the ground, the Avenger, its huge belly bulging with a ton of bombs, looked like some aberrant barnyard fowl," observed Bush biographer Joe Hyams. Because of its size and unusual shape, navy pilots nicknamed it "the Pregnant Turkey."

Bush fell in love with the plane immediately but found flying with instruments challenging. "Instruments are unbelievably hard," he wrote his parents. "You literally can't tell whether youre [sic] upside down or not unless you watch all instruments and watch them well." But once he learned how to use the dizzying array of switches and dials in the cockpit, he realized that despite its size, the plane handled well, responded to the lightest touch, and moved effortlessly through the sky.

Over the next month, Bush learned how to land on a carrier, using a runway created out of an open field that resembled the size of a carrier deck. By August, he had his first chance to land on a real aircraft carrier. "One can practice carrier landing on land forever without knowing the thrill of actually landing on a moving ship at sea," he reflected. "There's something about the isolation, the ocean, the tiny carrier below that gets the adrenaline flowing."

That same month, Bush was certified in aircraft landings, and the navy granted him a short leave. He and Barbara spent seventeen days at the Bush family home in Kennebunkport, Maine. Barbara got a chance to meet the entire Bush family, including aunts, uncles, and cousins. "I lived in very tight quarters with his immediate family," she recalled. "We swam, rode bikes, played tennis, picnicked, walked in the moonlight—and fell in love!" Not only did they fall in love; she and George also secretly got engaged.

After his leave, Bush reported to the navy base at Norfolk, Virginia, where he learned glide bombing, night flying, and how to fly in formation. On November 1 Bush almost lost his life when, while attempting to land, he had to swerve abruptly to avoid colliding with another aircraft. "This sent me careening sort of half sideway on one wing and the belly over the ground," he wrote his parents. The plane was "a total loss," but fortunately, neither he nor his crew members were hurt.

Although Bush was the youngest member of his group of pilots, the men respected him. They could tell by the way he spoke that he had received a good education, but Bush never mentioned his wealthy upbringing. He blended in as one of the guys. It was not until he invited a few friends to spend the weekend at a family-owned apartment in New York City that they realized just how privileged he was. One friend, Milt Moore, whose father owned a laundry, was impressed. "I realized that George was something more than I thought," he recalled, "but the members of his family that he introduced us to were real down-to-earth people."

In December 1943 Bush traveled to Philadelphia for the commissioning of the aircraft carrier to which he'd been assigned. Like the *Monterey*, the USS *San Jacinto* was a converted cruiser rushed to completion to replace the ships destroyed at Pearl Harbor and in the sea battles that followed. It was light, fast, and housed thirty-four planes: twenty-five fighters and nine torpedo bombers. (The ship was named in honor of Sam Houston's victory against Mexican dictator Antonio López de Santa Anna in April 1836 during the Texas Revolution.)

The ship left Philadelphia on March 25, 1944, sailed through the Panama Canal, and made a brief stopover in San Diego before arriving in Pearl Harbor on April 20, 1944. As it steamed into port, Bush saw the sunken hulls of the *Utah* and the *Arizona*. It was a powerful moment for the young man, who had joined the navy immediately upon hearing the news of the Japanese attack. Seeing the death and destruction firsthand only reinforced his desire to join the fight, regardless of personal risk.

While these events unfolded in the Pacific, the balance of power in Europe was starting to shift, too. Ever since the spring of 1943, Hitler's empire had begun showing signs of collapse under steady Allied pressure. After some initial setbacks, the Allies trapped one of Hitler's best generals, Field Marshal Erwin Rommel (nicknamed the "Desert Fox") in a giant pincer movement in North Africa. Finally, on May 13, 1943, the Allied army captured a quarter million Axis troops, including 125,000 Germans. Hitler had already faced significant losses on his Eastern front. Stalin's army surrounded a large German force at Stalingrad, and in February 1943, after six months of intense fighting, the Russians emerged victorious.

Despite these victories, Allied leaders remained divided over the wisdom of a cross-Channel attack on the French coast. Back in January 1943, Churchill and Roosevelt had met in the Moroccan city of Casablanca in northern Africa to discuss the next step in the European war. Eisenhower and Marshall urged Roosevelt to push ahead with the second front, both to aid the Soviets and to strike at the heart of German forces. But once again the British prime minister held sway, calling instead for a continuation of the Mediterranean campaign with an invasion of Sicily.

In July Allied troops assaulted the island. On July 22 General George Patton sliced through Italian defenses and entered the city of Palermo. Italy then arrested and imprisoned its fascist dictator, Benito Mussolini, who'd come to power in 1922, and surrendered to the Allies. Overnight, Italy was transformed from a German ally to a German-occupied country as Hitler poured sixteen divisions into the peninsula. A month later, in September, three British and four American divisions glided onto the beaches of Salerno, beginning the long, bloody struggle northward through Italy and toward Germany.

Despite bitter fighting in Italy, technological breakthroughs were giving the Allies a clear advantage. New radar allowed the Allies to track German submarines, while their destroyers and planes unleashed a deadly array of new, more powerful antisubmarine rockets and depth charges. Starting in May 1943, the Germans ordered all but a handful of U-boats out of the waters. "We had lost the battle of the Atlantic," noted a German commander. The Allies also gained control of the sky, launching the B-17 bomber, popularly known as the Flying Fortress, against strategic German targets: submarine yards, munitions factories, and railroad lines.

From 1943 to the war's end, Allied planes dropped more than two and a half million tons of explosives on occupied Europe and Germany.

As momentum shifted toward the Allies, Roosevelt traveled to Tunisia for a series of meetings with Churchill and Stalin to discuss whether to launch a second front in western Europe to relieve pressure on the Soviets and force Hitler to fight a war on two fronts. The question of who would lead such a campaign remained unsettled when Roosevelt arrived in the capital, Tunis—close to where Eisenhower was stationed—on Saturday, November 20, 1943. The assumption was that Marshall would get the job, and Eisenhower would return to Washington as the new army chief of staff. Roosevelt was torn: In theory, Marshall was the most qualified and had already demonstrated that he could handle the position. But FDR dreaded the idea of losing Marshall. A few months earlier, he had even tried floating Marshall's name—part of his favored strategy of testing ideas by leaking them to the press. By September, stories about Marshall's potential future had begun appearing in American newspapers. The public response was mixed, and it was clear that the armed services wanted Marshall to stay in his position. FDR's critics also claimed that Roosevelt would replace Marshall with someone who would manipulate war contracts to help ensure his victory in the 1944 presidential race.

Eisenhower was unhappy when he discovered that he would likely be chosen to replace Marshall. He said that if that happened, he would tell Roosevelt that the decision was a "tremendous mistake" because he was "not temperamentally fitted for the job." Although he had done a solid job handling Roosevelt and Churchill, Ike confessed that he did not like dealing with politicians and preferred to remain in the Mediterranean, where he had more independence. If he were to leave there, he would rather command American troops in Europe under Marshall's command. "The job of chief of staff does not appeal to Ike," observed his aide Harry Butcher, "and he believes he would be a failure in it because he is not a politician." Eisenhower had already grown weary of all the visiting politicians and moved his headquarters closer to the front lines, though that did little to slow the parade of visitors. "He didn't relish the idea of returning to a headquarters in London or Washington," Butcher noted.

By this time, Ike's name was also being floated for another government position: a Republican challenger to Roosevelt in 1944. But Eisenhower refused to dignify the rumors by making a statement. He had one doctrine and one doctrine only: He served the president, and "nothing could sway me from my purpose of carrying out faithfully his orders in whatever post he may assign me." Once again he made clear that he would "not tolerate the use of my name in connection with any political activity of any kind."

Roosevelt had planned to spend only one day in Tunis but ended up taking an additional day. He and Ike had met twice before briefly and hit it off instantly now. A "two-day lovefest," biographer Jean Edward Smith called it. They were both extroverts, quick to smile and easy to tell stories. As they traveled around looking at recent and ancient battlefields, FDR grilled the general. "The fact that Ike knew the details of each conflict pleased Father hugely," recalled his son Franklin, who accompanied them on the trip. "[I]t showed that Ike, like Father, had a bent for history and a love for knowledge."

After dinner that evening, Eisenhower accompanied FDR to the airport. Before he boarded the plane, the president indicated that he would be choosing Marshall. "Ike, you and I know who was the chief of staff during the last years of the Civil War, but practically no one else knows, although the names of the field generals . . . every schoolboy knows them. I hate to think that fifty years from now practically nobody will know who George Marshall was." Still, Roosevelt admitted how much he disliked the prospect of sending Marshall to Europe, concluding, "It is dangerous to monkey with a winning team."

Roosevelt's ambivalence about sending Marshall to Europe showed that he was starting to have second thoughts, so he invited Ike to join the scheduled conference with Churchill in Cairo, Egypt, where the general presented an impressive overview of the war. "He had demonstrated a firm grasp of the military situation, shown himself to be realistic about the possibilities, and in general added to the good impression he had previously made because of his conduct of affairs in the Mediterranean," observed biographer Stephen Ambrose.

Once again the most pressing decision concerned launching a second front. Churchill remained unconvinced about the wisdom of a frontal assault on the French coast. "We must take care that the tides do not run red with the blood of American and British youth or the beaches be choked with their bodies," the prime minister thundered. By this point, Stalin was furious with British reluctance on the matter. Eventually, under pressure from both Roosevelt and Stalin, Churchill relented and agreed to support a landing in northern France. "This battle has been forced upon us by the Russians and the United States military authorities," Churchill complained bitterly. The Allies gave the entire assault a code name—Operation Overlord—and scheduled it for May 1944.

On November 28, 1943, the American and British delegations traveled to Tehran, Iran, to meet with Stalin. Roosevelt and Churchill still faced the looming question of who should lead Operation Overlord. "The second front decision," observed Admiral William D. Leahy, a distinguished naval officer who now served as FDR's chief of staff, "overshadowed all other accomplishments of the Tehran meeting." Churchill deferred to Roosevelt, since the Americans would be committing far more in the way of men and materiel to the effort. Stalin, growing impatient with the delays, pressed FDR to appoint a supreme commander. When Roosevelt told him that he had not decided yet, Stalin erupted. "Then nothing will come out of these operations. One man must be responsible and one man must make decisions."

At the end of the conference, Roosevelt stopped over in Tunis again on his way back to Washington. While Eisenhower was sitting in the back seat of FDR's armored car, the president turned to him and announced casually, "Well, Ike, you're going to command Overlord." Driver Kay Summersby recalled that Eisenhower "was so happy I thought he would burst. That grin never left his face."

Eisenhower assumed command at the age of fifty-three, marking a turning point in his already illustrious career. The recognition and accolades he received from his management of the operation would make him one of the most recognized and respected men in the world. He would ride that wave of popularity into the White House precisely nine years later.

Why did FDR choose Eisenhower? While Ike complained about how much he disliked politicians, he was himself a talented politician who had proved himself capable of managing the enormous egos involved in the planning and execution of complicated maneuvers. He impressed everyone with his competent management of the troops as well as his strategic vision and discipline. British general Bernard Montgomery said of Eisenhower, "His real strength lies in his human qualities. . . . He has the power of drawing the hearts of men towards him as a magnet attracts the bit of metal. He merely has to smile at you, and you trust him at once." A staff member echoed Montgomery's estimation, writing that Eisenhower "was a living dynamo of energy, good humor, amazing memory for details, and amazing courage for the future."

Like FDR, Ike possessed a common touch and inspired trust in everyone, from heads of state to the common foot soldier. Stories circulated among the men about how he berated generals who put their own comfort ahead of the troops'. Once, on the Mediterranean island of Capri, an aide told Ike that two luxurious villas had been set aside for him and another general. Instead of basking in his good fortune, he shouted, "None of those will belong to any general as long as I'm boss!" Similarly, when he learned that the entire island had been reserved as a recreational facility for officers, he ordered that "all British and American personnel in this area, particularly from combat units, may be assured of proportionate opportunity in taking advantage of these facilities." His visits to troops on the front lines were legendary. Instead of using these visits as photo ops, he listened to his troops and did what he could to help. "His popularity with the men rested on his genuine concern for their welfare and on his common touch—they regarded him as one of them," noted Ambrose.

Eisenhower also managed to charm his driver, Kay Summersby, a thirty-four-year-old former model who was separated from her husband and engaged to another man. "I succumbed immediately to that grin which was to become famous," she reflected. The attraction was mutual. Kay started out as Ike's driver, but he soon promoted her to serve as his personal assistant. She accompanied him on trips to the combat zone and sat in on high-profile meetings, including those with Roosevelt and Churchill. "We have no secrets from Kay," Eisenhower told Churchill. General Omar Bradley called her "Ike's shadow." On those rare occasions when Eisenhower had free time, they spent evenings together, listening to music and playing poker.

Although he was twenty years her senior, Ike did little to disguise his affection for Kay. When asked if Ike and Summersby were intimate, a *Chicago Tribune* war correspondent observed, "You didn't often see a general kissing his chauffeur." After spending time with the two, Roosevelt told his daughter that he thought Ike was sleeping with Kay. In her memoir, Summersby wrote that while there was lots of passion, the general had difficulty consummating the affair. "Whether he and Kay were intimate remains a matter of conjecture," observed biographer Jean Edward Smith. "But there is no question they were in love."

Word of Ike's relationship with Summersby made its way back to Mamie, who was living alone in the couple's two-bedroom apartment in DC's fashionable Wardman Park Hotel. She understood Ike's need for female companionship but feared that Kay had become her surrogate in London. Those fears became especially acute after a *Life* magazine article profiled Kay, describing her as "Eisenhower's pretty Irish driver."

For his part, Ike did his best to reassure Mamie and to profess his love for her. "I just want to say that you're the greatest gal in the world," he wrote in February 1943. "I'll never be in love with anyone but you!"

MARSHALL INSISTED THAT IKE TAKE A SHORT VACATION BEFORE AS-suming his new command. Eisenhower balked, but Marshall was adamant, telling him, "You will be under terrific strain from now on. I am interested that you are fully prepared to bear the strain, and I am not interested in the usual rejoinder that you can take it. It is of vast importance that you be fresh mentally, and you certainly will not be if you go straight from one great problem to another." Reluctantly, Eisenhower acquiesced and made plans to return to Washington. Kay drove him to the airport in the Algerian capital, Algiers. "Two weeks seems like a long time," she said. "Especially when you are going to be so far away."

"Twelve days," responded Ike. "You'll be with me all the time." Before boarding the plane, he handed her a slip of paper. "Kay, can you take care of this for me?" he asked.

"Certainly, General. Have a safe trip."

After he boarded, she looked at the note. "Think of me," he'd written. "You know what I will be thinking."

Ike finally arrived in Washington at one in the morning on January 2, 1944. "Ike and Mamie had changed," observed biographer Jean Edward Smith, "and the divide between them was greater than ever." Mamie noticed that he was heavier, noticeably older, and more self-assured than he'd been eighteen months earlier. Her husband was now the confidant of Churchill and Roosevelt, a man who commanded armies of men. He seemed preoccupied, spoke abruptly, and had little patience for small talk.

What had changed most of all was that Ike was now sharing his heart with another woman. "I kept calling her Kay," Ike confessed to Summersby after he flew back to London. "Every time I opened my mouth to say something to Mamie, I'd call her Kay. She was furious." Each time, Ike blushed and reassured his wife that Kay meant nothing to him. Mamie remained unconvinced.

Ike now found himself facing one of the greatest undertakings in military history, described by Churchill as "the most complicated and difficult that has ever taken place." While Ike prepared to command the war in Europe, three other future presidents—Kennedy, Nixon, and Ford—were fighting in the Pacific, getting their first searing exposure to the hardships of war. Kennedy's experience was the most dramatic, but both Ford and Nixon also demonstrated great courage, putting their lives on the line to support their fellow soldiers and to secure victory in battle. Their time in combat would leave a lasting impression, shaping their character, and teaching lessons they would carry with them into the Oval Office.

======

CHAPTER 4

"Okay, Let's Go"

JUNE 6, 1944
NORMANDY, FRANCE

In January 1944 Dwight Eisenhower arrived in London to assume command of the long-awaited second front. For Eisenhower, the impending invasion represented more than a military operation; he called it "the Great Crusade." The goal was not just to win on the battlefield but also to destroy Nazism and put an end to a brutal war that had shattered a continent and killed tens of millions.

The enormity of the assault created a logistical nightmare that tested Ike's organizational and leadership skills. Military planners had to figure out how to land 150,000 men at the same time onto a fifty-mile beachhead in hostile territory—a nearly impossible task. But over the next few months, the general would demonstrate his impressive expertise, managing these many complexities while also defying the ingrained habits of the British and American air services.

By that point, military planners had already chosen Normandy as the site of invasion because it was remote enough to allow Allied airpower to sever its connection to German supply routes but still within the 175-mile radius of the British Spitfire fighter plane, which would provide air cover for the invading forces. Its beaches were wide enough to accommodate the massive number of troops and vehicles that would be landing. Just as important, Normandy was unexpected: While the Germans knew that the Allies were planning an invasion, they believed that it would come from farther north, around Calais.

The original Overlord plan called for a modest-sized initial landing force of three divisions, along with several airborne drops to secure the flanks. But neither Eisenhower nor Bernard Montgomery, the British commander of troops that would carry out the initial invasion, liked that plan. Preferring a more ambitious operation, they sent the planners back to the drawing board, insisting on five divisions. In order to cut off supply lines and prevent the Germans from reinforcing their troops on the beach, they also called for a simultaneous drop of three airborne divisions behind German lines.

Eisenhower could not supervise all the details of such an elaborate operation, but according to biographer Stephen Ambrose, he "was the funnel through which everything passed." It was Ike who had to tend to all the soldiers in southern England gathering for the invasion—amounting to almost 3 million Allied troops, including 1.7 million Americans, by the spring of 1944. "Never before had an American commanded so many men from so many nations or shouldered such an awesome burden of responsibility," wrote Cornelius Ryan in his classic *The Longest Day*.

All of these men needed to be housed, trained, and fed. There were so many of them that it took fifty-four thousand cooks to prepare their meals. More than fifteen million tons of supplies had to be unloaded on British wharves—a mishmash of prefabricated huts, tents, locomotives, ammunition, jeeps, and even dental fillings. "I stood on a bridge one day," recalled an Englishman, "and saw the largest train I had ever seen pass slowly by, packed with tanks. I thought it would go on forever."

The Allies also needed to create the infrastructure to support the troops as well as develop new weapons of war, such as amphibious tanks designed specifically for the invasion. They set about those tasks without delay. By the time of the invasion, the Allies had already constructed 163 new air bases and added 170 miles of new railroad lines. The most important innovation were two man-made, temporary harbors called "Mulberries," which would facilitate unloading supplies onto the beach quickly.

These advances would be useless, however, without the most precise timing. The Allies determined that a successful operation required a full moon, which happened only six days each month. Ideally, the sea would be calm for the landing craft and the sky clear for the bombers. On top of that, Eisenhower was receiving top-secret briefings about how the Germans were seeking to develop deadly new atomic and biological weapons. He had ordered air assaults on the German factories where intelligence reports indicated the weapons were being developed. But every day that he delayed launching the invasion gave the Germans more time to discover the Allied bases in England and launch a preemptive attack—potentially with these potent new weapons. For that reason, the planners chose early May for the assault.

But one big problem changed that entire calculus: The Allies could not manufacture enough landing craft to carry men from the mother ships in the Channel to the beach. Eisenhower needed 271 landing craft beyond what had already been allocated, a condition that eventually forced him to postpone D-Day to June 5. The situation puzzled Churchill. "How it is that the plans of two great empires like Britain and the United States should be so much hamstrung and limited by a hundred or so of these particular vessels will never be understood by history," he wrote Marshall.

Even under the best of conditions, however, amphibious operations were complicated, and few had ever been successful. To improve their odds, military planners relied on deception. They developed elaborate schemes to deceive the Germans into believing that the cross-Channel invasion would take place farther east. They even created a phantom army with eleven divisions consisting of forty thousand to sixty thousand imaginary men. To make the ruse even more believable, the army assigned one of its finest generals, George Patton, who had successfully led the US Seventh Army's campaigns in North Africa and Sicily, to command the phantom army group.

Operation Overlord may have had the advantage of surprise, but it still needed to contend with Field Marshal Erwin Rommel, the Desert Fox of Germany's defeat in North Africa. In December 1942 Hitler placed Rommel in charge of reinforcing the Atlantic Wall of heavily fortified German positions that ran up and down the northwestern European coast. "The enemy must be annihilated before he reaches our main battlefield," Rommel told his troops. "We must stop him in the water."

Rommel planned a bloody welcome for the invading forces regardless of where they landed. To prevent gliders from entering farther inland, he planted hundreds of heavy wooden posts that could tear a plane apart upon landing—obstacles that the Allies referred to as "Rommel's asparagus." Additionally, he flooded low-lying lands to prevent an inland invasion. Rommel then requested that his prized panzer tanks be moved closer to the coast so that they could respond more quickly. But Hitler vetoed that idea, believing it best to keep the deadly tanks closer to Paris until the Allies revealed the location of their efforts.

Meanwhile, Ike had to contend with political challenges that further complicated the logistical ones. One of the most pressing was how to handle France, which had fallen to Nazi rule in June 1940. Ike was convinced that General Charles de Gaulle, the leader of the Free France movement, was the only person who could rally the French against Hitler. Ike also needed the French Resistance to feed him intelligence and to engage in sabotage in the weeks leading up to the invasion. So, he pleaded for de Gaulle's help in liberating France and establishing a provisional government. Eisenhower did not have enough troops to both fight a war and govern a nation. "I must have your assistance, and I have come to ask for it," he told the French leader.

FDR, however, was dead set against supporting de Gaulle, insisting that the French people would never accept someone imposed on them by the Allies and that backing de Gaulle could spark a civil war in France. Only the French people, he argued, could choose their leader. Eisenhower said later that the difficulties imposed by Roosevelt's desire to ignore de Gaulle caused one of the most difficult problems he had to face before D-Day. For weeks, Ike pleaded with the president to no avail. Undeterred, he decided to enlist British prime minister Winston Churchill's help. Finally, FDR agreed to a compromise: De Gaulle would allow the Resistance to take orders from Ike; in return, Eisenhower promised to allow Free French troops to participate in the liberation of Paris. The entire episode showcased Ike's ability to turn on his charm to win people to his side and, when that failed, to muster his skills as a bureaucratic infighter.

Although Churchill helped defuse the de Gaulle dilemma, he was simultaneously throwing up his own roadblocks. Ike insisted that the strategic bombers be under his command so that he could execute the Transportation Plan, destroying the French railway system to prevent Germans from bringing reinforcements to the Normandy area. "It was vital that the entire sum of our assault power, including the two strategic air forces, be available for use during the critical stages of the attack," he observed. But the leaders of the British strategic air forces believed that Overlord was unnecessary and the war could be won by strategic bombing alone. They wanted to focus on hitting populated areas and German oil refineries—not bombing France's transportation system or participating in a pre-invasion bombardment of entrenched German forces in Normandy.

Eisenhower knew that the Allied forces would be outnumbered ten to one during the initial invasion and that air power was essential to improve their odds of success. Churchill, however, refused to surrender control of Bomber Command. This stalemate forced the general to draw a line in the sand, telling Churchill he would "simply have to go home" if the prime minister refused to change his position. Out of the dozens of disagreements Ike had with FDR and Churchill during the war, this was the only time he threatened to resign. Fortunately, his threat triggered a breakthrough. Ike would later tell his biographer Stephen Ambrose that his insistence on the Transportation Plan was his "greatest single contribution" to the success of the operation.

In April Eisenhower moved his headquarters to outside Portsmouth, the principal embarkation point for Overlord. With many of the details of the invasion settled, he now focused on inspiring the troops. Over the next few weeks, he visited twenty-six divisions and twenty-four airfields, along with hospitals and other military installations. Kay Summersby, who accompanied Eisenhower as his chauffeur, observed, "There was no military pomp about his visit. Ike got out and just started walking among the men. He went from group to group and shook hands with as many men as he could. He spoke a few words to every man, and he looked the man in the eye as he wished him success." He interacted with hundreds of men and made sure that as many others as possible could at least catch a glimpse of him. "Soldiers like to see the men who are directing operations," Eisenhower wrote in his memoirs. "Diffidence or modesty must never blind the commander to his duty of showing himself to his men, of speaking to them, of mingling with them to the extent of physical limitations." Yet despite his show of openness, Ike confessed later to Summersby, "It's very hard, really, to look a soldier in the eye when you fear you are sending him to his death."

As the operation loomed, the pressure increasingly weighed on Eisenhower. He slept less and smoked more. "The strain is telling on him," his aide Harry Butcher observed on May 12. "He looks older now than at any time since I have been with him." Though Ike exuded confidence in public, he expressed worries in private as the preparations consumed more of his time and energy. "No one who does not have to bear the specific and direct responsibility of making the final decision as to what to do," he wrote shortly before the invasion, "can understand the intensity of these burdens."

Ike still had two more consequential decisions to make in the lead-up to the invasion. On May 29 intelligence reports revealed that the Germans were reinforcing the area where American paratroopers were scheduled to land. One estimate indicated that 70 percent of the men would be killed. Eisenhower was shocked, saying later, "It would be difficult to conceive of a more soul-racking problem." Sitting alone in his tent, he went back and forth on the issue. A dreadful number of lives were at stake. But paratroopers were essential to the mission, and canceling them would gravely impact the chances of Overlord's success. In the end, he decided that the mission would go forward with paratroopers. But he knew that if things went south, he would be blamed for the unnecessary slaughter of hundreds of American airmen.

On June 2 Ike issued a statement to the members of the Allied Expeditionary Force upon whom the operation relied. "You are about to embark upon the Great Crusade, toward which we have striven these many months. The eyes of the world are upon you. The hopes and prayers of liberty-loving people everywhere march with you. . . . We will accept nothing less than full victory! Good luck! And let us beseech the blessing of Almighty God upon this great and noble undertaking." It was not simply a call to arms but a supplication. One soldier recalled hearing his captain read Eisenhower's words over the ship's public address system. "I can tell you it was a great moment," he said. "Goose pimples came out on almost everybody that listened."

Everything was now set for the June 5 invasion—except for the weather. Early on the morning of June 4 the general received a "discouraging" weather report. Low clouds and high winds made air support impossible, while high waves jeopardized the landings. His staff was split on whether to push back the mission. All eyes remained on Eisenhower as he deliberated the final decision. When he and his staff met again at three thirty in the morning on June 5, the wind was still howling and the rain torrential. The meteorologist told him that had they had gone ahead with the planned June 5 assault, it would have ended in disaster. If the storm did not clear up by the next day, Eisenhower would have to postpone the operation another two weeks before the tides at Normandy would be low enough to permit a landing. The pessimistic reports forced Eisenhower to push back the invasion until the next day, June 6.

But then, at the last minute, the meteorologist made an "astonishing declaration": There would be relatively good weather beginning the next morning that could last for up to thirty-six hours. Ike's staff erupted when they received the news. "You never heard middle-aged men cheer like that," noted one participant. Yet the final decision still rested solely on Ike's shoulders. He listened carefully to the advice of his staff, weighing the opinions of all those assembled. One general was struck by Eisenhower's "isolation and loneliness" as he sat, hands clasped, staring down at a table. After a few minutes of silence, he stated, "I am quite positive that the order must be given." Then, after another long, thoughtful pause, Ike made it official: "Okay, let's go."

Afterward, Eisenhower scrawled out a press release he hoped the world would never see but one that reflected his deep awareness of the perils ahead. "Our landings . . . have failed . . . and I have withdrawn the troops," it began, before concluding, "If any blame or fault attaches to the attempt it is mine alone." He then placed the backup note in his wallet.

That evening Eisenhower visited the American airborne regiments who would be the first to land in France. He stood, hands in his pockets, gazing up grimly at the massive formation of planes. As the last plane took off, a reporter glanced over at Eisenhower and saw his eyes filled with tears.

In the early morning hours of June 6, 1944, D-Day, the Allies finally launched the long-delayed second front. Operation Overlord ended up being the greatest amphibious assault in recorded history, employing over 5,000 ships, 11,000 airplanes, and 175,000 men. The first wave of landing craft carried American, Canadian, and British troops onto code-named beaches. The British and Canadian troops, who landed on Gold, Juno, and Sword Beaches, and the Americans who stormed Utah Beach, encountered light resistance. The 14,000 American soldiers who assaulted Omaha Beach, however, were not so lucky. A wall of German gunfire and artillery pinned them down—just as Field Marshal Rommel had planned so meticulously. More than 2,000 were killed or wounded in only the first two hours of combat. "The surface of the water was covered with thousands and thousands of helmets floating upside down," recalled one participant. After three hours, though, a few GIs managed to climb the beach cliffs and destroy the German positions.

Although Eisenhower had been involved in planning every aspect of the assault, he could now do little more than wait to see how it unfolded. He spent the morning pacing back and forth at his headquarters waiting for reports from Normandy. At nine thirty he learned that the landing had been successful and that Allied troops had established a secure, though tenuous, foothold on all five beaches. He then instructed his press aide to release a cautious statement: "Allied naval forces, supported by strong air forces, began landing Allied armies this morning on the northern coast of France."

By nightfall, the Allies had punched a five-mile gap in Hitler's Atlantic Wall and gained control of all five beaches, but not before losing a staggering 10,549 soldiers: 6,603 Americans, 3,000 British, and 946 Canadians. It was the bloodiest day in US military history since the Battle of Antietam during the Civil War. The next morning, Eisenhower visited the beachheads in person to get a firsthand view of the state of affairs. "I made a tour along the beaches," he recalled, "finding opportunities to confer with principal commanders."

Even though Allied troops had made their first significant advances into western Europe, it still took all summer for them to shatter the German defenses. By September, the Allies had liberated Paris and were marching toward Belgium but ended up getting bogged down again. Eisenhower had hoped the war in Europe would end before Christmas, but it dragged on for another six months.

The German offensive in December 1944, known as the Battle of the Bulge, would be Eisenhower's final test of leadership. Hitler sent a quarter million men into thinly defended Allied lines in the Ardennes Forest. Despite the slim odds, Eisenhower's coolheaded leadership prevailed once again. According to biographer Stephen Ambrose, the Battle of the Bulge proved to be "Ike's finest hour as a military commander." He "acted instantly and with great vigor," recalled his chief of staff, Lieutenant General Walter Bedell Smith.

German forces had forced a bulge in the Allied lines, but this left them vulnerable to counterattack, creating enough opportunity for Ike to turn the tables on the führer. "It is easier and less costly to us to kill Germans when they are attacking than when they are holed up in concrete fortifications," Eisenhower told his aide Harry Butcher. "The more we can kill in their present offensive, the fewer we will have to dig out pillbox by pillbox." Ike proved to be right; Hitler's last-gasp effort to win the war failed miserably. "If victory in Normandy had ensured the liberation of France," noted historian William Hitchcock, "victory in the Ardennes ensured the defeat of the Third Reich."

Just as the Allied side began gaining a clear edge, tragedy struck: The man who led the nation through the war would not live to see it end. On April 12, 1945, around noon, a gravely ill Franklin Roosevelt was posing for a picture at his home in Warm Springs, Georgia, when he suddenly slumped in his chair. "I have a terrific headache," he muttered. A few hours later, FDR was dead, leaving his successor, Harry S. Truman, not even three months into the vice presidency, with the gargantuan task of winding down the war and resolving the complicated challenges of postwar global security.

Three days after FDR's death, the Allied armies rolled up to the Elbe River, roughly fifty miles west of the German capital. There they joined hands with the Russians, who had been advancing from the east. As So-viet troops closed in on Berlin, Hitler proceeded to marry his mistress, Eva Braun, before shooting her, then himself, in a suicide pact on April 30. With Hitler finally gone, the new German government had no choice but to sign an unconditional surrender in Allied headquarters. Ike sent a typically low-key telegram to Washington to mark the milestone: "The mission of this Allied force was fulfilled at 0241 local time, May 7, 1945."

Eisenhower entered the war as a mid-level military officer; he emerged from it as a world leader universally acclaimed for his decisiveness and commitment to victory. The experience had taught him how to establish strategic priorities, manage difficult personalities, and make tough decisions—all while projecting confidence and remaining calm under the most challenging of circumstances.

The general returned home an esteemed national hero. On June 19 more than four million people turned out to greet Eisenhower as he rode in a ticker-tape parade down Fifth Avenue in New York. The mayor de-clared it "Eisenhower Day" and made it a holiday for city workers. De-spite the festivities, Eisenhower struck a somber note during an address at City Hall. "There is no greater pacifist than the regular officer," he pro-claimed. "Any man who is forced to turn his attention to the horrors of the battlefield, to the grotesque shapes that are left there for the burying squad—he doesn't want war. He never wants it." It would be a message that he would carry with him to the White House.

In May 1944, while Ike stood on the cusp of launching Operation Over-lord, Lieutenant Junior Grade George Bush and the USS *San Jacinto* joined the Allied island-hopping campaign in the Pacific led by Admiral Bill Halsey's Third Fleet Fast Carrier Task Force (TF-38). The *San Jacinto* was part of a massive armada—by some estimates the largest ever as-sembled in one place—consisting of nearly eighty ships, including fleet carriers, battleships, heavy cruisers, and destroyers. Bush flew his early missions as part of the Allied effort to regain control of Wake Island, a site located 2,500 miles west of Hawaii that had fallen into Japanese hands on the same day as the Pearl Harbor attack.

On his first mission, Bush was assigned to fly low over the Pacific and identify enemy submarines, but over the next few weeks, he would participate in bombing raids on Japanese communication stations. His plane, which he named *The Barbara*, also conducted photo reconnaissance, a recent innovation. The marines, frustrated with shoddy intelligence reports that had failed to identify entrenched Japanese positions, were demanding better photos to prevent more of the same type of carnage. Bush had learned the basics of aerial photography at Norfolk, Virginia, and now part of his job was to collect photos and forward that information to Pearl Harbor, where it was evaluated by the Joint Intelligence Center.

On June 12, his twentieth birthday, Bush and two crewmates, ordnanceman Leo W. Nadeau and radioman John Delaney, engaged in a bombing raid on an air base on the southern coast of Saipan, softening up Japanese defenses for an invasion scheduled three days later. Bush's orders were to drop his payload of four five-hundred-pound bombs on a fuel dump and the radio command center. He managed to avoid antiaircraft fire and release all his bombs, but he missed the target. Although he did temporarily sever some of the radio wires, the Japanese were able to get them working again by the end of the day. Bush also watched helplessly as antiaircraft fire shredded one of his twelve fighter escorts.

Bush's commander gave him the afternoon off to celebrate his birthday, but he was back in the cockpit the next morning for a predawn strike against Japanese fortifications on Saipan. Unfortunately, his plane developed a hydraulic problem, forcing him to scrap the mission. He pushed on through this string of bad luck, returning to the sky a few days later to carry out a raid on Rota Island, which Japan used to resupply bases on Guam, and another bombing raid on Saipan.

Japan now sent its main carrier group to track down and destroy the American fleet. On the morning of June 19, the ship's radar identified some four hundred enemy planes flying in their direction. Bush and his men rushed to the deck to get into the air. "Our plane was taxied to the catapult and tied down. We had to be catapulted instead of making a deck takeoff," recalled Nadeau. While they were waiting to take off, Japanese Zeros swarmed above. Since the ship had not been turned into the wind, the only thing Bush and his crewmates could do was sit and pray.

"It was hairy," he reflected. Once the wave of fighters passed, the ship catapulted *The Barbara* into the air.

As they climbed to around 1,500 feet, an errant piece of shrapnel severed Bush's oil line. "We are losing oil pressure," he said over the intercom. "I think the oil lines have sucked up shrapnel." There was not enough time to make it back to the carrier, so Bush told the men that he was ditching the plane. "Seconds later," Nadeau recalled, Bush "made a beautiful water landing."

As the plane floated on the water's surface, Bush climbed out onto the wing, pulling the life raft from the stowage area. The three men climbed in and started paddling to get away from the sinking plane. "We got into a rubber lifeboat, and Delaney and I started singing 'Over the Bounding Main,'" Nadeau remembered. Bush was not amused. "You guys had better shut up, or they're going to think we're having too good a time out here." An hour later, a nearby destroyer picked up the crew, returning them to the carrier a few days later.

With Allied forces moving closer each day to the mainland, Tokyo decided to draw a line in the sand at Chichi Jima, a small outpost 150 miles north of Iwo Jima and only 500 miles from the mainland. By August, fifteen thousand Japanese troops had assembled on the island. To beef up defense against an Allied assault, Japanese military leaders sent the imperial antiaircraft gunners to reinforce the island, creating a virtual fortress.

On Tuesday morning, August 1, Bush was briefed on his next mission. His target was Asahi Station 6, a high-frequency radio facility that guided pilots from Tokyo to air bases in the South Pacific and that also produced electricity for the entire complex. The radio tower sat on Mount Yoake, more than a thousand feet above sea level. Its summit and slopes were covered with powerful antenna towers protected by dozens of antiaircraft guns and radar facilities. The mission was to knock out the transmitter before the scheduled US Marine assault on the island of Peleliu. That morning, Bush scrambled to avoid the withering antiaircraft fire, but all his bombs again missed their intended target. "The antiaircraft fire on that island was the worst we had seen," Nadeau recalled.

At dawn the next day, Saturday, August 2, Bush was back in the small ready room on the *San Jacinto*. His instructions were as simple as they were brief: "The radio station is your primary target."

When the briefing ended, Lieutenant William Gardner "Ted" White approached Bush. Ted, who was six years older than Bush and a Yale graduate, maintained the plane's weapons system and wanted to see how it worked in combat. For weeks, he had been begging Bush to take him on a mission instead of his usual gunner, Nadeau.

"What are you hitting today, George?" White asked.

"The radio station on Chichi Jima."

"We're moving out later today, and this may be the last time I can go with you," White said. "How about it?"

"It could be a rough trip," Bush warned, but White persisted, and Bush eventually agreed.

At a quarter after seven in the evening, the Avenger, loaded with four five-hundred-pound bombs, lifted off from the carrier along with four F6F Hellcat fighter planes for the seventy-one-mile journey. Bush strapped the target approach map to his knee for quick reference. Along the way, the squadron met up with a dozen additional Hellcats from the USS *Enterprise*.

One hour later, after flying through haze and light fog, the bombers reached their target. Commander Don Melvin and wingman Doug West led the first dive, dropping all eight bombs on the radio station and nearby buildings. By the time it was Bush's turn, however, the Japanese antiaircraft guns had him in their sights. He picked up speed as he dived straight for the tower, plunging so steeply that it felt as if he were standing on his head. Puffs of black smoke from antiaircraft guns occasionally blocked his view, but he kept focus on the target. "You see the explosions all around you," Bush told the author James Bradley, "these dark, threatening puffs of black smoke. You're tense in your body, but you can't do anything about it. You cannot take evasive action, so you get used to it. You just think to yourself, 'This is my duty, and I've got to do it.'" Besides, he added, "You always thought someone else was going to get hit."

Suddenly a flash of light appeared, followed by an explosion. "The plane was lifted forward, and we were enveloped in flames," Bush recalled. "We were probably falling at a speed of one hundred and ninety miles per hour. Smoke was coming up from the engine; I couldn't see the controls. I saw flames running along the wings to the fuel tanks. I thought, 'This is really bad.' But I was thinking of what I was supposed to do. And what I was supposed to do was drop those bombs and haul ass out of there."

Although practically blinded by the smoke, Bush managed to release all four bombs. His flight leader wrote, "Bush continued his dive, releasing his bombs on the radio station to score damaging hits. He then turned sharply to the east to clear the island of Chichi Jima, smoke and flames enveloping his engine and spreading aft as he did so, and his plane losing altitude."

Bush knew that he would not make it back to the carrier, but he was determined to get as far away as possible from the island to avoid capture. He considered making a water landing, but the flames were spreading too fast, so he had no choice but to make an emergency parachute landing. Each of the three men was restricted to his own space and could not see the others, so they depended on the plane's intercom to communicate. "Hit the silk!" Bush shouted over the intercom, commanding White and Delaney to bail out. "Hit the silk!"

When he did not get a response, Bush assumed that both men had already bailed out. Now it was his turn to abandon the plane before it exploded in a giant fireball. He calmly leveled the plane, removed his headset, released his harness, and pushed himself out. "I unfastened my seatbelt and dove out and down to avoid the tail," he said. "But I pulled the cord too quickly, and the tail came up and hit me in the head." The fall also tore a few panels out of his parachute.

Bush plummeted toward the water at a high speed, but he still had the presence of mind to release his parachute about twenty feet above sea level. As he hit the water, he remembered that airmen would often get entangled in their chutes and drown. With his clothes and shoes weighing him down, he kicked frantically to stay afloat until he could inflate his life vest. Blood streamed down from his head wound. At first, he was not aware that a life raft had fallen with him from the plane and was floating on the surface about fifty feet away. A Hellcat swooped down and pointed its wings to the yellow one-man raft, roughly the size of a large sofa cushion. Bush swam toward it, inflated it, and struggled to get in.

At that point, Bush paused to assess his situation. It was not encouraging. He had crashed about four miles northeast of the island. The small container of water attached to the raft had cracked open. With no paddles, he sat helplessly as the wind blew him back toward Chichi Jima. "I could see the island," Bush said. "I started paddling with my hands, leaning over the front of the raft, paddling as hard as I could."

He tried to remain calm, but the circumstances were terrifying. By this point, rumors of Japanese atrocities, including the cannibalizing of downed Allied fliers, had spread throughout the fleet. In an effort to prevent these pilots from suffering a similar fate, the navy had ordered submarines into the area to serve lifeguard duty near each of the targeted islands. Making matters worse, Bush had swallowed mouthfuls of seawater as he swam to the raft, and, adding to his misery, a Portuguese man-of-war stung his arm, which was now throbbing. "I was crying," Bush admitted later. "I was twenty years old, and I was traumatized. I had just survived a burning plane crash. I was all alone, and I was wondering if I'd make it."

Yet despite the danger to his own life, Bush couldn't stop thinking about his crewmates, White and Delaney. He searched for the sight of another raft, but a hazy sky and choppy water obscured his vision. He assumed that they had escaped when he gave the order, but he could not know for sure.

Meanwhile, Doug West, who was circling above, providing air cover, noticed Japanese troops on the beach climbing into boats to capture Bush. "I saw those small boats heading his way, and I thought, 'Oh, he's a goner,'" remembered gunner Charles Bynum. "But at that instant, [Milt] Moore, who was my pilot, and Melvin in the adjoining bomber, took the initiative. Our two planes went down and strafed the boats and drove them off." Records show that the pilots fired 1,460 rounds of machine gun bullets, which managed to drive the Japanese away. But for how long? Bush's fellow pilots were running low on fuel and needed to return to their carriers. The flight leader radioed Bush's location to the rescue submarine USS *Finback*, which was standing by for just such an emergency.

Now Bush was once again all alone, bobbing in a small raft in enemy territory. It seemed that he would either die of thirst or be captured by the Japanese. But he controlled his terror by focusing on staying alive—which for now meant paddling as hard as possible to avoid being swept back to shore.

This struggle went on for nearly three hours before Bush spotted something miraculous: the conning tower of the *Finback*. At more than three hundred feet long and boasting two powerful diesel engines, the submarine was one of the largest and fastest in the US fleet. "At first, I thought maybe I was delirious," Bush reflected years later, "and when I concluded it was a submarine all right, I feared that it might be Japanese. It just seemed too lucky and too far-fetched that it would be an American submarine." But he knew he had been rescued when he spied American sailors on the deck. A team of four enlisted men dived into the water and swam toward him. Together they pulled the lanky future president out of the raft and onto the *Finback*.

The submarine's photographer, Ensign Bill Edwards, stood on the deck with a Ciné-Kodak 8 mm movie camera, recording the moment for posterity.

"Welcome aboard, sir," said Don Kohler, a torpedoman second class.

"Happy to be aboard," Bush replied.

"Let's go below," Kohler said. "The skipper wants to get the hell out of here."

Bush had narrowly escaped capture—or death—with a few minor cuts and bruises. But he was emotionally fragile. By now, he knew that his two crewmates had died in the crash. The next day, he sat down to pen a letter to his parents, telling them that he was "physically" fine but "troubled inside and with good cause." He felt "so terribly responsible" for the demise of his missing crewmates. "Perhaps as the days go by it will all change and I will be able to look upon it in a different light." The guilt would follow Bush for decades and serve as a personal reminder of the horrors of war. "I think about those two all the time," he told biographer Jeffrey Engel decades later.

Bush would spend the next thirty days trapped on the submarine as it completed its mission. On the surface, the twenty-year-old pretended to be lighthearted and entertaining. But he was plagued with survivor's guilt. He kept replaying the incident in his head, repeatedly questioning whether he had done all he could to save his men.

Even holed up in a submarine, Bush's brush with danger was still not over. Japanese ships dropped their deadly depth charges on the *Finback* twice. "We just had to sit in there and be still," he recalled. "That experience was far scarier than an airplane bombing run. At least in the plane you control your destiny to some extent: you could see puffs of smoke coming at you, and you knew what the problem was. But there, underwater, all you could do was hope like hell that the enemy wouldn't put an explosive on top of you. The real submariners weren't that worried about it; they'd been through it all before. But for me, there was a certain helplessness. Having no assigned duty made it even worse—waiting for one explosion and then the next. There were times when it felt as though the sub would shake apart. I felt trapped and scared, far more scared than I was being shot at in my plane."

After spending thirty days on the *Finback*, Bush could have gone home on leave. But he wanted to get back to his squadron instead. After undergoing some additional training, he flew a naval transport plane to Guam, where he was to meet up with his carrier. Since the *San Jacinto* was operating off Leyte Island, in the Philippines, he did not rejoin it until November 2. At that point, Bush and his new crew began targeting Japanese military positions around Manila Bay.

Bush flew his last mission on Monday, November 13, 1944, before being ordered to take a thirty-day leave, when he traveled home. "I arrived Christmas Eve, December 24, 1944. No reunion could have been scripted more perfectly," he reflected. "There were tears, laughs, hugs, joy, the love and warmth of family in a holiday setting." The celebration continued past Christmas. Two weeks later, he and Barbara were married at First Presbyterian Church in Rye, New York.

Bush was in Virginia Beach, Virginia, training for the eventual invasion of Japan, when he and Barbara learned that the war had ended. "Before going home, we went to a nearby church filled with others giving thanks and remembering those lost in the war," Bush said later. "After four years, it was finally over." Bush was officially discharged from the navy on September 18, 1945—after logging 1,228 hours of flying time, 126 carrier landings, and 58 missions. He would be awarded the Distinguished Flying Cross for bravery.

Bush was not a reflective man, and when the war ended, he moved on. "George lives his life in chapters," said his sister, Nancy. "The war was over, and he left it behind. Some people had trouble doing that. George didn't."

Like JFK, Bush was transformed by his service in World War II. His time as a pilot and while on the *Finback* proved to be the defining moments of his life. "As you grow older and try to retrace the steps that made you the person that you are," he reflected years later, "the signposts to look for are those special times of insight. I remember my days and nights aboard the *Finback* as one of those times—maybe the most important of them all." The experience, he admitted, gave him a "sobering understanding of war and peace."

Characterizing his life before the navy as "protected," Bush confessed that his "vision of the world was narrow" and that he was "a little judgmental at age eighteen." But the war enabled him to mature as a man and to relate to people from different classes and regions. While he emerged from the ordeal convinced of the righteousness of the Allied cause and of the importance of preparedness, he also appreciated the painful price of war. His service, Bush later claimed, taught him "the realities of death."

Those harrowing lessons stuck with him when he entered the White House. Like Eisenhower and JFK, Bush balanced his commitment to defending America's national interest with a genuine comprehension of the horrors of war. "When it came time for me to send their kids to Panama, and later to the Middle East, I thought back on my own experiences in combat and what it was like to be shot at," he reflected. "Those memories were constantly in my mind when we were discussing committing troops and estimating expected combat losses." It was the inhumanity of war that helped humanize Bush's understanding of the postwar world.

In December 1944, shortly after Bush flew his final mission, Admiral Bull Halsey's Carrier Task Force sat off the eastern Philippines providing air cover for General Douglas MacArthur's troops as they retook the Japanese island of Leyte. Among the light carriers in the armada were George Bush's *San Jacinto* and Gerald Ford's *Monterey*. Bush was at home for his thirty-day leave, but Ford stood in the eye of one of the most powerful typhoons in history.

Halsey showed little concern as the weather deteriorated on the morning of December 17, dismissing it as a "tropical disturbance." At the time, weather forecasters had no way to identify and track typhoons, and this one was especially deceptive. Powerful but compact, it gave little advance warning of its fury. The admiral made several attempts to maneuver the ships out of danger but inadvertently placed them directly in the storm's path, with its soaring seventy-foot waves and howling 145-mile-per-hour winds. By the afternoon, he was receiving word of men and fighter jets being swept off the decks of their ships.

Conditions were especially dire on lighter carriers such as the *Monterey*, which bobbed powerlessly in the water like a child's toy. At one point, the *Monterey*'s captain, Stuart Ingersoll, called Halsey, asking for permission to navigate a course away from the storm. Despite Ingersoll's pleas, Halsey replied dismissively that the rough seas would give his men the opportunity to practice their seamanship.

Conditions continued to deteriorate through the evening and overnight. Ford, who was the presiding officer on the bridge from midnight to four in the morning, noted that in his eighteen months at sea, he had never seen waves so big. When his watch ended, Ford went below deck and crawled into his bunk. Less than an hour later, the captain called general quarters, and Ford, smelling smoke, immediately jumped to his feet. As he raced to the bridge, a giant wave crashed against the ship, forcing it to pitch 25 degrees to port. Ford was knocked to the deck, where for about twenty seconds he slid "as if I were on a toboggan" across the 109-foot-wide deck. "It scared the hell out of me," he confessed later. "I was going overboard."

In a stroke of luck, Ford was rescued by a two-inch-high steel lip surrounding the deck. Its purpose was to prevent tools from sliding overboard, but that night it saved the life of a future president. The lip broke his slide and gave Ford the chance to regain his balance, climb to his knees, and force his way onto the catwalk. Undeterred, he turned around and inched back to the bridge. "Well, let me tell you," he recalled years later, "my second trip back from the catwalk to the bridge, I was much more careful."

As soon as Ford arrived on the bridge, Captain Ingersoll briefed him on the situation. Some of the planes on the hangar deck had broken loose and were smashing into one another, catching fire. The night before, Ingersoll had wisely ordered all of the planes to be drained of fuel, but the remnants had still ignited. To make matters worse, the carrier's ventilation system, which was supposed to transmit fresh air to the engine and boiler room, was instead pumping out deadly black fumes. One sailor was already dead, and thirty-three others were suffering from asphyxiation. With no one to tend them, three of the four boilers had stopped functioning. If the fourth failed, the ship would lose water pressure in the hoses that were necessary to fight the fire.

It looked as if the ship would not make it. An observer on a nearby vessel, seeing the *Monterey* engulfed by fire and heavy smoke, radioed, "Well, check off the *Monterey*." Finally recognizing the severity of the situation, Admiral Halsey instructed Ingersoll to abandon ship and ordered two cruisers and several destroyers to move alongside to rescue survivors. Ingersoll, however, was not yet ready to surrender. "Give us more time," Ford heard him say over the radio. "I think we can solve the problem." He then turned to Ford and entrusted him with the daunting task of saving the carrier.

Without hesitation, Ford put on a gas mask and led a fire brigade below. His first task was to retrieve the injured men, some of whom were unconscious. Ford described the burning planes as "darting around down there like trapped, terrified birds." He and his team of firefighters fought tenaciously to get the chaos under control. When a firefighter was overcome by smoke or burned, he would be replaced by another. After about forty minutes, the firefighters managed to extinguish the flames and save the fourth boiler. At 4:41 A.M. Ingersoll radioed, "Have fire under control."

Still, the ship was not completely out of danger, riding out the storm for another seven hours. By the time the storm subsided the following morning, the *Monterey* had lost 18 of its 34 aircraft—more than half. Three men were dead and another 40 injured, 10 critically. The fleet lost a total of 3 destroyers, 146 aircraft, and almost 800 men, with 80 injured.

Given the extent of its damage, the navy ordered the *Monterey* to Washington State for repairs. Ford, however, disembarked in Saipan and flew back to his hometown of Grand Rapids for leave. "I wish I could have stayed," he reflected years later. "I had no reason to get home. I had no family or anything. . . . [If] you believe in your cause and your country, you might as well be out there where things are going on."

But it would not be long before Ford jumped back into the fray. After spending a few weeks in Grand Rapids, he was assigned to a preflight program at Saint Mary's College of California, where he was again responsible for training recruits. While there, he was promoted to lieutenant commander. In April 1945 Ford was transferred to the Naval Reserve Training Command staff at Glenview Naval Air Station, near Chicago. But his heart still remained with his men. "I was anxious to get back out there," he recalled. "I was bored in Chicago." He applied for sea duty, but none was forthcoming.

While Ford waited in the States, the Allies continued their relentless drive toward Tokyo. In February 1945, US forces had captured Iwo Jima, a speck of an island that cost 4,189 American lives. Two months later, 11,260 US soldiers died in the successful assault on Okinawa. The fanatical resistance of Japanese defenders on Iwo Jima and Okinawa sent a clear message: The invasion of their home islands would be long and bloody. War planners estimated the conquest of Japan, scheduled to begin on November 1, 1945, could take a year and cost as many as one million American casualties. Unable to accept that prospect, the new president, Harry Truman, made a fateful decision that would change the international balance of power forever. He approved the deployment of a destructive new weapon that had never been used before.

On August 6, 1945, a B-29 named *Enola Gay* dropped the first atomic bomb on Hiroshima. The sky exploded into a mushroom cloud. Striking with the force of 12,000 tons of TNT, the atomic bomb killed about

80,000 of the city's 550,000 inhabitants instantly, and thousands more died later of burns or radiation poisoning. Two days later, on August 8, the Soviet Union declared war on Japan and invaded Manchuria and Korea. The next day, the United States dropped a second atomic bomb on Nagasaki, incinerating another 40,000 people and obliterating much of the city.

World War II came to an end shortly thereafter, on September 2, but Ford remained in uniform until January 1946. By the time he left the navy, at thirty-two years old, he had earned ten battle stars as well as something far more intangible: a firsthand perspective on both the promises and perils of war.

———

World War II proved to be the most transformative event of the twentieth century. The conflict devastated nations, crippled societies, and shattered the international system beyond recognition. When it ended, sixty million people had perished; more than half of those—thirty-six million— were Europeans. With typically powerful prose, Winston Churchill depicted postwar Europe as "a rubble heap, a charnel house, a breeding ground of pestilence and hate." Those wretched conditions precipitated a historic shift in American foreign policy. For the previous five hundred years, Europe had dominated the international system. Not anymore. The great European powers before the war—Germany, Britain, Italy, and France—were now left either defeated or crippled. Unable to feed their own people, these nations lacked the resources to sustain their far-flung colonial empires, providing an opportunity for nationalist movements in the Middle East and Asia to break away from their former masters. Amid this shifting landscape, the United States emerged as the world's sole superpower. The other Allied powers had been decimated by the war; the Soviets alone lost more than twenty million people.

While the United States was spared the massive casualties suffered by other nations, the war still served as a catalyst for major changes in American society. The most obvious change was a dramatic increase in the size and scope of the federal government. The growing centralization of power in Washington that began during the New Deal accelerated during World

War II. The cost of the war—more than $330 billion—was twice the sum of all government spending in US history up to that point. By comparison, Roosevelt's New Deal responded to the 1938 recession by spending $3 billion on public works.

The war also enhanced the power of the presidency over the other branches of government. Roosevelt's twelve years in office had been marked by various crises that demanded a robust executive response. During that time, FDR made the presidency the focus of the public's expectations. His skillful use of radio enabled him to build a personal relationship with millions of Americans desperate for help and hope. They would gather in their living rooms, listening intently to the president's rich, resonant voice as he explained how he would steer them through difficult times.

The war laid the foundation for social changes that would occur in the postwar era, partly by raising the country's expectations of what government could accomplish and the opportunities it could provide. Those who had participated in the war effort and helped secure victory now demanded that the government address their grievances. "The war changed our whole idea of how we wanted to live when we came back," explained a veteran. Americans who fought in the war felt they deserved "a good job, a respectable life." The war had made new employment opportunities available to women, who sought to build on those gains in the postwar period. Organized labor, which limited its strike activity during the war, now flexed its muscle to secure the benefits of prosperity for its members. Most of all, African American veterans who had risked their lives to preserve freedom abroad now came home demanding it for themselves. Unsurprisingly, when peace came in 1945, the poet Maya Angelou saw Black soldiers returning home treated "like forgotten laundry left on a back yard fence." This time, though, they felt more empowered to protest their perpetual mistreatment. In short, the war made more obvious the festering problems that future presidents would need to address.

World War II did not simply transform domestic and international politics on a structural level. It also reshaped the hearts and minds of those who survived it—including each of the future presidents. All but Reagan had seen the war as a critical test between freedom and tyranny and felt a personal responsibility to get close to the action. While LBJ spent only a few minutes in combat, Kennedy, Nixon, Ford, and Bush all showed remarkable personal courage, lobbying relentlessly to get near the front lines. Eisenhower lived with war every day and made critical decisions that led to the Allied victory in Europe.

The war would prove central to the political identity and popular appeal of both Ike and JFK. They emerged from the war as heroes, and their association with the war helped carry them to the White House. It is very likely that had there been no World War II, there would have been no President Eisenhower or President Kennedy.

In 1939 Ike was a forty-nine-year-old lieutenant colonel, admired by his peers for his organizational skills and planning brilliance but stuck in a dead-end job in the Pacific. By the time the war ended, he was the supreme commander of all Allied troops in Europe and one of the most recognizable and revered men in the world. Kennedy's fiery patriotism and romantic views of war motivated him, as they did many men of his generation, to join the Allied fight against Nazi Germany. But he showed genuine heroism, and his actions following the sinking of PT-109 were central to his public image and helped carry him into the White House in 1960. The author William Doyle noted that "the PT-109 incident made John F. Kennedy—both the man and the myth."

Other World War II veterans also tried to capitalize on their war experiences but with limited success. Lyndon Johnson spun exaggerated tales of his brief encounter with Japanese Zeros. The whole affair lasted only a few minutes, but you would not have known that if you listened to Johnson on the campaign trail, bragging about his role in shooting down enemy planes. Though the extent of his direct involvement was questionable, LBJ did gain one valuable lesson from the war: the necessity for civilian leadership to constantly question the claims of military men. Unfortunately, President Johnson would forget that lesson when Vietnam landed on his desk.

Similarly, Richard Nixon wore his naval uniform during his 1946 run for Congress, but unlike JFK, he did not have a compelling story to tell, and voters seemed to lose interest. Partly because of this, Nixon went searching for another issue to stir up the public: anti-Communism. Much of the fervor that he devoted to that cause arose from his brief time in Washington before heading for the Pacific theater. It was from that wartime experience that Nixon developed his abiding disdain for "the establishment"—the Ivy League liberals and left-leaning Jewish lawyers who implemented Roosevelt's domestic and foreign policy agenda. He still harbored that resentment when he entered the White House, and it ultimately led to his downfall.

Prior to the war, Gerald R. Ford had been convinced that the two oceans would protect America from the hostilities consuming Asia and Europe. "I'd been an isolationist," he confessed. "But now I had become an ardent internationalist. My wartime experiences had given me an entirely new perspective." He was now convinced that the United States "could no longer stick its head in the sand like an ostrich. Our military unpreparedness before World War II had only encouraged the Germans and Japanese." Like all the veterans of World War II who occupied the White House, Ford vowed "never again" to "allow our military to be anything but the best."

When the war came to an end, Ronald Reagan clearly felt that commuting to a Hollywood studio every day, just as he did before the war, entitled him to many of the same emotions as those veterans who were coming home from the battlefield. "By the time I got out of the Army Air Corps, all I wanted to do—in common with several other veterans—was to rest up a while, make love to my wife, and come up refreshed to a better job in an ideal world," Reagan wrote in his 1965 autobiography. In reality, he spent just about every night of World War II comfortably at home. He may not have seen his wife often, but that had nothing to do with where he was stationed. Jane Wyman was off making movies and participating in war bond drives.

Just as important, his role in the war transformed the way the public viewed him. "Ronald Reagan might have never left California during the war, but his military service projected him to America as a war hero," wrote biographer Bob Spitz. He appeared in public always wearing his uniform, while on the screen he displayed enormous courage in fighting and defeating the enemy. "Millions saw him in uniform onscreen and came to recognize his voice as the voice of those protecting America against aggression," observed biographer H. W. Brands. "They learned to associate him with American power and American patriotism." The public could not distinguish Reagan's celluloid heroism from that of Jimmy Stewart or Clark Gable, who actually saw real combat. "No twentieth-century president, with the exception of Dwight Eisenhower, had been seen in uniform by more people," remarked biographer Stephen Vaughn.

Reagan's military career came to an end on September 12, 1945, when he was officially discharged. The studio reinstated him at his full salary and promised to give him a leading role in a major film as soon as it received an acceptable script. Because he never left home, and experienced war only through Hollywood roles that he played in the 1940s, Reagan viewed war as an abstraction untethered by the reality of battle. He experienced war through characters such as Lieutenant Ames in *The Rear Gunner*, who engaged with Japanese pilots in the Pacific, and the hotshot pilot in *Recognition of the Japanese Zero Fighter*. Ironically, what brought the war home to Reagan was not how it was fought but how it ended. The bomb raised for him the unthinkable specter of a nuclear holocaust, and, like many liberals, he advocated for international control of nuclear weapons. Over the next few decades, he would abandon most of his liberal beliefs, but he never shed his deep personal fear of the destructive capability of nuclear weapons or of the need for international controls. The contradiction between Reagan's often bellicose rhetoric and his fear of nuclear Armageddon would be key to understanding his approach as president in dealing with the Soviets and the key role that he would play in bringing about a peaceful ending to the Cold War.

Unlike his predecessor, Bush had a personal comprehension of the pain and suffering that war required. Even as he continued to believe in the necessity of sacrifice for a noble cause, memories of World War II weighed heavily on him. On December 31, 1990, nearly five months after the country of Iraq invaded its tiny neighbor Kuwait, Bush wrote a letter to his family explaining his decision to confront Iraqi president Saddam Hussein with American troops should the dictator not withdraw his occupying forces by a January 15 deadline. "How many lives might have been saved if the appeasement had given way to force earlier on in the late 30s or earliest 40s?" he asked rhetorically. "How many Jews might have been spared the gas chamber, or how many Polish patriots might be alive today?"

All those who fought endured hardship and demonstrated enormous personal courage, but Eisenhower, Kennedy, and Bush faced the most searing experiences. Of those three, it was likely Eisenhower who would become most aware of the brutality of war. Following the D-Day invasion of Normandy, Eisenhower toured the front lines and talked to the wounded, seeing firsthand the anguished faces of the boys he'd sent into battle. Kennedy and Bush also knew what it was like to lose men under their command. Two sailors died when JFK's PT boat sank in the Pacific. Their bodies were never recovered. Similarly, Bush lost two crewmates when his plane was shot down. It haunted him for the rest of his life.

In a sobering reflection of war's pervasive consequences, Kennedy and Bush both mourned the death of George Mead, a distant Bush relative as well as a close Cape Cod friend of JFK's (although neither man realized the connection then). Mead was among the first casualties when Americans stormed the beaches of Guadalcanal in August 1942. While spending time in Guadalcanal, Kennedy visited Mead's grave. "He is buried near the beach where they first landed," he wrote to his girlfriend. "The whole thing was about the saddest experience I've ever had and enough to make you cry." Meanwhile, Bush was in Chapel Hill, North Carolina, training to be a pilot when his mother wrote to him about Mead's death. Bush remained stoic. "He died the way all of us would like to die when our time comes," he replied.

Tempered by their wartime experiences, the future presidents now had to adjust to the new realities of the postwar world. The war had taught them to remain vigilant and respond forcefully to perceived threats to the international order. Having won a titanic struggle against Nazism and Imperial Japan, these men, like many Americans, were filled with grand expectations for the future. They embraced what influential publisher Henry R. Luce termed "the American Century," in which the United States "must be the elder brother of the nations in the brotherhood of man."

There was, however, one major obstacle to this triumphalist American vision of the future. In 1945 Luce's *Life* magazine cautioned that the Soviet

Union "is the number one problem for Americans because it is the only country in the world with the dynamic power to challenge our own conceptions of truth, justice, and the good life." Each of these men would summon the lessons learned during World War II to respond to this new threat and avoid another world war. Unfortunately, they would end up trying to impose the "lessons of Munich" onto a far more complex world.

Part 2

INTO THE ARENA

CHAPTER 5

"My Mother Is a Gold Star Mother, Too"

JANUARY 23, 1946
CHARLESTOWN, MASSACHUSETTS

A frail, bone-thin, twenty-eight-year-old John F. Kennedy faced a packed house of Gold Star Mothers—those who had lost sons during the war—at the American Legion in Charlestown, Massachusetts. The former lieutenant was campaigning for a congressional seat in Boston's Eleventh District. The district included not only vote-rich Cambridge, home of Harvard and the Massachusetts Institute of Technology, but also the gritty working-class town of Charlestown as well as poor Italian and Irish enclaves such as Somerville. Since the district was heavily Democratic, winning the primary was tantamount to winning the election in November.

In some ways, Kennedy seemed out of place. He was the son of a millionaire with a Harvard degree running in one of the poorest districts in the state. He did not even live there and used his grandfather's sparsely furnished two-room suite at the Hotel Bellevue across the street from the state capitol as his residence. In addition, he was running against ten other primary candidates with deep roots in the area. The night before his campaign launch, a prominent Cambridge political figure reminded him of his outlier status by telling him, "You're not going to win this fight. You're a carpetbagger. You don't belong here."

While many biographers claim that his overbearing father forced him to run for Congress, JFK actually came to the decision on his own after reflecting on his wartime experience. Near the end of World War II, he wrote to a former Choate teacher that the savagery he had witnessed convinced him that armed conflict must be the last resort. "I should really like—as my life's goal—in some way and at some point to do something to help prevent another."

Politics provided an avenue toward achieving this ideal. Dave Powers, a popular political figure in Charlestown who joined the 1946 campaign and would be by Kennedy's side until his ill-fated 1963 trip to Dallas, believed that JFK, like other veterans, was drawn to politics by the "realization that whether you really like it or not, this was the place where you personally could do the most to prevent another war." This was also the appeal Kennedy made to other military veterans to join his campaign. "If we're going to change things the way they should be changed," he said, "we all have to do things we don't want to do."

It was a message that Kennedy would repeat numerous times on the campaign trail. "There are many pursuits which I could have followed," he told crowds, "but the war has taught me in clear and unmistakable terms the lesson that [it] is the duty of all of us to devote all our time and all our efforts to the preservation of the American way of life." He frequently described the "promise" he had made while a PT boat captain in the Pacific: "When ships were sinking and young Americans were dying . . . I firmly resolved to serve my country in peace as honestly as I tried to serve it in war."

Kennedy would grow into one of the most able and inspiring politicians of his generation, but his career did not start out that way. Initially awkward and shy, he often read directly from a text in his high-pitched voice. Tip O'Neill, who would later represent the district and go on to become Speaker of the House in 1977, was not impressed when he met Kennedy for the first time. "I couldn't believe the skinny, pasty-faced kid was a candidate for anything!"

Kennedy had delivered his first speech of the campaign back in September 1945 at a Rotary Club in Hyannis. A reporter covering the event wrote that Kennedy "more closely resembled a high school senior chosen as boys state representative . . . than a young man on the threshold of a political career. His loss of weight made the collar of his white shirt gape at the neck." His suit "hung slackly from his wide, but frail-seeming, shoulders and gave him the look . . . of a little boy dressed up in his father's clothes." According to the reporter, Kennedy projected "a quality of grave seriousness that masked his discomfiture. No trace of humor leavened his talk. Hardly diverging from his prepared text, he stood as if before a blackboard, addressing a classroom full of pupils who could be expected at any moment to become unruly."

To make matters worse, Kennedy avoided discussing the very thing that could have connected him to voters: his heroism during the war. When asked about PT-109, he usually responded with a quip: "I had no choice. They sunk my boat." He informed an aide that he had no desire "to parlay a lost PT boat and a bad back into political advantage." But private polls that Joe Kennedy Sr. commissioned revealed that most voters were more intrigued by "Jack Kennedy, the hero of PT-109" than "Jack Kennedy, the politician." Even Kenneth O'Donnell, a close friend of Bobby Kennedy's, confessed that he was "much more interested in meeting Bobby's war hero brother than I was interested in meeting Bobby's brother who is running for Congress."

The truth of this observation became apparent on that January night at the American Legion. According to Powers, Kennedy began by reading blandly from a prepared text. "He started to talk to all these wonderful ladies who all lost a son in World War II, and he was not a great speaker at that time," Powers reflected. But after about ten minutes, Kennedy paused, looked up at the faces of grieving mothers, and spoke directly from his heart. "I think I know how all you mothers feel because my mother is a Gold Star Mother, too." Powers noticed that with that sentence, Kennedy instantly established a "magical link" with everyone in the room. Although painfully shy, Jack was at last able to summon his experience of the war to connect with strangers. "Suddenly swarms of women hurried up to the platform, crowding around him and wishing him luck. And I could hear them saying to each other, 'Isn't he a wonderful boy, he reminds me so much of my own John' or 'my Bob.'" Powers had never witnessed anything like that moment.

Afterward, the campaign aggressively marketed Kennedy as a war hero. According to friend Billy Sutton, who traveled with JFK from morning to night, "The PT-109 was the great theme of the campaign. We did all we could to make sure every voter in the district knew that Jack had received the Navy and Marine Corps Medal as well as the Purple Heart for his service in the Solomons during World War II." By Election Day, he continued, "'Kennedy the war hero' and 'PT-109' were household phrases in the Eleventh District."

Although personally uncomfortable with the war hero label, Kennedy understood the political power of returning veterans. Roughly 10 percent of all Americans were veterans, and 75 percent of men born between 1919 and 1929 served in the military, although a much smaller number actually saw combat. Many veterans chose the same path as JFK upon returning home. According to the *Army Times*, a service publication, 183 World War II veterans survived the primaries to represent their party in the 1946 general election: 110 Democrats and 73 Republicans. Of these, 69 were elected, or about one out of every seven members of the new Congress.

Kennedy appealed directly to this new generation of veterans. Mark Dalton, Kennedy's 1946 campaign manager, observed that many older veterans felt that Kennedy was too inexperienced, but that the candidate formed "a real bond" with the younger cohort of World War II vets. "There was a tremendous ferment after the war," Dalton reflected. "The whole feeling of taking over—that it's a new era. The young veteran wanted to do something, and he was naturally attracted to John Kennedy."

JFK focused his campaign message squarely on this group. "I feel that I have earned the right to say that I know the problems of the veteran," he stated. At the top of his list of priorities was more money for housing and education. "Those who experienced the hardship and sacrifices of war, both here and abroad, are worthy of the best homes we can provide," he said. Although he supported the 1944 Servicemen's Readjustment Act—popularly known as the GI Bill—which provided veterans with a small stipend, low-cost mortgages, and tuition assistance, Kennedy was frustrated with the program's implementation. He complained that the money provided for education was an "empty gesture, for the gates of our schools and colleges remain closed to thousands and thousands of veterans due to inadequate facilities." Additionally, he called for improving and expanding hospital facilities for returning veterans. Though Kennedy acknowledged that these programs "will impose heavy tax burdens on the American people," he insisted that "a prosperous America with growing production and a mounting national income can carry these burdens."

Kennedy's foreign policy views had evolved in response to changing circumstances in Europe during the year before his campaign. As a college senior, JFK had been critical of England's unwillingness to arm itself, arguing that its lack of preparation had only whetted Hitler's expansionist plans. Now he contended the opposite, calling for a reduction in armaments due to fears that another arms race could produce a new world war. Like many Americans, Kennedy worried about the dangerous effects that massive defense spending—in competition with the Soviet Union—would have on our democratic institutions. If the United States tried to compete with "a dictatorship like Russia in maintaining large armies for an indefinite period, our democracy would probably collapse internally," he wrote. "Democracy sleeps fitfully in an armed camp."

As tensions increased between East and West, Kennedy would check his earlier optimism, but he remained hopeful of reaching some accommodation with the Soviets. Back in February 1945 Franklin Roosevelt had traveled to Yalta, a resort on the Black Sea coast, to meet with Winston Churchill and Joseph Stalin in hopes of resolving the thorny questions of control in Europe. The leaders reached compromises on many issues, but the postwar political status of Poland caused the most controversy at the conference. To avoid letting arguments over Poland undermine harmony, the Allies worked out an agreement that papered over significant differences with vague, elastic language. Stalin agreed to "free and unfettered elections," but refused to offer a specific date for when that might happen.

Roosevelt left Yalta convinced that he had laid the foundation for a peaceful postwar landscape. But with its Red Army of ten million men in control of most of Eastern Europe, the Soviets proceeded to impose their will by force. Within weeks of the Yalta Conference, despite his promise to hold "free and unfettered elections," Stalin installed a pro-Soviet puppet government in Poland. With that country firmly in his grasp, the Soviet leader then moved to effect a stranglehold on the rest of Eastern Europe.

Kennedy had a bird's-eye view of the next meeting of the Grand Alliance, which took place in Potsdam, Germany, from July 17 to August 2—following Germany's surrender but still a few weeks away from America's unleashing the Atomic Age, breaking Japan's will. He was one of three US presidents present: the current commander in chief, Harry Truman, and another future chief executive, Eisenhower.

After serving as supreme commander in Europe, Eisenhower had planned a quiet life of retirement, but he was wrong to think that he could slip out of the limelight. Shortly after the war, Ike returned to Europe as governor of occupied Germany. He soon realized what a challenging job he'd been tasked with. "The country is devastated," he wrote. "Whole cities are obliterated. And the German population, to say nothing of millions of former slave laborers, is largely homeless." It was, he wrote, "a bleak picture. In my wildest nightmares, I never visualized some of the things now thrown at me."

When Truman traveled to Potsdam, he asked Ike to join him. Eisenhower was not a formal member of the American delegation, but he used the opportunity to consult with both Truman and General George Marshall. One day he and General Omar Bradley took Truman for a tour of the devastation in Berlin. Ike was stunned when Truman, a Democrat, who was suffering from plummeting poll numbers, offered to support him for president in 1948. "Now, in the car, he suddenly turned toward me and said: 'General, there is nothing that you may want that I won't try to help you get. That definitely and specifically includes the presidency in 1948.'" Ike was stunned by the proposal and laughed it off. "Mr. President, I don't know who will be your opponent for the presidency, but it will not be I."

By this point, Eisenhower was making no effort to hide his relationship with his chauffeur, Kay Summersby. According to Truman, Ike wrote Marshall a letter saying that he wanted to be relieved of duty so that he could divorce Mamie and marry Kay. The president went on to say that Marshall was furious and told Ike that if he tried to do such a thing, he would "bust him out of the army." Truman recounted, too, that when he left office in 1953, he "got those letters from [Eisenhower's] file in the Pentagon, and I destroyed them." It may have been a moment of weakness, but Ike quickly realized that marrying Kay was not an option and broke off the relationship.

Meanwhile, Jack accompanied Navy Secretary (and family friend) James Forrestal to the conference. Though he did not attend the formal meetings, Kennedy had the chance to meet the major players, including Eisenhower. In a diary entry dated August 1, he described Ike as "an outstanding figure" who possessed "an easy personality, immense self-assurance, and gave an excellent presentation of the situation in Germany." The two men also had a brief encounter when Kennedy accompanied Forrestal on a plane trip to Frankfurt. When they descended the plane's ladder, Eisenhower was standing on the tarmac waiting. One photographer managed to capture the moment when Eisenhower greeted Forrestal, with twenty-eight-year-old JFK in the background.

The conference would be rocked by two shocking events: the British electorate turned Winston Churchill and his Conservative Party out of office, while scientists in New Mexico had successfully tested an atomic bomb. Ike was stunned when he learned of the weapon and voiced his "grave misgivings" about using it. In his words, "I disliked seeing the United States take the lead in introducing into war something as horrible and destructive as this new weapon was described to be." He believed that detonating the bomb was unnecessary because Japan was already defeated, making it more likely that the rest of the world would react unfavorably to such a massive use of force.

Despite these developments, Truman and Stalin managed to reach tentative compromises by the end of the conference. Russia agreed to permit Western observers in Eastern Europe and to withdraw its troops from Azerbaijan in Iran. In return, the West reluctantly acquiesced to Soviet occupation of German territory and accepted Russian control of eastern Poland. "I can deal with Stalin," Truman wrote in his diary. "He is honest—but smart as hell."

Eisenhower shared Truman's cautious optimism. In August, shortly after the end of the Potsdam Conference, he traveled to Moscow and was treated with enormous deference. Stalin was clearly impressed by the former supreme commander, describing him as a great man, "not only because of his military accomplishments but because of his human, friendly, kind, and frank nature." Eisenhower had warm feelings for Stalin as well, characterizing him as "benign and fatherly." He left Moscow "convinced that Russia and the United States must work together in a spirit of amity."

Unfortunately, Truman's and Eisenhower's hopes proved unfounded. The ink had barely dried before Stalin installed governments subservient to Moscow in Bulgaria, Hungary, and Romania. Refusing again to abide by his agreement at Potsdam, he denied Western observers access to Eastern Europe and continued his occupation of Azerbaijan. Stalin's actions in Poland and Germany were especially troubling to Truman. The Soviet dictator ignored the Yalta accords and brutally suppressed Polish democratic parties. In Germany, the Soviets stripped their zone of industry and started to make heavy demands for factories, power plants, and tools from the American and British zones. The Truman administration feared that the Soviets would cripple Germany, igniting a widespread famine that would require a massive infusion of American resources.

Both East and West heightened tensions further by engaging in a war of words. On February 9, 1946, Stalin declared that Communism and capitalism were incompatible and incapable of coexistence. Several weeks later, Winston Churchill returned fire, declaring, "From Stettin in the Baltic to Trieste in the Adriatic, an iron curtain has descended across the Continent." To counter this threat, Churchill called for "a fraternal association of English-speaking peoples" to always remain vigilant. Polls suggested that most Americans agreed with Churchill's assessment. Shortly after his "Iron Curtain" speech, a survey showed that 60 percent of the public believed that the United States was being "too soft" on the Russians; one in four supported going to war immediately to halt Soviet expansionism.

IN LIGHT OF THESE DEVELOPMENTS OVER THE PREVIOUS YEAR, KENnedy entered his campaign with a rather ambivalent foreign policy stance.

His original optimism about the potential of a constructive relationship with the Soviets had faded, but he also feared the consequences of an arms race. He had thought too deeply about these issues to be easily pigeonholed. Luckily, most voters shared his mixed opinion. His district included many Catholics from European backgrounds who were hostile to "godless Communism" and felt the Truman administration had been too accommodating toward the Soviet Union. Yet although they advocated for a stronger military, they still remained hopeful that disputes could be settled by working through the recently established United Nations.

In terms of domestic policy, Kennedy's platform stressed the "bread and butter" needs of his district's constituents. Many were poor or working-class union members who favored liberal economic programs such as public housing, rent control, minimum wage laws, unemployment benefits, the right to organize and strike, and expanded Social Security benefits.

Kennedy had a number of advantages over the other candidates. Not only was he a war hero, but also he had a father who was willing to spend whatever it took to get his son elected. "With what I'm spending, I could elect my chauffeur," the elder Kennedy once joked. Jack's campaign, buttressed by a large staff, could afford to conduct polls and flood the district with campaign posters and flyers. In its final days, Joseph Kennedy reprinted a hundred thousand copies of the *Reader's Digest* article on Jack and PT-109 and sent them to every registered voter in the district. Powers called the move "highly effective," while another campaign aide described it as "the clincher, a knockout blow." None of JFK's opponents had a war record to brag about, noted Dave Powers, and "his well-known display of incredible courage in the South Pacific" helped overshadow "the charges that he was a carpetbagger whose wealthy father was trying to buy him a seat in Congress."

The campaign climaxed on June 17, 1946, with the Bunker Hill Day celebrations. It was a holiday in Boston and an "event among the Boston Irish rivaled only by the St. Patrick's Day parade in South Boston," observed Powers. In a speech that morning, Kennedy spoke directly to returning veterans, urging the federal government to do more to provide jobs, housing, and other services to them. At one o'clock Kennedy and a large contingent of supporters, including veterans, joined the five-mile parade in Charlestown. Aides placed Kennedy banners on every other house along the parade route, and JFK marched as a representative of "the Lieutenant Joseph P. Kennedy Jr., Post 5880 of the Veterans of Foreign Wars," which Jack and his veteran friends had recently organized.

The day's activities, coming after an exhausting primary campaign, took a toll on JFK's health. The walk left him drained, forcing aides to take him to the home of a local politician, who recalled what happened next: "Jack was ill. He turned yellow and blue and collapsed. He looked like he had had a heart attack. We took him up to the second floor, took off his underwear, and sponged him over. I called his father, and I was instructed to wait until the doctor came. His father asked me if he had his pills. He did, and he took some pills. Then, after several hours, they took him from my residence."

Despite the health scare, Kennedy scored a clear victory in the next day's primary. He beat out ten candidates for the Democratic nomination, earning 41 percent of the vote in a crowded field. The nearest competitor scored less than 20 percent. As expected, he then breezed to victory in November, burying his Republican challenger with 73 percent of the vote, despite the fact that Republicans swept Massachusetts. In his district, Kennedy received thirteen thousand votes more than the well-known Democratic governor who lost to his Republican opponent.

═══════

Across the country, another navy veteran, Lieutenant Commander Richard Nixon, was also running for election to Congress.

Although the Twelfth Congressional District of California, which sat east of Los Angeles, was staunch Republican territory, it had elected Democrat Horace Jeremiah "Jerry" Voorhis in 1936 and kept reelecting him. A former Socialist who came into the Democratic fold as an avid supporter of Roosevelt's New Deal, the often rumpled, pipe-smoking Voorhis was well liked and popular with his constituents and respected by his peers and the press corps in Washington. Capitol Hill reporters voted him among the "most serious men in Congress" and the "hardest working," someone who put "national issues above local ones."

While liberal on most issues, Voorhis had earned a reputation as a fierce critic of Communism. In 1940 he sponsored an anti-subversive bill—the Voorhis Act—requiring the registration of political groups that accepted foreign money. This move placed him squarely on the right of the Communism issue. Voorhis also advocated for currency reform, the curbing of monopolistic practices, and the regulation of big banks. His willingness to tackle these tough issues earned him the respect of those on the Left but provoked anger on the Right despite his anti-Communist bona fides.

In 1940 the Republican-dominated legislature tried to gerrymander Voorhis out of office by redefining his district, slicing off two working-class communities where Voorhis had racked up impressive margins. But the effort failed, and Voorhis went on to win election again in 1942 by a thirteen-thousand-vote majority, and then again in 1944 by the same margin.

Determined to oust Voorhis in 1946 and convinced that the regular Republican Party had failed to find credible candidates, a group of successful business, industrial, and professional figures called the "Committee of 100" decided to get involved in selecting a Republican nominee who could possibly win the district. One of the group's leaders, Herman Perry, was an old Nixon family friend and influential banker, and he suggested that the committee interview Nixon for the job. Shortly afterward, Perry sent Nixon a telegram asking if he "would like to be a candidate for Congress on the Republican ticket in 1946." Nixon was then in the process of winding up the cancellation of wartime contracts in Baltimore.

On October 1, 1945, Nixon telephoned Perry, saying that he felt "honored" to have been chosen. Then, according to Nixon, Perry "poured some cold water on my enthusiasm," explaining that the ultimate decision was not his alone but the entire committee's. The next morning, Nixon sent Perry a letter confirming his interest in running. "I feel very strongly that Jerry Voorhis can be beaten, and I'd welcome the opportunity to take a crack at him," he wrote. "An aggressive, vigorous campaign of a platform of practical liberalism should be the antidote the people have been looking for to take the place of Voorhis's particular brand of New Deal liberalism." He concluded by noting that his "brief experience in Washington with the bureaucrats and my three and a half years in the Navy have given me a pretty good idea of what a mess things are in Washington."

The Committee of 100 sent Nixon the $300 he needed to fly back to California for a brief interview. On October 31, 1945, the thirty-two-year-old Nixon stood before the group, clad in his navy uniform. "There were two ways of looking at America's economic future," he said. "One, advanced by the New Deal, is government control and regulating our lives. The other calls for individual freedom and all that initiative can produce. I subscribe to the second view. I believe the returning veterans—and I have talked to many of them in the foxholes—will not be satisfied with a dole or a government handout."

The committee was clearly impressed, with one observer praising Nixon for his "electrifying personality." Member Roy O. Day, who was also chairman of the Republican Central Committee, wrote Nixon on November 12, two weeks before the November 28 meeting to vote on candidates, that "it looks like a landslide for you." He was right. On November 28 Nixon won sixty-three votes, while his nearest competitor got only twelve. The committee decided to make it unanimous in its second vote. At two in the morning, a member called Nixon to deliver the news. "Dick, the nomination's yours!" Nixon was so excited by the call that he and Pat could not fall back asleep.

In his letter to Day officially accepting the offer, Nixon sounded strikingly like JFK: "As a veteran of this war, I recognize the urgent necessity of adopting a practical, realistic foreign policy which will have as its primary purpose the avoidance of all future wars." He also made a clear statement of his domestic policy stance: "Economic dictatorship by irresponsible government agencies must never be allowed to become an accepted principle of our American system of government." Several days later, Nixon wrote another letter to Day, informing him that his "main efforts are being directed toward building up a positive, progressive group of speeches which tell what we want to do, not what the Democrats have failed to do." By presenting a concrete program for change rather than just critiquing the opponent, Nixon believed he could "build a fire under the district which won't die out until Jerry Voorhis's goose is cooked!"

Before returning to California, Nixon traveled to Washington to meet with congressional Republicans. They echoed his intended strategy, advising him to focus on Voorhis's voting record, saying that he "consistently votes with the most radical element of the New Deal group." But they also described Voorhis as "honest, conscientious, and able," and suggested that "our campaign should not be directed *against* Jerry Voorhis" and that Nixon should mostly focus on "selling" himself and "not even mention Jerry's name."

As part of the effort to sell himself, the committee asked Nixon to provide background material about his time in the war. Nixon sent the commendations that he received for his work establishing combat air transport facilities at Bougainville and Green Island, as well as terminating contracts after the war. He described his service accurately and without embellishment.

In January 1946, when Nixon returned to California, he and Pat were expecting their first child in a month. They had a $10,000 nest egg from her earnings during the war and his poker wins while in the service. They had planned to use it as a down payment for a house, but Richard wanted to split it, putting half of their savings down on the house and the other half on his political venture. Describing his first campaign as a "mom-and-pop" operation, they used their own money to rent a small office in downtown Whittier, filling it with borrowed furniture. Pat, who ran the office along with a former schoolmate, personally typed all of the campaign literature, had it printed, stuffed envelopes, and sent them out in the mail. Because of California's open primary laws, Nixon registered in both the Republican and Democratic primaries.

Promising "a fighting, rocking, socking campaign," Nixon kept a rigorous schedule, campaigned nearly all day, and attended as many civic organizations in his district as possible. His public relations advisor told him, "Just stand there in your uniform, keep your mouth shut, and I'll get you elected to Congress!" The political novice did exactly that, even wearing his navy uniform to events. Campaign literature advertised him as the "clean, forthright young American who fought in defense of his country in the stinking mud and jungles of the Solomons." Nixon also made sure to emphasize that his opponent did not boast the same record, but he failed to mention that Voorhis was already forty years old when the United States entered the conflict. "I am a veteran of this war, the only candidate for the office who is a veteran." When Voorhis produced a pamphlet saying that he was a strong supporter of veterans, the Nixon campaign fired back, "CONGRESSMAN VOORHIS IS NOT A VETERAN OF ANY WAR." While other members of Congress "resigned their official positions to serve in the armed forces during the war," Voorhis did not "follow [their] lead."

Though the basic distinction was true, Nixon's strategy failed. For one thing, his tales of the South Pacific lacked the key element of heroism that resonated so dramatically with voters. Because of this, he could not channel the same emotions as someone like JFK could when recalling his wartime experiences. Even wearing his uniform seemed to backfire. When one of his aides told him there were many enlisted men in the district and they did not particularly like officers, Nixon tossed the uniform and bought a gray pin-striped suit instead. The words "Dick Nixon" henceforth replaced "Lieut. Cmdr. Richard M. Nixon" on his literature.

Luckily, Nixon still had plenty of ammunition to work with in attacking an incumbent Democrat. At the time, the national political environment was largely hostile to Democratic rule. Within a month after the war ended, the government canceled $35 billion in war contracts and slashed war-related production by 60 percent. The cuts produced massive layoffs. Within ten days of the Japanese surrender, 2.7 million men and women lost their jobs. At the same time, a flood of servicemen returned home looking for civilian jobs. Inflation added to the economic anxiety. Steak increased in price from fifty-five cents to one dollar a pound. A headline in the *New York Daily News* screamed: "Prices Soar, Buyers Sore, Steers Jump over the Moon." As skyrocketing prices and job losses squeezed American workers, they went on strike for higher wages in record numbers. By October 1945, a half million workers were walking the picket line. This combination of unemployment, inflation, and labor unrest took a toll on Truman's popularity, which nosedived from 87 percent to 32 percent by the spring of 1946.

Sensing an opportunity amid the economic turmoil, Nixon promised a principled and forward-looking campaign based on new ideas. "We cannot win simply by being against the party in power," he stated. "If that is all we have to offer, we do not deserve to win." He positioned himself as a moderate who recognized that the federal government needed to play a role in modern life but that its bureaucratic machinery needed to operate more efficiently. "There is an increasingly powerful group in America who believes that our economy has become so complicated that government control of industry is necessary," he told voters. "There are others who say that our difficulties today stem mainly from too much government interference and control." Nixon claimed that he stood "somewhere between the two extremes."

In terms of foreign policy, Nixon downplayed growing tension with the Soviet Union, claiming in his memoirs that he had shown "general disinterest" in the Communism issue until he listened to Churchill's Iron Curtain speech. "I was jolted by these words," he confessed, "and at first I wondered if he had gone too far." He went on to say that it was not until Cold War tensions escalated in 1947 that he "realized that the defeat of Hitler and Japan had not produced a lasting peace, and freedom was now threatened by a new and even more dangerous enemy." For now, though, he believed that the United States should continue to sustain the wartime alliance and work to resolve issues through the United Nations. "We believe in peace—must work for it—through the UN," he told the Veterans Legion.

On June 4, 1946, Nixon, who appeared on both tickets due to California's open primary system, won the Republican nomination by a wide margin but lost the Democratic vote by an even wider margin. Initially, Nixon was discouraged by the results, until he was told that his opponent's total percentage was only 53.5 percent, which was down from 60 percent in 1944. Suddenly he realized that Voorhis was vulnerable and that taking a measured approach like in the primary would not suffice for the general election. He needed to find a way to shake up the race. "The results of the primary election definitely indicate that we can win," he wrote supporters. But victory required that the campaign "take advantage of every opportunity between now and November 5 to win voters away from the discredited policies of the New Deal Administration which Mr. Voorhis has consistently supported." Nixon's campaign manager, Roy Day, underscored the message, telling supporters, "From this point on, you will see a fighting, two-fisted candidate by the name of Nixon tearing into the weaknesses of the incumbent New Dealer with telling effect."

In the general election, the high-minded Nixon who articulated the grievances of his largely white, middle-class community competed with Nixon the barroom brawler. The whole tone and character of the campaign changed. Nixon may have shown little prior interest in the international threat posed by Communism, but he now decided to make anti-Communism the centerpiece of his general election message.

During the war, many Communists and liberals had worked together in various labor and political organizations under the umbrella of the Popular Front. However, as Cold War tensions escalated, some anti-Communist liberals began purging Communists from the ranks, convinced that their goals for the postwar world were no longer compatible. Voorhis had been highly critical of Communist influence in the liberal coalition, and for that reason, the Congress of Industrial Organizations Political Action Committee (CIO-PAC) executive board in California voted to endorse every Democratic congressman except Voorhis. "I believe the Communists are in substantial control of the CIO," Voorhis wrote friends, "and between you and me I think that is why I didn't get the endorsement." Instead, a liberal, anti-Communist faction in the Southern California branch of an auxiliary organization associated with the CIO pushed through a local endorsement of Voorhis.

But this fine distinction meant little to Nixon, who engaged in an aggressive red-baiting campaign, smearing his opponent with the taint of Communism. He unveiled his new strategy at the first rally of the general campaign on August 29 in Whittier. "I want you to know," Nixon said, "that I am your candidate primarily because there are no special strings attached to me. I have no support from any special interest or pressure group. I welcome the opposition of the PAC, with its Communist principles and its huge slush fund." Voorhis spent the remainder of the campaign helplessly denying charges that he was the CIO's errand boy. Nixon was not the only Republican candidate running that year who employed what one journalist called the "then developing technique of lightly smearing an opponent with Communism." But he soon proved to be one of the most skilled red-baiters in the nation.

Nixon hammered home the issue, distorting Voorhis's reputation by suggesting that his voting record proved his alignment with the CIO-PAC. Nixon counted many of the incumbent's votes twice, and even included among those Voorhis's support for ending the poll tax in the South and some—such as providing a postwar loan to Britain—that the Communists vehemently opposed. Not only was Voorhis supported by Communists, Nixon charged, but also he was a largely ineffective legislator who had passed only one piece of legislation in the previous four years—and that concerned transferring rabbits from one federal department to another.

Nixon relied on a foolproof formula among postwar conservatives: blurring the line between liberalism and Communism by blasting both as un-American. "There are those walking in high places in our country," he declared, "who would destroy our constitutional principles through socialization of American free institutions." His opponent was not just wrong on the issues, he was a traitorous dupe for the Communists who would sacrifice liberty to the state. "There are the people who front for un-American elements, wittingly or otherwise, by advocating increasing federal controls over the lives of the people. . . . Today the American people are faced with a choice between two philosophies of government; one of these, supported by the radical PAC and its adherents, would deprive the people of liberty through regimentation. The other would return the government to the people under constitutional guarantee, and, needless to say, that is the philosophy for which I will fight with all my power in Congress."

Nixon's hapless opponent never knew what hit him. "Voorhis had never run into anyone like Nixon," observed Stephen Ambrose, "and he was quite out of his league." Before Voorhis could respond to one attack, Nixon was already launching others. Ambrose described his campaign as one "characterized by a vicious, snarling approach that was full of half-truths, full lies, and innuendos, hurled at such a pace that Voorhis could never catch up with them." Well before the height of McCarthyism, the Nixon campaign was stirring up fears of domestic subversion in order to secure political victory.

WHEN ELECTION DAY FINALLY ARRIVED, NIXON REVERSED THE PRI-
mary result, winning 57 percent to 43 percent of the vote. He won every
town except three and even outpolled Voorhis in his home district. When
asked why he won the election, Nixon listed the most important issues as
"government controls, labor legislation, housing, and foreign affairs." He
said nothing about Communism or the CIO-PAC, and never acknowledged the mudslinging that he had engaged in.

Nixon's victory was only a microcosm of a much larger political shift.
Across the nation, Republicans running on a similar platform of anti-
Communism and public weariness over high prices and labor unrest
gained control of both houses of Congress for the first time since 1930.

For all of their differences in style, Nixon and Kennedy shared the common experience of being veterans, which they claimed afforded them
unique insight into both the specific problems plaguing veterans and the
general challenges America faced abroad. Both remained hopeful for
some accommodation with the Soviet Union, and they were not as far
apart on domestic issues as their rhetoric suggested. Nixon described himself as a "liberal Republican" and a "practical liberal"; Kennedy labeled
himself "a fighting conservative."

World War II shaped their views of the role that government should
play in the lives of Americans. Kennedy was not yet a Keynesian—that
would happen after he entered the Oval Office—but the enormous productivity of wartime convinced him that government had a responsibility
to help the few who were left behind by widespread economic growth.
This would emerge as a key difference between Democrats and Republicans in the postwar period. Those like Kennedy, who had been impressed
with wartime prosperity, were convinced that the nation's economy was
strong enough to handle higher taxes to pay for essential social services.
Republicans like Nixon and Eisenhower remained convinced that the
economy was fragile and feared that excessive federal spending would
stifle economic growth. Many Republicans also worried that expanded
government spending, whether to sustain a large standing army or to

fund social programs, would subsume individual rights to the power of the state. Not only did liberals *not* share that fear, but also they often believed the opposite: The United States needed a powerful military to protect freedom abroad and strong federal involvement to guarantee equal opportunity at home.

Both men tailored their messages to their respective districts. Nixon leaned right to appeal to his conservative constituents; Kennedy moved left to attract support from working-class voters. Their main focus was also shaped by the stifling anti-Communist consensus, which had taken hold by 1946 and would later limit their range of options in the White House. Kennedy, running in a district with many European immigrants, emphasized the international threat of Soviet expansionism but said little about the dangers of domestic Communism. Nixon showed little interest in the threat of international Communism but tapped into public frustrations among many middle-class voters with the dislocations caused by the war. He convinced voters that any politician who advocated for ongoing government regulation of the economy was simply doing the bidding of the Communist Party.

Beyond their opposing emphases on domestic or international Communism, Nixon and Kennedy lived in different worlds. Nixon, who grew up in modest circumstances, longed to gain the acceptance of the Eastern establishment that had rejected him in the past. He was disciplined, focused, and fiercely ambitious. Kennedy, while equally ambitious, had been born to great privilege and was thus able to glide through life buffered by his father's money and connections. They also spoke to different groups. Nixon represented the fears of many middle-class white voters regarding inflation, government regulation, and growing labor strife; Kennedy's constituents were mainly poor, first- and second-generation immigrants who needed government support.

Although separated by only a few years, Nixon seemed more mature than the boyish Kennedy. The California congressman, always neatly dressed and serious in his demeanor, appeared older than his actual age. Kennedy, with his rumpled clothes, tousled hair, and boyish grin, looked more like a congressional aide than a congressman. "Well, how about that?" he declared one morning with amusement as he entered his congressional office. "Some people got into the elevator and asked me for the fourth floor!"

Both were junior members in a Republican-controlled Congress determined to prosecute its case against the Truman administration and aggressively pursue a conservative agenda. Nixon, who always viewed himself as an outsider, eagerly embraced the opportunity to impress both Republican leaders and the Washington establishment. Kennedy, born into the establishment, did not feel the same fire to prove he belonged. Furthermore, as a member of the minority party saddled with an unpopular president, Kennedy saw little opportunity for the type of national leadership role that he craved. He was bored with many of the responsibilities of being a congressman and had little interest in pressing the flesh with locals or responding to their many demands. He was fiscally more conservative than the people he represented and grew tired of their constant demands for more government services. "I can't do it," he complained to his Boston staff after spending a day being besieged with requests and favors. "You'll have to call them off." Fortunately, JFK's father paid for a large and competent staff that managed to pick up the slack. Despite Kennedy's poor attendance, due to his myriad medical problems and a general lack of interest in the work of Congress, his father used his media connections to generate a stream of favorable news stories in major newspapers, including *The New York Times* and *The Boston Globe*. "I've never seen a congressman get so much press while doing so little work," grumbled Tip O'Neill.

Kennedy's poor health also limited his effectiveness, keeping him away from Congress for long periods of time. After meeting him in 1947, a fellow representative described JFK as a "frail, sick, hollow man." He did manage, however, to maintain an active social life, developing a well-deserved reputation for being a ladies' man. "Jack liked girls," fellow congressman George Smathers understated.

Yet for all their differences, the two men managed to develop a respectful relationship. Even if Nixon privately resented Kennedy's advantages and envied his Harvard degree, he chose instead to emphasize their similarities. "Neither of us was a back slapper, and we both were uncomfortable with boisterous displays of superficial camaraderie," he wrote in his memoirs. "He was shy. . . . But it was shyness born of an instinct that guarded privacy and concealed emotions. I understood these qualities because I shared them." While acknowledging that they "were too different in background, outlook, and temperament to become close friends," Nixon observed that "we were thrown together throughout our early careers, and we never had less than an amicable relationship." In short, they viewed each other "as political opponents but not political rivals."

Nixon admired Kennedy's grace and glamour, while Kennedy found Nixon knowledgeable and respectful. "Listen to this fellow," JFK told an aide. "He's going places."

Well before the famous 1960 Nixon-Kennedy debates, the two men faced off for the first time over the issue of labor. In April 1947 the twenty-nine-year-old Kennedy and the thirty-four-year-old Nixon traveled to the small steel town of McKeesport, Pennsylvania, just outside of Pittsburgh. A Pennsylvania Democrat had invited them, both junior members of the House Committee on Education and Labor, to debate a tough new Republican bill, the Labor-Management Relations (or Taft-Hartley) Act of 1947, which curtailed the power of unions. Only a small crowd came to see these two figures who would soon dominate American politics for the next quarter century. Nixon took a moderate stance, expressing support for workers but complaining how organized labor had grown "by leaps and bounds" over the past few decades. He went on to claim that the wave of strikes since the end of World War II threatened the nation's economic growth. Kennedy, on the other hand, was more conciliatory, stating that the legislation went too far in restricting the right of workers to unionize and, if enacted, would lead to a "war" between labor and management. Despite their obvious differences, the two men did share a common concern about the dangers of Communist influence in organized labor.

After the debate, Nixon and Kennedy ate together at a local diner, where they talked about baseball before catching the midnight Capitol Limited for the long overnight trip back to Washington. After boarding the train, they flipped a coin to see who would get the bottom berth. Nixon won. But instead of sleeping, the two men stayed up most of the night talking. They exchanged stories about their time in the South Pacific, discovering that they had both been stationed at Vella Lavella at the same time and may even have crossed paths.

They were most absorbed by the issue that related directly to their wartime experience: foreign policy. "There was a lot to discuss," Nixon recalled. Both men entered politics hopeful that the United States and the Soviet Union could peacefully coexist after the horrors of World War II. But by the spring of 1947, they had arrived at the same disappointing conclusion: The Soviet Union was bent on world domination, and the United States needed to remain vigilant.

The previous month, on March 12, 1947, President Truman had announced that the United States would be providing Greece and Turkey with economic and military aid in its fight against Soviet-supported insurgents. "I believe that it must be the policy of the United States to support free peoples who are resisting attempted subjugation by armed minorities or by outside pressures," he declared before Congress in what became known as the Truman Doctrine. Both men applauded the president's speech and voted in favor of Truman's request. It was a politically perilous position for Nixon to take, given the strong isolationist sentiment in his district. Yet he made the courageous decision to buck public opinion and side with a Democratic president. It was easier for Kennedy, whose constituents were staunchly anti-Soviet and opposed to isolationism. He told students at the University of North Carolina that it was imperative for the United States to avoid the mistakes of the 1930s, when it had engaged in a policy of appeasement. Aside from Kennedy's belief in the moral rightness of taking a tough stand against Stalin, he also wished to distance himself once and for all from his father's now-discredited isolationism.

In June, realizing that military assistance might deter the Soviets in Greece and Turkey but would not save war-torn western Europe from economic disaster, the new US secretary of state, George C. Marshall, announced a bold new initiative to provide economic aid to Europe: the Marshall Plan. Once again Nixon was inclined to back the president's policy but faced fierce resistance from within his district. Many of his allies, including Herman Perry, warned against supporting the plan, dismissing it as an extension of the New Deal. Republicans would be successful at home, Perry wrote Nixon, only if they were "wise enough to refuse to be drawn into support of a dangerously unworkable and profoundly inflationary foreign policy." They needed to ensure that "the Democrats do not succeed in so dividing our party by bipartisan internationalism that there is no longer any way to tell who is a Republican."

Despite Perry's warnings, Nixon decided that he needed to educate himself—and possibly his constituents—about the real situation in Europe. He managed to get appointed to a nineteen-member select committee, headed by Congressman Christian Herter of Massachusetts, that traveled to Europe to make recommendations about the Marshall Plan. What he witnessed there left him shocked. "Despite all of our briefings and studying, I do not think that any of us was really prepared for what we found in Europe," he scribbled on a yellow legal pad. "From the minute we stepped off the luxurious ship in Southampton it was clear that we had come to a continent tottering on the brink of starvation and chaos. In every country we visited the situation was the same: without American aid, millions would starve or die of diseases caused by malnutrition before the winter was over. The political facts were equally evident: without our food and aid, Europe would be plunged into anarchy, revolution, and, ultimately, communism."

The devastation Nixon saw in Europe convinced him, like Kennedy, of the necessity of avoiding the mistakes of the 1930s. "We learned to our sorrow in the events leading up to World War II that appeasement of a totalitarian aggressor eventually leads to war," Nixon wrote in his diary. "We must not fall into the same error in our dealings with another totalitarian aggressor at this time." At one point, he scribbled a note to himself: "One basic rule with Russians—never bluff unless you are prepared to carry through, because they will test you every time."

But this stance was a tough sell to his constituents who wanted lower taxes and less government—not a perceived handout to Europe. When he returned to the United States in October, Nixon conducted a poll and found that 75 percent of his constituents were opposed to the Marshall Plan. Nonetheless, he decided "after what I had seen and learned in Europe" that he had "no choice but to vote my conscience and then try my hardest to convince my constituents." At the end of October, he delivered fifty speeches around the district in support of the Marshall Plan.

In the end, the young congressman achieved a win-win. Nixon made the courageous decision to support an unpopular policy, swayed opinion in his district, and even saw his poll numbers go up. On April 2, 1948, the House approved the plan by a lopsided vote of 318–75. The Senate roared its approval by an overwhelming voice vote.

After the measure became law, Kennedy traveled to Europe to examine the progress of the Marshall Plan and to measure the extent of Communist infiltration in labor unions. He also planned to spend time with his sister Kathleen, who was living in London. But his poor health forced him to cut the trip short without ever going on his inspection tour. In September, while in London, he could barely stand up and was admitted to the London Clinic, where he was diagnosed with Addison's disease, a serious, often fatal illness of the adrenal glands. The doctor was pessimistic about Kennedy's diagnosis. "That American friend of yours, he hasn't got a year to live," he told family friend Pamela Churchill, who was with JFK at the time.

The Kennedy family went into crisis mode. Eager to dispel any rumors that Jack was seriously ill, they claimed that he was suffering from a recurrence of the malaria that he had contracted during the war. In October he spent the entire five-day voyage home in the sick bay of the ocean liner RMS *Queen Elizabeth*. Though "flat on his back, yellow as a pot of honey," Jack remained "cheerful as all get-out, and again asking questions," observed a friend.

On October 18, when the ship arrived in the United States, Jack's health had declined so dramatically that the family called a priest to administer the last rites of the Catholic Church. Afterward, he was carried off the ship on a stretcher and placed on a chartered flight to Boston. He would spend weeks in the Lahey Clinic, recovering his strength.

The Addison's diagnosis was not the only personal struggle that Kennedy would endure during his first term in Congress. On May 13, 1948, Kathleen's charter plane ran into a violent storm and smashed into the side of a mountain ridge in France. Out of all his siblings, Kathleen, nicknamed Kick, was closest to Jack. They possessed the same sense of humor and could often finish each other's sentences. He was devastated by her death and spent days holed up in his room in Hyannis Port, refusing to speak to anyone. Even after he returned to Congress, he had difficulty concentrating, and his mind often wandered.

Eventually, however, Kathleen's death, along with his illness, made him more aware of his own mortality and even more determined not to waste his time in Congress. "The point is," he told a colleague, "that you've got to live every day like it's your last day on earth." His plan was not to throw himself into his work in the House but rather to lay the groundwork for a campaign for the Senate, which he felt provided a better launchpad for his dream of becoming a national statesman.

Kennedy now embarked on a rigorous effort to expand his name recognition across the state by traveling nearly every week. He visited 39 cities and 312 towns in Massachusetts, often attending twelve events a day and speaking at civic organizations, including the VFW and American Legion chapters. According to Dave Powers, "Jack would try to get up here every Friday, Saturday, and Sunday to speak." He contemplated running for the Senate in 1948, but when private polls showed it would be an uphill fight, he decided to wait for another opportunity.

While Kennedy was shoring up support for a potential Senate run, Nixon managed to keep his name in the news through his work on the House Un-American Activities Committee, which was created in 1938 to investigate alleged subversion. House Speaker Joe Martin told Nixon when he appointed him that "we need a young lawyer on that committee to smarten it up." HUAC's membership, to say the least, was not distinguished. In fact, it was so dominated by anti-Semites and racists that it refused to investigate the Ku Klux Klan because it was, observed Mississippi's John Rankin, "an old American institution." "I don't think that committee could have located a Communist in Red Square in Moscow on May Day in front of Lenin's tomb," quipped reporter George Reedy, who would go on to become Lyndon Johnson's White House press secretary. Though his appointment aimed to make the committee appear more reputable, Nixon, observed biographer John A. Farrell, "was dwelling in a scoundrels' den, and it was difficult to escape the stain."

In the spring of 1948, Nixon and Karl Mundt of South Dakota

introduced a bill mandating that all members of the US Communist Party register with the government. The bill was contentious and even incurred the wrath of Republican governor and 1948 presidential nominee Thomas Dewey, who blasted it as "nothing but the method of Hitler and Stalin." *The New York Times* predicted that the bill "could be used to impose restraints on freedom such as the American people have not known for one hundred and fifty years." But the fight over the legislation, which failed to pass, kept Nixon's name in the public eye.

It was, however, the case of Alger Hiss that made Nixon a household name and one of the most controversial men in politics. "The Hiss case brought me national fame," Nixon wrote later. In August, Whittaker Chambers, a *Time* magazine editor, accused Alger Hiss, a high-ranking aide to Franklin Roosevelt at Yalta as well as to several other former government officials, of having Communist affiliations. It seemed unlikely that the charges would stick. Chambers was a confessed former Communist spy and a homosexual ("a pervert," according to FBI director J. Edgar Hoover). Hiss, a striking patrician, epitomized the Ivy League–educated foreign policy establishment, with degrees from Johns Hopkins University and Harvard Law School. But Nixon pursued the case relentlessly. For 134 days, from August 3 to December 15, 1948, Nixon's name dominated the headlines as he challenged Hiss's assertion that he had never been a member of the Communist Party. "I was a lawyer," he said later, "and I knew he was a lawyer, and I felt that his testimony was just too slick." After one mistrial, Hiss was found guilty in a second trial in 1950 and sentenced to five years in jail. More than any other event, the Hiss trial convinced many Americans that the Roosevelt and Truman administrations had been oblivious to the dangers of Communist espionage.

Nixon had been a workhorse during his first two years in Congress and had shown considerable guts in bucking popular opinion in his district to support the two major foreign policy initiatives of the Truman White House: the Truman Doctrine and the Marshall Plan. But it was his red-baiting 1946 campaign, and his dogged pursuit of Hiss, that would define his image as a ruthless and unscrupulous politician. While his antics won him the acclaim of the right wing of the Republican Party, they outraged the establishment whose approval he desired so desperately.

Kennedy, on the other hand, accomplished little in his first term in Congress. He showed scant interest in the details of legislating or in servicing the needs of his constituents. Because of his health, he was absent for long periods of time. But his father, who was instrumental in his election, now played a similar role in keeping Jack's name in the media, depicting him as a rising star in the party.

What the two men shared was ambition. Neither planned to stay in the House for long and early on set their sights on higher office.

Both Kennedy and Nixon cruised to victory in 1948, cementing their reputations as leading lights in their respective parties. That same year, another navy lieutenant, Gerald Ford, decided to run for Congress in Michigan's Fifth District against a popular incumbent and fellow Republican, sixty-three-year-old Bartel J. "Barney" Jonkman, then in his fourth term.

For Ford, the emerging anti-Soviet consensus forced him into the race. The reformed isolationist was now a committed internationalist, whereas Jonkman had won election in 1940 playing to the isolationist sentiment in his district. He was a hero to the America First Committee, opposed that year's Selective Training and Service Act, and, as a member of the House Foreign Affairs Committee, dismissed the Marshall Plan for its flagrant waste of tax dollars.

Jonkman may have been out of touch with the growing anti-Soviet sentiment nationwide, but he was popular in his district and had the support of leading Republicans. Historian Isaiah Berlin described Jonkman as "typical of the Michigan Republican Bloc." Ford's effort to defeat him was a long shot. Like Kennedy, he would be running in a noncompetitive district, so winning the Republican nomination was tantamount to winning the seat come November. Even Ford's former law partner, Philip Buchen, saw little hope in his candidacy. "You probably can't win," he told the political novice, "but lay the groundwork and see what happens."

Ford made foreign policy the centerpiece of his campaign to unseat Jonkman, correlating aid to Europe with the preservation of freedom. When asked whether the United States would be "spending vast sums overseas" while "neglecting many of our own citizens who are in need," Ford responded that the country "must spend money in Europe to try and dry up the Communist influence that threatens our freedom" and "give the common man of Europe a real basis for faith in free government." He flatly rejected complaints that the Marshall Plan would exacerbate economic inequality, insisting that it was "not designed to make the rich richer and the poor poorer." Furthermore, investing in a strong military would provide the necessary protection for the new world order. "We cannot convincingly carry the torch for freedom against the Russian bully," he insisted, "unless we are adequately prepared from a military point of view."

Ford waged an aggressive and energetic campaign. He helped with cancer drives and fundraisers, and even joined the local chapter of the National Association for the Advancement of Colored People (NAACP). He spoke at as many events as possible and on each occasion drew attention to his opponents' outdated isolationist views. To highlight his own war service, as well as the postwar housing shortage for veterans, Ford set up a rented Navy surplus Quonset hut emblazoned with the message "Jerry Ford, Jr. for Congress" in a parking lot next to a department store. The huts, common on military bases during the war, served as an obvious reminder of Ford's wartime service.

When discussing domestic policy, Ford often sounded more like a Democrat than a Republican. He advocated for expanding the educational benefits of the GI Bill. He also called for strengthening Social Security by "broadening the coverage where practical" rather than continuing the government's current trend of "neglecting to provide adequate payments to the people who are dependent on Social Security for a livelihood." Far from campaigning against Washington, Ford promised to do a better job of bringing federal dollars to his district, saying, "We must remember that the federal government won't step in and do things for us unless someone is aggressively pushing our needs to the front."

Ford's moderation resulted from wartime changes in his hometown of Grand Rapids. The furniture industry, which had dominated the local economy, was now joined by other industries. General Motors and a few auto parts manufacturers opened manufacturing plants in the city. Organized labor followed. While Nixon used anti-Communism to drive a wedge between Democrats and organized labor, Ford received the support of the regional representative of the CIO and the president of the United Auto Workers (UAW). In contrast, Representative Jonkman sounded more like Nixon, attacking Communists in government and blaming the State Department for being soft on Communism. Like JFK, Ford never played the Communism card at home and instead kept the focus on the threat of Soviet expansion abroad.

There was one secret that Ford kept from voters during the primary. In the fall of 1947, he had met Betty Bloomer Warren, a dancer who was in the process of getting a divorce. They dated for a few months, and in February 1948 he proposed. "He's a very shy man," Betty recalled, "and he didn't really tell me he loved me; he just told me he'd like to marry me." But Ford confessed that their wedding couldn't be held until the fall, she said, "because there was something else he had to do first." Even she was skeptical of his chances of winning the election. "I couldn't imagine this Dutch town turning out the incumbent, who was himself Dutch, who'd been in office for eight years, and who was as conservative as most of the voters in the Fifth District he represented," she recalled.

Given the conservative attitudes of the two Dutch Calvinist denominations that dominated western Michigan, Ford and his advisors feared the political implications of his marrying a divorcée. "I could see what would have happened," a campaign aide said. "On Sunday before the Tuesday primary, the opposition would have gone to all the Dutch churches and passed out handbills saying, 'Vote for Ford' and carrying a juicy tidbit about his intentions to marry a divorcée and ex-dancer."

Those fears went unrealized, because Ford scored a resounding victory in the primary. His message of toughness abroad and moderation at home appealed to many Democrats, who crossed over and voted in the Republican primary, giving him a surprisingly lopsided win over the incumbent. When all the ballots were counted, Ford secured 62 percent of the primary vote.

With the primary behind him, Gerald and Betty could finally prepare for their October 15 wedding at Grace Episcopal Church in downtown Grand Rapids. A few weeks later, Ford trounced his Democratic opponent, winning 60.5 percent of the vote.

―――

Although he had flirted with the idea of running for Texas governor in 1946, Lyndon Johnson decided instead to run for reelection to the House, easily defeating Hardy Hollers, a forty-five-year-old decorated army colonel and attorney. Johnson carried all ten counties in the district, beating his opponent by a large margin of 42,672 to 17,628 votes.

Like JFK, Johnson had set his sights on running for Senate in 1948 and began positioning himself to become more acceptable to conservative voters outside his Austin district. Rhetorically, he distanced himself from the New Deal and spoke more often about the importance of free enterprise and limited government. He supported the anti-labor Taft-Hartley Act and even voted with Republicans to override the president's veto. "Labor's not much stronger in Texas than a popcorn fart," LBJ quipped. He also opposed civil rights measures, including bills ending the poll tax and outlawing lynching. At the same time, he voted against tax cuts for the wealthy, and supported bread-and-butter programs such as aid for housing.

Like Nixon, LBJ's views of the Soviet crisis were shaped by his first-hand exposure to conditions in Europe after the war. The week after Germany surrendered in May 1945, Johnson traveled to Europe as part of a five-man subcommittee to evaluate naval properties. This was his first trip to the Continent, and what he saw shocked him: swaths of London destroyed by German bombs; drastic shortages of food and housing in Paris. Although he worried that the Soviets might try to capitalize on the instability in Europe, Johnson's initial solution to the problem was to re-affirm FDR's cooperative approach to the Russians. In January 1946 he told the League of Women Voters in Austin that America needed to get along with Russia. He even favored divulging the secret of the atomic bomb to Moscow.

His views evolved, however, not only because of growing tensions between the Soviet Union and the United States but also because he recognized the necessity of appealing to his constituents' fears. A tough stance against the Soviets abroad and Communism at home made sense in conservative Texas. By 1948, Johnson was enthusiastically backing Truman's anti-Soviet hard line, voting in favor of the Truman Doctrine and the Marshall Plan. Foreshadowing what Eisenhower would later describe as the "domino theory," Johnson proclaimed, "If Italy is lost, Greece will be cut off, and Turkey isolated. The bell has tolled for Romania, Yugoslavia, Czechoslovakia. It is tolling for Finland, Norway, Sweden. Each toll of the bell brings closer the day when they could call for you and me." He extended the same reasoning to the Marshall Plan, saying that it would represent "the first time in the history of the world a great nation will attempt to urge peace." Only by taking positive action to block Soviet aggression would America emerge as the world's leading superpower. "If despair is replaced by faith, if desolation is replaced by construction, if hunger is answered by food—if those things are done," Johnson declared, "we shall be directors in the battle."

Johnson warned against returning to the isolationism that had shaped American policy in the 1930s, challenging fiscally conservative Republicans who were reluctant to spend the money needed to prevent another war. "There is a budget hysteria afoot now to sink our ships, ground airplanes, and reduce the size of our army." But that was the sentiment, he argued, that led to World War II. The question now was whether they wanted to spend a modest amount of money "over the next four years in an attempt to stop the spread of Communism or to spend three hundred or four hundred billion dollars in another war from which nobody would emerge the winner." Recalling the lessons of Munich, Johnson told voters that the nation "must apply to dictator Stalin the same doctrine that we should have applied to the kaiser and to Hitler." Speaking as a veteran, Johnson warned that Americans needed to keep in mind how many young men had died in the war due to the lack of a strong military at its outset. "I'd rather save lives than money," he said. "It's either your boys' lives or tax rebates for millionaires."

Johnson went a step further by linking prosperity at home with preparedness abroad. The United States needed a strong federal government to spend on important domestic programs at home and on building "the world's most powerful air force, and army and navy adequate to any task."

He depicted opponents of federal power as old-fashioned isolationists reluctant to make the investments needed to meet the international obligations that would ensure stability at home. Yet Johnson also tried having it both ways, supporting increased domestic spending while also claiming that government needed to be respectful of free enterprise and states' rights.

The July primary featured ten candidates, but Coke Robert Stevenson, a towering figure in Texas politics who had served as Speaker of the House in the Texas legislature before running successfully for governor in 1942, emerged as LBJ's chief opponent. Stevenson, a fiscal conservative and states' rights advocate who opposed many of FDR's New Deal programs, won reelection as governor in 1944 with 85 percent of the vote. Nicknamed "Mr. Texas," Stevenson seemed unbeatable and, as expected, won 40 percent of the vote in the July primary, far ahead of Johnson's 34 percent. The nine other candidates dropped out, setting up a runoff between Stevenson and LBJ on August 28. Since Texas was a one-party state, the winner was almost guaranteed victory in the fall. In order to win the general election, Johnson needed to capture roughly two of every three votes that had been cast for another candidate. It was a tough task. "We thought we were going to come out of it winning or be really close to the top," Lady Bird said, "and we were overwhelmingly, vastly, horribly behind. . . . It looked hopeless."

Johnson realized that he could not win the runoff without appealing to intense anti-Communist and anti-labor sentiment. So, over the next few weeks, in preparation for the runoff, LBJ launched attacks against the "red menace" while depicting Stevenson as a pawn of northern Communist labor bosses. The *Johnson Journal*, a campaign publication distributed among rural voters, warned, "The big northern labor unions, with their leadership which includes admitted Communists . . . have aligned their forces against Lyndon Johnson and in favor of Coke Stevenson."

Johnson ran a modern campaign, employing sophisticated polling and flying around the state in helicopters, while Stevenson campaigned the old-fashioned way, appearing in parades and traveling by car. The helicopter allowed LBJ to visit as many as twenty towns a day, landing on tops of buildings, on baseball fields, and on open cow pastures, blaring his message over a loudspeaker to eager crowds. Before the campaign was over, Johnson had delivered 350 speeches in only sixty days. Not even a painful bout of kidney stones could keep him off the trail for long.

Although Johnson had made a calculated decision to appeal to more conservative voters, he never race-baited and even managed to gain support from Black voters who were able to participate in Texas elections for the first time. (The US Supreme Court had overturned the all-white Texas primary law in 1944 with the *Smith v. Allwright* decision.) Stevenson, on the other hand, was an avowed racist who lined up behind the Texas Regulars, a group of white supremacist, conservative Democrats who resented the New Deal, trade unions, and civil rights advances such as *Smith v. Allwright*.

Like the other veterans who would become president, Johnson made direct appeals to returning veterans and their families, arguing that his military experience in World War II made him better prepared to deal with growing tensions with the Soviet Union. He lambasted Stevenson for refusing to accept that the United States needed to play an active role in the postwar world. Stevenson had already alienated many veterans when he refused a wartime move to repeal the poll tax for Texans in uniform, and his isolationist views were clearly out of touch with evolving hard-line views of the Soviets in Texas and around the country.

LBJ went to almost comical lengths to highlight his "combat" experience. As biographer Robert Caro has pointed out, Johnson insisted that he be introduced by a veteran—ideally one who had been wounded or lost a limb during the war. "So successful was the Johnson campaign in locating pro-Johnson amputees for this task that the percentage of men introducing Johnson who still possessed all their limbs was surprisingly small," observed Caro.

Johnson showed little restraint in describing his time in uniform, using it to connect with voters who had lost sons during the war. "I shared your boys' experiences," he repeated often. "I said that if war was declared, I'd go to war beside them, and I did." He never missed an opportunity to highlight his Silver Star, which he displayed prominently on his jacket lapel. On some occasions, he would begin the ceremony by having the pin placed on his chest as if for the first time; on other occasions, he would take off his jacket and hold it in the air with the lapel stretched out so that everyone could see the pin. "That's the Silver Star!" he shouted. "General MacArthur gave it to me."

On Election Day, it appeared that Stevenson had won. But that was before the Thirteenth Election Precinct in South Texas, where, strangely enough, 202 Mexican Americans voted for Johnson—in alphabetical order—providing him with an 87-vote margin of victory. While much of the focus was on the illegal voting that boosted LBJ over the top, the fact was that Texas elections were notoriously corrupt. Johnson simply cheated better than his opponent. Stevenson contested the outcome, taking his case to the executive committee of the state Democratic Party, which upheld the Johnson victory by a slim 29-to-28 vote, and then to the federal courts. By this time, all the voting records had mysteriously gone missing, and the Supreme Court decided that it did not have jurisdiction. In November Johnson went on to win the seat in a landslide against his Republican opponent.

＝＝＝＝＝＝

Thus, by 1948, four men who would become president—Kennedy, Nixon, Ford, and Johnson—had positioned themselves in Congress with the shadow of their wartime service behind them. All four witnessed the brutality of war up close and emerged from the conflict convinced that the United States could never return to its isolationist past. The war was the most formidable experience of their lives, and they each came away convinced that the conflict had fundamentally altered America's role in the world. For three of them—Kennedy, Nixon, and Ford—postwar trips to Europe, where they viewed the destruction caused by the Nazi war machine, only reinforced these lessons. (Eisenhower, of course, had spent much of the war in Europe, so he was intimately familiar with the war's devastating impact.) For them, the Truman Doctrine—establishing a military shield against aggression—and the Marshall Plan—providing economic aid to nurture democratic institutions—forged a template that they would try to duplicate while in the White House. They would soon learn, however, that what worked in western Europe, with its strong democratic institutions, did not apply to other parts of the world, especially Southeast Asia.

CHAPTER 6

"You Boys Must Be Crazy"

Republican presidential candidate Dwight Eisenhower, along with a small group of close aides, had retreated to the manager's office above the Cleveland Public Auditorium, where Ike was scheduled to speak to a large crowd of Republicans that evening. Sitting on a sofa next to his wife, Mamie, surrounded by about twenty friends and staffers, the former supreme commander stared intently at a wooden cabinet television set with its rabbit ears antenna pointing toward the ceiling.

A week earlier, the *New York Post* revealed that his running mate, California senator Richard Nixon, had created a private fund so that wealthy donors could contribute to his campaign. It was perfectly legal, and other candidates, including Democratic presidential nominee Adlai Stevenson II, had similar arrangements, but the move undercut one of Eisenhower's primary messages: that he would end corruption in Washington. "Of what avail is it," Ike asked, "for us to carry on this crusade against this business of what has been going on in Washington if we ourselves aren't as clean as a houndstooth?"

The fact that Ike was even a candidate surprised many observers. His status as a war hero led both Democrats and Republicans to court him to run for president in 1948, but the supreme commander abhorred politics and remained steadfast in denying any interest in running for office. In October 1950, after a brief stint as the president of Columbia University, Eisenhower accepted President Truman's invitation to take the position of commander in chief of the recently formed North Atlantic Treaty Organization (NATO). But the move did little to dampen bipartisan calls for Eisenhower to run for president. Independent "Ike for President" clubs were springing up across the country. Everywhere, bumper stickers proclaimed, "I like Ike."

At first, Eisenhower, who had never even registered a party affiliation or voted in an election, expressed little interest, but he feared that if he did not run, the party would nominate Ohio senator Robert Taft. Though Taft enjoyed a large following among the party's Old Guard, his isolationist views and uninspiring manner limited his appeal to mainstream voters. When, in February 1952, Taft advocated bringing American troops home from Europe, Eisenhower finally decided to run. He resigned from NATO and entered his name for the Republican nomination.

After a bitter convention struggle, Eisenhower won the nomination and turned his attention to choosing a running mate. When his campaign manager, Herbert Brownell Jr., asked about his ideas for vice president, Eisenhower looked surprised. "I thought the convention had to do that," he said. "I didn't realize that was for me to decide." Eisenhower, thinking out loud, rattled off a few names—mainly of successful businessmen. Brownell interrupted, telling him that he needed someone who would rally the delegates on the floor. He then suggested a name: Richard Nixon. Brownell described Nixon as "an almost ideal candidate for vice president. He was young, geographically right, had experience both in the House and Senate with a good voting record, and was an excellent speaker."

"Fine," Eisenhower responded tersely. The next day, Brownell and two aides gathered around a phone and placed the call to Nixon. "We picked you," they said. Nixon recalled being "speechless."

Two years earlier, Nixon had won a highly contested California Senate seat against liberal actress Helen Gahagan Douglas, a three-term Democratic congresswoman, by using the same scorched-earth, red-baiting tactics that had secured him a seat in the House in 1946. He smeared her as a full-fledged Communist who was "pink right down to her underwear." Weaving together anti-Communism and patriotism, his campaign instructed voters, "Don't vote the red ticket, vote the red, white and blue ticket." His slashing style, along with his role in the Hiss case, earned him the admiration of those on the Right and the enmity of the press and many Democrats. Douglas, who was married to Hollywood leading man Melvyn Douglas, labeled him "Tricky Dick," and popular political cartoonist Herbert L. Block (better known by his nom de plume, Herblock) depicted him as a shady, unscrupulous character and a threat to civil liberties.

But Nixon offered diverse benefits to the ticket. Although an internationalist who supported both the Truman Doctrine and the Marshall Plan, he remained close to the Taft wing of the party. Eisenhower was an expert on foreign policy, while Nixon was primarily known for domestic politics. He hailed from an electorally rich state that added geographical balance to Eisenhower's New York residency. Eisenhower was nonpartisan; Nixon was ruthlessly partisan. His youth—he was thirty-nine years old and the youngest Republican in the Senate—was also a benefit, especially since Eisenhower was sixty-two.

The two men did not know each other well. Nixon recalled seeing Eisenhower for the first time on VE (Victory in Europe) Day in 1945. He was wrapping up navy contracts on the twentieth floor of a building in downtown Manhattan while Eisenhower was being greeted as a conquering hero in the streets below. Nixon could barely see him because of the "snowstorm of confetti" that filled the air. On two subsequent occasions, Nixon got to see the general close up, but they did not meet officially until May 1951, when both were in Paris. Nixon, in Europe attending a conference, met with Eisenhower at his NATO headquarters. Nixon recalled finding the general "erect and vital and impeccably tailored," while Eisenhower praised Nixon for his work on the Hiss case and his internationalist views of foreign policy. "Being strong militarily just isn't enough in the kind of battle we are fighting now," Ike said. Nixon was as impressed by the general's manner as he was by the substance of the conversation. "I felt that I was in the presence of a genuine statesman," he concluded.

But those early feelings of goodwill soon gave way to tension. When Eisenhower learned about the slush fund, he sent clear signals to his junior officer that he expected him to resign from the ticket, but Nixon refused and instead opted to deliver a live, prime-time television address on Tuesday, September 23—just six weeks before Election Day. The Republican Party reserved thirty minutes from nine thirty to ten o'clock EST immediately following *The Milton Berle Show*, one of the most popular programs on television. The stage at the El Capitan Theatre in Hollywood was set up to look like a typical suburban living room.

The address was viewed by sixty million people, making it one of the most-watched events in the early history of the medium. (Incidentally, it came to be dubbed the "Checkers" speech because of Nixon's awkward attempt to gain sympathy by saying he would never give back the black-and-white spotted cocker spaniel that their six-year-old, Tricia, had named Checkers.) The public response was overwhelmingly positive, but Eisenhower was furious that his running mate refused to follow his orders to step aside. Instead, Nixon announced that he would turn the decision over not to Eisenhower but to the party regulars at the Republican National Committee.

Eisenhower let Nixon twist in the wind for a few more days before deciding to keep him on the ticket. But the episode, as biographer John A. Farrell observed, "drove a wedge" between the two. From that point on—for the next eight years—the president would keep his vice president at arm's length. He rarely consulted Nixon on important policy decisions, and neither he nor Pat was ever invited to a social function at the White House or to Eisenhower's Gettysburg farm. That cold treatment made perfect sense to Eisenhower, who had spent most of his life in the military, where the chain of command was sacred. Junior officers never ignored or circumvented orders. General Ike knew he had made a mistake in allowing a subordinate to seize control of the campaign's first major crisis. Though he respected Nixon's fighting spirit, he learned to never truly confide in him again. "He had for me, I believe, fulsome respect for my abilities and my integrity and similar political persuasion," Nixon would recall. "But there was little personal feeling between us. I gathered that I was considered a trusted lieutenant to the commander, but with the differences in our age and temperament, I was not a personal friend."

The resentment ran both ways. Nixon was acutely aware of the gap in status between him and Ike. During the war, while Eisenhower was negotiating with Roosevelt and Churchill, Nixon was loading and unloading cargo planes in the steamy jungles of the Pacific. Nixon never forgave Eisenhower for not publicly supporting him and forcing him to endure the humiliation of revealing his family finances on national television. Pat, too, found the whole experience degrading. "Why do we have to tell people how little we have and how much we owe?" she pleaded with her husband.

"People in political life have to live in a goldfish bowl," he responded.

"But aren't we entitled to have at least some privacy?" she persisted.

Beyond just his relationship with the president, the scandal had a profound impact on Nixon's worldview. He admitted six years later that it "left a deep scar which was never to heal completely." With a deepened sense of grievance and paranoia, Nixon now saw that he would never be accepted within the Republican establishment. He also viewed himself as an innocent victim of vengeful Democrats who were out to get him for identifying "the Communists and crooks" in the Truman administration. He even felt betrayed by members of the press whom he had once considered friends. But among Eastern opinion makers and those in Eisenhower's inner circle, Nixon's self-pitying behavior only reinforced his image as a ruthless opportunist who was willing to do anything to gain power.

———

While most Democrats relished seeing Nixon flail, John F. Kennedy, who was seeking a Senate seat in Massachusetts, was not one of them. JFK had always enjoyed a close, even fawning, relationship with the press. Not only did he impress reporters with his wit and charm, but also he and his father consciously courted them. Kennedy knew Nixon well enough to recognize that he had not received fair treatment during the entire slush fund episode. He told a neighbor that Nixon "was a victim of the worst that ever hit a politician in this country," and described the media's attitude toward him as "disgusting."

The two men had maintained a cordial, even friendly, relationship. Back in 1950, when Nixon ran for the Senate, Kennedy strolled into his office (as he often did), sat in a chair, and pulled out an envelope from his breast pocket. "Dick, I know you're in for a pretty rough campaign," he said, "and my father wanted to help out." As Kennedy got up to leave, he said, "I obviously can't endorse you, but it isn't going to break my heart if you can turn the Senate's loss into Hollywood's gain." After he left, Nixon opened the envelope and discovered a check for $1,000.

After Nixon received the Republican nomination for vice president in July 1952, Kennedy wrote him a two-page handwritten letter. "I was tremendously pleased that the convention selected you for VP," he wrote. "I was always convinced that you would move ahead to the top—but I never thought it would come this quickly. You were an ideal selection and will bring to the ticket a great deal of strength."

But Kennedy had little time to focus on Nixon's travails in 1952, because he was trapped in a tough Senate race in Massachusetts. When friend George Smathers learned that Kennedy was planning to challenge popular incumbent Henry Cabot Lodge Jr., he went to talk him out of it, thinking it would be political suicide. The Florida congressman found JFK lying on a couch in the House cloakroom in excruciating pain. Smathers grabbed his legs and helped Kennedy to his feet. "My God, man, I don't see how you can possibly think about running when you can't even get up and down!" he exclaimed.

Like Kennedy, the tall, handsome, and aristocratic Lodge hailed from a storied Boston family. His grandfather, the first Henry Cabot Lodge, had spent two decades in the Senate and was perhaps best known for leading the fight against President Woodrow Wilson's failed effort to join the League of Nations. Lodge could have used his family connections to avoid fighting in World War II but instead volunteered and served with distinction. Unlike Lyndon Johnson, Lodge gave up his Senate seat to become a commissioned major with the US Sixth Army Group, ultimately receiving a Bronze Star for bravery. He was the first senator since the Civil War to voluntarily abandon his Senate seat to defend the nation.

Ironically, Kennedy attacked Lodge not for his actions during the war but for supporting the same isolationist views as his father in the years before America's entry into the conflict. Lodge had downplayed the threat posed by Hitler, claiming as late as October 1939—*after* Germany's surprise attack and occupation of Poland—"No European power can occupy or vanquish the United States, and it is fanciful to suggest that it could." Acting on this belief, Lodge opposed revising the 1935 Neutrality Act so as to allow the United States to offer aid to England. A month before Pearl Harbor, the senator voted against allowing American ships to deliver supplies to British ports in the war zone. "Is this the foresight of a statesman?" Kennedy asked.

LODGE'S STERLING TRACK RECORD OF MILITARY SERVICE DID NOT STOP Kennedy from playing up his own status as a war hero. Under his father's supervision, and with his almost limitless resources, the campaign produced ads that appeared in popular newspapers and magazines across Massachusetts. The campaign ran ads in major newspapers retelling the story of PT-109, concluding: "ITS HERO WAS LT. JOHN F. KENNEDY, U.S.N.R. CANDIDATE FOR THE U.S. SENATE." Joe Kennedy paid to print 1.2 million copies of a glossy, eight-page publication about his son's exploits in the Pacific. In addition, he sent reprints of John Hersey's 1944 *Reader's Digest* article about PT-109 to every home in the state.

Meanwhile, his mother and sisters organized teas for women voters, at which JFK's charm was on full display. "Unmarried, wealthy, Harvardishly casual in his dress, and with a distinguished war record in addition to his other attainments," observed *The New York Times*, "he just about bracketed the full range of emotional interests of such an all-feminine group—maternal at one end and romantic at the other." By the end of the campaign, an estimated seventy-five thousand women had attended these celebratory teas.

The battle between Lodge and Kennedy revealed a key legacy of World War II. Since the war had forged a broad ideological consensus that American institutions were fundamentally sound and that the nation needed to avoid the mistakes of Munich, candidates often struggled to draw clear ideological differences between each other. "Rarely in politics have hunter and quarry so resembled each other," wrote Kennedy biographer James MacGregor Burns. Both men were internationalists who supported the broad outlines of the Cold War while gravitating toward the center on domestic issues. Both favored increased spending on federal social programs, a higher minimum wage, rent control, and federal support for education and housing.

Thus, to put some distance between himself and Lodge, Kennedy moved to the right on foreign policy. Ironically, he tied the Republican Lodge to the outgoing President Truman, calling him weak in dealing with the Soviets and Communist China. Reversing his previous opinion, Kennedy now argued that the United States could "win" a military confrontation with the Soviets and warned about the possibility of another world war. "Most Europeans," he told an audience in Fall River, "believe that there will not be an open war with the Soviet Union, but every month of weakness that goes by is an invitation to war." He was also not above red-baiting, blasting Lodge for not taking the threat of domestic Communism seriously enough.

Kennedy grossly distorted Lodge's record. In many ways, the incumbent senator's positions on both domestic Communism and the Cold War were similar to the positions that Kennedy himself had already staked out. But JFK was desperate for votes and headlines, and nothing aroused the public quicker than the charge of being soft on Communism.

The postwar consensus also reinforced the politics of personality. With few substantive differences separating candidates, elections often turned on charm and personality, a trend that would grow even more important once television became the American people's principal medium for political news. Kennedy had plenty of charisma, captivating audiences with his good looks and sex appeal. His personal magnetism drew people to him and convinced them that he shared both their dreams and their fears. "There's something about Jack," remarked a former mayor of Pittsfield, "that makes people want to believe in him." The fifty-year-old Lodge, by contrast, was cold and aloof. "He wasn't the type of person you approached too easily," recalled a campaign aide.

Additionally, Kennedy's campaign was long on generalities and short on specifics, enabling him to tailor his message to different groups. "He was all things to all men," recalled a powerful Massachusetts Democrat. With his endless charm, he could adapt seamlessly to nearly any environment. He would shake hands at a factory gate in the morning, demonstrating his concern for working men. Later that night, he would kick back with conservative businessmen and party bosses. Women, especially, were enamored by his presence. "Jack was a dream lover to the young girls who waved their handkerchiefs and God's glory of a son to their mothers," wrote historian Laurence Leamer.

Polls showed a close election, but Kennedy received a boost on October 19 when *The Boston Globe* published a letter sent to him from Kohei Hanami, the captain of the Japanese destroyer that had sliced Kennedy's PT boat in half in 1943. "I take this opportunity," Hanami wrote Kennedy, "to pay my profound respect to your daring and courageous action in this battle and also to congratulate you upon your miraculous escape under such circumstances." Hanami went on to express his "wish" that Kennedy would be successful "in the coming election in your country." While Lodge received the endorsement of five of the state's six major newspapers, and the *Globe* kept to its tradition of not endorsing candidates, this letter from a former enemy served as a powerful reminder of Kennedy's wartime heroism at a critical juncture.

Lodge was so confident of victory that he spent most of the fall traveling the country as one of Eisenhower's campaign managers, which kept him away from the state for long periods of time. Kennedy took advantage by developing an efficient ground game and by reminding voters that Lodge was more interested in electing Ike than in representing Massachusetts. Lodge responded to these attacks by showcasing Kennedy's less-than-stellar attendance record in Congress. "Would you hire a man who came to work one-third of the time?" he asked. The charges wouldn't stick, though. Kennedy started out behind in the polls but quickly narrowed the gap.

Meanwhile, the race for the White House that fall was never close. The Democratic nominee, Illinois governor Adlai Stevenson II, delighted intellectuals with his eloquence but failed to connect with the working-class, Black-ethnic-urban coalition of the New Deal. He was burdened most of all by a stalemated war on the Korean peninsula, where, in June

1950, an unpopular Truman had committed American forces to repel Chinese-supported troops in the North that had swarmed over the 38th parallel to invade the democratic South. By contrast, Eisenhower endeared himself to the public with his serene, confident manner and what one reporter called a "leaping and effortless smile."

The GOP campaign correctly identified Korea, Communism, and corruption as the key issues in 1952. Complaining of "plunder at home, blunder abroad," Republicans vowed to "clean up the mess in Washington." Nixon served as Eisenhower's hatchet man, while Ike remained above the fray, the war hero unsullied by politics. It did not start out that way, however. Initially, Nixon, in an effort to expand his appeal, took the high road and avoided criticizing the Democratic ticket. Then on September 12, Ike issued a clear directive: He preferred the "old" slash-and-burn Nixon. "Of course, everybody is noting that you are talking the new high level," Nixon recorded Ike as saying. "However, I think today you ought to take notice of some of these attacks that have been made on the administration and me." Eisenhower wanted Nixon to respond to the attacks, "and if you have to praise me, that will be okay." Eisenhower even suggested a few lines: "Do you want to go back to war in order to have prosperity under the Democrats? . . . Do you want to go back to the casualty lists?" Nixon reflected later that Ike "knew that to maintain his above-the-battle position, he needed a running mate who was willing to engage in all-out combat, and I was good at it. In a sense, the hero needed a point man."

Nixon did not disappoint. He dismissed Stevenson as "Adlai the Appeaser" and a "PhD graduate" of the "cowardly College of Communist Containment." He even went so far as to label President Truman and other leading Democrats "traitors to the high principles in which many of the nation's Democrats believe." Truman never forgave him for that remark, privately blasting Nixon as a "shifty-eyed, goddamn liar."

While his running mate attacked the Democrats, Eisenhower played the role of balanced statesman, declaring just ten days before the election, "I shall go to Korea." Though he did not say what he would do when he got there, his pledge proved to be a masterful stroke. In a break with most presidential elections, which are decided primarily on domestic issues, more than one-half of the electorate in 1952 regarded the Korean War as the country's single most important problem. Furthermore, most people believed that Eisenhower's military background made him the best candidate to end the conflict.

Few people were surprised on Election Day when the Eisenhower-Nixon ticket won 55.1 percent of the popular vote while scoring a lopsided 442-to-89 advantage in the electoral college. The Republicans took control of both houses of Congress, 48–47 in the Senate (with one Independent) and 221–211 in the House. The election gave Republicans control of the White House and Capitol Hill for the first time since 1930.

Meanwhile, Kennedy bucked the Eisenhower landslide, winning by a narrow margin of seventy thousand votes. Many observers credited the teas for mobilizing women to go to the polls. "Everywhere," the *Boston American* reported on Election Day, "there was evidence that women for the first time were taking complete advantage of their political emancipation."

On January 3, 1953, the thirty-five-year-old Kennedy was sworn in as a United States senator and assigned room 362 in the Senate office building. A few weeks later, the forty-year-old Nixon took the oath as vice president. As president of the Senate, Nixon was assigned room 361, directly across the hall from JFK.

"My first day at President's Desk," Eisenhower recorded in his diary on January 21, 1953. "Plenty of worries and difficult problems. But such has been my portion for a long time—the result is that this just seems (today) like a continuation of all I've been doing since July '41—even before that!"

In referencing "July '41," Eisenhower was recalling his promotion to the chief of staff, Third Army, at Fort Sam Houston, Texas, and the beginning of his long climb to becoming supreme commander of Allied forces in Europe. It is revealing that Eisenhower would draw that parallel on his first day in the Oval Office, because his background and leadership in the army would not only shape the way he managed the presidency but also provide him with the skills needed to tackle the countless problems he would encounter. He applied many of the same management skills that he fine-tuned in the military to the White House, and his extensive travels and knowledge made him better prepared to deal with America's place in a complicated postwar world.

In organizing his administration, Eisenhower reflected on the advice that General George Marshall gave him in the days after the Japanese attack on Pearl Harbor. "Eisenhower," Marshall had said, "this department is filled with able men who analyze their problems well but feel compelled to always bring them to me for final solution. I must have assistants who will solve their own problems and tell me later what they have done." As president, Eisenhower adopted the same approach of appointing men who were not only successful but also independent. Millionaire businessmen and corporate lawyers dominated the Cabinet, holding every office except that of secretary of labor, which was reserved for the head of the plumbers' union. Liberals accused Eisenhower of filling his Cabinet with "eight millionaires and a plumber."

Eisenhower met with his Cabinet every Friday morning and made it clear that he expected them to debate issues, just as Generals Omar Bradley and George Patton had done during the war. The president would often sit silently, doodling on paper, while listening to the discussion. When it was over, he would ask for a vote and then either announce his position or return to his office before deciding.

Unsurprisingly, Ike ran the White House with military precision and discipline. He began his day at six o'clock by reading intelligence reports and a small number of major newspapers. Breakfast was served promptly at seven fifteen, and he was behind his desk in the Oval Office by eight. He took two breaks during the day: one for lunch and another in the afternoon to practice his golf swing on the South Lawn. He imposed a similar structure on those who worked for him. Everyone knew their place in the White House hierarchy. "The lines of authority were clear, the national interest was broadly defined, and there was no buck passing," observed biographer Jean Edward Smith.

Where did Ike's vice president fit in this organizational chart? Eisenhower viewed Nixon as a staff member, not an equal. There was no warmth to their relationship. "As personalities," recalled White House advisor Bryce Harlow, "they didn't blend well. Eisenhower would never have picked him as his favorite bridge partner." Nixon was too intense, too insecure to ever be a part of Ike's inner circle, which consisted almost exclusively of wealthy, confident businessmen. "Despite his great capacity for friendliness," Nixon noted, "Eisenhower also had a quality of reserve which, at least subconsciously, tended to make a visitor feel like a junior officer coming in to see the commanding general."

At the same time, Eisenhower did not want to repeat the mistake that FDR had made when he excluded his new vice president Harry Truman from major administration initiatives such as the Manhattan Project. At sixty-two, Eisenhower, who had been a lifelong smoker and suffered from numerous health issues, was only a year younger than Roosevelt had been when he died of a massive stroke. So, Ike made sure to include his vice president in important meetings with administration officials and congressional leaders, even if he did not always listen to Nixon's advice.

Few men had come to the presidency better prepared to deal with foreign policy and defense matters than Eisenhower. He had wide experience in both areas and maintained a personal relationship with many of the world's leaders. He understood military minutiae and kept himself informed about advances in military hardware and weapons systems. His extensive background, and the confidence that came with it, reassured a nation that was struggling to keep up with the dizzying array of problems that emerged in the years after World War II.

Eisenhower's top priority as president was ending the Korean War. In December 1952, while still president-elect, he fulfilled his campaign promise to travel to Korea. He had learned from his many trips to the front lines during World War II that it boosted morale if soldiers had a chance to meet those who were responsible for sending them into harm's way. Bundled in a thick jacket, a fur-lined hat, and thermal boots, he chatted with troops and ate meals in the mess while also assessing conditions on the ground. Nothing Ike witnessed or heard changed his view that the war needed to wind down as quickly as possible. In July 1953, over the grumbling of many Republicans, including his own outspoken secretary of state, John Foster Dulles, Eisenhower agreed to terms that called for the division of Korea at approximately the same line that had existed before the war—the 38th parallel—with a demilitarized zone separating the two Koreas.

Ending the war was important for Eisenhower's other priorities. During the campaign, he depicted the world as divided between tyranny and freedom, making clear his belief that the United States needed to defend free nations from Soviet adventurism. "Freedom," he said in his inaugural address, "is pitted against slavery; lightness against dark." Nevertheless, Eisenhower feared that unrestrained defense spending would cripple the economy and lead to a "garrison state" in which the attempt to spread democracy abroad would destroy the nation at home. His goal was thus to achieve "security without paying the price of national bankruptcy." Economic strength and military might were inseparable, he concluded, and if "these two are allowed to proceed in disregard one for the other, you then create a situation either of doubtful military strength, or of such precarious economic strength that your military position is in constant jeopardy." Excessive spending would lead to inflation, resulting in the need for greater government controls and a more regimented society. This idea, observed historian John Lewis Gaddis, "was probably the most persistent single theme of Eisenhower's public and private utterances while in the White House."

Eisenhower believed that one way to balance military readiness with domestic strength was to take advantage of America's overwhelming superiority in nuclear weapons, attacking enemy forces with small explosives or even striking at the source of aggression: Moscow or Beijing. Cheaper than conventional forces, nuclear weapons offered "more bang for the buck." The administration called its defense strategy the "New Look." The often bombastic Dulles spelled out this approach in a 1954 magazine article in which he called on "the free world" to "make imaginative use" of its powerful nuclear arsenal. "A potential aggressor," he wrote, "should know in advance that he can and will be made to suffer for his aggression more than he can possibly gain by it." To make credible the threat to use atomic arms, the Eisenhower administration dramatically increased the nation's nuclear stockpile. Between 1952 and 1959, the number of nuclear weapons in the American arsenal grew from around

1,500 to more than 6,000, including a formidable new hydrogen bomb, which was a thousand times more powerful than the Hiroshima bomb.

But it was not just nuclear deterrence that Eisenhower planned to employ in pursuit of his international objectives. Allen Dulles, the brother of Ike's secretary of state, transformed the Central Intelligence Agency from an intelligence-gathering vehicle into a secret branch of government that used its power to overthrow foreign regimes, engage in assassination attempts, and carry out sabotage—anything necessary to thwart Soviet ambitions and defend American interests abroad. Eisenhower, who had made effective use of intelligence capabilities during World War II—including depending on the French Resistance for information about German troop movements in the months before D-Day—embraced the CIA's covert operations.

The president believed that the Truman administration had allowed itself to get sucked into the Korean conflict, an unwinnable war that dramatically increased the defense budget to more than $50 billion a year. Ike's administration would take a different approach. Instead of responding to every conflict at a place and time of the opponent's choosing, the New Look called for an "asymmetrical response." It would employ a variety of means—negotiations, alliances, covert operations, and even nuclear weapons—to apply pressure precisely where the adversary was weakest. And instead of sending ground troops to places such as Korea, the administration could threaten to use nuclear weapons or poke the Soviets in Eastern Europe.

For Eisenhower, the goal was not to win wars but to prevent them by dangling the menace of nuclear annihilation. This would save American lives, protect interests abroad, and be more cost-effective. Eisenhower drew on his own military experience to highlight the point. "For forty years, I was in the army, and I did one thing: study how you can get an infantry platoon out of battle. The most terrible job in warfare is to be a second lieutenant leading a platoon when you are on the battlefield."

Despite the New Look's preemptive approach to war, Eisenhower understood that ultimately the best way to limit defense spending was to defuse Cold War tensions. In March 1953, only 121 days after Eisenhower's election, Soviet leader Joseph Stalin died, raising hopes of a thaw in relations between the two countries and an opportunity for genuine peace. Ike decided to deliver a speech titled "The Chance for Peace," even though both his secretary of state and his defense chief opposed it. "Every gun that is made, every warship launched, every rocket fired," Eisenhower declared, "signifies, in the final sense, a theft from those who hunger and are not fed, those who are cold and are not clothed." It was a bold stance that reflected Eisenhower's hatred of war and fear of an arms race. However, the Soviets showed little interest in conciliation, and the olive branch quickly died.

In July 1955 Eisenhower and the new Soviet leader, Nikita Khrushchev, along with their British and French counterparts, met in Geneva, Switzerland, for the first top-level conference among wartime allies since the 1945 Potsdam meeting. "The United States will never take part in an aggressive war," Eisenhower promised the Soviets. To further back this claim, Ike made an "Open Skies" proposal, which called for aerial surveillance of both countries' nuclear facilities. Though it proved to be a propaganda victory, the suggestion was neither as bold nor as innovative as many at the time thought. Since American skies were *already* open, Eisenhower was actually asking the Soviets to make a unilateral concession—something they refused to do. "In our eyes," Khrushchev told the president, "this is a very transparent espionage device. . . . You could hardly expect us to take this seriously."

Although Eisenhower returned from the summit with no tangible victory, he felt that the United States had taken an important first step toward a new era of coexistence with the Russians. He told the American public that "the prospects of a lasting peace" were "brighter" and the "dangers of the overwhelming tragedy of modern war are less." Voters certainly appreciated his efforts. His popularity rose to an impressive 79 percent in August 1955.

However, the friendly words and smiling faces at Geneva could not mask the serious differences dividing the two countries. The thaw ended on October 29, 1956, when 200,000 Soviet soldiers and 4,000 tanks swept into Budapest, Hungary, to repress a popular uprising. The Soviets killed 40,000 Hungarians and forced 150,000 refugees to flee the country. The invasion shocked the world. Eisenhower resisted calls to intervene in the conflict—even from members of his own administration—fearing that any such action might antagonize the Soviets and spark a wider war.

Eisenhower demonstrated similar restraint in dealing with other international flashpoints. When, in the fall of 1954, Communist Chinese exchanged fire with Western-supported Chinese Nationalists living on the offshore islands of Quemoy and Matsu, both controlled by Formosa, Eisenhower ignored calls for America to intervene. Instead, he signed a security agreement with the Nationalists that committed the United States to protect the strategically important island of Formosa but left ambiguous America's commitment to Quemoy and Matsu, which he believed to be of limited strategic value. When the Communist People's Republic of China renewed its bombing of Quemoy and Matsu later that spring, Ike issued public statements hinting about the possibility of using nuclear weapons to stem Communist attacks. "In any combat where these things [tactical nuclear weapons] can be used on strictly military targets and for strictly military purposes, I see no reason why they shouldn't be used, just exactly as you would a bullet or anything else," he stated. Chinese leaders, uncertain whether Eisenhower was bluffing, stopped the attacks instantly.

How would a generation accustomed to total war and total victory adjust to the new challenges of fighting limited wars? It was a question that members of the post–World War II generation would struggle to answer as a wave of decolonization swept the Global South. Between 1945 and 1960, almost forty nations with a combined eight hundred million people waged anti-imperialist struggles against their colonial rulers. Newly independent states in Asia, the Middle East, Latin America, and Africa became the fresh battlegrounds of the Cold War. The leaders of these countries tried to exploit superpower tensions to gain concessions from both Washington and Moscow. Henry Cabot Lodge, who'd become US ambassador to the United Nations after losing his Senate seat to JFK, aptly posed the question that plagued American policymakers in the years following World War II: "The US can win wars, [but] can we win revolutions?"

Vietnam would be the primary testing ground for that paradox. During the 1950s, Eisenhower and two future presidents—Nixon and Kennedy—stood at the center of the debate over how the United States should respond to the growing crisis in Indochina. All three men knew well the lessons of Munich, but each also had traveled abroad and thus been exposed to the power of nationalist revolutions as people struggled to cast off old colonial shackles. None of the other future presidents had spent time in Vietnam during the early years of French colonial rule. They thus had less sensitivity to the aspirations of local citizens or awareness of the complicated interaction between nationalism and Communism.

During World War II, Roosevelt had expressed support for Vietnamese nationalist forces led by Ho Chi Minh, a Communist educated in Paris and Moscow, and called for an end to French colonial rule. After Communists led by Mao Zedong came to power in China in 1949, however, American policy shifted. Fearing that a Communist "victory" in Indochina would result in a sweep of Southeast Asia and tilt the global balance of power, the United States openly endorsed French policy in Asia. In 1950, when the Soviet Union and China extended diplomatic recognition to Ho's government, Harry Truman responded by supplying military aid to the French.

But the war was going badly for the French. After suffering heavy casualties, they decided on a new strategy of amassing troops at a remote jungle fortress near the Laotian border at Dien Bien Phu. Yet by March 1954, the Communist Vietminh forces had completely surrounded the fortress, and its fall seemed imminent. The French pleaded for direct American intervention to rescue their troops. Eisenhower dismissed the idea, reflecting later that "any soldier that would argue for such a thing ought to have his head examined."

Eisenhower believed that the only way for the French to succeed was to make clear "that this is a fight between freedom and Communism." That required them to accomplish two things: "First, make the world believe it, and second, make the Vietnamese believe it." He went on to say that "no one's ever going to win in Vietnam until these people understand that they are to have their own government and run it themselves."

For weeks, the administration debated a course of action. Eisenhower was divided: He viewed the fighting in Vietnam as part of the global struggle against Communism, but he had also spent four years in the Philippines before the war and understood better than most of his advisors the power of nationalism. Sensitive to the terrors of war, Ike was determined not to lead the nation into another one unless as a last resort. But how could he maintain American credibility without committing the nation to another war? Like his successors, he would repeatedly try to thread that needle.

At a January 8, 1954, meeting of the National Security Council, Eisenhower was adamant that he would not send American troops to fight in Vietnam. Eisenhower said that he "simply could not imagine the United States putting ground forces anywhere in Southeast Asia. . . . There was just no sense in even talking about United States forces replacing the French in Indochina. If we did so, the Vietnamese could be expected to transfer their hatred of the French to us. I cannot tell you how bitterly opposed I am to such a course of action." Having just ended a war in Korea, Eisenhower could not imagine sending the 275,000 men the army had estimated would be necessary to quell the insurrection.

Though firm in his decision not to send American troops to Vietnam, Eisenhower was by no means willing to accept a Communist victory, and he planned to use every other tool in his arsenal to prop up the French. Although he possessed a sophisticated view of the struggle, Eisenhower could not escape the lessons of the past that taught him—along with the other men who fought in World War II and went on to become president—that appeasement only produces greater sacrifice down the road. In the postwar world, Communism had replaced Fascism as the chief threat to US interests, and the postwar generation was determined not to repeat the fatal error the West had made during the 1930s.

Eisenhower made clear that he did not want to commit resources, yet he also insisted that he would do so if the British agreed to support American intervention. Early in 1955 Eisenhower wrote a telegram to Winston Churchill, who'd returned as prime minister in 1951 after a six-year absence, to enlist British support by recalling the hard lessons of the 1930s. "We failed to stop Hirohito, Mussolini, and Hitler by not acting in unity and in time. May it not be thought that our nations have learned something from that lesson?" It was necessary, Ike stated, "to look some of these unpleasant facts squarely in the face and meet them exactly as our grand alliance of the 1940s met our enemies and vanquished them." Churchill, then seventy-nine and in poor health due to several strokes, was unmoved. He responded that the British people, who had granted India independence a few years earlier, had no interest in helping France maintain its empire.

With British backing out of the picture, Eisenhower reiterated his opposition to American intervention at a hastily called April 6 meeting of the National Security Council. According to notes of the meeting, Eisenhower was again emphatic that "there was no possibility whatever of US unilateral intervention in Indochina." His military advisors, along with his secretary of state, tried to leave open the possibility of military action, even if only as a last resort. But Eisenhower had made up his mind. He told them that he rejected the simplistic idea that "because we might lose Indochina we would necessarily have to lose all the rest of Southeast Asia."

Yet the day after privately assuring his advisors that the fall of Indochina would not seriously weaken American interests in the region, Eisenhower told the public something very different. When a reporter asked him at his weekly press conference about the strategic value of Indochina, Eisenhower announced his famous "falling domino" principle. "You have a row of dominos set up, you knock over the first one, and what will happen to the last one is the certainty that it will go over very quickly," he said. "So you could have a beginning of a disintegration that would have the most profound influences." This "possible sequence of events," Eisenhower warned, would lead to the loss of not only Indochina but also all of Southeast Asia. Directly contradicting his message the day before, he concluded that the "possible consequences of the loss are just incalculable to the free world."

While Eisenhower is properly credited with not sending ground troops to Vietnam, he missed an opportunity to educate the public about the complexity of the struggle. Instead, he appeared to waffle back and forth between restraint and intervention. If only he had told the American public what he expressed in private—that Vietnam was not vital to

US interests—he could have significantly reframed the conflict, limited America's commitment to its outcome, and provided breathing room to his successors. Polls showed that a large majority of Americans (68 percent) opposed sending ground troops to Vietnam, and Congress echoed that sentiment. Eisenhower's stature as the former supreme commander could have defused a tense situation by confirming what many people felt. Instead, he chose to create a rhetorical trap for himself and his successors. He put his credibility behind a flimsy theory that elevated a local conflict into a superpower confrontation.

That stance established a dangerous pattern: Every president going forward would harbor similar doubts about the wisdom of US involvement in an unwinnable conflict in Southeast Asia, yet each felt compelled to continue that conflict. Trapped by the Munich analogy, American policymakers viewed local struggles as worldwide symbols, confusing indigenous nationalist movements with Soviet-inspired aggression. America's attitude underscored the arrogance of power, a belief that national force could and should shape the internal affairs of distant countries. In time, the United States would pay a heavy price for that mistaken belief.

As the situation in Vietnam continued to deteriorate, and a Communist victory appeared inevitable, Eisenhower seemed more determined than ever to avoid committing troops. At a stormy NSC meeting on April 29, 1954, Dulles, who was in Geneva at the time, sent a cable urging Eisenhower to take strong action. Eisenhower flatly rejected the advice. The president then went on to say that in spite of the views of the secretary of state about the need for leadership to bring the French and British along, he did not see how the United States, together with the French, could intervene with armed forces in Indochina unless it did so in concert with some other nations and at the request of the Associated States themselves. This seemed quite beyond his comprehension. For the next two hours, Eisenhower debated the entire committee, which was unanimous in pushing for American intervention. Given his vast military experience, Eisenhower was comfortable taking on the experts. If the French indeed collapsed and the United States moved in, he told foreign aid director Harold Stassen, we would in the eyes of many Asiatic peoples merely replace French colonialism with American colonialism.

He then raised some practical questions. Where would the United States find the troops? Were they prepared for a full mobilization? What if China and the Soviet Union entered the conflict in response to our escalation? To go in unilaterally in Indochina and other areas of the world which were endangered, he continued, amounted to an attempt to police the entire world. If we attempted such a course of action, using our armed forces and going into areas whether we were wanted or not, we would lose all our significant support in the free world. Of course, Eisenhower avoided the elephant in the room: how this stance seemed to directly contradict the domino theory he had voiced only weeks earlier.

———

Vice President Richard Nixon had traveled to Indochina, but he developed little appreciation for the forces of nationalism sweeping the region. Back in October 1953, Richard and Pat went on a two-month tour of Asia and the Middle East. In Vietnam, he ventured into the countryside and witnessed a French attack on a Communist stronghold near the Chinese border. He returned home convinced that French arrogance would doom their efforts. Instead of writing off the region, however, he was convinced that all the French needed was American military and economic aid. Before leaving the country, he promised, "You shall not fight unaided."

"I told them," he recalled later, "that they were fighting on the very outpost of freedom and that the American people supported their cause and honored their heroism."

Not surprisingly, Nixon remained convinced that the United States could not allow the French to fail, and he emerged as one of the leading hawks in the administration. When asked during the crisis how the administration would react to a French loss, he said, "We must take the risk by putting our boys in." He later recalled being convinced that if the French were to pull out, "Vietnam—and possibly Laos and Cambodia as well—would fall like husks before the fury of the Communist hurricane." Based on his limited observations of Asia, he believed "that the United States would have to do everything possible to find a way to keep the French in Vietnam until the Communists had been defeated." In his estimation, more was at stake in Indochina than just the collapse of an obscure French outpost; this represented a global struggle for freedom and democracy. The Communists needed to see clearly "that so-called wars of liberation would be resisted by military means if necessary, [or] they would not stop until they had taken over Southeast Asia, just as they had in Eastern Europe."

Foreshadowing his position as president, Nixon was concerned that American prestige and credibility in the world would suffer if it allowed an ally to undergo a humiliating defeat. At the April 29 NSC meeting, Nixon suggested that the United States launch airstrikes to help the French wage a ground war. Even if air power might not change the outcome of the battle, he insisted, "the effect of such air strikes on the climate of opinion throughout the free world might well prove decisive." He continued, "It would amount to the United States saying to the Communists, 'This is as far as you go, and no further.'" In stark contrast to Ike, Nixon also expressed support for sending in ground troops to aid the French, insisting that America "must adopt the principle of uniting together to resist subversive aggression of the Indochina and Chinese Civil War type."

Eisenhower opposed his vice president's ideas forcefully. He knew from his time in the Philippines that air power could not win a war in that region and that using nuclear weapons was out of the question. "I certainly do not think that the atom bomb can be used by the United States unilaterally," he said. "You boys must be crazy. We can't use those awful things against Asians for the second time in less than ten years. My God." Disappointed by Eisenhower's reluctance to intervene, Nixon noted in his diary, "He seemed resigned to doing nothing at all unless we could get the allies and the country to go along with whatever was suggested, and he did not seem inclined to put much pressure on to get them to come along."

═══════

Surprisingly, during Eisenhower's first term, Senator Lyndon Johnson supported most of the president's foreign policy positions. As was often the case with Johnson, his decision to cooperate with Eisenhower was motivated by multiple reasons, "but above all," in his words, by "one strongly shared belief: that in our nation's relations with the outside world, partisanship should be left behind." The Texan's experience during World War II and the early Cold War convinced him that the president needed support and latitude in protecting American interests abroad. Furthermore, as a keen meteorologist of the public mood, Johnson recognized a fundamental fact: "Americans loved Ike." Attacking Eisenhower would be "like telling children that their father was a bad man." Johnson thus refused to be a martyr for Democratic legislation that he knew Ike would veto anyway, and he rejected the advice of other Democrats who wanted him to establish clear ideological lines between the two parties. Of course, an element of political calculation did play a role in Johnson's conciliatory approach. By uniting behind Eisenhower, Johnson had the advantage of exposing the fault lines within the Republican Party between internationalists and isolationists.

But Johnson deviated from this strategy when it came to the administration's Indochina policy. The Senate minority leader had little appreciation for the complicated situation on the ground in Vietnam and no real understanding of the Vietnamese people's desire to cast off French rule. Like Nixon, he resorted to boilerplate Cold War rhetoric. Even before Dien Bien Phu fell, Johnson denounced the administration, saying that "American foreign policy has never in all its history suffered such a stunning reversal." The United States, he continued, stood "in clear danger of being left naked and alone in a hostile world."

While Johnson used the crisis to score political points, JFK took a more measured approach and emerged as one of the most thoughtful critics of the White House policy in Vietnam. Overall, Kennedy took issue with Eisenhower's efforts to align the nation's defensive posture with his concern for balanced budgets. He stressed that the United States should instead "spend enough to give a clear margin of superiority over our enemies." Any other approach would be "dangerous, possibly fatal." Warning that the administration's plans to save money would limit the effectiveness of the nation's foreign policy, he lobbied to add more money to the defense budget. Kennedy firmly believed that while the administration talked tough with its rhetoric of massive retaliation, its approach actually hampered military effectiveness and worried our allies.

Back in October 1951, Kennedy, accompanied by his brother Bobby and sister Pat, had spent ten days in Indochina and came away skeptical of the possibility of a military solution to the conflict. In his diary, he noted that "we are more and more becoming colonialists in the minds of the people." He warned that the United States must avoid the mistakes of the crumbling European empires by recognizing that the real enemy was not Communism but "poverty and want," "sickness and disease," and "injustice and inequality." He understood how Communists like Ho Chi Minh manipulated nationalist sentiment to achieve their own goals of conquest. Most of all, he was skeptical that the French would fulfill their promise to allow self-rule and argued that future American aid should be tied to specific reforms that gave greater power to the Vietnamese people.

Unlike with Nixon, Kennedy's travels convinced him that the United States needed to align itself with nationalist sentiment in the region. In a speech delivered on the Senate floor on April 6, 1954, Kennedy questioned the underlying assumptions guiding Eisenhower's approach to the conflict. He supported the administration's position that any American action in the region needed to be coordinated with the British and French, but he questioned if even that would work. Unless the French fulfilled their promises to grant independence to the Vietnamese, victory—even with American support—was impossible. "To pour money, materiel, and men into the jungles of Indochina without at least a remote prospect of victory would be dangerously futile and self-destructive." He also doubted whether US aid could prove decisive in such a remote part of the world. "No amount of American military assistance can conquer an enemy which is everywhere and at the same time nowhere, 'an enemy of the people' which has the sympathy and covert support of the people," he declared.

Given Ho Chi Minh's popularity, even if the United States agreed to partition Vietnam into North and South, just as Korea had been divided in 1945, the result would soon be Communist domination. Kennedy suggested that the only way to win would be to organize a "native army" composed of soldiers from Indochina. He came away convinced that neither the French not the Americans could win a war in Vietnam using conventional means. The week after his Senate speech, JFK criticized

Nixon for suggesting that the United States should send ground troops. The country, he reiterated, "cannot save those who will not be saved," adding that Asian nations needed to play a major role in achieving their own independence.

That is not to suggest that Kennedy was ready to abandon Vietnam to Communism. In some ways, his interest in creating a "native army" and his growing fascination with counterinsurgency reflected his belief that the United States could preserve a non-Communist government in South Vietnam if only it adopted different strategies and tactics than the French. But it also revealed something more fundamental: Kennedy was slowly coming to the realization that World War II offered few lessons for fighting wars in a nuclear age and also that American military power had its limits. More than any future president, JFK thought deeply about these issues and was willing to grapple with the central conflict between the nation's desire to fight Communism around the globe and its limited ability to influence conditions on the ground.

He repeated that same message in numerous speeches and interviews. It was pointless, the senator said, to send American troops to prop up the French, and any American aid needed to be contingent on the French enacting democratic reforms. "There is no outright military intervention that the United States could take in Indochina which I believe would be successful." He further pointed out that US intervention could also provoke the Chinese, which would then leave the United States "in a much worse situation than we found ourselves in Korea."

That same month, Kennedy called Nixon to get a sense of what the administration was thinking. According to JFK's recollection of the conversation, recorded on a Dictabelt, the vice president was "very bitter against the British" and worried that the administration had appeared weak for not doing enough to prevent a French defeat. Nixon thus saw no viable option other than to support the French and hope they would be able to defend their territory. Both men then discussed actions short of intervention, including the creation of a coalition government, but Nixon dismissed all alternatives. For now, he told Kennedy, the administration could only provide support to the French, even though their efforts seemed doomed. Kennedy cautioned that if Nixon were right, "we are about to enter the jungle and do battle with the tiger."

By the time the French surrendered on May 7, 1954, their garrison had been reduced to the size of a football field. Shortly after, the foreign ministers of China, the Soviet Union, the United States, Great Britain, and France met in Geneva to work out a settlement. Ho Chi Minh was initially reluctant to participate, but Eisenhower used the threat of nuclear weapons to force him to the negotiating table. Under the Geneva Accords, the Great Powers agreed to divide Vietnam at the 17th parallel, with a northern zone led by Communist Ho Chi Minh and a southern zone headed by Emperor Bao Dai and Prime Minister Ngo Dinh Diem, a staunch anti-Communist and devout Catholic. The accords also stipulated that a free election would be held in July 1956 to reunify the country under one government. Meanwhile, John Foster Dulles set up an anti-Communist military alliance, the Southeast Asia Treaty Organization, in an effort to stem Soviet and Chinese influence in the area. SEATO also pledged the United States to defend Australia, New Zealand, Thailand, Pakistan, and the Philippines against Communist aggression.

With the bilateral division of Vietnam, the administration made obvious that it was not ready to accept a Communist victory in the country. In October 1955 Diem defeated Bao Dai in a government-controlled referendum and appointed himself president of South Vietnam. The United States subsequently flooded the South with economic and military aid in hopes of establishing a stable regime. But by 1956, after a military buildup in the North, Diem announced that the South would not participate in the free elections promised under the Geneva Accords. Publicly, he claimed that free elections would be impossible given the repressive nature of the North Vietnamese government. The real reason, however, was that he knew the North would win an overwhelming victory.

Diem skillfully manipulated the United States, accepting a total of $2 billion in aid between 1954 and 1961 while ignoring demands that he expand and democratize his government. Over the next few years, while he engaged in a campaign of repression and terror, the United States sat idly by. The Geneva Accords had given the Diem regime a fig leaf of respectability, but it was not enough to silence the administration's toughest critics. "Vietnam represents the cornerstone of the free world in Southeast Asia, the cornerstone in the ark, the finger in the dike," JFK now declared. "It is our offspring. We cannot abandon it, we cannot ignore its needs."

———

It is often argued that it was not the New Deal but World War II that decisively ended the Great Depression. In a related sense, World War II also seemed to validate the ideas put forth by British economist John Maynard Keynes in his landmark book *The General Theory of Employment, Interest, and Money*. By the 1950s, many young theorists, influenced by Keynes's theses, assumed positions at major universities and filtered into government jobs. Like their mentor, they questioned the prevailing economic orthodoxy that the free market contained self-correcting mechanisms. Instead, they believed that government should play a more proactive role in the economy, running deficits to spur growth and cutting spending when the economy overheated.

Keynesian ideas gained traction among liberals in the postwar era but would not be fully implemented until the Kennedy and Johnson presidencies. In the meantime, Eisenhower tried to find common ground between conservative faith in small government and liberal belief in federal activism.

Like many conservatives, Eisenhower railed against growing federal power and high taxes, but he also realized that it was wishful thinking for the party to expect to return to the days of Herbert Hoover. The New Deal had reconfigured the relationship between the people and the state, and World War II had only further institutionalized that close relationship. As he put it, "Should any political party attempt to abolish Social Security and eliminate labor laws and farm programs, you would not hear of that party again in our political history." Eisenhower labeled his approach "the middle way" or "modern Republicanism" because it chipped away at the dogma of limited spending and balanced budgets.

Indeed, Eisenhower's policies consolidated and strengthened the New Deal's economic and social programs. During his presidency, federal spending on social welfare programs rose steadily, and twice the president and Congress increased Social Security benefits and broadened the system to include an estimated ten million new workers. Congress and Eisenhower also compromised on a new law that increased the minimum wage from seventy-five cents to one dollar an hour and agreed to increase federal spending for slum clearance and public housing. Furthermore, instead of shrinking the size of government, the thirty-fourth president added a new Cabinet-level agency: the Department of Health, Education, and Welfare.

Eisenhower's most notable domestic achievement—the construction of a federal highway system—reflected his belief that government could play a positive role in postwar American life. For Ike, the idea of building a highway system that would connect big cities and small towns was born in 1919, when he was one of six officers assigned to lead the army's first transcontinental motor convoy from Washington to San Francisco. The three-mile-long caravan left DC in early July and did not arrive in San Francisco until September. The expedition assumed that it was traveling through "enemy country" and therefore had to be "self-sustaining throughout." The results were not reassuring. Over half the distance was made up of dirt roads, mountain trails, and desert sands, with nearly five hundred miles being "practically impassable" to heavy vehicles. The experience convinced him that the United States could not flourish without a more efficient form of transportation.

That idea was reinforced during World War II, when he witnessed the effectiveness of the German high-speed autobahns. Cold War fears further added to the need for improved roads, since they would allow for the evacuation of cities in the event of a nuclear attack. Finally, with millions of new cars on the road, Americans demanded better roads and highways.

In response to all these factors, Eisenhower backed the building of a nationwide network of four-lane highways, and Congress agreed in 1956 by passing the Federal-Aid Highway Act. The largest public works project in American history, this act appropriated $32 billion to build forty-one thousand miles of highway. The new system made travel easier, faster, and more convenient. By the end of the decade, the nation had more than three million miles of roads, almost 75 percent of which were paved.

Ironically, Eisenhower's approach to domestic issues angered both conservatives and liberals. Senator Barry Goldwater, a rising conservative star from Arizona, complained that Ike ran "a dime-store New Deal." At the same time, liberals accustomed to the take-charge leadership of FDR complained that Ike did not work hard at his job. "Eisenhower is no fire-eater," observed the liberal journalist I. F. Stone, "but seems to be a rather simple man who enjoys his bridge and his golf and doesn't like to be too much bothered." These critics often underestimated Eisenhower and failed to appreciate his strong bond with the American people. More than any specific policy position, it was Ike's engaging personality and dominating presence, as well as his modesty and sincerity, that endeared him to the public.

IKE'S WARMTH AND POPULARITY DID NOTHING TO DAMPEN WISCONSIN senator Joseph McCarthy's crusade to expel suspected Communists from government. For two years, the pugnacious McCarthy tormented the Truman administration with his outrageous tactics and unfounded claims. The fact that there was now a Republican in the White House meant little to McCarthy. Eisenhower tried to outflank him by implementing a tough new government loyalty program, but the junior senator persisted in his attacks, blasting the administration for conducting a foreign policy of "whiny, whimpering appeasement." Eisenhower, who believed that getting involved in a partisan battle with McCarthy would diminish the presidency, stayed in the background, delegating the dirty work of confronting McCarthy to Vice President Nixon. "I just won't get into a pissing contest with that skunk," Ike grumbled privately.

Eisenhower was not the only future president who struggled to deal with Joe McCarthy. Their generation had learned the lessons of Munich and was convinced that the United States had a mission to fight Soviet aggression abroad while uprooting Communist subversion at home. Politically, the Wisconsin senator was popular with many of their constituents. LBJ feared alienating many of the Texas oilmen who both funded his campaigns and supported McCarthy, while JFK's position was especially precarious. Not only was McCarthy popular with his staunchly anti-Communist, Catholic constituents, but the Wisconsin senator happened to be a family friend who vacationed at the Kennedy compound in Hyannis Port and even dated two of JFK's sisters, Pat and Jean. Privately, both LBJ and JFK detested McCarthy's methods, but they feared the political consequences of incurring his wrath.

With Eisenhower refusing to expend political capital to attack McCarthy, and with leading Democrats sitting on the sidelines, it was up to the old red-baiter himself, Richard Nixon, to take on the Wisconsin senator. Reluctantly, Nixon delivered a speech that used the odd metaphor of shooting rats to make his point. "When you go out to shoot rats, you have to shoot straight," he told the nation, "because when you shoot wildly, it not only means that the rat will get away more easily, you make it easier on the rat."

When McCarthy continued his attacks, the president leaked to the press an army report that documented attempts by McCarthy and his staff to win preferential treatment for a former staff member drafted into the army. The Senate, embarrassed by the army's accusations, decided to hold investigative public hearings that eventually led to McCarthy's downfall. In December 1954 the Senate voted to "condemn" McCarthy for bringing Congress into disrepute. Three years later, at the age of forty-eight, Joseph McCarthy—once the most feared man in America—died of hepatitis and other health problems caused by alcoholism.

Eisenhower was proud that he had taken down McCarthy without having to get into the gutter with him, but the truth was more complicated. He may have been the only political figure in America with the credibility to confront McCarthy and refute his outrageous charges. But Ike was unwilling to spend his enormous political capital—especially on a domestic issue about which he cared little. While he stayed on the sidelines, hundreds of Americans fell victim to vicious, inaccurate attacks, and many lost their federal jobs.

═══════

If Vietnam posed the greatest challenge to Eisenhower's worldview, civil rights exposed the limitations of Ike's "modern Republicanism" at home. It goes without saying that race would prove to be a complicated issue for each of the future presidents who fought in World War II. All would live in the wake of the enormous social and demographic changes produced by the war. It reordered social arrangements, aroused expectations, especially for those groups that had been marginalized, and transformed the relationship between citizens and the federal government. Before the war, the presidency was not central to the lives of ordinary Americans, but Franklin Roosevelt's leadership during the Depression and war changed all that. People now looked to the presidency to address problems that had been traditionally left to the states. The war had also raised the stakes of the social contract, making more urgent Black demands for an empowered federal government to address the enduring legacy of Jim Crow.

With the exception of the Black valet who laid out his clothes every morning, Eisenhower had little exposure to African Americans and thus little understanding of the challenges they faced. His whole life had been spent in a white world, from his youth in Kansas to his time in the segregated army. During the war, Blacks were relegated to separate units, where they largely served in support positions. The army was simply a microcosm of life in the American South, where Jim Crow forced African Americans to live in separate neighborhoods and attend segregated schools. Most of Ike's friends were successful white men, primarily from the South. Eisenhower thus accepted segregation and felt little need to question or challenge it, believing that he would be overstepping his constitutional powers if he were to uproot deeply ingrained racial customs and habits. "I have never yet given up my belief that the American people, faced with a great problem like this, will approach it intelligently and with patience and understanding, and we will get somewhere," he stated neutrally.

In May 1954 the unanimous Supreme Court decision in *Brown v. Board of Education of Topeka, Kansas*, which ruled that segregation in public schools was illegal, put Eisenhower's attitudes toward race to the test. Privately, Eisenhower opposed the *Brown* decision, telling his secretary he preferred a gradual approach that would begin by desegregating graduate schools, then colleges, high schools, and eventually elementary schools. Publicly, however, Eisenhower said nothing about the decision, a move that biographer Stephen Ambrose appropriately called "an abdication of responsibility."

Predictably, the historic decision triggered a wave of "massive resistance" among state and local politicians in the South at the same time that it quickened the pace of civil rights protests. In December 1955 a Black seamstress named Rosa Parks refused to give her seat on a public bus to a white person, in open defiance of segregation laws in Montgomery, Alabama. After police arrested Parks, Black leaders decided to boycott the city bus system and sought the support of Black ministers at the forefront of African American communities. Twenty-six-year-old Martin Luther King Jr., a pastor at the Dexter Avenue Baptist Church, agreed to head the Montgomery Improvement Association (MIA), which was established to promote and support the boycott.

As civil rights leaders used the momentum of *Brown* to empower their cause, Southern politicians continued to double down. In March 1956 nineteen senators and seventy-seven representatives signed the so-called Southern Manifesto, vowing to "use all lawful means to bring about a reversal of this decision which is contrary to the Court and to prevent the use of force in its implementation." The issue came to a head in September 1957 at Central High School in Little Rock, Arkansas, when nine Black students—to become known as the Little Rock Nine—attempted to enroll at the all-white school. Governor Orval Faubus sent the Arkansas National Guard to surround the school and prevent the students from entering. Eventually Eisenhower ordered 1,100 army paratroopers into Little Rock and federalized the Arkansas National Guard. In essence, Eisenhower employed the same strategy in dealing with angry whites in Little Rock as he used on D-Day. "In my career, I have learned," Ike said, "that if you have to use force, use overwhelming force and save lives thereby." Attorney General Herbert Brownell Jr., his former campaign manager, noted that Eisenhower "was acting as a military commander in chief, dealing with Faubus as a subordinate who had let him down in the midst of battle."

Eisenhower confessed to a reporter that sending troops to quell a revolt in Little Rock was the hardest decision he ever had to make, with the exception of D-Day. "But goddamn it, it was the only thing I could do." For Eisenhower, the choice had little to do with supporting desegregation or not. Faubus had shown insubordination toward the general, who had sworn to abide by the Constitution. "Simply put," Ike stated, "it was to enforce the law of the land."

Ike's tendency to equivocate on civil rights emerged as another key point of difference between him and Nixon. Like Eisenhower, Nixon grew up in a segregated world, but he had African American friends, including Brooklyn Dodgers star Jackie Robinson, who'd shattered the color barrier in professional baseball in 1947. He was an honorary member of the NAACP, and he impressed Black leaders with his three-week goodwill mission to Africa in 1957. Although he opposed racial discrimination and had a better understanding of Black aspirations than the president, Nixon, too, believed in a gradual approach to addressing the problem, largely because he was convinced that it would take decades for unskilled African Americans to compete with whites in the workplace. Change would be slow but inevitable and would not require aggressive federal action.

It is more difficult to track what George H. W. Bush and Ronald Reagan felt about the *Brown* decision. Bush had campaigned locally for Eisenhower in Texas in 1952, but his real focus was on his father's campaign for a Connecticut senate seat, which Prescott Bush won. But politics did not yet play a central role in George's life, partly because personal tragedy overshadowed all else. In 1953 George and Barbara were devastated by the loss of their three-year-old daughter, Robin, to leukemia. "One minute she was there, and the next she was gone," recalled Barbara. Over the next few years, George channeled his grief into building a successful oil business, cofounding Zapata Petroleum Corporation and drilling new wells in West Texas.

Meanwhile, in 1954 Ronald Reagan had left the movie business and landed a lucrative role as the host of the CBS-TV program *General Electric Theater*. By this point, he was moving away from his support for the Democratic Party. Six years earlier, he had endorsed Harry Truman and gave speeches on behalf of Hubert Humphrey, the energetic liberal mayor of Minneapolis who won election to the Senate in 1948. In 1952, however, Reagan cast his vote for a Republican for the first time. He supported Ike yet had nothing but disdain for Nixon, whom he dismissed as "a handpicked errand boy with a pleasing façade and naught but emptiness behind." He noted further that Nixon was "less than honest and [an] ambitious opportunist completely undeserving of the high honor accorded him." Reagan's animus stemmed partly from Nixon's vicious 1948 campaign against Helen Douglas, who was married to his acting friend Melvyn Douglas.

In addition to hosting *General Electric Theater,* Reagan pinballed around the country as a public relations spokesman for the company. Although he was too busy with speaking engagements to focus on national politics, his speeches revealed a man lurching dramatically to the right. The massive government intervention in the economy during World War II produced a backlash among many conservatives and business groups that resented higher taxes and more regulations. GE fed Reagan a steady diet of corporate propaganda that preached the importance of free markets and demonized government intervention. By the mid-1950s, Reagan was on the warpath against creeping Socialism, high taxes, and the dangers of international Communism. Given the rightward trajectory of his thinking, it is fair to assume that Reagan would have opposed the *Brown* decision on the grounds that it exemplified federal intervention in local and state affairs.

Gerald Ford was the only future Republican president who expressed outright support for the Supreme Court's decision, calling it "morally and constitutionally right." He viewed the decision through the lens of the Cold War as well as the internationalist lessons he had garnered from World War II. After *Brown*, he said, "No longer can Communists holler and scream that the United States legalizes racial discrimination in our public school system." He naïvely believed there would be a peaceful transition "if the extremists on both sides will hold their tongues and let the moderates implement the court's decision."

For Johnson and Kennedy, political calculation more than idealism shaped their responses to the growing demands for civil rights. In the postwar era, race had become an especially sensitive issue for Democrats. The Roosevelt coalition had consisted of northern liberals and white southern segregationists, as FDR pulled both groups under the umbrella of the Democratic Party in the face of the class anxieties of the Great Depression. World War II aroused the expectations of many African Americans—especially veterans who, having fought a war against Fascism, now refused to accept second-class citizenship at home. The growing demands by African Americans for change put leading Democrats in a bind. Intellectually, they supported those demands, but they also needed the electoral backing of southern whites to win national elections. As they eyed national office, both Johnson and Kennedy tried to straddle the fence. For the southerner Johnson, that required becoming more acceptable to northern liberals; for the northeasterner Kennedy, it necessitated winning the approval of the South.

———

The desire to prove himself a viable national candidate drove nearly all the major moves Kennedy made after his election to the Senate—including the decision to get married. His father warned that being a bachelor in his twenties was fine, but that being a bachelor in his thirties would lead people to suspect that he was a homosexual. Besides, voters expected leading politicians to conform with the standards of the time, which meant being married and having a family. After winning his Senate race in 1952, Jack told aides that he needed to get married—and soon. Not long afterward, he encountered a twenty-two-year-old George Washington University graduate named Jackie Bouvier at a dinner party. According to his recollection, he "leaned over the asparagus and asked her for a date." Jackie's beauty and style mesmerized John. "I've never met anyone like her," he told Dave Powers. "She's different from any girl I know." For her part, Jackie was fascinated by his good looks, sense of humor, wit, and charm. (It also did not hurt that he was fabulously wealthy.) They were married in a high-profile wedding in Newport, Rhode Island, on September 12, 1953.

With his family image intact, Kennedy started to position himself for a possible run for the White House. During his nine years on Capitol Hill, Kennedy had been a reliable vote—but never a voice—in support of civil rights. Now, however, he engaged in a careful remaking of his image to a racial moderate. His position was similar to Eisenhower's: He supported racial equality but called for slow, gradual change buttressed by the voluntary support of the southern wing of the party. When confronted with the apparent contradictions in his position, Kennedy, according to biographer Fredrik Logevall, "bobbed and weaved, avoiding unambiguous statements," while making it clear that the courts should have the final say in determining the pace of desegregation.

AS WAS OFTEN THE CASE, KENNEDY'S HEALTH INTERFERED WITH HIS political ambitions. Jack had spent most of 1954 in agonizing back pain and made his way around the Capitol on crutches. During the summer recess, he chose to undergo a risky surgery. "Jack was determined to have the operation," his mother, Rose Kennedy, said later. "He told his father that even if the risks were fifty-fifty, he would rather be dead than spend the rest of his life hobbling around on crutches and paralyzed by pain."

In October Kennedy entered the hospital for surgery. The day before, he told a friend, "This is it. . . . This is the one that cures you or kills you." He knew that the chances of success were slim, while the likelihood of dying was high because his treatments for Addison's disease compromised his ability to fight off infection. Three days after the surgery, his fever spiked, and he went into a coma. Doctors promptly summoned his family, and they surrounded him as a priest administered the last rites of the Catholic Church for a second time. Rumors floated across Capitol Hill that Jack was near death. Even Nixon dissolved into tears upon learning that Kennedy might not survive. "Oh, brave Jack is going to die. Oh God, don't let him die," he cried.

But like so many times before, Kennedy fought back. Although critically ill and forced to spend several weeks immobilized in a hospital bed, his chances of a full recovery were promising. Kennedy would use his convalescence to write another best-selling book: *Profiles in Courage*, a 266-page tribute to senators who had demonstrated courage while in office. The book shot to the top of *The New York Times* bestseller list and would receive the 1957 Pulitzer Prize for Biography. When Kennedy returned to the Senate, he found a basket of fruit with a card signed, "Welcome home. Dick Nixon." The vice president also offered the ailing JFK use of his official office near the Senate floor so that he would not need to walk back and forth to his own office.

Kennedy's critically acclaimed book, along with his tough criticism of Eisenhower's foreign policy and his maneuvering to make himself more acceptable to the South, paid off in 1956. The press began speculating that he might be a viable vice presidential candidate for the presumptive nominee, Adlai Stevenson. Kennedy believed that Lyndon Johnson would be the best nominee for the party, but he also realized that Eisenhower would defeat any Democrat. His father, however, did not want to take any chances. He reached out to Johnson and asked him to join Jack as his running mate. In return, Joe Kennedy promised to bankroll the entire campaign. Johnson, however, turned him down, realizing that the senior Kennedy was using him as a stalking horse. He assumed that an LBJ ticket would lose to Eisenhower and then establish Kennedy as the leading contender for the 1960 nomination.

As expected, Adlai Stevenson won the party's nomination again and, in a surprise move, allowed the convention to choose his vice president. Initially, JFK was ambivalent, fearing that his Catholicism would be blamed for a likely Stevenson loss. But his competitive nature would not allow him to walk away from a challenge, so he submitted his name for consideration. "This year, it's the only game in town," he told speechwriter Ted Sorensen. His father was dead set against the idea of him joining a Stevenson ticket, which he assumed would be a losing proposition. "Jack's a total fucking idiot!" he shouted over the phone to Bobby when told the news.

Kennedy managed to win over many southern delegates who were attracted to his racial moderation. But it was not enough to earn the prize. When the votes were counted, JFK finished second to Tennessee senator Estes Kefauver. Although he fell short of securing the second spot on the ticket, he left the Democratic convention—the first televised from gavel to gavel—as a rising star in the party. Historian Arthur Schlesinger Jr., then a speechwriter and aide to Stevenson, wrote Kennedy that "you clearly emerged as the man who gained most during the Convention. . . . Your general demeanor and effectiveness made you in a single week a national political figure." Kennedy's first political loss on the national stage would prove to be a blessing in disguise.

The real intrigue in 1956, however, unfolded on the Republican side. On the evening of September 23, 1955, while vacationing in Colorado, the sixty-four-year-old Eisenhower suffered a major heart attack. The news shocked the nation, with the stock market suffering its steepest plunge since the Great Depression. The White House hid the seriousness of his condition from the public. It was not until October 23 that Ike could stand on his own two feet. He walked for the first time three days later. After forty-nine days in a Denver hospital, he was finally well enough to return to Washington.

The president's shaky health only highlighted Nixon's exclusion rather than giving him a chance to shine. Over the next few months, while Ike recovered, White House aides kept Nixon at a distance and limited his authority. They viewed him as too inexperienced to run the government. While the vice president was constitutionally mandated to assume power if the president died or was incapacitated, aides stressed that Eisenhower was still alive and mentally alert but simply needed rest. The Cabinet decided that not Nixon but Sherman Adams, the powerful White House chief of staff, should travel to Denver, where the president was recovering, to take charge, control the information that reached Ike, and act as the "sole official channel of information between Eisenhower and the world."

The only person who felt a sense of relief from Ike's heart attack was Lyndon Johnson. Three months earlier, Johnson, too, had suffered a massive heart attack. Initially in critical condition, he remained in Bethesda Naval Hospital for six weeks, then had to spend four months convalescing at his Texas ranch. The heart attack plunged LBJ into depression. He had survived—but barely—and assumed that his political career was over. But now he realized that if Eisenhower could have a heart attack and continue to function as president, then surely he could remain a powerful player in the Senate and possibly make a run for the White House.

Eisenhower's poor health led him to reconsider having Nixon remain on the ticket in 1956. The president appreciated Nixon's loyalty and considered him able, but he did not think that Nixon was mature enough to serve as president. Eisenhower believed that Nixon was still the partisan scrapper who lacked a larger vision for the country. He seemed consumed by smaller, tactical issues—how to win congressional seats, tossing red meat to the party faithful, and attacking his opponents—while also advancing his own career. Furthermore, Nixon seemed to have little political appeal beyond his association with the president.

As a result, Ike wanted Nixon to vacate the vice presidency and move into a top Cabinet post. He rationalized the move by convincing himself that it would be in Nixon's best interest, providing him with executive experience in government and thus preparing him for the presidency. Nixon was shocked. He understood correctly that such a proposal coming shortly after Ike's heart attack insinuated that the president did not fully trust him. "I was taken aback by this suggestion," he reflected.

The two men found themselves in a position similar to the one they had faced during the 1952 fund scandal, with Nixon refusing to relinquish power and Ike unwilling to force his hand.

Just as in the past, Eisenhower left Nixon to twist in the wind before finally acquiescing.

Throughout the process, Eisenhower was unfair—even cruel—to Nixon. He had asked him to join the ticket precisely because he was a bulldog who freed Ike from engaging in the messy demands of partisan politics. Nixon did exactly what was asked of him, but now his boss wanted to essentially fire him for doing his job. The president's treatment of his vice president angered JFK, who complained that Eisenhower "won't stand by anybody. He is terribly cold and terribly vain. In fact, he is a shit."

At the end of the day, Ike's running mate did not actually matter because Ike himself remained enormously popular. The Republican ticket won 57.4 percent of the popular vote, the second highest in US history at the time, exceeded only by FDR's 60.8 percent in 1936. Ike even carried Democratic strongholds such as Chicago and Jersey City. What's more, he secured a majority of the Catholic vote and even did well among African Americans, despite his moderate civil rights stance. It was an endorsement, however, of Eisenhower—not of his party. The Democrats increased their majorities in Congress and in governorships, thus inching closer to the edge of a new frontier.

CHAPTER 7

"I'm Forty-Three Years Old. I'm Not Going to Die in Office."

OCTOBER 4, 1957
GETTYSBURG, PENNSYLVANIA

President Eisenhower always enjoyed spending time at his 496-acre farm in Gettysburg, Pennsylvania, located next to one of the bloodiest battlefields of the Civil War. He and Mamie had purchased the land in 1950 after thirty-four years of marriage without a home of their own. At Mamie's insistence, Ike tore down the old, dilapidated house and constructed a new one, making it ready for his eventual retirement. The peaceful setting, with its scenic view of South Mountain, served as a retreat from the pressures of the White House. Ike spent a total of 365 days there during his eight years in office, watching over his herd of Black Angus cattle, practicing on the putting green, trapshooting, and barbecuing for friends. His favorite spot in the house was the glass-enclosed back room, where he could look out on his rose gardens or spend hours painting while Mamie watched television.

On Friday, October 4, 1957, Ike returned to Gettysburg anticipating a long, relaxing weekend of golf. But the calm was shattered at six thirty that evening, when he received a telephone call informing him that the Soviet Union had launched a satellite into space. The 187-pound device, called Sputnik, or "artificial fellow traveler around the Earth," was the size of a beach ball, with four metal antennae protruding from its aluminum surface. It was fairly basic, consisting of a radio transmitter, batteries, and temperature gauges. But the Soviets designed the satellite for maximum publicity, giving it a shiny surface that could be seen as it orbited 550 miles above Earth and installing a recording of a distinctive *beep-beep-beep* that could easily be heard by amateur radio operators.

Despite the big news, Eisenhower saw no reason for panic. He decided to remain at his farm and keep his regular tee time, leaving it to other administration members to reassure the nation. Press Secretary James Hagerty dismissed Sputnik as an event "of no security or defense significance." Ike's chief of naval research echoed that sentiment, questioning why there was such excitement over a "hunk of iron almost anybody could launch."

They and Eisenhower, however, seriously misread the public's mood: The launch stunned American scientists and shocked the nation. Never before, not even during World War II, had the country's airspace been violated; now a Soviet satellite passed overhead every ninety minutes at a speed of eighteen thousand miles per hour. The satellite made the front page of every major American newspaper, highlighted by screaming headlines alongside diagrams and maps of Sputnik's flight over the United States. *The New York Times* announced that Sputnik represented "one of the world's greatest propaganda—as well as scientific—achievements." *Time* featured the story on its cover with the headline "Red Moon over the U.S.," along with a warning that the Soviets had taken the first step "toward the conquest of outer space." The liberal *New Republic* compared Sputnik to "the discovery by Columbus of America," while fretting that the Soviets demonstrated "a commanding lead" in "the race for world scientific and technological supremacy." Physicist Edward Teller, father of the hydrogen bomb, opined that the United States had "lost a battle more important and greater than Pearl Harbor." Collectively, all these declarations stood in stark contrast to the administration's official stance.

Most worrisome, many Americans believed that if the Soviets had rockets powerful enough to propel a satellite into space, they were not far from the capability of launching nuclear warheads at the United States. Pundits and politicians now fretted about a looming "missile gap" that threatened national security. "We Middle Westerners are sometimes called isolationists," declared the normally staid Gerald Ford. "I don't agree with the label; but there can be no isolationists anywhere when a thermonuclear warhead can flash down from space at hypersonic speed to reach any spot on Earth minutes after its launching."

Eisenhower tried to calm the nation's nerves when he returned to the White House at the end of his weekend respite. In his first press conference after Sputnik, he again minimized the scientific achievement as nothing more than putting "one small ball in the air." He acknowledged that the Russians had achieved a great psychological victory, but that did not seem "to be a reason for just trying to grow hysterical about it." He went on to say that the satellite did not raise his apprehensions—"not one iota." The Soviets were still a long way from being able to use satellites for reconnaissance or as weapons of war, Ike insisted, before concluding that Sputnik "imposes no additional threat to the United States."

Because of his military experience, Eisenhower knew that launching a rocket at a specific target thousands of miles away was far more complicated than shooting a metallic ball into space. He also knew from top-secret information procured by American U-2 spy planes that no missile gap existed: The Soviets lagged far behind the United States in nearly every weapons category. While the Soviet Union was building more rockets, it had yet to develop a sophisticated guidance system that would transform them into effective weapons. Ike thus found himself in a frustrating position: He knew that the panic over a missile gap was unwarranted, but going public would have compromised America's chief covert intelligence-gathering operation. And so, in the absence of a missile gap, Eisenhower was inclined to maintain his policy of fiscal conservatism and avoid excessive defense spending, even rejecting pleas from his military advisors to invest larger sums of money into America's space program.

EISENHOWER HAD BEEN SUCCESSFUL DURING THE WAR BECAUSE HE was both a skilled strategist and an adept politician. But his political instincts failed him in dealing with Sputnik. From a military perspective, Eisenhower was right: Sputnik did not alter the balance of power between the two nations. But he seriously misjudged the politics of the moment. After Sputnik, wrote a White House advisor, Democrats finally "had a focus and a theme." Ike's perceived complacency provided them with an opening to attack the popular president. They began portraying Eisenhower as indifferent and out of touch. The Soviets, Lyndon Johnson warned, "will be dropping bombs on us from space like kids dropping rocks onto cars from freeway overpasses." LBJ clearly grasped the political opportunity in sending such a strong message. His press secretary, George Reedy, advised the Senate majority leader that Sputnik was an issue "which, if properly handled, would blast the Republicans out of the water, unify the Democratic Party, and elect you president."

The White House's own surveys underscored the political benefit that the Soviets reaped from the launch. They concluded that one week later, the belief that the Russians had gained "scientific and technological superiority over the West and especially the US [has] won greatly widened acceptance." More importantly, American prestige in the world had "sustained a severe blow" and caused concern among US allies that "the balance of military power has shifted or may soon shift in favor of the USSR."

If Johnson had any chance of winning the Democratic nomination in 1960, he needed to abandon his earlier policy of accommodation with the Eisenhower administration and forge an independent record as a foreign policy statesman. As part of his strategy, LBJ pushed to become a national spokesman on the US space program. After hearing from more than two hundred witnesses, his subcommittee released a report in January 1958 that advocated for building larger rockets and establishing what would become the National Aeronautics and Space Administration (NASA). To his fellow senators, Johnson proclaimed, "Control of space means control of the world."

Meanwhile, Richard Nixon recognized the political damage that Sputnik had inflicted on the administration as well as on his prospect of winning the 1960 election. He shared the fears of many Democratic critics that the Soviets were winning the arms race. "We can make no greater mistake than to see this as just a Soviet stunt," the vice president warned.

"We've got to pull up our socks and get with it and make sure that we maintain our leadership." Unlike Eisenhower, Nixon wanted a vigorous response and was frustrated by the president's flaccid reaction. One member of Eisenhower's Cabinet recalled seeing "Nixon get up from the table after Cabinet meetings so tense that beads of sweat were standing out on his brow. The cause of his tension was that he had to keep his mouth shut while decisions were taken that he knew would erode his political base for 1960."

Eisenhower had the stature to stand firm and not overreact to Sputnik or to Democrats' attacks; Nixon did not. He desperately wanted the administration to announce a bold step in weapons technology before the 1960 campaign. Publicly, however, he defended Ike's approach, telling reporters that the problem lay with the *previous* administration for its failure to invest in basic scientific research. The problem with that argument, however, was that the Eisenhower administration had also failed to make a concerted effort to advance missile technology. Nixon privately lobbied Eisenhower to create a centralized agency similar to the Manhattan Project, which would coordinate research and development. Predictably, Eisenhower vetoed the idea. "Only Eisenhower could have gotten away with saying no," observed Stephen Ambrose. "His unique prestige among his countrymen made him unassailable on the question of national defense."

But as Democrats increasingly denounced Eisenhower for his passive approach to the "missile gap," Nixon started to push harder. He began discreetly leaking to reporters that he was "taking a stronger line on the satellite situation than some people in the administration." It was clear that by "some people," Nixon meant the president. He also urged Eisenhower's speechwriter to incorporate stronger language in some of his speeches, such as this statement: "Regardless of the cost in money or effort, I intend to see that the United States maintains superior strength so that we can always be in a position to defend our freedom without compromising with slavery." Instead, Eisenhower said the opposite, denouncing calls for more military spending as "unjustifiable."

No one channeled public apprehension into a potent attack on the administration more effectively and powerfully than John F. Kennedy. He managed to synthesize the accumulated Democratic grievances into a compelling message that pierced Ike's political armor. On August 14, 1958, Kennedy fired the first salvo of the 1960 presidential election when he stood before the Senate and delivered the most important speech of his Senate career. While others focused almost exclusively on the missile gap, Kennedy launched a sweeping and sophisticated critique of the assumptions that informed Eisenhower's approach to the world. Ever since Hiroshima, one of those assumptions had been that the United States "possessed a capacity for retaliation so great as to deter any potential aggressor from launching a direct attack upon us." That premise, he said, "will soon no longer be correct" because the Soviets could launch a first strike and destroy the nation's ability to retaliate.

But a more urgent danger resulted from "Sputnik diplomacy," where the Soviets would use nuclear fear and intimidation to advance their interests in the underdeveloped world. "The periphery of the free world will slowly be nibbled away," Kennedy declared. As the Soviets infiltrated and dominated remote parts of the world, he warned, "The balance of power will gradually shift against us. Each such Soviet move will weaken the West; but none will seem sufficiently significant by itself to justify our initiating a nuclear war which might destroy us."

In light of this dangerous prospect, Kennedy called for a new approach that emphasized military imperatives over balanced budgets. In order to thwart Soviet adventurism, the nation needed to bolster its nonnuclear capabilities—including more air tankers to refuel bombers, an increase in the number of air-to-ground missiles, a bolstered continental defense system, and greater sealift and airlift necessary to intervene in a limited war. Most of all, the United States needed to use its current advantages to recruit new allies and build goodwill in underdeveloped parts of the world. Instead of opposing nationalist movements, America must exploit its "ideological advantage" by exporting "the revolutionary ideas of the Declaration of Independence" to inspire those challenging imperialist powers.

With this assertive stance, Kennedy made it clear that he was the one to watch in the upcoming presidential race.

The 1960 presidential race featured five World War II veterans: JFK, Lyndon Johnson, Richard Nixon, Henry Cabot Lodge, and the outgoing president, Dwight Eisenhower. It represented the coming of age of the junior officers of World War II. Both Nixon and Kennedy were the first contestants for the White House who were born in the twentieth century, entered World War II as young men, and left it having learned similar lessons.

Kennedy's reelection victory in the 1958 Senate race foreshadowed what was to come in 1960. The question had not been whether he would win but by how wide a margin. Since he viewed the election as a stepping stone to the presidency, Kennedy wanted to make a statement with his victory. And he did, winning 73.6 percent of the popular vote—the largest margin in the history of the state. He scored the victory even though he spent much of his time traveling around the nation campaigning for other candidates, building relationships, and seeking future endorsements. In July *The New York Times,* which described Kennedy as "the handsome, well-endowed young author-statesman from Massachusetts," opined that he was the man "many Democrats regard as their surest bet in the campaign to 'Stop Nixon in '60.'" Even more promising, Kennedy's victory was part of a Democratic tidal wave that year. In the congressional election, Democrats collectively won 56 percent of the vote, their best showing since the heyday of the New Deal in 1936. The party gained forty-seven seats in the House and thirteen in the Senate.

Events in the final years of the Eisenhower presidency provided additional ammunition for Democrats in 1960. At home, unemployment, which had held steady at 4 percent from 1955 to 1957, jumped to 8 percent in 1959. Since fewer people were working and paying taxes, the floundering economy produced huge budget deficits. Potentially the greatest threat to American pride, however, occurred miles off the coast of Florida on the small island of Cuba. On January 1, 1959, a young lawyer-turned-revolutionary, Fidel Castro, led a successful insurrection against the American-supported dictatorship of Fulgencio Batista. Castro then began to break up large cattle ranches and sugar plantations, sparking concern among US business interests. When the United States threatened to cut off economic aid, Castro responded by declaring his support for Communism and confiscating about $1 billion in US property. In February 1960 the Cuban leader solidified his defiance by signing a trade agreement with the Soviet Union. This turn of events would prove to be one of the most hot-button issues of the election season.

Meanwhile, as it became apparent that Nixon would likely be his opponent in 1960, Kennedy's feelings toward him cooled considerably. Although they had shared offices across the hall from each other for nearly eight years and socialized on occasion, Kennedy now told reporters that he barely knew the vice president. In October 1958 he went further, criticizing Nixon directly. "When Mr. Eisenhower talks about the party of the future," he told reporters, "he is talking about the party of Richard Nixon. And I cannot believe that the majority of American voters would want to entrust the future to Mr. Nixon." Senator George Smathers, who worked with both men, described their relationship as "cordial," claiming that "Nixon had a greater admiration for Kennedy than Kennedy had for Nixon." Smathers felt that Kennedy did not see Nixon as "a man of great strength of character," and instead viewed him as "a total opportunist."

Kennedy admired Nixon's intellect but expressed reservations about his personality, and those concerns only grew as they moved closer to becoming opponents. "Nixon is a nice fellow in private, and a very able man," JFK commented behind closed doors. "I worked with him on the Hill for a long time, but it seems he has a split personality, and he is very bad in public, and nobody likes him." Yet oddly enough, despite their obvious differences in temperament, Kennedy was ideologically closer to Nixon than he was to the liberal members of his own party. He even told his friend Charles Bartlett that if he did not win the Democratic nomination, he would likely vote for Nixon in the general election.

Kennedy's strategy for winning the Democratic nomination was to sweep a handful of primaries and head into the party's Los Angeles convention in July with an insurmountable lead in delegates. It was a risky bet, as only a handful of states held primaries, with most of the delegates still chosen by party bosses. They were "largely symbolic exercises," reflected JFK speechwriter Richard Goodwin. "But that was just what John

Kennedy needed: a symbol. A demonstration that—contrary to the established wisdom—people would vote for a young, inexperienced Catholic candidate for president of the United States." Winning the primaries would go a long way toward convincing skeptical party bosses that they should nominate a Catholic candidate.

His chief primary opponent was liberal Minnesota senator Hubert Humphrey, best known for his impassioned speech in favor of a strong civil rights plank at the 1948 Democratic convention. Given his background, the neighboring state of Wisconsin should have been friendly ground for Humphrey, but he got steamrolled by the Kennedy machine. Members of the Kennedy family descended on the state like locusts, visiting any county with more than three hundred residents. "I feel like an independent merchant competing against a chain store," Humphrey complained. Yet even though Kennedy won 56 percent of the vote, he still fell short of expectations, especially because he failed to carry the three heavily Protestant counties in the western part of the state. "It means that we have to do it all over again," Kennedy said. "We have to go through every primary and win every one of them: West Virginia and Maryland and Indiana and Oregon, all the way to the convention."

In May 1960 the campaign moved to West Virginia, an overwhelmingly Protestant state that was unfriendly turf for a Catholic candidate. While Humphrey traveled around the state in a bus, Kennedy purchased nightly television time and flew around the state in a $385,000 turboprop Convair, which was later named the *Caroline* after his daughter. West Virginia, having sent more men per capita into service after Pearl Harbor than any other state—and a similar percentage to Korea—proved fertile ground for Kennedy to flex his hero status. Campaign workers flooded the state with PT-109 souvenirs. The campaign also recruited Franklin D. Roosevelt Jr., himself a decorated navy combat veteran, to remind voters of Kennedy's military record. "You know why I'm here in West Virginia today?" Roosevelt Jr. asked. "Because Jack Kennedy and I fought side by side in the Pacific. He was on the PT boats, and I was on the destroyers."

But that was not the only message the Kennedys wanted Roosevelt Jr. to deliver. He was also there to question Humphrey's courage and patriotism. That Humphrey, who was married with a son and who suffered from a double hernia, qualified for an exemption during the war meant little to the Kennedys. "Nightly," Roosevelt recalled, "I received calls from Bobby, asking me, 'When will you lower the boom?'" Reluctantly, Roosevelt Jr. went along with the scheme, and when the press picked up on the story, Kennedy denied any knowledge of the attack. "Of course Jack knew," Roosevelt Jr. admitted years later. "But I always regretted my role in the affair. Humphrey, an old ally, never forgave me for it."

There were other dirty tricks, too. The Kennedy campaign hired a worker to distribute anti-Catholic literature and then blamed it on Humphrey, making him appear to be a religious bigot. The Kennedys also used their vast wealth to buy votes. On one occasion, a local boss asked for $3,500 to hand out to workers driving voters to the polls. The campaign, however, misunderstood the request and sent $35,000, delivered in two large suitcases—roughly the equivalent of $360,000 in 2024.

Eventually the Kennedy machine overwhelmed Humphrey, winning by 20 percentage points. Humphrey withdrew but did not endorse Kennedy. He would hold a grudge against JFK and his brother for the rest of his life.

Kennedy's strategy seemed to be working. In July he sailed into the convention with 600 of the 761 delegates needed for the nomination. But he had not counted on Lyndon Johnson, who announced his candidacy at the last minute. LBJ dismissed Kennedy and his ambition to run for president, poking fun at his inexperience and his privilege and referring to him as "sonny boy." Although he respected Kennedy's intellect and his eloquence, he resented his cavalier attitude toward the hard work of the Senate. In the Senate, he said, there were "workhorses" and "show horses." Kennedy was a "show horse."

The Kennedys felt betrayed by Johnson's intervention. In the late fall of 1959, JFK had dispatched his brother Bobby to LBJ's Texas ranch to sound him out on a number of issues regarding the upcoming presidential election. Johnson had assured Bobby that he would not be a candidate, nor would he endorse a candidate, in 1960. But now LBJ planned to deny Kennedy the additional votes he needed to secure the nomination on the first ballot. The Texan assumed that he could win the nomination the same way he ran the Senate: by making deals and winning the endorsements of influential Washington insiders. Mocking the primaries as "beauty contests," Johnson insisted that "when it gets down to the nut-cuttin', [Kennedy] won't have the old bulls with him."

As the Democratic convention opened on July 11, 1960, Johnson openly challenged Kennedy for the nomination—and he made it personal. "I can't stand to be pushed around by that forty-two-year-old kid," Johnson complained. Unable to add to his delegate count, LBJ tried to force defections from JFK by spreading rumors about his health, telling one reporter that Kennedy was a "little scrawny fellow with rickets." Johnson surrogates revealed that Kennedy was suffering from Addison's disease. Although true, Kennedy vehemently denied the claim, releasing a statement insisting, falsely, that the candidate "does not now have nor has he ever had an ailment described classically as Addison's disease." But somebody was looking for proof of Kennedy's health issues. Burglars even broke into his physicians' office in Manhattan. "All the Ks were spread around the floor, but nothing was missing," recalled one of the doctors. Luckily, Kennedy's records had been filed under "another letter far from K."

JOHNSON DID NOT HOLD BACK, JUMPING FROM ONE DELEGATION TO another, trying to swing delegates away from Kennedy. He even went after JFK's father. "I was never any Chamberlain umbrella policy man," he told Washington State delegates. "I never thought Hitler was right." He also criticized JFK's life of easy privilege. "I haven't had anything given to me," LBJ said. "Whatever I have and whatever I hope to get will be because of whatever energy and talents I have." Nothing was too sensationalistic for Johnson. According to one reporter, an LBJ friend even offered "pictures of Jack and Bobby Kennedy in drag at a party in Los Angeles if I would promise to publish them."

Yet despite his best efforts, the Texas senator's last-minute antics failed to move the convention to abandon Kennedy. The biggest problem Johnson faced was that polls showed Kennedy the overwhelming favorite among Democratic voters, as well as the strongest candidate against Nixon—two facts that the party bosses simply could not ignore.

Johnson's combative behavior made it all the more shocking when

JFK turned around and chose him as his running mate—and did so over the strong objections of his closest advisors, including Bobby. The move startled the convention, especially liberals, who felt the selection of a conservative southerner betrayed the party's New Deal heritage. In fact, Kennedy's decision represented a brilliant political stroke that revealed both his pragmatism and his moderation. Kennedy believed that adding Johnson to the ticket improved his odds of winning the election. When close advisor Kenneth O'Donnell objected, saying that Johnson was a political hack who should not be a heartbeat away from the presidency, Kennedy responded, "I'm forty-three years old; I'm not going to die in office. So the vice presidency doesn't mean anything."

Kennedy's choosing Johnson was one thing, but why did Johnson accept? He enjoyed a comfortable perch as the Senate majority leader, and Eisenhower's passivity had enabled him to accumulate great power. He knew, however, that neither Kennedy nor Nixon would agree to a similar arrangement. Also, although he understood that being vice president could be a thankless job, he was convinced that he could transform the office. "Power is where power goes," he explained to a friend. Besides, he was banking on the fact that he might not even remain vice president for long. The relentlessly ambitious Johnson was making some actuarial calculations of his own. "I looked it up," he told a friend. "One out of every four presidents has died in office. I'm a gamblin' man, darlin', and this is the only chance I got."

Meanwhile, having served Ike loyally for eight years, Nixon emerged as the natural heir for the Republican nomination. The vice president had tried to recruit New York's liberal governor Nelson Rockefeller as his running mate but had to settle for Henry Cabot Lodge. As the United Nations ambassador, Lodge would highlight the campaign's focus on foreign policy while underscoring the theme of experience. In the end, however, Lodge proved a liability. He refused to participate in more than one event a day and always took weekends off. He even insisted on taking a nap every afternoon.

As they began the fall campaign, each man faced different challenges: Nixon needed to win election in a largely Democratic nation; the Catholic Kennedy had to convince Protestants to vote for him. But Nixon faced an additional handicap. Making experience the centerpiece of his campaign, and having been vice president for eight years, he had to defend the past, whereas Kennedy's emphasis on getting America "moving again" focused on the future.

Nixon stumbled right out of the gate, letting his arrogance overtake his better judgment. He made the unwise decision to be his own campaign manager and pledged to visit all fifty states instead of prioritizing the battleground states that he needed to win. It was an almost impossible task, given that there were only nine weeks between Labor Day and Election Day. Refusing to listen to the advice of Ike's television advisors, he insisted, "Look, I am going to be Nixon. I will not change to please TV or Madison Avenue. I'm going to be what I am, for good or bad." The journalist David Halberstam observed that "Nixon had changed in a decade from a reasonably approachable young man to a political megalomaniac. No one could tell him anything. He decided he was the ultimate politician." He wore himself down, was frequently moody, and occasionally exploded in anger. At one point, he was sitting in the back seat of a car on a lonely Iowa road when he became so frustrated that he began violently kicking the front seat. A few weeks later, Nixon lost his temper again and struck an aide. "I had had a rib removed where I had had open heart surgery, and that is where he hit me," recalled the aide, who quit the campaign immediately.

Nixon was determined to win the presidency on his own terms. Having lived in Eisenhower's shadow for the past eight years, he decided he would try to win without accepting any help from his popular boss. But the complicated relationship between the two men came into full view within weeks of Nixon's nomination. In the two previous elections, Eisenhower had tried to nudge Nixon off the ticket and remained ambivalent about his vice president. "Well, the fact is, of course, I've watched Dick a long time, and he just hasn't grown," he complained to a friend. "So I haven't honestly been able to believe he *is* presidential timber." What bothered him most was that he found Nixon's personality cold and aloof. "I can't understand how a man cannot have any friends," Ike said privately.

At his first press conference following the convention, Eisenhower made clear that electing Nixon was not a top priority. He promised to "promote" the Nixon-Lodge ticket, but that did not mean that he would "be out on the hustings and making partisan speeches." A week later, when pressed by reporters, the president described the Republican ticket as "fine" but said that he planned to be "just a spectator."

It went downhill from there. On the campaign trail, Nixon took pains to highlight his influence as vice president and the many important decisions he had been involved in making. But when a reporter asked Eisenhower if he "could give us an example of a major idea of his [Nixon's] that you adopted in that role," Ike, impatient to end the press conference, responded: "If you give me a week, I might think of one. I don't know." What Eisenhower meant to say was to wait for next week's press conference to ask the question. But that was not the way it came out—or the way journalists reported it. He immediately called Nixon to apologize, but the damage was already done. With that answer, Eisenhower undercut the central premise of Nixon's campaign: that his vast experience in government made him better qualified than Kennedy to lead the nation.

AS ALL THIS UNFOLDED ON THE REPUBLICAN SIDE, KENNEDY WAS RUN-ning a nearly flawless campaign: focused, disciplined, and well financed. Kennedy was a masterful campaigner who only gained more confidence as time progressed. As he had suspected, the selection of Johnson provided the perfect geographical balance to the ticket. In his campaign swings in the South, LBJ reassured white southerners that Kennedy was a racial moderate who had no plans to assault their way of life. At the same time, he tried to neutralize the religion issue by telling the story of Jack's brother Joe Kennedy, the bomber pilot, pointing out that no one had asked the young man his religion before he volunteered for the dangerous mission that would end his life. On September 12 Kennedy himself tackled the religion question head-on with a powerful speech before a hostile crowd of three hundred white Protestant ministers in Houston. "I am not the Catholic candidate for president, I am the Democratic Party's candidate for president who happens also to be a Catholic," he said.

As was the case with each of Kennedy's campaigns, few substantive differences actually separated Kennedy and Nixon. The war had forged a superficial consensus among leading members of both parties that American institutions were fundamentally sound and that economic growth had alleviated the need for social conflict. More than anything else, their time in the service reinforced the lessons of Munich: that the United States needed to play the role of global superpower, confronting the Soviets the way they believed the allies *should* have dealt with Adolf Hitler.

So once again personality played a decisive role. Kennedy understood better than Nixon the public's desire for dynamic leadership. Throughout the campaign, he struck the right tone with his calls for positive leadership, public sacrifice, and a bold effort to "get America moving again." "I run for the presidency because I do not want it said that in the years when our generation held political power . . . America began to slip," Kennedy declared with his crisp Boston accent.

It also helped that many of Kennedy's fellow PT-109 survivors rode in parades and were more than willing to share stories about their skipper with local reporters. Their presence in the campaign was a constant reminder of JFK's hero status. At one point, Kennedy joked about the many people who claimed to have been survivors of the accident. "[I]f I get the votes of everybody that claims to have been on your boat that night of the pickup, I'll win this election easy," he told William Liebenow, the navy officer who helped rescue Kennedy and who campaigned with him in his hometown of Grand Rapids. Although Kennedy's status as a war hero was already baked into his image by 1960, the campaign never missed an opportunity to mention it. (Meanwhile, the Kennedy people seemed to put the brakes on LBJ's tales of heroism in the Pacific. The campaign's official ten-page biography of Johnson made only passing mention of his wartime experience, calling him "an outstanding soldier" who received "the Silver Star for gallantry in action on a flight over New Guinea.")

Oddly, despite Richard Nixon's popularity with fellow sailors while in the navy, he'd left them behind when he returned to civilian life. There is no evidence that any of the men who knew him in the service played a role in his campaigns for office. This detail reveals a greater difference between the men. Kennedy's magnetism attracted people to him, and they stayed by his side. Although he was a very private person, he had layers of friends: old family friends along with people he met in college and the navy. He was naturally more affable and outgoing than the often brooding Nixon, who preferred long periods of solitude to hard days of campaigning and schmoozing with strangers. With the exception of a Miami businessman named Charles "Bebe" Rebozo, Nixon had no close friends.

Since he ran on his experience as vice president rather than as a veteran, Nixon rarely mentioned his time in the navy during World War II. He had learned in his first campaign for office in 1946 that without a compelling story of personal valor or courage, most voters were not moved by his record in the Pacific. It was seemingly more advantageous to stress his role as a key advisor to the popular Eisenhower.

Kennedy also benefited from a close relationship with—and the sometimes-fawning admiration of—the reporters who covered his campaign. According to the *Washington Post*'s Benjamin Bradlee, who spent time with both campaigns and later became a close Kennedy friend, the contrast between covering JFK and Nixon was "the difference between night and day." The people around Nixon, he observed, "cordially disliked the press and simply spoke a different language, where the men around Kennedy genuinely liked the press and spoke the same language." The reporter could get access to any of the key members of the Kennedy campaign, "often for a drink, always for a bull session." On the other hand, "It took an all-day siege to get a few minutes with the men around Nixon, and they made reporters feel like lepers during those few minutes." It helped that Kennedy genuinely liked reporters, enjoyed their company, and took an interest in their work. Nixon, on the other hand, was uncomfortable with the press. When he tried to be "one of the boys," journalists sensed that "he was putting on an act." If reporters questioned the Kennedy campaign's exaggerated crowd numbers, JFK would often joke that his press secretary counted "the nuns, and then multiplies by a hundred." Doubting the Nixon crowd numbers, Bradlee noted, "usually brought a lecture about bias."

Despite Kennedy's appeal, the election remained close. Nixon skillfully played to public concern about Kennedy's inexperience, especially in foreign affairs. Surprisingly, though, he wanted to campaign as a statesman and transcend his reputation as a partisan hack—even though many Americans remained reluctant to vote for a Catholic for president. For that reason, Nixon never unleashed his trademark scorched-earth tactics against his opponent's Catholicism. The Kennedy campaign was convinced that Nixon would give a "Checkers speech" on the religion issue by accusing JFK of appealing to "Catholic religious prejudice." The attacks never came, but ironically, that self-restraint only added to the perception of Nixon's immaturity. JFK told the economist John Kenneth Galbraith that he "felt sorry for Nixon because he does not know who he is, and at each stop he has to decide which Nixon he is at the moment, which must be very exhausting."

An unfortunate accident forced Nixon off the campaign trail at a critical moment. On Wednesday, August 17, he slammed his left knee against his limousine door. A few days later, it became dangerously infected and required hospitalization. Nixon was forced to check into Walter Reed Army Medical Center, where he would spend the next two weeks. Doctors released him on Friday, September 9. By that time, Kennedy, who had been campaigning and dominating the airwaves, had achieved a small lead.

The turning point in the campaign came in a series of four televised debates between September 26 and October 24. The debates were crucial for Kennedy, who needed to prove that he possessed the stature and the knowledge to compete with a skilled debater and experienced vice president. Kennedy took the challenge seriously, reading briefing books that the campaign referred to as "Nixopedia" because they recorded all of the GOP candidate's statements over the past few years. Meanwhile, Nixon was so consumed with fulfilling his promise to visit all fifty states that he had little time left to prepare. The night before the debate, he landed in Chicago tired, unrehearsed, and still sporting a 101-degree temperature.

It was ironic that Nixon, who had enjoyed a lifetime of good health, would spend weeks off the campaign trail while the sickly Kennedy seemed the picture of vitality. Just to make sure that he had the energy to compete, Kennedy received an added boost from Dr. Max Jacobson, also known as "Dr. Feelgood." On Wednesday, September 14, twelve days before the first debate, Kennedy slipped into Jacobson's New York office, where the doctor injected him with a mysterious concoction of drugs, including amphetamines. "After his treatment," Jacobson recalled, "he told me his muscle weakness had disappeared. He felt cool, calm, and very alert. I gave him a bottle of vitamin drops to be taken orally."

Kennedy arrived for the first debate on Monday night, September 26, tanned and well rested. He ducked into his dressing room, where an aide applied "a little drugstore makeup" to his cheeks and forehead. Nixon, on the other hand, looked ragged and pale. "My God, they've embalmed him before he even died," said Richard Daley, Chicago's Democratic mayor. Nixon's face, with its deep-set eye sockets, pronounced jowls, and dark features, was not made for television. To make matters worse, he wore a gray suit that blended into the studio's background.

Beyond their contrasting appearances, the first debate highlighted the basic ideological similarities between the two men. Kennedy took command, and Nixon passively concurred with whatever JFK said. Nixon would take a tougher line in the subsequent debates, but no one cared. The die had already been cast.

Ultimately, image triumphed over substance. In 1960 roughly 90 percent of homes had televisions, and a majority of the nearly seventy million Americans who watched—the largest television audience recorded to date—believed that Kennedy emerged the winner. Radio listeners, on the other hand, divided evenly on who had won the debate. "That night," the journalist Russell Baker reflected, "image replaced the printed word as the natural language of politics."

By the time of the debate, Dave Powers noted that Kennedy "had lost respect for Nixon as a political adversary" and "paid little serious attention to anything he said." The two men had shared a warm relationship in their early years in politics, but over time, especially under the pressures of the campaign, Kennedy saw in Nixon many of the same shortcomings that Eisenhower had observed. He now viewed Nixon as a deeply flawed man who lacked character and integrity. "He's a filthy, lying son of a bitch, and a very dangerous man," JFK told his aides. Speechwriter Richard Goodwin believed that Kennedy had "come to sense that the man was truly dangerous" and "that his unique blend of intelligence and amorality might have devastating consequences for the country."

What infuriated Kennedy most was not what Nixon said during the debate, but his actions afterward. While they were making small talk about the weather and the difficulty of getting a good night's sleep during the campaign, Nixon noticed a photographer about to take their picture. His expression suddenly grew serious, and he poked his finger in Kennedy's chest as if he were driving home a serious point. Later that night, Kennedy told aides that it was his patriotic duty to win the election in order to keep Nixon out of the White House.

As the campaign progressed, both men could boast recognizable names backing their tickets. Kennedy had a host of Hollywood actors supporting his candidacy, including the members of the so-called Rat Pack: Frank Sinatra, Dean Martin, Sammy Davis Jr., Joey Bishop, and Kennedy brother-in-law Peter Lawford. Surprisingly, one of Nixon's biggest supporters was the forty-nine-year-old Ronald Reagan, who just a few years earlier had been so dismissive of him. It was the vice president's performance in the impromptu "kitchen debate" with Soviet leader Nikita Khrushchev that turned Reagan around. Afterward, the GE spokesman wrote Nixon a letter congratulating him for emphasizing that "'Communism or Marxism' is the only system with aggression advocated as an essential part of it's [*sic*] dogma."

Reagan not only endorsed Nixon, but he also considered switching parties at that time. It was not an easy decision for him. As his second wife, the former Nancy Davis, put it, "I discovered that changing party affiliation could be as difficult as changing one's religion." But Nixon convinced Reagan to remain a registered Democrat, believing that his endorsement would have more power if it came from a member of Kennedy's own party. When Joseph Kennedy learned of Reagan's possible defection, he asked for a meeting. "He tried to persuade me to change my mind and support his son, but I turned him down."

Reagan was no fan of Joe's son. "Under the tousled boyish haircut," Reagan said of JFK, "it is still all Karl Marx—first launched a century ago. There is nothing new in the idea of a government being Big Brother to us all. Hitler called his 'State Socialism,' and way before him it was 'benevolent monarchy.'" He found JFK a dangerous figure because he was "a powerful speaker with an appeal to the emotions. Unfortunately, his message was wrong."

"He leaves little doubt," Reagan wrote Nixon shortly after the Democratic convention, "that his idea of the 'challenging new world' is one in which the Federal Govt. will grow bigger and do more and . . . of course spend more."

Throughout the campaign, both candidates engaged in a delicate balancing act on the issue of race, trying to win Black votes without alienating southern whites. African Americans had switched from the party of Lincoln to that of Roosevelt in the 1930s, but in 1956 Eisenhower had managed to make serious inroads, receiving 39 percent of the Black vote and winning fourteen of twenty-one southern cities. The Black vote was thus up for grabs in 1960. Kennedy's public courting of southern politicians, and his decision to choose Johnson as his running mate, raised doubts in the Black community about whether the Democrat was on their side.

An opportunity for both candidates to define their stances came in October, when Martin Luther King Jr. was arrested in Atlanta for participating in a protest against segregation. A racist local judge sentenced King to four months of hard labor for not having a proper Georgia license plate. Desperate, his wife, Coretta Scott King, reached out to Kennedy aide Harris Wofford. "They are going to kill him!" she cried. "I know they are going to kill him." As news of King's arrest spread, the Southern Christian Leadership Conference, along with twenty other civil rights organizations, sent a petition to both candidates asking them to speak out against the arrest. The Nixon camp decided that it was too politically risky to get involved. Kennedy, on the other hand, called Georgia's Democratic governor and asked if he could get King released. He also took the bold step of personally phoning Mrs. King. "I just wanted you to know that I was thinking about you and Dr. King," he reassured her. "If there is anything I can do to help, please feel free to call on me."

Kennedy's outreach paid off: About thirty hours later, King walked out of jail a free man. The civil rights leader thanked Kennedy for his help, describing it as "morally wise." While most major newspapers paid little attention to the story, it spread like wildfire in the African American community. On Election Day, Kennedy would win roughly 70 percent of the Black vote.

As the campaign moved into its final weeks, a restless Dwight Eisenhower grew increasingly angry about Kennedy's attacks on his administration. Ike was still a popular figure who could easily have won a third term had Congress not passed the Twenty-second Amendment in 1951 limiting presidents to two terms. "Listen, dammit," Eisenhower told an Oval Office visitor, "I'm going to do everything possible to keep that Jack Kennedy from sitting in this chair." With that, he decided to go out on the campaign trail—not so much to help Nixon but to defend his own record.

On October 28 Ike delivered a powerful thirty-minute television address that produced the highest ratings of any TV spot during the campaign. This new circumstance worried Kennedy. "With every word he utters," he told a friend, "I can feel the votes leaving me. It's like standing on a mound of sand with the tide running out. If the election were held tomorrow, I'd win easily, but six days from now, it's up for grabs." Political winds were fickle, Kennedy knew, and Ike's intervention could shift their direction substantially.

On Monday, October 31, Nixon planned to discuss the possibility of expanding Eisenhower's role in the final days with stops in the battleground states of Illinois, Michigan, and New York. But Mamie intervened, telling Pat Nixon that Ike's health would not allow such a burst of activity. She begged Pat to warn Richard, but not to reveal to Ike that she had called. Eisenhower's doctor also reached out to Nixon with a similar message: "I know what he wants to do, and he usually won't take my advice. Please, either talk him out of it or just don't let him do it—for the sake of his health." Although Nixon knew that having Eisenhower on the campaign trail could mean the difference between winning and losing, he reluctantly agreed. "Mr. President, you've done enough," he said. According to one witness, Eisenhower looked "like somebody had thrown cold water over him." Knowing nothing of the backdoor communications, he was puzzled by Nixon's refusal to accept his offer to campaign. "Goddamn it," he complained, "he looks like a loser."

Still, Eisenhower made two more campaign stops in the final days—and he did not mince words. Massive crowds estimated at more than a hundred thousand turned out in both places to see and hear from the outgoing president. Dismissing Kennedy as an inexperienced "young genius," he warned that the Massachusetts senator would lead the nation to "self-destruction." Surprisingly, Ike leveled the kinds of personal attacks that Nixon used to make on *his* behalf. "Strength cannot be conjured out of glittering generalities and promises; out of fanciful pictures of a life of ease—devoid of labor, sacrifice, and self-dedication; out of a grab bag of easy answers for hard questions," he stated.

Despite Eisenhower's intervention, a number of forces ultimately nudged Kennedy across the finish line ahead of Nixon. Not only did he run a disciplined campaign, but also he entranced the voting public with his charm and youthful appeal. Although Nixon managed a good campaign and kept the election close, he remained hamstrung by nagging concerns over his personality and temperament. Reporters from *The Wall Street Journal* who interviewed voters were struck by the repeated refrain of "I don't know why, but I just don't like him." The liberal journalist Morris H. Rubin observed that despite his many obvious talents, Nixon came across as "a mechanical man with a forced smile and contrived manner."

Yet he almost pulled off a victory. Of the nearly 68,500,000 popular votes cast, Kennedy won 34,226,731, Nixon 34,108,157. Kennedy's popular majority of two-tenths of 1 percent was the slimmest since 1880. His win in the electoral college was only more convincing, 303–219. Although there was evidence of voter fraud in heavily Democratic Illinois and Texas, Nixon chose not to put the nation through the ordeal of a recount. "We won, but they stole it from us," he told staffers a month after the election. He had few options, though. A legal challenge would probably fail, and even if it succeeded, overturning the election would likely cripple his presidency and make him appear to be a sore loser.

———

Just because he did not challenge the outcome did not mean that Nixon accepted the results. Never having lost an election, he spent the weeks afterward analyzing the reasons for his loss and drawing up plans for a rematch. The setback tapped into his underlying insecurities: his inflated sense of grievance, his belief that he would never be accepted by "the Establishment." It tapped into his disdain for the Washington elite forged during the early days of the war when he worked at the Office of Price

Administration. Convinced that JFK's campaign had bugged his head-quarters, Nixon resolved never to be outdone by an opponent's "dirty tricks" again. He also directed his anger at the press corps, blasting them as "suckers for style." Nixon would keep a mental note of all his enemies and swear never to allow them to defeat him again.

The loss hit Eisenhower especially hard. The day after the election, he sat slumped in his Oval Office chair, staring out the window. "I rarely saw him so depressed," observed his son, John. "All I've been trying to do for eight years has gone down the drain," Ike muttered. Reflecting years later, he identified Nixon's defeat as the "principal political disappointment" of his presidency. For the next two weeks, Eisenhower tried to process the election loss over games of golf and bridge. He could not get it off his mind. "I felt like I had been hit in the solar plexus with a ball bat," he wrote a friend.

Kennedy, too, was disappointed by the election results—but for a different reason. "How did I manage to beat a guy like this by only a hundred thousand votes?" he asked Kenny O'Donnell.

Though he had to prepare for the transition, what Kennedy needed most in the weeks after the election was rest. The long campaign had taken a toll on his delicate health. At his first post-victory press conference, Kennedy's hands shook. A reporter, concerned by JFK's appearance, asked whether the rumors of his poor health were true. The president-elect avoided answering, then retreated to his family estate in Palm Beach, Florida, to recover out of sight of the media. But his recuperation was slow. When speechwriter Ted Sorensen traveled to Palm Beach two weeks after the election, he noticed that JFK "still seemed tired then and reluctant to face up to the details of personnel and program selection."

Joe Kennedy, concerned that reports of election fraud would undermine his son's presidency before it began, lobbied for JFK and Nixon to appear together as a sign of unity. He reached out to former Republican president Herbert Hoover and asked him to pressure Nixon to agree to the meeting. "This is a generous gesture on his part," Hoover told the defeated candidate, "and you ought to meet it." With Nixon onboard, the elder Kennedy arranged for his son to travel from Hyannis Port back to Palm Beach, where Nixon was vacationing.

As usual, Kennedy was late for the meeting, forcing Nixon to stand waiting for him amid an army of reporters and curious bystanders. After Kennedy pulled up in a convertible, they walked together to Nixon's vacation villa. Following navy protocol, Kennedy, who now outranked Nixon, stood on the right. JFK's press secretary told reporters that the purpose of the meeting was to "resume the cordial relations with Vice President Nixon that existed between them during the fourteen years they served in Congress." In reality, Kennedy had little interest in reforging a relationship with his former opponent. What he needed was a photo op to prove to the nation that he had won the election.

At home on his Texas ranch, Lyndon Johnson was thrilled that he had skillfully kept much of the South, including Texas, in the Democratic column, but he was also disappointed that it was Jack Kennedy and not him who'd been elected president. One of his secretaries recalled that on election night, after it was clear they had won, LBJ "looked as if he'd lost his last friend on earth. . . . I don't think I ever saw a more unhappy man."

Despite the anger and bitterness of the campaign, both Kennedy and Eisenhower were committed to a smooth transition. The sitting president congratulated JFK on his victory and later extended an invitation for him to come to the White House, which the president-elect accepted quickly. "I was anxious to see [Eisenhower]," Kennedy noted, "because it would serve a specific purpose in reassuring the public as to the harmony of the transition. Therefore strengthening our hand."

The two men decided on December 6 for their first face-to-face meeting. Shortly before nine in the morning, Kennedy's cream-colored limousine pulled up to the North Portico of the White House, where seventy-year-old Eisenhower was waiting for him at the top of the stairs. Ike had planned to walk down the stairs to meet his forty-three-year-old successor, but the lean and tanned president-elect stepped out of the car before it had even come to a complete halt and rushed up to shake Ike's hand. "Good morning, Mr. President," a smiling Kennedy said.

"Senator," an unsmiling Ike responded as photographers snapped pictures and a marine band played "The Stars and Stripes Forever."

Inside, Eisenhower guided Kennedy to meet chief usher J. B. West and Secret Service chief James Rowley before taking the elevator down to the ground floor to view the physician's office, kitchen, and swimming pool. Afterward, they entered the Oval Office, where Ike settled behind his desk and JFK sat in a chair to his side. For the next hour and forty-five minutes, they discussed a wide range of topics, from crisis spots in Laos, the Congo, Algeria, Cuba, and Latin America, to the organization of the White House, to disarmament. Eisenhower wrote afterward that he urged the president-elect "to avoid any reorganization" of the National Security Council "until he himself could become well acquainted with the problem." (Ike underlined the phrase in his notes.) He recommended "earnest study and thinking before making radical changes."

Kennedy was eager to hear Ike's impressions of foreign dignitaries— French president Charles de Gaulle and British prime minister Harold Macmillan in particular. Eisenhower gave measured responses, mindful that JFK would need to form his own opinions. Most of the conversation focused on national security issues, but Ike did not pass up the opportunity to impress upon his successor the importance of a balanced budget.

After their private meeting, the two men walked into the Cabinet Room to meet with Ike's key lieutenants. Christian Herter, who replaced John Foster Dulles as secretary of state in 1959, talked about "danger spots" around the globe, describing Berlin as "acute and dangerous" as the Soviets struggled with preventing East Germans from fleeing to democratic West Germany. He said that Laos, where the United States had supported a right-wing coup to prevent Communist rebels from assuming control of the government, was "not of great importance in itself," but he described it as "the strategic gateway to Southeastern Asia." In light of a recent report from Kennedy's Senate colleagues calling for an overhaul of the Defense Department, Eisenhower once again urged caution, indicating that improvements could be made but that he opposed "anything extreme."

Both Eisenhower and Kennedy came away from the meeting with a greater respect for each other. "Eisenhower was better than I had thought," JFK confided to his brother Robert, adding that he could now grasp "why he was president of the United States." Ike, he concluded, was not the befuddled old man that the Kennedy campaign had depicted while on the campaign trail. For his part, Eisenhower also reconsidered his harsh judgment of Kennedy as a "young whippersnapper." Herter reported back to Clark Clifford, the urbane, silver-haired leader of Kennedy's transition team, that the president was "overwhelmed" by JFK. "What impressed the president most," Herter said, "was your man's understanding of world problems, the depth of his questions, his grasp of the issues, and the keenness of his mind." The reassessment went only so far, however. Ike still found Kennedy arrogant, impatient, and naïve, while Kennedy viewed Ike as lacking the imagination and energy to substantively address the problems the nation faced. Kennedy's staff held Ike in even lower estimation. According to Clifford, they looked on Eisenhower with "something bordering on contempt."

Years later, when asked about his impression of the young Kennedy, Eisenhower noted that his biggest concern was that "he looked upon the presidency as not only a very personal thing, but as an institution that one man could handle with an assistant here and another there. He had no idea of the complexity of the job." The former general organized and ran the White House the same way that he led troops during World War II. He delegated responsibility to staff, relied on teamwork, and established lines of authority. Kennedy, whose only executive experience was as a PT boat captain, was impatient with bureaucracy and planned to dismantle the White House hierarchy while depending on a few close, trusted aides to run the White House.

The day before the inauguration, the two men met again to discuss the dangerous situation that was developing in Laos. Despite having shown considerable restraint in dealing with the Communist victory over the French in Vietnam, Ike now invoked the domino theory to convince Kennedy that he should use force to support the new pro-Western regime. "If we permit Laos to fall," he said with uncharacteristic emotion, "then we will have to write off the entire area. We must not permit a Communist takeover." If a political settlement was not possible, Ike cautioned, then the United States "must intervene in concert with our allies. If we were unable to persuade our allies, then we must go it alone."

If the situation was so critical, Kennedy wondered, then why had Ike not mentioned it at their first December 6 meeting? There had also been no sense of urgency in Herter's briefing on the subject. And why had Eisenhower not already committed troops? Ike insisted that he did not want to make such an important decision in the final days of his administration—an unsatisfactory answer for the new president. Kennedy knew that inheriting a war he could blame on his predecessor would be less damaging than having to launch one himself. But an even bigger question loomed: When did Ike the dove, who adamantly refused to get involved in a land war in Asia, turn into a hawk? In 1954 he had disregarded his senior military advisors and his vice president when they recommended committing American resources to defeating the Communist insurgency in Vietnam. Drawing on his own military expertise and experience in the Philippines, the president warned that the United States could never win a war in Asia. Now, on his last day in office, he was telling Kennedy the exact opposite. The moment foreshadowed Eisenhower's stance throughout the 1960s, when he emerged as a forceful proponent of using military force in Vietnam.

Clifford described the mood of the meeting as grim, noting that the outgoing president's warning not only "had a profound effect on Kennedy" but also actually "did a disservice to the incoming administration." Kennedy may have believed that Eisenhower had failed as president, but he still respected the military acumen that Ike had demonstrated as supreme commander in Europe. If the normally reserved Eisenhower was so adamant about his willingness to use force, then surely the situation in Indochina must be grave. Afterward Kennedy dictated, "I came away from that meeting feeling that the Eisenhower administration would support intervention—they felt it was preferable to a Communist success in Laos." Ultimately, Eisenhower's forceful position on Laos would "cast a shadow," in Clifford's words, over the early decisions that Kennedy made regarding Vietnam and Cuba. (Ike made sure to raise the latter topic as well, saying that the United States should support "to the utmost" any credible opponent to Fidel Castro. He also informed JFK of his efforts to train anti-Castro guerrillas as part of a plan to overthrow the Cuban dictator.)

Before officially turning over the reins of power, Ike wanted to give a farewell speech to the nation modeled after George Washington's 1796 address. Like Ike, America's first president had warned the country against "overgrown military establishments" that were "inauspicious to liberty." After spending weeks poring over drafts, Eisenhower was ready to address the nation in a prime-time TV slot on January 17, 1961, three days before leaving office. He began by reassuring viewers that the United States remained powerful and productive. But, he warned, a "hostile ideology" had pushed the country to build "a permanent armaments industry of vast proportions" that would have "grave implications" for democracy at home. Ike then delivered the line containing a soon-to-be notorious term: "In the councils of government, we must guard against the acquisition of unwarranted influence, whether sought or unsought, by the *military-industrial complex*."

In some ways, the farewell address communicated nothing surprising. Eisenhower had emphasized a similar message in his "The Chance for Peace" speech early in his presidency. As recently as 1958, he had lamented the growing arms race, saying: "All of us deplore this vast military spending. Yet in the face of the Soviet attitude, we recognize its necessity." But Eisenhower likely felt a special urgency now because he was convinced that the defense industry was pushing the "missile gap" story in order to gain even greater federal outlays. (At the time of the speech, defense contractors made up thirty of the fifty largest industrial corporations in America, and spending on national security constituted 50 percent of the federal budget.) It is also likely that he did not trust his young successor, who had been lobbying for increased defense spending for most of the decade, to exercise similar discipline over the budget. Ironically, Ike did not seem bothered by the contradiction between warning about the military-industrial complex and supporting a hawkish foreign policy.

Before leaving office, Eisenhower had one final request: He wanted Congress to restore his five-star rank as general of the army, which he had relinquished when he ran for president in 1952. The request mystified Kennedy. Why, he asked his military assistant Brigadier General Ted Clifton, would Eisenhower want to replace the title of "Mr. President" with "General"? Clifton explained that Eisenhower was at heart a military man who had spent nearly his entire life in uniform. "Besides," he told the new president, "if he is a five-star general, he needs no favors from you or the White House." Kennedy got the point, and Congress passed the bill unanimously in March 1961.

Part 3

LESSONS OF THE PAST

CHAPTER 8

====

"The 1930s Taught Us a Clear Lesson"

TUESDAY, APRIL 17, 1961
11:58 P.M.
OVAL OFFICE
WASHINGTON, DC

President John F. Kennedy was in a solemn mood when he left a White House reception for members of Congress and other distinguished guests at 11:55 P.M. Three minutes later, still wearing his long dress coat and white bow tie, he strode into the Oval Office, where the members of his administration's "best and brightest" awaited him: Deputy National Security Advisor Walt Rostow, a Rhodes scholar and bespectacled MIT economics professor; National Security Advisor McGeorge Bundy, a forty-one-year-old former Harvard dean and a Republican; Secretary of Defense Robert McNamara, a past president of Ford Motor Company with a passion for systems analysis and organizational management; and Secretary of Defense Dean Rusk, also a Rhodes scholar and a former diplomat. Also present were CIA Director Allen Dulles and his deputy director of plans, Richard Bissell; Chief of Naval Operations Admiral Arleigh A. Burke; and close aides Kenny O'Donnell and Press Secretary Pierre Salinger. Anticipation filled the room as these "whiz kids" prepared to confront a fiasco none had seen coming.

What followed, Rostow said later, was "a session in the Oval Office no one present is likely to forget." According to special assistant Arthur Schlesinger Jr., that session marked the end of "a long and grim day" that would be one of the first real tests of Kennedy's presidency.

As president-elect, Kennedy had learned of a secret plan, approved by President Dwight Eisenhower in the spring of 1960, that called for American forces to join with refugees who were training in Guatemala for an invasion of Cuba and the overthrow of Communist prime minister Fidel Castro.

JFK had been skeptical of the operation from the beginning. His wartime experience taught him to distrust military brass, many of whom he found incompetent. On March 11 he made clear that he did not want his first act on the world stage to be the invasion of a sovereign nation, which would constitute a violation of international law. Kennedy dismissed the original plan, which included US airpower to destroy Castro's forces. "It sounds like D-Day," he told the generals. "You have to reduce the noise level of this thing." He feared that if the United States invaded Cuba, Soviet leader Nikita Khrushchev would respond by invading Berlin or, worse, launching nuclear weapons. To avoid this risk, Kennedy insisted that America would not provide direct military assistance or "become overly engaged with Castro's armed forces," but rather make the foray "appear as an internal uprising."

The CIA planners acquiesced to the president's demands and continued to insist that the operation would succeed. Privately, however, they believed that even if it went south, Kennedy would have no choice but to send American military forces to guarantee victory. They guessed that Kennedy would not be willing to accept a humiliating failure so early in his presidency. But they underestimated JFK's resolve.

Despite his concerns, Kennedy allowed the mission to go forward. How could he do otherwise? During the campaign, he had criticized the Eisenhower administration for allowing Castro to establish a Communist state ninety miles off the coast of Florida. Once again he could not expose himself to the charge of being soft on Communism. He and his advisors perceived the testy situation in Cuba as part of a larger strategic scheme.

Just a few months earlier, Khrushchev had announced support for "wars of national liberation" in the Third World. The speech had terrified Kennedy, who believed that it signaled a bold new phase in the competition between superpowers. Like Vietnam and Asia, surrendering in Cuba would spell disaster for the United States across the entire Latin American continent.

Kennedy was also in a bind because of his reluctance to abandon a mission that Eisenhower had already agreed to. "He was very in awe of Eisenhower," reflected Undersecretary of State George Ball, "and I think he felt he had no option but to go through with it." Schlesinger, who, like Ball, forcefully opposed the mission, agreed that Eisenhower's shadow loomed over Kennedy's decisions. In the United States, Schlesinger later wrote, "the notion that a fellow who had been a lieutenant JG [junior grade] in the Second World War would overrule a plan agreed to by the commander of the greatest amphibious invasion in history would not have gone down." Schlesinger concluded that JFK "was really trapped by what he inherited."

Almost from the beginning, everything that could possibly go wrong went wrong. On the morning of Monday, April 17, 1961, more than 1,400 CIA-trained Cuban exiles landed on the island's southern coast at Bahía de Cochinos (Bay of Pigs). The invasion was supposed to be a surprise, but Castro's army was waiting in ambush. His planes sunk ships carrying essential communications equipment and ammunition, while his well-trained army prevented the invaders from establishing a beachhead. Instead of inspiring an insurrection, the invasion aroused Cuban nationalist sentiment, reinforced Castro's control over the nation, and pushed him closer to the Soviet Union.

Throughout the day, the CIA, which oversaw the operation, pressured Kennedy repeatedly to salvage the mission by allowing US Navy jets to provide cover. Each time, Kennedy said no. Now, with the brigade marooned on a narrow beachhead, the pleas for help growing louder and more desperate, the CIA again urged the president to use American planes.

At two in the morning, Kennedy finally relented and allowed Admiral Burke to use six unmarked US Navy jets to provide air cover for one hour.

But it was too little, too late. More than a thousand exiles were forced to surrender. The shocked brigade commander sent one final message: "How can you people do this to us?"

The weight of the day's disaster hit Kennedy in the early morning hours. At four o'clock, while talking to aides, he paused midsentence, walked through the French doors leading to the Rose Garden, and spent forty-five minutes pacing around the West Lawn alone, still wearing his formal reception clothes. "He must be the loneliest man in the world," said Kenny O'Donnell. Sorensen made a similar observation, noting, "He seemed to me a depressed and lonely man."

Afterward, JFK returned to the private residence. "He came back to the White House to his bedroom, and he started to cry," Jackie Kennedy told Schlesinger later. "Just put his head in his hands and sort of wept. It was so sad, because all his first hundred days and all his dreams, and then this awful thing to happen."

The following day, Kennedy managed to collect his thoughts. He explained to a national television audience that direct intervention would have been "contrary to our traditions and to our international obligations," and promised "to profit from this lesson." Much to JFK's surprise, his poll numbers went up after the speech, soaring to 83 percent—the highest of his presidency.

Kennedy knew that public opinion was fickle, though, so he also worked to neutralize his two biggest potential critics: Richard Nixon and Dwight Eisenhower. On the morning of April 20, JFK invited his vanquished foe to the White House. When Nixon arrived, he found the president at his desk in the Oval Office talking to Vice President Lyndon Johnson. "The atmosphere was tense," Nixon reflected. After Johnson left the room, Nixon sat on one of the sofas near the fireplace while Kennedy reclined in his rocking chair. But soon Kennedy was up again, pacing back and forth, his fists clenched tightly. "His anger and frustration poured out in a profane barrage," Nixon recalled. "Over and over, he cursed everyone who had advised him: the CIA, the chairman of the Joint Chiefs of Staff, members of his White House staff."

"What would you do now in Cuba?" Kennedy asked. Nixon responded that he would "find a proper legal cover, and I would go in."

Kennedy obviously rejected the advice. He repeated what he had been saying all along: "If we move on Cuba, Khrushchev will move on Berlin." Nixon, a true Cold Warrior, responded that he saw Cuba "in the larger context of Communist ambitions around the world. Khrushchev would probe and prod in several places at the same time, and as soon as we showed any weakness, he would create a crisis to take advantage of us."

Nixon then advised that Kennedy take some military action not only in Cuba but also in Laos. Kennedy demurred. "I just don't think we ought to get involved in Laos," he said, "particularly where we might find ourselves fighting millions of Chinese troops in the jungles."

Eisenhower had also warned him of the importance of preventing a Communist victory in Laos, but Kennedy opted not to pursue a military option there. "I don't think there are probably twenty-five people [in the United States] other than us in the room who know where it is," he told Kenny O'Donnell. His entire presidency would be jeopardized, he said, if he were forced "to explain how in my first month in office [I] embarked on a military venture." Publicly, he continued to maintain a hard line. At a March 23 news conference, for example, he had declared that "the security of all Southeast Asia will be endangered if Laos loses its neutral independence." Behind the scenes, however, he was quietly searching for a diplomatic solution to the problem, eventually supporting a coalition government that included Communist officials.

Nixon was struck by this contradiction between Kennedy's words and his actions. Rhetorically, Kennedy had been saying that the Communist threat was "indivisible, and, unless it was resisted everywhere, there was really no point in resisting it anywhere." But his actions in his first months in office revealed a more practical man who refused to be bound by his own proclamations.

This gap between Kennedy's bellicose rhetoric, which hearkened back to the lessons of appeasement in the 1930s, and his more deliberate actions in office, is key to understanding the Kennedy presidency. He had not fully abandoned the basic assumptions of the Cold War, but he was already questioning them—and those questions would grow more profound as his term progressed. His thinking about America's role in the world evolved even as his spoken words did not. He understood the emotional power of tough anti-Communist rhetoric to rally public support for his agenda even as he searched for compromise solutions that would defuse a potential confrontation with Moscow.

Despite their differences, Nixon promised Kennedy his full backing, saying, "I will publicly support you to the hilt if you make such a decision in regard to either Laos or Cuba, and I will urge all other Republicans to do likewise." Kennedy remarked that the way things were going for him, it was likely he would not be in office after 1964. "It really is true that foreign affairs is the only important issue for a president to handle, isn't it?" he asked. "I mean, who gives a shit if the minimum wage is $1.15 or $1.25, in comparison to something like this?"

After wrapping up their meeting, Kennedy walked Nixon out to his car. The former vice president watched Kennedy as he ambled up the path back to the White House. "His hands were thrust in his jacket pockets, but his head was bowed, and his usually jaunty walk seemed slow. At that moment, I felt empathy for a man who had to face up to a bitter tragedy that was not entirely his fault but was nonetheless his inescapable responsibility."

Nixon's empathy did not last long. Although he had vowed to support JFK publicly, he gave a speech on May 5 that explicitly criticized the president for not being tough enough on Communism. "The worst thing that could flow from our failure in Cuba," Nixon declared, "is not the temporary drop in prestige which seems to obsess too many observers, but that this failure may discourage American policymakers from taking decisive steps in the future because there is a risk of failure." Foreshadowing what would be his own aggressive approach to Vietnam, Nixon warned, "Whenever American prestige is to be committed on a major scale, we must be willing to commit enough power to obtain our objective even if all of our intelligence estimates prove wrong. Putting it bluntly, we should not start things unless we are prepared to finish them."

Nixon's criticism did not bother Kennedy, however. The person he worried about most was Eisenhower. The two men had maintained a cordial, professional relationship during the transition and the early months of the new administration. On his first day in the Oval Office, Kennedy wrote Ike to thank him "for your many acts of cordiality and assistance during the weeks since the election," and for helping ensure "one of the most effective transitions in the history of the Republic." Eisenhower responded by offering his "profound hope that under your leadership the country will be peaceful, prosperous, and happy." But the relationship remained tense. Robert Kennedy, the young administration's attorney general, explained later that his brother "always felt that Eisenhower was unhappy with him," that he was too young and inexperienced to handle the weighty duties of the office.

Kennedy knew that no one could sink his presidency faster than the former supreme commander, who exerted outsize influence when it came to foreign policy, so he planned to appeal to Ike's sense of patriotic duty. Needing a photo op showing the general supporting his administration, Kennedy invited Eisenhower to confer with him at Camp David on April 22, five days after the Bay of Pigs fiasco. It was JFK's first visit to the presidential retreat, located in Maryland's Catoctin Mountain Park and named after Ike's grandson.

Over a meal of fried chicken, the thirty-fifth and thirty-fourth presidents of the United States dissected the failed invasion. Eisenhower asked Kennedy many of the questions that should have been posed to military brass.

"No one knows how tough this job is until he has been in it a few months," Kennedy sighed.

Ike could not resist a small moment of triumph: "Mr. President, if you will forgive me, I think I mentioned that to you three months ago."

"I certainly have learned a lot since," Kennedy admitted. "Well, I just approved a plan that had been recommended by the CIA and by the Joint Chiefs of Staff. I just took their advice."

"Mr. President," Eisenhower responded, "were there any changes in the plan that the Joint Chiefs of Staff had approved?"

"Yes there were. We did want to call off one bombing sally."

"Why was it called off? Why did they change plans after the troops were already at sea?"

"Well, we felt it necessary to keep our hand concealed in this affair;

we thought that if it was learned that we were really doing this rather than these rebels themselves, the Soviets would be very apt to cause trouble in Berlin."

"Mr. President, that is exactly the opposite of what would really happen. The Soviets follow their own plans, and if they see us show any weakness, then is when they press us the hardest. The second they see us show strength and do something on our own, then is when they are very cagey."

Ike then went on to predict that Kennedy's actions in the Bay of Pigs "will embolden the Soviets to do something that they would not otherwise do," to which Kennedy responded defensively, "Well, my advice was that we must try to keep our hands from showing in the affair."

Eisenhower claimed later to be "astounded" by Kennedy's response.

"Mr. President, how could you expect the world to believe that we had nothing to do with it? Where did these people get the ships to go from Central America to Cuba? Where did they get the weapons? Where did they get all the communications and all the other things that they would need? How could you have kept from the world any knowledge that the United States had been involved in the invasion? I believe there is only one thing to do when you go into this kind of thing. It must be a success."

Kennedy then brought up the situation in Laos, telling Ike that "there was no possibility of saving Laos by unilateral military action." Eisenhower was vague, refusing to give specific advice, but he suggested that "in order to keep your position strong at the conference table, you had constantly to let the enemy see that our country was not afraid. We believe in what is right and attempt to insist upon it."

After wrapping up their discussion, the two men met with the press. Eisenhower assured reporters that he was "all in favor of the United States supporting the man who has to carry the responsibility for our foreign affairs." Kennedy got the photo op that he wanted. The next day, *The New York Times* published a picture of the two men together under the headline "Eisenhower Urges Nation to Back Kennedy on Cuba."

Unlike Nixon, Ike was true to his word. The following week, when Republican congressional leaders pressed him to criticize the administration, he told reporters, "Don't go back and rake over the ashes, but see what we can do better in the future."

Privately, however, Eisenhower expressed his contempt. In a diary entry, he speculated that there would be a public outcry "if the whole story ever becomes known to the American people," and concluded that Kennedy's handling of the affair "could be called a 'Profile in Timidity and Indecision.'"

In the days that followed, Kennedy berated himself for having agreed to the plan. "How could I have been so stupid?" he repeated to friends and advisors. "How could I have done it?" Ever since his experience in the Pacific, he had harbored a lingering skepticism of top military brass, but in the early days of his administration, he sidelined those doubts. Now he was paying the price. "I don't think he ever believed anything the Joint Chiefs told him again," observed Schlesinger. The president bluntly confessed to friend and journalist Ben Bradlee: "The first advice I'm going to give my successor is to watch the generals and to avoid feeling that just because they were military men their opinions on military matters were worth a damn."

Though the affair represented a humiliating disaster for the Kennedy administration, the president and his brother remained determined to get rid of Castro. Within six months, they launched Operation Mongoose, a secret CIA-coordinated program to destabilize the Cuban government. Operatives hatched various plans to humiliate Castro, including placing a special powder in his shoes that would make his "magical" beard fall out, and even pumping LSD into his radio booth to make him sound crazy on the air. There were also more sinister plots to assassinate Castro, such as providing him with poisoned cigars or harpooning him while he went snorkeling at a resort. Though they did not realize it at the time, their obsessive efforts to topple Castro's regime actually set the stage for the Soviet decision to send offensive weapons to the island—sparking what would be the Cold War's most dangerous superpower confrontation.

Over the next few months, Khrushchev tested Kennedy's mettle, manhandling him at a summit in Vienna, Austria, and building a wall separating East and West Berlin.

For all the visual drama of the Berlin Wall, Khrushchev's boldest and most reckless challenge came in Cuba. Following the Bay of Pigs, and the Kennedy administration's medley of illegal efforts to kill him, Castro begged both the Soviets and the Chinese for nuclear weapons. Eventually Khrushchev gave in to the pressure. Between July and September 1962, he secretly deployed intermediate-range, medium-range, and short-range nuclear missiles, along with nearly forty thousand Soviet troops. Khrushchev's plan was to conceal the buildup until after the November US midterm elections and then make the shocking announcement at a meeting of the United Nations General Assembly. He hoped that he could then use the weapons as bargaining chips to force American concessions on Berlin and Cuba.

But Kennedy learned of the missile buildup earlier than Khrushchev wanted—on the morning of October 16, 1962, when National Security Advisor McGeorge Bundy showed him reconnaissance photos of the missile sites. The president set up a meeting in the Cabinet Room and then called his brother, Attorney General Robert Kennedy. "We have some big trouble. I want you over here," the president told him.

The group that assembled that day was officially called the Executive Committee of the National Security Council, or ExComm. It included the members of the National Security Council and the Joint Chiefs of Staff, along with others whom Kennedy invited, including Dean Acheson, the hard-line secretary of state in the Truman administration who was one of the architects of America's postwar policy of containment. Over time, the group grew to about eighteen people.

It soon became obvious that there were no good options. Initially, ExComm leaned toward a military response: an air assault to knock out the missiles and a ground invasion to clean whatever remained of the weapons. JFK agreed with that approach when Bundy first showed him the photographs, saying, "We are probably going to have to bomb them." That evening, RFK came to the same conclusion. "If we go in, we go in hard," he scribbled on a piece of paper.

But as the discussion proceeded, it became clear that an air strike followed by an invasion carried enormous risk. General Maxwell Taylor, chairman of the Joint Chiefs of Staff, cautioned that the air force could not guarantee knocking out all the missiles in a surgical strike. "It'll never

John F. Kennedy sitting in the cockpit of PT-109 shortly before it was sliced in half by a Japanese destroyer on the night of August 1–2, 1943. Kennedy's heroics that night and in the days that followed would help boost his campaigns for political office.

ALAMY

Lieutenant Commander Gerald R. Ford in uniform in 1945.

ALAMY

Lieutenant George H. W. Bush in uniform during World War II. The photo has no date but it is most likely from 1942.

GEORGE H. W. BUSH PRESIDENTIAL LIBRARY

Lieutenant Commander Richard M. Nixon in 1945.

NAVAL HISTORY AND HERITAGE COMMAND

Second Lieutenant Ronald Reagan in uniform during World War II.

ALAMY

General Dwight Eisenhower talking with paratroopers on June 5, 1944, just hours before the D-Day invasion. ALAMY

Four past and future presidents—all veterans of World War II—are captured in this photo of JFK's inauguration. They would govern the United States from 1953 to 1974. (Left to right: Eisenhower, Kennedy, Johnson, and Nixon.) ALAMY

After the disastrous Bay of Pigs episode, a shaken JFK invited former president Dwight Eisenhower to Camp David. While Ike publicly supported Kennedy, privately he was deeply critical of JFK's actions.

Lyndon B. Johnson takes the oath of office on Air Force One following the brutal assassination of President Kennedy on November 22, 1963.

In late 1967, Bush traveled to Vietnam to get a firsthand look at the war. Based on his own experience in World War II, he believed it was important to personally deliver a message to the troops that the government supported their efforts.

GEORGE H. W. BUSH PRESIDENTIAL LIBRARY

LBJ (center) with Secretary of Defense Robert McNamara (right) and Secretary of State Dean Rusk (left). Both men, leftover from the JFK administration, were prisoners of the past, convinced that the "lessons of Munich" required the United States to stop the spread of communism in Vietnam.   ALAMY

Johnson and Nixon meet in the Oval Office on December 18, 1968, a month after the Republican defeated Hubert Humphrey in the election. It was an awkward meeting: Nixon had sabotaged LBJ's last-minute peace efforts in Vietnam, and Johnson knew all about it. Instead of going public with the information, Johnson passed it on to Humphrey who refused to use it in his campaign.   LBJ PRESIDENTIAL LIBRARY

Following his "silent majority" speech on November 3, 1969, Nixon ushered reporters into the Oval Office to reveal the many telegrams he received in support of the speech. His appeal to the silent majority was popular, but the White House orchestrated the letter-writing campaign.

ALAMY

Ronald Reagan challenged incumbent Gerald Ford in the 1976 Republican primaries. Ford eked out a victory, but Reagan established himself as a powerful force in American politics.   ALAMY

World War II had instilled in Ronald Reagan a profound fear of nuclear weapons. That fear made the old cold warrior open to negotiation with Soviet leader Mikhail Gorbachev. In a series of meetings, both men agreed in principle to limit the number of intermediate-range nuclear weapons in their arsenals.   ALAMY

In June 1984, President Reagan addressed the aging veterans of D-Day on the fortieth anniversary of the assault. He highlighted the courage and sacrifice of the Army Rangers who climbed the steep cliffs of Pointe du Hoc and knocked out powerful German cannons.   ALAMY

British Prime Minister Margaret Thatcher meets with Bush at the White House (no date). World War II also shaped Thatcher's view of Saddam Hussein's invasion of Kuwait. "Aggression must be stopped," she told the president.   GEORGE H. W. BUSH PRESIDENTIAL LIBRARY

be one hundred percent," he warned. If the Cubans managed to launch even one missile, it could lead to the destruction of an entire US city. A massive bombing campaign could also kill hundreds of Soviet troops on the island.

The lessons of World War II hung over the debates as the committee struggled to formulate an appropriate response. For RFK and George Ball, the reference point was Pearl Harbor. Less than twenty-four hours after suggesting a ground assault, RFK passed a slip of paper to speechwriter and counsel Theodore Sorensen: "I know now how Tōjō felt when he was planning Pearl Harbor." On Friday morning, with the committee deadlocked, RFK again raised the specter of Pearl Harbor. According to notes taken by a State Department official, the attorney general declared that a "sneak attack was not in our traditions. Thousands of Cubans would be killed without warning, and a lot of Russians too." He recognized that the United States needed to respond, and forcefully, "but he thought the action should allow the Soviets some room for maneuver to pull back from their overextended position in Cuba."

Ball, who initially supported military action before changing his mind, also embraced the Pearl Harbor analogy. "If we act without warning," he said, "without giving Khrushchev some way out . . . That's like Pearl Harbor. It's the kind of conduct that one might expect of the Soviet Union. It is not conduct that one expects from the United States." He reminded the other members that America "tried the Japanese as war criminals because of the sneak attack on Pearl Harbor." A surprise attack carried out by the United States, "far from establishing our moral strength . . . would in fact alienate a great part of the civilized world by behaving in a manner contrary to our traditions."

Being against military action was one thing. But how would they get Khrushchev to dismantle the weapons and stop the shipments of new ones? Those who drew the Pearl Harbor comparison gravitated toward a position first articulated by Robert McNamara: Impose a blockade on future shipments of missiles. To them, the blockade was the best of the bad options. While it would stop short of triggering a military exchange, it would do nothing to remove the weapons already in place. At best, it would slow down the process and give Khrushchev time to reconsider his next step. The defense secretary also made clear early in the discussions that the United States would likely need to propose a trade-off: Soviet missiles in exchange for removing American nuclear missiles that had recently been installed in Turkey.

To former secretary of state Dean Acheson and US Air Force chief of staff Curtis LeMay, Munich, not Pearl Harbor, was the appropriate metaphor. The cocksure Acheson saw this crisis as a battle of wills between Khrushchev and Kennedy, and advised the president to prove his strength by launching a military strike immediately and without warning.

Acheson received support from the cigar-chomping LeMay, who had earned widespread praise for his leadership during the firebombings of Japan during World War II and the Berlin airlift in 1948–49. LeMay believed that Khrushchev would never engage in a nuclear exchange with the United States because he knew he would "lose." America, he told the group, had "the Russian bear" by the balls. "Now that we have gotten him in a trap, let's take his legs off right up to his testicles," he insisted. "On second thought, let's take off his testicles, too."

LeMay repeated his argument in the presence of the president on October 19, but Kennedy explained that the Russians would likely respond to air strikes against the Cuban missiles by moving against Berlin. Few scenarios existed that did not end in a nuclear exchange, Kennedy said, "which leaves me with only one alternative, which is to fire nuclear weapons—which is a hell of an alternative." LeMay retorted that the opposite was true. "If we don't do anything to Cuba, then they're going to push on Berlin and push *real hard* because they've got us *on the run*." When Kennedy asked the general how he thought Moscow would respond, LeMay said they would do nothing. Then he zeroed in on the blockade idea. "This blockade and political action, I see leading into war," he said in a slow, patronizing tone, as if he were lecturing a dimwitted student. "I don't see any other solution. It will lead right into war. This is almost as bad as the appeasement at Munich, [which] would be seen by a lot of our friends and neutrals as being a pretty weak response."

The Munich reference was greeted by stunned silence. According to one witness, Kennedy, who viewed the mention of Munich as a direct reference to his father's policies toward Hitler in the 1930s, looked "cho-leric." JFK had spent most of his public life distancing himself from his father's isolationist views. He understood the lessons of Munich as well as anyone, even writing a book, *Why England Slept*, that highlighted the failure of the West to respond to Hitler's aggression. His travels after the war and his exposure to nationalist revolutions had convinced him of the limits of the lessons of Munich. While it was a powerful rhetorical device that could easily arouse the public, it was too blunt an instrument for dealing with the complexity of the modern world. Unlike during the Bay of Pigs, Kennedy was not going to allow the generals to stampede the nation into war. He relied on the counsel of his closest aides, especially his brother, and his own instincts.

Kennedy once again found himself torn. On the one hand, he took personally Khrushchev's bold move, was convinced that he was being tested, and was determined not to be an appeaser. For those reasons, he believed that a forceful response was necessary. On the other hand, he was not willing to risk a nuclear war. No winner would emerge from any nuclear exchange—in fact, as many as seventy million Americans would perish. Having witnessed the horrors of war firsthand, the thought of igniting a nuclear World War III overwhelmed Kennedy. "If you could think only of yourself," he said, sitting in his undershorts on Air Force One on the flight home from Vienna, "it would be easy to say you'd press the button. And easy to press it, too. You can't just think about yourself. There are generations involved. It really doesn't matter as far as you and I are concerned. I've had a full life. What really matters is all the children."

The next morning, Kennedy called Eisenhower, who was relaxing on the porch of his Gettysburg farm. The president told his predecessor that he planned to establish a "quarantine"—the word *quarantine* legally dif-ferentiating the action from *blockade*, which indicated a state of war. Eisenhower again pledged his full support. "I think you're really making the only move you can," he said. Ike echoed the view of the Joint Chiefs who did not believe that the Soviets would respond by moving on Berlin. "The damn Soviets," he said, "will do whatever they want, what they fig-ure is good for them. And I don't believe they relate one situation to an-other."

Kennedy then raised his ultimate fear: that the Soviets would respond by using nuclear weapons. Ike was dismissive of that prospect as well. "Oh, I don't believe they will," he assured Kennedy. When Kennedy told him that he planned to promise not to invade Cuba if the offensive missiles were removed, Eisenhower cautioned, "Don't sign a blank check. Other conditions might come up when you would have to enter Cuba sometime, and I think you ought to define the circumstances in which you might go in."

On Sunday evening, John McCone, who took over as head of the CIA following the Bay of Pigs fiasco, had briefed LBJ on these developments. The vice president had been attending ExComm meetings when he was in town, but he rarely spoke at them, so there is little record of what he thought. "I don't recall anything he said that had a major impact upon the rest of us," said one participant. Johnson told McCone that he favored a surprise strike, complaining that "we are telegraphing our punch" and "locking the barn after the horse was gone." Yet he reluctantly supported the blockade after learning that Eisenhower had signed off on the approach.

On October 24 Kennedy took his case to the American people in a seventeen-minute Oval Office address. "Good evening, my fellow citizens," he told a television audience of one hundred million—the largest ever to tune in for a presidential address. "This government, as promised, has maintained the closest surveillance of the Soviet military buildup on the island of Cuba. Within the past week, unmistakable evidence has established the fact that a series of offensive missile sites is now in preparation on that imprisoned island. The purpose of these bases can be none other than to provide a nuclear strike capability against the Western Hemisphere."

After describing the nature of the weapons, Kennedy spoke of the threat they posed to nations in the West and the rationale behind his response. In doing so, he turned the Munich analogy on its head. Throughout the ExComm discussions, hard-liners like LeMay used Munich to defend their efforts to launch an invasion, criticizing Kennedy's support for a blockade as akin to appeasing Hitler in the 1930s. Now Kennedy skillfully co-opted the Munich reference to bolster his more measured response. America would not adopt the tactics of the enemy. "The 1930s taught us a clear lesson," he said. "Aggressive conduct, if allowed to go unchecked and unchallenged, ultimately leads to war. This nation is op-posed to war. We are also true to our word. Our unswerving objective, therefore, must be to prevent the use of these missiles against this or any other country, and to secure their withdrawal or elimination from the Western Hemisphere."

For the next few days, the world teetered on the brink of nuclear war until October 27, when Khrushchev agreed to dismantle all nuclear weapons on the island. In return, Kennedy pledged not to invade Cuba. Over the strong objections of nearly all his advisors, Kennedy agreed to a secret deal to remove all the NATO and US medium-range Jupiter missiles from Turkey—an exchange that he even misled Ike about. The public was not made aware of this quid quo pro until 1982, when several of Kennedy's top advisors wrote an article for *Time* magazine because the Kennedy Presidential Library was about to release the secret tapes that recorded their meetings during the conflict.

In the short run, the missile crisis set the stage for a gradual improvement in US-Soviet relations. Both nations, traumatized by their close brush with nuclear war, appeared ready to lessen tensions. In June 1963 Kennedy used the commencement speech at American University to propose a thaw between the two nations. "In the final analysis," he said, "our most common link is that we all inhabit this small planet. We all breathe the same air. We all cherish our children's future. And we are all mortal." The historian Robert Dallek called the speech "one of the great state papers of any twentieth-century American presidency." The following month, the United States and the Soviet Union agreed to sign a nuclear test ban treaty, which banned atmospheric and underwater nuclear testing.

Also that June, Kennedy traveled to Europe to build support for negotiations for the test ban treaty and to reassure NATO allies that the United States remained committed to protecting them from Soviet aggression. In Berlin, two to three million people turned out to greet him. It was the largest crowd that Kennedy had ever seen. Arthur Schlesinger recalled that the people were "clapping, waving, crying, cheering, as if it were the second coming." Kennedy did not disappoint, giving one of the most memorable speeches of his presidency. "Two thousand years ago," he declared, "the proudest boast was '*civis Romanus sum.*' Today, in the world of freedom, the proudest boast is '*Ich bin ein Berliner.*'" The enthusiastic crowd roared with approval as JFK denounced the evils of Communism and highlighted West Berlin as an example of the superiority of Western values.

The speech once again exposed the tension between Kennedy's words and actions. He was in Europe to drum up support for a peace treaty with the Soviets that was designed to reduce animosity between the two countries. Swept up in the fervor of the crowd, however, he ad-libbed some of his toughest anti-Soviet lines. This was a constant pattern in the Kennedy presidency. He often reverted to simplistic Cold War rhetoric, knowing that it was guaranteed to stir an audience. But certainly by 1962, the rhetoric failed to reflect his more nuanced view of the world and his practical sense of the limits of American power.

Later that day, Kennedy flew to his ancestral homeland of Ireland. He was still euphoric from the Berlin crowd's reaction. "We will never have another day like this one, as long as we live," he told Ted Sorensen wistfully.

Unlike crisis spots in Cuba and Berlin, Vietnam was largely a back-burner issue for Kennedy until the final months of his presidency. Furthermore, since his involvement with the conflict was episodic, there are few records documenting his thoughts, and the ones that exist are often contradictory. But here, as with all the major issues Kennedy faced, his public pronouncements invoking the lessons of Munich diverged from the modest actions he took to preserve a non-Communist Vietnam. What resulted was a policy of caution, ambiguity, and indecision.

On the one hand, Kennedy faced considerable pressure to expand America's commitment and introduce troops if necessary. Having compromised on Laos, he felt that he needed to prove US power and credibility—and the place to do it seemed to be Vietnam. Politics also weighed heavily on his mind. He remembered the drubbing that Truman had received for "losing China," and worried that a similar backlash would cripple his administration's priorities and perhaps cost him reelection in 1964.

Most of all, the long shadow of Munich darkened his approach to Vietnam. Kennedy was still convinced that the United States needed to contain Soviet adventurism, and he embraced the overall thrust of the domino theory: that it was not just Vietnam but the entire continent at stake. As RFK recalled a few years later, his brother feared "the loss of all of Southeast Asia if you lost Vietnam. I think everybody was quite clear that the rest of Southeast Asia would fall."

On the other hand, ever since France's defeat at Dien Bien Phu, Kennedy believed that the United States could not win a war in Asia. According to Schlesinger, JFK was convinced that if the conflict in Vietnam "were ever converted into a white man's war, we would lose the way the French had lost a decade earlier." Roger Hilsman, the assistant secretary of state for Far Eastern affairs, claimed that the president told him "over and over again" that his "job was to keep American involvement at a minimum, so that we could withdraw as soon as an opportunity presented itself."

Kennedy chose Vice President Johnson to deliver a message of support to the regime of Ngo Dinh Diem, whom the United States had helped assume power in 1955.

Kennedy had Johnson spend two weeks in Asia, with Saigon as the primary destination. "The purpose of the trip," recalled Johnson press secretary George Reedy, "was to convince Diem that he simply had to institute some social and fiscal reforms if he were to survive." LBJ carried with him a letter from the president promising increased military advisors and aid. But though he tried to stick to the plan, Johnson's exuberance still boiled over. He compared South Vietnam's struggle against Communist insurgents to Britain's fight against Hitler during the 1930s. In one arm-waving speech in Saigon, he even drew a parallel between Diem and Winston Churchill.

Reflecting on his trip years later, Johnson claimed that he wanted to combine the administration's recommendations for Diem to make his government more democratic with a pep talk about the importance of standing up to aggression. His reference point was the 1930s. When Hitler threatened Europe, LBJ recalled, "a great many people started by compromising and by trying to mediate the situation. And Chamberlain came back and thought he had obtained peace in our time," Johnson lectured Diem, "but it remained for Churchill . . . to rise to the occasion . . . and provide the inspiration and the courage to keep his people in the war." Johnson was convinced that Diem confronted a similar situation in Asia and that he needed to follow Churchill's example. Paraphrasing the prime minister's June 4, 1940, speech to the House of Commons, Johnson told the Vietnamese leader "that we'll meet them on the beaches, and we'll meet them in the alleys, and we'll meet them in the streets, and if everything else fails, before we'll let Fascism succeed, we'll use our beer bottles on them."

Upon his return, Johnson, invoking the domino theory, warned Kennedy that if the United States did not resist Communist encroachment in Southeast Asia, it would have to "surrender the Pacific and take up our defenses on our own shores." He insisted that the administration "must decide whether to help these countries to the best of our ability or throw in the towel in the area and pull back our defenses to San Francisco and a 'fortress America' concept." Yet despite his bombastic rhetoric, the vice president did not recommend sending more troops, only more advisors.

Kennedy found Johnson's recommendation too simplistic. Though he realized the risks of restraint, he also recognized that Southeast Asia was not Europe, and that the challenges in the 1960s were different from those in the 1930s. Publicly, he spoke about the evils of Communism and the importance of preventing the fall of Vietnam, but privately he harbored doubts. He did not want to lose Vietnam, but he was also determined not to commit American troops. After all, he had gotten involved in politics precisely because he envisioned a world where the scale of force used during World War II would be exceedingly rare. "I think Kennedy's view was that he very much wanted to avoid getting in deeply in the war," George Ball recalled. "At the same time, he didn't want to be regarded as a coward."

Kennedy believed, as he had argued during the 1950s, that the only way to stop Communist aggression was to train a local army to fight its own battles. So, in May 1961, JFK sent 400 Green Berets to train South

Vietnamese troops; by the end of 1962, he'd sent 11,500 military advisors to the country. That number would grow to roughly 18,000 by the time of his assassination. He also supported a massive counterinsurgency plan that included a "strategic hamlet" program designed to protect small villages from the Vietcong while convincing them to support their government's efforts to rid the nation of Communists.

Yet despite the massive American aid, few signs of progress emerged. Though effective in the past, Diem grew more remote from his people and less tolerant of dissent. He stoked grassroots anger by ignoring calls for reforms that would reduce his power. Kennedy thus found himself in another bind over how to respond. He felt frustrated that the information he was receiving about what was taking place on the ground was either incomplete or contradictory. "The two of you did visit the same country, didn't you?" Kennedy quipped after reading two reports that offered diametrically different views of the conflict. With his advisors split, Kennedy sought the advice of General Douglas MacArthur, whom he respected for his military judgment if not necessarily his leadership abilities. Aide Kenny O'Donnell recalled MacArthur telling Kennedy, "There was no end to Asia, and even if we poured a million American infantry soldiers into that continent, we would still find ourselves outnumbered on every side." Another observer noted that MacArthur's opinion "made a very deep impression on the president." For the rest of his time in office, MacArthur's views "tended to dominate very much the thinking of President Kennedy with respect to Southeast Asia." Unable to reconcile his desire to save South Vietnam with his commitment to avoid getting trapped, Kennedy therefore adopted a middle position. He sent more advisors and more military aid, while also pressuring the Diem regime to expand its support.

While publicly committed to defending South Vietnam, Kennedy suggested privately more than once that his goal was to withdraw after the election. In July 1962 he directed McNamara to plan for a phased withdrawal that would stretch through the end of 1965 and transition South Vietnam's troops, as trained by American advisors, to assume all on-the-ground responsibility. Once again Kennedy was trying to balance his antiwar ideals with the political realities of strong anti-Communist sentiment. "If I tried to pull out completely now from Vietnam," he told O'Donnell, "we would have another Joe McCarthy Red Scare on our hands, but I can do it after I'm reelected. So we had better make damn sure that I am reelected."

Kennedy knew full well that if he were to withdraw, Republicans would pounce, accusing him of appeasement. He was able to keep Eisenhower and Nixon somewhat on his side following the Bay of Pigs, but both would likely rally opposition if they heard any talk of exiting Vietnam. Even Congressman Gerald Ford, who supported most of Kennedy's foreign policy agenda, opposed any effort to compromise with the Communists and advocated sending US troops to prop up the Diem regime. "What right does this generation of Americans have not to expect to have to make sacrifices?" he asked. The syntax was garbled, but the message was clear: World War II had taught that appeasement anywhere in the world led to greater sacrifice down the road.

Although Ronald Reagan did not show up on the White House radar screen, the politically ambitious Hollywood actor used his celebrity status to launch broadsides against JFK's New Frontier domestic program. With his acting career stalled, Reagan had lots of time to devote to politics. Kennedy's election sent him spiraling to the right. He disapproved of nearly every major New Frontier initiative, from JFK's muted response to the construction of the Berlin Wall, to the food-stamp program, and to raising the minimum wage. He traveled around the country warning like-minded Republicans of the evils of state Socialism, claiming that Communists had infiltrated "all phases of the government."

There was also no subtlety to Reagan's view of the Cold War. Those future presidents who had seen combat, even if they shared similar general views, balanced abstract notions of the conflict between capitalism and Communism with a concrete fear of the trauma of war. But Reagan's views of the world were shaped by World War II Hollywood caricatures of "good guys" versus "bad guys," along with reading right-wing propaganda. Reagan was no warmonger, and he feared the consequences of a nuclear confrontation with the Soviets, but it was hard to know that from his often bellicose rhetoric. In March 1961 he reminded the Phoenix Chamber of Commerce that the United States was engaged in an ideological war with Marxism-Leninism, which was determined to conquer the world. "The inescapable truth is we are at war, and we are losing the war simply because we don't or won't realize that we are in it," he said. He blamed JFK for his failure to stand up to Communist aggression and for his efforts to reach accommodation with the enemy. "Even now," he told the appreciative crowd, "it would appear we are preparing to drink the bitter cup of capitulation in Laos only partly diluted by face-saving devices," while Cuba "is a Soviet beachhead." For Reagan, withdrawal from Vietnam would be unthinkable, representing appeasement comparable to that of the 1930s.

The actor also saw a clear connection between events at home and abroad. He charged that liberal efforts to expand federal power would extinguish individual freedom and push the nation from "capitalism to Communism." Efforts to provide medical care to the aged, aid to education, and even the progressive income tax, he believed, were part of a plot to subvert freedom and democracy. For now, Reagan's right-wing views survived on the far fringe of American politics, but over time, he would tone down some of his more extreme positions and emerge as a major force in American politics.

Reagan's hostility toward the Kennedys was personal. Robert Kennedy's Justice Department launched a grand jury to investigate possible sweetheart deals between MCA, then the largest talent agency in Hollywood, and the Screen Actors Guild, where Reagan had once served as president. When *GE Theater* dropped him as host because of sagging ratings, Reagan blamed RFK and the long arm of government. In 1962 Reagan officially switched from Democrat to Republican, claiming that his former party had become captive to Communists and Socialists.

THE SITUATION IN VIETNAM CONTINUED TO DETERIORATE IN THE spring of 1963, when Diem's Roman Catholic government decided to enforce a previously ignored nationwide ban on the public display of religious flags. This crackdown happened in the run-up to an important Buddhist celebration, igniting a clash between the army and celebrants that left nine citizens dead. Soon after, Buddhist monks and nuns organized protests across the country. These culminated on June 11, when a monk set himself on fire in a busy Saigon intersection. An American photographer captured the gruesome image, which soon landed on the front pages of most major US newspapers and became a ubiquitous symbol of protest against a corrupt government. After seeing the photo, Kennedy observed, "No news picture in history has generated so much emotion around the world as that one."

The administration pleaded with Diem to de-escalate the crisis, but he did the exact opposite. His brother, Ngo Dinh Nhu, who oversaw security, argued that Communists had orchestrated the protests. Madame Nhu, Diem's sister-in-law, callously described the Buddhist self-immolations as a "barbecue," adding, "Let them burn, and we shall clap our hands."

The Diem government's intransigence prompted Kennedy to start losing faith in the entire effort. That skepticism was apparent in August, when Ball asked JFK to clear an outgoing State Department cable. It pointed out that Diem's government had "instituted serious repressive measures against the Vietnamese Buddhists," highlighting that the United States "deplores repressive actions of this nature." Yet the final sentence backtracked: "We shall continue to assist Viet Nam to resist Communist aggression and maintain its independence." Kennedy responded, "Why don't you leave that last sentence out?" Once again split between considerations of morality versus realpolitik, the president seemed to be subtly downgrading America's unequivocal support for South Vietnam. On November 1, frustrated with Diem's refusal to reform his government and worried about the possibility of a Communist victory, Kennedy greenlighted a coup to replace him. While Kennedy had assumed that Diem and his brother would be given safe passage back to the West, Vietnamese army officers assassinated both men.

On November 21, the day before his death, Kennedy was leaving for Texas when he told an aide that at the start of 1964 he wanted to "organize an in-depth study of every possible option we've got in Vietnam, including how to get out of there. We have to review this whole thing from the bottom to the top."

It is impossible to know what Kennedy would have done had he lived.

He did not face the imminent fall of Saigon; that would be left to his successors. But Kennedy's approach of straddling the line was remarkably consistent for more than a decade: He wanted to defeat the Communists, yet he opposed transforming the conflict into a US war. His administration ultimately enlarged America's presence in the country, but the president never wavered from his belief that US combat forces should not be on the ground. For many members of his administration, and most of the foreign policy establishment, Munich was a conceptual prison. But not for Kennedy, whose views of the world were too sophisticated to be bound by rigid ideology. By 1963, he was questioning many of the basic assumptions that had guided him—as well as an entire generation of American policymakers—since World War II.

The war's impact extended far beyond the way future presidents viewed America's role in the world. Especially for liberals, it fundamentally altered their perception of the economy and the role the federal government should play in promoting growth. While all of the seven presidents accepted the notion that economic growth was essential to a healthy society, they disagreed on the best way to achieve that goal. Republicans such as Eisenhower, Ford, and Bush remained faithful to balanced budgets and limited spending, while liberals embraced the ideas of John Maynard Keynes. Keynes challenged the classical belief in balanced budgets, arguing that deficit spending could lift the economy during downturns, while monetary policy could cool the economy during inflationary periods. While Franklin Roosevelt had adopted some of Keynes's ideas in the final years of the New Deal, it was the massive government spending and extraordinary economic growth that occurred during World War II that seemed to prove the viability of Keynesian economics.

By 1961, the Keynesian emphasis on economic growth through government action had become the defining feature of postwar liberal thought. It served as a panacea for liberals who believed that everyone, regardless of class status or race, would benefit from that expansion. Kennedy came to office embracing many of the tenets of classical economics, but over the next few years, he would emerge as a dedicated disciple of Keynesianism. Walter Heller, a little-known but highly respected University of Minnesota economics professor, would serve as JFK's guide and teacher.

The two men had met briefly while JFK was campaigning in Wisconsin. Kennedy liked Heller instantly, viewing him as the type of "action intellectual" that he wanted to bring into his administration. The tall, slender, forty-five-year-old Heller had shuttled between the University of Minnesota and government throughout his career, serving as an advisor to many Democrats, most notably Senator Hubert Humphrey. For Heller, economics was not simply a body of abstract theory but also a practical means to shape public policy. In particular, understanding and explaining the causes of the Great Depression enabled economists to develop policies that would prevent similar downturns from occurring again.

Heller diagnosed the state of the American economy in the early 1960s by elaborating on the concept of "performance gap." The gap, he stated, represented the difference between the economy operating at full employment, which he defined as under 4 percent, and the current rate of about 5.5 percent. According to his calculations, the performance gap in 1961 amounted to $50 billion and five million jobs. The task of the government was to restore full employment and close this gap, but, Heller argued, the commitment to a balanced budget was exacerbating "chronic slack," thus causing the economy to slow and unemployment to remain higher than it should. The best way to take up this "slack" between the economy's actual versus ideal performance was for the federal government to cut taxes and produce a deficit, which in turn would put money in people's pockets and spur economic growth.

On December 16, 1960, Kennedy invited Heller to his Georgetown home to offer the economist a job as chairman of the Council of Economic Advisers (CEA), a small agency established by the Employment Act of 1946 to advise the president on policies that would provide for "maximum production, employment, and purchasing power." JFK assured Heller of his commitment to policy changes. "You'll find that I am a good deal more interested in economics than my predecessor—and maybe a little bit better informed on it!" JFK told him. To hedge his bets,

Kennedy had just offered the job of secretary of the Treasury to Douglas Dillon, an Eisenhower holdover, who was sitting in the other room. Dillon had said he needed to confer with Ike before he could accept. "I think Dillon will accept," JFK told Heller. "I need you as a counterweight to him. He will have conservative leanings, and I know that you are a liberal."

Over the next several years, Heller would emerge as the chief theoretician of the Kennedy administration's economic program. "Heller's achievement in the early 1960s was to engineer a revolution in federal macroeconomic policy," observed Yale economist James Tobin, who served on the council. The media labeled his approach "the New Economics," with its emphasis on maximizing economic growth through "fine-tuning." Kennedy asked Heller to "use the White House as a pulpit for public education in economics, especially on the desirable effects of the federal deficit in a recession," while also making sure to "always make clear that the recession started *last year*." Soon enough, the reserved Heller became something of a media sensation, even landing on the cover of *Time* magazine twice during the Kennedy years.

Heller's favorite teaching tool was the memo. Over the next few years, he and the council sent Kennedy nearly three hundred easily digestible memos—brief, colorful, full of facts, and devoid of jargon. They began by outlining the problem, before offering a solution and rebutting potential criticism. According to Tobin, Heller also "knew how to get them read." He befriended Ken O'Donnell, who would often slip Heller's memos into the briefcase that Kennedy took with him on weekends to Hyannis Port.

Heller was not the only Keynesian who had Kennedy's ear. Economist John Kenneth Galbraith, now ambassador to India, had been arguing since the publication of his book *The Affluent Society* (1958) that the government needed to impose taxes on consumer goods and use that money to fund public needs such as schools and playgrounds. He acknowledged the benefits of deficits, but unlike Heller, he alleged that additional government spending, not tax cuts, was the best way of creating them. Galbraith penned his own witty memos to the president, criticizing Heller and advocating for expanded public works spending. "No tax cut has the slightest chance of having the slightest effect on the economy by November," he wrote Kennedy in 1962. An outlier among liberal thinkers, Galbraith believed that the redistribution of wealth, not economic growth, should be the goal of federal policy. "Most Americans," he charged, "can't remember whether growth rate is three per cent, six per cent, or ten per cent."

Galbraith also didn't shy away from using intimidation, reminding Heller of his close relationship with the president and Mrs. Kennedy. "If I disagree with you, I'll slit your throat," he warned Heller. "I won't hesitate to slit your throat from ear to ear, but I'll come over and tell you about it afterwards." Heller's council grew so concerned about Galbraith's influence that the members set up an informal "Galbraith Early Warning System" to get the word out when the ambassador was in Washington.

Galbraith may have been wittier and more aggressive, but Heller ended up being more persuasive. In the spring of 1962, when the economy sputtered and the stock market dropped, Heller repeated his case to the president, insisting that the "measures so far taken and proposed by the administration will help, but they are not likely to bring unemployment down to acceptable levels." In fact, Heller predicted, unemployment might end up being higher than in "any other postwar presidential term." He made sure to remind Kennedy that the economic recovery remained weak, so the nation would likely be in a recession by the time he ran for reelection in 1964. "I'm told," Heller wrote, "that Nixon said last winter (somewhat bitterly) that your chances of reelection were linked in considerable part to whether Dr. Heller can avoid poorly timed recessions."

Kennedy did not understand the intricacies of economic thought, but he knew how to win elections. Heller's appeal convinced him that sluggishness and slack prevented the economy from functioning at its full potential and, furthermore, that a tax cut offered the best solution to achieving that potential. Though Kennedy had already asked for a temporary cut, the proposal was languishing in Congress. Now he wanted to take an even bigger political risk, reforming the tax structure and making cuts permanent. This would be a revolutionary usage of fiscal policy—not in *response* to an imminent downturn but in order to *avoid* a future one. As Heller wrote later, "These are profound changes. What they have wrought is not the creation of a 'new economics,' but the completion of the Keynesian Revolution—thirty years after John Maynard Keynes fired the opening salvo."

On June 11, 1962, Kennedy used his commencement speech at Yale University to articulate this new economic message as well as the social philosophy that undergirded it. He spoke about the titanic struggles faced by previous generations as they grappled with deeply controversial issues such as slavery. He then noted that while "these old sweeping issues very largely have disappeared," the nation now faced a more insidious challenge: "The central domestic issues of our time are more subtle and less simple. They relate not to basic clashes of philosophy or ideology but to ways and means of reaching common goals—to research for sophisticated solutions to complex and obstinate issues." To address these new problems, Kennedy stated, the public must "disenthrall itself from the inheritance of truisms and stereotypes."

One of the first truisms in need of reevaluation concerned the scope of the government's responsibilities toward its people. According to Kennedy, "The myth here is that government is big, and bad—and steadily getting bigger and worse." In fact, the president pointed out, for the past fifteen years, the federal government had grown more slowly than the overall economy. Related to this myth of "big, bad government" was another deeply rooted fear of government debt. Here Kennedy drew upon the core Keynesian principles advocated by Heller. "The myth persists that federal deficits create inflation and budget surpluses prevent it," he said. "Yet sizeable budget surpluses after the war did not prevent inflation, and persistent deficits for the last several years have not upset our basic price stability. Obviously, deficits are sometimes dangerous—and so are surpluses. But honest assessment plainly requires a more sophisticated view than the old and automatic cliché that deficits automatically bring inflation."

At its core, the "more sophisticated view" that Kennedy spoke of accounted for the new realities of the postwar world. "What is at stake in our economic decisions today is not some grand warfare of rival ideologies which will sweep the country with passion," he argued, "but the practical management of a modern economy." Rather than relying on outdated labels, the country required a "more basic discussion of the sophisticated and technical questions involved in keeping a great economic machinery moving ahead." In other words, the economic challenges this generation faced required "technical answers, not political answers," and Kennedy would not hesitate to find them.

As promised, JFK submitted his tax proposals to Congress in January 1963. The $13.6 billion cut included $11 billion for individuals and $2.6 billion for corporations—a massive amount that was projected to produce $3.4 billion in additional revenue, leaving a deficit of $10.2 billion.

His plan encountered fierce opposition, even among members of his own Cabinet who feared less money for their departments. Republicans blasted Kennedy's proposal as "both morally and fiscally wrong." Gerald Ford predicted that Kennedy did not "have a prayer of getting tax reform and tax reduction in the same bill," even suggesting that House Republicans would block both proposals unless there were "a bona fide reduction in spending."

While Eisenhower had been reluctant to publicly criticize Kennedy's foreign policy, he felt no such tentativeness with regard to domestic issues. He told *The Wall Street Journal* that "my sense of duty as a citizen" demanded that he "speak out bluntly" about Kennedy's proposal, because it posed "a clear danger which could threaten our free way of life and our security as a nation." Although a tax cut would be "highly desirable," it could not be instituted without a corresponding reduction in federal expenditures. Failure to do so, Ike argued, was "unwise, undesirable, and certain to damage our currency and the nation."

But Kennedy would not budge. He responded by famously insisting that "a rising tide lifts all boats" and that tax cuts would only encourage widespread economic growth. It had taken almost two decades, but the Keynesian revolution inspired by World War II would find a reluctant convert in JFK. His successor, however, would unabashedly embrace Keynes to justify launching a bold new plan to transform American society.

━━━━━

Kennedy's fight over tax reduction and reform illustrated several core beliefs that had been birthed by the West's victory in World War II: that ideology was dead; that the problems facing America were technical, not moral; and that economic growth would solve most social problems. The African American freedom struggle, however, posed the fiercest challenge to each of these beliefs.

As president, Kennedy took clear albeit limited steps to underscore his commitment to civil rights. For the most part, JFK's strategy was to offer rhetorical support and symbolic gestures to the Black community. Early on, he knew that little chance existed to get Congress to support meaningful legislation and that pushing for civil rights would divide his caucus, prevent passage of his entire domestic agenda, and damage his reelection chances. For all Kennedy's inherent idealism, his political initiatives stopped short of robust civil rights reform. As Arthur Schlesinger noted, "The Kennedy civil rights strategy, however appropriate to the congressional mood of 1961, miscalculated the dynamism of a revolutionary movement."

Neither Kennedy nor anyone else fully anticipated how the movement would continue to grow and gain support. Beginning in February 1960, young African Americans organized sit-in demonstrations at lunch counters across the South in defiance of Jim Crow. Beginning in May 1961, "freedom riders" began testing the administration's commitment to enforcing a Supreme Court decision barring racial segregation in interstate transit. They often found themselves brutalized by angry whites along the way.

The following year, James Meredith, a twenty-eight-year-old Black US Air Force veteran, tried to break down another barrier by attempting to register at the all-white University of Mississippi. When the state's Democratic governor, Ross Barnett, whipped up a white mob to block Meredith, Kennedy was forced to order thirty thousand regular army troops and federalized National Guardsmen to restore peace. Tensions only escalated from there. In June 1963 Alabama's pugnacious governor, George Wallace, fulfilled a campaign promise to "stand in the schoolhouse door" if the courts ordered the integration of his alma mater, the University of Alabama.

Wallace's resistance inadvertently provided Kennedy with the opportunity to submit bold new civil rights legislation to Congress. On the evening of June 11, Kennedy delivered one of the most eloquent, moving, and important speeches of his presidency. He became the first president in American history to refer to civil rights as a moral issue, one that was, he said, "as old as the scriptures and as clear as the American constitution."

Four hours after his speech, Medgar Evers, a veteran of D-Day, pulled into his driveway in Jackson, Mississippi. He was walking toward his house when he was suddenly shot in the back by a gunman hiding in a nearby bush. Evers bled to death in front of his wife and children.

Evers's brutal murder capped off a long list of tragedies that undermined Kennedy's naïve faith in the power of postwar prosperity to solve social ills. JFK could no longer allege that economic growth and promises of gradual reform would ameliorate the plight of Black Americans. Eight days after his historic civil rights speech, he asked Congress to enact a law ensuring any citizen with a sixth-grade education the right to vote. It also called for outlawing job discrimination, as well as expanding the powers of the attorney general to enforce court-ordered school desegregation. Perhaps the most controversial provision requested the end of discrimination in all places of public accommodation. Martin Luther King praised the president's civil rights agenda as "the most sweeping and forthright ever presented by an American president," and predicted that it would "take the nation a long, long way toward the realization of the ideals of freedom and justice for all people."

The legislation was still languishing in Congress when JFK left for Dallas in November 1963.

Kennedy's private indiscretions continued during his three years in the White House. The president had affairs with numerous women, including Jackie's personal secretary, Pamela Turnure. He became involved with two recent college graduates, dubbed "Fiddle and Faddle," who worked in the White House despite their limited skills. In the summer of 1962 he seduced Mimi Beardsley, a nineteen-year-old college student interning at the White House. Dave Powers served as wingman, lining up Hollywood stars and call girls for the president's enjoyment. Similarly, when hosting parties at his Georgetown home, journalist Joe Alsop recruited young, attractive women from as far away as New York to entertain the president.

In a few instances, Kennedy's reckless behavior had risky political ties. He engaged in an ongoing affair with Judith Campbell Exner, who worked as a courier for the Mob. (In 1975 she testified before the US Senate Select Committee to Study Governmental Operations with Respect to Intelligence Activities about Mafia involvement in CIA assassination attempts on Castro.) He was also rumored to have been intimate with a suspected East German spy, Ellen Rometsch, whom the White House rushed out of the country before she could be called to testify before the committee. Unsurprisingly, the president's many affairs placed a strain on his marriage. Jackie was aware of her husband's philandering but chose to look the other way, just as she had for their entire marriage.

But the tragic death of their newborn son, Patrick, in August 1963 seemed to bring them closer together. Born at thirty-seven weeks and weighing only 4 pounds, 10.5 ounces, the infant suffered from hyaline membrane disease and lived for only thirty-six hours. Patrick's death signaled a turning point in the president's relationship with his wife. Those around the couple noticed that after the tragedy, JFK grew more affectionate with Jackie and spent more time with both John and Caroline.

The president's health remained precarious, however. Historian Richard Reeves noted that "Kennedy was more promiscuous with physicians and drugs than he was with women." A physician who reviewed Kennedy's medical records observed that he "was being treated with narcotics all the time." According to Robert Dallek, who was the first historian to gain access to Kennedy's medical records, his doctors used a Medication Administration Record (MAR) catalog to keep track of his many medications. He received oral corticosteroids for his adrenal insufficiency and shots of the anesthetic procaine to relieve his back pain. In addition, he took a host of pills daily to deal with diarrhea and abdominal discomfort, along with antibiotics for urinary infections and medication to help him sleep.

Aside from his private behavior and delicate health, the JFK who traveled to Dallas in November 1963 was very different from the one who took the oath of office in January 1961. Kennedy was questioning many of the assumptions that had grown out of World War II. The possibility of nuclear war, brought home in dramatic fashion by the Cuban Missile Crisis, led to a softening of Cold War attitudes and a new emphasis on cooperation. Under the tutelage of Walter Heller, Kennedy embraced Keynesian economics, taking the unprecedented step of intentionally running a deficit to stimulate economic growth. Finally, the confrontation between the Black freedom struggle and the intransigence of southern whites forced Kennedy to realize that only more direct federal intervention could guarantee equal opportunity for all Americans.

The one theme that runs through Kennedy's presidency is his capacity for evolution. Abroad, JFK had always revealed a more sophisticated view of the world than many of his colleagues, but the searing events of his presidency—the Bay of Pigs, Berlin, the Cuban Missile Crisis, and Vietnam—led him to question the reductionist logic of Munich. While he believed that the United States needed to deter Soviet aggression, he no longer perceived the lessons of the 1930s as a straitjacket. His speeches, eloquent and powerful, were designed to tap into Cold War fears to build support for his programs in the face of a limited mandate. However, they rarely reflected his private doubts and concerns.

Kennedy's tragic death in November 1963 cut short this evolution, leaving future generations to continually ponder the unanswerable: "What if he had lived?"

CHAPTER 9

"We Have Learned That Munichs Win Nothing"

NOVEMBER 22, 1963

12:30 P.M. CST

DALLAS

In November 1963 President John F. Kennedy began laying the foundation for his 1964 reelection campaign by visiting the key state of Texas. Shortly after noon on the twenty-second, his entourage arrived at Dallas Love Field airport. Kennedy, handsomely attired in a gray suit and pin-striped shirt, exited Air Force One with his wife, Jacqueline, who was wearing a strawberry-pink wool outfit and matching pillbox hat and cradling a bouquet of red roses. After shaking a few hands, the president, the First Lady, and Texas governor John Connally and his wife, Nellie, hopped into the back of their open-top Lincoln limousine.

Friendly onlookers greeted the president's motorcade as it traveled along a ten-mile route through downtown Dallas. As the cars turned onto Main Street and moved westward toward Dealey Plaza, the crowds grew denser. People were everywhere, waving from office buildings, filling the streets, cheering. At the corner of Main and Houston, the motorcade turned right and headed north. As it approached Elm Street, Nellie Connally remarked, "Mr. President, you can't say Dallas doesn't love you." Kennedy answered, "That's obvious." The time was twelve thirty.

The vice president's limousine, a light-blue 1961 Lincoln convertible, rolled along behind the Secret Service vehicle that trailed the president. Even when driving through the less populated areas, Johnson was struck by "the visible enthusiasm of the people along the route and their obvious good wishes." But he was in a sour mood that day. According to Texas senator Ralph Yarborough, who was in the back seat with LBJ and Lady Bird, Johnson never acknowledged the well-wishers; instead, he "stared glumly, straight ahead." Only a few times did he raise his right hand, offering a routine wave of his large white Stetson hat. Yarborough was not the only observer to comment on Johnson's sullen demeanor. According to Ken O'Donnell, the vice president "sulked all through the trip." Hugh Sidey, Washington bureau chief for *Time* magazine, recalled seeing LBJ earlier in the day. "Johnson was very dour and perfunctory, mechanically shaking hands," he told author William Manchester. "Johnson was a changed man as vice president. He didn't have anything to do, and he became much less vital and more mechanical."

Suddenly the sound of gunfire ripped through the air. "Oh no!" Jackie Kennedy cried. The president clutched his neck with both hands and slumped down in his seat. One bullet had passed through his throat; another had shattered his skull. Governor Connally had also been hit, seriously but not mortally. The driver pulled the limousine out of the motorcade line and sped to nearby Parkland Hospital.

Johnson remembered hearing "an explosion," but he did not know what it was and was not initially alarmed. "I just thought it was firecrackers or a car backfiring," he recalled. "I had heard those all my life. Any politician—any man in public life—gets used to that kind of sound." Within seconds, Johnson was on the floor of the car, covered by his Secret Service agent.

When they arrived at Parkland, more Secret Service agents swarmed around Johnson and rushed him into a private room. He waited there for forty-five minutes before learning that JFK was dead. "I found it hard to believe that this nightmare had actually happened," Johnson recalled. "The violence of the whole episode was unreal, shocking, and incredible."

After a hurried race to Air Force One, LBJ took the oath of office from a local justice of the peace, with Mrs. Kennedy standing next to him in her blood-stained suit.

OFFICIAL WASHINGTON, AND MUCH OF THE NATION, TUNED INTO CBS'S coverage of events. CBS News anchorman Walter Cronkite broke into the afternoon soap opera *As the World Turns* with an audio announcement: "In Dallas, Texas, three shots were fired at President Kennedy's motorcade in downtown Dallas. The first reports say that President Kennedy has been seriously wounded by this shooting." A few minutes later, Cronkite appeared on camera relaying live reports from Dallas and reading news bulletins from the Associated Press and CBS Radio.

Never before had a news story spread so fast. Thirty minutes after the shots rang out at Dealey Plaza, two out of three Americans had heard of the assassination attempt. Most people learned of the shooting from friends or colleagues. A study in Denver found that only 13 percent heard the news from radio and 9 percent from television. The majority learned of the shooting from "a good friend" (30 percent), from "a casual acquaintance" (35 percent), or "a stranger" (11 percent).

Arriving in Washington later that evening, Johnson walked past the Oval Office and went directly to his suite in the Executive Office Building (EOB), where he worked the phones. In an effort to forge a sense of national unity, Johnson wanted to reach out to the three living presidents and invite them to the White House. Harry Truman promised to come to Washington on Sunday, but Herbert Hoover was too ill to answer the phone. The next call was to Dwight Eisenhower. "I need you more than ever now," Johnson told the general. Eisenhower replied, "Anytime you need me, Mr. President, I will be there." LBJ asked Ike to come visit him the next morning and offered to send a government aircraft to pick him up, but Ike said he would use his private plane.

Shortly after eleven o'clock the next morning, after viewing JFK's casket in the East Room of the White House, Johnson walked with Eisenhower to his office in the EOB—making sure that photographers were present to record the moment. His meeting with Ike was scheduled for later in the afternoon, but Johnson wanted the world to see him conferring with the former supreme commander of NATO, and the man whom JFK had replaced in office. Their joint appearance sent a reassuring signal to allies, a warning to potential enemies, and a comforting bipartisan message to many Americans.

After attending church services with Lady Bird, LBJ returned to the EOB, where Ike was waiting for him. The two men already knew each other well, having worked closely together when Johnson was majority leader and Ike was president. As Johnson recalled in his memoirs, "I had tremendous respect for the opinions of this wise and experienced man who knew so well the problems and the burdens of the presidency." Ike noted later how respectfully Johnson acted toward him, saying that the new president "was kind enough several times to express implicit confidence in my objectivity and dedication to the country." But even with Ike's calming presence, Johnson seemed anxious and fidgety. "He was, as he always is, nervous—walking around, and telephoning everyone. He loves to phone, and he was phoning all the time. I would mention someone in the conversation, and he would snatch up the telephone and call the person."

Johnson wanted Eisenhower's advice on a host of issues, especially foreign affairs. "As far as I could see at that time, Lyndon Johnson's only intention was to find out what was going on and to carry policy through," Ike reflected. "He suggested nothing new or different. He wanted to talk about Laos, Cuba, and so forth. He seemed to be less informed about foreign policy than about domestic policy." Eisenhower's observation was astute: When it came to twisting arms in the Senate cloakroom, LBJ had no equal, but he was less sure when it came to handling delicate foreign policy issues and understood—like JFK had—the importance of maintaining Eisenhower's support in this arena. The generation of presidents who emerged from World War II shared a similar mindset when it came to America's view of the world. They experienced the war in different ways and disagreed on strategy and tactics, but all agreed that preventing World War III required standing firm against Communist aggression. Kennedy was convinced that Eisenhower's policy of relying on the threat of using nuclear weapons prevented the nation from responding to simmering conflicts in developing nations, especially in Southeast Asia. The goal, however, was the same: to avoid repeating the mistakes of the 1930s.

The same could not be said about domestic policy. For liberals, the greatest domestic legacy of the war was to prove that Keynesian economics worked. Kennedy had been a reluctant convert, but Johnson fully embraced the notion that government now possessed the power to end the cycle of boom-and-bust and guarantee a steady stream of widely shared economic growth. This is where Republicans and Democrats differed. Johnson believed that a growing economy could support greater government spending on new social initiatives, while the fiscally conservative Eisenhower possessed less faith in the healing power of economic growth and remained wedded to the traditional belief in limited spending and balanced budgets. Even before Kennedy was laid to rest in Arlington National Cemetery on Monday, November 25, LBJ was talking to aides about expansive new domestic programs, but he chose not to share these ambitions with the former president.

Johnson also discussed with Eisenhower how to handle the issue of staff resignations. Despite LBJ's urging Kennedy staff members to stay on the job, it was still unclear whether most would respond to his pleas. "Few of us were well acquainted with our new leader," Undersecretary of State George Ball observed. "As vice president, he had been an unhappy, brooding, sometimes irascible man. Nothing a vice president did was important, yet no one wanted to cross Johnson for fear of eruption." Now, with LBJ firmly in charge, those who had so closely identified with and adored JFK were again unsure about how to proceed. "Could they happily function under a Texan who had made his way by slicing through the political sagebrush with a machete and was burdened by the baggage of regional attitudes and prejudices?" Ball asked. "How many of us would stay once we had tested the new leader and he had tested us? No one could say."

As LBJ and Ike continued their discussion, an aide entered the room with the names of ambassadors who had submitted their resignations. "The president said he needed these men and did not want them to resign," Ike recalled. Urging LBJ to reconsider, Eisenhower suggested that he instead send out word that "there would be no immediate changes." The nation needed time to reflect and rest. "Such few changes that the president might desire to make," Ike remembered, "would be effective after the present period of emotional shock had passed."

But Eisenhower was not the only president whose support LBJ needed. Always the political tactician, Johnson realized that the outpouring of grief that followed Kennedy's death provided him with a powerful opportunity to build political support for a bold liberal agenda. Johnson planned to recruit both the Kennedy myth and memory in service of his domestic ambitions. Over time, however, his predecessor's legacy proved to be a double-edged sword. Johnson would be haunted by the tragic circumstances that forged his presidency. "I always felt bad for Harry Truman and the way he got the presidency," LBJ once said. "But at least his man wasn't murdered." In the wake of the horrible tragedy that unfolded in his home state, Johnson feared that the American people, and many members of the Kennedy staff, would not accept him. "I took the oath," Johnson told historian Doris Kearns Goodwin. "I became president. But for millions of Americans, I was still illegitimate, a naked man with no presidential covering, a pretender to the throne, an illegal usurper."

In the immediate moment, however, these insecurities took a back seat to LBJ's domestic priorities. Despite all the postmortem praise of Kennedy as a great leader, the former president's legislative program had been stalled in Congress for months. Kennedy had submitted a tax reduction bill calling for $13.5 billion in cuts. Congress had already whittled that down to $11 billion, and both the House and the Senate were in no hurry to pass the measure. His civil rights bill was also tied up in House committees and facing the prospect of a Senate filibuster. LBJ thus knew that one of his first tasks as president was to jump-start the process.

"I'm going to get Kennedy's tax cut out of the Senate Finance Committee, and we're going to get this economy humming again," Johnson told aides on the night of the assassination. "Then I'm going to pass Kennedy's civil rights bill, which has been hung up too long in the Congress," aide Jack Valenti recalled him saying. "And I'm going to pass it without changing a single comma or a word. After that, we'll pass legislation that allows everyone anywhere in this country to vote, with all the barriers down. And that's not all. We're going to get a law that says every boy and girl in this country, no matter how poor, or the color of their skin, or the region they come from, is going to be able to get all the education they can take by loan, scholarship, or grant, right from the federal government."

Six months later, on May 22, 1964, Johnson used the commencement address at the University of Michigan to give a name to his ambitious agenda. Americans, he told the appreciative audience of eighty thousand who interrupted him twenty-nine times to applaud, had conquered a continent and mastered the levers of prosperity. Now it was time to address the vexing problems of poverty and racial injustice. The challenge, he charged, was "to move not only toward the rich society and the powerful society, but upward to the Great Society." In this "Great Society," people would be "more concerned with the quality of their goals than with the quantity of their goods."

Johnson's speech that day captured the essence of the liberal mindset that arose from World War II. At the heart of the Great Society was a belief that economic growth provided all Americans, regardless of age, race, or economic status, with the historic opportunity to forge a new national consensus. He had reason to be optimistic. Spurred by federal laws, especially the GI Bill, a postwar baby boom, and explosive consumer spending, the nation experienced unprecedented growth in the decades following World War II. The gross national product more than doubled between 1940 and 1960, skyrocketing from $227 billion to $488 billion. Every economic measure—family income, wages, and employment—increased. "Never had so many people, anywhere, been so well off," the editors of *U.S. News & World Report* concluded in 1957.

Growth, Johnson believed, would eliminate the need for higher taxes, while also producing a surplus that would replenish new social programs. Johnson was convinced that the social conflicts—labor versus management, Black versus white—that had characterized American politics from the early days of the republic would fade painlessly in the wake of unprecedented prosperity. Walter Heller, who stepped down as chairman of the Council of Economic Advisers a year after the assassination, gave Johnson the confirmation that he needed. Heller told the president in June 1964 that the economy was "showing new vitality and promise," with "no inflation in sight." If there was ever a time for liberal hopes to be realized, it seemed to be now.

The Keynesian revolution that began under JFK culminated during the Johnson presidency. In December 1965 a *Time* magazine cover story declared triumphantly, "We Are All Keynesians Now." Gardner Ackley, who replaced Heller as CEA chairman, stated: "The new economics is based on Keynes. The fiscal revolution stems from him." The figures buoyed Johnson's faith that the federal government could care for those who could not care for themselves. "I'm sick of all the people who talk about the things we can't do," he said. "Hell, we're the richest country in the world, the most powerful. We can do it all."

Unimpeded growth both defined and justified Johnson's vision of the Great Society. According to historian Robert M. Collins, "It fueled the basic optimism that made such a grandiose conception appear reasonable." White House domestic policy advisor Joseph Califano recalled that Johnson "considered a robust, noninflationary economy so critical to his domestic program that he spent more time on economic matters than on any other subject." Furthermore, domestic success energized his overseas ambitions. As Heller observed later, prosperity put at the president's "disposal, as nothing else can, the resources needed to achieve great societies at home and grand designs abroad." It allowed Johnson to dream of rebuilding American cities while also facing down Communist expansion worldwide.

Events over the next few years, however, would expose deep cracks beneath the superficial consensus. The rosy postwar liberal worldview underestimated the profound structural barriers to equal opportunity at home, while overestimating the ability of the United States to shape the world in its own image. Communism, they would discover, was not a monolithic force, and the methods used to stem Soviet advancement in western Europe at the end of the war had little relevance to challenges in the developing world. Growth infused the Johnson administration—and an entire generation of liberals—with a sense of hubris that they could manipulate the mechanisms of government to provide for needs at home and fight threats abroad. If this generation could win a global war against Fascism, liberals reasoned, then surely they could prevent Soviet adventurism while providing opportunity for all Americans at home. Journalist Theodore White captured the mood in Washington when he observed the rise of "a new generation of Americans who saw the world differently from their fathers. [They were] brought up to believe, either at home or abroad, that whatever Americans wish to make happen, would happen."

No domestic program exposed the hubris that emerged from the war more than Johnson's much-heralded War on Poverty, which he launched within months of assuming the presidency. "Conquest of poverty is well within our power," Johnson declared. His proposals called for spending almost a billion dollars on a wide range of anti-poverty programs, including Head Start for preschoolers and the Job Corps for urban youth. Convinced that most poor people would benefit from economic growth, the administration developed a program that emphasized opportunity and promised to help the poor help themselves—giving "a hand up, not a handout." The centerpiece of the new initiative was the Community Action Program (CAP), which aimed to stimulate sustained involvement among the poor by calling for the "maximum feasible participation" of local community members in shaping anti-poverty programs.

As the Council of Economic Advisers pointed out in its 1964 annual report, the traditional belief was that poverty could be resolved simply by transferring money to the poor by way of taxes and income supplements. But Johnson's War on Poverty represented a significant departure from this economic thinking. LBJ opposed any redistributive scheme because it would produce the type of political backlash he was trying to avoid. As columnist Walter Lippmann observed, the goal of the War on Poverty was not just to transfer money to the poor but to provide them with the skills to participate in society.

Ultimately, however, the irony of the War on Poverty was that a program launched as the result of renewed faith in the power of government would eventually undermine public faith in Washington's ability to solve social problems. "Perhaps no government program in modern American history promised so much more than it delivered," noted the historian James T. Patterson. The contrast between promise and performance ended up infuriating many Americans. By 1967, more than two-thirds of the public would complain that the administration had gone "too far."

The War on Poverty represented a key piece of Johnson's agenda, but before he could push the rest of it any further, he needed to win reelection in 1964. LBJ chose liberal Minnesota senator Hubert Humphrey as his running mate, while the Republicans nominated Arizona senator Barry Goldwater, an outspoken critic of liberal reform who hoped to rally millions of conservative voters in the South and the West with his calls for smaller government and aggressive anti-Communism. Goldwater's extremism energized the party's vocal right wing, but it also alienated Republican moderates and liberals. "Extremism in the defense of liberty is no vice," he proclaimed infamously. "Moderation in the pursuit of justice is no virtue." By waging a campaign to win over the Right, Goldwater conceded the broad middle ground to Johnson, who brilliantly exploited the opportunity. He played the role of the fatherly figure committed to continuing the policies of the nation's fallen leader. Campaigning eighteen hours a day, he reminded voters of his party's past accomplishments and promised to carry the nation to new heights.

By numbers alone, the election was never close. Johnson won 61 percent of the popular vote, matching Roosevelt in 1936. Carrying all but six states, the incumbent gathered 486 electoral votes to Goldwater's 52. The president's coattails carried many congressional Democrats to victory, providing the administration with commanding majorities in both chambers: 68–32 in the Senate and 295–140 in the House. Yet what no one noticed at the time was that Goldwater had begun laying the foundation for a growing Republican groundswell that both Richard Nixon and Ronald Reagan would soon capitalize on.

Following his victory over Goldwater in November, Johnson moved ahead with launching the Great Society. "Hurry, boys, hurry," he told his aides. "Get that legislation up to the Hill and out. Eighteen months from now, ol' Landslide Lyndon will be Lame Duck Lyndon."

The administration's top priorities were to rescue two staples of the Democratic agenda since Truman's Fair Deal that had been held hostage by congressional conservatives: medical insurance for the elderly and education funding for the young. Johnson and his new allies in Congress overwhelmed the opposition. Along with providing medical assistance to people on Social Security (Medicare), the legislation included a Medicaid program that would pay the medical expenses of the poor, regardless of age. The president also managed to quiet opponents of federal aid to education and convince Congress to pass his Elementary and Secondary Education Act of 1965. Its heart was Title I, which provided more than a billion dollars for textbooks, library materials, and special educational programs for poor children.

TOPPING THE LONG LIST OF JOHNSON'S PRIORITIES WAS JFK'S STALLED civil rights legislation. Using the skills he had honed from years on the Hill, the president assumed personal control of the fight to secure this landmark package. Finally, on July 2, 1964, LBJ signed into law the Civil Rights Act of 1964, the most far-reaching legislation of its kind since Reconstruction following the Civil War. The act ended segregation in public places and forbade employment discrimination on the basis of race, color, religion, sex, or national origin.

But Johnson did not stop there; he knew that having access to public accommodations meant little if African Americans could not exercise political power. Many members of the World War II generation, liberals and conservatives, hoped that removing legal barriers would allow Black people to integrate into American society, just as immigrants from Europe had done at the beginning of the twentieth century. But passing laws did little to soften de facto segregation—deeply ingrained racial attitudes and habits that confined African Americans to the poorest urban areas, with limited access to jobs, health care, and quality education. In 1964 only two million of the South's five million voting-age Blacks were registered to vote. The Fifteenth Amendment, passed almost a century earlier, had guaranteed the right to vote, but America's federalist system enabled states to deny voting privileges through measures such as the poll tax, literacy tests, and grandfather clauses (the latter until 1939). In March 1965, in Selma, Alabama, when a phalanx of police officers wearing helmets and gas masks assaulted peaceful protestors demanding voting rights, Johnson used televised images of the violence to make his case for a powerful new voting rights bill.

Finally, on August 6 he signed into law the Voting Rights Act of 1965, which empowered federal officials to register voters, and it banned the use of literacy tests. On the night that Congress passed the act, a somber Johnson told an aide: "I think we've just handed the South over to the

Republican Party for the rest of our lives." The prediction proved painfully accurate.

Yet five days after LBJ signed the Voting Rights Act into law, the Watts section of Los Angeles exploded. The uprising, and those that followed over the next four summers, served as a reminder that racism in America—as well as anger over it—persisted. The belief that the combination of an expanding economy and the removal of legal barriers would quickly improve the plight of African Americans proved illusory. The success of the civil rights movement in the South did not address the dire living conditions faced by those in northern ghettoes, where many young African Americans rejected Martin Luther King's calls for nonviolence and instead embraced the Black nationalist message of activists such as Stokely Carmichael and Malcolm X.

After all that he had accomplished on their behalf, LBJ could not understand how young African Americans could still turn against him. According to Califano, during the Watts riots LBJ went into hiding, refusing to even answer the phone. "He just wouldn't accept it." When the president finally decided to confront the problem, he wallowed in self-pity. "How is it possible? After all we've accomplished? How can it be?" According to NAACP head Roy Wilkins, LBJ "seemed to take the riot as a personal affront, a rejection of all he had done for black Americans."

"What do they want?" Johnson implored. "I'm giving them boom times and more good legislation than anybody else did, and what do they do? Attack and sneer. Could FDR do better? Could anybody do better? What do they want?"

―――――――

For more than a decade, two American presidents had essentially punted when it came to the Vietnam conflict, sending in enough aid and offering just enough advisors to prevent the total collapse of the South Vietnamese government. Johnson did not have that luxury. One month after the JFK assassination, Defense Secretary Robert McNamara described the situation in South Vietnam as "very disturbing," warning that unless current trends were "reversed in the next 2–3 months," the best the administration could hope for was a neutralization, although the more likely outcome would result in "a Communist-controlled state." The Kennedy administration had removed the authoritarian Ngo Dinh Diem from power in hopes of facilitating a more cooperative government; instead, chaos had ensued. In 1964 alone, a total of seven different regimes attempted to govern Saigon. Military leaders would come to power with the "life span of June bugs," in the words of George Ball. Frustrated over the inability to establish a secure government, Johnson at one point sent a blunt message to Saigon: "No more of this coup shit."

Without a stable government in South Vietnam, the North Vietnamese made continued progress. In March 1964 North Vietnam sent twenty-three thousand fresh recruits south to join forces with the National Liberation Front (NLF), swelling the ranks of the Vietcong. They also improved and extended the Ho Chi Minh Trail, a network of roads on which supplies flowed south. This increased military pressure exacerbated political instability in the South. Desertions from South Vietnam's military, the Army of the Republic of Vietnam (ARVN), reached epidemic levels, exceeding six thousand a month in 1964. The CIA estimated that the Vietcong controlled up to 40 percent of the territory of South Vietnam and more than 50 percent of the people. Washington responded to the volatility in Saigon by waging a more aggressive campaign in the North, hoping that doing so would motivate the South Vietnamese government to function more effectively. Johnson also instructed the Joint Chiefs to prepare a contingency program of graduated military pressure against the North.

As he ramped up the American presence, Johnson came to see any hostile event as an opportunity to justify further involvement. On August 2, 1964, a North Vietnamese torpedo boat attacked the destroyer USS *Maddox,* which was on a covert mission to gather intelligence in the Gulf of Tonkin. LBJ responded by ordering a second destroyer, the USS *Turner Joy,* into the area. On August 4 both ships reportedly came under attack. It is, however, unlikely that the second attack actually took place and was instead the result of bad weather and faulty sonar. Johnson quipped later, "For all I know, our navy was shooting at whales out there."

But LBJ never shared his doubts with Congress or the public. Instead, he continued to portray the North as the aggressor, using the attack to neutralize criticism from the Right and to secure congressional backing for a wider war. With little debate and strong public support, Congress overwhelmingly ratified the Tonkin Gulf Resolution, which authorized the president to take "all necessary measures to repel any armed attacks against the forces of the United States and to prevent further aggression." The resolution provided the legislative foundation for a vast expansion of the Vietnam War. As Johnson observed, it was "like Grandma's nightshirt—it covers everything."

By the end of 1964, LBJ had agreed to a phased escalation but was waiting for the right opportunity to implement his new strategy. In February 1965, after a Vietcong mortar attack against Pleiku, a mountain town about two hundred miles north of Saigon, the White House organized air strikes against Vietcong targets. By April, after the Vietcong almost succeeded in blowing up the American embassy in Saigon, Johnson sent more ground troops.

Yet even as he heightened the war effort, Johnson continued to talk peace. That same month, at a speech at Johns Hopkins University, he claimed that the United States was prepared to enter into "unconditional discussions" with the North. In truth, there was nothing unconditional about his offer. LBJ insisted that the North withdraw its forces from the South before the United States would cease bombing. He also rejected any plan that allowed the NLF to participate in a coalition government in South Vietnam.

Less than two weeks after the attack on Pleiku, Johnson invited Eisenhower to the White House again. It's hard to know whether the president really sought Ike's advice or if he simply needed the photo op with the former supreme commander before he announced plans to expand America's role in the war. Whatever the case, Ike delivered. Although he had warned against sending ground troops to Vietnam when he was president, Eisenhower showed no such restraint in advising both JFK and now LBJ to win the war at all costs. Ike's drastic departure shows how those who fought in World War II and who then went on to the presidency reinforced one another. Because of Eisenhower's military status, both Kennedy and Johnson deferred to him and his judgment. When it came to Vietnam, Ike provided political cover for escalating the war. One is left wondering whether America would have pursued an entirely different course in Vietnam had Ike been as restrained in his advice out of office as he had been while president.

In a wide-ranging, two-hour discussion with Johnson and his national security team, Eisenhower reaffirmed that the purpose of American policy "was that of denying Southeast Asia to Communists." While Ike admitted that stopping the infiltration was a job best left to the Vietnamese, he still insisted that the United States must "play a major part in destroying the will of the enemy to continue the war." The goal, Eisenhower stated, "must be to destroy the enemy's morale" while buttressing the morale of the South. "In his judgement," the meeting notes state, "air strikes against the north cannot deny the ability of the DRV to infiltrate. The strikes can, however, discourage the north, and can make them pay a cost for continuing their aggression."

In this meeting, Ike reinforced one of the major misperceptions that would guide America's approach to the Vietnam War early on. Despite the South Vietnamese government's repeated failures to rally public support against the North, he was convinced that its people wanted to be "saved"—even if they did not know it. Ike blamed the current predicament on JFK's decision to overthrow Diem, whom the general described as "a capable man." According to a memo of the meeting, Eisenhower expressed the opinion that, "Despite [Diem's] nepotism, he would have been effective, and [Eisenhower] felt that the removal of Diem resulted in a great setback for our cause." He then suggested that Johnson end the war the same way that he had negotiated an end to the Korean conflict: by sending word to Russia and China "that if a satisfactory armistice were not signed promptly, we would remove the limits we were observing as to the area of combat and the weapons employed."

Johnson, hanging on to Ike's every word, next asked how the United States should handle a recent British peace proposal that called for a bombing halt in return for a North Vietnamese promise to stop sending men and materiel to the South. Ike responded by referencing the way Abraham Lincoln had handled the Emancipation Proclamation in 1862: The sixteenth president had waited for a decisive Union victory at Antietam before releasing his executive order freeing all slaves in the rebel South as of January 1, 1863. Similarly, Ike advocated gaining a position of strength first to increase leverage at the negotiating table later. Once again equating negotiation with appeasement, the general noted, "We have learned that Munichs win nothing." He suggested that Johnson tell the British, "'Not now, boys,'" because the administration "should be sure that the enemy does not lack an appreciation of our stamina and determination to keep nations free by whatever means required." America, Eisenhower noted, had "put its prestige onto the proposition of keeping Southeast Asia free." He expressed hope that it would not take six to eight divisions to achieve that goal, "but if it should be necessary, so be it."

Then Johnson asked what he should do if the Chinese sent in troops. Eisenhower recommended using nuclear weapons. McNamara asked him to elaborate. In a matter-of-fact tone, Eisenhower confirmed that the weapons "should be used when the enemy comes in large strength as organized formations."

The contrast between Eisenhower's actions when he was president and the advice he gave LBJ was striking. In 1954, when the French fortress at Dien Bien Phu was collapsing, Ike explicitly ruled out the nuclear option, fearing the world's reaction if the United States used the weapon for a second time in Asia. He had also forcefully opposed deploying ground troops in Vietnam and expressed private doubts over the strategic significance of the country. Now he was lecturing another president about America's responsibility to save Vietnam using any means necessary.

On the surface, it would appear that Eisenhower's views had changed, but the truth was more complicated. In 1954 the French were fighting a colonial war, but after the Geneva Accords and the massive US investment in the country, it was in America's vital interest to defend the Republic of Vietnam from a Communist attack. Failure to defend an ally, he reasoned, would embolden the Soviets, undermine support from allies, and lead to another Munich moment. For better or worse, the United States had placed its credibility on the line, and now it had no choice but to achieve "victory." World War II had taught Eisenhower about the importance of using overwhelming force to defeat an enemy. Avoid war if possible, but if you are going to fight, employ all the resources at your disposal to crush the enemy. "The tragedy," observed Eisenhower biographer Will Hitchcock, "was that Ike was applying a strategic doctrine that had fit the US Army from the Civil War to the end of [World War II], but no longer was adequate" to fighting a limited war in Vietnam.

Two weeks after the meeting with Eisenhower, Johnson launched Operation Rolling Thunder, the sustained bombing of North Vietnam that would last until 1968. US ground troops were sent to protect air bases, but their role soon expanded to leading combat operations. Once again the administration believed that bombing in the North would stabilize the regime in the South. And once again it was proved wrong. McGeorge Bundy offered a dark assessment of the future of Saigon: "The situation in Vietnam is deteriorating, and without a new US action, defeat appears inevitable." LBJ's national security advisor estimated that this defeat would occur within the next year.

Despite such dire warnings, Johnson kept Ike close, often invoking his name in meetings with members of Congress and expressing "my hearty thanks" directly to the former president. "The members," he wrote Ike, "are pleased and reassured, I believe, to know that we have been talking together and that I have the benefit of your seasoned judgement on this difficult challenge." For his part, Eisenhower continued to provide the White House with both public and private support for its efforts to expand the war. On March 12, 1965, he once again endorsed Johnson's decision to send troops to defend American bases, saying, "I think you had every right—indeed the obligation—to protect our important bases with some of our own troops." Less than two weeks later, Eisenhower informed a Republican gathering that "In Vietnam, the way the president is conducting operations is very good indeed for the United States." On April 30 Ike again reassured Johnson that whenever he was asked about Vietnam, he would reply that there "is only one spokesman for America in conducting" foreign policy and that LBJ was "employing a policy well calculated to serve the best interests of the United States."

In July, with the situation growing increasingly desperate, Johnson made the critical decision to send American ground troops to Vietnam. But first, he wanted to consult with Ike again. During a seven-minute phone call on July 2, 1965, LBJ explained how he had arrived at his reasoning. The general reiterated his support for more aggressive action. According to his notes of the conversation, Ike told Johnson that "when you go into a place merely to hold sections or enclaves, you are paying a price and not winning. When you appeal to force in an international situation involving military help for a nation, you have to go all out! This is a war, and as long as they are putting men down there, my advice is 'do what you have to do!'" Johnson then asked, "Do you really think we can beat the Vietcong?" Eisenhower admitted that it was hard to say for sure because he did not know how many enemy forces were local rebels and how many were invading from the North. But either way, the mission of saving South Vietnam remained paramount. "We are not going to be run out of a free country that we helped to establish," he said firmly. Ironically, that statement overlooked the fact that Ike's own administration had ignored the Geneva Accords by refusing to support free elections and by installing a pro-Western government with little connection to the broader populace.

With the situation in Saigon at a crisis point, Johnson held a series of meetings in July to finalize his plans to expand the war. During all-day meetings on July 21, the president's national security team met to discuss McNamara's recommendations to deploy thirty-four battalions, bringing the total US commitment to between 175,000 and 200,000, and to call up 235,000 men in the Reserves and National Guard. If the United States did not send additional forces, the defense secretary argued, "the VC will push the GVN [government of Vietnam] into small enclaves and [the GVN will] become increasingly ineffective." The United States should either increase its forces or "get out." Most of Johnson's advisors supported the thrust of McNamara's advice. Bundy told the group, "A non-Communist society is struggling to be born," while Secretary of State Dean Rusk "emphasized that the nature and integrity of the US commitment was fundamental. It makes the US stance with the USSR credible." General Earle Wheeler, chairman of the Joint Chiefs of Staff, also left no doubt as to where he stood. "You must take the fight to the enemy," he said. "No one ever won a battle sitting on his ass." Yet while they supported escalation, most of LBJ's advisors, including McNamara, admitted that the war would be hard-fought and victory uncertain.

Only George Ball dissented. In a brilliant sixty-page, single-spaced memorandum, he systematically challenged every argument used to support America's commitment to South Vietnam. He took special aim at the logic for bombing. "Once on the tiger's back," he observed, "we cannot be sure of picking the place to dismount." The undersecretary of state insisted that "the more forces we deploy in South Viet Nam—particularly in combat roles—the harder we shall find it to extricate ourselves without unacceptable costs if the war goes badly." He did not believe that the United States could win a war in Vietnam and recommended instead that the administration "cut our losses" now despite the "almost irresistible" pressures to move toward a larger war.

Despite the strength of Ball's argument, his colleagues forcefully rejected it, including Bundy, Rusk, and Henry Cabot Lodge, the US ambassador to South Vietnam. It was Lodge who offered the most revealing response, telling the group, "I feel there is a greater threat to start World War III if we don't go in. Can't we see the similarity to our own indolence at Munich?" No one present at the meeting questioned the historical parallel underlying this statement. Lodge went on to assert that the United States could not count on stability in South Vietnam. "We shouldn't take the government too seriously," he declared. "If the area is important to us, we must do what is necessary regardless of the government." Officially, American policy dating back to Eisenhower had been focused on establishing a free South Vietnamese government, but according to Lodge, the wishes of the local government were, in fact, irrelevant. The lessons of World War II required the United States to prevent the spread of Communism, not because we cared about the desires of the Vietnamese people but because doing so was in America's own national interest.

Instinctively, Johnson expressed skepticism over the policy recommended by the majority of his national security team. In another top-secret meeting with his foreign policy advisors, he suggested giving the South Vietnamese leaders an ultimatum. "Why not say, 'This is it!'" he exclaimed. The cryptic, handwritten notes of the meeting captured LBJ's opposition to expanding the effort. "Not send Johnson City boys out to die if they acting as they are," he wrote. Privately, Johnson expressed anguish over the war, often questioning whether the United States could win a military struggle in Southeast Asia and describing himself as "depressed" and "scared to death" about the conflict. At one point he cried to Lady Bird, "I can't get out [of Vietnam], and I can't finish it with what I have got. And I don't know what the hell to do!" Trying to decide on the best course of action, he told her, is "like being in an airplane, and I have to choose between crashing the plane or jumping out. I do not have a parachute."

Throughout these crucial meetings, the president asked all the right questions. He raised concerns that McNamara's proposal "gives no sense of victory, but rather of continuing stalemate. Why can't we get more third-country troops?" He peppered his team with queries: "What are the alternatives available to us? We could tell the GVN that we are leaving, but is this an option we wish to pursue at this time? If we pull out of Vietnam now, will we have to call up more troops and suffer more casualties at some later date?" Finally, he asked, "What will this increased force accomplish?" Was the entire effort inherently doomed to fail? How could America wage war effectively in collaboration with a government that changed so frequently?

Johnson's anguish was real and palpable. "Among all the top command," Ball recounted, "President Johnson was the most reluctant to expand America's involvement." McNamara described his boss as "very depressed" and in "constant turmoil" as he struggled to find either a "plan for victory" or an honorable way out of the conflict. At night, he roamed the halls of the White House, often ending up in the Situation Room, where surprised military aides updated him on events.

Some of Johnson's reluctance to expand the war stemmed from worry over the fate of his cherished Great Society programs. In describing the early weeks of 1965, Johnson told Doris Kearns Goodwin, "I knew from the start that I was bound to be crucified either way I moved. If I left the woman I really loved—the Great Society—in order to get involved with that bitch of the war on the other side of the world, I would lose everything at home. All my programs. All my hopes to feed the hungry and shelter the homeless. All my dreams to provide education and medical care to the Browns and the Blacks and the lame and the poor. But if I left that war and let the Communists take over South Vietnam, then I would be seen as a coward, and my nation would be seen as an appeaser, and we would both find it impossible to accomplish anything for anybody anywhere on the entire globe." Johnson seemed to be facing an irresolvable contradiction that had emerged after World War II, one that pitted his domestic policy vision against new foreign policy prerogatives.

Why then, if Johnson instinctively wanted to avoid a wider war and even his most hawkish advisors believed that a war would be long and costly, did he choose to Americanize the war?

In the end, the lessons that Johnson and his advisors learned from Western appeasement in the 1930s took precedence, compelling them to believe that America needed to defend South Vietnam from Communist aggression. LBJ did not escalate the war because he had a strategic vision for future success, but because he was burdened by the weight of the past. He confessed later to Doris Kearns Goodwin that "everything I knew about history told me that if I got out of Vietnam and let Ho Chi Minh run through the streets of Saigon, then I'd be doing exactly what Chamberlain did in World II. I'd be giving a big, fat reward to aggression."

Johnson also feared that abandoning Vietnam would lead to a political backlash similar to the one that Truman had faced by "losing" China. "And I knew that if we let Communist aggression succeed in taking over South Vietnam, there would follow in this country an endless national debate—a mean and destructive debate—that would shatter my presidency, kill my administration, and damage our democracy." Like many members of the World War II generation, Johnson was convinced that the United States needed to expand the war in order to maintain its credibility, even as he expressed doubts about whether the nation could even win. "If you let a bully come in and chase you out of your front yard," he said, "tomorrow he'll be on your porch, and the next day he'll rape your wife in your own bed." Yet even as he accepted this slippery-slope logic, Johnson also worried that the United States could not defeat the Vietcong "bully" without resorting to the unthinkable: deploying nuclear weapons and "kicking off World War III."

Part of the reason why Johnson took the 1930s analogy so seriously was because the "best and brightest" who remained from the Kennedy administration reinforced his own instincts. "Johnson," White House advisor Clark Clifford reflected, "encountered practically unanimous sentiment among his senior advisors. And they all said, the domino theory is unquestionably so. You will remember if we'd known then what we know now, we never would have permitted Hitler to get started when Hitler went into the Low Countries and into Czechoslovakia and Austria; if he'd been stopped, then we might have prevented World War II . . . so all of this was very much in their minds."

The lessons that Johnson learned from the 1930s were clear, but so too were the lessons unlearned. Johnson had emerged from his time in World War II deeply skeptical of the military brass, whom he described in a radio broadcast shortly after returning home to the States as "indecisive, stupid, selfish, and incompetent." Later, LBJ declared from the House floor that his experience in the war taught him to be skeptical of everything the military said. He went on to call for a "purge" of incompetent generals and others in senior military positions. By the time he arrived in the White House, however, Johnson—who lacked confidence in his own understanding of world events—had abandoned much of his early skepticism and deferred to the military and to JFK's senior advisors. But LBJ learned another lesson from World War II that would shape his Vietnam policy. His success in transforming a brief, though dramatic, military encounter into a tale of personal courage had convinced him that he could alter public perception and control narratives.

Later that month, the president announced that he was increasing US fighting strength in Vietnam from 75,000 to 125,000 and would send additional forces if field commander General William Westmoreland requested them. "Three times in my lifetime, in two world wars and in Korea," Johnson told the nation, "Americans have gone to far lands to fight for freedom. We have learned at a terrible and brutal cost that retreat does not bring safety and weakness does not bring peace." This lesson, Johnson asserted, taught that the United States must defend Vietnam. Surrender was not an option "because we learned from Hitler at Munich that success only feeds the appetite of aggression. The battle would be renewed in one country and then another country, bringing with it perhaps even larger and crueler conflict, as we have learned from the lessons of history."

Ultimately, America's military failure in Vietnam underscored the fundamental problem with invoking Munich to rationalize Cold War decisions. For this generation, any mention of Munich produced a reflexive response, like a tap below the knee. Not only did it allow policymakers to avoid asking the tough questions about America's role in the world, but it became an easy way of explaining the war to the broader public. Blinded by the lessons of the past, US officials rejected the nationalist impulse behind the Vietnamese revolution and transformed a local struggle into a superpower conflict. Only three decades later, in 1995, did a contrite McNamara admit, "We both overestimated the effect of South Vietnam's loss on the security of the West and failed to adhere to the fundamental principle that, in the final analysis, if the South Vietnamese were to be saved, they had to win the war themselves."

After the escalation, Johnson continued to court Ike, showering him with praise and affection. "History will record," he wrote Ike in August 1965, "that President Dwight D. Eisenhower, both in and out of office, never swerved from what he believed to be the truth nor from giving his courage and his energy to the people he serves as patriot, soldier, President, and now as wise counselor to the nation." When Eisenhower was hospitalized in December 1965 after suffering a major heart attack, LBJ and Lady Bird showered him with heartfelt messages, flowers, and phone calls.

This outreach stemmed as much from political calculation as it did from goodwill: Johnson recognized that he could use Eisenhower as cover for his own missteps. At one news conference, he asserted that in carrying out his Vietnam policy, he felt compelled to honor the past commitments of both JFK and Eisenhower. He cited a letter that Ike had written Diem in 1954 pledging to "help these people help themselves." Publicly, Eisenhower pushed back gently, saying that he was "not talking about military programs, but foreign aid." But privately he reminded Johnson of the larger issues at stake. "If I may refer again to history; we failed to halt Hirohito, Mussolini, and Hitler by not acting in unity and in time," he wrote. "That marked the beginning of many years of stark tragedy and desperate peril. May it not be that our nations have learned something from that lesson?"

While outwardly supporting the administration, Eisenhower complained behind closed doors that Johnson still was not aggressive enough in prosecuting the war. "It is important to avoid acting by 'driblets,'" he told an aide. "If we want to win, we should not base our action on minimum needs or a weak strike program against the North, but should swamp the enemy with overwhelming force." It was absolutely necessary, Ike emphasized, for the administration to communicate to the international community that it would "do whatever is needed to defeat Communism" in Southeast Asia.

AT LEAST PART OF JOHNSON'S GOAL IN COURTING EISENHOWER WAS TO have him play a moderating role in keeping other Republicans in check. No matter how much LBJ expanded the war, leading Republicans, including future presidents Richard Nixon, Gerald Ford, and Ronald Reagan, attacked him for not doing enough. Unburdened by having to take responsibility for the actions they advocated, they called for more bombs and, later, more troops. They embraced many of the same flawed assumptions that guided LBJ's policy in Vietnam: that the struggle was part of a worldwide Communist conspiracy; that negotiation was tantamount to appeasement; that the United States had an obligation to "save" South Vietnam; that the objectives could be achieved with little pain or sacrifice; and that American military might would force the North into submission. In essence, they promised to do what LBJ was doing—but better.

Initially, Congressman Ford expressed optimism about the Johnson presidency, remembering LBJ as an "extraordinarily effective" Senate majority leader and a competent vice president. "I was confident that he could lead the nation through this difficult time," Ford stated. Shortly after assuming office, Johnson entrusted Ford with an important and politically delicate job serving on a bipartisan blue-ribbon commission to investigate the assassination of President Kennedy.

Following the disastrous Goldwater campaign, House Republicans chose Ford as their minority leader. Although he positioned himself as a centrist who opposed the influence of "zealots" in his party, he quickly became one of LBJ's toughest critics. He supported both civil rights acts but attacked most other Great Society initiatives, complaining that they cost too much money. The nation, he declared, could not afford both guns and butter. But Ford reserved his toughest criticism for Johnson's Vietnam policy, charging the president with "shocking mismanagement" of the war. Following the Gulf of Tonkin incident, Ford told reporters that the United States should immediately "take command of the forces in Vietnam and not simply remain advisors."

No matter what Johnson did, Ford challenged and critiqued him for not doing enough. Following Johnson's decision to order air strikes after the attack on Pleiku, Ford and GOP leaders in Congress released a statement complaining that the president should have started bombing "more frequently since the [Gulf] of Tonkin decision." In June 1965 Ford accused the administration of playing "geo-political footsie with the power-mad Communist leaders in Southeast Asia." He demanded "that the administration immediately take the wraps off our military forces in Southeast Asia by unleashing devastating air and sea power against all significant military targets in North Viet Nam." At the same time, he deemed "illogical" the idea of sending ground troops to Vietnam, claiming that air and sea power alone would convince the Vietcong to end their aggression.

That same month, Ford explained why the nation was involved in Vietnam to a group of young Republicans. He said it was for the same reasons that the nation was "on the beaches of Normandy, at Iwo Jima, on Guadalcanal, at Midway, [and] crossing the Rhine, in North Africa." Both then and now, the United States stood "on the side of freedom, fighting the good fight, seeking peace on earth." He rejected the calls of those suggesting that America withdraw, claiming that it would only force the nation to fight another war "on a broader and bloodier scale, and from a much more difficult and far more dangerous line of defense." Most of the speech consisted of a history lesson educating the younger generation about the failure of appeasement. "The situation in Vietnam today bears many resemblances to the situation just before Munich," he said. "Then, too, there were student protests for peace. Senators and representatives sponsored resolutions for negotiations. The president campaigned on the premise America would never go to war." But Winston Churchill understood that "the appeasement of a compulsive aggressor simply whetted the enemy's appetite for further expansion and made war more likely."

In many ways, Ford asserted publicly what Eisenhower said privately, arguing that the United States should assume a more decisive role by using air power to seal South Vietnam's borders, with limited risk to American troops. "If that doesn't work, then we should engage in hot pursuit and bomb the supply lines and bases in North Vietnam," he said. In July, when LBJ was planning to announce sending in ground troops, he was so concerned about the House minority leader's response that he personally asked Eisenhower to intervene—unaware that Ike essentially agreed with Ford. Eisenhower noted that during a July 2 phone call LBJ worried his decision "will stir up such people as Ford—who is for continued bombing but not ground troops—and the president states we cannot even defend our air bases without ground troops."

Despite Ford's barrage of criticism, Johnson's charm offensive toward Eisenhower appeared to be working. Sidelining his private concerns, Ike refused to publicly criticize the administration. In August, following LBJ's decision to send troops, Ford and House Republicans released a white paper that criticized Kennedy and Johnson for pursuing a policy that had been "uncertain, providing a basis for miscalculation by the Communists." Ford pleaded with Eisenhower to stand with the House GOP, but the former president replied that his approach was to "keep still while we are in a condition of crisis."

Ford was not the only Republican whom Johnson was trying to neutralize. Former vice president Richard Nixon had not adjusted well to becoming a private citizen following his humiliating loss to Democrat Edmund "Pat" Brown in the 1962 race for governor of California. "You won't have Nixon to kick around anymore, because, gentlemen, this is my last press conference," he famously told reporters on election night. But he quickly grew tired of private life. "If I have to play golf one more afternoon, I'll go out of my mind," he complained to a friend. Deciding to jump back into the political arena, Nixon moved to New York, where he became a senior partner in a respected Wall Street law firm, using the opportunity to travel, make connections, hone a more compelling message, and craft a new Nixon.

Over the next few years, Nixon, like Ford, lambasted Johnson repeatedly for not doing enough to "win" the war—though his critiques were more reactive than proactive. "Nixon aspired to be a geopolitical genius," observed biographer John A. Farrell, "but his stance on Vietnam in the early 1960s was never more than ordinary." Biographer Stephen Ambrose agreed, writing, "Whatever move Johnson made in the direction of escalation, Nixon was always one step ahead of him, demanding more."

For all his knee-jerk criticism, Nixon—just like Johnson—viewed Vietnam through the distorted lens of Western appeasement in the 1930s. "What had been true of the betrayal of Czechoslovakia to Hitler in 1938 was no less true of the betrayal of South Vietnam to the Communists," he wrote in his memoirs. "The fall of free Vietnam to outside aggression would have sent shockwaves throughout Asia." He compared bargaining with Hanoi without achieving success on the battlefield with "negotiating with Hitler before the German armies had been driven from France." In oversimplified terms, he insisted, "There can be no substitute for victory when the objective is the defeat of Communist aggression."

While Ford focused his criticism narrowly on the tactics Johnson employed in Vietnam, Nixon obsessed over the larger issue of US credibility. After a trip to Asia in the spring of 1964, including a stopover in Saigon, Nixon claimed that everywhere he traveled, he "heard about America's declining prestige" and "expressions of dismay that the world's strongest nation was showing so little positive leadership." The problem, he declared, was that Washington was *limiting* the actions of military personnel on the ground. "Both the Americans and the Vietnamese military leaders were distressed that Washington was holding them back from launching air raids into North Vietnam as well as ground raids into Laos to cut off the pipeline of Vietcong arms and supplies known as the Ho Chi Minh Trail," he declared.

Like Ford, Nixon was convinced that the United States could win the war by using air and sea power to "quarantine" the enemy, blocking outside interference from Laos and North Vietnam. The key to victory, he claimed, was instituting bombing raids and expanding the war to "the sources of the trouble, whether in North Vietnam or Laos." After the attack on Pleiku, Nixon called on Johnson to "follow up" bombing raids "with similar decisive action to prevent further infiltration of arms and men into South Viet Nam." At a party fundraiser in Philadelphia, he repeated that failing to engage in an aggressive "day-by-day and night-by-night" bombing campaign would "mean loss of the war . . . to imperial Communism. . . . The choice today is not between this war and no war, but this war and another, much bigger war."

Ultimately, the biggest hurdle in Nixon's eyes was the lack of political resolve in Washington. If only the administration had "the will to win," then "victory is entirely within our grasp," he argued. Not even Johnson's decision to deploy ground troops satisfied Nixon, who continued to complain that LBJ was attempting "to achieve a precarious balance of not-quite-winning and not-quite-losing." In his heated opposition to Johnson's Vietnam policy, Nixon was beginning to reveal what would become the foundation of his own approach to the conflict years later. He believed that American leaders needed to project toughness and be willing to expand the war in order to end it.

Meanwhile, Johnson worried that Nixon planned to use the upcoming 1966 midterm elections as a launching pad for another run for the presidency in 1968. So, he assigned an aide, Jake Jacobsen, to keep tabs on his potential rival. On November 4 Jacobsen noted that the president "rather likes Nixon personally," but complained that Nixon was "utilizing the war in Vietnam as a political issue" and "has been talking out both sides of his mouth in his speeches, at one time saying 'escalate,' and the next time 'seeking peace.'" At one point Nixon told a television audience, "The Republicans generally take a stronger position on resisting aggression in Vietnam than do the Democrats." Therefore, he claimed, the election of forty or more Republicans to the House "will serve notice to the enemy in Vietnam that the US is not going to do what the French did ten years ago: cut and run." With that statement, Nixon put a partisan gloss on what had seemed to be a postwar foreign policy consensus, identifying Democrats with appeasement and Republicans with decisiveness.

Eisenhower, too, was determined to keep Vietnam front and center as the election approached. During an October 3, 1966, phone call with LBJ, the former president suggested that poverty programs and other Great Society initiatives needed to take a back seat to winning the war in Vietnam. He reiterated that while he would not speak out publicly against the administration, this did not prevent him from encouraging others to do so. In fact, in a letter shortly after this conversation, Eisenhower urged Nixon to "keep hitting" the Johnson White House for its "hesitation, indecision, and even timidity" in conducting the war.

Meanwhile, as Gerald Ford traveled around the country in support of other GOP congressional members, he continued adding to the chorus of criticism of Johnson's domestic and foreign policy. "The American people are recognizing the Great Society, Lyndon Johnson style, for what it is: the Great Illusion," he said on September 26. A few days later in Ridgefield, Connecticut, he announced, "War has become a household word in America under the Johnson administration." America, he said, was "mired down" in a struggle with a nation "about the size of Oregon, with dim prospects for victory or an honorable peace." There was also "guerilla war being waged in the streets of our cities," coupled with a failed war on poverty. As expected, Ford's needling got under Johnson's skin. At one point, LBJ told reporters that "there's nothing wrong with Jerry Ford except he played football too long without a helmet" and that the Michigan congressman "couldn't fart and chew gum at the same time."

Johnson may have been so defiant precisely because he knew Republican critics had plenty of ammunition to use against his administration. At home, a backlash was building against the expansion of federal power and especially LBJ's civil rights agenda. One July 1966 survey of twelve thousand people revealed that 90 percent opposed additional civil rights legislation. This reaction should not have been surprising. Two years earlier, voters in California who had elected Johnson in a landslide nevertheless passed by a 2–1 margin Proposition Fourteen, which repealed the state's new fair housing act. "The essence of freedom is the right to discriminate," contended a leader of the repeal movement.

Beginning in 1964 the nation experienced a series of so-called long, hot summers characterized by heightened racial unrest. Images of young Black men looting stores sent shock waves throughout white society.

Nearly every week produced new images of violent clashes between police and protestors. Tensions peaked in 1967, when African Americans in dozens of major cities revolted, producing massive property damage, while leaving dozens dead. For many white Americans, the urban violence appeared to be part of a crime epidemic sweeping the country in the 1960s. Their fears were partly justified—both property crime and violent crime spiked during the decade. The complication was that these crimes became linked in many white Americans' minds with the racial issue, divorced from historical context. Against this volatile backdrop, domestic concerns shaped the outcome of the 1966 midterm elections more than anything else.

But foreign affairs virtually ensured disaster for the Democrats. As *The New York Times* editorialized, the administration also faced "widespread dissatisfaction and uneasiness about the course and the prospects of the Vietnam War." A 1966 Gallup poll found that the percentage of Americans who believed the war was a mistake jumped to 36 percent in June, up from 25 percent in March. A survey the same month showed that 44 percent of local Republican leaders considered Vietnam the issue where Democrats were most vulnerable in 1966. An Alabama county chairman reflected broader GOP sentiment when he opined that a "stand against Communist world domination must be made," and Vietnam was as good a place as any to make it. Nearly half (47 percent) of local GOP leaders believed that the administration should be more aggressive in waging the war.

Given the powerful headwinds, Democrats suffered a crushing defeat on election night in 1966, as Republicans gained forty-seven House seats and three in the Senate. The Democrats actually lost more seats that year than they had won in LBJ's 1964 landslide. Across the nation, Republicans added 557 state legislative seats. Altogether, the party received four million more votes than the Democrats in races across the country. Two years after respected political commentators had wondered openly if the GOP was finished as a national party, the Republicans seemed poised to form a new majority in American politics. Republicans interpreted the results as a mandate to undo the Great Society. "I view this election as a repudiation of the president's domestic policies," declared Ford. Even leading Democrats could read the political tea leaves. Senate Majority Leader Mike Mansfield of Montana said the slogan of the new Congress was "Stop, look, and listen." House Majority Leader Carl Albert of Oklahoma warned, "We've run the gamut on new programs. Why, we've passed most of the bills we talked about for the past thirty years. Now we need to slow down."

By 1967, Johnson's utopian hopes were under assault, undermined by the false belief that economic growth would solve vexing social problems, and ripped apart by a conservative backlash against the dramatic expansion of federal power. Vietnam only exacerbated this nationwide discontent. The war sapped the president's energy, eroded public support for his presidency, and further divided Americans into rival camps of hawks and doves. The decade had begun with Kennedy criticizing Eisenhower for not being aggressive enough in fighting Communist expansion. Now, with Democrats divided among themselves regarding Vietnam, Republicans positioned themselves as the defenders of freedom and the Democrats as the party of appeasement. Ironically, World War II had united the nation in its opposition to a Fascist threat, but the assumptions that grew out of that conflict now trapped policymakers in an unwinnable war in Southeast Asia.

CHAPTER 10

"This Is Treason"

JANUARY 4, 1966
LOS ANGELES, CALIFORNIA

On the evening of January 4, 1966, Ronald Reagan, the ruggedly handsome fifty-four-year-old Hollywood actor, announced his candidacy for governor of California in a prerecorded thirty-minute television appearance carried by more than a dozen local stations. For those who had been following Reagan's career over the past few years, the announcement came as no surprise, nor did the themes he highlighted: an unrepentant faith in free enterprise, strident criticism of rising crime rates and soaring taxes, and a populist disdain for government.

With a wood-paneled study as his backdrop, Reagan strolled comfortably across the room, sitting briefly on a desk and using props like a bottle of ketchup to underscore how "social tinkering" had led to a loss of farm jobs needed to make the product. In the wake of widespread campus unrest against the Vietnam War, he called on universities "to teach self-respect, self-discipline, and respect for law and order." Taking aim at the misguided policies of the Johnson administration, he declared, "A great society must be a free society. And to be truly great and really free, it must be a creative society, calling on the genius and power of its people." The problem with liberals, he charged, was that they were "dedicated to a belief in rule by administrative edict with more and more control and regulation of the economy and our lives."

Reagan invoked his service during World War II to respond to critics who claimed that he lacked the administrative experience necessary to run the state. "During World War II," he told the television audience, "I was called to active duty as a lieutenant in the cavalry reserve and ended up a captain and adjutant of an air force installation. Now, as many of you know, that was an administrative post." Reagan, however, never made it clear that he fought the war from the comfort of his own home. He went on to talk about his other experience, including his six terms as president of the Screen Actors Guild, from 1947 to 1952, and 1959 to 1960. It was during those earlier years that Reagan shifted from being a self-proclaimed "New Deal liberal" to a staunch anti-Communist conservative. He saw no tension between his leadership of the 1960 SAG strike and his role as a confidential informant for FBI agents seeking to identify "subversive" elements in Hollywood. Taken together, his wartime duties and SAG presidency seemed proof of Reagan's credentials.

Reagan had burst onto the national political scene in October 1964 when he delivered a speech to eight hundred Los Angeles powerbrokers packed inside the Cocoanut Grove supper club at the Ambassador Hotel. By his count, he had given the speech "hundreds of times before," but this time it got attention—and lots of it.

For Reagan, all the social ills facing America resulted from a decline of morality and a disrespect for authority. He elevated discussion about a host of problems—rising crime, high taxes, social unrest on campuses and in cities—into a larger cultural critique that tapped into the anxiety of many white, middle-class suburbanites who believed their values and privileges were under assault. He also fingered a culprit responsible for all the problems plaguing the state and the nation: a big, impersonal government and the liberal bureaucrats who staffed it. "This is the issue of this election," he said many times. "Whether we believe in our capacity for self-government, or whether we abandon the American Revolution and confess that a little intellectual elite in a far-distant capital can plan our lives for us better than we can plan them ourselves."

Although he spoke primarily about state issues, Reagan made clear that he hated international Communism just as much as bloated bureaucracy. He told audiences that it was immoral for the United States not to liberate Eastern Europe from the Soviets, because the alternative would be subjugation. Since he was not in the Oval Office making policy, Reagan did not have to confront the obvious contradiction between his strident anti-Communism and his equally strong fear of nuclear war. The United States, he declared, should never tell "a billion human beings now enslaved behind the Iron Curtain, 'Give up your dreams of freedom because in order to save our own skins, we're willing to make a deal with your slavemasters.'"

Reagan's Cocoanut Grove speech made such an impact that afterward a friend told him, "We've got to get that speech on television." But Barry Goldwater's camp resisted, worried that Reagan would steal the thunder from its candidate. They were right to be concerned. The Republican Party purchased airtime on October 27, 1964, and Reagan delivered the speech, titled "A Time for Choosing," before a live studio audience. With that speech, it became clear that Reagan—not Goldwater—was conservatism's true heir apparent. "Those who watched came to the same conclusion as those at the Cocoanut Grove," observed biographer Bob Spitz. "Ronald Reagan was a far better conservative advocate and came across as more reasonable and statesmanlike than Barry Goldwater." The journalist David Broder described Reagan's address as "the most successful national political debut since William Jennings Bryan electrified the 1896 Democratic convention with his 'Cross of Gold' speech."

The timing of Reagan's "A Time for Choosing" speech coincided with wider political currents in his adopted state. Two months after Johnson's 1964 landslide, a group of wealthy Californians started plotting to find a candidate to challenge the incumbent governor, Pat Brown, who would be running for an unprecedented third term in 1966. Grassroots conservative activists were excited about Reagan, so a few leading Republicans approached him about running.

Reagan was intrigued, but he needed to make money to support his family. In the spring of 1962 General Electric, fearing his political views were too controversial, had fired Reagan as a corporate spokesman. He was still hosting the popular TV Western series *Death Valley Days*, but he would be forced to give up that position if he announced his candidacy. His wealthy benefactors solved the problem. They formed a group, Friends of Ronald Reagan, that provided financial support so that Reagan could travel across the state, testing his appeal to party regulars while also measuring his own interest in running for office.

Reagan had proved that he could excite conservatives, but could he win over more moderate Republicans? The primary pitted him against George Christopher, a moderate former two-term mayor from San Francisco, who initially led Reagan by 17 points. Over the next few months, however, Reagan narrowed the lead. He was given a further boost when the chairman of the California Republican Party, Gaylord Parkinson, announced the so-called Eleventh Commandment: "Thou shalt not speak ill of another Republican." The unofficial rule frustrated Christopher, making it difficult for him to criticize Reagan for some of his past controversial positions, such as abolishing Social Security. But even without the commandment, Reagan's personal style—his ease in front of the camera, self-deprecating humor, and genial demeanor—combined with his reassuring message, made him a charismatic figure to many voters. "He exudes warmth and enthusiasm, his simplified statements about fiscal problems come across to the people, and he is not doctrinaire like Goldwater," remarked one self-described liberal Republican.

On primary day, Reagan crushed Christopher and three other minor candidates, winning an impressive 65 percent of the vote. Afterward, he traveled to Gettysburg to secure Dwight Eisenhower's endorsement as well. "Here in a brick house on a shaded lawn," wrote *The Washington Post*, "he humbly paid his respects to General Eisenhower, respectfully listening and eagerly posing for photographs with him." Reagan understood the significance of the photos and of Ike's words of support. "Your generous comments and the fact of our meeting have done more than you could ever know to unify the Party here in California," Reagan wrote the general. His meeting with Ike also revitalized Reagan's own spirit. The day after, he spoke to a capacity crowd at the National Press Club in Washington, where a *Los Angeles Times* reporter observed that he gave a "witty, deft, engaging performance in his debut in one of the capital's chief forums."

Brown, a gregarious, old-school politician, supported LBJ's Great Society and, during his two terms in office, had expanded California's freeway system and poured money and resources into expanding the state's university system. A strong advocate for civil rights, he signed a statewide fair employment act, instituted affirmative action and job training programs, and successfully lobbied the legislature to pass a controversial fair housing bill that outlawed discrimination. His liberal positions made him vulnerable from the Right, leading Los Angeles's tough-talking mayor, Sam Yorty, to challenge Brown in the primaries. Yorty lost, but he managed to win nearly a million votes by attacking Brown for coddling criminals and tolerating campus unrest.

Yorty's campaign exposed the daunting obstacles that Brown faced. The mood in California was sour, and many blamed the governor for the myriad problems plaguing the state. According to *The Wall Street Journal*, voters were "angry or uneasy over high property taxes, the demands of Negro militants, campus demonstrators, and rising welfare costs." Brown could have reined in any one of these issues, but together they produced an angry electorate. "Pat's problem," said a leading Democrat, "is that he is fighting a mood, not an issue. Sometimes you can refute an issue, but how do you refute a mood?"

It turned out that Reagan knew exactly how to appeal to this mood. He was not only able to lob ideological grenades in Brown's direction but also nimble enough to avoid getting tied down on specifics. To help with his image, Reagan hired a political consulting firm that ironed out some of the rough ideological edges, toned down some of his conservative views, and instructed him to "play the role of the bland good guy." He played the part so well that Brown's efforts to label Reagan an extremist—"the crown prince of the extreme Right"—fell flat. "Reagan speaks with flawless Hollywood diction and looks the way most wives wish their husbands looked at the age of 35, let alone 55," wrote one reporter.

Reagan was more than just a handsome former actor, however. He could subsume diverse issues under one anti-government, anti-Communist umbrella by channeling the discontent of middle-class, suburban white voters. As small property owners, these voters fought to maintain the racial homogeneity of their communities and resisted Washington's efforts to force integration. "Something has to be done about the way they keep raising taxes and giving in to the Negroes on everything," said one small business owner. Although the federal government supplied the loans used to pay their mortgages and helped build the roads that tied their communities together, many suburban residents saw no contradiction in their virulent hatred of Washington's intervention in racial matters. Furthermore, since they were heavily dependent on military contracts for their survival, these voters supported an aggressive anti-Communist stance and opposed any efforts to negotiate with the Soviets.

The genius of Ronald Reagan was his ability to co-opt liberal goals while denouncing their tactics. He understood that government had a responsibility to care for the poor but dismissed the war on poverty as "just a new pork barrel and a rehash of old ideas that do not work." He supported equal opportunity for all but objected to specific provisions of the Civil Rights Act of 1964, claiming it was "badly written" and trampled on individual rights. He said that everyone should have the right to vote but then opposed the Voting Rights Act, calling it "humiliating to the South." He believed in medical care for the elderly but criticized some of the provisions of Medicare. When journalists tried to pin down Reagan on what steps he would take as governor to address these exact issues—civil rights, poverty, and the medical needs of the elderly—he resorted to generalities about the evils of big government while refusing to offer concrete alternatives.

Over time, Reagan would redefine conservatism, moving it away from Eisenhower's obsession with balanced budgets and toward a new gospel of growth. Like many liberals after World War II, Reagan believed that the primary focus of government should be to promote economic growth. However, by the 1960s, Kennedy and Johnson, along with an entire generation of liberals, had come to the realization that promoting growth was not enough; government needed to play a role, albeit a small one, in offering aid to those left outside the system. Reagan rejected that move leftward, with its Keynesian emphasis on using government controls to manipulate the economy, and instead preached the wonders of free enterprise. The best way to unleash growth, he argued, was to limit government power and allow the creative force of capitalism to uplift the poor through equal opportunity. Reagan was convinced that there was no problem that free enterprise could not solve.

Since he was running for a state office, Reagan addressed foreign policy issues only occasionally, but he made clear that the United States was already engaged in an ideological war with international Communism, even if most Americans refused to acknowledge it. "This war was declared a century ago by Karl Marx and reaffirmed by Lenin when he said that Communism and capitalism cannot exist side by side," he declared. While rhetorically Reagan resembled Kennedy when describing the Cold War, privately he lacked the sophistication that could come only from direct experience in war. He showed little interest in strategy and rarely spoke about the human consequences of war. For those presidents who'd seen combat up close and understood the horrors of the battlefield, especially Eisenhower and Kennedy, war was more than an abstraction—it was an actual place where young men lost their lives under ghastly conditions. Their firsthand involvement grounded their understanding of the role that America played in the world and impressed on them the limits of American power—nuances that Reagan lacked.

On Vietnam, Reagan spouted many of the same positions as the other Republican critics of the Johnson administration. "Once the killing starts and we send young American boys over there to die, the nation has a moral obligation to impose its full resources to end it as soon as possible," he said. He called for more bombing of North Vietnam, especially weapons depots, and he endorsed an invasion of the region, led by the South Vietnamese and "supported logistically by the United States." America needed to defend the sovereignty of South Vietnam regardless of the costs—even if that meant using nuclear weapons. The problem with Johnson's policy, he argued, was that gradual escalation failed to take into account "that the so-called enemy nations have not retreated one step from their announced intention to impose their system on the world." In that situation, he declared, compromise amounted to delusion.

On the campaign trail, Reagan drove home this message, insisting that Johnson should go to Congress to obtain a formal declaration of war against Vietnam. Privately, however, he left open a side door, saying that if Vietnam had defense treaties with China and Russia, a declaration would be "inadvisable." In that case, he wrote a constituent, Congress could adopt a resolution "short of a declaration of war."

As Reagan touted the need for war in the abstract, critics charged that his own efforts to shrink government would actually hurt programs for veterans. Reagan reacted defensively to that accusation, referring to himself in one constituent letter as "a veteran of four years of World War II." He cited his time in service in a similar way in campaign flyers: "As a World War II Veteran, I am well aware of the problems of Veterans' benefits that have been hard won in California. . . . As a second lieutenant in the US Cavalry reserve, I was called to active duty in 1942 and was discharged as a Captain in 1946. I served with the Air Force and under the command of Air Force intelligence." While true, the claim exaggerated Reagan's connection to the war effort, never mentioning that he slept in his own bed most nights—a luxury not afforded to most veterans, especially those fighting in a war zone.

Yet the exaggeration did little harm, because as Election Day drew near, Reagan represented the most exciting story in American politics. In October his face was featured on the cover of *Time* magazine as part of a long, glowing profile titled "California: Ronald for Real." In November Reagan crushed Brown, piling up a one-million-vote margin while leading the Republicans to a near sweep of statewide offices. Reagan scored 72 percent of the vote in conservative-leaning Orange County, even though half the voters were still registered Democrats.

―――――

Reagan was not the only future president elected in the backlash year of 1966. Two years earlier, the forty-year-old George H. W. Bush had challenged Democrat Ralph Yarborough for a Texas Senate seat. Many people expected that Bush, like his father, would campaign as a liberal Republican. Instead, he ran as a Goldwater conservative—a move that years later Bush suggested had more to do with political calculation than ideological purity. "I was a *Texan*," he protested, "I was running for office in *Texas*." Like Goldwater, Bush opposed the Civil Rights Act of 1964, saying that it infringed on states' rights. Reflecting on his position later, Bush admitted it was "a difficult issue" because he opposed "discrimination of any kind," but he still believed that the legislation "threatened more rights than it protected." Like Goldwater, Bush opposed most of the major initiatives of Johnson's Great Society, including Medicare (he called it "socialized medicine") and the war on poverty. However, he spoke sympathetically about the plight of the urban poor and about the need for Republicans to reach out to minority communities. He was a practical, pro-business conservative who lambasted as "nuts" the right-wing ideologues surrounding Goldwater. One constituent observed that Bush "wants the same things as Goldwater, but he's not reckless."

Even though Texas remained a Democratic stronghold, Bush liked his chances. He assumed that John F. Kennedy, whose popularity in the South had cratered due to his support for civil rights, would be running for reelection. Instead, due to the tragedy in Dallas, it ended up being the widely popular LBJ heading the Democratic ticket. Although the new president disliked Yarborough, he was determined to keep the seat in the Democratic column. (In 1961 Republican John Tower had filled the seat left vacant when Johnson became vice president.) On election night, Bush ran two hundred thousand votes ahead of Goldwater, but that still was not enough to defeat Yarborough, who scored 56.2 percent of the vote.

Bush immediately regretted some of the conservative positions he had advocated during the campaign. "I took some of the Far Right positions to get elected," he confessed to his pastor in 1965. "I hope I never do it again." Shortly after the election, Bush wrote to Richard Nixon, thanking him for making a campaign appearance on his behalf. He complained that the massive turnout among African Americans, 98.5 percent of whom supported his opponent, doomed his campaign. He also placed blame on the "bunch of 'nuts'" who ran the Goldwater campaign in Texas, but he refused to castigate the candidate himself. "Goldwater's philosophy was not rejected," he wrote, "it was the false image that people had about Goldwater." Nixon seemed to agree with this assessment, writing back that the "fact that the Negro vote was almost 100% against us made it impossible to win in several states where that vote is a decisive number."

In 1966 Bush ran again, this time for a newly created congressional seat representing Houston's affluent west side, where he lived. His campaign differed significantly from that of his peers. The first generation of

World War II veterans who ran for office in the immediate aftermath of World War II—Eisenhower, Kennedy, Ford, LBJ, and Nixon—bonded with voters by highlighting their wartime experiences. By 1966, however, this aspect failed to resonate as strongly, so Bush downplayed his wartime service, rarely discussing it on the campaign trail and making only passing mention of it in pamphlets and literature. Instead, he portrayed himself as a man of "action" who would get things done in Washington. Eschewing ideology, he made ambition and energy the centerpiece of his message. One commercial showed Bush walking the streets of Houston as a voiceover stated, "People sympathize with a man who tries hard." Avoiding Goldwater's rigid ideological language, Bush appealed to the thriving business community in his district, which was more interested in the traditional Republican message of lower taxes and less regulation.

Like Reagan, Bush saw a lack of respect for authority and traditional values as a major source of social turmoil. Events during the decade—antiwar protests, racial unrest, the loosening of sexuality—only exacerbated those concerns. Bush was especially alarmed about changing sexual mores. In the 1960s, the countercultural embrace of sexual expression had seeped into the mainstream. The media offered extensive coverage of "Summer of Love" festivals, and music, which once celebrated the wonders of dating, now made explicit reference to sex acts. In 1964 the Beatles topped the charts with the comparatively tame "I Want to Hold Your Hand." By 1968, they were singing, "Why Don't We Do It in the Road?" Meanwhile, the development in 1960 of the birth control pill—which soon became known as just "the pill"—gave women a greater sense of sexual freedom than any previous contraceptive device. By divorcing sex from the danger of unwanted pregnancy, the pill enabled women to choose to have sex when and where they wished and made contraception widely acceptable.

In a theme that dated back to his time in service during World War II—when he critiqued the loose morals of women who lived near his base and the married men who enjoyed their company—Bush complained often of America's declining moral standards. "I felt," he reflected, "that too many young people use the war as an excuse to break the law, practice free sex, take drugs, and eschew responsibility of any kind. The personal values I had been taught as a child were threatened and, at least for a time, seemed lost." Like Reagan, Bush was articulating the fears of an increasingly potent political force: the New Right.

Yet while he took conservative positions on most issues—supporting the Vietnam War and calling for cutbacks on Great Society spending—Bush worked hard to win over African American voters. His efforts paid off. On Election Day he boasted a coalition of traditional Republicans and Democrats that included 34 percent of the African American vote, crushing his Democratic opponent, District Attorney Frank Briscoe. George H. W. Bush racked up 57.1 percent of the total votes cast to become the first Republican to represent Houston since Reconstruction.

Perhaps the biggest winner on election night was Richard Nixon, who had stumped tirelessly for Republican candidates. In his memoirs, Nixon said that the 1966 election was "a prerequisite for my own comeback." Indeed, the White House was watching. A Johnson aide observed that Nixon's "standing with the professional politicians in one party is as high as it ever was. His standing with the Goldwaterites is very good indeed, and though he is disliked, he is not completely unacceptable to the moderates."

———

By 1967, despite the presence of more than 450,000 American combat troops, the situation in Vietnam continued to deteriorate as US casualties mounted.

As the war dragged on, some students at large state universities and elite private colleges held mass demonstrations, burned their draft cards, and chanted angrily, "Hey, hey, LBJ, how many kids did you kill today?" Although they attracted considerable media attention, these young people actually remained a minority even among college students. One study concluded that between 1965 and 1968, only 20 percent of college students participated in antiwar demonstrations. Yet, over time, such overt resistance chipped away at America's policy of global containment, raising widespread skepticism over the nation's anti-Communist obsession. Soon the "lessons of Vietnam"—that American values are not universal, its resources not unlimited, or Communism monolithic—would compete with the lingering lessons of Munich.

The lessons of Munich meant little to many young people who came of age after World War II. Communism, they argued, was not synonymous with 1930s Fascism, Ho Chi Minh was not Hitler, and grainy images of goose-stepping Nazi soldiers storming into the Sudetenland region of Czechoslovakia seemed far removed from the complex issues faced by developing countries struggling to break the bonds of colonialism. Over time, this new generation came to see a connection between the war and seemingly intractable social problems at home. "There is something sick," commented the University of Michigan daily paper, "about a nation that can deploy thousands of soldiers to go off shooting Vietcong . . . but can't spare a few hundred to avert the murder" of civil rights workers in the South.

Many establishment figures also began raising tough questions about US involvement in Vietnam. Back in 1966, Democratic senator J. W. Fulbright (whom LBJ dubbed "Senator Halfbright"), the powerful chairman of the Senate Foreign Relations Committee, had held nationally televised hearings that skewered the administration's Vietnam policy. According to historian Charles DeBenedetti, the hearings "made dissent all the more legitimate and the public questioning of U.S. war policy all the more acceptable."

In the hearings, Fulbright charged that by displaying an "arrogance of power," the United States was "not living up" to its "capacity and promise as a civilized example for the world." One of the star witnesses, George Kennan, considered the father of America's containment policy, attacked the relevance of the Munich analogy that the Johnson administration used to justify America's involvement in the war. "I think that no episode, perhaps, in modern history has been more misleading than that of the Munich conference," said Kennan. "It has given too many people the idea that never must one attempt to make any sort of political accommodation in any circumstances. This is, of course, a fatally unfortunate conclusion. Hitler was, thank heaven, a unique phenomenon."

By the spring of 1967, even Robert McNamara, who had once forcefully argued for American intervention in Vietnam and dismissed those like George Ball who argued for caution, had lost hope that the United States could win the war. He now told the president that he saw "no attractive course of action," fearing that further escalation would forever tarnish America's image in the world. "The picture of the world's greatest super-power killing or seriously injuring 1,000 noncombatants a week while trying to pound a tiny backward nation into submission on an issue whose merits are hotly disputed is not a pretty one," he wrote. The Joint Chiefs of Staff echoed McNamara's pessimism, admitting that the "bombing campaign in the North has not and cannot succeed in cours-ing the North Vietnamese into a settlement or reduce the flow of men and material to the South to the extent that victory is possible." But still John-son persevered, buoyed by reports from Walt Rostow, who had taken over as national security advisor, that victory was in sight. "Hanoi is moving towards negotiations," Rostow reassured the president on June 28.

Compounding the problem, LBJ's repeated distortions about Ameri-ca's involvement in the conflict, and the prospect for victory, further un-dermined public trust in his presidency. Journalists now referred to LBJ's "credibility gap," which the *Los Angeles Times* defined as "a phrase in-vented by Washington newsmen who didn't want to come out and call any public official a liar." In 1967 presidential speechwriter and advisor Harry McPherson lamented that "the President is simply not believed."

At the same time, Johnson's decision to wage a war against poverty at home and Communism abroad without raising taxes threatened to un-dermine the Keynesian revolution that he had triumphantly celebrated just a few years earlier. The faith in continuous, noninflationary growth had fueled LBJ's ambitions to enact a wide-ranging liberal agenda. By 1966, however, an overheated economy led to a spike in inflation that threatened a recession. Now back in private life, Walter Heller argued for the necessity of a tax hike to cool down the economy. Still the president resisted. Despite troubling signs of inflation, Johnson refused to raise taxes or scale back his efforts. "Anybody who wanted to slow things down was a killjoy," said the CEA's Arthur Okun. Johnson knew that a pro-posed tax hike would provide ammunition to critics who wanted to scale back his Great Society.

Not until January 1967 did Johnson finally relent and propose a temporary 6 percent surcharge on corporate and individual income taxes. "So, Johnson hesitated on taxes and fudged on the cost of the war," observed historian Robert M. Collins. He did not send a proposal to Congress until August. By then, it was too late. Congress made clear that it preferred cuts in domestic spending to increases in taxes.

By October 1967, only 31 percent of the nation approved of Johnson's handling of the war. As his problems mounted, the president became more withdrawn, paranoid, and defensive. According to one witness, when a reporter pressed him on why the nation was fighting in Vietnam, "LBJ unzipped his fly, drew out his substantial organ, and declared, 'This is why!!'"

Much of LBJ's paranoia (and vulgarity) was directed at Robert F. Kennedy, now a senator from New York. It was not so much RFK that Johnson feared as it was the mythology surrounding Bobby's brother Jack. Johnson resented his slain predecessor even as he tried to emulate him. In 1966, while discussing the 1968 campaign over dinner with Arthur Krim, the head of United Artists movie studio and a major Democratic fundraiser, and Robert Kintner, who ran both ABC and NBC before joining the administration as Cabinet secretary, Johnson raised the idea of producing a big Hollywood film based on his World War II experiences.

Filmmakers had turned JFK's adventures on PT-109 into a movie; why not do the same for LBJ's time in the Pacific? According to notes of the conversation, Johnson "said he didn't understand why a movie company couldn't make a film about his activities in navy planes showing the various missions that he flew." Johnson went on to say that the movie could help "the soldiers that are serving in Vietnam now . . . to see that the president wasn't 'just talking' about war games—that he had actually been in one himself and, therefore, could understand the hazards and sacrifices that are met by a soldier." Both Kintner and Krim were initially enthusiastic about the idea, but the project never got off the ground.

Robert Kennedy, now the standard-bearer of the Camelot legacy, was making headlines across the country, drawing large and enthusiastic crowds while being surrounded by an adoring press contingent. Johnson, already insecure about the shadow that JFK cast over his presidency, loathed the attention showered on the senator. The two men were so openly hostile that they had difficulty even being civil with each other. "I can't stand the bastard," RFK told an aide. Johnson reciprocated the resentment by dismissing RFK as "that little shit." Obsessed with the Kennedy "myth making machine," Johnson believed it was out to destroy him and his presidency to make room for RFK. Of course, the president had only himself to blame for this predicament, because it was he who had helped transform JFK into a martyr in order to build support for his Great Society agenda.

To differentiate himself from the president, Robert Kennedy staked out positions to the left of LBJ. On Vietnam, he announced his support for a negotiated solution, similar to the one his brother had set up in Laos, even if it meant Communists eventually coming to power. In response, Johnson ordered his supporters to attack Kennedy, charging that NLF participation in a coalition government was like putting "a fox in the chicken coop" or "an arsonist in the fire department." But RFK shot back, connecting Johnson's foreign policy mishaps with his domestic policy misses. Johnson was so preoccupied with the war, RFK charged, that he was failing to address pressing social needs.

The approaching publication of William Manchester's book about the Kennedy assassination, *The Death of a President*, became another flash point in LBJ's strained relationship with the slain president and his younger brother. Johnson viewed the book as part of RFK's effort to undermine support for his presidency. Manchester made little effort to hide his contempt for Johnson, but after reading a draft of the manuscript, Jacqueline Kennedy insisted that the author remove personal details of the assassination, especially her graphic personal recollection of that day, and tone down his criticism of LBJ. When Manchester made only minor changes, she filed a lawsuit to block publication. Eventually the two sides reached a settlement, but not before Manchester acceded to many of her demands. Despite the controversy, Manchester's book was a national bestseller.

Although Johnson complained that he was not able to compete with the well-oiled Kennedy public relations machine, he followed their example and cooperated with a friendly writer to tell *his* side of the story. He turned to the popular author Jim Bishop, whose book *The Day Kennedy Was Shot* represented the flip side of the Manchester book. In his account, the Kennedys "were effete Europeans, in manner and address," while the Johnsons "were earthy Americans." The book, however, achieved only modest success.

In the tumultuous year of 1968, the nation experienced a series of shocks that not only sealed the demise of Johnson's presidency but also challenged the basic assumptions that had emerged from World War II.

On January 31, 1968, the Vietcong invaded the US embassy compound in Saigon and waged bloody battles in the capitals of most of South Vietnam's provinces during the lunar New Year, called Tet in Vietnamese. Sixty-seven thousand enemy troops poured into more than one hundred of South Vietnam's cities and towns. From a military perspective, the Tet Offensive was a disaster for the North Vietnamese. They suffered heavy casualties and failed to gain new ground or incite a popular rebellion against the United States. But what may have been a military defeat for the North simultaneously represented a striking *psychological* victory. Televised images of US Marines desperately defending the embassy grounds stunned the nation. Voicing the shock of many Americans, CBS news anchorman Walter Cronkite declared that the United States was now "mired in stalemate." At that moment, Johnson turned to an aide and said, "It's all over." If he had lost Cronkite, he had lost "Mr. Average Citizen."

The Tet Offensive dealt Johnson's credibility a final, debilitating blow. In the month after Tet, those Americans describing themselves as "hawks" dropped from 60 percent to 40 percent. For the first time, the number of self-described "doves" (42 percent) outnumbered hawks. Democratic senator Eugene McCarthy of Minnesota, who managed to galvanize both hawks and doves critical of Johnson's Vietnam policy to score a psychological win over Johnson in the New Hampshire primary on March 12, was the chief political beneficiary of this shift. (McCarthy lost by a margin of 48 percent to 42 percent but scored much better than anyone expected.) Four days later, LBJ's worst nightmare came true when his nemesis Robert Kennedy entered the race for the Democratic nomination.

While the Tet Offensive doomed any lingering hope of public support, Johnson's path forward still seemed unclear. General Westmoreland now asked the president to call up 206,000 additional troops, warning him that "a setback is fully possible if I am not reinforced, and it is likely we will lose ground in other areas." Johnson felt trapped. Looking for a way out, he asked Clark Clifford, who had recently replaced McNamara as secretary of defense, to consider alternatives and make a recommendation. After a week of study, Clifford reported that he was "convinced that the military course we were pursuing was not only endless, but hopeless." He suggested that Johnson reconvene the "Wise Men," a group of senior statesmen who had previously urged Johnson to stay the course in Vietnam. A month later, in March, they informed the president that "There has been a very significant shift in most of our positions since we last met," before recommending that "we must begin to take steps to disengage." Given all the challenges facing Johnson, they now saw no option other than to pursue what was unthinkable just a few months earlier: a negotiated settlement. "We seem to have a sinkhole," Clifford said. Reluctantly, Johnson agreed.

A few days later, on March 31, Johnson announced his new policy to the nation. There were no longer any references to Munich or appeasement. Instead, he wanted to talk about "peace in Vietnam and Southeast Asia"—meaning an immediate unilateral halt to the bombing of North Vietnam. His face gaunt and tired from years of strain, Johnson then concluded his speech by announcing that he would not seek reelection. A few weeks later, Vice President Hubert Humphrey threw his hat into the ring.

As opposition to the war intensified, Republican hard-liners softened their rhetoric. Leading into the 1968 presidential year, Nixon backed away from his militant positions on Vietnam, rejecting his previous statements that the United States should expand the war into the North or Laos. He addressed Vietnam in general terms, refusing to commit to a specific policy. To attract doves, Nixon emphasized his commitment to peace; for hawks, he stressed his vow to preserve a non-Communist South Vietnam.

In a February 15, 1968, speech in Boston, he reaffirmed his belief that "there shall be no reward for armed aggression" but also asserted, "We must be equally firm in our insistence that peaceful progress for the people of that beleaguered country must be pressed with a sense of compelling urgency." One month later, speaking to a Republican gathering in New Hampshire, Nixon reiterated his stance by pledging to "end the war and win the peace." He developed a new mantra that attempted to capture this ambiguity: "Peace with honor." Ironically, for someone so steeped in the lessons of Munich, Nixon failed to see that his call for "peace with honor" echoed Neville Chamberlain's "peace for our time" message in the 1930s.

Even his own staff noticed the obvious contradiction in Nixon's approach to the war. A speechwriter said that Nixon's strategy was not designed to propose a serious solution to the Vietnam crisis but rather "to find the least unassailable middle ground." William Safire, another Nixon aide, dismissed the candidate's public statements as "a grab bag of phrases, from which audiences could draw whatever general conclusions they please."

But there was an even bigger underlying problem. Nixon confessed to speechwriter Richard Whalen that he, too, had privately concluded there was "no way to win the war." He continued, "We can't say that, of course—in fact, we have to seem to say the opposite, just to keep some degree of bargaining leverage," but he knew deep down that the war "can't be brought to a successful military conclusion." Nixon's confession reveals how, at key moments in the evolution of the nation's involvement in the war, a gap existed between what presidents said in private and what they told the public. Nixon's position was reminiscent of when, in 1954, Eisenhower had privately told his staff that Vietnam was not vital to America's national interests but then the next day announced to the world the "domino theory," claiming that the loss of Vietnam would lead to a string of unacceptable losses to Communism. Similarly, both Kennedy and Johnson expressed private doubts about whether the United States could win the war but never shared their concerns with the public.

By 1968, Gerald Ford had also changed his tone, talking more about peace than about escalation. In a rare moment of agreement, he characterized Johnson's decision to initiate a bombing halt as "sound" and supported the president's call for "an early and honorable peace in Vietnam." Any increase in troop strength, he said, "should come from South Vietnamese manpower." But Ford could not completely abandon his hawkish views. He qualified his calls for conciliation by pointing out that starting peace talks would mean that the United States would "be approaching the bargaining table at a time when most of South Vietnam's countryside is in Communist hands as a result of the Tet Offensive." He made no effort to address the contradiction between supporting negotiations and suggesting that the United States keep fighting to improve its negotiating position.

While both Ford and Nixon recognized that the war was going badly, George Bush retained an overly optimistic view of the conflict. On December 26, 1967, he embarked on a two-week trip to Vietnam, traveling to Saigon, Da Nang, and eleven of the forty-four provinces, as well as twenty-one villages and hamlets. He met with soldiers and marines, top American military and diplomatic officials, and ARVN troops and locals. What he saw and heard impressed him. "I am totally convinced that we are not involved in a stalemate," Bush said naïvely on January 11, 1968, less than three weeks before the Tet Offensive. "I am further convinced that we are winning; and, further, that our rate of progress is accelerating." The morale of the fighting men was high, he claimed, and "[m]ore and more we are taking the battle to the enemy," as the Vietcong were "suffering disproportionately larger losses." Overall, he returned to America in *support* of LBJ's policy in Vietnam and simply counseled greater patience. Whether touring the combat zone reminded Bush of his own experiences in World War II and underscored the connection between the two conflicts is unclear. But he wasted little time in applying the lessons of the past to the present. "If we stay steadfast, Hanoi will stop misreading the dissent in this country, and when it does, the progress that I am telling you about tonight will be translated into a message that Hanoi reads loud and clear that its plan of aggression cannot succeed," he wrote in his prepared remarks. He then scribbled, "Then the war will end." The next day, Bush reiterated the points in a letter to a constituent. "I do feel things are going better in Viet Nam than one would think from reading the papers here," he wrote.

In March Bush engaged in a remarkably revealing exchange with Richard Mack, his former Yale classmate and a fellow member of the university's Skull and Bones senior secret student society. By this point, Mack had soured on the war and explained his disillusionment in a long letter to Bush. The war, he claimed, had eroded the faith of young people in their elected leaders, including Bush. He wrote that "the youth of our nation don't trust you, don't believe in you, and perhaps even worse, don't even give a damn about you." He then followed up with a rhetorical question: "How long do you think a nation can survive without trust and inspiration of its youth?" Losing Vietnam did not worry him, he told his old friend, because he was not "scared of Communism." He questioned the morality of a nation that was trying to impose its will on a nation that refused to accept it. The war, he concluded, "makes me ashamed as an American."

Bush responded a few weeks later with a full-throttle defense of the war. He rejected the argument about the immorality of the war, which he claimed was part of a "blind willingness" to criticize the actions of the South Vietnamese government "while totally overlooking the terror of the VC and the past slaughters by Ho." He argued, as many historians would later, that the Tet Offensive represented a psychological victory for the North but a military defeat. He repeated many of the arguments put forth by the Johnson administration: The North Vietnamese would soon be forced to the peace table; journalists offered distorted and pessimistic accounts of what was taking place on the ground; the South Vietnamese troops were brave and committed to winning the war; and protests at home "have definitely strengthened Hanoi's will." Surprisingly, he defended LBJ from the "mean" criticism of critics. "I detest this suggestion that the president really doesn't care about human lives."

Bush offered no hint as to what he would do differently other than to point out that "there is no easy answer" to ending the conflict. "I'm no 'Communism is monolithic' man," he concluded, "but nor am I one who feel [*sic*] the Communists have renounced their clearly stated goals for world revolution or world takeover."

Despite his slightly more nuanced view of Communism, Bush offered no realistic solution to ending the war. As long as he continued to believe that the lessons of Munich and the domino theory applied to Southeast Asia, he could not accept a Communist victory. The best he could do was to call for the unification of North and South Vietnam under the rules established by the Geneva Accords. "I urge free and supervised elections in both North and South," he wrote. Ironically, this statement ignored the fact that it was South Vietnam, with support from the United States, that refused to allow free elections in 1956 out of fear that Ho Chi Minh would win in a landslide. Despite America's romantic notion that most people living in South Vietnam wanted to be "saved" from Communism, holding elections in 1968 likely would have resulted in a Communist victory. Bush never addressed that critical point: Would he support the outcome of a free election if the Communists won?

Reagan was the only future president who did not alter his message or tone down his calls for total victory even as the situation devolved. The details on the ground were of little interest to him, and he was indifferent to the complex nature of fighting a guerrilla war in Southeast Asia. In November 1967 Reagan asserted that elected leaders needed to accept that "we are in Vietnam because our national interest demands that we take a stand there now so we won't have to take a stand later on our own beaches." The war, he declared, "must be fought through to victory"—and that meant maintaining a non-Communist Vietnam.

Reagan's stubborn stance echoed that of post-presidency Eisenhower, who never wavered in his commitment to winning the war. While many other critics shifted to discussions of peace, Ike told Johnson that "now may be the time to increase our combat effort." He made clear that "if any Republican or Democrat suggests that we pull out of Vietnam and turn our backs on the more than 13,000 Americans who died in the cause of freedom there, they will have me to contend with." He promised to oppose any candidate who advocated "capitulation and the abandonment of South Vietnam."

Eisenhower delivered the same hawkish message to the White House. During a January 22, 1968, personal briefing by General Andrew Goodpaster, a World War II combat veteran who'd served as an advisor in the

Eisenhower administration and who would later be named commander of NATO, he stated that a coalition government as advocated by many liberal critics of the administration "would be undesirable and dangerous, and we should oppose it." Instead of pulling back, he recommended that "now is the time to hit" the enemy harder, including using the B-52 to bomb "enemy forces and bases in SVN." Ike then told Goodpaster bluntly that he "wants to see the president win the war."

As the debate over the Vietnam War grew increasingly heated, developments at home added more fuel to the fire. On April 4, a lone gunman assassinated Martin Luther King, who was in Memphis supporting a strike by sanitation workers. After learning of King's death, Johnson lamented, "Everything we've gained in the last few years we're going to lose tonight." With the Black community reeling, riots engulfed more than a hundred cities and towns across the nation. Rioters burned twenty blocks in Chicago, where Mayor Daley ordered police to "shoot to kill." The worst violence occurred in Washington, DC, where seven hundred fires burned and nine people lost their lives. For the first time since the Civil War, armed soldiers guarded the steps to the Capitol. The turmoil capped four straight summers of unrest, including massive riots in Newark and Detroit the previous year.

Any hope of racial conciliation, of convincing a majority of white people to accept responsibility for the plight of poor Blacks, died that night. The violence that ensued in the wake of King's death made many white Americans even less sympathetic to appeals for racial justice and more sympathetic to calls for "law and order" that Nixon, Reagan, and Bush would make central to their presidencies.

Following the assassination, the Johnson administration made a new push to pass a fair housing bill, which LBJ had first introduced in 1966. Conservatives among both Democrats and Republicans had opposed the legislation. North Carolina senator Sam Ervin, a Bible-quoting constitutional conservative who would earn fame and admiration a few years later as chairman of the Senate Watergate Committee, claimed that the legislation was designed "to bring about equality by robbing all Americans of their basic rights of private property." The reception among the future presidents was more mixed. Ford voted for the measure without hesitation.

Nixon opposed it initially but later voiced tepid support—even though he rarely mentioned it on the campaign trail for fear of antagonizing suburban white voters.

Race was an especially difficult issue for Bush, a Republican in the Deep South, where there was scant support for open housing. But he made the courageous decision to vote his conscience, knowing that he would pay a high political cost. Afterward, he wrote that his office was flooded with angry letters: "I voted for the bill and the roof is falling in—boy does the hatred surface. [H]ave had more mail on this subject than on Viet Nam and Taxes and sex all put together." Of the future Republican presidents, only Reagan spoke out against the legislation on the basis of what he framed as individual freedom. "If an individual wants to discriminate against Negroes or others in selling or renting his home," the governor said, "he has a right to do so."

The shocks kept coming. Two months after the King assassination, Robert Kennedy was felled by an assassin's bullet after winning the crucial California primary. With Kennedy gone and Johnson out of the race, Humphrey quickly emerged as the nominee, but the party could not come together to agree on a platform. At the Democratic convention in Chicago that August, hawks and doves clashed over whether to include a plank supporting the president's Vietnam policies. The hawks won in a close vote. The real drama, though, was outside the convention hall, as police assaulted peaceful antiwar protestors in full view of the national media. "These are our children," *New York Times* columnist Tom Wicker cried out as the violence played out in front of him.

There was plenty of intrigue on the Republican side as well. Nixon had emerged as the leading candidate for the nomination, but Reagan hoped to deny him the prize. In his memoirs, Reagan claimed that he only allowed his name to be put forward at the convention as a "favorite son" candidate of the California delegation. That was not true. Less than two weeks after winning election as governor in 1966, Reagan had met with a group of political advisors to discuss a run for the presidency. His aides developed a detailed campaign plan that had him traveling across the country building support for his candidacy. His strategy was to siphon off enough votes to deny Nixon the nomination on the first ballot.

At that point, Reagan hoped to re-create his magic from 1964 by addressing the convention and igniting a move toward him.

Nixon, however, knew what Reagan was up to and outmaneuvered him. He went straight to Reagan's strongest supporters—Southern conservatives—and secured their support by promising to choose a conservative vice president. When the convention opened on August 5 in Miami Beach, Nixon made sure that Reagan did not have an opportunity to address the hall until *after* he had secured the nomination—which he did on the first ballot, thus crushing Reagan's hopes of becoming the party's standard-bearer. Only then did Nixon allow his rival to speak from the podium. Instead of wooing delegates, however, Reagan made a motion that Nixon's nomination be made unanimous.

Congressman Ford was among the candidates whom Nixon considered for the vice presidential role that had been central to his bargain with Southern conservatives. On the night of his nomination, Nixon invited a dozen Republicans, including Ford, to his hotel suite to discuss a possible running mate. "I know that in the past, Jerry, you have thought about being vice president. Would you take it this year?" What Ford did not know was that Eisenhower had already nixed the idea, believing that Ford would not be able to inspire voters. So instead Nixon surprised the convention by choosing Spiro Agnew, the little-known, tough-talking, law-and-order governor of Maryland. When Nixon divulged the news to Ford, the congressman burst out laughing. Ford thought Agnew was shockingly unqualified for the job. According to a witness, after Ford's outburst, a Nixon aide stared at him "as if he had farted at the communion rail." George Bush, on the other hand, described the choice of Agnew as "pretty darn sensible."

Part of Nixon's strategy for the general election was to keep Johnson on the sidelines. He knew there was no love lost between Humphrey and LBJ, so he calculated that by promising to protect the president's legacy, he could keep Johnson from hitting the campaign trail, especially in the Democratic South, where Nixon hoped to make inroads. He told reporters, knowing that it would get back to the president, that LBJ "should have the respect of all citizens" and that he "would do nothing to destroy that respect."

He echoed that theme again on September 8, when he used evangelist Billy Graham to deliver a "private and confidential message" to Johnson. While Graham scribbled notes, Nixon dictated that he would "never embarrass" Johnson after the election. "I respect him as a man and as a president," he said. Nixon went on to say that he wanted "a working relationship" with Johnson and planned to "seek his advice continually." He promised that after the war ended, he would give LBJ "a major share of credit" and would "do everything" to preserve Johnson's well-deserved place in history.

On September 15 Reverend Graham flew to Washington to deliver the message to Johnson in person. After a brief meeting, Graham reported back to Nixon that Johnson "was touched" by his gesture and responded with "warmth and appreciation." Johnson told Graham that he intended "to loyally support Mr. Humphrey, but if Mr. Nixon becomes the president-elect," he would "do all in my power to cooperate with him." Despite his stated intention to support Humphrey, LBJ was ultimately won over by Nixon's flattery. When asked to campaign for Humphrey in key battleground states where the president remained popular, Johnson refused. "You know that Nixon is following my policies more closely than Humphrey," he stated.

Running against an embattled Democratic administration, Nixon continued to tone down his tough rhetoric and emphasize instead his desire to "Bring Us Together." He hammered away at the Democrats for "cities enveloped in smoke and flame" and for "Americans dying on distant battlefields." His subdued populist message appealed to the angry white middle class but avoided the direct racial appeals of third-party candidate Governor George Wallace of Alabama. Populism came naturally to Nixon, who always viewed himself as an outsider—a feeling that was reinforced when he was working at the Office of Price Administration in the early years of the war. While in the Pacific, his time as the operator of Nick's Snack Shack helped him realize that he could relate to men from many different backgrounds and regions. Now Nixon promised to listen to "the voice of the great majority of Americans, the forgotten Americans, the nonshouters, the nondemonstrators." He called for "a new beginning," even as he remained intentionally vague and noncommittal about his plans for addressing the nation's problems.

Ironically, given his earlier critique of Johnson's Vietnam policy, Nixon now spoke more often of peace than war. Peace, he said, "requires strength of will, strength of arms, and strength of purpose." While he continued to insist on the necessity of maintaining America's military strength and international prestige, he did signal a willingness to engage in conversation with both the Soviet Union and China to reduce tensions.

Former Johnson White House press secretary George Reedy picked up on Nixon's mixed messaging. In a memo to Humphrey, Reedy pointed out that Nixon was "presenting himself to the voters as a man who will bring about change—but he is keeping the nature of that change a deep, dark secret." He was telling audiences that he would never "pull out of Vietnam" while also promising to get the war "over with in a hurry."

It would, however, become more and more difficult to continue waffling on Vietnam. On September 30 Humphrey, whose campaign was floundering, decided to make a dramatic break with LBJ, announcing his support for a unilateral bombing halt. "I believe it could lead to success in the negotiations and thereby shorten the war," he said. Nixon immediately called the White House to find out if Humphrey was announcing a new administration policy or simply speaking for himself. Johnson reassured him that Humphrey was not speaking for him. "I have not read his speech," the president said. "It has not been discussed with me."

By early October, the polls gave Nixon a comfortable lead, and there seemed little that could derail his drive to the presidency. But on October 16, Johnson used a conference call to inform the three major candidates—Nixon, Humphrey, and Wallace—of dramatic new developments in the Paris Peace Talks between the United States and North Vietnam, which had commenced in May. The Soviets, fearing a Nixon presidency, had pressured North Vietnam to agree to all the conditions the administration had established to begin the talks. South Vietnamese president Nguyen Van Thieu, an army general who'd headed the country since 1965, "fully agreed" with the arrangement. If the details could be worked out, Johnson would announce a bombing halt on October 31 and commence talks on November 4—just one day before the election. Nixon seemed to take the news in stride, even though the prospect of peace could strengthen Humphrey's chance of winning. "I've made it very clear that I will make no statement that would undercut the negotiations," he told LBJ, concluding that he hoped "this thing works out."

Nixon was not surprised by the news—he had spies in the White House warning him that something was brewing. Bryce Harlow, a former Eisenhower staff member who was now a Nixon advisor, bragged that he had "a double agent working in the White House." Harlow claimed that he "knew about every meeting they held. I knew who attended the meetings. I knew what their next move was going to be." And he kept Nixon informed of every detail. Nixon also had a direct line to Harvard professor Henry Kissinger, a member of Johnson's negotiating team who was playing both sides of the fence to secure a high-level White House job regardless of who won. He, like Harlow, had sent word to Nixon that "something big was afoot."

On October 25 Nixon released a statement supporting the peace talks, but not before pointing out that some people believed the "spurt of activity is a cynical, last-minute attempt by President Johnson to salvage the candidacy of Mr. Humphrey." Having introduced the criticism, Nixon then claimed disingenuously, "This I do not believe." He promised to "facilitate the president's pursuit of an agreement that will save American lives and lay the foundation for stability and a just peace in Vietnam and throughout Southeast Asia."

As negotiations moved forward, Nixon's public statements increasingly contradicted his private thoughts—and covert actions. On the afternoon of October 31 Johnson called Nixon to inform him that he was announcing a bombing halt. "I could feel my anger and frustration welling up," Nixon recalled years later. "Johnson was making the one move that I thought could determine the outcome of the election. Had I done all this work and come all this way only to be undermined by the powers of an incumbent who had decided against seeking reelection?"

Publicly, Nixon supported the president's initiative. That same night, at a rally in New York City's new Madison Square Garden, the former vice president said that neither he nor his running mate "will destroy the chance of peace. We want peace." But Nixon had no intention of allowing LBJ's last-minute maneuvers to cost him the cherished presidential prize for a second time. He had convinced himself that his loss in 1960 stemmed from Democratic dirty tricks in key electoral states, especially Texas and Illinois. (While there were irregularities, especially in Texas, it is unlikely that they changed the outcome of the election.) The Kennedys had stolen one election from him; he was not going to allow that to happen again. He had already seen his once formidable lead shrink, as many Democrats returned to the fold following Humphrey's call for a unilateral bombing halt. Nixon knew full well that the announcement of a possible peace deal could doom his candidacy.

Thus began one of the most sordid affairs in the history of American politics. "To him, it was a very personal thing," Nixon aide Tom Huston recalled. Nixon conspired with a prominent Republican lobbyist named Anna Chennault—the China-born widow of a famous American World War II general—and South Vietnam's ambassador to the United States, Bui Diem, to convince President Thieu to refuse to participate in the talks. They promised Thieu that South Vietnam would get a better deal if they waited for a Nixon administration.

But the game was being played by both sides. Although Nixon's team thought it was operating in secret, Johnson had been tipped off to the possible plot and ordered the FBI to wiretap Chennault's and Diem's phones. In one call, they overheard Chennault telling the ambassador that "she had received a message from her boss" that the ambassador was to "hold on, we are gonna win."

Obviously, Johnson was furious over Nixon's subterfuge. He shared what he had learned with his old friend Republican senator Everett Dirksen of Illinois. "This is treason," Johnson said. "I know," the longtime Senate minority leader agreed. Dirksen then contacted Nixon. Several days later, on November 3, Nixon called Johnson to swear that reports that he had tried to sidetrack the discussions were untrue. "My God," he insisted, "I would never do anything to encourage . . . Saigon not to come to the table. . . . We've got to get them to Paris, or you can't have a peace."

Johnson seemed somewhat appeased, especially since he lacked concrete proof of Nixon's personal involvement. According to some reports, though, after hanging up, Nixon collapsed with laughter.

At the time, Johnson worried that treason was too serious a charge to level against a presidential candidate in the final days of the campaign, especially without tangible evidence tying Nixon directly to the sabotage. That evidence wouldn't emerge until much later. In 1997, three years after his death at the age of eighty-one, Anna Chennault acknowledged that Nixon and his campaign chairman, John Mitchell, knew everything. "I was constantly in touch with Mitchell and Nixon," she said. Years later, historians would discover the smoking gun in Nixon aide H. R. Haldeman's notes from the 1968 campaign. They showed Nixon personally orchestrating the effort to sabotage the peace effort by engaging in illegal negotiations with a foreign country. "Keep Anna Chennault working on SVN," Nixon ordered Haldeman. Elsewhere in his notes, Haldeman quoted Nixon asking, "Any other way to monkey wrench it? Anything RN can do?"

Unsure how to proceed, Johnson decided to share the information with Humphrey and his campaign so that they could handle it themselves. The Democratic candidate then made a fateful mistake: He chose not to drop the political bombshell that most likely would have won him the election. The vice president feared that the revelations would only further divide an already riven nation. Besides, the move could backfire by forcing the administration to disclose how it uncovered the secret negotiations. As Nixon hoped, Thieu refused to participate in the talks, and the possibility of peace quickly evaporated. Biographer John A. Farrell best summarized Nixon's role in the affair: "Given the lives and human suffering at stake and the internal discord that was ripping the United States apart, it is hard not to conclude that, of all Richard Nixon's actions in a lifetime of politics, this was the most reprehensible."

The weekend before the election, Humphrey pulled even with Nixon in many polls. But on Election Day, Nixon won by a razor-thin majority in the popular vote, receiving 31,770,222 votes to Humphrey's 31,267,744. Less than seven-tenths of 1 percent separated the two candidates. Nixon took only 43 percent of the popular vote, the smallest share of a winning candidate since Woodrow Wilson in 1912. He scored a more decisive triumph in the electoral college, amassing 301 votes to Humphrey's 191. George Wallace carried five states, receiving 9.9 electoral votes and 13.5 percent of the popular vote—the best showing for a third-party candidate in forty-four years.

These narrow results demonstrated just how divided the nation had become as it grappled with the complicated legacy of World War II.

By 1968, all seven presidents who had served in World War II had entered the political arena. JFK was dead, but his mystique lingered. Eisenhower, though he no longer held public office, continued to exercise considerable influence on foreign policy decisions. Ford and Nixon, part of the first generation to join politics shortly after the war ended, were now reaching their peaks. Reagan and Bush, who didn't enter politics until the 1960s, would soon confront a new set of issues that challenged many of the assumptions that the first generation had adopted from the war.

An important generational difference separated the two groups. Eisenhower, Kennedy, Nixon, and Johnson came of age in the afterglow of victory, when the United States emerged as a world superpower. Living in the oppressive shadow of the lessons of Munich and the domino theory, they were determined to avoid any hint of appeasement that might hasten the spread of Communism around the globe. But as the Vietnam War dragged on with no victory in sight, a younger generation with no memory of Munich started to articulate an alternative worldview that stressed the limits of American power and challenged the belief in a monolithic international Communist conspiracy.

The turbulent decade of the 1960s also called into question the previous generation's unbridled faith in the healing power of economic growth that had emerged from World War II. While Ike and Nixon remained committed to limited federal spending and balanced budgets, Kennedy (slowly) and Johnson (enthusiastically) embraced the Keynesian faith in growth, and convinced themselves that prosperity would mute ideological differences and lessen social unrest. But Johnson's decision to escalate the war without raising taxes sparked an inflationary period that would spiral into a new phenomenon called stagflation: the combination of a recession and inflation for which Keynesian economics offered few answers. In the short run, the end of the age of Keynes signaled a return to the fiscal conservatism of the Eisenhower years, although Nixon's economic philosophy would prove malleable and often unpredictable.

The generation of presidents who came to power in the 1960s—Bush and Reagan—and those who returned—Nixon—confronted a far more complex world. The Sino-Soviet split undermined the myth of a monolithic Communist bloc, just as a cohort of young Americans began questioning the dubious assumption that the United States had a mission to battle international Communism. Nixon would once again try to straddle the line, accounting for this ideological shift while also expanding America's involvement in the war. In the end, however, he would be undone by his private demons. Meanwhile, although he did not enter politics until 1966, Reagan was closer in age to the first generation of World War II veterans, and despite all the upheaval of the 1960s, he clung to many of the original assumptions that emerged after the war. But Bush—Reagan's vice president for eight years—was a very different leader. At home, he defied the Reagan wing of his party and fought for balanced budgets, while abroad he struggled to maintain American credibility at the end of the Cold War, developing an approach to the world that sought to balance the lessons of Munich with those of Vietnam.

Perhaps the defining feature of the 1960s—and the one that would shape American politics for decades to come—was backlash. World War II had united the nation in a common cause against Fascism. Now social unrest at home and a bumbling war abroad divided Americans into rival groups.

On one side of the divide were those who challenged the status quo, demanding new rights while questioning old verities. They would spearhead a cultural revolution that continued to intensify in the years ahead. Over time, the social movements of the 1960s expanded the range of individual choices people had about the way they lived their lives. The civil rights movement not only advanced the cause of African Americans, but it also inspired other empowerment movements, especially for women and members of the LGBTQ community, that would transform the entire cultural and political landscape.

Meanwhile, these dramatic changes angered traditionalists who believed that as countercultural values became normalized, respect for institutions and godly authority eroded. Many white, middle-class Americans living in the sprawling suburbs were appalled that students had turned college campuses into seedbeds of radical thought and that Black people were rioting in the streets. Republicans, eager to win over disaffected Democrats, especially in the South, tapped into the frustrations of this group by articulating a language of cultural populism, blaming liberal elites and big government for the problems plaguing society. While campaigning for Republican candidates in 1966, Nixon claimed that the Democratic Party had "become the party of the backlash." He went on to say, "I don't know one Republican candidate who is riding the backlash." A White House aide scoffed at Nixon's statement, noting that the former vice president "should ask Pat Brown to name one."

Indeed, as the seventies dawned, it grew increasingly apparent that the backlash came less from the counterculture than from the traditionalists, and that a major conservative revival was starting to unfold. It would be Nixon, Ford, and Reagan who appealed to the nostalgia of these people, advocating a return to the time immediately after World War II, when America stood strong in the world and their social status in society remained unchallenged. They would lead a successful counterrevolution, but their victory would produce its own complicated legacy.

CHAPTER 11

"The Great Silent Majority"

NOVEMBER 3, 1969
9:30 P.M.
OVAL OFFICE

President Richard M. Nixon sat at his Oval Office desk, staring grimly into the bright lights from the cameras of the three major television networks. More than seventy million Americans had tuned in to hear what he would say about the Vietnam War and domestic dissent. When he took the oath of office the previous January, Nixon had inherited 536,000 American troops in Vietnam. More than 30,000 men had already been killed in the war, nearly half of those in just the previous year. The war had destroyed his predecessor's presidency, and Nixon was determined not to suffer the same fate. "I'm not going to end up like LBJ, holed up in the White House, afraid to show my face in the street," Nixon told an aide. "I'm going to stop that war. Fast."

Yet for all his talk of peace with honor and promises to end the protracted conflict quickly, Nixon still found himself trapped in the same predicament as LBJ. By 1969, references to the domino theory seemed outdated, replaced by an obsession with "American credibility." The threat now seemed far greater than before—not just one defeat sweeping across the Southeast Asian continent but also the threat of losing allies and emboldening enemies around the globe, especially in Africa and Latin America. National Security Advisor Henry Kissinger voiced this fear when he warned that "displays of American impotence in one part of the world . . . would inevitably erode our credibility in other parts of the world." He, along with Nixon, claimed that while it had been a mistake to Americanize the war, now that US prestige was on the line, it was even more essential to win. "For nearly a generation, the security and progress of free peoples had depended on confidence in America," Kissinger wrote in his memoirs. "We could not simply walk away from an enterprise involving two administrations, five allied countries, and thirty-one thousand dead as if we were switching a television channel."

But the challenge was the same no matter the justification: Nixon was fighting one war on two fronts. He needed to reassure Hanoi of his determination to win at all costs while simultaneously defusing the antiwar movement at home by appearing to wind down the conflict. Kissinger reinforced this belief, advising the president: "We must convince the American people that we are eager to settle the war, and Hanoi that we are not so anxious that it can afford to outwait us."

Nixon believed that he could win in Vietnam by escalating bombing throughout Southeast Asia—a conclusion influenced at least partially by his time in the Pacific, when he witnessed how Japan's bombs could undermine American troop morale. The United States was mired in Vietnam not because of faulty assumptions or an exaggerated fear of Communism, he argued, but because Lyndon Johnson had simply not dropped enough bombs. It was now time for decisive military action. Nixon explained his approach as "the Madman Theory." "I want the North Vietnamese to believe I've reached the point where I might do *anything* to stop the war," he confided. Once again Kissinger echoed the president, telling his staff, "I refuse to believe that a fourth-rate power like North Vietnam doesn't have a breaking point."

Nixon implemented his new policy within weeks of entering the White House, ordering the air force to start bombing the Communist camps and supply lines in neutral Cambodia as part of Operation Menu. Over four months, US pilots flew 3,875 sorties and dropped 108,823 tons of bombs. At the same time, fearing the backlash that would ensue if the public learned that he had expanded the war, Nixon ordered the air force to tamper with the navigational system on the planes to obscure the fact that they were bombing in Cambodia. Additionally, in the event that the initial round of bombing did not force the North to the conference table, Nixon instructed NSC staffers to begin working on Operation Duck Hook, which would involve a massive escalation of the conflict, including the use of tactical nuclear weapons; blocking the ports of Hanoi and Haiphong; bombing power stations, bridges, and railways; and destroying the levee system in the Red River that irrigated the rice fields that fed the nation.

While dramatically expanding the bombing campaign, Nixon announced a policy of Vietnamization, believing that by reducing the number of US combat troops, he could cut the casualties that fueled home front protest. In June the White House announced the withdrawal of twenty-five thousand troops in the first large-scale reduction of troop strength. "In the previous administration, we Americanized the war in Vietnam," the president said. "In this administration, we are Vietnamizing the search for peace."

Nixon's strategy also involved convincing the Soviet Union to use its influence to force Hanoi to end the war. Despite his deviousness in waging war, Nixon did forge a new relationship between the United States and the rest of the world. He was steeped in the lessons of Munich, yet he accepted the new reality that the United States was no longer the preeminent nuclear or economic power that it had been since the end of World War II. The Soviets had gained nuclear parity, Europe had recovered from the devastation of the war, and Asia was emerging as a global economic player. Since each superpower had the capacity to destroy the other, both nations by then shared an interest in self-preservation. Nixon called this strategy of lessening tensions with the Soviet Union détente, proclaiming in his inaugural address that "we are entering an era of negotiation." At the same time, his administration skillfully manipulated growing Sino-Soviet tensions to achieve rapprochement with China.

In his first press conference, Nixon announced that America's goal was to diminish the potential of a costly arms race by committing to "sufficiency, not superiority." Several months later, in October 1969, the

United States agreed to participate in arms control talks in Helsinki, Finland, and in Vienna. The negotiations, which dragged on for two years, resulted in a "conceptual breakthrough" that would culminate in two groundbreaking treaties: the Strategic Arms Limitation Talks (SALT) and the Anti-Ballistic Missile Treaty (ABM). Although the treaties covered only a small fraction of missiles, they nonetheless laid the foundation for future efforts at reconciliation between the two nations.

The president also laid out a new strategy—the so-called Nixon Doctrine—to prevent the United States from being sucked into another debilitating foreign conflict. He confirmed that the United States would uphold protecting nations considered essential to American security that were threatened by another nuclear power. But "in cases involving other types of aggression"—such as Vietnam—the United States would provide military and economic assistance, but it would not send troops into combat. Those nations would be responsible for their own defense. In some ways, Nixon's approach hearkened back to the Eisenhower and Kennedy policy of sending advisors but refusing to commit ground troops to Vietnam.

Although Nixon showed remarkable skill in reorienting America's approach to the world, he and Kissinger remained stubbornly committed to achieving an elusive victory in Vietnam. Yet nothing they tried worked. The bombings not only failed to intimidate the North Vietnamese, but also they did nothing to improve the morale or fighting ability of the South Vietnamese army (ARVN). Furthermore, while Moscow had some influence over Hanoi, it ultimately could not control its ally. The biggest obstacle was that the North Vietnamese remained committed to one simple goal: a united Vietnam under Communist control.

More troubling for Nixon, by the fall of 1969, the dormant peace movement was showing new signs of life. By September, 57 percent opposed and only 35 percent supported the president's policies. On October 15, the Vietnam Moratorium Committee, formed by young activists from Democratic senator Eugene McCarthy's 1968 presidential campaign, attracted more than twenty-four million protestors in more than two hundred cities who demanded an end to the Vietnam War. The largest gathering took place in Boston, where one hundred thousand protestors packed the Common. In Washington, more than twenty thousand held candles as they marched past the White House. The protest was so widespread that when a Kissinger aide stepped out of the southwest gate to light a cigarette, he spotted his own wife and three daughters walking past.

Media reports of the moratorium emphasized the peaceful and middle-class nature of the telegenic rallies and prayer vigils. "Historic in its scope," pronounced Walter Cronkite on the *CBS Evening News*. "Never before have so many demonstrated their hope for peace." *Life* magazine described the moratorium as "the largest expression of public dissent ever seen in this country," and *Time* magazine wrote that the protest was "an unmistakable sign to Richard Nixon that he must do more to end the war and faster." Nixon got the message. "In style and content, it was everything the organizers could have hoped for," White House counselor Daniel Patrick Moynihan wrote the president. "The young white middle-class crowds were sweet-tempered and considerate, at times even radiant. . . . I believe the administration has been damaged. . . . If we are going to get through this period, we are going to have to act a lot smarter than we have done lately."

With a second moratorium scheduled for November 15, Nixon needed to regain control of the narrative, and he believed the best way to accomplish that was with a presidential address. Later, he recalled shuttling back and forth between the White House and Camp David, working "12 to 14 hours a day" drafting a speech that he considered the most important of his career. He often quoted from a conversation he had had with British prime minister Winston Churchill's son and biographer, Randolph: "My father spends the best hours of his life writing out his extemporaneous speeches." Indeed, Nixon spent whole days alone scribbling on yellow legal pads, working through a dozen drafts, keeping secret what he planned to say from even his closest advisors. Finally, at eight in the morning on November 1, he telephoned an aide to say, "The baby's just been born." Nixon remained secluded for another day memorizing the speech.

On the night of November 3, nine months after his inauguration—when he had promised to "bring us together"—Nixon gave one of the most willfully polarizing speeches ever delivered by a US president. He started off with a brief history of America's involvement in the conflict before proclaiming that it had been "wrong" for LBJ to Americanize the war—conveniently ignoring that he had repeatedly criticized the administration for not fighting the war aggressively enough. But now that American credibility was on the line, the nation could not simply withdraw. A "precipitate withdrawal" would be a "disaster," he told the TV audience, leading almost inevitably to a "bloody reign of terror" in South Vietnam and producing "the first defeat in our nation's history." He promised to remove American troops at an undisclosed time—but not now. "It is not the easy way," he added, but "it is the right way. It is a plan which will end the war and serve the cause of peace."

Then, as his speech drew to a close, Nixon acknowledged that it was not "fashionable to speak of patriotism or national destiny these days," before proceeding to do just that. "The survival of peace and freedom will be determined by whether the American people have the moral stamina and the courage to meet the challenge of free world leadership. Let historians not record that when America was the most powerful nation in the world, we passed on the other side of the road and allowed the last hopes for peace and freedom of millions of people to be suffocated by the forces of totalitarianism." He then made a personal appeal to "the great silent majority" to fall in line and support his approach. "Let us be united for peace. Let us also be united against defeat. Because let us understand: North Vietnam cannot defeat or humiliate the United States. Only Americans can do that."

As the networks began removing their equipment, Nixon told an aide to produce one hundred letters from Republican leaders complaining about the media coverage of the speech—even before the editorials had been written. Dining alone afterward in the Lincoln Sitting Room, Nixon refused to watch the TV. His family did, however, and they were "livid," Nixon recalled. The news commentators were not impressed. ABC anchor Frank Reynolds told viewers that Nixon's speech communicated "no new initiative, no new proposal, no announcement of any new troop withdrawals." Reynolds's assessment echoed the general sentiment of his peers. After the negative coverage, Tricia entered the room and said to her father, "They talked as if they had been listening to a different speech than the one you made."

Reynolds and the other pundits did, in fact, miss the significance of Nixon's speech. With his urgent plea to "the silent majority," the president managed to tap into deep cultural and class resentments that shaped attitudes toward the Vietnam War and antiwar protestors. Americans, by a 55–31 majority, called themselves "doves," and nearly 80 percent said they were "fed up and tired of the war." Yet as frustrated as Americans were with the war, they disliked protestors even more. Polls showed that more than half of all those who favored immediate and total withdrawal from Vietnam had negative feelings toward those who *publicly* advocated this same position. Not only did most Americans resent the organized peace movement's open displays of dissent, but they also viewed the war itself differently. Antiwar protestors tended to oppose the war for moral reasons, condemning it as an indictment of the entire political system. Most Americans, however, saw the war more narrowly as a foreign policy mistake and a waste of valuable resources.

The polarizing debate over Vietnam exposed the fault lines in American society that had been smothered by the celebration of consensus forged during World War II. That consensus had always been fragile, held together by a shared fear of repeating the mistakes of the 1930s and a naïve optimism about the power of economic growth. Nixon's genius was in his ability to expose those fault lines and then use them for his own political advantage. By appealing directly to white resentment, Nixon forged one of the foundations of the modern Republican Party. Overnight, this stalwart member of the Republican establishment managed to transform himself into an angry populist channeling the frustrations of the struggling white middle class. "My source of strength," he once observed, "was more Main Street than Wall Street." He hoped to reach out to the two-thirds of the country he called the "constituency of uneducated people." They were the angry voters who had flirted with George Wallace's antiestablishment populism in 1968. "These are my people," Nixon said. "We speak the same language."

Since the days of the New Deal, Democrats had been the ones to use the language of economic populism to cement the loyalties of the working class, charging that an economic elite was out of touch with the concerns of average voters. Ironically, World War II, by providing unprecedented economic opportunities to the white middle class, eroded that sense of class solidarity and allowed a Republican president to articulate a new lexicon of populism, arguing that a cultural elite associated with the Democratic Party had lost touch with the mainstream values of average Americans.

The day after his "silent majority" speech, Nixon herded reporters into the Oval Office to view the mounds of positive telegrams that numbered, he said, in the "high thousands." In reality, the White House had orchestrated the massive letter-writing campaign, largely from Republican officials around the country. Despite the smoke and mirrors, the public did, in fact, rally behind Nixon's message. A Gallup telephone survey showed that 77 percent of those who had watched the speech supported Nixon's policies, and his approval rating shot up from 52 percent to 68 percent. Another poll showed that nearly 75 percent of the public considered themselves part of the silent majority.

Nixon was not yet finished winning over that newly identified contingent. Patrick Buchanan, the president's pugilistic speechwriter, had another idea for keeping the momentum on their side: Attack the news media. "Let Agnew go after these guys!" he told Nixon. Vice President Spiro Agnew had been largely marginalized in the White House thus far, but now Nixon viewed him as a powerful messenger for his appeals to the silent majority. On November 13 in Iowa, Agnew dismissed the media machine as an "unelected elite" that manipulated reality. "A small group of men, numbering perhaps no more than a dozen anchormen, commentators, and executive producers, settle upon the film and commentary that is to reach the public," he charged. "They decide what forty or fifty million Americans will learn of the day's events in the nation and in the world."

In the short run, Nixon and Agnew's offensive worked. It took the steam out of the planned November 15 moratorium. Although half a million people attended the demonstration, the media, cowed by Nixon's threats to pull their broadcast licenses, devoted little attention to the events, instead highlighting the small group of protestors who broke windows and provoked riots. "[W]e've got those liberal bastards on the run now," Nixon gloated. "We're going to keep them on the run."

━━━━━━

Having gained a tactical victory at home, Nixon was ready to send another message to the North Vietnamese. With the war going badly and peace talks stalled, he started to envision making a "bold move" in Cambodia, which US military officials believed Hanoi was using as a staging ground for attacks on South Vietnam. Nixon could not shed his World War II mindset that the United States could bludgeon its enemy into submission. And by "bold," Nixon meant a decisive military strike that would prove to the American people and the world that the United States was winning in South Vietnam. He instructed Kissinger in no uncertain terms: "They have got to go in there, and I mean really go in. I want the gunships, I want the helicopter ships. I want everything that can fly to go in there and crack the hell out of them. There is no limitation on mileage, and there is no limitation on budget. Is that clear?" Kissinger faithfully relayed the president's message to his assistant General Alexander Haig: "He wants a massive bombing campaign in Cambodia. . . . Anything that flies or anything that moves."

As final preparations began, Nixon began to drink heavily. He spent most of the day in his darkened office with a bottle of booze and a yellow legal pad, writing another television address. In phone calls to Kissinger, his speech sounded slurred. He did not sleep for days. In the days leading up to the invasion, Kissinger recalled, "Richard Nixon was virtually alone, sitting in a darkened room in the Executive Office Building, the stereo softly playing neoclassical music—reflecting, resenting, collecting his thoughts and his anger."

On April 30, 1970, American and South Vietnamese forces crossed the international border and attacked Communist sanctuaries in Cambodia. That evening, a visibly nervous president explained his decision to a war-weary public. Nixon, who insisted on giving his speech from the White House Map Room, where FDR had conducted World War II, stressed that American aims were limited in scope and duration, and that the United States had no intention of occupying Cambodia. He nevertheless spoke in apocalyptic terms. "My fellow Americans," he said, expanding on the rhetoric of his silent majority speech, "we live in an age of anarchy, both abroad and at home. We see mindless attacks on all the great institutions which had been created by free civilizations in the last five hundred years. Even here in the United States, great universities are being systematically destroyed." He then built to his conclusion, with a warning for the American people: "If, when the chips are down, the world's most powerful nation, the United States of America, acts like a pitiful, helpless giant, the forces of totalitarianism and anarchy will threaten free nations and free institutions throughout the world." Secretary of State William P. Rogers, watching the speech on the seventh floor of the State Department headquarters, turned off the television, muttering, "The kids are going to retch."

Unsurprisingly, the raids turned out to be a strategic failure. The North Vietnamese knew in advance of the assault and moved their forces farther into the heartland of Cambodia—a development that so destabilized the government there that it produced the conditions that would ultimately lead to the Khmer Rouge genocide in the mid- to late 1970s.

The invasion also re-inflamed antiwar sentiment and eroded support for Nixon's policy in the Senate. Shortly after the bombing, South Dakota senator George McGovern told his colleagues, "This chamber reeks of blood." In a dramatic challenge to presidential authority in wartime, the Senate passed—but the House rejected—an amendment to cut off all funds for the Cambodian operation after June 30. The Senate also repealed the 1964 Tonkin Gulf Resolution, which LBJ and then Nixon had used to justify their right to wage war without congressional approval.

Just as Secretary of State Rogers had predicted, college campuses erupted in marches and protests. On May 4, at Kent State University in Ohio, panicked National Guardsmen fired into a crowd of student protestors, killing four and wounding nine. A week later at Jackson State College in Mississippi, two Black students were killed and eleven wounded when police fired indiscriminately into a dormitory. Student protests reached a fever pitch in the weeks that followed. At least 440 colleges experienced strikes or closures, with some even shutting down for the remainder of the academic year because it was no longer possible to conduct classes. "The overflow of emotion seemed barely containable," observed *The Washington Post*. "The nation was witnessing what amounted to a virtual general and uncoordinated strike by its college youth." Nixon did not aid his cause when on May 1, while walking through the Pentagon, he criticized the protestors as "bums blowing up the campuses."

In public, Nixon made a deliberate effort to appear nonchalant about the growing signs of discontent with his policies. Whenever he had doubts, he watched the movie *Patton*, released early in 1970, drawing inspiration from the controversial general who led his troops into the bloodiest battles of World War II. Behind the confident facade, however, Nixon was becoming increasingly isolated and embattled, paranoid that his enemies in the Congress, the press, and the antiwar movement were conspiring to destroy him. "Within the iron gates of the White House, quite unknowingly, a siege mentality was setting in," a Nixon aide recalled. "It was now 'us' against 'them.' Gradually, as we drew the circle closer around us, the ranks of 'them' began to swell." *Shell-shocked* was the word Kissinger used to describe the psychological state of the administration after Cambodia.

Yet the overall public response to the protests highlighted the long-term effectiveness of Nixon's silent majority appeal. A Gallup poll found that 50 percent of Americans held the protestors responsible for the Kent State shootings, while only 11 percent blamed the National Guardsmen. One local resident even told the town newspaper that the guardsmen "should have fired sooner and longer." On May 8 a wave of construction workers charged into an antiwar demonstration in downtown Manhattan, shouting "All the way, U-S-A!" and "Love it or leave it!" Along the way, they used metal pipes covered with the American flag to bludgeon protestors and several bystanders. Rather than condemning the violence, Nixon relished the cultural divide he had helped inflame and even hosted the construction workers at the White House.

The same day as the Manhattan clash, Nixon called a White House press conference at the unusually late hour of ten o'clock. Afterward, he returned to the family quarters, feeling "agitated and uneasy." He made fifty phone calls over the next few hours. A few minutes before four, still unable to sleep, Nixon informed his valet that he wanted to go to the

Washington Monument, where a group of protestors had gathered. Accompanied by a few nervous Secret Service agents and his valet, Nixon left the White House and was motored instead to the Lincoln Memorial, just southwest of the White House, on the banks of the Potomac River, to speak directly to the crowd. (He was also trailed by military staffers carrying the nuclear "football.") Nixon, who was always uncomfortable in personal interactions, tried making small talk, asking the students where they were from and discussing college football. However awkward, the meeting offered a glimpse into the emerging generational divide in America.

According to a long memorandum he dictated after returning to the White House, Nixon said that he shared with the students how his view of the world—including his Vietnam policy—was shaped by his experiences during World War II. "I know that probably most of you think I'm an SOB, but I want you to know that I understand just how you feel," he remembered saying. "I recall that when I was just a little older than you, right out of law school and ready to get married, how excited I was when Chamberlain came home from Munich and made his famous statement about peace in our time. I had heard it on the radio. I had so little in those days that the prospect of going into the service was almost unbearable, and I felt that the United States staying out of any kind of conflict was worth paying any price whatever." As a Quaker and a pacifist, he thought "that Chamberlain was the greatest man alive, and when I read Churchill's all-out criticism of Chamberlain, I thought Churchill was a madman." But events proved him wrong. "I think now that Chamberlain was a good man, but that Churchill was a wiser man and that we in the world are better off than we would be because Churchill had not only the wisdom but the courage to carry out the policies that he believed were right even though there was a time when both in England and all over the world he was extremely unpopular because of his 'anti-peace' stand."

Nixon's history lesson was lost on the fervent young protestors. After he left, they belittled his remarks, and the press eagerly highlighted their criticism. "Nothing he was saying was coherent," recalled one of the students. But they missed the point. What Nixon believed may not have seemed relevant to their lives, but it embodied a very coherent—if outdated—worldview, and one that was shared by all the men who were in uniform during World War II and went on to become president. They never questioned the beneficence of American values or doubted the power of its military. They viewed their motives—fighting for freedom and democracy—as noble. For them, Vietnam, like Korea, was another testing ground for their convictions.

Meanwhile, the youth gathered at the Memorial that day had been nurtured on a very different generational experience. They had no memories of Hitler and lacked the pervasive fear of Communism that branded Nixon's generation. In this war, America stood as the aggressor, a global superpower using brute force to impose its values on a distant country engaged in a civil war. These young people could not articulate an alternative paradigm to counter the lessons of Munich; at this point, they simply wanted the war to end. Underscoring their determination, one student told the president, "I hope you realize that we are willing to die for what we believe in." Nixon responded adroitly, "Many of us when we were your age were also willing to die for what we believe in. The point is, we are trying to build a world in which you will not have to die for what you believe in."

While trying to appease his young critics, Nixon also had to keep a watchful eye on his right flank, as conservatives continued pressuring him to wage war more aggressively. One of those conservatives was California governor Ronald Reagan. Several weeks after the moratorium, Reagan traveled to Eisenhower College in Seneca Falls, New York, to offer his views on the war. He expressed support for the president's Vietnam policy, praising his efforts to win and condemning protestors for their shallow understanding of the situation. "Those entrusted with the awesome responsibility of the leadership of our nation deserve not only our support," Reagan declared, "but our rejection of those in our midst who would arrogantly kibitz in a game where they haven't even seen the cards with which the game is played."

Unlike Nixon, who viewed the peace movement through the lens of politics and occasionally expressed sympathy for the protestors, the governor viewed the antiwar movement through the prism of morality. Protests against the war were just one sign of a much broader assault on

America's moral standards. Those who participated, Reagan argued, were dupes of the Communists in Hanoi, "less concerned with peace than they are with the welfare of the enemy." Everywhere he looked, Reagan believed he saw evidence of American moral decline reminiscent of the factors that led to the fall of ancient Rome. In his view, the Roman Empire crumbled because of "a welfare system not unlike our own." As its citizens became more affluent, young men started avoiding military service, "finding excuses to remain in the soft and sordid life of the city." Men "took to using cosmetics and wearing feminine-like hairdos and garments," he warned, making it difficult "to tell the sexes apart." Crime was so rampant it "became unsafe to walk in the countryside or the city streets. Rioting was commonplace, and sometimes whole sections of towns and cities were burned." If such signs were not recognized and averted, Reagan cautioned, America would share the same fate as Rome.

Despite his words of support for the president, Reagan was already positioning himself to win the nomination in 1972 if Nixon were to falter. According to a newspaper report, Reagan's staff circulated a memorandum calling for a plan to "take the national leadership in opposing Nixon." The goal was to "keep pressure on President Nixon from the right in the hope disaster in Vietnam and increasing violence at home will cause the Republican National Convention in 1972 to dump the president and turn to Reagan." The governor denied knowing anything about the memo, but rumors of it served as a reminder to Nixon that he needed to keep a close eye on the right wing of his party.

Meanwhile, the president received support from an unlikely ally: Lyndon Johnson. The night after Nixon announced the invasion of Cambodia, Johnson delivered his first speech since leaving office, at a Democratic fundraiser in Chicago. In the speech, LBJ placed the blame for the violence not on US intervention but on Hanoi. "This nation can only have one president at a time," he stated, before urging all Americans to support "our president."

Nixon had been especially solicitous of LBJ since assuming the presidency, fearing that his predecessor might someday release information implicating him in the effort to undermine peace talks in 1968. In fact, Nixon worried so much about Johnson that he created a position especially for him: special assistant to the president for liaison with former presidents. Johnson took full advantage of the new role, pestering the White House for briefings and travel arrangements. He called so often for housing in Washington that the White House purchased a home next to Blair House, the president's official guest residence, that would be reserved just for former presidents. Every Friday, Nixon dispatched a plane to LBJ's ranch carrying classified national security briefing papers. Cabinet members also often called the former president with updates. Even Henry Kissinger occasionally visited in person to discuss the progress of the peace talks.

Their relationship also had an emotional element to it. The previous September, Nixon had thrown a lavish sixty-first birthday party for his predecessor, flying him to his elegant fourteen-room mansion, situated on twenty-eight acres overlooking the Pacific in San Clemente, California. After a briefing by top administration aides on domestic and foreign policy issues, they boarded Air Force One and made a brief stop in Sacramento to pick up Governor Reagan, before reaching their destination in Redwood National Park near Crescent City, California. Lady Bird had dedicated the park as part of her conservation efforts, and Nixon signed a proclamation naming a three-hundred-acre grove of redwoods in her honor. LBJ gave a short speech thanking his successor. "My father told me one time, when I was a little boy," Johnson told Nixon, "that I'd never know what it meant to be a father until I was a father. And one never knows what it is to be a president until you are a president." With empathy, he continued: "We are very proud to stand behind you and to support you in your earnest quest for peace in the world and for prosperity at home. No man occupied the place that you occupy who didn't want to do the best he could. Some have succeeded, and some have had less success. But of this you can be sure: If all of your days are as successful as today in bringing happiness to your predecessor, you will have a most successful presidency."

Dwight Eisenhower died ten weeks into Nixon's presidency at the age of seventy-eight. Nixon, who was meeting with aides in the Oval Office when he learned the news shortly after noon on March 28, stared out the window and "started to cry, just standing there," observed an aide. The two men had developed a closer personal relationship since Ike's only grandson, David, had married Nixon's twenty-year-old daughter Julie in December 1968. Feeling ill, the president headed to Camp David, where he spent hours reminiscing about Ike's unparalleled leadership skills. What set Ike apart, Nixon believed, was his personality. "Everybody loves Ike," Nixon said. He would highlight that point in his eulogy, praising Ike as "one of the giants of our time," a man who was "loved by more people in more parts of the world than any president America has ever had."

Ironically, Nixon himself was not an easy man to love. Stephen Ambrose, who wrote biographies of both men, observed that Eisenhower's approach "was to calm a crisis; Nixon's to play it up. Ike's instinct was to put salve on a wound after a political dispute, Nixon's to rub in some salt." Nixon had learned a great deal from Eisenhower during the eight years serving as his vice president, but he could never imitate Ike's appeal. Where Ike was friendly and outgoing, Nixon was a loner, telling aides in the early days of his presidency, "I must build a wall around me." At one point he confided in an aide, "It would be goddamned easy to run this office if [I] didn't have to deal with people."

Nixon depended on only three aides to limit his interactions with people. All three possessed an uncritical devotion to the president and shared his fears of big government at home and Communist expansion abroad. H. R. Haldeman, his chief of staff, was a successful former Los Angeles advertising executive who had been working for Nixon since 1956. Haldeman now functioned as Nixon's gatekeeper, once bragging that "every president needs a son of a bitch, and I'm Nixon's. I'm his buffer, I'm his bastard." John Ehrlichman, who had been Haldeman's classmate at the University of California, Los Angeles, served as assistant to the president for domestic affairs. Because of their stern demeanor and imperious manner, journalists referred to Haldeman and Ehrlichman as the "Germans" or the "Berlin Wall." The third member of the troika was John Mitchell, a former law partner who successfully managed Nixon's 1968 presidential campaign and whom Nixon now appointed attorney general.

Despite having been in national politics for more than two decades, Nixon still remained inscrutable to most people. "There was no true Nixon," Kissinger remarked, "several warring personalities struggle for preeminence in the same individual. One was idealistic, thoughtful, generous; another was vindictive, petty, emotional. There was a reflective, philosophical, stoical Nixon; and there was the impetuous, impulsive, and erratic one." James Farmer, assistant secretary at the Department of Health, Education, and Welfare, delivered a blunter assessment: "He believed in nothing. He was neither moral nor immoral, but amoral; he made decisions based on how they would affect him politically, not based on whether they were right or wrong."

The one consistent theme that coursed through Nixon's life was a deeply rooted paranoia, an abiding fear that the Washington "establishment" was out to destroy him. It was baked into his personality and only metastasized over the decades. Nixon believed that "it was 'me against the world,'" recalled Counselor to the President Robert Finch.

During his time working at the Office of Price Administration, Nixon developed a pointed disdain and distrust of the liberal Jews who populated the Washington establishment. That resentment carried over into his presidency, as he would frequently complain that the "government is full of Jews" and that "most Jews are disloyal." At one point he told Haldeman, "Bob, generally speaking, you can't trust the bastards." On July 2, 1971, Nixon read a story quoting an anonymous official at the Bureau of Labor Statistics, who explained that a recent dip in the unemployment numbers was a statistical fluke. Nixon found out that the official was Assistant Commissioner of Labor Statistics Harold Goldstein. According to Haldeman, Nixon then asked, "[I]s it all Jews?"

"Yes, every one of them is a Jew," Haldeman replied.

"I want a look at any sensitive areas around where Jews are involved. . . . The Jews are all through the government, we have got to get in those areas. Got to get a man in charge who is not Jewish to control the Jewish. . . . Do you understand?"

A few months later, when Nixon learned that the Internal Revenue Service was investigating the evangelist Billy Graham, he went off on another one of his anti-Semitic rants. "The IRS is battering the shit out of him," he told Haldeman. "Some son of a bitch came to him and gave him a three-hour grilling. . . . Now here's the point. Bob, please get me the names of the Jews—you know, the big Jewish contributors of the Democrats. . . . All right. Would you please investigate some of the cocksuckers?"

Yet for all his deep-seated bigotry, Nixon, like Eisenhower, sought to govern from the center—much to the dismay of many of his fellow conservatives. His approach arose less out of firm principles than political calculation. Nixon was the first president since 1849 forced to work with a Congress controlled by the opposition party—and the margin was substantial, with Democrats holding the edge in the Senate by 57–43 and the House by 243–192. Nixon also had little interest in domestic issues, which he compared to "building outhouses in Peoria." He once told a journalist, "I've always thought the country could run itself domestically without a president. You need a president for foreign policy."

The pressure to compromise with Democrats, coupled with his relative indifference to domestic policy, meant that Nixon adopted moderately progressive positions during his early years in office. "The size of government under Nixon grew immensely," economist Alan Greenspan recalled. "His reasoning was always, 'Well, if we don't do it, they'll do more.'" In addition to signing Democratic bills that increased spending on mandated social welfare programs, especially Social Security, Medicare, and Medicaid, he declared a war on cancer that included a massive infusion of medical research money. He signed into law the 1970 Occupational Safety and Health Act (OSHA), establishing a federal agency to protect American workers. His most innovative and surprising proposal was the Family Assistance Plan (FAP), which provided a guaranteed minimum annual income of $1,600 to every US family. Although the bill died in the Senate, it revealed Nixon's capacity for domestic innovation.

Nixon, however, was not so much interested in achieving legislative success as in creating a new Republican majority. In August 1970 he read a book titled *The Real Majority,* written by Democratic-leaning social scientists Richard M. Scammon and Ben J. Wattenberg. The book reinforced Nixon's desire to divide Americans along cultural lines and seemed to complement his "silent majority" strategy. Winning elections meant capturing the center, the authors contended, and the center was up for grabs. The centrist voter, they said, was a mythical "47-year-old housewife from the outskirts of Dayton, Ohio, whose husband is a machinist." Since the New Deal, the Democrats had secured her vote on the economic issue, but the disturbances of the 1960s birthed a new issue—the social issue—which presented the Republican Party with a historic opportunity. If the Republicans successfully combined conservatism on the social issue with liberalism on the economic issue, they would win over the housewife from Dayton and become the new majority party. The book's argument impressed Nixon greatly. "P hot about real majority and need to get that thinking over to all our people," Haldeman recorded in his diary on August 28. "Wants to really ram this home and make all decisions based on . . . Wants to hit pornography, dope, bad kids."

Nixon first put this strategy to the test during the 1970 midterm campaign. Though he came to office on a tough law-and-order platform, Nixon had always been a racial moderate, and in the tense political atmosphere of the late 1960s, he had looked for ways to demonstrate his goodwill. During his first two years in office, he had reached out to Black voters, dramatically expanded government enforcement of desegregation, and institutionalized racial quotas in all government contracts. But now he saw the advantage of using race to divide Democrats and win over white, working-class voters to the Republican Party. He denounced racial quotas, appointed conservative southern justices to the Supreme Court, and capitalized on white resistance to court-ordered busing. According to the journalist Thomas Edsall, it was busing, more than any other issue, that allowed Nixon to convince working-class white Democrats that the federal government had abandoned them.

Cleverly playing to the public's mood, Nixon wrapped himself in the flag and questioned the patriotism of those who challenged his policies. His combative strategy reached a fever pitch in the final weeks of the 1970 midterm elections. In a desperate attempt to unseat Democrats and increase Republican power in Congress, Nixon engaged in a campaign that the historian James T. Patterson described as "among the most aggressive and divisive" in modern politics. Campaigning frantically in twenty-three states during the final days, Nixon orchestrated confrontations with protestors in order to further arouse the indignation of his cherished "Middle Americans." But this time the public failed to respond to Nixon's shrill rhetoric. The Democrats gained nine House seats, lost two in the Senate, and gained eleven governorships. Overall, Democrats received 4.1 million more votes than their Republican challengers.

George H. W. Bush was one of those Republicans who lost his election in 1970. He had been pushed by Nixon to run for the Senate against liberal Democrat Ralph Yarborough, but the decision was risky. Bush would be giving up a safe House seat and a long, secure future in the chamber. Seeking to diminish the risk, Nixon promised to find a place for Bush in the administration were he to lose. Bush remained unsure, however, so he sought out the advice of none other than Lyndon Johnson. On April 9, 1969, he flew to meet LBJ at his ranch outside Austin. Bush knew that LBJ despised Yarborough and likely hoped to sideline the still-popular Texan. "Mr. President," he said, "I've still got a decision to make, and I'd like your advice. My House seat is secure—no opposition last time—and I've got a position on Ways and Means. I don't mind taking risks, but in a few more terms, I'll have seniority on a powerful committee. I'm just not sure it's a gamble I should take, whether it's really worth it." Johnson replied: "Son, I served in the House. And I have been privileged to serve in the Senate, too. And they're both good places to serve. So I wouldn't begin to advise you what to do, except to say this: that the difference between being a member of the Senate and a member of the House is the difference between chicken salad and chicken shit." With that vivid piece of advice, Bush seemed to have his answer.

But Democrats threw Bush a curveball. Instead of nominating a liberal in increasingly conservative Texas, they chose Lloyd Bentsen, another oilman with a distinguished war record and centrist views. *The Dallas Morning News* observed, "There is not two cents' worth of difference in their basic political philosophies." On the one hand, Bush still believed that he could ride Nixon's coattails into the Senate. On the other, he worried that because he and Bentsen had similar voting records, the White House would not get actively involved in the race. In May he requested a meeting with the president to explain that "Bentsen is *not* for you," pointing out that Bentsen had attacked the administration on a host of issues, including inflation and the war. Bush then asked for the president's help in persuading "[k]ey newspaper people" and "big business people" that he would be the most effective in carrying out the Nixon agenda. For unclear reasons, the meeting never happened.

On Election Day, Democrats in heavily populated East Texas turned out in larger than expected numbers, driven to the polls by a local measure that would have legalized the sale of liquor by the drink. "Like Custer, who said there were just too many Indians, I guess there were just too many Democrats," Bush said drily. Bentsen prevailed by roughly a 7 percent margin.

On Wednesday, December 9, 1970, the newly defeated Bush reported to Haldeman's West Wing office to see which position Nixon would offer him in his administration. Before escorting him into the Oval Office, Haldeman informed him that he could become an assistant to the president. Bush made clear that he did not want to be a White House staffer and instead made a case to become the US ambassador to the United Nations. "I felt I could really put forward an image there that would be very helpful to the administration," Bush said. According to Haldeman's notes: "He explained that the reason for his interest in the U.N. was his feeling that for too long the president had not been represented there by anyone who was a strong advocate. . . . There was a dearth of Nixon advocacy in New York City." Nixon seconded the idea, telling Haldeman, "Wait a minute, Bob, this makes some sense."

Critics, however, complained that Bush lacked the credentials to serve as UN ambassador. "The appointment of a political loser," editorialized *The Washington Star*, and "a lame-duck congressman with little experience in foreign affairs and less in diplomacy—would seem a major downgrading of the U.N. by the Nixon Administration." *The New York Times* expressed a similar concern, noting, "There seems to be nothing in his record that qualified him for this highly important position." Even a Democratic friend was puzzled by the appointment. "George," he said, "what the fuck do you know about foreign affairs?" Bush responded: "You ask me that in ten days."

Like other members of his generation who witnessed the enormous productivity unleashed by World War II, Nixon believed, as he'd announced in his inaugural address, that "we have learned at last to manage a modern economy to ensure its continued growth." Liberals such as JFK and Johnson had embraced the Keynesian approach that had emerged from World War II, convinced that with minor tinkering, government could guarantee a constant stream of economic growth. By contrast, Eisenhower, whose economic views were shaped before World War II, had remained fearful that the economy's continued fragility required balanced budgets. Nixon combined elements of both views: a liberal belief in the curative powers of economic growth but a conservative faith that it could be achieved by way of small government and tax cuts.

The global economy had changed dramatically since World War II, and Nixon faced a new and troubling phenomenon that confounded his approach: stagflation. LBJ's decision to fight the Vietnam War without cutting social programs or significantly raising taxes had produced spiraling inflation. Early on, Nixon and his economic team decided that the most important goal was "cooling down the overheated economy." He pressured the Federal Reserve to tighten the money supply through a process called gradualism. As expected, the reduced money supply restrained economic growth, but unexpectedly, it did not stop prices from rising. By 1970, unemployment had risen from 3.6 percent to 4.9 percent, while the consumer price index rose by 11 percent.

Nixon feared that the fight against inflation would lead to a spike in unemployment that could damage his chances of winning a second term. In fact, he blamed Republican losses in the 1970 elections on rising unemployment. "A Republican administration with any kind of economic slowdown is a disaster," he told Haldeman two days after the election. "Without economic drag, [we] would have carried both House and Senate." Haldeman reported in his diary on November 18 that the president "doesn't want to take any chances on screwing up 1972."

Nixon also had another earlier precedent to draw upon: When he was vice president in 1958, the Federal Reserve drove the economy into a recession, hurting Republicans at the polls. "We cooled off the economy and cooled off fifteen senators and sixty congressmen at the same time," he stated. He would not allow history to repeat itself—and evidence was suggesting already that the economic downturn was costing him support. In early 1971 Nixon's approval rating had dropped to a low of 52 percent, and Maine senator Edmund Muskie, the Democratic front-runner for 1972, had pulled even with him in the national polls. *Newsweek* warned in January 1971, "If there is not sustained pickup in the months ahead, the economy could turn out to be Richard Nixon's 'Vietnam.'"

Nixon revealed his new approach three months after the midterm elections, when he appointed the silver-haired and silver-tongued former Texas governor John Connally as secretary of the Treasury. There was a small problem with Connally's appointment, though: He knew nothing about economics. (But, he often joked, "I can add.") What would guide him more than economic know-how was sheer nationalism. As he once said, "My view is that the foreigners are out to screw us, and therefore it's our job to screw them first." He quickly became one of the most powerful and influential members of Nixon's Cabinet.

In early August 1971 Connally faced his first big test. Mired in recession and plagued by rising inflation and unemployment, the United States was running a trade deficit for the first time since 1895. Meanwhile, the international monetary system adopted after World War II was under serious threat. Under that system, other countries could convert the dollars they accumulated into gold at a fixed price of $35 an ounce. The fear had always been that someday the Europeans and the Japanese, who held $7 for every $1 of gold in Fort Knox, might begin buying gold. That's exactly what happened beginning in the spring of 1971, when Belgium, the Netherlands, and France traded $400 million for gold. On August 9 London, grappling with its own economic troubles, insisted that its $3 billion in dollar reserves likewise be reimbursed in gold. Nixon now faced a dilemma. If more countries followed, a run on gold would ensue. On the other hand, if the United States went off the gold standard and let the dollar float against all other national currencies, the dollar would weaken. The effect would likely be inflationary; imports would become more expensive.

On August 13 Nixon gathered his economic team at Camp David for what one aide described as the "most important weekend in economics" since FDR closed the banks in 1933. Connally took the lead in developing the administration's response, proposing what Nixon described as "a bold stroke." With the United States facing a trade deficit and a gold drain, Connally advocated for abandoning the gold standard to devalue the dollar and thus give US exports a competitive edge. He also recommended imposing a freeze on wages and prices as a buffer against inflation. In addition to the ninety-day freeze, the proposal—initially dubbed the New Economic Plan until someone realized that Vladimir Lenin had once used the same label—called for lifting the excise tax on automobiles to encourage sales, along with cutting spending and offering an investment tax credit.

Connally's package of reforms contradicted everything Nixon claimed to believe. For one, he had always vehemently opposed wage and price controls. During his campaigns for Congress after the war, Nixon held up the OPA as a vivid example of government waste and fraud. He spoke out often about the evils of government interference in the economy, while praising the free market. Now he was advocating for the same Keynesian solutions that Kennedy and LBJ had once championed. "I am now a Keynesian," he declared. Commenting on Nixon's dramatic switch, journalist Howard K. Smith quipped, "It's a little like a Christian crusader saying, 'All things considered, I think Mohammed was right!'"

Nixon announced his new policy on the night of Sunday, August 15, 1971, preempting an episode of the hit TV Western *Bonanza*. The immediate public reaction to Nixon's economic plan was positive, with 73 percent of those polled approving of wage and price controls. Wall Street seemed pleased as well, as the Dow Jones Industrial Average jumped almost 33 points on Monday, August 16, the largest one-day increase in its history to that point. America's allies were less thrilled; the move sent shock waves throughout their economies.

In the short term, this unorthodox solution achieved Nixon's political and economic goals. During the 1972 election year, the GNP grew by 7.2 percent and the unemployment rate dropped from 6 percent to 5.1 percent. In the long run, however, Nixon's policies proved disastrous. By ignoring clear signs of inflation and intentionally expanding the economy, he contributed to a cycle of spiraling inflation that would soon cripple the economy. Wage and price controls were popular and gave the economy a boost—at first. But inflation eventually burst loose, reaching double digits by the end of the decade. In his memoirs, Nixon admitted that his "bold" move turned out to be a short-term boom but a long-term bust. "The piper must always be paid," he wrote.

The other issue that Nixon needed to neutralize before the election was Vietnam. He had reduced US troops in South Vietnam from more than a half million in 1969 to fewer than seventy thousand in 1972, but victory remained elusive. The more Vietnamization failed to deter the North or inspire the South, the more bombings Nixon ordered.

In March 1972, when North Vietnam's forces launched a massive invasion of the South, Nixon announced Operation Linebacker, ordering B-52s to drop their deadly cargo on targets near Haiphong, only sixty-five miles west of Hanoi. US bombers had never struck that far north. The move was risky not only because it might further inflame opinion at home, but also because it might jeopardize a planned summit with the Russians. Yet the gamble succeeded. Even though American bombs inadvertently hit Soviet ships, the Soviet Union offered only tepid protest, and most Americans supported the president's tough stance.

At last, the North Vietnamese invasion and Nixon's forceful response created an opportunity for negotiations. Both sides had reason to seek accommodation. The North Vietnamese wanted to end the punishing American bombings; the United States needed to end the war quickly. Since early 1971, Henry Kissinger had been holding private meetings in a suburb of Paris with his North Vietnamese counterpart, Le Duc Tho. The key stumbling block had been Hanoi's insistence that South Vietnam's president Thieu be removed from power and that North Vietnamese troops be allowed to remain in the South. For a year, neither side budged.

In September 1972 Kissinger finally made the first move by agreeing to allow North Vietnamese soldiers to remain in South Vietnam. Tho responded by dropping the long-standing demand regarding Thieu. A settlement appeared imminent. The following month, Kissinger announced confidently at a televised press conference that "peace is at hand." Initially Nixon congratulated Kissinger, but he remembered quickly that the phrase was eerily similar to what Chamberlain had said at Munich. Nixon also worried that achieving peace before the election might actually *hurt* his chances by focusing public attention on domestic issues, where Democrats held an advantage. So, ironically, he refused to pressure President Thieu to accept the terms Kissinger had negotiated. Nixon had now twice intervened for political reasons to allow the war to continue. In 1968 he'd sabotaged Johnson's plans, and now, four years later, he undercut his own secretary of state.

Despite his paranoia, Nixon's victory was never in doubt. By November, everything seemed to be falling in place for him. The economy was booming, the war was winding down, and he achieved a great foreign policy triumph by exploiting the Sino-Soviet rivalry to develop closer ties with both countries.

Nixon also had the fortune of facing off against the perfect foil for his new politics of resentment. The Democrats nominated the outspoken liberal senator George McGovern of South Dakota. His nomination revealed the deep divisions even among the World War II generation about the legacy of that war. McGovern, like Nixon, volunteered for service in the war, and as a B-24 Liberator pilot, flew thirty-five bombing missions over Nazi-occupied Europe, earning a Distinguished Flying Cross. But McGovern aligned himself with young critics of the Vietnam War, arguing that the lessons of Munich were irrelevant to what he viewed as a civil war in a faraway nation that represented no threat to American national security. McGovern's affiliation with the peace movement, and his support for expanding the Great Society, left him susceptible to red-baiting, and no one red-baited better than Richard Nixon.

Throughout the campaign, Nixon played on public fear of urban violence and social disorder by implying that a McGovern victory would be a slippery slope. The party of FDR, he told wavering Democrats, had been hijacked by antiwar protestors and New Left radicals. "The time has come," Nixon declared in a campaign speech, "to draw the line . . . for the Great Silent Majority . . . to stand up and be counted against the appeasement of the rock throwers and the obscenity shouters in America." Nixon's shrewd appeals to the silent majority touched a responsive chord with many working-class Democrats who felt their party had abandoned them in pursuit of more liberal voters and Black people.

Almost ten million Democrats—nearly one-third of all registered Democrats—and an overwhelming 70 percent of the white working class voted for Nixon. On Election Day the incumbent scored a resounding victory, winning 60.7 percent (47,165,234) of the popular vote. McGovern received only 29,170,774 votes, or 37.5 percent. Nixon carried every state except Massachusetts and the District of Columbia, by a margin of 521–17 in the electoral college.

After his landslide victory, a newly emboldened Nixon decided to re-shuffle his Cabinet, ordering Haldeman to "eliminate the politicians." Bush was the one exception. "He'd do anything for the cause," Nixon remarked. Bush had been enjoying his time at the United Nations and only reluctantly accepted his new role as the chairman of the Republican National Committee. It was a decision he would soon regret.

On January 23, 1973—three days after Nixon's inauguration—the Paris Peace Accords officially ended US involvement in the Vietnam War. To persuade President Thieu to sign the accords, Nixon secretly promised to employ American military power "with full force" against North Vietnam if Hanoi violated the agreement. This was, in fact, a false promise: Nixon knew that neither the nation nor Congress had any appetite left to continue the fight.

The praise for Nixon was universal, but it would soon prove to be misplaced. Telling a national television audience that the United States had achieved "peace with honor," Nixon claimed that the "agreement will ensure a stable peace in Vietnam and contribute to the preservation of lasting peace in Indochina and Southeast Asia." Nothing could have been further from the truth. Back in the spring of 1972, Nixon and Kissinger had analyzed the South's chances of stability. "I must tell you honestly," Kissinger said to the president. He did not think South Vietnam would survive "beyond 1974." And, just as the secretary of state predicted, the North violated the ceasefire within a few months and continued its relentless drive south. It would be left to Nixon's successor to oversee the humiliating end of the war two years later.

Lyndon Johnson would not witness that end. Two days after Nixon's second inaugural—what would have been the end of Johnson's second term had he run and won in 1968—LBJ died alone at his home in Texas at the age of sixty-four. Nixon later said that Johnson died "of a broken heart," pointing out that he had "longed for the popular approval and affection that continued to elude him." Despite a few flare-ups, Nixon and Johnson had grown close in recent years, talking on the phone and exchanging visits frequently. "Tell the president I love him," Johnson said shortly before he died.

Even though JFK had been dead for nearly ten years, his ghost haunted the Nixon White House. One of Nixon's first acts was to purge the White House and the Executive Office Building of all reminders of Kennedy. His larger objective was to destroy the Camelot legacy entirely. When a poll showed that young people held both John and Robert Kennedy in higher regard than him, it only confirmed a deep resentment that Nixon had long harbored. He became determined to "expose" JFK, convinced that the slain president's media-savvy advisors had manufactured a false image of a bold, imaginative leader, while the ever-compliant media overlooked his many flaws.

In September 1969 Nixon ordered Haldeman to find files on Ngo Dinh Diem, the South Vietnamese leader who was assassinated a few weeks before Kennedy in 1963. The president was looking for evidence that JFK had conspired to have Diem murdered. At one point, the White House hired former spy E. Howard Hunt to investigate. Hunt located a CIA agent who knew of the plot and invited him to his office, hoping to secure a taped confession. Hunt hid a tape recorder beneath his seat cushion and, to help loosen the agent's tongue, offered to share a bottle of scotch. But after the agent left, Hunt realized he had crushed the recording device and was so drunk that he could not remember anything that had been said. That still didn't deter Nixon's operatives from forging a cable claiming that JFK had denied asylum to the South Vietnamese leader and his brother.

The president saw another opportunity to shatter the Kennedy image in June 1971, when *The New York Times* began publishing the Pentagon Papers. Commissioned by Defense Secretary Robert McNamara in 1967, this study described explicitly how officials in the Kennedy and Johnson administrations had been lying to one another—and to the American people—about the nature of the war. While fighting to keep the material under seal, Nixon ordered his aides to covertly circulate only the Kennedy administration chapters of the Pentagon Papers. "Leak it to some other paper," Nixon said, and, without any sense of irony, added: "The public is entitled to know." (Ultimately, the Supreme Court ruled 6–3 against the administration, citing the First Amendment freedoms of speech and the press.)

Aside from his personal vendetta against JFK, Nixon sought to undermine support for the slain president's youngest brother, Massachusetts senator Edward "Teddy" Kennedy, whom Nixon saw as his toughest possible challenger in 1972. "During most of my first term," Nixon would confirm years later, "I had assumed that my opponent in 1972 would be Kennedy, Muskie, or Humphrey. I thought that I could probably beat Muskie or Humphrey. A campaign against Teddy Kennedy would be much more difficult to predict because it would involve so many emotional elements." Kennedy's reckless private life resulted in the death of a young woman passenger who drowned when the senator drove off a bridge in the middle of the night on the Cape Cod island of Chappaquiddick in July 1969. Ultimately, it was Nixon's obsession with the Kennedys that would precipitate his downfall. His concern intensified when he learned in the winter of 1970 that the Democratic National Committee had selected former Kennedy aide and 1960 campaign manager Lawrence O'Brien as its chairman. The president viewed O'Brien as a stalking horse for Edward Kennedy's plan to run in 1972. Haldeman recorded in his diary that Nixon wanted to "move hard on Larry O'Brien now that he is back as DNC chair." It is unclear whether the White House was looking for dirt on O'Brien or trying to find what damaging information the DNC had on Nixon.

Either way, on June 17, 1972, a security guard caught burglars breaking into the DNC headquarters on the sixth floor of the Watergate Office Building in Washington, DC. The situation unraveled quickly. In February 1973, when it emerged that one of the men involved in the break-in had once worked for the president's reelection committee, Congress created a bipartisan select committee to probe further into the Watergate affair. Over the next few months, the committee, headed by North Carolina Democrat Sam Ervin, uncovered a trail of corruption leading to higher and higher levels of the White House staff.

Events soon spiraled out of control. On June 25 White House counsel John Dean described in detail an unscrupulous administration committing crimes under the cover of national security. Soon afterward, former aide Alexander Butterfield revealed to the Ervin Committee that Nixon had installed a secret taping system to record, "for posterity," his private conversations in the White House and the Executive Office Building. The special prosecutor, Harvard Law School professor Archibald Cox, whom Nixon had dismissed as "that fucking Harvard professor," asked the court to order Nixon to release the tapes. Nixon refused. What ensued on the evening of October 20, 1973, would soon become known as the "Saturday Night Massacre." Nixon demanded that his attorney general, Elliot Richardson, fire Cox, but he refused and resigned. Nixon then turned to Deputy Attorney General William Ruckelshaus to carry out his order, but he too resigned in protest. Finally, Nixon found someone who would carry out his order: Solicitor General Robert Bork. That evening, NBC reported that "the country tonight is in the midst of what may be the most serious constitutional crisis in its history."

Ten days later, the House of Representatives, for the first time since 1868, began formal proceedings to impeach the president of the United States. Only then did Nixon's lawyer announce that the White House would turn over the tapes and appoint a new special prosecutor, Leon Jaworski, who had been chairman of Texas Democrats for Nixon in 1972.

In the early days of the investigation, Nixon had tried to enlist LBJ's support to quiet congressional Democrats. When Johnson refused, the White House threatened to release damaging information about LBJ's own wiretapping activities during the 1968 campaign. When Johnson learned from a reporter what Nixon was up to, he called the FBI's deputy assistant director, Deke DeLoach. "If they try to give me any trouble," Johnson warned, "I'll pull that cable from my files and turn the tables on them." After that call, DeLoach warned Haldeman not to mess with Johnson. "LBJ got very hot," Haldeman recorded, "and called Deke and said to him that if the Nixon people are going to play with this, that he would release [redacted]." Decades later, it was revealed that the deleted material referred to Nixon's role in persuading South Vietnam to postpone peace talks until after the 1968 election. Nixon backed off.

The Saturday Night Massacre was only one of a series of scandals that kept the administration and the American public reeling. Just ten days before, Vice President Spiro Agnew had appeared in federal court and pleaded "no contest" to one felony count of tax evasion and resigned from the vice presidency.

Nixon now needed to choose a replacement. After getting input from party leaders, members of Congress, the Cabinet, and White House staff, two candidates emerged in a tie for first: Nelson Rockefeller, the liberal Republican governor of New York, and Ronald Reagan. Nixon feared that picking either the liberal Rockefeller or the conservative Reagan would divide the party. He was especially critical of Reagan, convinced that he lacked the work ethic necessary to do the job and describing him as "a lightweight and not someone to be considered seriously or feared." In a May 1971 conversation with Kissinger, Nixon summed up Reagan as being "pretty shallow" and "a man of limited mental capacity." If nominated and confirmed, the former actor would be a heartbeat away from the presidency, a prospect Kissinger deemed "inconceivable."

The man who came in third—John Connally, who'd switched parties in May, becoming a Republican—was Nixon's top choice. Eventually Nixon accepted that Connally could never be confirmed, a point underscored by Senate Majority leader Robert Byrd of West Virginia, who warned the president, "If you send down Connally, there'll be blood on the floor." Nixon realized that with all the problems he faced regarding Watergate, the last thing he needed was a partisan bloodbath.

Nixon initially showed little enthusiasm for Gerald Ford, who ranked fourth on the list. Although the men had been friends since the years following World War II—at least as much as Nixon was capable of friendship—the president had little regard for Ford's intellect and thought he would be overwhelmed by the demands of the office. Ultimately, however, Ford was the practical choice. House Speaker Carl Albert told the White House that "if the president wants to know who would be the first choice of the House, it would be Jerry Ford." According to Kissinger, Nixon calculated that naming Ford would slow the push for impeachment because "Congress would not want to run the risk of placing a supposedly inexperienced man in charge of foreign affairs." According to an aide, Nixon claimed that he picked Ford "because he thought Jerry would be confirmed [as vice president], but that *nobody would want him to be president!*"

The news came as a surprise to the congressman himself, who had just promised his wife that he would retire in 1976, to devote his time to practicing law and playing golf. Not surprisingly, given his cordial relations with congressional Democrats and Republicans, Ford was quickly confirmed by overwhelming majorities in the House and Senate and assumed office on December 6, 1973.

But Nixon was sorely mistaken if he thought Ford's appointment would slow down the impeachment drive. All attention turned now to the secret tapes. The president agreed only to release edited transcripts; the special prosecutor insisted on reviewing all of them. On the morning of July 24, 1974, a unanimous Supreme Court ruled against Nixon. Just as John Dean had contended, the tapes revealed that Nixon had personally intervened to stifle an FBI investigation into the Watergate break-in and authorized payments of more than $460,000 in hush money to keep the Watergate burglars from implicating higher-ups in the administration. Three days later, by a vote of 27–11, with six Republicans joining all twenty-one Democrats, the Watergate Committee passed the first article of impeachment against the president. Two days later, they passed the second article of impeachment by an even stronger vote, 28–10. Both Ford and George H. W. Bush, who had vigorously defended Nixon in the past, felt betrayed when the tapes exposed the president's lies. When Bush learned of the so-called smoking gun tape, he realized that Nixon had been lying to him the whole time. "This was proof the president had been involved, at least in the cover-up," he wrote in his diary. "This was proof the president had lied. After this, I lost faith in Nixon. I could not forgive him this time." An equally flabbergasted Ford recalled Nixon's repeated professions of innocence over the previous months. "We had been friends for twenty-five years," he reflected later. "We had campaigned for each other, and there had never been a time when I felt he wasn't telling me the truth." Yet despite the rude awakening, Ford still felt obligated as vice president to continue supporting Nixon. "If I did anything else, people would charge that I was undercutting him in order to acquire the presidency myself," he noted.

On Friday, August 9, 1974, facing certain impeachment, a disgraced Richard Nixon became the first American president to resign from office. The previous evening, in the White House East Room, he had delivered a raw, emotional farewell to his staff. Wiping sweat from his upper lip, he rambled on about his mother and father before offering advice: "Always remember, others may hate you, but those who hate you don't win unless you hate them, and then you destroy yourself." Bush, who was in the room, remarked that the president "looked just awful." But he described the speech as "masterful" and agreed with "that argument about hating—only if you hate do you join the haters."

The next day, just before noon, Nixon walked across the South Lawn of the White House and climbed on board the presidential helicopter. At noon, the sixty-one-year-old Ford was sworn in as the country's new chief executive, promising to heal "the nation's wounds" and to restore a sense of confidence in government. Initially, the press hailed both the message and the messenger, finding the down-to-earth Ford a refreshing break from the imperious Nixon. "He's superbly average," observed *U.S. News & World Report*. "He's like Ike. He gives you an impression of solid dependability." The honeymoon, however, would prove brief.

Bush was thrilled that Gerald Ford was now president. Echoing *U.S. News & World Report*, he described him as a "latter-day Eisenhower. He is an Ike without the heroics, but he has the decency the country is crying out for right now."

During their four years in Congress together, Ford and Bush had developed a respectful relationship. Because of their leadership positions—

minority leader and chairman of the Republican Party, respectively—they were among Nixon's most outspoken defenders. But in the end, the two men trusted each other in a way that they didn't necessarily trust Nixon. They both possessed similar temperaments and style: warm, outgoing, and honest, with a deep-seated belief in the importance of decency and civility in politics. "I will take Ford's decency over Nixon's toughness because what we need at this juncture in our history is a certain sense of morality and a certain sense of decency," Bush noted in his diary.

Two days after Nixon's resignation, Ford invited Bush to the Oval Office. Bush knew that he was among the top candidates Ford was considering for vice president. At Ford's request, Bush walked through his résumé. "Phi Beta Kappa economics, Yale, East and West, successful in business, Ways and Means, finances in order, knowing the business community, press relations, politics, UN." Surprisingly, Bush never mentioned his war record. Ford remained coy, asking him his opinions on other possible vice presidents, including Barry Goldwater and Nelson Rockefeller. While Bush later recalled expressing his concern about "divisions in the party from either right or left," he "kept coming down on the middle ground." As he left, he assured Ford, "No matter [whom] you pick, you will have my total support."

During Ford's first week in office, Bryce Harlow, a Republican wise man who had worked in the Eisenhower White House, presented an analysis of sixteen possible vice presidential candidates. Harlow ranked them based on several qualities: experience, geography, image, loyalty, age, and the ability to broaden Ford's political base. Bush led all contenders. Of Bush, Harlow wrote: "Strongest across the board; greatest weakness—regarded as intellectually 'light' by many top leaders in the country." In the end, however, Harlow believed that a Bush appointment would be too conventional, "foretelling a presidential hesitancy to move boldly in the face of known controversy." He convinced Ford that the more liberal Rockefeller would be a stronger choice. Not only would it represent a break from Nixon, but it could help Ford attract moderate Democrats in 1976.

With the vice presidency filled, Bush decided to lobby for another high-profile position in the administration, and Ford wanted to reward him for faithfully defending Nixon and the Republican Party throughout the Watergate crisis. Bush initially expressed interest in becoming White House chief of staff, but the president said that he was redefining the position in order to have direct access to more people. Bush then raised the possibility of a foreign affairs position. "I indicated that way down the line, maybe 1980, if I stayed involved in foreign affairs, I conceivably could qualify for secretary of state," he reasoned. Ford proposed the ambassadorship to London, but Bush said that he could not afford it because the ambassador was expected to host lavish gatherings, with only a small portion of the costs covered by the State Department. In the end, Bush wished to be the liaison with China. (Since the two nations did not yet have full diplomatic relations, only the position of liaison existed.) "Never in our lives," Bush wrote, "have Barbara and I craved change more."

No matter how hard he tried, Ford could not escape Richard Nixon's dark shadow. At his confirmation hearing for vice president in the fall of 1973, Ford had said that if he became president, he would not issue a pardon because the country "wouldn't stand for it." But now that he was president, Ford believed that a criminal indictment and trial would take months if not years to reach a conclusion and would serve as an endless distraction preventing him from making his own mark.

In early September, after less than a month in office, Ford secretly sent his private attorney, Benton Becker, to San Clemente to negotiate a pardon. The Supreme Court had ruled that acceptance of the federal pardon represented an admission of guilt, but Nixon still did not believe he was guilty of anything more than stupidity. Ford told Becker that while a statement of guilt was "not a precondition to pardon," it would be his preference. For two days, Nixon's advisors fought with Becker over the statement the former president would sign. "I can tell you right now," declared Ronald Ziegler, Nixon's combative press secretary, "that President Nixon will make *no* statement of admission of complicity in return for a pardon from Jerry Ford." Becker, angry that Ziegler referred to the president as "Jerry Ford," decided to call his bluff.

"Can you tell me how to reach the air force pilot that brought me here, so that I can instruct him to take me back to Washington?"

That did the trick. Both sides now went back and forth on a draft of the statement, with Becker again pushing for Nixon to admit his responsibility. At last, they got a statement in which Nixon would finally concede that he "was wrong in not dealing with Watergate more forthrightly and directly, particularly when it reached a judicial stage."

Once they had worked out the details, Ziegler led Becker to Nixon's office. Becker had never met him before, and what he saw left him shocked. "As I entered the office, he was seated behind a desk in a room that was very sparsely adorned," he reflected in a detailed memorandum of the meeting. "My first impression, and the one that continues with me to this day, was, unhappily, one of freakish grotesqueness. His arms and body were so thin and frail as to project an image of a head size disproportionate to a body. . . . I met a man whom I might more reasonably expect to meet at an octogenarian nursing home. He was old. . . . I would have estimated his age to be 85. The famous Nixon jowls were exaggerated, the face highly wrinkled, the hair disheveled, and the posture and comportment all reminiscent of advanced age."

On September 8, 1974, one month into his presidency, Ford granted an unconditional pardon to the disgraced former president. He ended up paying a heavy political price for that decision. His popularity tumbled 22 points in a Gallup poll, the largest single drop in history.

Despite his hopes that pardoning Nixon would allow his own achievements to shine, Ford struggled to develop a coherent economic message. He inherited soaring inflation, skyrocketing interest rates, and a stagnant economy with high unemployment. In October Ford declared inflation "domestic enemy number one," and called for budget cuts and a tax increase. Rumors that Ford was considering raising taxes troubled Ronald Reagan, whose second term as governor was coming to an end and who was again waiting in the wings for Ford to stumble. The day before Ford was scheduled to deliver an economic speech before a joint session of Congress on October 7, Reagan sent him a telegram: "Dear Mr. President, I am concerned that the press reports indicate you will propose tax increases tomorrow in an effort to curb inflation. The 1972 election mandate was clear: no new taxes for four years, and reduce the size of the federal government."

Ultimately, as much as Ford disliked Reagan, he ended up agreeing with the California governor. Even as unemployment jumped from 5.8 percent to 7 percent during the fall, and leading economic indicators signaled a steep recession, Ford switched gears, announcing a tax *cut* to stimulate growth. His press secretary, making light of the situation, told reporters that the president's new policy was only a "179-degree shift" from his October anti-inflation program. The president's flip-flop on the economy and taxes contributed to a growing public perception that Ford was out of his depth in the White House.

The president's early stumbles, along with a public desire to punish Republicans for Nixon's crimes, produced a massive Democratic victory in the 1974 midterm elections. Democrats won forty-three seats in the House and the two-thirds majority required to override presidential vetoes. Energized Democrats used their majority to pass legislation for expanded social programs, but Ford held the line, vetoing many of the bills. During his brief term in office, Ford blocked legislation calling for increased federal spending on education and health care. When he refused to approve a federal bailout of New York City in 1975, the headline of the *New York Daily News* screamed: "Ford to City: Drop Dead." After his first year in office, White House aides Donald Rumsfeld and Dick Cheney offered Ford a blunt assessment of his biggest challenge: "Among the public-at-large, the president is perceived as decent and honest. They like you. However, there are growing questions about your leadership, capabilities, and competence."

Ford also had the misfortune of presiding over the messy end of the Vietnam War. On January 7, 1975, North Vietnamese troops, freshly provisioned by the Soviet Union and China, struck from their bases in Cambodia and moved relentlessly toward Saigon. As South Vietnam's armies retreated in disorder—a clear sign that the war was over—Ford nevertheless persisted in his support of the South. From the beginning of the conflict, Ford had viewed Vietnam through the lens of World War II. For him, losing to the Communist government in Hanoi was comparable to surrendering to Nazi Germany. That was not going to happen on his watch. He assured Congress that "With adequate United States military assistance," the South could still win the war, repeating the tired mantra "If we do not stand up to aggression, we would lose our credibility around the world."

On some level, however, Ford knew the end was near and was likely setting up Congress to take the blame for losing the war. He pleaded with Congress to provide emergency military and economic aid to South Vietnam, but both Congress and the American people had already moved on. On April 30, 1975, North Vietnamese troops captured Saigon. The chaotic image of American helicopters evacuating staff from the roof of the US embassy became an enduring and humiliating symbol of American impotence.

———

Ultimately, the United States dropped more than seven million tons of bombs on Southeast Asia during the Vietnam War—more than triple what had been dropped during World War II. Yet it remains unclear what lessons, if any, these veterans of World War II learned from the Vietnam debacle. Was it a mistake to invest American prestige in Southeast Asia, or was it the noble thing to do, no matter how poorly executed? Did America lose the war because of a hostile press and a spineless Congress? Or did the war reveal that the US view of the world was fundamentally flawed? This inability to fully confront the tragedies of Vietnam—and its underlying World War II–era assumptions—ensured that the end of one war would have little bearing on future aggression.

Ford never questioned the relevance of the lessons of World War II or doubted America's motives for entering Vietnam. "From the beginning of our involvement in the area, I have always thought that we were doing the right thing," he professed. "Our policy was a natural outgrowth of decisions we had made at the end of World War II." The failure, he argued, had been a tactical one, proving one key lesson: "If you commit to war, commit to win. Don't let any war drag on. Go in with the will and manpower and weapons to succeed. Reach your objective. Declare victory. Pull out."

Even at the bitter end, Ford—like his predecessor—believed that the answer to preventing a North Vietnamese victory was to drop more bombs. As an analogy, he used the dubious example of America's having dropped two atomic bombs on Japan at the end of World War II. "Yes, the bombs did terrible things to the Japanese people. But by not having to invade Japan, we saved lives on both sides." He acknowledged other problems—a weak government in the South that never gained the support of the people and growing congressional opposition at home—but he clung to the illusion that despite these hurdles, increased bombing could have eventually achieved victory.

Ford relied heavily on the advice of Henry Kissinger to formulate his views on the meaning of Vietnam. A month after the fall of Saigon, Kissinger, continuing as secretary of state, wrote the president a long memo dismissing the significance of America's defeat and reasserting the lessons from World War II: "Vietnam represented a unique situation, geographically, ethnically, politically, militarily, and diplomatically. We should probably be grateful for that and should recognize it for what it is, instead of trying to apply the 'lessons of Vietnam' as universally as we once tried to apply the 'lessons of Munich.'" Kissinger concluded: "I do not believe our soldiers or our people need to be ashamed."

While he had once claimed that it was a mistake to Americanize the war, Kissinger now blamed the defeat on Congress, declaring that he was convinced that "even at the end," the United States could have preserved a non-Communist government in South Vietnam. In fact, Kissinger stated unapologetically, America's involvement in Vietnam, despite its defeat, "prevented Indonesia from falling to Communism and probably preserved the American presence in Asia." This assertion was clearly fiction, but it was the story that many conservatives told themselves to avoid the serious soul-searching that Vietnam demanded.

Meanwhile, George Bush watched the fall of Saigon from his diplomatic perch in China. The most thoughtful of the future presidents, Bush spent years trying to reconcile his deeply ingrained belief in American values and the importance of US military power with the recognition that the nation had just lost its first war. As the United Nations ambassador, Bush had seen firsthand the changing nature of international power as new nations emerged and demanded to be treated as equals. The days when the United States could dictate terms to other countries were over; multilateralism needed to replace America's penchant for unilateralism. But there were limits to Bush's efforts to integrate Vietnam into his worldview. "I have complete conviction that there is such a thing as a domino theory," he wrote in his diary. He never questioned America's motivations for getting involved in Vietnam and resented critics who accused the United States of imperialism.

In many ways, Bush's position was similar to what Nixon had announced early in his presidency: that the United States needed to exercise prudence in how it expended its resources. "We have got to be realistic," Bush observed. "We have to have our eyes open." By establishing priorities, the United States could ensure that "we are not committed in wars we shouldn't be involved in, where we'd have no support from the American people." Yet Bush admitted that while this sounded good in the abstract, he did not have a clear plan for implementing this sort of approach. "[I]f somebody said to me today what would you declare" to be America's vital interests, he conceded, "I'd be damned if I know how I'd define it."

Ronald Reagan was the only future president who showed no desire to rethink his views of the world in light of Vietnam. Now a private citizen, Reagan reassured the nation that its values (as well as its mission to spread those values) remained noble, that Communism remained as dangerous in the 1970s as it had been in the 1940s, and that the lessons of Munich remained relevant. He rejected détente, convinced that the Soviets, like Hitler's Germany, could not be trusted to keep their commitments. Speaking to a veterans convention a few months after the fall of Saigon, Reagan described the American withdrawal from Vietnam as more disgraceful "than any single event in our nation's history." As veterans cheered, Reagan declared that the United States should "never again . . . ask young men to fight and die for their country unless the goal is a complete victory."

Instead of questioning assumptions, Reagan searched for scapegoats, blaming the loss on a biased news media, spineless politicians, entitled students, and a weak president who failed to wage the war more aggressively.

"I have taken the position that an irresponsible Congress has, for the first time in 200 years, held the United States up to view as an untrustworthy country, capable of breaking its pledge to our allies," he wrote Nixon in April 1975. Reagan's solution was not to revise lessons learned during World War II but to grasp them more tightly. Ironically, his language echoed JFK's strident denunciations of Communism and calls for America to defend freedom around the world. Kennedy, however, had already begun questioning many of those assumptions by the time of his death in 1963. A decade later, Reagan revived the call for national greatness—a message that resonated with many Americans who wished to return to the days of US hegemony immediately following World War II.

Reagan molded his critique of Vietnam into a powerful message of nostalgia: The United States would move forward by returning to its glorious past. After the political and cultural shocks of the 1960s and early 1970s, Reagan understood that many Americans longed for stability and a return to "traditional values." They no longer wanted to feel guilty over Vietnam or apologetic for demanding law and order at home. Reagan reassured them that the goals that emerged from World War II could still be achieved: greater economic growth without inflation and the vigilant defense of freedom abroad.

Coming to terms with Vietnam was only one of the challenges the nation faced in the mid-1970s. The United States stood at a critical juncture in its history that challenged many of the core beliefs and institutions forged during World War II and its immediate aftermath. The two pillars of thought that emerged from World War II—that the country had discovered the tools to guarantee economic growth and that it had a responsibility to defend freedom around the globe—now lay in ashes. Vietnam, Johnson's dishonesty in justifying it, and Nixon's illegal behavior in the Watergate affair—all these issues contributed to a grave erosion of public faith in the integrity of elected leaders. Polls showed that trust in government declined from 80 percent in the late 1950s to only 33 percent in 1976.

At home, broader economic and political changes conspired to undermine confidence in economic growth. American productivity reached new lows, while inflation exploded to nearly 10 percent by the end of 1973. In 1974 retail prices increased by 11 percent and wholesale prices by 18 percent. The end of "cheap oil" also exacerbated the nation's economic woes. In response to American support for Israel in the October 1973 Yom Kippur War, Saudi Arabia cut oil production, leading to gas rationing and long lines at the pump. Additionally, for the first time since the end of World War II, American business encountered stiff competition from other countries as the industrial economies of western Europe and Japan finally recovered from the war. The US share of world trade declined by 16 percent between 1960 and 1970 and dropped another 25 percent during the 1970s. The surge in foreign competition offered consumers quality products at lower prices. But it also threatened jobs that had for years offered Americans high wages and dependable employment.

For all his personal failures, Nixon had taken the first step in accommodating these global changes. Abroad, the Nixon Doctrine, which made clear that the United States would not be dragged into another war like Vietnam, stressed the limits of American power. At home, he lectured Americans about the imperative of adjusting to an age of limits. The nation, he said, had to accept "a very stark fact: we are heading into the most acute energy shortage since World War II." Americans needed to sacrifice by cutting back on their energy demands: "less heat, less electricity, less gasoline," he told the nation.

Nixon may have declared himself a Keynesian out of political expediency, but he had at least tried to accommodate new economic realities. Ford, however, refused to acknowledge that the global environment had changed and that the United States needed to rein in its economic ambitions. His lifetime in Congress had left him unprepared for the challenges he faced as president. Neither a deep thinker nor a political visionary, he showed little willingness to challenge conventional wisdom. He replaced Nixon's wage and price controls with a voluntary program called Whip Inflation Now (WIN), which asked Americans to cut back on spending to slow inflation. His solution to the global oil crisis was to call for a tariff on oil imports, while cutting the price of domestic oil to spur production.

On foreign policy issues, Ford relied heavily on Kissinger, who pushed for continuing Nixon's policy of détente with the Soviets by agreeing to the outline of a SALT II treaty. "Anything that would bring the arms race under control would be a plus for the entire world," Ford declared. In the summer of 1975 he signed the Helsinki Accords, which called for peaceful settlements of disputes and greater scientific and economic co-operation between the two countries, and formally recognized the boundary settlements in Eastern Europe that the United States and the Soviet Union had agreed to at Yalta thirty years before as "legitimate." Two weeks earlier, the US Apollo and Soviet Soyuz manned spacecrafts achieved an apparent "détente in space" by linking 142 miles above the Earth.

Critics pointed out that the treaties left the Soviet Union with more nuclear missiles than the United States and that the Soviets were acting more aggressively in places such as Africa. Kissinger turned the argument on its head, saying that the rise of a new generation of Soviet leaders like Leonid Brezhnev made it even more important to keep a lid on the arms race by negotiating. "With him [Brezhnev]," Kissinger argued, "will go the entire age group that has such a morbid fear of war, based on the World War II experiences."

Meanwhile, Reagan rejected the Nixon-Ford emphasis on détente and touted a return to the glory days of American military superiority. He criticized the arms control agreements, claiming that the Helsinki Accords "put the seal of approval on the Red Army's World War II conquests." In a March 31, 1976, radio address, he pushed the point further, arguing that the Soviets had surpassed the United States in just about every military category. "The Soviet army outnumbers ours more than two to one and in reserves, four to one. They outspend us on weapons by fifty percent. Their navy outnumbers ours in surface ships and submarines two to one. We're outgunned in artillery three to one, and their tanks outnumber ours four to one," he said. Nixon's and Ford's efforts to maintain détente had left the United States "number two in a world where it's dangerous, if not fatal, to be second best." Once again he warned about the fate of other toppled empires: "I don't believe the people I've met in almost every state of this union are ready to consign this, the last island of freedom, to the dustbin of history, along with the bones of dead civilizations of the past."

Ironically, Reagan, who had long advocated for the international control of atomic weapons, feared that a nuclear imbalance would make the Soviets more likely to launch a nuclear strike. He planned to build up the nation's stockpile to give it the leverage needed to force Russia to engage in what he considered to be more meaningful agreements.

Reagan's message tapped into the frustrations of the growing conservative movement in America. Conservatives applauded his emphasis on morality, believing that the country's problems represented a crisis of the spirit, one instigated by the federal government and the liberals who staffed it. They were traumatized by many of the events of the previous decade—violent protests, demands for civil rights and women's rights, and the Supreme Court's 1973 decision legalizing abortion—all of which they viewed as signs of America's moral decline. Many felt humiliated by developments overseas as well. The outcome in Vietnam convinced them that the United States had become weak and lost its nerve to fight Communism.

Ford's immediate concern was to flex US military muscle in the wake of Vietnam, sending a clear signal that the United States would not withdraw from its international responsibilities despite its defeat in Asia. That thinking produced a major blunder. On the morning of May 12, 1975, the White House learned that Khmer Rouge rebels had seized an American merchant ship, the SS *Mayaguez,* along with its thirty-nine passengers, in international waters off the coast of Cambodia. Information was scarce and sometimes conflicting. "I knew from my own experience in the navy in World War II that specific information is hard to come by," Ford reflected. Regardless of the facts, he was determined to use the incident to demonstrate American resolve.

At a National Security Council meeting that afternoon, the president's advisors debated a response. Kissinger explained that two problems existed. The first was "how to get the ship back"; the second was "how the US appears at this time." He advocated for a "show of force" and even suggested that the United States "seize a Cambodian ship on the high seas." Vice President Nelson Rockefeller was the most outspoken hawk at the meeting. "I think a violent response is in order," he insisted. "We have to show that we will not tolerate this kind of thing. It is a pattern. If we do not respond violently, we will get nibbled to death. The world should know we will act and that we can act quickly." The others in the room fell right in line. Kissinger told the group, "We should give the impression that we are not to be trifled with," emphasizing that "the issues at stake go far beyond the seizure of the ship" and involved "international perceptions of US resolve and will."

Even before the incident, Kissinger was looking for an opportunity to "carry out some act somewhere in the world which shows [US] determination to continue to be a world power."

Kissinger now had his opportunity. "You must establish a reputation for being too tough to tackle," he told the president. "If you use force, it should be ferociously." This was not a time for delicate diplomacy; the United States needed to take decisive military action to preserve its prestige. Ford agreed: "We wanted them to know that we meant business." So, he sent more than a thousand marines to invade the Cambodian island of Koh Tang, where he believed the hostages were being held, and ordered the bombing of mainland Cambodia. From his perch in China, Bush applauded the action. "It shows our spine," he recorded in his diary. "It shows our unwillingness to be pushed around."

But it was all unnecessary. Ford ordered the attack after the sailors had already been released and then continued the bombing even after he had been informed that the crew was safe. The operation was once again costly. When the mission ended two days later, thirty-eight American servicemen were dead, and three marines had been left in Cambodia alive. A study by the US General Accounting Office concluded that "certain US actions probably" contributed to the Cambodian desire to free the crew but "the final marine assault and the bombing of the Cambodian mainland did not." That meant, the report declared, "41 American lives were lost unnecessarily" in a "futile" raid.

Nevertheless, Ford continued to believe he had rescued the crew, US credibility, and his own reputation. "Many people's faith in their country was restored, and my standing in the polls shot up 11 points," he recounted in his autobiography. The story made the cover of every news-magazine, with *Newsweek* deeming the mission "a daring show of nerve and steel."

———————

All of the events swirling around Ford worried Reagan, who shrugged off speculation that he would challenge the president in the 1976 GOP primaries. "I had never in my life thought of seeking or holding public office, and I'm still not quite sure how it all happened," said the man who ran for governor twice, tried to snatch the presidential prize from Nixon in 1968, stood ready if Nixon faltered, and now was considering a challenge to an incumbent president of his own party. "A candidate doesn't make the decision whether to run for president," he wrote in his autobiography, "the people make it for him." It also helped to have wealthy and influential friends who allowed Reagan to take advantage of a loophole in the election laws that enabled him to continue making a living while secretly campaigning for president.

His protestations to the contrary, Reagan maintained a high profile after leaving the Governor's Mansion in Sacramento. Within three months, he was making eight to ten speeches a month at an average fee of $5,000 per speech. His column appeared in 174 newspapers, and his commentaries aired on more than 200 radio stations. As governor, Reagan had balanced his ideological leanings with pragmatic tendencies, but on the lecture circuit, he was surrounded by impassioned conservatives yearning for ideological comfort. Reagan gave them what they wanted, rousing audiences with his diatribes against the federal government. He used colorful, often apocryphal, anecdotes drawn from letters he received and from crackpot publications to highlight his themes. For instance, he blasted subsidized housing projects in New York City, claiming that "if you are a slum dweller, you can get an apartment with eleven-foot ceilings, with a twenty-foot balcony, a swimming pool and gymnasium, laundry room and playroom, and the rent begins at $113.20, and that includes utilities." His favorite image was of the "welfare queen" who "has eighty names, thirty addresses, twelve Social Security cards, and is collecting veterans benefits on four nonexistent deceased husbands," and a "tax-free cash income [of] over $150,000." It did not matter that most of these stories were untrue. They resonated with the frustrations of the same members of the silent majority who had once rallied around Nixon.

Ford did not think highly of Reagan and was dismissive of his "superficial remedies for all the ills that affected America." "I hadn't taken those warnings seriously because I didn't take Reagan seriously," he reflected later. To Ford, the "one characteristic" that ruled Reagan out as a possible president "was his penchant for offering simple solutions to hideously complex problems." Ford also heard that Reagan was lazy—"a nine-to-five governor." "That alone would disqualify him from ever being president," Ford said. Despite the noise the ex-governor was making on the campaign trail, Ford "never thought Reagan would run."

The truth soon emerged. On the afternoon of November 19, 1975, Reagan called the White House to let Ford know that he had decided to enter the Republican primaries. "Well, Mr. President, I am going to make an announcement, and I want to tell you about it ahead of time. I am going to run for president. I trust we can have a good contest, and I hope that it won't be divisive."

"I'm sorry you're getting into this," Ford responded. "I believe I've done a good job, and that I can be elected. Regardless of your good intentions, your bid is bound to be divisive."

"I don't think it will harm the party," Reagan replied defensively.

"Well, I think it will," Ford snapped before slamming down the receiver. "It burned the hell out of me," he said later.

With Reagan posing the most serious challenge to an incumbent Republican in the Oval Office since 1912, when former president Theodore Roosevelt tried snatching the prize from William Howard Taft, Ford decided to shake up his team to prepare for a tough primary season. In mid-September 1975 he had seen a poll showing that 25 percent of Republicans would not vote for him if Rockefeller were the vice presidential nominee, because they considered him too liberal. Ford considered the poll an "ominous" warning. As Reagan biographer Lou Cannon wrote, "More than any other single act of Ford's, or indeed all of them combined, it was the selection of Rockefeller that fueled national interest among conservatives in a Reagan candidacy."

So, to appease conservatives, Ford privately pressured Rockefeller to remove himself from the 1976 ticket, a decision that he later described regretfully as "one of the few cowardly things I did in my life."

In addition to dropping Rockefeller, Ford shook up his Cabinet, replacing many Nixon appointees with men he knew would be loyal to him. At the end of October, Ford asked Bush to return to the States as head of the CIA. It was a challenging moment for the agency. In December 1974 *The New York Times* revealed that the CIA had spied on American citizens and monitored their political views, which was especially shocking given that the intelligence agency was barred from engaging in domestic affairs. In January 1975 the Senate set up a special committee, headed by Idaho senator Frank Church, which exposed secret wiretaps, bugging, and harassment of reporters, government officials, and private citizens, as well as facilitating a violent military coup against the democratically elected leader of Chile.

Bush was as surprised as most other people that Ford chose him, especially since he had no background in intelligence. It seems likely that the move was orchestrated by presidential aides Donald Rumsfeld and his deputy, Dick Cheney, who viewed Bush as a rising star, and thus a threat to their careers, and conspired to damage his career. That was certainly how Bush viewed it, believing that running the CIA would be a thankless, dead-end job that would mark the end of his political career. "I do not have politics out of my system entirely, and I see this as the total end of any political future," he noted in his diary. "I would not have selected this controversial position if the decision had been mine . . . [but] one should serve his country and his president. And so if this is what the president wants me to do, the answer is a firm 'yes.'"

In the end, despite opposition from liberal Democrats, who complained about having a political appointee run the spy agency, Bush won approval by a vote of 64–27.

Over the next few months, Reagan and Ford fought it out in the Republican primaries. When it was over, Ford ended up on top and won the nomination on the first ballot. Reagan was hardly gracious in defeat, telling *The New York Times* that Ford won because of manipulation in the "the machine states" and blaming "party bosses" for his loss. "There is no place in America for some of the things we saw happen to us," he declared.

After delivering an unmemorable acceptance speech, Ford, knowing many delegates remained sympathetic to Reagan, waved him up to the platform in a show of unity. To the cheers of the emotionally drained delegates, Reagan walked to the platform and gave a dramatic, six-minute speech that was more a call to battle than a concession. He speculated about how Americans a century from now would view this time. "Will they look back with appreciation and say, 'Thank God for those people in 1976 who headed off that loss of freedom? Who kept us now a hundred years later free? Who kept our world from nuclear destruction'?" The answer to those questions depended, Reagan insisted, "on what we do here." As delegates wept, he concluded by citing the late Douglas MacArthur: "We must go forth from here united, determined, that what a great general said a few years ago is true: 'There is no substitute for victory.'"

After the speech, Ford called on Reagan at his hotel room. It was an awkward moment. Despite the bitter campaign, Reagan would have been a logical choice for Ford to choose as his vice presidential nominee. However, a Reagan aide sent Ford a message saying that the governor did not want to be asked to join the ticket because it would be embarrassing to the president if Reagan rejected his offer. Instead, Ford chose Kansas senator Robert Dole. Years later, Reagan denied ever sending that message to Ford. James Baker III, a Bush ally who became a key aide in the Reagan White House, questioned the president about whether he would have accepted the nomination. "Look," Reagan responded, "I really did not want to be vice president, and I said so at the time. But I don't have any recollection of telling anyone to pass a message to President Ford not to offer me the spot. If he had asked, I would have felt duty bound to say yes."

A few weeks later, Reagan received a letter from Nixon consoling him about his defeat. "Having won a few and lost a few, I can say that winning is a lot more fun!" Nixon wrote, before congratulating him for conducting himself "magnificently" at the convention. "The millions who saw and heard you on T.V. during the convention had to conclude—even if they in some cases did not agree with your philosophy—that you were an eloquent and persuasive advocate of your point of view." Nixon then quoted from his wife, Pat, who had turned to him after Reagan had addressed the convention and said, "Ronald Reagan, in defeat, was as great as he was in victory." In his reply, Reagan assured the former president that he and Nancy were "at peace with ourselves." Yet he still insisted that he had been the victim of a rigged process, pointing out that "where delegates had freedom to vote, we did well. Defeat came in those three Northeast states where the party structure controlled the vote."

Reagan may not have won that year, but he continued to lay the groundwork for victory in the long term. According to biographer Craig Shirley, the 1976 campaign "marked the point when conservatives took over the Republican Party and changed its message and its ideology." He was right: Ford would be the last "moderate" to head the GOP ticket, and his ultimate defeat by Georgia's little-known governor, Jimmy Carter, set the stage for Reagan's second campaign for president in 1980.

Vietnam, social unrest, and a stagnant economy dealt the final blows to the institutions and worldviews that had emerged from World War II. While the fight against Nazism and Japanese imperialism had unified the nation in a common cause, events in the 1960s and 1970s did the opposite, splintering the United States into competing factions that could agree on little. For some leaders, the events of the previous decade required Americans to rethink the assumptions inherited from World War II and to instead recognize the limits of US military and economic power. Richard Nixon, for all his failures, acknowledged these changes and tried to nudge the country in a new direction aligned with the realities of the postwar world. At the same time, however, he skillfully manipulated the fears of white Americans who perceived social disorder and the Communist menace at every turn.

Reagan followed in Nixon's footsteps, not only channeling these cultural anxieties but also weaving a nostalgic vision that emerged from World War II: America as the dominant superpower, with a booming economy and white, heterosexual men standing atop the social pyramid. So it was that by 1976, two major elements—cultural resentment and nostalgia—formed the soul of the modern Republican Party.

═══

CHAPTER 12

"Make America Great Again"

JUNE 6, 1984
NORMANDY, FRANCE

President Ronald Reagan traveled to Normandy, France, as part of a ten-day trip that included a sentimental visit to his ancestral home of Ireland and to an economic summit in London. Since his trip coincided with the fortieth anniversary of D-Day, he planned to give a speech honoring the Americans who fought in that pivotal World War II battle. The original plan involved French president François Mitterrand greeting Reagan in the afternoon before the speech, but his US counterpart's media-savvy team insisted that Reagan's speech take place earlier in the day so that it could be covered live by the American morning television programs.

Most Americans associated World War II with the tragedy of Pearl Harbor or President Harry Truman's controversial decision to end the war by dropping the atomic bomb on Japan. Reagan's team looked instead for an event that commemorated a simpler story of heroism. But rather than marking D-Day by memorializing the well-known, bloody assault on Omaha and Utah Beaches, Reagan traveled to Pointe du Hoc, where, early on the morning of June 6, 1944, before the Allied assault on the beaches, Army Rangers had climbed the heavily defended hundred-foot cliffs, dodging German grenades and bullets to dismantle the 155 mm guns pointing below. Had their mission failed, it's likely that Nazi Germany's guns would have wreaked lethal havoc on the invading Allied forces and thus forestalled the invasion that would entirely change the war's direction.

On this cloudy, blustery day, Reagan stood in front of a monument that was situated atop a craggy piece of land jutting into the English Channel. Here the president did what he did best: He told a moving story of the brave men who had risked their lives to save the world from the scourge of Nazism. Sixty-two of the surviving Rangers sat facing him, dressed in dark blazers and gray slacks. "Behind me is a memorial that symbolizes the Ranger daggers that were thrust into the top of these cliffs," Reagan declared in a soft but firm voice that perfectly matched the cadence of his speech. "And before me are the men who put them there. These are the boys of Pointe du Hoc. These are the men who took the cliffs," he said, as he nodded to the veterans surrounding him. "These are the champions who helped free a continent. These are the heroes who helped end a war." His powerful words brought tears to the eyes of many of those in attendance, even hardened veterans and cynical reporters.

For the millions who watched or listened to Reagan's speech, the moral was clear: The United States should not repeat the mistakes of the 1930s by appeasing the Soviets in the 1980s. The monument at Pointe du Hoc provided the nation with a visual reminder of the dangers of appeasement and the need to stand strong against a ruthless enemy. It was, Reagan told the aging veterans of World War II, "better to be here ready to protect the peace than to take blind shelter across the sea, rushing to respond only after freedom is lost."

With this lesson in mind, Reagan came to office in 1981 preaching "peace through strength" and advocating for the largest peacetime increase in defense spending in history. He even made a surprising historical reference, citing FDR as a leader who stood on the right side of history. "I remember when Hitler was arming and had built himself up," Reagan told CBS news anchor Walter Cronkite shortly after becoming president. "Franklin Delano Roosevelt made a speech at the dedication of a bridge over the Chicago River. And in that speech, he called on the free world to quarantine Germany. Can we honestly look back now and say that World War II would have taken place if we had done what he [Roosevelt] wanted us to do back in 1938? I think there is a very good chance it wouldn't have taken place."

No World War II veteran who went on to the presidency was more wedded to the lessons of Munich than Ronald Reagan. At his first press conference in 1981, the fortieth president claimed that to achieve world domination, Soviet leaders "have openly and publicly declared that the only morality they recognize is what will further their cause, meaning they reserve unto themselves the right to commit any crime, to lie, to cheat, in order to attain that." He echoed this message again shortly afterward, telling the National Security Council, "The Soviets have spoken as plainly as Hitler in *Mein Kampf*." The battle between the United States and Soviet Union, he argued, was a "struggle between right and wrong and good and evil." Reagan firmly believed that the Kremlin was not simply immoral but that it commanded an "evil empire," one locked in a Manichean struggle against America.

Even before the word *détente* became part of the American vocabulary, both Democratic and Republican presidents had accepted the necessity of finding ways to coexist with the Soviets. Not Reagan. He longed for the days of American hegemony in the immediate aftermath of World War II, when the United States possessed sole ownership of the bomb and stood as a military Goliath over the ruined empires of Europe. Détente, he said dismissively, was "a French word the Russians had interpreted as a freedom to pursue whatever policies of subversion, aggression, and expansion they wanted anywhere in the world." For Reagan, uncompromising opposition to Communism—*not* détente—would be the defining feature of both his domestic and foreign policies.

Not surprisingly, the Soviets viewed Reagan's bellicose rhetoric and military buildup in the light of their own experiences during World War II. "The beginning of the Reagan presidency calls to mind the Fascist seizure of power," recalled a Soviet official, who recounted how the surprise Nazi invasion of 1941 led to twenty million Russian deaths. Ironically, the Soviets—like the Americans at Pearl Harbor—believed they had let down their guard and were thus determined not to commit the same mistakes. Moscow refused to show that it could be easily cowed, sending a warning to its Warsaw Pact allies that Washington "has declared a 'crusade' against Socialism as a social system."

Like his predecessors, however, Reagan possessed more complicated views than his simplified public pronouncements would suggest. Reagan never saw actual combat during World War II and understood the horrors of war only through celluloid depictions of death. But like most Americans, he was shocked by the destructive power of the atom bomb that swiftly brought about an end to the war. He agreed with Truman's decision, but, worried about the long-term consequences of nuclear weapons, he joined many liberals after the war to call for international control of the deadly weapons. Many of his beliefs had evolved since his early days as a Hollywood liberal, but on this point, he remained steadfast: The United States needed to create a world free from the threat of nuclear annihilation. That fear made him receptive to the overtures of the reform-minded Mikhail Gorbachev, a new breed of Soviet leader, and set in motion a process that would ultimately end the Cold War.

Before Reagan could implement his hard-line policies, however, he first needed to win the 1980 election. He had been running for president every election cycle since 1968, but now the stars finally seemed aligned. By 1980, the public had grown disillusioned with the leadership of Jimmy Carter, a 1946 graduate of the US Naval Academy who broke the string of successive World War II veterans occupying the White House since 1953.

Carter managed to squeak out a victory in 1976 by tapping into public anger over Watergate and high interest rates, as well as promising to lessen Cold War tensions. Once in office, however, Carter proved surprisingly ineffectual. At home, he never developed a consistent message for how to deal with crippling stagflation, and he struggled to get legislation passed, even though Democrats controlled both chambers of Congress. He preached the politics of austerity, lecturing Americans about the need to adjust to a new age of limits. With gasoline and heating prices soaring, Carter called the energy crisis the "moral equivalent of war" and proposed a comprehensive program to cut energy consumption. When Congress refused, Carter gave a dramatic speech in July 1979, describing a so-called crisis of confidence that "strikes at the very heart and soul and spirit of our national will." To address this crisis, he urged the development of alternative energy sources, higher oil and natural gas taxes, and tougher automobile fuel-efficiency standards. Carter had brilliantly dissected the public mood, but critics pounced, calling it the "malaise" speech, even though the president had never used the word.

Despite a few notable foreign policy successes, Carter also failed to convince the American public that he could protect the country's global interests from an aggressive Soviet Union. He came to office promising to move beyond the "inordinate fear of Communism" that had shaped American foreign policy since the beginning of the Cold War, but that promise soon went up in flames. In November 1979, Iranian nationalists, angry that Carter had allowed the now-exiled repressive shah of Iran, Mohammad Reza Shah Pahlavi, into the United States for cancer treatment, seized fifty-two American soldiers and diplomats and held them hostage in Tehran. Then, the following month, the Soviets invaded neighboring Afghanistan to prop up a bumbling regime. Carter responded by calling the invasion the "most serious threat to world peace since World War II"—and moving decisively away from détente. The public initially rallied around the embattled president, allowing him to fend off a spirited challenge from Senator Edward Kennedy, but he still entered the general election with dangerously low approval ratings.

Carter was clearly vulnerable, but before Reagan could challenge him, he needed to defeat another World War II veteran to secure the Republican nomination. Having almost topped an incumbent president in 1976, Reagan appeared to be the front-runner. But George H. W. Bush believed that the former governor was too conservative to win a general election. After leaving the CIA in 1976, Bush had returned home to Houston but soon found himself bored with private life. "I went home and couldn't figure out what the hell to do," Bush recalled. He had been thinking about running for president since his first foray into politics in the 1960s. Now he finally saw an opportunity. He spent the next few years delivering speeches to influential groups across the country. In 1979 alone he traveled an astonishing 246,000 miles.

For all of his experience in Washington and success in business, Bush twice lost a statewide race in Texas and had little national name recognition. For most of his career, he had been dependent on the generosity of more powerful men for his various government roles. Because he had always served under other presidents, Bush lacked a clear political identity. He belonged to a dying breed of establishment Republicans who were moderate on social issues such as abortion, conservative on fiscal issues, and hawkish on foreign policy—a mishmash that may have made sense in practice but did not translate well to political campaigns. "When asked why he was running," observed historian Timothy Naftali, "Bush recited a résumé instead of a rationale."

By contrast, no questions hovered around Reagan's political identity. The governor's message was as simple as it was compelling: love of country, fear of Communism, and scorn of government. Telegenic features, combined with extensive experience in front of a camera, made Reagan a master craftsman of the new art of technological campaigning. Calling for a "new beginning" that included large reductions in personal taxes, cuts in unnecessary social spending, and massive increases in defense spending, Reagan promised to "renew the American spirit and sense of purpose." His sunny optimism resonated with a nation tired of stagflation, daily reminders of hostages held in Iran, and Carter's gloomy austerity lectures. Polls showed that between 1973 and 1980, less than 30 percent thought the country was on the "right track." For the first time, a generation of Americans worried that their children might not have the same opportunities in life that they had enjoyed. Amid this fraught context, according to historian Garry Wills, Reagan became a "symbol of America" and a figurative "angel of our better natures."

Reagan tapped into two powerful currents that were beginning to transform American politics in the 1970s. The first was the rise of Christian fundamentalism. Between 1963 and 1978, the number of Americans who identified themselves as "born again" increased from 24 percent to nearly 40 percent. America, they preached, confronted a crisis of the spirit brought on by the pervasive influence of "secular humanism," which stressed material well-being and personal gratification over religious conviction and devotion to traditional Christian values. In their minds, the federal government—and the liberals who staffed it—were responsible for America's moral decline. The second current of historical change arose from vociferous anti-tax sentiment. In 1978, voters in Reagan's home state of California overwhelmingly approved Proposition Thirteen, which reduced assessments, limited property taxes to 1 percent of full value, and prevented the easy passage of new taxes. As the tax cut wildfire spread throughout the states, Prop 13's congressional cousin—the Kemp-Roth tax bill calling for a one-third slash in federal income taxes—gained converts in Washington as well. "This isn't just a tax revolt," insisted President Carter's pollster, Pat Caddell. "It's a revolution against government."

Part of the problem was that voters had lost faith in government and did not trust it to spend their tax dollars wisely. In addition, stagflation challenged old economic assumptions and exposed the limits of Keynesian economics, which had held sway in policymaking circles since World War II. Not only had Keynesians argued that the government should manipulate aggregate demand through taxing and spending, but also they assumed that a trade-off existed between inflation and unemployment. When one went down, the other went up. But during the 1970s, both increased at the same time. The failure of Keynesian theory to explain or solve this unprecedented economic crisis created a vacuum that conservatives filled with their own radical theory: supply-side economics.

The challenge facing conservatives in 1980 was that while Americans demanded tax relief, they still embraced popular and expensive entitlement programs. To square the circle of cutting taxes while maintaining those programs, supply-side advocates argued—with no evidence—that by lowering taxes on the wealthiest Americans, the government would provide an incentive for them to reinvest, creating new businesses and more jobs. Even though tax rates would be lower, supply-siders reasoned, revenues would actually increase, since more people would be willing to pay taxes. Supply-side theory allowed conservatives to have the best of both worlds: They campaigned as tax reform crusaders but also claimed they would be able to dramatically expand spending on defense, while protecting popular government entitlements such as Social Security.

Reagan's personal disdain for taxes dated back to World War II when he had to pay a 91 percent income tax on his $3,500 per week earnings. Supply-side theory seemed to be the solution he had long waited for. Though the math never added up, Reagan clung to his convictions. Herbert Stein, who served as chairman of the Council of Economic Advisers under Nixon, dismissed Reagan's program as "the economics of joy"— completely divorced from reality. Stein had a point: Ironically, Reagan's utopian dreams of providing for everyone were more reminiscent of the spirit that animated Lyndon Johnson's Great Society than the staid conservatism of Dwight Eisenhower.

As primary season commenced, Bush scored a surprising upset in the Iowa caucus, but squandered his momentum with a disastrous performance at a debate in New Hampshire. The two men agreed to a debate organized by the *Nashua Telegraph* editorial staff but paid for by the Reagan campaign. The newspaper invited only Reagan and Bush, the two front-runners. When the debate opened, both men were seated on the stage, but Reagan insisted that the other candidates, who were gathered next to the stage, be permitted to participate. As Reagan voiced his objection, the moderator ordered the sound technician to turn off his microphone, prompting booing from the crowd. Reagan was furious, declaring, "I am paying for this microphone, Mr. Green!" (His real name was Breen.) The audience erupted. Bush remained still, staring straight ahead like a deer caught in headlights. According to one observer, Bush "looked like his mother had dropped him off at the wrong birthday party." Reagan also recognized that the debate marked a turning point in the campaign, exposing a seemingly cowardly side to Bush. "I may have won the debate, the primary—and the nomination—right there."

Reagan went on to secure New Hampshire in a landslide. Over the next few weeks, the two men sharpened their attacks. Bush dismissed Reagan's embrace of supply-side economics as "voodoo economics," and suggested repeatedly that the sixty-nine-year-old Reagan lacked the vigor to be president due to his age. He also ran ads comparing Reagan's inexperience to Carter's, asking, "Can we afford the same mistake twice?" For his part, Reagan told primary voters that Bush was too Ivy League for the GOP's new grassroots base and that he lacked true conservative principles. Voters clearly believed that Reagan had the best argument, as he racked up victories in South Carolina, Alabama, Florida, Georgia, and Illinois.

By the spring, it had grown clear that Bush could not secure enough delegates to win the nomination. Reluctantly, he dropped out, hoping that the gesture would earn him a place on the ticket as Reagan's running mate.

Bush seemed the logical choice because he added geographical and ideological diversity to the ticket. However, Reagan was not convinced. Not only did the governor's most conservative advisors consider Bush too liberal, but Reagan remained angry over Bush's criticisms during the campaign, especially the "voodoo economics" remark and his suggestion that Reagan was too old. Then there was Bush's performance at the Nashua debate, which left Reagan with the impression that Bush did not respond well under pressure. While some in his campaign lectured the former governor about how Bush would complement the ticket, especially in swing states and with more moderate voters, Reagan continued to resist. "I can't take him," Reagan snapped when an aide suggested that he choose Bush. "That 'voodoo economic policy' charge and his stand on abortion are wrong."

The Reagan campaign's internal polls revealed that Gerald Ford was the only vice presidential nominee who scored better than Bush. So, he tried to woo his former opponent to join the ticket.

Since Reagan had come to him, Ford assumed he could negotiate certain conditions on personnel and White House structure. Through intermediaries, Ford made clear that "his primary interest in the Congress had been national security" and that "he would like to advise" Reagan "on national security and foreign policy issues." Ford made personnel demands as well, insisting that Reagan bring back Henry Kissinger as secretary of state—a choice that would be difficult for Reagan to swallow, since he had based his campaign on attacking détente, the centerpiece of Kissinger's strategy for dealing with the Soviets. Furthermore, Ford envisioned himself functioning as the de facto White House chief of staff. A joke began circulating on the Republican convention floor: "Ford will be president before nine, after five, and on weekends."

Not surprisingly, Reagan balked at Ford's demands. But it was a television interview that the former president granted to CBS anchor Walter Cronkite that turned Reagan's irritation into outright revulsion. When Cronkite asked whether "it's got to be something like a co-presidency," Ford responded obliquely: "That's something Governor Reagan really ought to consider." All that Reagan heard was the word *co-presidency*— and it was too much. "Did you hear what he said about co-presidency?" Reagan asked in disbelief.

"As far as Ronnie was concerned, that did it," recalled Nancy. The suggestion that Reagan would be sharing the sovereignty of the office with the vice president was simply unacceptable.

With Ford out, Bush now became the logical choice, but Reagan still resisted the idea. Reagan aide Richard Allen, who supported Bush, asked the governor whether he would reconsider if Bush agreed to all of the positions in the platform. Reagan had put his stamp of approval on the most conservative Republican platform in recent memory. For the first time in four decades, the Republican Party did not endorse the Equal Rights Amendment, which guaranteed all Americans equal rights regardless of sex. The platform came out in favor of a pro-life constitutional amendment and backed supply-side economics—positions contrary to what Bush had campaigned on. Reagan mulled over Allen's suggestion before declaring, "Well, if you put it that way, I would agree to reconsider." At precisely 11:38 P.M. on July 16, Reagan called his new running mate. "George," he said, "I would like to go over there and tell them that I am recommending you for vice president. Could I ask you one thing: Do I have your permission to make an announcement that you support the platform across the board?" As he had done in the past, Bush effortlessly switched his position on issues in order to gain the political prize that he sought.

In many ways, Reagan and Bush were vastly different politicians. During World War II, Reagan wore the uniform but never left the United States; Bush served as a combat veteran and nearly lost his life. Reagan was a product of Hollywood; Bush, although living in Texas, never shed his privileged East Coast upbringing. Reagan was a conservative ideologue who understood the importance of using symbols and rhetoric to sway voters; Bush was a political pragmatist, uncomfortable with the media and shy about articulating broad themes. Reagan was aloof and reserved in private but knew the power of television and how to project warmth on camera; Bush was outgoing, gregarious, and enjoyed the company of others but never learned how to use television to inspire voters.

Those differences, however, would mean little in the heat of the campaign. In his acceptance speech to an upbeat and boisterous convention in Detroit, Reagan framed the essential issue of the campaign in attractively simple terms. "The major issue of this campaign is the direct political, personal, and moral responsibility of Democratic Party leadership—in the White House and in Congress—for this unprecedented calamity which has befallen us," he told the enthusiastic crowd. "They say that the United States has had its day in the sun; that our nation has passed its zenith. They expect you to tell your children that the American people no longer have the will to cope with their problems; that the future will be one of sacrifice and few opportunities. My fellow citizens, I utterly reject that view." With cheerful confidence, Reagan promised to restore America's influence in the world and revive a struggling economy, urging the nation to join his "great national crusade to make America great again."

Throughout his campaign for president in 1980, Reagan repeated the mantra that he would "make America great again." The phrase, emblazoned on campaign cups and posters, captured the essence of Reagan's worldview. His mission was to purge the nation of the social unrest of the 1960s and return to the sureties of the 1940s and 1950s. "If I could be elected president, I wanted to do what I could to bring about a spiritual revival in America," he reflected. Although he talked about a revolution, what he really wanted was a restoration. The civil rights struggle of the 1960s and the empowerment movements that grew out of the 1970s had challenged the old social and racial orders. Reagan wanted to put back together what he and his fellow conservatives perceived as broken.

By mid-July, Reagan held a commanding 30-point lead over Carter in the polls. The race tightened over the ensuing months as Democrats closed ranks around their nominee, and the president's verbal assaults took their toll on the governor. In his acceptance speech, Carter depicted Reagan as someone who lived in "a world of tinsel and make-believe." Not only would Reagan "launch an all-out nuclear arms race," but also he would attack "everything that we've done in the achievement of social justice and decency in the last fifty years." Carter claimed that the nation faced "a choice between two futures": a democratic one of "security and justice and peace" and a Reagan future marked by "despair," "surrender," and "risk." The 1980 presidential race was complicated by the presence of a third-party candidate: Illinois congressman John Anderson, a white-haired fiscal conservative and culturally liberal Republican.

Reagan opened his campaign in Philadelphia, Mississippi, where, sixteen years earlier, the Ku Klux Klan had murdered three civil rights activists. He wasted little time summoning the coded phrase that every white southerner understood. "I believe in states' rights," he told the raucous, uniformly white crowd. As *New York Times* columnist Bob Herbert observed, "Reagan may have been blessed with a Hollywood smile and an avuncular delivery, but he was elbow deep in the same old race-baiting Southern strategy of Goldwater and Nixon." Reagan's racial appeals may have been subtler than those of Goldwater and Nixon, but they were no less effective. With his support for "states' rights," along with his attacks on "welfare queens" and school integration, Reagan connected with voters who opposed civil rights advances. These voters perceived themselves as victims of "government actions that cost them the privileges their whiteness once afforded them," wrote historian Rick Perlstein.

In the hopes of countering Carter's strident attacks against Reagan as a warmonger, the campaign tried to humanize him by producing a mini biographical film. It told the story of a boy raised "in America's heartland, small-town Illinois," who went on to build a successful career in Hollywood. As Reagan and his handlers would do throughout his time in politics, the biography straddled the truth in describing his experience during World War II. Just like the early fan magazines published during the war, the film created the false impression that Reagan had wartime experience comparable to that of other GIs stationed overseas. Reagan, it declared, had been "a peacetime volunteer army officer, and with the outbreak of World War II, he signed on for active duty." It failed to mention the great lengths to which Warner Bros. had gone to secure deferments for him so that he could spend the war making films in Culver City, California.

The race remained deadlocked until late October, when the nation turned its attention to the lone debate between the two presidential candidates, to be held a week before Election Day. Among those anticipating the showdown was Richard Nixon, who sent Reagan an unsolicited letter offering both practical and strategic advice. On a practical level, he suggested that Reagan rest for at least two days before the debate, and that on the day of the debate, he should have nothing on his schedule other than keeping up with breaking news stories. "You know that I learned the hard way in 1960—that how you look is if anything more important than what you say," Nixon wrote.

Ironically, Nixon also recommended following the example of his archnemesis, JFK: Instead of responding to the question asked, simply repeat talking points. "I would suggest you ask your smartest advisors . . . to list eight or ten points they would like to see you make. Then make them even if the questions do not call directly for that kind of answer." Additionally, he suggested that Reagan use human stories to dramatize the pain of inflation. "In the final analysis, in a close election it comes down to how people look at the two men. You come over on T.V. like gangbusters, and despite his glibness with the facts and figures, he comes over like a little man. That is why I have told people that while he might win the debate, which I would question, you will certainly win the audience."

On October 28 nearly half of all Americans—120 million people—tuned in for the Cleveland debate. For most of the broadcast, the two men held their own. But in his closing remarks, Reagan focused public attention on Carter's responsibility for double-digit inflation, the Americans still being held hostage in Iran, and Soviet troops in Afghanistan. "Are you better off than you were four years ago?" he asked. "Is America as respected throughout the world as it was?" By appearing calm and thoughtful, as well as deflecting many of Carter's attacks with good humor, Reagan effectively erased his image as a trigger-happy warmonger and emerged the clear winner. His lead widened considerably in the days after the debate.

On Election Day, Reagan trounced Carter, winning 51 percent of the vote to Carter's 41 percent. Only 7 percent of voters chose Anderson. The Democrats, moreover, lost not only thirty-four House seats but also twelve Senate seats, thus losing control of the upper chamber by a margin of 53–47. Postelection surveys showed that Reagan received overwhelming support—71 percent—from those who opposed government actions to improve the lives of African Americans. Since Carter received 93 percent of those backing those same policies, and there was no diminution of support for other social programs, it is appropriate to conclude that much of Reagan's victory stemmed from racial resentment that had been pent up for decades.

On January 20, 1981, two weeks before his seventieth birthday, Ronald Reagan took the oath of office to become the fortieth president of the United States. For the first time in the history of the presidency, he stood on a podium that overlooked the National Mall and faced symbolically westward toward the Potomac and the Sun Belt beyond. In keeping with that spirit, Reagan used his inaugural address to evoke a sense of rebirth and new directions, calling for "an era of national renewal." Abandoning Carter's message of limits, Reagan gestured toward a future of unlimited possibilities led by "a strong, prosperous America at peace with itself and the world." At home, Reagan pledged, a growing economy would "provide equal opportunities for all Americans, with no barriers born of bigotry or discrimination." Abroad, the United States would "again be the exemplar of freedom and a beacon of hope for those who do not now have freedom." Yet Reagan also had a warning for the nation: These grand expectations could be realized only if Americans scaled back the power of the federal government. To the delight of conservatives, Reagan declared, "In this present crisis, government is not the solution to our problem; government *is* the problem."

For many on the Right, the 1980 election represented the long-awaited triumph of Richard Nixon's conservative majority. "Like a great soaking wet shaggy dog, the Silent Majority—banished from the house during the Watergate storms—romped back into the nation's parlor this week and shook itself vigorously," observed the columnist William Safire. Indeed, the conservative movement only emerged stronger after a brief period of licking its wounds, and the new president rode the cultural and political backlash against the 1960s straight into the White House. His message of traditional values and smaller government appealed to Americans rocked by the resignation of a president, the painful experience of a lost war, the trials of stagflation, and the humiliation of Americans being held hostage in Iran.

Along with confronting the Soviets, Reagan's other priority in the White House was to revive a struggling economy. This would be no easy task. He came to office during one of the steepest downturns since the Great Depression, with unemployment at 7.4 percent and the cost of living soaring by more than 20 percent. On February 18, 1981, Reagan announced his economic plan before Congress, promising "to put the nation on a fundamentally different course, a course leading to less inflation, more growth and a brighter future for all of our citizens." Two days later, the headline in *The New York Times* declared, "Trying to Repeal Keynes—President's Plans Considered as Revolutionary as Those Espoused by the New Deal in the 30's." It was clear that the Reagan administration saw itself as making history, guiding the nation boldly toward an economic renaissance.

But those plans came to a screeching halt on March 30, 1981, when a would-be assassin shot and seriously wounded the new president as he left the Washington Hilton Hotel. A bullet that ricocheted off the presidential limousine struck Reagan, puncturing his lung before lodging within an inch of his heart. Press Secretary James Brady took a bullet to his head that left him permanently disabled; a Secret Service agent and a policeman were also injured. Throughout the ordeal, Reagan showed courage and spirit. "Honey, I forgot to duck," he quipped to Nancy as he was wheeled into the operating room. Humor aside, Reagan was in serious condition. His deputy press secretary took notes as the doctors briefed the Reagan team. "Doctors believe bleeding to death," he wrote. "Can't find a wound. Think we're going to lose him. Touch and go."

While the commander in chief lay unconscious on the operating table, the White House should have temporarily transferred presidential authority to the vice president. But Reagan's inner circle worried that doing so would alarm the country and its allies—and, perhaps most of all, remind people of Reagan's age. So instead Bush, who was in Texas when he learned of the shooting, rushed back to Washington, knowing that he needed to carefully manage the situation without appearing overly eager to assume Reagan's responsibilities. He disregarded suggestions that his helicopter land on the South Lawn of the White House and instead landed at the vice president's mansion at six thirty. "Only the president lands on the White House lawn," he replied humbly. He then traveled by motorcade to the White House. Upon arriving in the Situation Room at seven o'clock, roughly four and a half hours after the shooting, Bush immediately exerted a calming effect on Reagan's jittery Cabinet. By then, the president was out of danger.

In the short run, the assassination drama only heightened Reagan's popularity and swayed Congress into accepting his radical economic plan. An ABC News/Washington Post survey indicated that the president's rating soared 11 points, to 73 percent, immediately following the assassination attempt. "The bullet meant to kill him," observed *Newsweek*, "made him a hero instead, floating above the contentions of politics and the vagaries of good news or bad." In May dispirited Democrats joined Republicans in passing a budget resolution that called for deep cuts in many social programs and increased spending for the military. "The people have been heard," Reagan said triumphantly after the vote. Three months later, Congress rubber-stamped the administration's massive tax cut, providing for across-the-board reductions of 5 percent the first year and an additional 10 percent in each of the succeeding two years. He also gave tacit support to the Federal Reserve's policy of applying monetary brakes on the economy to wring out inflation. The strategy worked, but at a high cost. Raising the federal funds rate to 20 percent strangled growth and produced an unemployment rate of 9.5 percent— the highest since 1941.

Budget director David Stockman, a precocious Michigan congressman with an affinity for numbers, had warned Reagan early on that his policies would produce massive deficits. "We are facing potential deficit numbers so big that they can wreck the president's entire economic program," he told Reagan. Stockman estimated that the deficit would top $80 billion by fiscal year 1983 and $110 billion by 1986. "The president was stunned," Stockman recalled, but he refused to acknowledge the reality. "No, we can't give up on a balanced budget," Reagan insisted. "Deficit spending is how we got into this mess." Reagan refused to listen to Stockman's recommendation that the administration slow the pace of defense spending to balance the budget. "There must be no perception by anyone in the world that we're backing down an inch on the defense budget," he declared.

"I'm being stubborn," Reagan wrote in his diary. "I think our tax cuts will produce more revenue by stimulating the economy. I intend to wait and see some results."

In the long run, the goodwill following Reagan's attempted assassination started to run dry. In 1982 Congress not only rejected some of the president's cuts in social programs but also forced Reagan to raise taxes again to address the deficit. The legislation doubled the excise tax on tobacco and boosted taxes by nearly $100 billion over three years. But the president continued to deny that he had raised taxes. "To . . . refer to this as a tax increase, I think was wrong. It was an adjustment." Ironically, at the same time that he was blowing a hole in the budget, Reagan campaigned for a balanced-budget amendment. One columnist aptly described Reagan's approach as "a classic example of the drunk preaching temperance."

Despite the high interest rates and ballooning deficit, the economy began showing signs of life by 1984, when the GNP increased by an impressive 4.3 percent. Inflation fell from 12.4 percent to 4.1 percent; interest rates dropped from 21.5 percent to 12 percent; and unemployment, still high at 7 percent, had declined from a high of 10 percent. Nearly 60 percent of voters gave Reagan credit for the improvement.

This good economic news virtually sealed Reagan's reelection in 1984, when he crushed former vice president Walter Mondale. Riding a wave of personal and organizational confidence, Reagan exhorted citizens "to make America great again and let the eagle soar." On Election Day voters returned Reagan to office with 59 percent of the popular vote and the biggest electoral vote total in history: 525. Mondale received only 41 percent and 13 electoral votes. Reagan swept the entire nation except for Minnesota and the District of Columbia. Rarely had America seen such an all-encompassing landslide. In every region, in every age group, in virtually every demographic slice of a heterogeneous nation, the message was clear: "Four more years."

At the start of Reagan's second term, relations between the two super-powers had hit rock bottom. Reagan had spent the last few years not only talking tough but also backing up that talk with concrete actions. He took a hard line on discussions with the Soviets to limit both Intermediate-Range Nuclear Forces (INF) and Strategic Arms Reduction Talks (START), demanding that the Soviets make a disproportionate share of the cuts. Reagan complicated matters when he announced in March 1983 that the United States would develop the Strategic Defense Initiative (SDI), a missile defense system that in theory would use lasers to destroy enemy missiles before they could strike their targets. In his mind, the initiative would move the world closer to nuclear disarmament by making nuclear weapons obsolete. He even promised to share the technology with the Soviets. But the Kremlin feared that the deployment of the system—dubbed "Star Wars" by critics—would destabilize relations between the two countries by providing the United States with a first-strike capability.

US-Soviet relations were thus already tense when, in September 1983, a Soviet interceptor aircraft shot down a Korean Air Lines plane, killing all 269 people on board, after the Boeing 747 strayed into Soviet air space on a flight from Anchorage, Alaska, to Seoul, South Korea. American intelligence suggested the tragedy was the result of confusion and incompetence on the part of Soviet military officials who believed the civilian airliner was a spy plane, but Reagan, genuinely outraged by the incident, called it "an act of barbarism, born of a society which wantonly disregards individual rights and the value of human life." Reagan's moralistic condemnation, coupled with the stalemate on arms control, stoked the Soviet Union's fears that the United States was preparing for war. For the first time since the Cuban Missile Crisis, Moscow sent a message to its stations in Western capitals, warning staff to prepare for an imminent attack.

Convinced that negotiations with the United States were futile, Soviet diplomats walked out of the INF talks. The United States responded by deploying new missiles in West Germany, Britain, and Italy. The Soviets then moved new rockets into Czechoslovakia and East Germany. Fears of a nuclear Armageddon rapidly swept through western Europe and the United States. "The second cold war has begun," shrilled an Italian newspaper.

By 1984, World War II had faded into a distant memory for many Americans. The deep psychic wounds of Vietnam were fresher, and they taught a different set of lessons: that the United States needed to abandon its fear of Communism and limit the use of force. As the historians Fredrik Logevall and Kenneth Osgood pointed out, Reagan saw a common theme uniting the two conflicts: "One war began because of weakness; another was lost because of it," they observed. "Both taught the very same lesson: the importance of standing firm in the face of aggression." For Reagan, Vietnam taught not the value of restraint but the necessity of revitalizing and remoralizing America's power. That was why he felt comfortable telling a convention of the Veterans of Foreign Wars that Vietnam was "a noble cause . . . a war that was necessary to check the expansionist designs of the Soviet Union and its client states and to uphold the global position of the United States."

Like many of his conservative supporters, the president believed that the "liberal media," antiwar protestors, and incompetent Washington bureaucrats were responsible for America's defeat in Vietnam because they forced the military to fight with "one hand tied behind their backs." While Reagan did fear the costs of war, he also believed that only through war could the United States ensure peace. "If we are forced to fight, we must have the means and the determination to prevail, or we will not have what it takes to secure the peace," he stated. "And while we are at it, let us tell those who fought in that war that we will never again ask young men to fight and possibly die in a war our government is afraid to let them win."

Reagan now applied that interpretation—with disastrous results—to simmering conflicts in Central America, where left-wing insurgents were seeking to overthrow dictatorial regimes. Hearkening back to the early days of the Cold War, Reagan revived the domino theory, claiming that the Soviets were behind these new efforts to challenge the status quo. For Reagan and his advisors, any leftist victory in Latin America would give rise to another Cuba that could serve as a staging ground for Soviet expansion throughout the rest of the Western hemisphere. "Let us not delude ourselves," he advised the American people. "The Soviet Union underlies all the unrest that is going on. If they weren't engaged in this game of dominos, there wouldn't be any hot spots in the world."

In language reminiscent of Lyndon Johnson, Reagan claimed that America's objective in Central America was to preserve the freedom and right of self-determination of the peoples living there. In El Salvador, a poor country where 2 percent of the population controlled nearly all of the wealth, a coalition of leftist guerrillas had been attempting to topple the government. Reagan, convinced that the rebels represented Soviet influence, spent lavishly on military and economic aid to the government. Similarly, in an effort to overthrow the leftist Sandinista government in Nicaragua, the CIA spent hundreds of millions of dollars training guerrilla soldiers known as contras, whom Reagan glorified as "freedom fighters" and the "moral equivalent of our Founding Fathers."

Reagan believed that critics who compared his approach to Latin America to President Johnson's policy in Vietnam were mistaken. Once again the former actor chose to stick to his version of reality, seeing no difference between the lessons of World War II and those of Vietnam. His advisors, however, were forced to develop policies that made sense in a post-Vietnam world. Given that discrepancy, divisions soon began to crop up among them, and Reagan never imposed discipline on the contentious process. Chief of Staff James Baker recalled that policymaking within the administration was "a witch's brew of intrigue, elbows, egos, and separate agendas," adding, "You never had a day when the secretary of state and the secretary of defense weren't at each other's throats."

On one side stood the pragmatists, such as Baker, Defense Secretary Caspar Weinberger, and the Joint Chiefs of Staff. In 1984 Weinberger, believing that it was a mistake to send American ground troops to Vietnam without popular support or a clear strategy for victory, spelled out tests "to be applied when we are weighing the use of US combat forces abroad." Weinberger was determined to prevent American servicemen from falling prey to another ill-conceived mission. His goal was to establish reasonable criteria that would navigate a course between policy extremes. Weinberger argued that US forces should be used only if (1) the nation's vital interests were at stake; (2) the country was willing to commit the necessary number of troops to achieve victory; (3) the military was given clear and specific objectives to achieve; (4) the policy had the support of the American people and Congress; and (5) all other diplomatic efforts had failed. The press quickly dubbed this approach the "Weinberger Doctrine," which *The Washington Post* opined was "simply distilling the post-Vietnam consensus."

Other conservatives in the administration, whose worldviews remained shaped by World War II, objected vehemently to the limits that Weinberger placed on the use of force. United Nations ambassador and neoconservative Jeane Kirkpatrick, Secretary of State Alexander Haig and his successor George Shultz, and CIA Director William Casey feared that the new doctrine would represent a retreat from America's global commitments and create a power vacuum that the Soviets would eagerly fill. Openly disdainful of Congress and public opinion, they believed that the use of force was a legitimate presidential prerogative. In his memoirs, Secretary Shultz claimed that the Weinberger Doctrine "was the Vietnam syndrome in spades, carried to an absurd level, and a complete abdication of the duties of leadership."

Ironically, for all of his combative rhetoric, Reagan did recognize the public's deep-seated fears of military intervention abroad and expressed remorse over any loss of life. In 1982 he sent US Marines on an ill-conceived multinational peacekeeping mission to war-torn Lebanon that resulted in the deaths of 241 servicemen, when, on October 23, 1983, a terrorist suicide bomber drove an explosive-laden truck into the four-story US barracks in Beirut, demolishing the building. Reagan later called it the "saddest day of my presidency, perhaps the saddest day of my life." Perhaps that memory partially explains why he deployed military power only twice in his eight years in office. The most dramatic use of force came two days after the Beirut barracks bombing, when Reagan ordered 1,900 marines to invade the tiny Caribbean island nation of Grenada. The eight-day campaign, Operation Urgent Fury, was initiated to evacuate nearly six hundred American students who were attending school there, as well as to reinstall the pro-American government that had been overthrown by militant Marxists. Although US casualties were considered relatively light, nineteen lives were lost in the fighting. Then in April 1986, during Reagan's second term, Libyan agents blew up a Berlin nightclub that was popular with American soldiers. The president ordered a retaliatory air strike that killed an estimated thirty-seven Libyans, including the infant daughter of Libyan strongman Muammar al-Qaddafi.

Nevertheless, the Reagan administration's tendency to provide indirect support to anti-Communist puppet regimes resulted in a confused foreign policy, simultaneously interventionist and restrained.

By the time he spoke at Pointe du Hoc in the summer of 1984, Reagan was beginning to rethink his hard line toward the Soviets. Changing political currents pushed him to adjust course. His strident opposition to arms control and his tough Cold War rhetoric revived a nascent peace movement in the United States and Europe. Polls showed that nearly 60 percent of Americans favored an immediate freeze on the testing, production, and deployment of nuclear weapons. At the same time, critics questioned the wisdom of the administration's policies. "Cease this madness," implored George Kennan, the father of containment. Reagan's own pollsters were telling him to tone down his belligerent language, as evidence indicated that a large number of voters believed Reagan was "more likely" than his Democratic opponent in 1984, Walter Mondale, "to start an unnecessary war."

At the same time, the threat of global annihilation seeped into the realm of popular culture. On November 20, 1983, more than one hundred million US viewers anxiously tuned in to the ABC movie of the week: *The Day After,* a riveting and terrifying two-hour drama that portrayed the effects of a nuclear exchange between the Soviet Union and the United States on Lawrence, Kansas. Reagan was so concerned that the movie would frighten Americans from his efforts to increase the nation's nuclear arsenal that he asked for an advance copy, which he watched at Camp

David on October 10, 1983. "It is powerfully done, all $7 million worth," he reflected in his diary. "It's very effective and left me greatly depressed." Shortly afterward, he met with military leaders to discuss how America would respond to a nuclear attack. The briefings, he reflected, were "a most sobering experience" that "paralleled those in the ABC movie." He found it hard to believe that if the Soviets launched a nuclear weapon, he would have only six minutes "to unleash Armageddon!"

A letter from Nixon that arrived shortly after Reagan's landslide victory in 1984 also nudged the president to negotiate with the Soviets. The two men had maintained cordial relations over the years. Reagan had been a fierce defender of Nixon during Watergate and felt that he was unfairly forced from office by the liberal media and partisan Democrats. During the 1970s, Nixon recognized Reagan as a rising star in the party and, perhaps, someone who could use his foreign policy advice.

Although there had been little warmth between the two men, Reagan was unusually emotional when he learned that Nixon had been hospitalized just a few months after leaving office and that his life hung in the balance. He called Nixon's home and spoke with his daughter Tricia. Her sister Julie left the following message for her father: "Dear Daddy, Gov. Reagan called [and] told Tricia, 'Just hope your father knows how many people love him and are pulling for him.' He and Nancy have been praying for him." She then added: "What we want to tell you about the call is that Gov Reagan could hardly speak because he was so emotional—really crying."

Perhaps some of that closeness motivated Nixon to pen a five-page memo to Reagan, titled "A New Approach for the Second Term." In it, he advised the current chief executive that in a second term, "even after a landslide," a president "has a much briefer honeymoon and a less effective mandate than after his first election." He offered a brief history lesson going back to FDR and suggested that in order to avoid repeating the past, Reagan "needed to move on three fronts: new men, new ideas and new drive. . . . What is required is to give the new administration a sense of purpose and drive toward great new goals rather than being satisfied with continuing the policies of the past, even though they have just received an overwhelming vote of approval. . . . What he should recognize is that he will have won on his own. He will owe his victory to *no one* and *everyone*." The ambitious goal that he had in mind was for Reagan to take the lead in "establishing a new, less dangerous relationship with the Soviet Union." In doing so, Nixon assured, the president could "become the preeminent post–World War II foreign policy leader."

Nixon was not the only insider encouraging Reagan to soften his approach to the Soviets. Nancy, concerned about her husband's legacy, and angered by depictions of him as a warmonger, pushed him to find common ground with the Soviets. "More than anything else," recalled an aide, "she wanted him recognized as a man of peace." Throughout her husband's second term, improving relations with the Soviets became Nancy's mission. "Although few thought of her as a peaceful force," journalist Lou Cannon observed wryly, "she became a force for peace within the White House."

Timing also proved to be a decisive factor. During his first four years in office, Reagan struggled to forge any kind of relationship with his counterparts in the Soviet Union. "They kept dying on me," he quipped later. But just two months into his second term, the Soviets installed a new leader: fifty-four-year-old Mikhail Gorbachev, the youngest head of the Soviet Communist Party since Joseph Stalin. Less ideological than any of his predecessors, Gorbachev advocated perestroika (restructuring) and glasnost (transparency), both policies aimed at reforming the Soviet Union's economic and political systems and making its society more open. Gorbachev also expressed his determination to close the "bleeding wound" in Afghanistan, by then in its fifth year, and ease Cold War tensions, thus diverting resources to domestic needs and helping gain access to Western technology. Indeed, the freshness of Gorbachev's changes was dramatized by a single statistic: The average age of Central Committee members dropped from seventy-one to fifty-eight.

While the American intelligence community was divided over how to handle Gorbachev, Reagan followed his own instincts. British prime minister Margaret Thatcher—a hard-liner like Reagan—reassured the president that Gorbachev was "someone we could deal with." So, Reagan kept an open mind despite his initial doubts. He yearned for peace and detested nuclear weapons; now he had a chance to act in a way that aligned with his feelings. Through a series of letters to his Soviet counterpart, Reagan came to understand "something surprising," as he recalled later: "Many people at the top of the Soviet hierarchy were genuinely afraid of America and Americans. Perhaps this shouldn't have surprised me, but it did." Reagan thus calculated that he could ease tensions between the two countries by giving the Soviets fewer reasons to fear the United States.

As he mulled over how to handle Gorbachev, Reagan was also reminded of the long memory of World War II. In the spring of 1985, German chancellor Helmut Kohl invited him to pay his respects at a military cemetery in Bitburg in honor of the fortieth anniversary of the end of the war. It was soon revealed, however, that more than three German soldiers buried there had been members of the brutal Waffen-SS, which had slaughtered seven hundred French civilians as well as ten Americans. Pressure built for Reagan to cancel, but he refused. Instead, he accepted Kohl's compromise suggestion that they visit the infamous death camp at Bergen-Belsen before visiting Bitburg. The entire episode reminded Reagan of how delicately he needed to tread.

All of these developments culminated in a series of four Reagan-Gorbachev summits beginning in 1985. In preparation for their first meeting in Geneva in November, Reagan dictated a five-page memo to himself that captured his open mind: "Let there be no talk of winners and losers." Despite his conciliatory tone and his support of a plan to eliminate all intermediate-range nuclear missiles in Europe, Reagan refused to compromise on his cherished SDI program, and the two men left disappointed that they had not been able to agree on arms reductions.

When Reagan and Gorbachev met again in Reykjavík, Iceland, only SDI prevented them from agreeing to a historic deal that would end the Cold War. Gorbachev boldly proposed the elimination of all nuclear weapons by the year 2000. The idea appealed to Reagan's anti-nuclearism, but he rejected Gorbachev's insistence that SDI never be deployed. With the negotiations near collapse, the Soviet leader pleaded with Reagan: "If you will agree to banning tests in space, we will sign the document in two minutes." Reagan replied, "I'm very sorry." Although he rejected the proposal, Reagan recognized that Gorbachev was a new kind of Soviet leader. However, with the exception of George Shultz, none of the president's senior advisors, including Vice President Bush, shared Reagan's optimism. The same was true on the other side: Gorbachev was under pressure from hard-liners to crack down on dissent, but he sensed Reagan's genuine desire not to win the Cold War but to end it.

After Reykjavík, Soviet scientists convinced Gorbachev that SDI was not as threatening as it seemed, largely because they did not believe that it would ever work. When the Soviet leader dropped his objections, the United States and the Soviet Union finally agreed to the Intermediate Nuclear Forces (INF) Treaty, which, for the first time, called for the destruction of existing missiles and allowed for on-site inspections to verify compliance. In December 1987 Gorbachev traveled to Washington amid great fanfare to sign the treaty in the East Room of the White House. Reagan later deemed the event "a grand historical moment."

Ironically, Reagan—who had viciously attacked his predecessors' efforts to negotiate with the Soviets—now found himself the target of conservative critics. The Conservative Caucus, a lobbying group founded in 1974, ran a newspaper ad comparing Reagan to Chamberlain and Gorbachev to Hitler. William F. Buckley Jr. of the conservative magazine *National Review* claimed that Reagan misunderstood the malevolent intentions of the Soviet Union under Gorbachev: "To greet it as if it were no longer evil is on the order of changing our entire position toward Adolf Hitler," he wrote.

Nixon—despite his earlier memo urging Reagan to develop a more conciliatory Soviet policy—was also upset by the president's recent moves. The old Cold Warrior was deeply distrustful of Gorbachev, and this time he went public with his concerns, issuing a series of public broadsides against the administration.

Worried that Nixon's public criticism might dampen Soviet enthusiasm for a deal, Reagan summoned him to the White House for a meeting that included his new chief of staff, Howard Baker, and Secretary of Defense Frank Carlucci. Nixon understood the purpose of the meeting, noting that Baker was trying "to get us to back down from our public criticism." Based on his notes of the meeting, the former president did most of the talking. He began with a simple observation: The Soviets always wanted to limit summits to a discussion of nuclear arms control. "This was not in our interest," Nixon declared. "We should insist that regional issues and disputes—such as Central America and Afghanistan—be considered at the same level or given an even higher priority, because these issues could lead to the use of arms."

Nixon continued hammering home the point that since Gorbachev could not be trusted, any deal needed to include a wide range of topics and not just the arms race. "Political issues and regional issues and human rights issues should be at the top of the agenda," he insisted. Meanwhile, Reagan defended his administration, telling Nixon that he held a positive view of Gorbachev for being "a different kind of Russian leader"—although it was unclear if he had ever actually met another Soviet leader.

Studying Reagan closely during the meeting, Nixon was not impressed by what he witnessed. "Reagan, candidly, does not seem to be on top of the issues," he observed. He described Reagan as being "fuzzy" on some topics and not understanding others. "I fear he simply does not realize what I'm trying to get across," he reflected. The president, he said, "seemed tired, particularly so as the hour drew to a close. He was simply having difficulty concentrating, even though I made the presentation as simple and direct as possible. As I've already indicated, he was courteous throughout, but I think I sensed a certain coolness on his part. . . . In summary, I must regretfully observe that Reagan looks far older, more tired, and less vigorous in person than in public. There is no way he can ever be allowed to participate in a private meeting with Gorbachev."

Nixon may have questioned Reagan's capacity to grasp the issues, but his advice went unheeded. In the final year of his presidency, Reagan stood in the middle of Moscow's Red Square and publicly retracted his earlier criticism of the Soviets. When a reporter asked if he stood by his earlier description of the Soviet Union as an "evil empire," Reagan replied frankly: "They've changed. . . . That was another time, another era." Another reporter then asked whether the two were now old friends. "Da! Da!" Gorbachev said, with Reagan adding, "Yes."

———

Having come to office in 1980 on a groundswell of public outrage over Iran's seizure of American hostages, Reagan proudly emphasized that he would never negotiate with terrorists. "The United States gives terrorists no rewards," he said in June 1985. "We make no concessions. We make no deals." Reagan's tough talk, however, masked the fact that, behind the scenes, he was negotiating to sell Iran high-tech US arms in exchange for the release of seven American hostages taken in Beirut, Lebanon.

The plot had an added twist. After the February delivery of missiles to Iran, the administration had taken between $3 million and $4 million from the proceeds and diverted it to aid the Contras, the anti-Communist rebel group fighting the Sandinista government in Nicaragua. The move was an unambiguous violation of the Boland Amendment, which Congress had passed in 1984 to prevent the Reagan administration from future covert meddling in Nicaraguan affairs. When it passed, Reagan had told his national security advisor, "I want you to do whatever you have to do to help these people keep body and soul together." As was often the case, he left the details to his aides.

The flow of money continued through November 1986, when a Lebanese newsmagazine exposed the scheme. At first, the administration denied that it had violated its own policy by offering incentives for the release of the hostages. Over the next few months, however, reporters dug up the sordid details of the arms sales and the funneling of money to the Contras. Congress opened an investigation, but the White House stonewalled and refused to turn over key documents.

The scandal, which consumed Reagan's final two years in office, damaged the president's reputation as an effective leader. A congressional committee charged that he had abdicated his "moral and legal responsibility to take care that the laws be faithfully executed," but stopped short of accusing him of intentionally breaking the law. Far more damaging was the report of Independent Counsel Lawrence E. Walsh, who concluded that the White House successfully constructed a "firewall" to protect Reagan, allowing lower-level officials to take the blame for an illegal policy approved by the president. But, Walsh emphasized, "President Reagan created the conditions which made possible the crimes committed by others."

Despite the damage done by Iran-Contra, Reagan still left office with the highest public approval rating of any president since Franklin Roosevelt: an astounding 68 percent, according to a New York Times–CBS poll.

The evidence is mixed on whether Reagan deserves credit for ending the Cold War. His supporters claim that Reagan forced the Soviets to the negotiation table through a combination of tough rhetoric and a massive military buildup. In fact, the Soviet Union responded to Reagan's early policies by *increasing* the money it spent on weapons. It was Reagan's deep-seated fear of nuclear weapons, and his willingness to discuss arms control, that convinced the Soviets that the United States was a reliable partner. Furthermore, as George Kennan had predicted in the late 1940s, the Soviet Union ultimately collapsed due to Communism's inherent instability, as well as the weight of America's bipartisan containment policy—authored by Kennan himself—dating back to the Truman Doctrine and the Marshall Plan. "The United States did not win the Cold War so much as the Soviet Union gave up," observed historian Jeffrey Engel.

At home, Reagan's economic policies produced a remarkable period of sustained growth. Between 1983 and 1990, unemployment fell to 5.2 percent, the economy grew by one-third and produced nineteen million new jobs, and inflation remained stable at less than 4 percent. Yet alongside this growth and stability was a ballooning federal deficit. Reagan's inability to reconcile his tax-cutting policies with his spending priorities, especially the massive military increases, caused the federal deficit to soar. By the time he left office in January 1989, the federal government was spending $206 billion more per year than it was receiving in tax revenues. In just eight years, the national debt rose from $908.5 billion to nearly $2.7 trillion.

While Reagan restored respect for the presidency, he also heightened expectations of what it could accomplish. In 1980 only 22 percent of people polled said they could trust government "most of the time." But after eight years of Republican rule, the percentage had increased to 38 percent, and nearly half said they favored increased government spending. Reagan came to office preaching a message of limited government and individual initiative. Ironically, his success over the next eight years helped to restore public faith in government at the same time that the massive deficits he created limited Washington's ability to address the public's demand for greater services. He would leave it to his successor to solve that paradox.

═══════

George H. W. Bush spent most of his eight years as vice president trying to prove to conservatives that he was the natural heir of the Reagan legacy. His greatest asset was the respectful working relationship he had developed with the president. Bush presided over several domestic task forces on deregulation and drugs and attended daily briefings in the Oval Office. When possible, he and the president met privately for weekly lunches, eating Mexican food, telling dirty jokes, and discussing sports. Like most vice presidents, Bush represented the president on many foreign trips, ultimately traveling 1.3 million miles and visiting sixty-five countries. He spent so much time flying to funerals that James Baker coined the slogan "You die, I'll fly."

There was, however, little personal chemistry between the two men. "Reagan treated his vice president the way he treated everyone else," observed historian Richard Reeves, "as a hired hand." Bush also never managed to win over the First Lady, who was a powerful force in the White House. Their son Michael described the difference between Nancy and Ronald this way: "Dad looks at half a glass of water and says: 'Look at this! It's half full!' Nancy is always trying to figure out: 'Who stole the other half from my husband?'" She had opposed Bush's selection as vice president, believing him weak, and also didn't like Bush's wife, Barbara. In fact, Nancy was so worried that the Bushes would upstage her and the president that she had an aide deliver a message to them shortly after the 1980 election. The message, as Bush remembered it, was "stay out of the paper, get a lower profile, back down." Over the course of two terms, she never warmed up to the Bushes and remained formal, distant—even cold. At one point, despite the warnings of deputy White House chief of staff Michael Deaver, she even made sure to exclude the Bushes from the famed November 1985 dinner that she and Ronald hosted for Princess Diana and Prince Charles. For their part, the Bushes resented that the Reagans invited them to the private quarters of the White House only once and never to Camp David.

Perhaps partly because the Reagans kept their distance, Bush occasionally overstepped in his efforts to prove his loyalty to the president. For example, Bush was well aware that the administration was trading arms for hostages. He had been present in many meetings where the initiative had been discussed, including the Oval Office session in which both Shultz and Weinberger strenuously opposed the idea. Still, Bush stuck to the script, going on national television to say it was "inconceivable" that the United States would partake in such a scheme—a claim that one historian described as "a bald-faced lie." Bush also misled veteran *Washington Post* reporter David Broder when he said that he would have opposed the policy had he known that Shultz and Weinberger expressed concerns.

By this point, Bush was preparing to run for president in 1988 and worried that the scandal would damage his image. He stonewalled the investigation and refused to turn over his diaries to investigators. According to biographer Jon Meacham, Bush's "denial of the details of the Iranian arrangement and his subsequent efforts to minimize his knowledge about the arms sales was an instance in which duty and ambition conflicted with and trumped his obligations to the full truth."

Bush compromised his principles to demonstrate loyalty to the president and to fulfill his own ambitions, but he received no reward from the conservative faithful, who always viewed him as a closet moderate. Both televangelist Pat Robertson and Kansas senator Robert Dole, a World War II veteran who had suffered injuries in Italy in April 1945, challenged Bush in the primaries.

After finishing third in the Iowa caucus behind both Dole and Robertson, Bush decided to wholly change his message and his tactics. As he had done at other times in his career to win elections, Bush repudiated his own moderate views on social issues and suppressed his commitment to fiscal responsibility and balanced budgets in an all-out effort to convince conservatives that he was one of them. He also rewrote his stump speech to express how fully he embraced the Reagan legacy. The strategy worked. He sailed to victory on Super Tuesday and secured the nomination, winning sixteen of seventeen states with 55 percent of the total vote.

Before Bush addressed the delegates at the August Republican convention, held in the New Orleans Superdome, the campaign revealed a biographical video narrated by conservative actor Charlton Heston. The film honored the character and strength of the World War II generation by highlighting Bush's time in the Pacific. A campaign aide had managed to locate the original, grainy video of Bush being rescued and pulled aboard the USS *Finback*. It was the first time that the public had a chance to see the dramatic footage. The clip concluded with another member of that generation, Ronald Reagan, declaring, "I trust George Bush. America can trust him too."

In his acceptance speech, Bush tried to articulate a message that would retain the loyalty of Reaganites without alienating moderates. The highlight of the speech was a carefully scripted promise not to raise taxes. "Read my lips," he proclaimed. "No new taxes." The vice president also appealed to moderates by emphasizing his support for education and the environment. Then, in a move that puzzled observers and many of his closest advisors, Bush picked the untested and lightly regarded Dan Quayle, a conservative senator from Indiana, as his running mate. Richard Nixon was the first person to call to congratulate Quayle, seeing parallels between them. "Vice President Bush did the same thing Eisenhower did," Nixon told him. "He picked a young senator with a foreign policy background."

The following month, Democrats nominated Massachusetts governor Michael Dukakis, who tried to avoid addressing the controversial social issues that had divided the party since the 1960s by declaring that the campaign was about "competence, not ideology." During the primaries, Dukakis bragged about his success in creating jobs and lowering taxes in his home state—the so-called Massachusetts miracle. He promised "good jobs at good wages," clean air, childcare, and increased federal support for education, but he never suggested how the additional spending would affect the gargantuan deficit. To underscore his new centrist message, he chose Bush's nemesis, Texas senator Lloyd Bentsen, as his running mate.

Bush was determined to tar the Democrats with the stigma of social liberalism—in other words, to frame the campaign as a battle for the cultural legacy of the 1960s. On cue, the Bush campaign concentrated on convincing the public that Dukakis was soft on crime, weak on defense, and an enemy of family values. In red-baiting language reminiscent of

Wisconsin senator Joseph McCarthy, Bush called Dukakis "a card-carrying member of the ACLU," and used the governor's position against requiring the Pledge of Allegiance in schools to question his patriotism. "Michael Dukakis on crime is standard old-style sixties liberalism," Bush charged.

While appealing to voters' fears of big government and high taxes, Bush also exploited racial tensions. This strategy built on trends that the Right had been cultivating for years, from Nixon's emphasis on "law and order" to Reagan's expansion of the carceral state and privatization of criminal justice. The Bush campaign's most effective advertisement depicted Willie Horton, an African American who had raped a white woman while on leave from a Massachusetts prison during Dukakis's governorship. Once again Bush contorted his principles to serve his political ambitions. While Bush appealed to the values of the white middle class, Dukakis traveled the country offering detailed proposals for student aid, health care, and a jobs program.

But Bush took nothing for granted. A close student of Republican politics, he remembered what had happened to Nixon in 1960 when Eisenhower seemed to offer only a tepid endorsement of his former VP. Bush would not make the same mistake. His campaign took full advantage of Reagan's popularity by sending him out on the hustings in the final weeks. Reagan had his own reasons for wanting a Bush victory. He told aides that his legacy would last less than one hundred days if Dukakis took over the White House.

On Election Day, Bush became the first sitting vice president since Martin Van Buren in 1836 to be elected directly to the presidency. He won 53.2 percent of the popular vote and carried forty states with 426 electoral votes. Dukakis won only ten states and the District of Columbia for a total of 112 electoral votes and 46 percent of the popular vote. Nevertheless, Democrats added two seats in the House and one in the Senate.

Having secured his victory, Bush wasted no time in putting distance between himself and his predecessor. "I'm going to be a wake-me, shake-me president," he told supporters on election night—an oblique shot at Reagan's tendency to snooze through Cabinet meetings as well as overnight crises. Even before taking the oath of office, Bush asked for the resignation of all Reagan political appointees. In their place, he staffed his administration with many moderate veterans of the Ford White House. He also made clear that he would no longer be supporting the Contras or spending money on Star Wars, which he deemed too impractical. Bush's bold moves caught the attention of *The New York Times*, which published a headline declaring, "Reagan Doesn't Work Here Anymore." The press began reporting a general revolt against Reagan worship, a desire to tell all about the man whom Bush aides characterized as ill-informed, lazy, and detached. One article recounted that several aides "had been quietly critical of Reagan's personality and style for years but suffered in silence." Now that Bush was in the Oval Office, they felt "liberated to speak" their minds.

At the top of Bush's list of priorities was developing an approach for dealing with the dramatic changes taking place in the Soviet Union. The new president lacked Reagan's enthusiasm for Gorbachev. He was suspicious of Gorbachev's intentions and feared instability in the region. Bush also worried over an important, unresolved question: Who would control the powerful Soviet nuclear arsenal if the nation fragmented into a number of small, independent republics?

As the Bush administration debated how to approach this delicate situation, the unraveling of the Soviet Empire in Europe began to accelerate. In the early months of Bush's presidency, Lech Walesa, a shipyard electrician and founder of the independent trade union Solidarity, led a series of strikes against the Soviet-controlled government in Poland. In the past, such an uprising would have brought a swift reprisal from the Soviet Union, but this time Gorbachev ordered the regime to negotiate with the reformers. The result was an agreement to hold free elections in 1990, the first in Poland in sixty-eight years. Soon enough, the seed of revolution spread rapidly from Poland to other Soviet Bloc countries. In Hungary, reformers adopted a new constitution, called for elections, and disbanded the Communist Party. In Czechoslovakia, playwright and populist Vaclav Havel helped orchestrate a nonviolent "Velvet Revolution" that resulted in the resignation of the Soviet-installed regime and free elections that carried Havel to the presidency.

The revolutionary fervor was not confined to Communist regimes in Eastern Europe but also soon swept into the Soviet Union itself. The Baltic states of Estonia, Latvia, and Lithuania had lived under Soviet rule since 1939, when Stalin seized control as part of the Nazi-Soviet Non-Aggression Pact. Now, a half century later, in December 1989, the Lithuanian Communist Party formally broke ties with the Soviet Union. The following year, Lithuania and Latvia declared their independence. These developments followed on the heels of the Soviet Union's first free elections since 1917, which resulted in hundreds of party officials going down in defeat.

Only China bucked the trend toward reform that was sweeping across the globe. Bush, who had served briefly as liaison to China under Nixon, came to office confident that he understood the Chinese leadership and could forge closer economic ties with the country while also nudging its leaders to enact democratic reforms. Instead of opening up its society, however, China cracked down on dissent. The most notorious instance occurred in the spring of 1989, when the Chinese army attacked a pro-democracy rally in Beijing's Tiananmen Square. The army brutally suppressed the protestors, killing as many as three thousand and wounding roughly ten thousand more in a naked display of military power. Perhaps the most iconic image from the massacre was that of a lone Chinese protestor attempting to stare down a line of tanks—a moving symbol of defiance.

While Bush condemned the assault, he did not want it to derail efforts to develop a closer strategic relationship with Chinese leaders. So, he imposed sanctions and stopped arms sales, but within weeks, he sent his national security advisor to China and began a gradual move toward normalizing relations. Then, less than a year after the slaughter at Tiananmen Square, Bush accorded China most-favored-nation status. Bush's policy of straddling the divide received support from none other than Nixon, who as the first US president to visit the People's Republic of China, in 1972, had been instrumental in thawing relations between the two countries. "What's happening [is being] handled badly and is deplorable," the former president said of the crackdown, "but take a look at the long run."

The events in China helped Bush make up his mind about how to handle Gorbachev—once again not committing fully to either side. Throughout the year, the United States found itself in an awkward position: Since the beginning of the Cold War, it had provided rhetorical support for pro-democracy movements in the Soviet Bloc, but at the moment when the democracy movements were succeeding, US leaders offered only tepid praise. The main reason was that the administration did not want to undermine relations with Gorbachev by appearing to exploit his troubles. "We're not there . . . to poke a stick in the eyes of Mr. Gorbachev," Bush said during a visit to Poland in June 1989, but to "encourage the very kind of reforms he is championing, and more reforms."

This diplomatic approach, however, became increasingly irrelevant in light of the dramatic change taking place in Germany. Since its construction in 1961, the Berlin Wall stood as the ultimate embodiment of the Cold War. Harrowing images of barbed wire, watchtowers, vast minefields, snarling patrol dogs, and well-armed sentries served as stark reminders of a divided Berlin, of two Germanys, and of a world separated between East and West. But shortly after midnight on November 9, 1989, East Germany's Communist government yielded to the growing demands for freedom by opening the Berlin Wall, symbolically raising the Iron Curtain and elevating hopes for an end to the Cold War.

Bush was nearly alone among world leaders in lobbying for a unified Germany as a member state of NATO. The president viewed German reunification as representing the true end of not just the Cold War but also World War II. Europeans, however, remained unconvinced. Gorbachev, Thatcher, and Mitterrand made clear that they all strongly opposed German unification. Referring to the lingering trauma of World War II, Thatcher advised Bush that "history here is living history."

"If we are not careful," she warned, "the Germans will get in peace what Hitler couldn't get in the war."

Gorbachev echoed Thatcher's sentiments, claiming that the deaths of twenty-seven million Russians during World War II gave the Soviet

Union a say in the discussion over a unified Germany. Bush understood their fears, but he did not want to be a prisoner of the past, confiding to his diary, "I don't think we can be naive about history, but I don't think we need to let history and the problem with World War I and World War II control Germany's fate in the future."

In December 1989 the president met Gorbachev aboard a ship off the island of Malta as a howling storm and twenty-foot waves swirled around them. While they negotiated little of substance, the summit was notable for what was said. Gorbachev made the astonishing declaration that the Soviet Union was prepared "no longer to regard the United States as an adversary." Bush responded, "We stand at the threshold of a brand-new era in US-Soviet relations." Gorbachev agreed, saying at a news conference after the summit, "We stated, both of us, that the world leaves one epoch of cold war, and enters another epoch."

Now that the United States and the Soviet Union had agreed to embark on the road toward peace, an opportunity emerged to continue the progress in arms control that began under Reagan. In 1989 Bush declared that it was time to "move beyond containment" by integrating the Soviet Union into "the community of nations." He backed up his rhetoric with actions, agreeing to slash conventional forces in Europe while cutting in half the number of strategic nuclear weapons on the Continent. Additionally, the two leaders signed agreements to open trade, expand cultural exchanges, and reduce chemical weapons.

Some of the president's advisors were worried about his close embrace of Gorbachev—a skepticism that Nixon shared. "I don't want to be the skunk at the lawn party," he said, "but I do not share the views of those who believe that because Gorbachev is tearing down a wall that should never have been built when he had no other choice, and because he often speaks of his devotion to freedom and human rights, that he is deep down a closet democrat." Nixon believed that Gorbachev was simply "making a virtue out of necessity," and that his objectives were no different from those of his predecessors. "His long-term goal is to get the United States out of Europe," he wrote. Because of this view, Nixon also did not agree with Bush's recent advances in arms control, saying that the president should instead "continue to insist that since Soviet superiority in conventional arms is the primary reason we had nuclear arms, an agreement on eliminating that superiority must take precedence over START."

As much as he advised against dealing with Gorbachev, Nixon was also prescient in predicting the Soviet leader's downfall. In August 1991, Soviet hard-liners hoping to re-create the former Soviet Union placed Gorbachev under house arrest at his vacation spot in the Crimea and moved to take over the government. With Gorbachev now powerless, a defiant Boris Yeltsin, the newly elected chairman of the Russian parliament, climbed atop an armored truck, denounced the coup, and demanded Gorbachev's reinstatement as president of the USSR. The military backed down, and Gorbachev survived the coup, but Yeltsin emerged as the most potent force for reform. By the end of the year, Russia proclaimed its independence from Soviet control and, along with Ukraine and Belorussia (now Belarus), formed the Commonwealth of Independent States. On Christmas Day 1991 a weary Gorbachev resigned as president of the Union of Soviet Socialist Republics, which by now had ceased to exist.

Now that a new leader was in power, Nixon pleaded with the White House to provide enough economic aid to allow Yeltsin's government to succeed. "Gorbachev is Wall Street, and Yeltsin's mainstream," he told Bush. "The stakes could not be higher." If Yeltsin succeeded, the future would bring reduced tensions and robust international trade. But if he failed, Nixon wrote, "the prospects for the next 50 years will turn grim. The Russian people will turn back to Communism. But a new, more dangerous despotism based on extremist Russian nationalism will take power."

Nixon's argument for more money for Russia could not have been more poorly timed. "We had bent over backwards to scrape together the money we were providing," National Security Advisor Brent Scowcroft recalled, "and here Nixon was pushing—pushing hard—for more." The White House believed that Russia needed to win its own revolution and that financial support from the United States would not tip the balance. Nevertheless, perhaps partly influenced by Nixon, Bush would eventually announce a $24 billion aid package for Russia.

The end of the Cold War was as earth-shattering as World War II in its potential to reshape global alliances. While Gorbachev deserved the lion's share of credit for initiating reforms, Reagan and Bush played important roles as well. They both overruled their hard-line advisors, followed their own instincts, and took advantage of an unprecedented opportunity. As the Cold War wound down, Bush began envisioning a "new world order" rooted in a close partnership between the United States and Russia.

At 4:32 A.M. on Thursday, August 2, 1990, Brent Scowcroft knocked on the president's bedroom door and informed him that Iraqi president Saddam Hussein had invaded neighboring Kuwait. Hussein, who had nearly bankrupted his country during a bloody eight-year war with Iran, needed Kuwait's vast oil reserves, which accounted for 20 percent of the world's oil supply, to pay for the conflict. The move represented a serious threat to the oil-dependent global economy. Even more worrisome, if Hussein used Kuwait as a launching pad for an invasion of Saudi Arabia, he would control more than 45 percent.

After meeting with his national security team early that morning, Bush traveled to Aspen, Colorado, to fulfill a long-standing commitment to deliver a major address on US foreign policy. He would have preferred to stay in Washington to manage the crisis, but British prime minister Margaret Thatcher would be attending the same conference, and he wished to consult with her in private. Thatcher was adamant that Hussein needed to be expelled from Kuwait. "I told him my conclusions in the clearest and most straightforward terms," she recounted. "Aggressors must never be appeased. We learned that to our cost in the 1930s." Perhaps stiffened by Thatcher's resolve, Bush subsequently made his strongest statement yet on the crisis. "It has to be withdrawal and the restoration of the Kuwaiti government," he told reporters.

Over the next few months, Bush rallied world opinion against "Saddam." When United Nations Security Council economic sanctions failed to force Hussein out of Kuwait, it authorized use of force for the first time since the Korean War. The resolution gave the Iraqi leader until January

15, 1991, to remove all troops from Kuwait or face military action. Bush sent five hundred thousand American troops to lead a multinational force to enforce the UN resolution.

While some leaders used the Munich analogy to justify force even when they harbored private doubts, that was not the case with Bush. From the beginning, the president viewed the crisis in light of the lessons of the 1930s. He repeated in his diary and in private letters to his children the same message that he was communicating to the American people. Bush told the public that there was "a parallel between what Hitler did to Poland and what Saddam Hussein has done to Kuwait. . . . We do not need another Hitler in this time of our century." His diary entry around the same time echoed this outlook: "[Hussein] is clearly bad and evil as Hitler and as the Japanese war machine that attacked Pearl Harbor. And I say, check him now, check him now." These historical parallels weighed heavily on Bush's mind, for if Hussein was akin to Hitler, then countless lives and human morality itself were at stake. On the last day of 1990, just weeks from the Security Council deadline, Bush wrote to his children: "How many lives might have been saved if the appeasement had given way to force early on in the late 30s or earliest 40s? How many Jews might have been spared the gas chamber, or how many Polish patriots might be alive today? I look at today's crisis as 'good' vs 'evil'—yes, it is that clear."

As a young man, Bush had been forced to put aside his personal ambitions, join the military, and risk his life to pay the price for appeasement in the 1930s. The lessons of the past were not an abstraction; they were ingrained into his personality and worldview. The problem was that Bush, like his predecessors, substituted an analogy for critical thinking. Hussein was a ruthless, bloodthirsty tyrant, but he was not Hitler, and Iraq, bankrupt from years of fighting Iran, lacked the resources and the ambition to become a world power. That is not to say that Bush was wrong to force Hussein out of Kuwait; in fact, he probably made the right decision—but not because the conflict in the Persian Gulf had anything to do with the 1930s.

In many ways, the Gulf War became the testing ground for the lessons that conservatives took away from the Vietnam debacle. As Bush ramped up pressure on Hussein, he reassured the American public that he would not commit the same errors as Johnson had in Vietnam. Like many conservatives, Bush believed that the mistakes made in Vietnam were tactical, not strategic. It was not wrong for the United States to have tried to save an independent nation (albeit one that it had created). The policy failed simply because policymakers refused to employ the full range of American military power, and then bowed to pressure from student radicals and a liberal media. Bush sought to correct all of those mistakes in his handling of the Gulf War. "I know that there are fears about another Vietnam," he said. "Let me assure you, should military action be required, this will not be another Vietnam. This will not be a protracted, drawn-out war." He explained that a war with Iraq would be very different from the conflict in Vietnam. "The forces arrayed are different," he declared. "The opposition is different. The resupply of Saddam's military would be very different. The countries united against him in the United Nations are different. The topography of Kuwait is different." He pledged that America would also pursue a very different strategy. "I want peace, not war," he concluded. "But if there must be war, we will not permit our troops to have their hands tied behind their backs. And I pledge to you: There will not be any murky ending. If one American soldier has to go into battle, that soldier will have enough force behind him to win and then get out as soon as possible, as soon as the UN objectives have been achieved. I will never—ever—agree to a halfway effort."

The public debate around the crisis in the Gulf focused on competing historical analogies. When *The New York Times* polled the public on what analogy they found most relevant, 61 percent agreed with the statement "Saddam Hussein is like Adolf Hitler of Germany in the 1930s, and it is important to stop him." Only 33 percent disagreed. Only 42 percent agreed with the assertion that "the current situation in the Middle East is a lot like Vietnam in the 1960s." A majority, 52 percent, disagreed. Importantly, while a majority of Americans agreed with the similarities to Hitler, they were *not* willing to go to war to punish Hussein's aggression. Polls showed that a majority of Americans wanted to continue to rely on economic sanctions, even if those sanctions failed to prod the Iraqis out of Kuwait.

In January the Senate and the House vigorously debated a joint resolution that would authorize the use of military force. Many doubted that the invasion represented a threat to American interests. "All that's happened is that one nasty little country invaded a littler but just as nasty country," declared the influential New York senator Daniel Patrick Moynihan. Like him, most Democrats strongly opposed the use of military force—no matter how tempting it might be to draw parallels with World War II. Minnesota senator Paul Wellstone told his colleagues that he was often asked if he would be willing to send his draft-age children to fight. "I'm the son of a Jewish immigrant from the Soviet Union, and if I believed that Saddam Hussein was a Hitler," he said, "I could accept the loss of life of one of my children." But Wellstone insisted that this was not a comparable case, so he could not send his own children to battle.

Still, the comparison between Hussein and Hitler was a potent one precisely because it demanded preemptive and decisive action. Waiting for more proof of the analogy's accuracy might end up being too late. Illinois Republican Robert Michel, a combat veteran of World War II, articulated the reasoning behind the urgent need to confront Hussein: "Those of our generation know from bloody experience that unchecked aggression against a small nation is a prelude to an international disaster. Saddam Hussein today has more planes and tanks and, frankly, men under arms than Hitler had at the time when Prime Minister Chamberlain came back from Munich with that miserable piece of paper—peace in our time. I'll never forget that replay of that movie in my life," Michel said. "Either we stop him now, and stop him permanently, or we won't stop him at all."

The president eventually won his resolution by a close vote in the Senate (52–47) and a more comfortable margin in the House (250–183). Now armed with congressional approval and sustained by strong international support, Bush ordered American air forces to commence the assault on Iraqi positions. At three in the morning Iraqi time on January 17, 1991, just five days after Congress gave authorization, Bush launched Operation Desert Storm, a daunting display of modern military power in which the air force and the navy would pound Iraq for five weeks.

In his speech on the evening of January 16, 1991, announcing that American planes had begun attacking Iraq, Bush once again made the

Vietnam parallels explicit. "I've told the American people before that this will not be another Vietnam," he said, "and I repeat this here tonight. Our troops will have the best possible support in the entire world, and they will not be asked to fight with one hand tied behind their back. I'm hopeful that this fighting will not go on for long and that casualties will be held to an absolute minimum."

Three weeks into the air war, Bush met with his national security team to discuss the impending ground offensive. On February 23 the Allies, under the command of US general H. Norman Schwarzkopf, launched this second phase of the war. Bush believed in its necessity, but he continued to worry over repeating the mistakes of Vietnam. "The president was torn," Scowcroft remembered. "He did not want to appear to be second-guessing the military experts. Still vivid in his mind was the image of Lyndon Johnson during Vietnam, hunched over aerial charts selecting individual targets for air strikes." The historian George Herring, noting Bush's frequent references to Vietnam, observed: "Such was the lingering impact of the Vietnam War that the Persian Gulf conflict appeared at times as much a struggle with its ghosts as with Saddam Hussein's Iraq."

Meanwhile the military, also scarred from its Vietnam experience, helped maintain public morale by restricting media access to the battlefront and establishing regular news briefings. In the Gulf War, the media operated under far stricter rules of censorship than even in World War II. Recalling how bloody battlefield images eroded support for the war in Vietnam, military leaders restricted press access to the war zone and forced reporters to submit all dispatches to military censors. They even limited press access to ceremonies honoring the return of the remains of those soldiers killed in the conflict. "It's okay to die for your country," columnist James McCartney observed caustically. "The Pentagon just doesn't want anyone to know about it." While imposing this rigid censorship, the military made no real effort to disguise its hostility toward the media. When reporters asked hard questions at press conferences or wrote critical stories, they were denied access to officers, troops, and the other favors the military had to bestow on journalists. The government, according to the venerable Walter Cronkite, whose nightly newscasts had molded public opinion on Vietnam, "trampled on the public's right to know."

After coalition forces liberated Kuwait on February 27, the president called off the attack, declaring a ceasefire only a hundred hours after ground operations had begun. By that time, Iraqi forces had already fled Kuwait. The United States suffered only 184 dead, compared with nearly 100,000 Iraqi deaths, mostly casualties of the bombing.

Meanwhile, though Bush had publicly likened Hussein to Hitler, the administration declined to continue on to Baghdad and overthrow the Iraqi leader. The obvious question now arose: If he was as evil as Hitler, then why did Bush allow him to remain in power? The coalition that Bush assembled included Arab states that opposed regime change. If Iraq crumbled, it would create a power vacuum that Iran could then move to exploit. The CIA predicted that the Iraqis would revolt against Hussein's government or his own generals would execute him. While Bush offered verbal support for a coup, he did nothing when Hussein used helicopter gunships and poison gas to suppress an uprising. In that sense, the Vietnam parallel did apply: The United States left a sovereign country devastated and destabilized, and it would be Bush's own son who would have to grapple with the long-term consequences.

In the short run, though, the war renewed America's faith in the military and produced a surge of patriotism. It appeared that the country had confronted evil and prevailed. "It's a proud day for America," Bush declared as the fighting ended. "And, by God, we've kicked the Vietnam syndrome once and for all."

─────────

The war boosted Bush's popularity to astronomical levels—*USA Today* estimated as high as 91 percent—but events at home soon brought him crashing back to earth. Ironically, although Republicans took credit for ending the Cold War, it was Democrats who reaped the political benefits. The breakup of the Soviet Union removed anti-Communism from the arsenal of weapons conservatives had used to undermine support for Democrats. With the Cold War over, and with no clear foreign threat to distract them, Americans were beginning to focus more attention on

problems at home. The anti-tax revolt of the 1970s and 1980s had temporarily receded, as many Americans said they would be willing to pay
higher taxes if doing so led to improved medical care and education. Bush
responded to the evolving public mood by breaking with conservatives
and supporting two important pieces of domestic legislation: the Americans with Disabilities Act and the Clean Air Act Amendments. But he
never established a clear sense of domestic priorities or articulated a compelling vision for where he wanted to move the nation.

The most pressing issue facing the administration was a ballooning
budget deficit created by the false promises of supply-side economics. Two
ways existed to address the deficit: raise taxes or cut spending. Like Eisenhower and Ford, Bush had always embraced the traditional Republican
faith in fiscal responsibility and balanced budgets. He never caught the
Keynesian fever, and despite his public statements, he privately ridiculed
Reagan's supply-side approach. But now, trapped between a crippling
budget deficit and growing demands for more social services, Bush was
forced to abandon his "Read My Lips: No New Taxes" pledge, made in
dramatic fashion at the 1988 Republican convention. He justified the
switch by claiming that he learned about the severity of the budget deficit
only after assuming the presidency. "I've started going into the numbers,
finally," Bush said, "and they're enormous."

In 1990 Bush agreed to a deficit reduction compromise with congressional Democrats that included $133 billion in new taxes. He worked
courageously across the aisle, spurning the right wing of his own party,
to pass legislation that would serve as a cornerstone of nineties prosperity.
As expected, the move infuriated Reaganite conservatives, who saw it as
proof that Bush had never been one of them. The *New York Post*'s front
page screamed "READ MY LIPS . . . I LIED." As the historian Timothy Naftali observed, "Bush's problem was that while he was held responsible for
the financial mess left by Reagan, no one seemed to give him credit for
trying to fix it."

In the short run, Bush's efforts failed to boost a struggling economy,
which dipped into a brief recession at the end of his term. By 1992, many
Americans had concluded that Bush was a decent man but a bad president, out of touch with the concerns of everyday Americans. His approval

rating sagged to 34 percent, with less than 20 percent of the public supporting his handling of the economy.

Politically weaker than in 1988, the sixty-seven-year-old president faced a more formidable Democratic challenger in the youthful forty-six-year-old Arkansas governor Bill Clinton. A party moderate, Clinton cast himself as a "new Democrat" who understood the concerns of the struggling middle class. Hoping to neutralize complaints that he was soft on crime and a typical tax-and-spend liberal, Clinton campaigned as a cultural conservative who supported capital punishment and vowed to "end welfare as we know it" and make the streets safer. For the party faithful, he offered a message of economic populism, promising to soak the rich and fight to preserve popular social programs. His strategist James Carville posted a sign on the wall of campaign headquarters to encapsulate Clinton's platform—"It's the economy, stupid!"—which would soon become their slogan.

It was Clinton's private life, not his public positions, that caused the most controversy. Throughout his public career, Clinton had been shadowed by accusations of womanizing. The issue resurfaced a few weeks before the New Hampshire Democratic primary, when a former state of Arkansas employee named Gennifer Flowers announced that she had been Clinton's mistress for years—and produced taped phone conversations to prove it. No sooner had he dodged that bullet than *The Wall Street Journal* fired another one. Less than two weeks before the primary, the *Journal* challenged Clinton's story about how he had managed to avoid the draft during the Vietnam War. Clinton claimed that he had voluntarily placed himself in the draft in the fall of 1969 while a Rhodes scholar at Oxford University, but that his number was never called. However, the *Journal* produced a letter written by a twenty-three-year-old Clinton in December 1969 thanking the director of the ROTC program for "saving me from the draft." (Joining the Reserve Officers' Training Corps provided a draft deferment.) Of his later decision to enter the draft, Clinton described being torn between his opposition to Vietnam and his future ambitions: "I decided to accept the draft in spite of my beliefs for one reason: to maintain my political viability within the system." The letter suggested that manipulation, not luck, had allowed Clinton to avoid the draft, and that later he entered the draft only to burnish his political image.

Yet the lingering doubts over Clinton's integrity did not prevent him from winning the nomination earlier than any Democrat in more than two decades. At the party's convention in New York City, Clinton underscored the "new Democrat" theme by choosing fellow baby boom southerner Al Gore, a senator from Tennessee, as his running mate.

Meanwhile, Bush asked his close friend James Baker to take charge of his faltering campaign after the Republican convention. Baker initially sketched a high-minded strategy: Having spent his first term addressing world problems, Bush would now devote the same energy to addressing domestic needs. When that message failed to resonate, Bush switched gears and decided that the only way to win was to attack his opponent just as he had in 1988. "For the rest of the way, we're going one hundred percent negative," said a Bush campaign official.

Bush employed many of the "wedge issues" that Republicans had used so effectively against Democrats in the past. Clinton, Bush said, was an "elitist," an "Oxford-educated . . . social engineer" who preferred European-style Socialism to the rugged individualism that Bush had learned firsthand from the Texas oilfields. Both Bush and his surrogates drew a sharp distinction between the World War II hero who volunteered for service and the draft-dodging baby boomer. Bush was genuinely disturbed by Clinton's actions during the Vietnam War and saw the draft controversy as representative of the differences between two generations. "I'm tired of the guy lying and ducking on the draft and not coming clean," Bush wrote in his diary on September 9, 1992. For Bush, the incident reflected not only Clinton's shaky integrity but also his unpatriotic refusal to fight when the nation was at war. Bush could have used his family's connections to avoid fighting in World War II, but he insisted on volunteering and went on to participate in dangerous missions in the Pacific. He bitterly came to recognize that while he and many members of his generation found avoiding service "offensive," Clinton and "the new generation" did not.

Gerald Ford also joined in the effort to hammer home this message, contrasting Clinton's actions in the 1960s with Bush's heroism in the 1940s. He penned a letter in response to a *Denver Post* editorial claiming that while both candidates were "trying to be the new Truman, George Bush has the lesser claim." Ford pointed out that in World War II, "President Bush was the youngest combat navy pilot and was shot down by enemy forces in the Pacific War. Governor Clinton and several of his relatives, in contrast, manipulated and maneuvered so he did not serve in the Armed Forces while the United States was at war. Both Truman and Bush obviously believed that military service in wartime was an obligation of citizenship and an act of patriotism. Governor Clinton did not." It was a blunt indictment coming from a former president.

While the charges carried some truth, the end of the Cold War made Republican attacks on Clinton's patriotism appear shrill, and the public backlash forced the Bush campaign to retreat. This unexpected response underscored a key difference between 1988 and 1992: The wedge issues that had been shaped by the immediate aftermath of World War II had now lost their bite. "Wedge issues don't work on Clinton because he's taken positions that inoculate him," observed a centrist Democrat. The Democratic nominee routinely mentioned his work-oriented welfare views, posed with police officers and their widows at law-and-order events, and emphasized his support for the death penalty. Bush persisted in attacking Clinton's values, despite overwhelming poll evidence showing that voters were more interested in the economy. "Every time Bush used some of these issues," a frustrated Republican observed, "it would reaffirm with some voters that he was out of touch with the most important issue."

On election night, Clinton won 43 percent of the popular vote, compared to 38 percent for Bush, but his victory in the electoral college, where he won thirty-one states and 357 electoral votes, proved decisive. (A third-party candidate, Ross Perot, received 18.9 percent of the popular vote but failed to carry a state.) The Democrats' all-South ticket secured eight southern and border states, sweeping the coasts and the industrial heartland. Clinton also won a larger percentage of white voters than any Democratic nominee since Jimmy Carter in 1976. And in a final sign that a new generation of leadership had emerged, the Clinton-Gore ticket ran ahead of the Republicans in every age group but scored especially well with young voters.

―――――――

Bush would be the last of the World War II veterans to occupy the White House. He would also be the last president to have seen military action. Those two facts illuminate an important distinction: Every president who directly witnessed World War II shared a unifying experience with ambiguous lessons. Oftentimes, they would exaggerate and misapply those lessons, condoning actions that contradicted their private hesitations. They understood the costs of violence but also feared the threat of inaction—a quandary that reached a tipping point during the Cold War era with the birth of nuclear weapons.

These presidents also had to grapple with the conflicted legacy of a federal government that had expanded vastly during wartime, raising expectations among its citizens about the scope of the social contract; expectations that reached a fiery peak throughout the 1960s and 1970s. In the face of emboldened social movements, the White House had to strike a delicate balance: a state that exerted great power on the international stage and one that *appeared* carefully limited at home.

While World War II acted as a catalyst for a robust anti-Communist policy at home and abroad, these prerogatives lost their urgency with the end of the Cold War. For the subsequent generation, it was the legacy of the 1960s—not the Second World War—that loomed large. That legacy of division ushered in a period of centrist, pragmatic, and moderate politics for roughly the next quarter century. Nevertheless, World War II continued to exert a powerful sway over the nation's collective consciousness— and its memory would be summoned periodically by the new generation of presidents striving to navigate a complex post–Cold War world.

Epilogue

The fall of the Berlin Wall may have marked the final battle of World War II, but it did not stop the next generation of presidents from invoking Munich and Hitler to build public support for their policies. Bill Clinton, the first man elected to the White House after the Cold War, struggled to articulate a new vision for America's role in the world. Early in his presidency, when eighteen US Army Rangers were killed in a bloody firefight while on a misguided mission in Somalia, Clinton quickly retreated, withdrawing the remaining American forces. "Gosh, I miss the Cold War," Clinton remarked, alluding to the fact that competition with the Soviets had provided an organizing framework—albeit a flawed one—for America's role in the world.

The searing experience in Somalia left Clinton reluctant to use force in other parts of the world, including the former Yugoslavia, where, between 1992 and 1995, Serbian nationalists engaged in a campaign of "ethnic cleansing" against the newly formed Republic of Bosnia and Herzegovina. Eventually, however, Clinton rallied an international coalition that forced Serbian leader Slobodan Milosevic to the negotiating table while committing American troops to Bosnia as part of a multinational force to keep the peace.

Boxed in by NATO troops in Bosnia, Milosevic turned his war machine against the province of Kosovo, where ethnic Albanians were struggling for independence. This time, Clinton took a tough line, largely because of the influence of his new secretary of state. Madeleine Albright, the first woman to serve as the nation's top diplomat, possessed a different generational mindset than the baby boomer Clinton. Born a diplomat's daughter in Prague, Czechoslovakia, in 1937, she fled Nazi occupation with her family and spent most of World War II living in London. "Some people's historical context is Vietnam; mine is Munich," she told reporters. "For me, America truly is the indispensable nation." Clinton now told the American people that it was necessary to punish Serb atrocities in Kosovo. "What if someone had listened to Winston Churchill and stood up to Adolf Hitler earlier?" he asked a national television audience in an address from the Oval Office. "Just imagine if leaders back then had acted wisely and early enough, how many lives could have been saved, how many Americans would not have had to die?"

While Clinton belatedly embraced the lessons of Munich, he repudiated another legacy of the war: Keynesian economics. Clinton ran for president as a classic Keynesian, calling for increased government spending for education, health, and the environment, and a tax cut for the middle class to end the recession. But even before he took office, Clinton began reconsidering his priorities. In December Federal Reserve chairman Alan Greenspan convinced the president-elect that reducing the deficit would have a greater long-term impact on the economy than a modest program of tax cuts and spending increases. Greenspan's advice directly contradicted Keynes, who had argued that deficits were good because they added money to the economy, translating into more jobs and increased production. Clinton, however, accepted the new logic, which claimed that deficits drained capital from the private sector, pushed up interest rates, and strangled the economy. "You mean to tell me that the success of my program and my reelection hinges on the Federal Reserve and a bunch of fucking bond traders?" he complained to his staff.

After the Republicans gained control of the House and Senate in 1994, Clinton moved further away from Keynesian economics by accepting the Republican goal of balancing the budget in ten years or less. "The era of Big Government is over," he announced in Reaganesque language. White House liberals fought against the move, and many congressional

Democrats complained afterward that the president lacked a clear ideological compass. But his policies worked. By 1998, a bustling economy combined with fiscal restraint filled the nation's coffers, erasing the budget deficit that had swelled under Reagan. The federal government reported a $70 billion surplus for fiscal year 1998—the first in three decades—and projected a $4.4 trillion surplus over the next fifteen years.

Texas governor George W. Bush squeaked out a victory in the 2000 presidential election by promising a new "compassionate conservatism." But the administration—and the nation—was rocked on September 11, 2001, when terrorists flew hijacked commercial airliners into the World Trade Center and the Pentagon. Before nightfall, 2,813 civilians were dead, making it the bloodiest day on American soil since September 17, 1862, when 6,300 Union and Confederate soldiers were killed or mortally wounded in the Civil War Battle of Antietam.

On the evening of the attacks, a shaken President Bush declared war on global terrorism. The United States took aim at Osama bin Laden and the radical Taliban government of Afghanistan, which provided a safe haven for his operations. In the weeks leading up to the actual military assault on Afghanistan, Bush, like his father, built an impressive international coalition to bolster military action and quickly disposed of the Taliban government.

Even while American troops were fighting in Afghanistan, Bush and his advisors began drawing up plans to send troops into Iraq. Convinced that Iraqi strongman Saddam Hussein possessed "weapons of mass destruction," the administration decided to launch a preemptive strike to topple the regime and destroy the stockpiles of deadly agents. Defense Secretary Donald Rumsfeld justified the war by comparing the Iraqi leader to Hitler. "Think of the prelude to World War II. Think of all the countries that said, 'Well, we don't have enough evidence,'" Rumsfeld told reporters. "*Mein Kampf* has been written. Hitler had indicated what he intended to do. Maybe he won't attack. Maybe he won't do this or that. There were millions of people dead because of the miscalculations." The administration also believed naïvely that the United States could reconstruct Iraq the same way it had Germany and Japan after World War II.

Bush and his advisors were wrong on both points. The United States failed to uncover the promised stockpiles of chemical and biological weapons, and even after Bush declared the end of "major combat operations" in Iraq on May 1, 2003, US soldiers were subject to daily deadly attacks. By May 2006, the war had claimed more than 2,400 American lives and left another 18,000 wounded, while tens of thousands of Iraqis had died. The relative restraint of Bush's father in exercising military power had been lost on him.

In the early months of his administration, Bush also repudiated his father's commitment to fiscal responsibility and balanced budgets in favor of the siren call of supply-side economics. Most armchair economists familiar with Keynes knew that he called for the government to put money in the hands of consumers during a downturn by cutting taxes, spending more, or both. What they often failed to appreciate was that the British economist also offered advice for prosperous times: Government, he argued, should *save* money so that it had resources to contend with a downturn. Although Bush inherited a booming economy, he pushed aggressively for a $1.6 trillion, ten-year tax cut package. The Senate trimmed the package, but it still represented a major legislative victory for the new administration, and was the first of two major tax cuts during his first term in office.

At the same time, Bush ironically presided over an expansion of federal power unseen since the days of Lyndon Johnson's Great Society. Within the first few weeks following the September 11 attacks, the president approved $55 billion in federal spending, including a massive federal relief package for New York. He also abandoned the traditional conservative faith in deregulation when he orchestrated a federal bailout of the airlines. Then, in June 2002, Bush called for the creation of a new Department of Homeland Security that would oversee the areas of anti-terrorism, border security, cybersecurity, and disaster management. The proposal represented the largest reorganization of the federal government since Harry Truman signed the National Security Act of 1947. Finally, in 2003, Bush added a new unpaid-for entitlement—prescription drug coverage— to Medicare. During times of crisis, all presidents become Keynesians.

After just three years, Bush's combination of tax cuts and additional spending produced massive deficits. The administration watched a $236 billion federal budget surplus dissolve into a $400 billion annual deficit. Overall, government spending increased by 16 percent. Although post–September 11 defense needs accounted for much of the increase, domestic spending also grew by 11 percent.

Bush confronted another crisis in the final years of his presidency. After the attacks on September 11, the Federal Reserve slashed the interest rate, but the move fueled a housing boom that eventually went bust in 2007. Global stock prices plummeted, many banks stopped lending money, and the world faced the prospect of a financial meltdown. The administration proposed a $700 billion plan that would allow the government to buy bad assets from the nation's biggest banks. While the effort may have avoided an economic catastrophe, it failed to spur lending or restore confidence.

Bush left it to his successor, Barack Obama, a former Illinois senator and the first African American to win the presidency, to pick up the financial pieces. The new president confronted the greatest economic crisis since Franklin Roosevelt took office in the depths of the Great Depression. The collapse of the housing market pushed the banking system to the brink of disaster. Unemployment soared, and two major automotive companies neared bankruptcy.

Unlike his predecessor, Obama made no apologies about being a Keynesian. In 2009 he pressured Congress to pass a $787 billion spending bill designed to stimulate the economy. But Republicans who had opened the spending spigot for Bush turned it off once Obama came to office. The bill passed the House with no Republican votes and with only three in the Senate. The administration also forced struggling General Motors and Chrysler into bankruptcy and then invested more than $60 billion in federal money to revive the ailing auto industry. Ultimately, Obama's policies helped turn around the economy. By the end of his second term, just about every economic indicator revealed an American economy on the rebound, and growth far outpaced that of other developed nations.

In the realm of foreign policy, Obama carefully avoided using the Munich analogy, realizing that it had become a cliché; his critics did not.

During the 2008 presidential campaign, Bush chastised then-candidate Obama for saying that he would negotiate with both friends and enemies. "Some seem to believe," Bush said, "that we should negotiate with the terrorists and radicals. . . . We have heard this foolish delusion before. As Nazi tanks crossed into Poland in 1939, an American senator declared: 'Lord, if I could only have talked to Hitler, all this might have been avoided.'" Later during his presidency, when Obama negotiated a nuclear deal with Iran, South Carolina Republican senator Lindsey Graham invoked Munich as well in order to accuse Obama of naïveté. "He's the Neville Chamberlain of our time who believes that over the next fifteen years, Iran is going to change their behavior, because this deal doesn't require them to do a damn thing in terms of changing their behavior."

In the 2016 presidential race, New York real estate baron and reality television star Donald Trump defeated former secretary of state Hillary Clinton in a shocking upset. Trump tapped into the anger of white, conservative Christians who opposed increased government spending and who resented the nation's growing demographic diversity. Since the 1960s, conservatives had used the message of moral decay and individual responsibility to rally their base. Although conservative leaders claimed to be addressing the economic ills of a declining white middle class, the reality was that their grievances stemmed largely from cultural and racial factors.

Trump announced his candidacy by attacking Mexican immigrants, labeling them rapists and drug dealers, as well as Muslims, calling for a ban on their entry into the United States. He then widened his reach by using well-tested racial "dog whistles"—a form of coded language—to appeal to white voters. Like most demagogues, Trump divided the nation into two groups: real Americans who supported him and a disgraced economic and cultural elite who backed his opponent. "The Silent Majority is back," Trump told audiences in 2016, "and we're going to take our country back."

Though Trump's foreign policy was riddled with contradictions, his overall approach was to tear up international agreements and chastise the nation's closest allies, while coddling tyrants. "From this moment on, it's going to be America First," Trump vowed in his inaugural address, referencing the discredited isolationist movement that had praised Hitler and opposed US entry into World War II.

In June 2017 he withdrew from the landmark Paris Agreement on climate change designed to slow global warming. He ripped up a comprehensive treaty signed by most major powers, including Russia, to curtail Iran's nuclear program in exchange for sanctions relief. He threatened to withdraw from NATO if the other member countries did not increase defense spending. In February 2019 he made a trip to North Korea, posed for pictures with Supreme Leader Kim Jong Un, and immediately nominated himself for the Nobel Peace Prize. The photo op did not, however, translate into diplomatic gains, and Kim continued his missile program. Playing to his base, Trump engaged in a trade war with China that only ended up driving up costs for American consumers. In June 2020, without consulting any of the nation's European allies, Trump withdrew US troops from Germany. In the Middle East, he abandoned decades of American policy by moving the US embassy to Jerusalem, recognizing Israeli sovereignty over the Syrian Golan Heights, and supporting illegal Israeli settlements in the occupied West Bank. Shortly before leaving office, he announced a troop drawdown in Iraq and Afghanistan, again without consulting allies.

Meanwhile, at home Trump borrowed Ronald Reagan's "Make America Great Again" to summon memories of a heroic past before feminists, immigrants, African Americans, and members of the LGBTQ community started demanding new rights. World War II played a key role in this imagined past because the war represented a time when the United States stood united in a common struggle, respected by its allies and feared by its enemies, a military behemoth that towered over all the other countries on earth. Ironically, while Trump longed for the sense of solidarity that the war produced, he employed political methods that were deliberately designed to divide America into competing groups.

By 2020, Trump's gross mishandling of the COVID-19 virus overshadowed everything else. The pandemic, a global health crisis without precedent in modern times, triggered the most severe economic recession in nearly a century. By the time Trump left office, more than 450,000 Americans had died from COVID-19.

In the 2020 election, Democrat Joe Biden, who after decades in the Senate had served as Obama's vice president, managed to clinch a close victory over Trump. But Trump did not leave the White House voluntarily. On January 6, 2021, as part of a concerted effort to overturn a free and fair election, Trump invited an angry mob to Washington and then stirred them up with repeated false claims about a stolen election. After a violent clash at the nation's Capitol, the peaceful transfer of power finally proceeded—but not without long-standing repercussions that would continue to play out for years to come.

Just as George W. Bush handed his Democratic successor an economy in ruins, Trump's failed response to the pandemic produced an economic crisis that Biden had to fix. Perhaps no president since LBJ embraced the teachings of Keynes more than Biden. In the first few months of his presidency, he forced Congress to pass a handful of major reforms. The $1.9 trillion American Rescue Plan Act of 2021 sent stimulus checks to roughly 90 percent of households, while boosting jobs in an effort to counter the financial impact of the pandemic. Biden followed that by signing a $1.2 trillion, bipartisan Infrastructure Investment and Jobs Act, the largest long-term investment in infrastructure in the nation's history. In 2022 he pushed through Congress the Inflation Reduction Act, which aimed to curb inflation by lowering the cost of prescription drugs and investing in clean energy.

The memory of Hitler and World War II reemerged in February 2022, when Russian leader Vladimir Putin approved the unlawful invasion of Ukraine. Biden rallied the nation and its allies to provide Ukraine with much-needed military and economic aid. However, after taking control of the House in the 2022 midterm elections, conservatives aligned with Trump temporarily blocked shipments. Biden, using some of the toughest language since the height of the Cold War, reminded Congress in his fiery 2024 State of the Union address of the lessons of the past.

Biden began his hourlong speech with a historical comparison, invoking FDR's address to the nation in January 1941 amid Hitler's aggression in Europe. "In January 1941 President Franklin Roosevelt came to this chamber to speak to the nation," he said. "Hitler was on the march. War was raging in Europe." Biden called attention to the chilling historical parallel. "Putin of Russia is on the march," he thundered, "invading Ukraine and sowing chaos throughout Europe and beyond." Invoking the specter of appeasement, Biden warned, "If anybody in this room thinks Putin will stop at Ukraine, I assure you: He will not."

Not only did Biden invoke Hitler in condemning Putin, but he also attacked his predecessor (who supported Putin) for using inflammatory language reminiscent of Hitler. In December 2023, as he prepared for a rematch against Biden, Trump told an overwhelmingly white rally of supporters that undocumented immigrants were "poisoning the blood of our country" and referred to immigrants as "vermin." If reelected, he promised to "root out the Communists, Marxists, Fascists, and the radical Left thugs that live like vermin within the confines of our country, that lie and steal and cheat on elections"—once again repeating his lie that fraud had cost him the 2020 presidential election. He even went so far as to compare his political opponents at home to the Nazis in the 1930s. "Our country was at war with the enemy, and they wanted to extinguish our way of life forever," the ex-president told a cheering audience of religious broadcasters. "This time, the greatest threat is not from the outside of our country. . . . It's the people from within our country that are more dangerous."

Even more troubling, Trump's longest-serving chief of staff, General John Kelly, a retired US Marine, claimed that Trump often praised Hitler. Kelly recalled Trump saying, "Well, but Hitler did some good things," like "[rebuilding] the economy." Kelly replied, "But what did he do with that rebuilt economy? He turned it against his own people and against the world." Trump did not respond. Trump's ignorance of the sacrifices made to stop Hitler shocked Kelly: "It's pretty hard to believe he missed the Holocaust, though, and pretty hard to understand how he missed the four hundred thousand American GIs that were killed in the European theater."

━━━━━━━

World War II represented the defining event in the lives of seven men who would go on to the presidency. With the exception of Ronald Reagan, all of them served with distinction, showing great courage along the way. The war shaped their personalities, fed their political ambitions, and influenced their actions in the White House. The war instilled in many of those who saw combat—Eisenhower, Kennedy, and Bush in particular—an appreciation of the hardship of battle that made them more reluctant to use military force when they occupied the Oval Office. Lyndon Johnson came away from the conflict with a deep skepticism of the military—a lesson that he would later forget when waging war in Vietnam. Nixon's time working in the Office of Price Administration fed his sense of grievance, while his time in the Pacific refined his ability to relate to ordinary Americans—the same people who would later form the backbone of his silent majority. It is easy to dismiss stay-at-home Reagan, but Hollywood shaped the simplistic view of the world he carried with him into the White House, while the US's dropping the atom bomb on Japan imbued in him a deep fear of nuclear weapons—a fear that led him to ignore the advice of most of his advisors and follow his own instincts when forging a new relationship with the Soviet Union.

But total victory in World War II also instilled a sense of hubris in that generation; a belief that the United States could guarantee economic growth at home and defend against threats abroad. The nation experienced unprecedented prosperity in the years after the war and remained a powerful force in world affairs, but eventually stagflation proved resistant to Keynesian economics, and Vietnam exposed the fallacy of the lessons of Munich. Even after the war had faded into a distant memory, a new generation of presidents invoked its lessons to arouse support for their policies. Every future president, whether he served or not, lived in the long shadow of World War II.

That was certainly true of the eighty-one-year-old President Joe Biden, who was born eighteen months before the D-Day invasion. In June 2024 Biden marked the eightieth anniversary of that day by traveling to Pointe du Hoc, where 225 Army Rangers had scaled the steep slopes in the decisive battle of World War II. Like Reagan forty years earlier, Biden drew parallels between the historic fight against Nazism in the 1930s and the current struggle against Russian aggression abroad and isolationism at home. "As we gather here today, it's not just to honor those who showed such remarkable bravery on that day," Biden declared. "It's to listen to the echoes of their voices. To hear them. Because they are summoning us, and they're summoning us now. They ask us, what will we do? They're not asking us to scale these cliffs," he continued. "But they're asking us to stay true to what America stands for."

Ironically, the threats facing America in the third decade of the twenty-first century are very real and in many ways similar to the challenges the nation confronted in the 1930s. By 2024, however, many Americans had grown weary of foreign adventurism, cynical of democratic institutions, and distrustful of their political leaders. But they would do well to heed the lessons of the past, reject the siren call of isolationism and the odious pleadings of demagogues, and adopt a new, chastened view of America's role in the world that balances global responsibility with a recognition of the limits of US power. If not, the democratic values for which these seven men—and all veterans of World War II—fought will be lost.

ACKNOWLEDGMENTS

===

It is often said that it takes a village to raise a child. The same could be said about writing a book. I depended on the hard work and dedication of many people to complete this manuscript. Andrina Tran, an exceptionally talented historian, read every chapter, offering insightful comments and suggestions while also skillfully editing early drafts. Rick Loessberg read the manuscript and made many helpful comments. A number of research assistants fanned out to the presidential libraries that I could not get to. They are Lilyan Rock (Nixon), Kade Kahanek (Bush), Severina Scott (Ford), and Bradley Galka (Eisenhower). I am grateful to all the archivists at these libraries, as well as the John F. Kennedy and Lyndon B. Johnson Presidential Libraries, for all their assistance. A special thanks to Allen Fisher at the LBJ Library who is retiring this year after more than thirty years of service. Over the past few decades, Allen has helped guide me through the massive collections at the LBJ Library, and he has always done so with a warm smile and good cheer.

The idea for this book grew out of a conversation between my wonderful editor, Jill Schwartzman, and talented agent, Steve Troha (Folio Literary Management), and myself. I had just finished a book about World War II and we were brainstorming ways of combining the war with my interest in the modern presidency. I can't remember who first came up with the idea that resulted in this book, but getting there was a team effort. I am grateful to Jill for her understanding, patience, and skill, and to the entire Dutton team, especially Charlotte Peters, John Parsley, Stephanie Cooper, Amanda Walker, and Alice Dalrymple. I don't think I have ever had a copy editor as thorough as Philip Bashe. He managed to save me from many embarrassing mistakes.

While writing this book, I retired from teaching after forty years, including the last twenty-seven years at the University of Oklahoma. I also stepped down from my role as scholar in residence at the History Channel after more than two decades. As always, I am indebted to Abbe Raven, former CEO of AETN, for providing me with opportunities that I never dreamed of having, and probably did not deserve.

I am blessed to have many people in my life who sustain me with their support, encouragement, and laughter. You know who you are. My spouse, Vantuir Borges, has enriched my life in countless ways. Our cats, Jack and Rio, showed their support by sleeping on every page.

Nearly forty years ago, I dedicated my first book to my mom and dad. My dad passed recently, but my mom is still going strong at ninety-three. From the day my older brother, Franny, was born sixty-nine years ago, my mom has devoted her life to loving, caring, nurturing, and worrying about Franny and me, as well as my younger siblings, Mike and Karen. She deserves a dedication all her own.

NOTES

LIBRARY OR COLLECTION ABBREVIATIONS

DDEPL: Dwight D. Eisenhower Presidential Library

FDRPL: Franklin D. Roosevelt Presidential Library

GHWBPL: George H. W. Bush Presidential Library

GRFPL: Gerald R. Ford Presidential Library

JFKPL: John F. Kennedy Presidential Library

LBJA: Lyndon Baines Johnson Archives Collection

LBJPL: LBJ Presidential Library

RNPL: Richard Nixon Presidential Library

RRPL: Ronald Reagan Presidential Library

WCOH: Whittier College Oral History

PREFACE

1 **To his right sat:** For two excellent accounts of the inauguration, see Richard Reeves, *President Kennedy: Profile of Power* (New York: Touchstone, 1993), and Thurston Clarke, *Ask Not: The Inauguration of John F. Kennedy and the Speech That Changed America* (New York: Penguin, 2005), Kindle.

2 **Nixon reflected later that:** John Farrell, *Richard Nixon: The Life* (New York: Vintage, 2018), 211; William Hitchcock, *The Age of Eisenhower: America and the World in the 1950s* (New York: Simon & Schuster, 2018), 80; Jean Edward Smith, *Eisenhower in War and Peace* (New York: Random House, 2012), 757–58.

2 **Kennedy also worried about leaving:** Robert Caro, *The Years of Lyndon Johnson: Master of the Senate* (New York: Knopf, 2002), 624; Jeff Shesol, *Mutual Contempt: Lyndon Johnson, Robert Kennedy, and the Feud That Defined a Decade* (New York: W. W. Norton, 1998), 34.

3 **The election had chilled:** Chris Matthews, *Kennedy & Nixon: The Rivalry That Shaped Postwar America* (New York: Free Press, 2011), 79, 90.

3 **"The war made us get serious":** William Doyle, *PT 109: An American Epic of War, Survival, and the Destiny of John F. Kennedy* (New York: William Morrow, 2015), xiii.

4 **A generation of Western leaders:** Stephen R. Rock, *Appeasement in International Politics* (Lexington: University Press of Kentucky, 2000), 1–23, https://www.jstor.org/stable /j.ctt130jjpn.5; Jeffrey Record, *The Specter of Munich: Reconsidering the Lessons of Appeasing Hitler* (Washington, DC: Potomac Books, 2006), 11–15; Fredrik Logevall, *JFK: Coming of Age in the American Century* (New York: Random House, 2020), xii–xiii.

4 **Kennedy was witness to:** Logevall, *JFK*, xii–xiii.

5 **"From the experience of World War II":** Doris Kearns Goodwin, *Lyndon Johnson and the American Dream* (New York: Open Road Media, 2015), 118, Kindle.

5 **"Invocations of the Munich analogy":** Jeffrey Record, "Retiring Hitler and 'Appeasement' from the National Security Debate," *Parameters* 38, no. 2 (Summer 2008), doi:10.55540/0031-1723.2416. See also: Record, *Making War, Thinking History: Munich, Vietnam, and Presidential Uses of Force from Korea to Kosovo* (Annapolis, MD: Naval Institute Press, 2002); Fredrik Logevall and Kenneth Osgood, "The Ghost of Munich: America's Appeasement Complex," *World Affairs* 173, no. 2 (July/August 2010): 13–26; Robert J. Beck, "Munich's Lessons Reconsidered," *International Security* 14, no. 2 (Fall 1989): 161–91; Hal Brands and Jeremi Suri, eds., *The Power of the Past: History and Statecraft* (Washington, DC: Brookings Institution Press, 2016), 1–26.

6 **"They do not relate to":** President John F. Kennedy, "Commencement Address at Yale University, June 11, 1962," JFKPL, https://www.jfklibrary.org/archives/other-resources /john-f-kennedy-speeches/yale-university-19620611.

6 **"A rising tide lifts all boats":** For a discussion of Kennedy's use of the phrase, see Donald Lazere, "A Rising Tide Lifts All Boats: Has the Right Been Misusing JFK's Quote?," *History News Network* online, accessed December 21, 2022, https://historynewsnetwork .org/article/73227.

7 **gap between American ideals:** Steven M. Gillon and Cathy D. Matson, *The American Experiment: A History of the United States* (Boston: Houghton Mifflin, 2009), 977.

8 **According to Robert Kennedy:** Nancy Gibbs and Michael Duffy, *The Presidents Club: Inside the World's Most Exclusive Fraternity* (New York: Simon & Schuster, 2012), 124.

8 **"You must have a hot speech":** Herbert S. Parmet, *JFK: The Presidency of John F. Kennedy* (New York: Doubleday, 1983), 4.

9 **Convinced that economic growth:** Clarke, *Ask Not*, 1136, Kindle.

10 **The war exposed those like Nixon:** Parmet, *JFK*, 98; Jon Meacham, *Destiny and Power: The American Odyssey of George Herbert Walker Bush* (New York: Random House, 2015), 53.

CHAPTER 1

17 **At three o'clock the same day:** Hearings Before the Joint Committee on the Investigation of the Pearl Harbor Attack, 79th Congress, 2nd session, Document 244, Final report, "The Last Hours," 441.

18 **Only Republican congresswoman Jeannette Rankin:** William C. Murphy Jr., "U.S. Declares War on Japs," *Philadelphia Inquirer*, December 9, 1941, 1.

19 **"Is there objection to the request?":** Martin Caidin and Edward Hymoff, *The Mission: The Untold Story of Lieutenant Commander Lyndon B. Johnson's Secret Combat Mission in the South Pacific During WWII* (New York: Popular Library, 1964), 12–14; Merle Miller, *Lyndon: An Oral Biography* (New York: G. P. Putnam's Sons, 1980), 92.

19 **"A vote for Johnson is":** Robert Dallek, *An Unfinished Life: John F. Kennedy, 1917–1963* (New York: Little, Brown, 2003), 147–48.

19 **FDR telephoned aide Tommy Corcoran:** "Lyndon Baines Johnson," February 5, 1964, Franklin D. Roosevelt Presidential Library (abbreviated hereafter as FDRPL), President's Personal File, Lyndon B. Johnson (6106–6153). This appears to be a breakdown of all the meetings between Johnson and FDR. It is unclear why it is dated February 5, 1964. Robert Caro, *The Years of Lyndon Johnson: Means of Ascent* (New York: Vintage, 2011), 10.

20 **"He embodies the spirit":** Lyndon B. Johnson, "It Is Later Than We Think," San Jacinto Day Speech, April 21, 1941, joint session Texas Legislature, Henry A. Wallace Papers, FDRPL, General Correspondence, box 38.

20 **Though he never made it:** Caro, *Means of Ascent*, 19.

20 **"He had everyone working":** Miller, *Lyndon*, 92; Caro, *Means of Ascent*, 29.

21 **"He was excessively thin":** Caro, *Means of Ascent*, 29.

21 **"I hope sometime you run":** Caro, *Means of Ascent*, 20–21; Robert Dallek, *Lone Star Rising: Lyndon Johnson and His Times, 1908–1960* (New York: Oxford University Press, 1992), 231–33.

21 **Australia, New Zealand, and India:** Dallek, *Lone Star*, 236, Kindle; Caro, *Means of Ascent*, 24.

22 **"Today I am here":** Caro, *Means of Ascent*, 31–32.

22 **In desperation, he headed back:** Caro, *Means of Ascent*, 31–32.

22 **He had even suggested:** Caro, *Means of Ascent*, 33; McCabe to Hopkins, April 23, 1942, FDRPL, President's Personal File, "Lyndon Johnson"; Hopkins to McCabe, April 25, 1942, FDRPL, President's Personal File, "Lyndon Johnson"; Dallek, *Lone Star*, 233; Jonathan Daniels, *White House Witness, 1942–45* (New York: Doubleday, 1975), 28–29.

22 **"President Roosevelt wanted his eyes":** Caro, *Means of Ascent*, 32–33; Miller, *Lyndon*, 94–95.

22 **FDR may have wanted:** Dallek, *Lone Star*, 236.

23 **He was finally on his way:** Caro, *Means of Ascent*, 33.

23 **That moment galvanized him:** Logevall, *JFK*, 298.

23 **The evaluation described him:** "Kennedy, John Fitzgerald—Applicant for Commission as Ensign," September 8, 1941, JFK Personal Papers, John F. Kennedy Presidential Library (referred to hereafter as JFKPL), JFKPP-011-030-p0007.

24 **He knew that the rigorous:** Dallek, *Unfinished Life*, 82; Logevall, *JFK*, 288–91.

24 **"Reading the report of his exam":** Dallek, *Unfinished Life*, 82; Logevall, *JFK*, 293–94; Herbert S. Parmet, *Jack: The Struggles of John F. Kennedy* (New York: Dial Press, 1980), 86–87.

24 **After Pearl Harbor, the work:** Logevall, *JFK*, 304; Dallek, *Unfinished Life*, 83.

25 **With the direct approval of:** Logevall, *JFK*, 296, 306; Dallek, *Unfinished Life*, 83–84.

25 **"They shagged my ass":** Dallek, *Unfinished Life*, 83–84; Parmet, *JFK*, 91.

25 **His friend Lem Billings:** Logevall, *JFK*, 311; Parmet, *JFK*, 91–92.

25 **hospitals in Charleston and Boston:** Parmet, *Jack*, 92.

26 **"We are at war, mister!":** Richard Nixon, *RN: The Memoirs of Richard Nixon* (New York: Simon & Schuster, 2013), 37.

26 **"I thought at this time":** John A. Farrell, *Nixon: The Life* (New York: Vintage, 2017), 75.

26 **"seemed a good opportunity":** Nixon, *Memoirs*, 36; Farrell, *Nixon*, 75.

26 **"In her whole life":** Stephen E. Ambrose, *Nixon*, vol. 1, *The Education of a Politician, 1913–1962* (New York: Simon & Schuster, 2014), 47.

27 **The award came with:** Ambrose, *Education*, 50.

27 **His debate coach remembered:** Robert Dallek, *Nixon and Kissinger: Partners in Power* (New York: HarperCollins, 2009), 7.

27 **He described feeling "bitterly defeated":** Farrell, *Nixon*, 4; Dallek, *Nixon and Kissinger*, 11.

28 **she loved to ice-skate:** Will Swift, *Pat and Dick: The Nixons, an Intimate Portrait of a Marriage* (New York: Threshold Editions, 2014), 18–21; Roger Morris, *Richard Milhous Nixon: The Rise and Fall of an American Politician* (New York: Henry Holt, 1990), 221.

28 **"Our greatest hopes":** Morris, *Rise and Fall*, 236.

28 **It was tedious work:** Swift, *Pat and Dick*, 45–46; Morris, *Rise and Fall*, 236; "Business, Professional and Administrative Experience," Record Group 24: Records of the Bureau of Naval Personnel—Series: Official Military Personnel Files. Official Military Personnel File for Richard M. Nixon—September 1930–September 1970, National Archives, Washington, DC.

29 **The supervisor admitted to:** J. H. Beuscher to Director, Naval Officer Procurement, May 4, 1942, Record Group 24: Records of the Bureau of Naval Personnel—Series: Official Military Personnel Files. Official Military Personnel File for Richard M. Nixon—September 1930–September 1970, National Archives, Washington, DC.

29 **One of his supervisors said:** Morris, *Rise and Fall*, 238, 242–43.

29 **But he also praised:** Speech File: Campaign, Bureaucracy and RN's Experiences with OPA. Speech File (PPS 208), 1:15, Richard Nixon Presidential Library (referred to hereafter as RNPL), Yorba Linda, CA.

30 **"But I don't need a staff":** Nixon, *Memoirs*, 37; Morris, *Rise and Fall*, 243.

30 **"I would have felt mighty uncomfortable":** Nixon, *Memoirs*, 37–39.

30 **"It is believed his exceptional":** H. Beuscher to Director, Naval Officer Procurement, May 4, 1942, Record Group 24: Records of the Bureau of Naval Personnel—Series: Official Military Personnel Files, Official Military Personnel File for Richard M. Nixon "First Endorsement," May 8, 1942, National Archives.

31 **With that shining endorsement:** Nixon, *Memoirs*, 37–39.

31 **"Your country's attacked":** Meacham, *Destiny and Power*, 38; Robert B. Stinnett, *George Bush: His World War II Years* (Washington, DC: Brassey's, 1992), 1.

31 **"If the government fails":** Meacham, *Destiny and Power*, 39.

32 **George then invited Barbara:** Ellie LeBlond Sosa and Kelly Anne Chase, *George and Barbara Bush: A Great American Love Story* (Camden, ME: Down East Books, 2018), 188; Meacham, *Destiny and Power*, 41–43.

32 **"I knew what I wanted":** Joe Hyams, *Flight of the Avenger: George Bush at War* (New York: Harcourt, 1991), 32; Meacham, *Destiny and Power*, 40; Jeffrey A. Engel, *When the World Seemed New: George H. W. Bush and the End of the Cold War* (Boston: Houghton Mifflin Harcourt, 2017), 28, Kindle.

32 **"Got on the train":** Meacham, *Destiny and Power*, 46.

32 **"Powerful figures in Washington":** Hitchcock, *Age of Eisenhower*, 16.

32 **"My dreams were of":** Dwight D. Eisenhower, *Crusade in Europe: A Personal Account of World War II* (New York: Vintage, 2013), 15, Kindle.

33 **"four-year panoramic view":** Daniel Vermilya, "A Day When Everything Changed—Dwight Eisenhower and the Attack on Pearl Harbor," National Park Service, last modified December 7, 2020, https://www.nps.gov/articles/000/a-day-when-everything-changed-dwight-eisenhower-and-the-attack-on-pearl harbor.htm#:~:text=One%20of %20those%20who%20had,outside%20of%20San%20Antonio%2C%20Texas.

33 **"Tell your boss that":** Eisenhower, *Crusade*, 16.

33 **Eisenhower described Marshall:** Stephen E. Ambrose, *Eisenhower: Soldier and President* (Simon & Schuster, 2014), 61; Smith, *Eisenhower in War and Peace*, 180; "General George C. Marshall," *American Experience* online, accessed September 10, 2023, https://www.pbs.org/wgbh/americanexperience/features/macarthur-general-george-c-marshall/.

33 **Major General Charles Thompson:** Smith, *Eisenhower in War and Peace*, 173.

34 **When bad weather grounded:** Eisenhower, *Crusade*, 16.

34 **She embraced her role:** Smith, *Eisenhower in War and Peace*, 33–35; "Mamie Eisenhower," Miller Center, University of Virginia, accessed June 10, 2023, https://millercenter.org/president/eisenhower/essays/eisenhower-1953-firstlady.

35 **"My orders to France":** Smith, *Eisenhower in War and Peace*, 45–48; Hitchcock, *Age of Eisenhower*, 9.

35 **He spent the next two years:** Hitchcock, *Age of Eisenhower*, 16.

35 **He had just stepped off:** Eisenhower, *Crusade*, 20–21.

36 **"Do your best to save":** Dwight D. Eisenhower, Diaries (January 1–July 6, 1942), DDEPL, https://www.eisenhowerlibrary.gov/sites/default/files/file/DDE%20Diary%20JanJuly%201942.pdf.

36 **Eisenhower recalled that he:** Smith, *Eisenhower in War and Peace*, 176.

36 **In February 1942:** Smith, *Eisenhower in War and Peace*, 185–86.

37 **"We've got to go to Europe":** Hitchcock, *Age of Eisenhower*, 17–18; Eisenhower, Diaries, January 22, 1942, https://www.eisenhowerlibrary.gov/sites/default/files/file/DDE%20Diary%20JanJuly%201942.pdf.

37 **Though she managed to move:** Smith, *Eisenhower in War and Peace*, 187; Eisenhower, Diaries, January 4, March 11, 1942, 1, 10; Ambrose, *Eisenhower: Soldier and President* (New York: Simon & Schuster, 1991), 63–64; Vermilya, "A Day When Everything Changed."

37 **"Eisenhower and Marshall made":** Smith, *Eisenhower in War and Peace*, 182; Ambrose, *Soldier and President*, 63; Hitchcock, *Age of Eisenhower*, 16.

38 **He walked into his home:** James Cannon, *Gerald R. Ford: An Honorable Life* (Ann Arbor: University of Michigan Press, 2013), 57.

38 **Like JFK, Nixon, and Bush:** Gerald R. Ford, *A Time to Heal: The Autobiography of Gerald R. Ford* (New York: Harper and Row, 1979), 57.

38 **In April 1942:** Michael E. Unsworth, "'The Best Officer of the Deck': Gerald R. Ford's World War II Experience," *Michigan History,* January/February 1994, 8–9.

38 **In his senior year:** John Robert Greene, "Gerald Ford: Life in Brief," Miller Center, University of Virginia, accessed November 10, 2023, https://millercenter.org/president/ford.

39 **"I wanted desperately":** Unsworth, "'Best Officer of the Deck,'" 9; Ford, *A Time to Heal*, 57–58.

39 **Corwin responded quickly:** Ford to Corwin, December 22, 1942, Gerald R. Ford Presidential Library (referred to hereafter as GRFPL), box 1.

40 **When the bombs fell:** Lou Cannon, "Ronald Reagan: Life in Brief," Miller Center, University of Virginia, accessed November 10, 2023, https://millercenter.org/president/reagan/life-in-brief.

40 **"Let's get what we can":** Stephen Vaughn, *Ronald Reagan in Hollywood: Movies and Politics* (Cambridge: Cambridge University Press, 1994), 105.

41 **A few more deferments followed:** Marc Eliot, *Reagan: The Hollywood Years* (New York: Crown Archetype, 2008), 146–47; Vaughn, *Reagan in Hollywood*, 106–7.

41 **Hershey therefore instructed:** Vaughn, *Reagan in Hollywood*, 107.

41 **Thanks to Warner and Hershey:** Eliot, *Hollywood Years*, 161; Vaughn, *Reagan in Hollywood*, 107.

42 **Jack Warner made sure:** Eliot, *Hollywood Years*, 162.

CHAPTER 2

43 **They also landed on New Guinea:** George C. Herring, *From Colony to Superpower: U.S. Foreign Relations Since 1776* (New York: Oxford University Press, 2008), 539.

44 **Strategically, however, the battle:** John Winton, *War in the Pacific: Pearl Harbor to Tokyo Bay* (Leeds, UK: Sapere Books, 2022), 49–51.

44 **They soon formed a close bond:** Dallek, *Lone Star*, 237.

44 **For years after:** Caidin and Hymoff, *The Mission*, 25, 52–53; Miller, *Lyndon*, 94–95; LBJ Diary, Subject File, Johnson Papers, LBJPL, Lyndon Baines Johnson Archives Collection (referred to hereafter at LBJA) File, box 73.

45 **"Give us planes":** Miller, *Lyndon*, 98–99.

45 **"from the SWPA [Southwest Pacific Area]":** Caidin and Hymoff, *The Mission*, 30.

45 **In the Fiji Islands:** LBJ Diary, LBJA, Subject File, box 73.

46 **"Ground forces were in excellent shape":** LBJ Memo, n.d., LBJA, Subject File, n.d., Johnson Papers, LBJA-LBJPL, Subject File, box 74.

46 **Although MacArthur could use:** Dallek, *Lone Star*, 237; Caidin and Hymoff, *The Mission*, 25, 29, 54–55.

47 **Sometimes pilots would fly low:** Caidin and Hymoff, *The Mission*, 56, 66.

47 **LBJ insisted, though:** Caidin and Hymoff, *The Mission*, 55.

47 **"Find yourself another plane":** Hymoff to General Clifton, March 7, 1964, LBJPL, LBJA, Subject File, box 74; Caidin and Hymoff, *The Mission*, 83–84.

47 **The rest of the men all:** Caidin and Hymoff, *The Mission*, 84.

47 **"Down there at the time":** Caidin and Hymoff, *The Mission*, 85.

48 **"It's at least twice as bad":** Caidin and Hymoff, *The Mission*, 87.

48 **"planes as his headquarters":** Miller, *Lyndon*, 97.

48 **why a congressman would want:** Caidin and Hymoff, *The Mission*, 85–86.

49 **"He was absolutely determined":** Caidin and Hymoff, *The Mission*, 86; Miller, *Lyndon*, 97.

49 **did not have to wait long:** Caidin and Hymoff, *The Mission*, 88–89.

49 **fell back and out:** Caidin and Hymoff, *The Mission*, 105–6.

49 **"The Zeros stayed with us":** Caidin and Hymoff, *The Mission*, 109.

50 **"I'm always scared up here":** Miller, *Lyndon*, 97–98. In 1964 Martin Caidin and Edward Hymoff published *The Mission*, which chronicled LBJ's actions, telling the story of his bravery in the face of battle. In 1993 two aviation experts, Henry Sakaida and Barrett Tillman, wrote a book that poked holes in the Johnson narrative. They claimed *The Mission* was full of factual inaccuracies and essentially manufactured the myth of Johnson's plane coming under attack. They claim that the *Heckling Hare*'s generator stopped working long before they reached the drop site and that it never came under attack from Japanese Zeros. As proof, they interviewed Bob Marshall, a nineteen-year-old gunner on Johnson's plane that day, who charged that the entire story was "made up." Their plane, he said, "was never attacked. There was nothing." They also interviewed Saburo Sakai, the Japanese ace who supposedly fired at the plane. "Could a single-engine B-26 outrun a Zero?" they asked. Sakai responded, "On a clear day? Definitely not!" See Tillman and Sakaida, "LBJ's Silver Star—The Mission That Never Was," in *Pacific Air Combat WWII: Voices from the Past*, ed. Sakaida (Saint Paul, MN: Phalanx, 1993). A number of news outlets picked up on the story and published articles casting doubt on Johnson's mission. See Jamie McIntyre, "Another Undeserved Military Honor for LBJ," *Washington Examiner*, last modified May 10, 2019, https://www.washingtonexaminer.com/policy/defense-national-security/another-undeserved-military-honor-for-lbj, and "Navigator's Son Disputes LBJ Ever Saw Combat," CNN online, last modified July 9, 2001, http://www.cnn.com/2001/US/07/09/lbj.silverstar/index.html.

It's hard to reconcile these two narratives, especially when there are crew members from the same plane telling completely different stories. In my opinion, however, the circumstantial evidence at the LBJ Library leans in favor of the account in *The Mission*.

On July 3, 1964, shortly after the publication of *The Mission*, former members of the *Heckling Hare*'s crew gathered for a reunion. As reported in the Twenty-Second Bombardment Group newsletter, many crew members present supported the story told in the book. "It sure renews my memory," recalled one crew member. "Some good and some that I'd rather have left among the forgotten." The men offered minor criticism, mainly about the way the authors describe the inside of the plane, but none questioned the veracity of the story.

That same year, Sakai gave an interview to the Associated Press that offers even more convincing evidence. He pointed out that the American planes appeared "quite unexpectedly" out of the clouds. "We were totally unprepared," he recalled. According to the Japanese pilot, he tried to shoot down the damaged B-26 carrying LBJ "because I felt it was a stray sheep before a lion." He fired cannon shells at the plane but broke off in pursuit of the "main formation." He said that the story told in *The Mission* was true "judging from my wartime memory and diary." See Ken Sembon, Associated Press, February 26, [1964], Johnson Papers, LBJA-LBJPL, Subject File, box 74.

50 **"nonchalant in the face":** Caro, *Means of Ascent*, 46.

50 **Colonel Stevens and the entire crew:** Caro, *Means of Ascent*, 43; Caidin and Hymoff, *The Mission*, 113.

50 **third-highest combat decoration:** Caro, *Means of Ascent*, 44–45; Dallek, *Lone Star*, 240; Miller, *Lyndon*, 99.

51 **By July 10:** Miller, *Lyndon*, 100; Caidin and Hymoff, *The Mission*, 130–31.

52 **wounded during the exchange:** In the letter, Johnson wrote that he "cannot in good conscience receive this decoration and wear the coveted medal." He went on to say that he "cannot accept a citation of recognition for an inconsequential part I played for a short time in learning and facing with them the problems which they are encountering all the time." LBJ to Adjutant General, July 15, 1942, Johnson Papers, LBJA File, box 74.

52 **"Silver Stars in American military":** Caro, *Means of Ascent*, 48–49, 51; Ronnie Dugger, *The Politician: The Life and Times of Lyndon Johnson* (New York: W. W. Norton, 1982), 251–53.

52 **derisively referred to as:** Caro, *Means of Ascent*, 53.

52 **harshest criticism for military:** Japanese planes were faster and more lethal, and their pilots better trained than their American counterparts. "I'd just as soon try to weather a storm riding on the rail of a box kite as I would to face the fighting Jap Zero with one of those navy PBY crates some of those boys are now flying," he told a reporter. Johnson Papers, LBJA File, n.d., box 74; Dallek, *Lone Star*, 242.

53 **told another radio audience:** Dallek, *Lone Star*, 243–44.

54 **a hormonal imbalance:** Logevall, *JFK*, 317, 320.

54 **more attractive to him:** Joan Blair and Clay Blair Jr., *The Search for JFK* (New York: Berkeley, 1976), 175–76; Parmet, *Jack*, 93–95; Logevall, *JFK*, 321–22.

55 **He made one final request:** Logevall, *JFK*, 322–32; Doyle, *PT 109*, 29.

55 **"damn plywood board":** Logevall, *JFK*, 323.

55 **a second time to Walsh:** Doyle, *PT 109*, 34. Years later, after he'd learned about JFK's health problems, Harllee said that his "pulling strings" was an example of "his stubborn, indomitable courage," but it was "also reckless and irresponsible and somewhat selfish."

55 **ferocious battle for control:** Logevall, *JFK*, 324–26; Blair and Blair Jr., *Search for JFK*, 186.

56 **an intensive ten months:** Hyams, *Flight of the Avenger*, 32–33.

56 **exhilaration of coming in low:** "World War II Correspondence, 1942–48," George Bush Personal Papers, George H. W. Bush Presidential Library (referred to hereafter as GHWBPL), box 1. The individual letters are not dated, but the library has organized them based on where Bush was stationed. All the quotes that follow are from the following places: Chapel Hill, Minneapolis, Corpus Christi, and Fort Lauderdale.

57 **pilot, gunner, and radioman:** Stinnett, *Bush: World War II Years*, 12.

57 **how to control them because:** Bush to Mum, n.d., Bush Personal Papers, GHWBPL, box 1.
58 **"of a civilized community":** Bush to Mum, n.d., Bush Personal Papers, GHWBPL, box 1.
58 **painted on the side:** Bush to Mum, n.d., Bush Personal Papers, GHWBPL, box 1.
58 *"loves all of you":* Stinnett, *Bush: World War II Years,* 245.
58 **Naval Air Station Ottumwa:** The Chief of Naval Personnel to Nixon, October 9, 1942, Official Military Personnel File for Richard M. Nixon—September 1930–September 1970, Record Group 24: Records of the Bureau of Naval Personnel—Series: Official Military Personnel Files, National Archives (NA) 70.
58 **uncompleted runway stopped abruptly:** Nixon, *Memoirs,* 38–39.
59 **harsh Midwest winter:** Farrell, *Nixon,* 76–77.
59 **He and Pat discussed:** Nixon, *Memoirs,* 39.
59 **"coast of Southern California":** Navy Personnel to Chief of Naval Personnel, March 30, 1943, Official Military Personnel File for Richard M. Nixon, Record Group 24: Records of the Bureau of Naval Personnel, National Archives.
60 **evils posed by Germany and Japan:** Nixon, *Memoirs,* 39. On May 2, 1943, Nixon received his orders to report to San Francisco "for first available transportation to Noumea, New Caledonia, and upon arrival report to the Commander Fleet Air, Noumea, for duty." Chief of Naval Personnel to Nixon, May 2, 1943, Official Military Personnel File for Richard M. Nixon, Record Group 24: Records of the Bureau of Naval Personnel, National Archives.
60 **father sobbed uncontrollably:** Nixon, *Memoirs,* 40.
61 **plan with only a few:** Smith, *Eisenhower in War and Peace,* 190–91.
61 **Eisenhower presented his plan:** Eisenhower, *Crusade,* 58–59.
61 **"in command of the European theater":** Smith, *Eisenhower in War and Peace,* 198–99.
61 **eighteenth among all:** Smith, *Eisenhower in War and Peace,* 200.
62 **"being jovially outspoken":** Ambrose, *Soldier and President,* 72, Kindle; Hitchcock, *Age of Eisenhower,* 17.
62 **"straightforward, and very modest":** Ambrose, *Soldier and President,* 72–74.
62 **"bones and the exhaustion":** Eisenhower, Diaries, June 25, 1942, https://www.eisen howerlibrary.gov/sites/default/files/file/DDE%20Diary%20JanJuly%201942.pdf.
63 **"habit of passing the buck":** Eisenhower, Diaries, June 25, 1942, https://www.eisen howerlibrary.gov/sites/default/files/file/DDE%20Diary%20JanJuly%201942.pdf.
63 **Respect needed to apply:** Ambrose, *Soldier and President,* 75.
63 **July 22, 1942:** Smith, *Eisenhower in War and Peace,* 209; Ambrose, *Soldier and President,* 75.
64 **mission a success and proving:** James Bradley, *Flyboys: A True Story of Courage* (Boston: Little, Brown, 2003), 160.
64 **two men who mattered most:** Smith, *Eisenhower in War and Peace,* 248; Hitchcock, *Age of Eisenhower,* 19.
64 **"But we made so many":** Smith, *Eisenhower in War and Peace,* 265.
65 **"studios usually got behind":** Eliot, *Hollywood Years,* 168.
65 **industry popularity polls:** Eliot, *Hollywood Years,* 171; Bob Spitz, *Reagan: An American Journey* (New York: Penguin, 2018), 200; Ronald Reagan with Richard G. Hubler, *Where's the Rest of Me?: The Ronald Reagan Story* (New York: Duell, Sloan and Pearce, 1965), 121.
65 **the local recruitment office:** Spitz, *Reagan,* 199.
66 **$75 a week:** Eliot, *Hollywood Years,* 166; Spitz, *Reagan,* 199.
66 **American bases in the Pacific:** Reagan with Hubler, *Where's the Rest of Me?,* 118–19; Spitz, *Reagan,* 203–4.
66 **was receiving preferential treatment:** Eliot, *Hollywood Years,* 163–65.
67 **fighting in the trenches abroad:** Eliot, *Hollywood Years,* 166–67.

67 **her heroic husband:** Spitz, *Reagan*, 201–22.

67 **"living under the same roof":** Eliot, *Hollywood Years*, 179.

67 **a breezy style filled with:** Spitz, *Reagan*, 200–201.

68 **"morning, noon, and night":** Spitz, *Reagan*, 201; Vaughn, *Reagan in Hollywood*, 105.

68 **a Republican before the war:** Reagan would later claim that he remained a staunch liberal at the end of the war. "At the end of World War II, I was a New Dealer to the core," he wrote in his memoirs. But it was clear that his wartime experience exposed cracks in his liberal faith. Ronald Reagan, *An American Life: The Autobiography* (New York: Simon & Schuster, 1990*)*, 105.

68 **"are being unjustly denied":** Reagan to Shaw, January 14, 1961, Governor's Office Files, Research Files (Molly Sturgis Tuthill), Ronald Reagan Presidential Library (referred to hereafter as RRPL), box GO199.

69 **"process for empire building":** Reagan with Hubler, *Where's the Rest of Me?*, 124–25.

CHAPTER 3

70 **Japanese operations in:** David M. Kennedy, *Freedom from Fear: The American People in Depression and War, 1929–1945* (New York: Oxford University Press, 1999), 545.

71 **matériel flooded the island:** Kennedy, *Freedom*, 557.

71 **"certainly be a wonderful experience":** "Dear Children," March 4, 1943, Joseph P. Kennedy Private Papers, JFKPL, Family: Family Correspondence, 1938–October 1943, box 2.

71 **"screw up everything they touch":** Doyle, *PT 109*, 41–42, 55–57.

72 **37 mm antitank gun:** Nigel Hamilton, *JFK: Reckless Youth* (New York: Random House, 1992), 554.

72 **George "Barney" Ross:** Parmet, *Jack*, 100–101; Doyle, *PT 109*, 46–48, 77.

72 **servants and chauffeurs:** Doyle, *PT 109*, 44.

73 **army PX stations for candy:** Hamilton, *Reckless Youth*, 544, 527; Doyle, *PT 109*, 43, 50.

73 **He then corrected himself:** "Dear Dad & Mother," May 14, 1943, JFK Personal Papers, Correspondence, 1943–62, Personal, 1943, JFKPL, box 2; Dallek, *Unfinished Life,* 91; Logevall, *JFK*, 333–34.

73 **"bull coming out of chute three":** Logevall, *JFK*, 334.

74 **"you were in a closet":** Doyle, *PT 109*, 59, 81, 109; Parmet, *Jack*, 101; "John F. Kennedy and PT-109," n.d., JFKPL, accessed September 3, 2023, https://www.jfklibrary.org/learn /about-jfk/jfk-in-history/john-f-kennedy-and-pt-109; John Hersey, "Survival: Long Before He Became President, J.F.K. Battled to Save Himself and His Men While Adrift in the South Pacific," *New Yorker*, June 10, 1944, 2–3, https://www.newyorker.com/maga zine/1944/06/17/survival-jfk-second-world-war.

74 **hoping to catch the Express:** Stephen Plotkin, "Sixty Years Later, the Story of PT-109 Still Captivates," *Prologue* 35, no. 2 (Summer 2003), National Archives, https://www .archives.gov/publications/prologue/2003/summer/pt109.html; Hersey, "Survival," 3.

74 **one of their three motors:** Doyle, *PT 109*, 92–93; B. R. White and J. G. McClure, *Narrative on Sinking of PT-109 and Rescue, 22 August 1943*, JFK Personal Papers, JFKPL, Correspondence, 1943–1952, 1–2, https://www.jfklibrary.org/asset-viewer/archives/jfkpp -006-011#?image_identifier=JFKPP-006-011-p0003. The report was coauthored by Byron White, whom JFK would later appoint to the Supreme Court.

74 **"It all happened so fast":** White and McClure, *Narrative on Sinking of PT-109*, 2; Marc Lancaster, "PT-109: John F. Kennedy Fights to Survive in the Solomons," World War II on Deadline, last modified August 8, 2020, https://ww2ondeadline.com/2020/08/08 /pt-109-jfk-john-f-kennedy-world-war-ii-navy/.

74 **"Sound general quarters!":** Doyle, *PT 109*, 93–95.

75 **"and probably both halves sank":** Doyle, *PT 109*, 7.

75 **The only sound and smell:** Hersey, "Survival," 4.

75 **men swam back and clung:** Doyle, *PT 109*, 108; Hersey, "Survival," 5.

75 **"I hurt my leg":** Hersey, "Survival," 5.

75 **"I will not allow you to die!":** Doyle, *PT 109*, 110–11.

76 **back to the wreckage:** Plotkin, "Sixty Years Later"; Doyle, *PT 109*, 95–96; Dallek, *Unfinished Life*, 96.

76 **their waterlogged clothes:** Doyle, *PT 109*, 107.

76 **"Those sons of bitches ran":** Doyle, *PT 109*, 112.

76 **"just a foot above water":** Doyle, *PT 109*, 115; Hamilton, *Reckless Youth*, 581.

77 **in the ocean for fifteen:** Logevall, *JFK*, 343; Parmet, *Jack*, 104.

77 **outline of an enemy-held:** Doyle, *PT 109*, 118.

77 **discovered by a Japanese destroyer:** Logevall, *JFK*, 344; Doyle, *PT 109*, 123.

77 **PT boats were not traveling:** Doyle, *PT 109*, 124, 134; White and McClure, *Narrative on Sinking of PT-109*, 3–4.

77 **would never allow pain:** White and McClure, *Narrative on Sinking of PT-109*, 4; Hersey, "Survival," 11.

78 **never complained about the pain:** Hersey, "Survival," 12; Plotkin, "Sixty Years Later."

78 **dubbed the place Bird Island:** Hersey, "Survival," 12; Plotkin, "Sixty Years Later."

78 **"tow this island back!":** Doyle, *PT 109*, 140.

78 **Ross and Kennedy were Japanese:** White and McClure, *Narrative on Sinking of PT-109*, 4; Logevall, *JFK*, 345; Parmet, *Jack*, 105; Doyle, *PT 109*, 140–41. Kennedy believed it was Naru Island but it was actually Cross Island.

79 **"locals have found us!":** Plotkin, "Sixty Years Later"; Doyle, *PT 109*, 142.

79 **The ordeal of PT-109:** Hersey, "Survival," 14. Kennedy also kept in touch with Kumana and Gasa, often exchanging letters with them. He invited them to his inauguration, but they were unable to attend. The two were scheduled to meet with Kennedy in November 1963, but when they arrived at the airport, they were told the trip was canceled. Only after they got home did they learn why: JFK had been assassinated. "I was in the garden when the family heard the news on the radio," Kumana recalled. "I came back inside the house and found the photo of him, and I cried. I sat down with the picture and cried." See Hamilton, *Reckless Youth*, 602, and Kat Eschner, "Why JFK Kept a Coconut Shell in the Oval Office," *Smithsonian* online, last modified August 2, 2017, https://www .smithsonianmag.com/smart-news/why-jfk-kept-coconut-shell-white-house-desk -180964263/.

79 **insisted on getting back:** Dallek, *Unfinished Life*, 99–100.

79 **"they should measure their words":** Dear Mother & Dad, September 12, 1943, JFK Personal Papers (JFKPP), Correspondence, 1943–62, Personal, 1943, JFKPL, box 2.

80 **"keeping your bowels":** Jack to Dad, n.d., and Jack to Dad, October 30, 1943, JFKPP, Family: Family Correspondence, 1938–October 1943, JFKPL, box 2.

80 **"group of islands":** Logevall, *JFK*, 354; Hamilton, *Reckless Youth*, 621.

80 **PT-109 incident also qualified:** Dallek, *Unfinished Life*, 100.

80 **safety of the Kennedy bubble:** Logevall, *JFK*, 366; Plotkin, "Sixty Years Later."

81 **condensed version that August:** Parmet, *Jack*, 110; Blair and Blair Jr., *Search for JFK*, 379; Lancaster, "PT-109: Kennedy Fights to Survive in the Solomons."

81 **"where the hell was your radar?":** Doyle, *PT 109*, 205. Jack's PT boat was not equipped with radar, but that did not stop the new commander of the PT boat squadron, J. E. Gibson, from blaming Kennedy for the loss of PT-109, saying, "He lost the 109 through very poor organization of his crew." A few revisionist historians have made similar accusations. They could not be more mistaken. The collision resulted from the inherent problems with the boats themselves, especially their lack of radar, but also a refusal

among navy leadership to change tactics and strategy even after it became clear that the boats were ineffective against Japanese metal barges. Hamilton, *Reckless Youth*, 567–69.

81 **shared a room with him:** Blair and Blair Jr., *Search for JFK*, 325.

82 **The plane exploded eighteen minutes:** Doyle, *PT 109*, 206.

82 **rear of the shifting battle lines:** Morris, *Rise and Fall*, 247.

83 **two and four in the morning:** Carl J. Fleps, oral history, June 9, 1972, 2–3, Richard Nixon Oral History Project, Whittier College Archive, hereafter referred to as WCOH, June 9, 1972, 2–3.

83 **"the SCAT detachment":** Fleps, oral history, 4–5; Swift, *Pat and Dick*, Kindle, 52; Farrell, *Nixon*, 77.

83 **"ammunition, foodstuffs, medical supplies":** Hollis Dole, oral history, January 26, 1973, WCOH, 3, 13–14.

83 **"Our tent had been completely":** Nixon, *Memoirs*, 28.

84 **"hours in this particular area":** Dole, oral history, 4.

84 **"hospital from the centipede":** Dole, oral history, 3–4.

84 **"My poker playing":** Nixon, *Memoirs*, 29; Farrell, *Nixon*, 78.

84 **with him from Whittier:** Morris, *Rise and Fall*, 249.

85 **"really much more humble":** Morris, *Rise and Fall*, 251–52.

85 **Australian beer, and cold juice:** Swift, *Pat and Dick*, 53; Nixon, *Memoirs*, 28.

85 **basics of business law:** Ambrose, *Education*, 110.

85 **"never lost his cool":** Ambrose, *Education*, 108–9; Fleps, oral history, 6.

85 **Letter of Commendation:** J. H. Newton, "Lieutenant Richard M. Nixon, United States Naval Reserve," n.d., Record Group 24: Records of the Bureau of Naval Personnel—Series: Official Military Personnel Files Official Military Personnel File for Richard M. Nixon—Covers September 1930–September 1970, NAID: 57301209; Ambrose, *Education*, 111.

86 **"he became quite animated":** Dole, oral history, 6–7, 11; Farrell, *Nixon*, 78.

86 **"anxious to do something more":** Fleps, oral history, 6; Nixon, *Memoirs*, 28; Morris, *Rise and Fall*, 251.

86 **"States to get a bath":** Speech File: Reminiscences of WWII Experiences on Green Island, 1:30. Speech File (PPS 208), Richard Nixon Library and Birthplace Foundation, Yorba Linda, CA.

87 **recall of the bodies:** Farrell, *Nixon*, 78; Ambrose, *Education*, 110; Nixon, *Memoirs*, 29. Oddly, Nixon made no mention of this dramatic scene in his early reminiscences about his time on Green Island.

87 **confidence to believe:** Morris, *Rise and Fall*, 252.

87 **December 31, 1945:** Duane T. Hove, *American Warriors: Five Presidents in the Pacific Theater of World War II* (Shippensburg, PA: Burd Street Press, 2003), 124–25.

88 **sent into battle faster:** Office of the White House Press Secretary, "Information on the USS *Monterey*, May 23, 1975," Press fact sheet prepared by the Ford White House; Office of Naval Records and History, "History of the USS *Monterey*," n.d.; Joe Mayrose, "Gerald Ford on the USS *Monterey*," Military History of the Upper Great Lakes (MHUGL), Michigan Technical University, last modified October 16, 2016, https://ss.sites.mtu.edu/mhugl/2016/10/16/ford-on-the-uss-monterey/.

88 **He found that basketball:** James Cannon, *Honorable Life*, 59.

88 **the United States could launch:** Kennedy, *Freedom from Fear*, 610.

89 **drop its deadly cargo:** Unsworth, "'Best Officer of the Deck,'" 8–9; James Cannon, *Honorable Life*, 59.

89 **"throw his weight around":** James Cannon, *Honorable Life*, 60. Edward B. Camlin, "President Ford Was Cool as Battle Raged, Says a World War 2 Shipmate," *National Enquirer*, n.d., n.p., Ford Vertical File, GRFPL, box 1.

89 **"best Officer of the Deck":** Hove, *American Warriors,* 139–41; Unsworth, "'Best Officer of the Deck,'" 14.

90 **poorly trained substitutes:** Unsworth, "'Best Officer of the Deck,'" 12; Hove, *American Warriors,* 141–42.

90 **for twenty-four consecutive hours:** Hove, *American Warriors,* 143–47; Office of Naval Records and History, "History of the USS *Monterey,*" n.d., Ford Vertical File, GRFPL.

90 **"Our guns blasted away":** Bruce Michaels, "Jerry Ford USN," *Sea Classics* 23, no. 11, November 1990, 67–68; Ford, *A Time to Heal,* 58–59.

91 **youngest commissioned pilot:** Hyams, *Flight of the Avenger,* 47; Meacham, *Destiny and Power,* 54.

91 **its size and unusual shape:** Hyams, *Flight of the Avenger,* 51; Meacham, *Destiny and Power,* 56–57.

91 **effortlessly through the sky:** "World War II Correspondence, 1942–48," George Bush Personal Papers, GHWBPL, box 1.

91 **"gets the adrenaline flowing":** Hyams, *Flight of the Avenger,* 53.

91 **secretly got engaged:** Hyams, *Flight of the Avenger,* 54.

92 **neither he nor his crew members:** "World War II Correspondence, 1942–48," George Bush Personal Papers, GHWBPL, box 1; Hyams, *Flight of the Avenger,* 60.

92 **"real down-to-earth people":** Hyams, *Flight of the Avenger,* 64.

92 **Mexican dictator Antonio López de Santa:** Hyams, *Flight of the Avenger,* 70.

94 **who would manipulate:** Stephen E. Ambrose, *The Supreme Commander: The War Years of Dwight D. Eisenhower* (New York: Anchor Books, 2012), 296, Kindle.

94 **"a headquarters in London":** Harry C. Butcher, *My Three Years with Eisenhower: The Personal Diary of Captain Harry C. Butcher, USNR, Naval Aide to General Eisenhower, 1942 to 1945* (New York: Simon & Schuster, 1946), 421, 428.

95 **"connection with any political":** Ambrose, *Supreme Commander,* 300.

95 **"a bent for history":** Smith, *Eisenhower in War and Peace,* 293.

95 **"monkey with a winning team":** Smith, *Eisenhower in War and Peace,* 309.

95 **"conduct of affairs":** Ambrose, *Supreme Commander,* 305.

96 **entire assault a code:** Smith, *Eisenhower in War and Peace,* 391.

96 **"one man must make decisions":** Kennedy, *Freedom from Fear,* 680; Smith, *Eisenhower in War and Peace,* 404.

96 **"grin never left":** Smith, *Eisenhower in War and Peace,* 318.

96 **wave of popularity:** Hitchcock, *Age of Eisenhower,* 21–22; Ambrose, *Supreme Commander,* 308.

97 **"you trust him at once":** Patterson, *Grand Expectations,* 244, 271.

97 **on his common touch:** Ambrose, *Supreme Commander,* 320–21.

98 **listening to music and playing:** Smith, *Eisenhower in War and Peace,* 273, 350; Hugh A. Mulligan, "War's End Made a Non-Person of Eisenhower's Devoted 'Shadow,'" *Los Angeles Times,* May 28, 1995, 1; John Kifner, "Eisenhower Letters Hint at Affair with Aide," *New York Times,* June 6, 1991, 1.

98 **"no question they were in love":** Smith, *Eisenhower in War and Peace,* 404; Mulligan, "War's End," 1. Merle Miller recorded Harry Truman saying that "right after the war was over," Eisenhower told Marshall of his plans to divorce Mamie and marry Kay. "Marshall wrote him back a letter the like of which I never have seen," Truman recalled. "He said if Eisenhower ever came close to doing such a thing, he'd not only bust him out of the army but see to it that never for the rest of his life would he be able to draw a peaceful breath." Truman also claimed that "one of the last things" he did as president was to

remove the letter from Ike's file and have it destroyed. See Merle Miller, *Plain Speaking: An Oral Biography of Harry S. Truman* (New York: Berkley Books, 1973), 390, Kindle.

98 **"pretty Irish driver"**: Smith, *Eisenhower in War and Peace*, 218–19.

98 **"love with anyone but"**: Smith, *Eisenhower in War and Peace*, 218–19.

99 **"will be thinking"**: Smith, *Eisenhower in War and Peace*, 418–20.

99 **and had little patience**: Smith, *Eisenhower in War and Peace*, 421–22; Ambrose, *Soldier and President*, 120.

99 **Mamie remained unconvinced**: Smith, *Eisenhower in War and Peace*, 424; Ambrose, *Soldier and President*, 120.

CHAPTER 4

100 **shattered a continent**: Cornelius Ryan, *The Longest Day: The Classic Epic of D-Day* (New York: Simon & Schuster, 1994), 54. Kindle.

100 **demonstrate his impressive expertise**: Steven M. Gillon, *Len Lomell: D-Day Hero* (New York: Caliber, 2023), 69.

101 **from farther north**: Gillon, *Lomell*, 68.

101 **simultaneous drop of three**: Gillon, *Lomell*, 68.

101 **Cornelius Ryan in his classic**: Ryan, *Longest Day*, 52.

101 **"ever seen pass slowly by"**: Geoffrey C. Ward and Ken Burns, *The War: An Intimate History, 1941–1945* (New York: Knopf, 2007), 175–78; Ryan, *Longest Day*, 52, 57.

101 **unloading supplies onto the beach quickly**: Ryan, *Longest Day*, 54–55.

102 **planners chose early May**: Eisenhower, *Crusade*, 269, Kindle.

102 **"never be understood by history"**: Ambrose, *Soldier and President*, 127; Gillon, *Lomell*, 69–70.

102 **North Africa and Sicily**: Gillon, *Lomell*, 71.

103 **"stop him in the water"**: Gillon, *Lomell*, 79.

103 **Allies revealed the location**: Ryan, *Longest Day*, 30.

103 **"I must have your assistance"**: Smith, *Eisenhower in War and Peace*, 418–19, 422.

103 **the liberation of Paris**: Smith, *Eisenhower in War and Peace*, 427, 432–33; Ambrose, *Soldier and President*, 121.

104 **entrenched German forces in Normandy**: Eisenhower, *Crusade*, 222.

104 **the success of the operation**: Eisenhower, *Crusade*, 222; Smith, *Eisenhower in War and Peace* 431; Ambrose, *Soldier and President*, 121.

105 **"look a soldier in the eye"**: Smith, *Eisenhower in War and Peace*, 437, 499–50; Eisenhower, *Crusade*, 286–87; Ambrose, *Soldier and President*, 138.

105 **"the intensity of these burdens"**: Ambrose, *Soldier and President*, 127; Hitchcock, *Age of Eisenhower*, 22.

105 **unnecessary slaughter of hundreds**: Ambrose, *Soldier and President*, 133–35.

106 **"Goose pimples came out"**: Ambrose, *Soldier and President*, 136–39.

106 **"Okay, let's go"**: Eisenhower, *Crusade*, 299–300; Ambrose, *Soldier and President*, 137–39.

106 **placed the backup note**: Ambrose, *Soldier and President*, 140.

107 **his eyes filled with tears**: Ambrose, *Soldier and President*, 138; Ryan, *Longest Day*, 101.

107 **"northern coast of France"**: Ryan, *Longest Day*, 254.

107 **Battle of Antietam**: Ward and Burns, *The War*, 210.

107 **"confer with principal commanders"**: Eisenhower, *Crusade*, 303.

108 **"victory in the Ardennes"**: Hitchcock, *Age of Eisenhower*, 23.

109 **carry with him to the White House**: Hitchcock, *Age of Eisenhower*, 27.

109 **the Pearl Harbor attack:** Meacham, *Destiny and Power*, 58; Stinnett, *Bush: World War II Years*, 30. Along with Meacham, much of the account that follows comes from three sources. Hyams, *Flight of the Avenger*, is the definitive account of Bush's time in the Pacific. Also helpful is Bradley, *Flyboys*.

110 **the Joint Intelligence Center:** Stinnett, *Bush: World War II Years*, 25–26.

110 **twelve fighter escorts:** Stinnett, *Bush: World War II Years*, 62.

110 **resupply bases on Guam:** Stinnett, *Bush: World War II Years*, 62–63.

111 **wave of fighters passed:** Timothy J. Christmann, "Vice President Bush Calls WWII Experience 'Sobering,'" *Naval Aviation News*, March/April 1985, 14.

111 **"made a beautiful water landing":** Christmann, "'Sobering,'" 14; Stinnett, *Bush: World War II Years, 73*.

111 **destroyer picked up the crew:** Stinnett, *Bush: World War II Years*, 73–74.

111 **Japanese military leaders sent:** Stinnett, *Bush: World War II Years*, 125.

111 **"the worst we had seen":** Meacham, *Destiny and Power*, 60; Stinnett, *Bush: World War II Years*, 115, 138; Christmann, "'Sobering,'" 12.

112 **"radio station is your primary":** Bradley, *Flyboys*, 345.

112 **he had been begging Bush:** Bradley, *Flyboys*, 345; Hyams, *Flight of the Avenger*, 104–5.

112 **a dozen additional Hellcats:** Hyams, *Flight of the Avenger*, 105–6.

112 **"You always thought someone else":** Bradley, *Flyboys*, 348–49; Christmann, "'Sobering,'" 12.

113 **"haul ass out of there":** Hyams, *Flight of the Avenger*, 106; Bradley, *Flyboys*, 349.

113 **"his plane losing altitude":** Bradley, *Flyboys*, 348–50; Hyams, *Flight of the Avenger*, 106.

113 **"Hit the silk!":** Hyams, *Flight of the Avenger*, 107; Stinnett, *Bush: World War II Years*, 26.

113 **tore a few panels:** Hyams, *Flight of the Avenger,* 108; Bradley, *Flyboys*, 350.

114 **and struggled to get in:** Stinnett, *Bush: World War II Years*, 147.

114 **"I was all alone":** Bradley, *Flyboys*, 351–53; Hyams, *Flight of the Avenger*, 108–10, 118; George H. W. Bush, *All the Best: My Life in Letters and Other Writings* (New York: Scribner, 2013), 52.

115 **rescue submarine USS *Finback*:** Bradley, *Flyboys*, 352; Stinnett, *Bush: World War II Years*, 147.

115 **swept back to shore:** Hyams, *Flight of the Avenger*, 115.

115 **pulled the lanky future president:** Hyams, *Flight of the Avenger*, 118. According to the *Finback*'s captain, Bush was mistaken: The sub had been cruising on the surface. He believed that Bush's vision was obscured by the choppy waters. See Stinnett, *Bush: World War II Years*, 198n11.

115 **Ciné-Kodak 8 mm movie camera:** Stinnett, *Bush: World War II Years*, 156.

115 **"The skipper wants to get":** Meacham, *Destiny and Power*, 62.

115 **he told biographer Jeffrey Engel:** Bush, *All the Best*, 49–52; Engel, *When the World Seemed New*, 29, Kindle.

116 **"I felt trapped and scared":** Hyams, *Flight of the Avenger*, 125.

116 **First Presbyterian Church:** Stinnett, *Bush: World War II Years*, 165.

117 **logging 1,228 hours:** Stinnett, *Bush: World War II Years*, 185; Hyams, *Flight of the Avenger*, 156.

117 **"The war was over":** Engel, *When the World Seemed New*, 29, Kindle.

117 **"understanding of war and peace":** Bradley, *Flyboys*, 355; Meacham, *Destiny and Power*, 63–64; Christmann, "'Sobering,'" 12.

117 **"the realities of death":** Hyams, *Flight of the Avenger*, 158.

117 **Bush's understanding of the postwar world:** Hyams, *Flight of the Avenger*, 158–59.

118 **Ford stood in the eye:** Samuel J. Cox, "Typhoon Cobra—The Worst Natural Disaster in U.S. Navy History, 14–19 December 1944," *Naval History and Heritage Command*,

last modified December 26, 2019, https://www.history.navy.mil/about-us/leadership
/director/directors-corner/h-grams/h-gram-039/h-039-2.html.

118 **fighter jets being swept off:** Bob Drury and Tom Clavin, *Halsey's Typhoon: The True
Story of a Fighting Admiral, an Epic Storm, and an Untold Rescue* (New York: Atlantic
Monthly Press, 2007), 190–91; Cox, "Typhoon Cobra."

118 **practice their seamanship:** Drury and Clavin, *Halsey's Typhoon,* 181.

118 **"I was going overboard":** Drury and Clavin, *Halsey's Typhoon,* 191–93.

119 **"I was much more careful":** Drury and Clavin, *Halsey's Typhoon,* 193–94; "The U.S.S.
Monterey and the Great Typhoon," US Naval Communications Service CINCPAC and
CINCPOA, December 17, 1944, GRFPL, Vertical File.

119 **the ship would lose water pressure:** Drury and Clavin, *Halsey's Typhoon,* 194–96;
Unsworth, "'Best Officer of the Deck,'" 13; Michaels, "Jerry Ford USN," 68.

119 **He then turned to Ford:** "U.S.S. *Monterey* and the Great Typhoon"; Michaels, "Jerry
Ford USN," 69; Drury and Clavin, *Halsey's Typhoon,* 196.

119 **"Have fire under control":** There are conflicting accounts of Ford's actions during the
fire. It is unclear whether he participated in extinguishing the flames or if he simply
supervised men who were engaged in the effort.

120 **"I wish I could have":** Unsworth, "'Best Officer of the Deck,'" 13; transcript of interview
with James Cannon, 1989–94, GFPL, box 1. A court of inquiry blamed Halsey for the
damage and ship losses but found no negligence, only the "stress of war operations" and
"a commendable desire to meet military commitments." Halsey defended himself by
pointing out that he never received a "timely warning" of the typhoon and placed blame
with the fleet's meteorologists. The court disagreed, placing the "preponderance of responsibility" on Halsey, citing his "large errors" in predicting the path of the storm. See Michael D. Hull, "Two Typhoons Crippled Bull Halsey's Task Force," *WWII History,*
August 2015, 50–55, available on Warfare History Network, https://warfarehistorynetwork
.com/article/two-typhoons-crippled-bull-halseys-task-force-38/.

121 **promises and perils of war:** Michaels, "Jerry Ford USN."

121 **more than twenty million people:** Steven M. Gillon, *The American Paradox: A History
of the United States Since 1945* (Boston: Wadsworth, Cengage Learning, 2007), 25.

122 **$3 billion on public works:** Gillon, *Paradox,* 2.

122 **presidents would need to address:** Steven M. Gillon and Cathy D. Matson, *The American Experiment: A History of the United States* (Boston: Houghton Mifflin, 2006), 1046.

123 **"the PT-109 incident made":** Hitchcock, *Age of Eisenhower,* 16, 196–97; Smith, *Eisenhower in War and Peace,* 615–16; Doyle, *PT 109,* xii.

124 **ultimately led to his downfall:** Matthews, *Kennedy & Nixon,* 36.

124 **"be anything but the best":** Ford, *A Time to Heal,* 61.

124 **Wyman was off making movies:** Reagan with Hubler, *Where's the Rest of Me?,* 138.

125 **"No twentieth-century president":** H. W. Brands, *Reagan: The Life* (New York: Anchor Books, 2015), 57; Vaughn, *Reagan in Hollywood,* 118; Spitz, *Reagan,* 204.

125 **The studio reinstated him:** Eliot, *Hollywood Years,* 176.

125 **"How many Jews?":** George H. W. Bush, *All the Best,* 497.

126 **"He died the way":** Bush, *All the Best,* 25.

CHAPTER 5

131 **winning the election in November:** Parmet, *Jack,* 142–43.

132 **"You're a carpetbagger":** Kenneth P. O'Donnell and David F. Powers, *"Johnny,
We Hardly Knew Ye": Memories of John Fitzgerald Kennedy* (New York: Open Road,
2013), 82, Kindle.

132 **"something to help prevent another"**: Logevall, *JFK*, 405.

132 **"If we're going to change"**: O'Donnell and Powers, *"Johnny,"* 79.

132 **"I firmly resolved to serve"**: Logevall, *JFK,* 405; Joseph C. Goulden, *The Best Years 1945–1950* (Mineola, NY: Dover, 2019), 228.

132 **"skinny, pasty-faced kid"**: Matthews, *Kennedy & Nixon*, 3; Logevall, *JFK*, 414–15.

133 **"a classroom full of pupils"**: Blair and Blair Jr., *Search for JFK*, 461.

133 **"meeting Bobby's war hero brother"**: O'Donnell and Powers, *"Johnny,"* 105.

134 **Powers had never witnessed**: Blair and Blair Jr., *Search for JFK*, 494–95; Logevall, *JFK*, 420; O'Donnell and Powers, *"Johnny,"* 90.

134 **"in the Eleventh District"**: Blair and Blair Jr., *Search for JFK*, 501; Matthews, *Kennedy & Nixon*, 31–32.

134 **one out of every seven**: Mark D. Van Ells, "Hear Only Thunder Again: The Readjustment of World War II Veterans to Civilian Life in Wisconsin" (dissertation, University of Wisconsin at Madison, 1999), v–vii; Goulden, *Best Years*, 229.

134 **"naturally attracted to John Kennedy"**: Mark J. Dalton, oral history, interview 1, August 4, 1964, 1, 7, John F. Kennedy Oral History Collection, JFKPL.

135 **"a prosperous America"**: JFK, "Public Responsibility for the Veteran," Remarks to Massachusetts Taxpayers Association, September 11, 1946, JFKPL, Pre-Presidential Papers, box 98.

135 **"Democracy sleeps fitfully"**: Lieut. John F. Kennedy, U.S.N., "Let's Try an Experiment in Peace," 1945, David F. Powers Personal Papers, JFKPL, https://www.jfklibrary.org/asset-viewer/archives/DFPPP/021/DFPPP-021-002?image_identifier=DFPPP-021-002-p0001.

136 **"In my wildest nightmares"**: Hitchcock, *Age of Eisenhower*, 29.

136 **"Mr. President, I don't know"**: Hitchcock, *Age of Eisenhower*, 28–29; Smith, *Eisenhower in War and Peace*, 572.

137 **marrying Kay was not an option**: Smith, *Eisenhower in War and Peace*, 563–65.

137 **Eisenhower greeted Forrestal**: Logevall, *JFK*, 402–3.

137 **a massive use of force**: Goulden, *Best Years*, 254; Smith, *Eisenhower in War and Peace*, 450–51, 573.

138 **"a spirit of amity"**: Smith, *Eisenhower in War and Peace*, 576.

139 **right to organize and strike**: Blair and Blair Jr., *Search for JFK*, 525–26.

139 **"he was a carpetbagger"**: O'Donnell and Powers, *"Johnny,"* 112–13; Joan and Clay Blair, *In Search of JFK*, 540; Logevall, *JFK*, 421–22. Tip O'Neill estimated that Joseph Kennedy spent $300,000 on the race. One of Kennedy's opponents pinned a $10 bill to his shirt, calling it his Kennedy campaign button. See: David Pietrusza, *1960: LBJ vs. JFK vs. Nixon: The Epic Campaign That Forged Three Presidencies* (New York: Diversion Books, 2008), 34, Kindle. The Kennedys were not above using hardball tactics. Fearing that Third Ward councilman Joseph Russo would poll well among Italians in the district, the Kennedys recruited another Joe Russo, a janitor, to confuse voters and split the Russo vote. Pietrusza, *1960*, 35.

140 **"Lieutenant Joseph P. Kennedy Jr."**: O'Donnell and Powers, *"Johnny,"* 112–13. The night before, Kennedy had included remarks that struck a different tone. The nation, the speech read, must "have the courage and the determination to oppose that great force of evil which is emanating from the Kremlin." It continued: "Study the map of the world today, and you will find that the Hammer and Sickle is flying over nearly all of Europe and most of Asia." The remarks are crossed out in the original draft, so it is unlikely that he said them. It was revealing of Kennedy's dilemma: He was privately hopeful of maintaining close US-Soviet relations, but he also recognized that most of his constituents wanted him to take a hard line against Stalin. See: "Bunker Hill Knights of Columbus, Charlestown, Massachusetts, June 16, 1946," and "Bunker Hill

Day, Charlestown, Massachusetts, June 17, 1946," David F. Powers Personal Papers, Series 9, John F. Kennedy Speeches and Notes, 1942–1963, DFPPP-028-024, JFKPL.

140 **"took him from my residence":** Blair and Blair Jr., *Search for JFK*, 541.

140 **well-known Democratic governor:** O'Donnell and Powers, *"Johnny,"* 113.

140 **Capitol Hill reporters voted:** Morris, *Rise and Fall*, 258–59.

141 **his anti-Communist bona fides:** Morris, *Rise and Fall*, 260–61.

141 **thirteen-thousand-vote majority:** Morris, *Rise and Fall*, 287.

141 **"Republican ticket in 1946":** Morris, *Rise and Fall*, 271; Earl Mazo and Stephen Hess, *Nixon: A Political Portrait* (New York: Popular Library, 1968), 34–36.

142 **"what a mess things are":** Morris, *Rise and Fall*, 271–72.

142 **"a government handout":** Matthews, *Kennedy & Nixon*, 34; Ambrose, *Education*, 120; Morris, *Rise and Fall*, 281.

142 **Pat could not fall back:** Day to Nixon, November 12, 1945, Correspondence 1945, Congressional Campaign (CC), 1946, RNPL, 1.1 Correspondence, 1945.

142 **"Jerry Voorhis's goose is cooked!":** Nixon to Day, November 19 and December 4, 1945, RNPL, Correspondence, 1945, CC, 1946, 1.1 PPS 1.

143 **"not even mention Jerry's name":** Nixon to Perry, December 17, 1946, 11 Correspondence 1945, CC, 1946, RNPL, PPS 1. (Nixon mistakenly dated the letter 1946.)

143 **sent them out in the mail:** Ambrose, *Education*, 118, 121–22, 125; William Costello, *The Facts About Richard Nixon: An Unauthorized Biography* (New York: Viking Press, 1960), 50. There were always questions, however, about whether his campaign was the mom-and-pop operation that he claimed. In his memoirs, Nixon denied the charge that he was "the hand-picked stooge of oil magnates, rich bankers, real estate tycoons, and conservative millionaires." He claimed that what united his supporters was "no special vested interest but the fierce desire of average Americans to regain control of their own lives." But many biographers, including Roger Morris, have argued that wealthy donors, especially powerful oil companies, poured money into the campaign. There is some evidence in the Nixon Papers to support this claim. In November 1945 Nixon received a letter from Thomas Bewley saying, "They are really in the big money and Roy [Day] is pretty sure that they have already gotten $5,000.00 for campaign expenses and they plan on at least $10,000.00." Bewley to Nixon, November 7, 1945, RNPL, PPS 1.2.

144 **"serve in the armed forces":** Nixon to Day, December 26, 1945, 1.1 PPS 1, Correspondence, 1945, CC, 1946, PPS 1, box 1. Correspondence July–November 1946, 1.6; Goulden, *Best Years*, 228; Ambrose, *Education*, 123.

144 **"Lieut. Cmdr. Richard M. Nixon":** Ambrose, *Education*, 122–23; Morris, *Rise and Fall*, 288.

144 **32 percent by the spring:** Morris, *Rise and Fall*, 265.

145 **"somewhere between the two extremes":** "Modern Political Talk, The Economy," 1.2 Speech File (PPS 208); 1.14 Speech Files "America's New Frontiers II" (PPS-208), RNPL.

145 **he told the Veterans Legion:** Nixon, *Memoirs*, 45; 1.32 Speech File (PPS 208), RNPL.

146 **"New Dealer with telling effect":** Ambrose, *Education*, 130; Morris, *Rise and Fall*, 303–4; Nixon to Friends, July 12, 1946, PPS 1204; Roy newsletter, June 11, 1946, PPS 1, box 1, Correspondence May/June 1946, RNPL.

146 **a local endorsement of Voorhis:** Matthews, *Kennedy & Nixon*, 37–38.

147 **one of the most skilled:** Costello, *Facts About Nixon*, 52; Ambrose, *Education,* 130. Truth was a subtlety that Nixon chose to ignore. In 1955 he told a reporter, "Communism was not the issue at any time in the '46 campaign. Few people knew about Communism then, and even fewer cared." That was a gross distortion and part of his effort to rewrite history. When accused of lying, Nixon admitted that he knew his opponent

was not a Communist. "I had to win. That's the thing you don't understand. The important thing is to win." Ambrose, *Education*, 140.

147 **transferring rabbits:** Ambrose, *Education*, 134–35.

147 **"fight with all my power":** Costello, *Facts About Nixon*, 57–58.

147 **to secure political victory:** Ambrose, *Education*, 138.

148 **never acknowledged the mudslinging:** Nixon to Hause, January 21, 1947, PPS 1, 1.18, RNPL. Historian Irwin F. Gellman, an ardent Nixon defender, rejects the claim that Nixon's red-baiting helped him win the election. "The claim," he wrote, "that Nixon began his political career using unsavory practices belies the more likely explanation: Voorhis simply ran a lethargic campaign." See Gellman, *Campaign of the Century: Kennedy, Nixon, and the Election of 1960* (New Haven, CT: Yale University Press, 2021), 2.

150 **"for the fourth floor!":** Logevall, *JFK*, 437.

150 **"while doing so little work":** Dallek, *Unfinished Life*, 443–44; Pietrusza, *1960*, 44.

150 **"Jack liked girls":** Parmet, *Jack*, 165–66.

151 **"opponents but not political rivals":** Nixon, *Memoirs*, 43; Farrell, *Nixon*, 84.

151 **"He's going places":** Logevall, *JFK*, 446; Dalton, oral interview, August 4, 1964, 16.

151 **Communist influence in organized labor:** Matthews, *Kennedy & Nixon*, 51; Logevall, *JFK*, 446. Kennedy was one of 106 opponents of the Taft-Hartley bill. They were swamped by 308 Republicans and conservative Democrats who voted in favor. Dallek, *Unfinished Life*, 145.

152 **may even have crossed paths:** Gellman, *Campaign of the Century*, 4.

152 **needed to remain vigilant:** Logevall, *JFK*, 446–47.

152 **his father's now-discredited isolationism:** Dallek, *Unfinished Life*, 148–49.

153 **"who is a Republican":** Morris, *Rise and Fall*, 363–64.

153 **"Europe would be plunged":** Nixon, *Memoirs*, 49.

153 **"One basic rule with Russians":** Morris, *Rise and Fall*, 365; Farrell, *Nixon*, 90.

154 **an overwhelming voice vote:** Nixon, *Memoirs*, 51; Ambrose, *Education*, 156; Morris, *Rise and Fall*, 366. In April the SS *John H. Quick* sailed from its port in Galveston, Texas, with nineteen thousand tons of wheat for starving Europeans. Within months, it was joined by 150 ships carrying food and fuel to Europe every day. Between 1948 and 1951, American aid to Europe amounted to a staggering $12.5 billion. Thanks in part to the plan, European industrial production increased 200 percent between 1948 and 1952. Perhaps the Marshall Plan's greatest export was hope. British foreign secretary Ernest Bevin called it "a lifeline to a sinking man."

154 **family friend Pamela Churchill:** Logevall, *JFK*, 453–54.

154 **"cheerful as all get-out":** Logevall, *JFK*, 454.

154 **He would spend weeks:** Dallek, *Unfinished Life*, 153; Logevall, *JFK*, 454–55.

155 **he had difficulty concentrating:** Dallek, *Unfinished Life*, 153–54; Logevall, *JFK*, 457.

155 **becoming a national statesman:** Dallek, *Unfinished Life*, 154.

155 **wait for another opportunity:** Dallek, *Unfinished Life*, 155; Logevall, *JFK*, 459.

155 **"difficult to escape the stain":** Nixon, *Memoirs*, 44; Farrell, *Nixon*, 96–97, 101.

156 **kept Nixon's name:** Nixon, *Memoirs*, 44; Costello, *Facts About Nixon*, 189.

156 **dangers of Communist espionage:** Nixon, *Memoirs*, 47–48; Costello, *Facts About Nixon*, 192; Tim Weiner, *One Man Against the World: The Tragedy of Richard Nixon* (New York: Henry Holt, 2015), 14. Hiss and his supporters denied vehemently that he was a spy, but the release of new documents in 2009 offered convincing evidence that Nixon was right. See Harvey Klehr, John Earl Haynes, and Alexander Vassiliev, *Spies: The Rise and Fall of the KGB in America* (New Haven, CT: Yale University Press, 2009).

157 **dismissed the Marshall Plan:** Smith, *Eisenhower in War and Peace*, 124.

157 **"see what happens"**: Smith, *Eisenhower in War and Peace*, 125.

158 **"a military point of view"**: Smith, *Eisenhower in War and Peace*, 129.

158 **Ford's wartime service**: Jeremy M. Teigen, *Why Veterans Run: Military Service in American Presidential Elections, 1789–2016* (Philadelphia: Temple University Press, 2018), 184; "Ford Interviews," September 1948, Ford Congressional Papers, Press Secretary and Speech File, GRFPL, box D37.

158 **"aggressively pushing our needs"**: "Ford Interviews," September 1948, Ford Congressional Papers, Press Secretary and Speech File, GRFPL, box D37.

159 **the threat of Soviet expansion**: Parker James Ince, "Before Their Destiny: The Early Lives of Harry Truman, Lyndon Johnson, and Gerald Ford" (PhD dissertation, George Washington University, May 2011), 96–102.

159 **"I couldn't imagine this"**: Betty Ford, with Chris Chase, *The Times of My Life* (New York: Harper & Row, 1978), 53–55.

159 **"to marry a divorcée"**: Connie to Ron, March 3, 1978, Ron Nessen Papers, GRFPL, "President—Campaign for Congress, 1948," box 18.

160 **winning 60.5 percent**: Smith, *Eisenhower in War and Peace*, 133–34.

160 **42,672 to 17,628 votes**: Dallek, *Unfinished Life*, 279.

160 **supported bread-and-butter programs**: Dallek, *Unfinished Life*, 286–89; Pietrusza, *1960*, 59.

160 **He even favored divulging**: Dallek, *Unfinished Life*, 271, 274.

161 **"directors in the battle"**: Kearns Goodwin, *Lyndon Johnson and the American Dream*, 120–22.

161 **"It's either your boys' lives"**: Caro, *Means of Ascent*, 230; Dallek, *Unfinished Life*, 290–92.

162 **ensure stability at home**: Dallek, *Unfinished Life*, 299–303.

162 **"It looked hopeless"**: Dallek, *Unfinished Life*, 318.

162 **"in favor of Coke Stevenson"**: Dallek, *Unfinished Life*, 324.

163 **painful bout of kidney stones**: Kearns Goodwin, *Lyndon Johnson and the American Dream*, 126; Pietrusza, *1960*, 60.

163 **Stevenson, on the other hand**: Patrick Cox, "'Nearly a Statesman': LBJ and Texas Blacks in the 1948 Election," *Social Science Quarterly* 74, no. 2 (June 1993): 241–63.

163 **"still possessed all their limbs"**: Caro, *Means of Ascent*, 229.

164 **"MacArthur gave it to me"**: Caro, *Means of Ascent*, 229.

164 **Johnson went on to win**: Studies have shown that LBJ won because he was able to motivate his voters to go to the polls, while many of those who supported Stevenson in the primary failed to show up. An estimated 113,523 voters who supported Stevenson in the primary did not vote in August. "The quantitative evidence suggests that if Stevenson had mobilized just eight of every ten of his initial supporters, he would have won the Texas senatorial seat," concluded political scientists Dale Baum and James L. Hailey. See Baum and Hailey, "Lyndon Johnson's Victory in the 1948 Texas Senate Race: A Reappraisal," *Political Science Quarterly* 109, no. 4 (Autumn 1994): 599.

CHAPTER 6

165 **"clean as a houndstooth?"**: Smith, *Eisenhower in War and Peace*, 534; Morris, *Rise and Fall*, 833.

166 **"We picked you," they said**: Nixon, *Memoirs*, 86–87; Grant Madsen, *Sovereign Soldiers: How the U.S. Military Transformed the Global Economy After World War II* (Philadelphia: University of Pennsylvania Press, 2018), 215.

167 **a shady, unscrupulous character**: Farrell, *Nixon*, 158–59; Spitz, *Reagan*, 288–89. Throughout the campaign, Douglas complained that Nixon was "throwing up a smoke screen of smears, innuendos and half-truths to try and confuse and mislead" voters.

After the election, she wrote that "there was no question in my mind or of those working with me and supporting me that the entire Nixon campaign was deliberately designed to create the impression that I was a Communist or at least quote Communistic unquote." Douglas to Edson, September 19, 1956, box 164, Helen Gahagan Douglas Papers, Carl Albert Center, University of Oklahoma.

167 **Eisenhower was sixty-two:** Hitchcock, *Age of Eisenhower*, 71–72; Introduction, *The Papers of Dwight Eisenhower*, vol. 14, pt. 1, chap. 1, xix, Johns Hopkins University Press, https://eisenhower.press.jhu.edu/.

167 **"presence of a genuine statesman":** Nixon, *Memoirs*, 82.

168 **a typical suburban living room:** Smith, *Eisenhower in War and Peace*, 538; Hitchcock, *Age of Eisenhower*, 78.

168 **the Republican National Committee:** Ambrose, *Education*, 290; Pietrusza, *1960*, 83.

169 **"I was not a personal friend":** Farrell, *Nixon*, 183; Hitchcock, *Age of Eisenhower*, 80.

169 **"But aren't we entitled?":** Farrell, *Nixon*, 211; Morris, *Rise and Fall*, 813; Smith, *Eisenhower in War and Peace*, 542.

169 **do anything to gain power:** Ambrose, *Education*, 278. Matthews, *Kennedy & Nixon*, 85–86; Jeffrey Frank, *Ike and Dick: Portrait of a Strange Political Marriage* (New York: Simon & Schuster, 2013), 62.

169 **Nixon "was a victim":** Farrell, *Nixon*, 208.

170 **discovered a check for $1,000:** Nixon, *Memoirs*, 75. But that might have been the tip of the iceberg. Joe Kennedy once bragged to Tip O'Neill that he contributed more than $150,000 to the Nixon campaign. See Pietrusza, *1960*, 77.

170 **"a great deal of strength":** Nixon, *Memoirs*, 91.

170 **"My God, man!":** Laurence Leamer, *The Kennedy Men, 1901–1963: The Laws of the Father* (New York: William Morrow, 2001), 281.

170 **first senator since the Civil War:** Logevall, *JFK*, 503.

171 **"Is this the foresight?":** "Draft for Kennedy Speech on Foreign Affairs," n.d., Pre-Presidential Papers, JFKPL, box 102.

171 **every home in the state:** Revised Ad, September 3, 1952, JFKPL, Pre-Presidential Papers, box 103; Logevall, *JFK*, 511.

171 **seventy-five thousand women:** "The Making of JFK," *Boston College Magazine*, Fall 2000, 1.

172 **blasting Lodge for not taking:** Thomas J. Whalen, *Kennedy Versus Lodge: The 1952 Massachusetts Senate Race* (Boston: Northeastern University Press, 2000), 56–57.

172 **"He wasn't the type":** Whalen, *Kennedy Versus Lodge*, 7, 103–4.

173 **"Jack was a dream lover":** Logevall, *JFK*, 514; Leamer, *The Kennedy Men*, 298–99.

173 **heroism at a critical juncture:** Whalen, *Kennedy Versus Lodge*, 132–33.

173 **Kennedy started out behind:** Emilie Haertsch, "Lodge, Kennedy, and the 1952 Massachusetts Senate Election," *The Beehive* (blog), last modified May 22, 2013, https://www.masshist.org/beehiveblog/2013/05/lodge-kennedy-and-the-1952-massachusetts-senate-election/.

174 **"hero needed a point man":** "Memo to the file," September 12, 1956, "DDE Requires," Pre-Presidential Papers, Special Files: DDE, RNPL, box PPS 324: 1–103. See also Pietrusza, *1960*, 78; Farrell, *Nixon*, 202.

175 **first time since 1930:** Steven M. Gillon, *Politics and Vision: The ADA and American Liberalism, 1947–1985* (New York: Oxford University Press, 1987), 102.

175 **"taking complete advantage":** Whalen, *Kennedy Versus Lodge*, 3.

175 **Nixon was assigned room 361:** Matthews, *Kennedy & Nixon*, 90.

175 **"even before that!":** Diary, January 21, 1953, *The Papers of Dwight David Eisenhower*, vol. 14 (Baltimore: Johns Hopkins University Press, 1996), pt. 1, chap. 1, 5.

176 **"eight millionaires and a plumber":** Gillon, *Politics and Vision*, 104–5.

176 **When it was over:** "Ike's First Term as President," Eisenhower Foundation, accessed December 1, 2023, https://www.eisenhowerfoundation.net/ikes-life/ikes-first-term-president-1953-1957.

176 **"The lines of authority were clear":** "Ike's First Term as President," Eisenhower Foundation; Smith, *Eisenhower in War and Peace*, 176, 550–51, 567.

177 **"feel like a junior officer":** Farrell, *Nixon*, 211; Hitchcock, *Age of Eisenhower*, 72–73.

177 **Ike made sure to include:** Farrell, *Nixon*, 212.

177 **the dizzying array of problems:** James T. Patterson, *Grand Expectations: The United States, 1945–1974* (New York: Oxford University Press, 1996), 248.

178 **separating the two Koreas:** Ambrose, *Soldier and President*, 294; Madsen, *Sovereign Soldiers*, 218.

178 **"the most persistent single theme":** Patterson, *Grand Expectations*, 278; John Lewis Gaddis, *Strategies of Containment: A Critical Appraisal of Postwar American National Security Policy During the Cold War* (New York: Oxford University Press, 1982), 146–48.

179 **a thousand times more powerful:** Hitchcock, *Age of Eisenhower*, 114, 148–49.

179 **embraced the CIA's covert operations:** Hitchcock, *Age of Eisenhower*, 153.

179 **threaten to use nuclear weapons:** Gaddis, *Strategies of Containment*, 134.

179 **"The most terrible job":** Smith, *Eisenhower in War and Peace*, 641.

180 **the olive branch quickly died:** Smith, *Eisenhower in War and Peace*, 575.

181 **antagonize the Soviets:** Patterson, *Grand Expectations*, 308, Kindle.

182 **interaction between nationalism and Communism:** Before becoming president in 1963, LBJ made a brief trip to Saigon, where he reassured the anti-Communist government that the Kennedy administration would support its efforts. There is no evidence that he learned anything about local conditions during his visit.

182 **Eisenhower dismissed the idea:** Dwight D. Eisenhower, oral history, July 20, 1967, OH-11, DDEPL, 66.

182 **"Vietnam until these people":** Dwight D. Eisenhower, oral history, July 20, 1967, 65–66.

183 **Eisenhower could not imagine:** Hitchcock, *Age of Eisenhower*, 185–86.

184 **helping France maintain its empire:** Hitchcock, *Age of Eisenhower*, 194; Gaddis, *Strategies of Containment*, 131.

184 **"the rest of Southeast Asia":** Hitchcock, *Age of Eisenhower*, 195–96.

184 **"incalculable to the free world":** Hitchcock, *Age of Eisenhower*, 196–97.

185 **the United States would pay:** Farrell, *Nixon*, 227.

185 **stormy NSC meeting:** "Memorandum of Discussion at the 194th Meeting of the National Security Council, Thursday, April 29, 1954, 10 a.m.," "Foreign Relations of the United States, 1952–1954," Indochina, Volume XIII, Part 2, https://history.state.gov/historicaldocuments/frus1952-54v13p2/d818.

186 **lose all our significant support:** Farrell, *Nixon*, 228–29.

186 **"supported their cause and honored":** Nixon, *Memoirs*, 124.

187 **"they would not stop":** Farrell, *Nixon*, 218; Nixon, *Memoirs*, 125–26, 151–52; Gregory A. Olson, George N. Dionisopoulos, and Steven R. Goldzwig, "The Rhetorical Antecedents to Vietnam, 1945–1965," in *World War II and the Cold War: The Rhetoric of Hearts and Minds*, ed. Martin J. Medhurst (East Lansing: Michigan State University Press, 2018), 303–51.

187 **"and Chinese Civil War type":** Nixon, *Memoirs*, 151; Frank, *Ike and Dick*, 94.

187 **"He seemed resigned":** Ambrose, *Education*, 361.

188 **between internationalists and isolationists:** Richard N. Goodwin, *Remembering America: A Voice from the Sixties* (New York: Open Road, 2014), 196–99; Thomas M. Gaskin, "Senator Lyndon B. Johnson, the Eisenhower Administration and U.S. Foreign Policy, 1957–60," *Presidential Studies Quarterly* 24, no. 2 (Spring 1994): 341–61; Thomas

I. McInerney, "Eisenhower Governance and the Power to Command: A Perspective on Presidential Leadership," *Presidential Studies Quarterly* 11, no. 2 (Spring 1981): 262–70.

188 **"alone in a hostile world":** Dallek, *Lone Star*, 444.

188 **hampered military effectiveness:** Parmet, *Jack*, 276.

189 **power to the Vietnamese people:** Parmet, *Jack*, 277.

189 **" 'an enemy of the people' ":** Logevall, *JFK*, 576.

190 **Asian nations needed to play:** Parmet, *Jack*, 284–85.

190 **could also provoke the Chinese:** Dallek, *Unfinished Life*, 187.

191 **"do battle with the tiger":** Farrell, *Nixon*, 227; Gellman, *Campaign of the Century*, 8.

191 **would win an overwhelming victory:** Patterson, *Grand Expectations*, 297–98, Kindle.

192 **"It is our offspring":** Hitchcock, *Age of Eisenhower*, 440–41; Matthews, *Kennedy & Nixon*, 95.

192 **tried to find common ground:** Leon H. Keyserling, "For a National Prosperity Budget," *New York Times Magazine*, March 25, 1956, 12–13.

192 **spending and balanced budgets:** Steve Neal, "Why We Were Right to Like Ike," *American Heritage* online, December 1985, https://www.americanheritage.com/why-we-were-right-ike.

193 **a new Cabinet-level agency:** Gillon, *Politics and Vision*, 105.

193 **the United States could not flourish:** "Principal Facts Concerning the First Transcontinental Army Motor Transport Expedition, Washington to San Francisco, July 7 to September 6, 1919," Presidential Personal File, DDEPL, box 967.

193 **allow for the evacuation of cities:** Smith, *Eisenhower in War and Peace*, 651–52; Hitchcock, *Age of Eisenhower*, 261–62.

194 **"get into a pissing contest":** Patterson, *Grand Expectations*, 265; Frank, *Ike and Dick*, 84–85.

195 **consequences of incurring his wrath:** Larry Tye, "How Wealthy Texans Helped Create Joe McCarthy," *Texas Monthly* online, last modified July 7, 2020, https://www.texasmonthly.com/being-texan/texans-helped-create-joe-mccarthy/.

195 **"make it easier on the rat":** Patterson, *Grand Expectations*, 265; Frank, *Ike and Dick*, 84–85.

196 **"we will get somewhere":** Smith, *Eisenhower in War and Peace*, 708–10, 714.

196 **"an abdication of responsibility":** Eisenhower to "Swede," July 22, 1957, Hazlett Papers, DDEPL, box 2; Farrell, *Nixon*, 249; Ambrose, *Education*, 367.

197 **"in the midst of battle":** Patterson, *Grand Expectations*, 414; Smith, *Eisenhower in War and Peace*, 719, 721–22.

198 **Change would be slow:** Farrell, *Nixon*, 250–51.

198 **Zapata Petroleum Corporation:** Meacham, *Destiny and Power*, 94–107.

199 **Reagan's animus stemmed partly:** Spitz, *Reagan*, 288.

199 **it exemplified federal intervention:** Spitz, *Reagan*, 279–89.

199 **"moderates implement the court's decision":** Richard Norton Smith, *An Ordinary Man: The Surprising Life and Historic Presidency of Gerald R. Ford* (New York: Harper, 2023), 165.

200 **September 12, 1953:** Matthews, *Kennedy & Nixon*, 93.

201 **determining the pace of desegregation:** Logevall, *JFK*, 629.

201 **"paralyzed by pain":** Logevall, *JFK*, 585.

201 **"Jack is going to die":** Farrell, *Nixon*, 261–62.

201 **offered the ailing JFK:** Logevall, *JFK*, 587–88, 621–22; Gellman, *Campaign of the Century*, 9.

202 **contender for the 1960 nomination:** Evan Thomas, *Robert Kennedy: His Life* (New York: Simon & Schuster, 1980), 96.

202 **"Jack's a total fucking idiot!":** Logevall, *JFK*, 612, 634; Ted Sorensen, *Counselor: A Life at the Edge of History* (New York: HarperCollins, 2008), 169.

202 **"you clearly emerged as the man":** Logevall, *JFK*, 640–41.

203 **After forty-nine days:** Logevall, *JFK*, 611.

203 **he could remain a powerful player:** Pietrusza, *1960*, 62.

204 **"I was taken aback":** Farrell, *Nixon*, 231; Pietrusza, *1960*, 85.

204 **"In fact, he is a shit":** Farrell, *Nixon*, 241.

204 **the edge of a new frontier:** Gillon, *Politics and Vision*, 102.

CHAPTER 7

205 **while Mamie watched television:** Yanek Mieczkowski, *Eisenhower's Sputnik Moment: The Race for Space and World Prestige* (Ithaca, NY: Cornell University Press, 2013), 1, Kindle.

206 ***beep-beep-beep:*** Robert A. Divine, *The Sputnik Challenge: Eisenhower's Response to the Soviet Satellite* (New York: Oxford University Press, 1993), xxi, Kindle.

206 **"hunk of iron":** Divine, *The Sputnik Challenge*, xiv.

206 **"greater than Pearl Harbor":** Divine, *The Sputnik Challenge*, xiv, 24; Paul Dickson, *Sputnik: The Shock of the Century* (New York: Walker, 2007), 24, 108, Kindle.

207 **"hypersonic speed to reach":** Mieczkowski, *Sputnik Moment*, 17; Divine, *Sputnik Challenge*, xiv.

207 **into America's space program:** Divine, *Sputnik Challenge*, 7. In a 1988 letter, speechwriter Arthur Larson confirmed Eisenhower's position: "I can say with complete confidence that Eisenhower personally did not believe that the orbiting of Sputnik was an occasion for alarm." Larson to Mieczkowski, November 22, 1988, Larson Papers, DDEPL, box 21.

208 **"unify the Democratic Party":** Dallek, *Lone Star*, 529; Mieczkowski, *Sputnik Moment*, 16.

208 **"in favor of the USSR":** "Reaction to the Soviet Satellite: A Preliminary Evaluation," n.d., box 35, White House Office of the Staff Research Group, DDEPL.

208 **National Aeronautics and Space Administration (NASA):** "Reaction to the Soviet Satellite."

209 **"erode his political base":** Mieczkowski, *Sputnik Moment*, 31.

209 **"the question of national defense":** Ambrose, *Education*, 491–94.

209 **denouncing calls for more military spending:** Ambrose, *Education*, 494–95.

210 **"the Declaration of Independence":** Papers of John F. Kennedy, Pre-Presidential Papers, Senate Files, "U.S. Military Power," Senate floor, August 14, 1958, JFKPL, box 901.

211 **entered World War II as young men:** There was only one other election where all the candidates had served in the war. That was 1972, when Nixon and Agnew, the latter of whom was drafted into the army after Pearl Harbor, opposed George McGovern, who flew bombing missions for the US Army Air Forces, and Sargent Shriver, who volunteered for the navy after Pearl Harbor and served in the South Pacific. McGovern's first VP choice, Thomas Eagleton, served in the navy after the war.

211 **The party gained forty-seven seats:** Parmet, *Jack*, 458–60; Jack Doyle, "JFK's Early Campaign, 1958," The Pop History Dig, last modified August 21, 2013, https://pophisto rydig.com/topics/tag/jfks-1958-campaign/.

212 **Smathers felt that Kennedy:** George Smathers, oral history, July 10, 1964, pt. 3, 18, John F. Kennedy Oral History Project, JFKPL.

212 **told his friend Charles Bartlett:** Pietrusza, *1960*, 87, 93.

213 **should nominate a Catholic candidate:** Richard N. Goodwin, *Remembering America*, 81.

213 **"all the way to the convention":** O'Donnell and Powers, *"Johnny,"* 182–83; Arthur M. Schlesinger Jr., *Robert F. Kennedy and His Times* (Boston: Houghton Mifflin, 1978), 194–96. When the Humphrey campaign pointed out accurately that JFK's father had once donated money to Nixon, and that the candidate himself had supported Nixon over Helen Gahagan Douglas in his 1950 Senate race, the Kennedy people simply denied the charge and accused Humphrey of engaging in personal attacks. See "Nixon Aid by Father of Kennedy Denied," *Milwaukee Journal*, March 25, 1960, and Richard N. Goodwin, *Remembering America*, 83.

213 **"He was on the PT boats":** O'Donnell and Powers, *"Johnny,"* 189.

214 **"never forgave me for it":** Pietrusza, *1960*, 204.

214 **roughly the equivalent of $360,000:** Thomas, *Robert Kennedy*, 94–95.

214 **Kennedy was a "show horse":** Steven M. Gillon, *The Kennedy Assassination—24 Hours After: Lyndon B. Johnson's Pivotal First Day as President* (New York: Basic Books, 2009), 9.

215 **"down to the nut-cuttin'":** When RFK fired a rifle, the recoil sent him to the ground. "Son," LBJ boasted, "you've got to learn to handle a gun like a man." Pietrusza, *1960*, 113; Gillon, *24 Hours After*, 8.

215 **Kennedy's records had been filed:** Pietrusza, *1960*, 266. No one knows for sure who broke into the office, but there were obvious similarities to what Nixon's aides did years later when they rummaged through the files of Daniel Ellsberg's psychiatrist's office in search of damaging medical information. After the convention, Kennedy's doctor, Janet Travell, offered talking points on how he should talk about his health. She advised that he tell reporters that he did "not have classical Addison's disease." She suggested that he blame his adrenal insufficiency on the "extraordinary stress and malaria" that he encountered during the war. See Travell to Kennedy, July 29, 1960, Pre-Presidential Papers, Presidential Campaign Files, 1960, JFKPL.

215 **"Jack and Bobby Kennedy in drag":** Pietrusza, *1960*, 269.

216 **"vice presidency doesn't mean anything":** Pietrusza, *1960*, 312, 340.

216 **"I'm a gamblin' man, darlin'":** Pietrusza, *1960*, 312, 340; Richard N. Goodwin, *Remembering America*, 206.

217 **quit the campaign immediately:** Pietrusza, *1960*, 593; Farrell, *Nixon*, 280–81.

217 **"I can't understand how":** Mieczkowski, *Sputnik Moment*, 32.

218 **"just a spectator":** Hitchcock, *Age of Eisenhower*, 479.

218 **Eisenhower undercut the central premise:** Hitchcock, *Age of Eisenhower*, 479–80.

219 **"the Silver Star for gallantry":** "Biographical Sketch of Lyndon B. Johnson," August 1960, JFK Pre-Presidential Papers, JFKPL, box 1061.

220 **Charles "Bebe" Rebozo:** William Liebenow, oral history, February 15, 2005, 16, John F. Kennedy Oral History Project, JFKPL.

220 **"usually brought a lecture":** Benjamin C. Bradlee, *Conversations with Kennedy* (New York: W. W. Norton, 1975), 18–20.

221 **"felt sorry for Nixon":** Pietrusza, *1960*, 415; Richard N. Goodwin, "Memorandum on the Last 9 Days of Campaigning," JFK Pre-Presidential Papers, 1960 Campaign, JFKPL, box 1076.

221 **achieved a small lead:** Pietrusza, *1960*, 494.

221 **sporting a 101-degree temperature:** Richard N. Goodwin, *Remembering America*, 112; Sorensen, *Counselor*, 189.

222 **"I gave him a bottle":** Pietrusza, *1960*, 503.

222 **he wore a gray suit:** Edward M. Kennedy, *True Compass: A Memoir* (New York: Twelve, 2009), 155–56; Roman Puchinski, quoted in Gerald S. Strober and Deborah H. Strober, *Let Us Begin Anew: An Oral History of the Kennedy Presidency* (New York: HarperCollins, 1993), 31.

222 **The die had already been cast:** Sidney Kraus, *The Great Debates: Kennedy vs. Nixon* (Bloomington: Indiana University Press, 1973), 350–53. Washington attorney Clark Clifford, who would eventually run JFK's transition, was impressed with his candidate's performance. "You clearly came out the winner," he wrote JFK. "You were clear, concise and very convincing." See "Clifford, "Memorandum on Television Debate with Vice President Nixon, September 26," Clifford Papers, JFKPL, Series 2.

222 **"the natural language of politics":** Richard N. Goodwin, *Remembering America*, 116; Richard N. Goodwin, "Memorandum on the Last 9 Days of Campaigning," n.d., JFK Pre-Presidential Papers, 1960 Campaign, JFKPL, box 1076.

222 **"devastating consequences for the country":** Richard N. Goodwin, *Remembering America*, 105–6.

223 **out of the White House:** O'Donnell and Powers, *"Johnny,"* 244–45.

223 **"aggression advocated":** Reagan to VP, September 7, 1959, Ronald Reagan 87:9, RRPL, HCF: Garment 1968 Political Campaign File, box 21.

223 **"I turned him down":** Pietrusza, *1960*, 418.

224 **"the Federal Govt. will grow":** Reagan to VP, July 18, 1960, Ronald Reagan 87:9, WHCF: Garment 1968 Political Campaign File, RNPL, box 21.

224 **"feel free to call on me":** Steven Levingston, "John F. Kennedy, Martin Luther King Jr., and the Phone Call That Changed History," *Time* online, last modified June 20, 2017, https://time.com/4817240/martin-luther-king-john-kennedy-phone-call/.

225 **out on the campaign trail:** Hitchcock, *Age of Eisenhower*, 495.

225 **"it's up for grabs":** Hitchcock, *Age of Eisenhower*, 496–97; Pietrusza, *1960*, 586.

225 **"he looks like a loser":** Pietrusza, *1960*, 587–88.

226 **"grab bag of easy answers":** Felix Belair Jr., "Eisenhower Gibes at 'Young Genius' in Campaign Tour," *New York Times*, November 5, 1961, 1.

226 **"a mechanical man":** Christopher Matthews, "Great Debate," *San Antonio News* online, April 28, 1996, https://www.mysanantonio.com/magazine/article/GREAT-DEBATE-3499888.php; Morris H. Rubin, "The Case Against Nixon," *Capital Times* (Madison, WI), October 24, 1960, 32.

227 **keep a mental note:** Farrell, *Nixon,* 298–300. According to Sorensen, Henry Kissinger told him later that "Nixon's plan to bug the Democratic headquarters at the Watergate may have stemmed from Nixon's unwarranted suspicion that the Kennedys had somehow bugged his 1960 campaign plane and headquarters." See Sorensen, *Counselor,* 192.

227 **"hit in the solar plexus":** Hitchcock, *Age of Eisenhower*, 493.

227 **"How did I manage?":** Robert Dallek, "As Camelot Began: The Unseen Portraits of the Kennedys by Richard Avedon," *Vanity Fair*, November 2007, https://www.vanityfair.com/news/2007/11/jfk_avedon200711.

227 **JFK "still seemed tired then":** Dallek, *Unfinished Life*, 299–300.

227 **Kennedy arranged for his son:** Gibbs and Duffy, *Presidents Club*, 111–13.

228 **he had won the election:** Gibbs and Duffy, *Presidents Club,* 114.

228 **"I don't think I ever":** Dallek, *Lone Star*, 588.

228 **"Therefore strengthening our hand":** Eisenhower sent a perfunctory note to Kennedy simply offering his congratulations "for the victory you have just won at the polls." See Eisenhower to Kennedy, November 9, 1960, Eisenhower Papers, Anne Whitman File, DDE Diary Series, box 55; Dallek, *Unfinished Life*, 302.

228 **"The Stars and Stripes Forever":** Dallek, *Unfinished Life*, 302–33; Hitchcock, *Age of Eisenhower*, 497–98; Russell Baker, "Big Moment at the White House Turns Out to Be Unmomentous," *New York Times*, December 7, 1960, 46; Felix Belair Jr., "Meeting Cordial," *New York Times*, December 7, 1960, 1.

229 **He recommended "earnest study":** Eisenhower notes on meeting with JFK, December 6, 1961, Eisenhower Papers, Anne Whitman File, DDE Diary Series, box 55.

229 **Ike did not pass up:** Clark Clifford organized the meeting for Kennedy, pulling together the items that the outgoing and incoming presidents wished to discuss. See: "Informal List of Subjects to Be Discussed at Meeting of President Eisenhower and Senator Kennedy," December 6, 1961, Clark Clifford Papers, Series 1, JFKPL, Presidential Transition Files; Dallek, *Unfinished Life*, 303; Hitchcock, *Age of Eisenhower*, 498–99. Eisenhower's recollection of the meeting can be found in Anne Whitman File, DDE Diary Series, box 55. Clifford's handwritten notes of the meeting can be found online at the JFKPL, https://www.jfklibrary.org/asset-viewer/archives/CCPP/MF03/CCPP -MF03-006.

229 **he opposed "anything extreme":** "Memorandum for Record," December 6, 1960, Eisenhower Presidential Papers, Anne Whitman File, Presidential Transition Series, DDEPL, box 2. See: "Informal List of Subjects to Be Discussed at Meeting of President Eisenhower and Senator Kennedy," December 6, 1961, Clark Clifford Papers, Series 1, JFKPL, Presidential Transition Files. Dallek, *Unfinished Life*, 303; Hitchcock, *Age of Eisenhower*, 498–99.

230 **According to Clifford:** Hitchcock, *Age of Eisenhower*, 499–500; Dallek, *Unfinished Life*, 303; Clark Clifford, with Richard Holbrooke, *Counsel to the President: A Memoir* (New York: Anchor Books, 1991), 342.

230 **dismantle the White House heirarchy:** Eisenhower notes on meeting with JFK, December 6, 1961, Eisenhower Papers, Anne Whitman File, DDEPL, Diary Series, box 55; "Interview with President Dwight D. Eisenhower," November 8, 1966, Eisenhower Papers, Anne Whitman File, DDEPL, Diary Series, box 55.

230 **"we must go it alone":** Clifford with Holbrooke, *Counsel*, 343–44. Robert McNamara, who would serve as JFK's secretary of defense, also attended the meeting and came away with a different impression than Clifford. He believed that Eisenhower was sending a mixed message and was clearly uncertain about how to handle the challenges in Southeast Asia. Eisenhower "advised against unilateral action," but he also "stated without qualification, 'If Laos is lost to the Free World, in the long run we will lose all of Southeast Asia.'" See Robert McNamara, *In Retrospect: The Tragedy and Lessons of Vietnam* (New York: Vintage Books, 1996), 36. Unfortunately, McNamara's original notes have gone missing. See also Yuen Foong Khong, *Analogies at War: Korea, Munich, Dien Bien Phu, and the Vietnam Decisions of 1965* (Princeton, NJ: Princeton University Press, 1992), 81. Clifford's handwritten notes of the meeting can be found online at the JFKPL, https://www.jfklibrary.org/asset-viewer/archives/CCPP/MF03/CCPP-MF03 -005#folder_info.

231 **He also informed JFK:** Clifford with Holbrooke, *Counsel*, 343–44; Hitchcock, *Age of Eisenhower*, 501–2.

232 **"the *military-industrial complex*":** See Arthur Larson Memo, April 5, 1960, Larson and Moos Records, DDEPL, box 16; Hitchcock, *Age of Eisenhower*, 507–8; Felix Belair Jr., "Vigilance Urged," *New York Times*, January 18, 1961, 1.

232 **Ike did not seem bothered:** John T. Correll, "Eisenhower's Farewell Warning," *Air & Space Forces* online, last modified June 28, 2018, https://www.airandspaceforces.com /article/eisenhowers-farewell-warning/.

232 **Congress passed the bill unanimously:** Smith, *Eisenhower in War and Peace*, 959, Kindle; Ambrose, *Soldier and President*, 535; Kennedy to Eisenhower, March 22, 1961, Eisenhower Papers, Anne Whitman File, DDEPL, Diary Series, box 55; Eisenhower to Kennedy, March 24, 1961, Eisenhower Papers, Anne Whitman File, DDEPL, Diary Se-

ries, box 55. At the time, the pension for a general was substantially lower than that of a former president. The new law gave Ike the best of both worlds: the title that he desired and the pension that he'd earned as president.

CHAPTER 8

236 **"a long and grim day":** Arthur M. Schlesinger Jr., *A Thousand Days: John F. Kennedy in the White House* (Boston: Houghton Mifflin, 2002), 277, Kindle.

236 **Communist prime minister Fidel Castro:** According to General Andrew Goodpaster, Eisenhower's staff secretary, Ike had authorized the training of the refugees but had not signed off on the actual invasion plans. Goodpaster recalled saying to Eisenhower, "There is always the danger that this will develop a momentum of its own." Ike snapped back, "Not as long as I'm here." Goodpaster responded: "Yes, sir. That's just the problem." He argued that the plan presented to Kennedy was very different from the one that Eisenhower had approved. See Strober and Strober, *Lets Us Begin Anew*, 323–25.

236 **Kennedy insisted that America:** Gibbs and Duffy, *Presidents Club*, 129; Dallek, *Unfinished Life*, 42.

237 **"trapped by what he inherited":** Schlesinger, *Thousand Days*, 337; Strober and Strober, *Let Us Begin Anew*, 349.

238 **The shocked brigade commander:** Gibbs and Duffy, *Presidents Club*, 133; Jim Rasenberger, *The Brilliant Disaster: JFK, Castro, and America's Doomed Invasion of Cuba's Bay of Pigs* (New York: Scribner, 2012), 285. Bissell, one of the CIA architects of the mission, blamed the failure on a shortage of ammunition and a stronger than expected Castro response, but he refused to fault the CIA. "Although the intelligence was not perfect . . . we do not feel that any failure of intelligence contributed significantly to the defeat." He pointed a finger at JFK for his refusal to supply air cover for the rebels. The operation leaders, he wrote, "were obligated to fit their plan inside changing ground rules laid down for non-military considerations, which often had serious operational disadvantages." Bissell Memo, May 10, 1961, Sorensen Papers, JFKPL, box 48.

238 **"a depressed and lonely man":** Rasenberger, *Brilliant Disaster*, 286; Ted Sorensen, *Kennedy* (New York: HarperCollins, 2009), 308.

238 **"It was so sad":** Gibbs and Duffy, *Presidents Club*, 133.

238 **soaring to 83 percent:** Kennedy, "Address to American Society of Newspaper Editors," April 20, 1961, President's Papers, President's Office Files, JFKPL; "The Bay of Pigs," *The President's Desk: A Resource Guide for Teachers—Grades 4–12*, 74, JFKPL, https://www.jfklibrary.org/asset-viewer/archives/JFKPOF/034/JFKPOF-034-018?image_identifier=JFKPOF-034-018-p0015; Parmet, *JFK*, 179.

238 **"Over and over, he cursed":** Nixon, *Memoirs*, 232–34.

239 **"fighting millions of Chinese troops":** Nixon, *Memoirs*, 234–35.

239 **he was quietly searching:** Reeves, *President Kennedy*, 376; Dallek, *Unfinished Life*, 467.

240 **"wage is $1.15 or $1.25?":** Nixon, *Memoirs*, 235.

240 **"I felt empathy for a man":** Nixon, *Memoirs*, 235–36.

240 **"we should not start things":** Nixon, *Memoirs*, 236.

241 **to handle the weighty duties:** Kennedy to Eisenhower, January 21, 1961, Eisenhower Papers, Anne Whitman File, DDEPL, Diary Series, box 55; Eisenhower to Kennedy, January 30, 1961, Eisenhower Papers, Anne Whitman File, DDEPL, Diary Series, box 55.

241 **"recommended by the CIA":** Eisenhower did not mention the exchange in his official notes of the meeting, but much later, in 1966, when he reflected on the meeting with a

reporter. See "Interview with President Dwight D. Eisenhower," November 8, 1966, Eisenhower Papers, Anne Whitman File, DDEPL, Diary Series, box 55.

242 **"It must be a success":** "Interview with President Dwight D. Eisenhower," November 8, 1966, Eisenhower Papers, Anne Whitman File, DDEPL, Diary Series, box 55. At one point, the transcript mistakenly states, "Mrs. Kennedy," when identifying the president.

242 **"We believe in what is right":** "Notes by General Eisenhower in Luncheon Meeting with President Kennedy at Camp David," April 22, 1961, Eisenhower Papers, Anne Whitman File, DDEPL, Diary Series, box 55. Eisenhower would send mixed signals to the White House. In March 1962, after Kennedy said at a press conference that "the security of all Southeast Asia will be endangered if Laos loses its neutral independence," Eisenhower told a journalist, "That boy doesn't know what the hell he's doing. He doesn't even know where Laos is." After publicly criticizing the president for saying in public what the general had been saying in private, Eisenhower privately communicated a very different message to Kennedy. He told McCone, who reported back to Kennedy, that he considered the situation in Laos so central to the fate of Thailand and Vietnam that "extreme measures, including the commitment of US forces to combat in Laos, were justified." He again referenced the domino theory, pointing out "consequences of losing Southeast Asia" and saying that "nothing would stop the southward movement of Communism through Indonesia, and this would have the effect of cutting the world in half." See "Discussion with General Eisenhower: Mr. McCone and Mr. Forrestal present," May 10, 1962, JFKPL, POF, Special Correspondence.

242 **"Eisenhower Urges Nation to Back":** W. H. Lawrence, "Eisenhower Urges Nation to Back Kennedy on Cuba," *New York Times*, April 23, 1961, 1.

242 **"do better in the future":** Parmet, *JFK*, 176–77.

243 **"'Profile in Timidity and Indecision'":** Hitchcock, *Age of Eisenhower*, 512–13; Parmet, *JFK*, 175–77; JFK to President, May 9, 1961, Eisenhower Papers, Anne Whitman File, DDEPL, Diary Series, box 55.

243 **"The first advice":** Strober and Strober, *Let Us Begin Anew*, 347; Bradlee, *Conversations with Kennedy*, 122.

244 **American concessions on Berlin:** Dallek, *Unfinished Life*, 711.

244 **"We have some big trouble":** Reeves, *President Kennedy*, 368; Dallek, *Unfinished Life*, 721–22.

244 **the group grew:** Strober and Strober, *Let Us Begin Anew*, 382.

244 **"If we go in":** Reeves, *President Kennedy*, 370; Thomas, *Robert Kennedy*, 213.

245 **kill hundreds of Soviet troops:** Thomas, *Robert Kennedy*, 213.

245 **allow the Soviets some room:** Thomas, *Robert Kennedy*, 218; Reeves, *President Kennedy*, 386.

245 **"contrary to our traditions":** Reeves, *President Kennedy*, 386; Dallek, *Unfinished Life*, 731–32.

246 **strike immediately and without warning:** Thomas, *Robert Kennedy*, 215–16.

246 **"take off his testicles, too":** George M. Watson Jr. and Herman S. Wolk, "'Whiz Kid': Robert S. McNamara's World War II Service," *Air Power History* 50, no. 4 (Winter 2003): 8; Michael Dobbs, *One Minute to Midnight: Kennedy, Khrushchev, and Castro on the Brink of Nuclear War* (New York: Knopf, 2008), 21.

247 **He relied on the counsel:** Ernest R. May and Philip Zelikow, eds., *The Kennedy Tapes: Inside the White House During the Cuban Missile Crisis* (Cambridge, MA: Belknap Press of Harvard University Press, 1997), 177–79; Mark Rathbone, "Appeasement & the Cold War: The Munich Effect," *History Review*, no. 64, September 2009.

247 **"I've had a full life"**: Lawrence J. Haas, *The Kennedys in the World: How Jack, Bobby, and Ted Remade America's Empire* (Lincoln: University of Nebraska Press, 2021), 11; Dobbs, *Minute to Midnight*, 22.

248 **"I think you ought to define"**: There is some confusion over when Kennedy called Eisenhower. Some records indicate he placed the call on Monday morning, but Eisenhower recalled that it took place on Sunday evening. "Interview with President Dwight D. Eisenhower," November 8, 1966, Eisenhower Papers, Anne Whitman File, DDEPL, Diary Series, box 55; Gibbs and Duffy, *Presidents Club*, 148–49.

248 **he reluctantly supported the blockade**: Strober and Strober, *Let Us Begin Anew*, 384; May and Zelikow, *Kennedy Tapes*, 215.

248 **"a nuclear strike capability"**: John F. Kennedy, "Radio and Television Address to the American People on the Soviet Arms Build-up in Cuba, 22 October 1962," JFKPL, audio, 17.46, https://www.jfklibrary.org/asset-viewer/archives/jfkwha-142-001, and transcript, https://www.jfklibrary.org/learn/about-jfk/historic-speeches/address-during -the-cuban-missile-crisis.

249 **"to secure their withdrawal"**: Kennedy, "Radio and Television Address to the American People on the Soviet Arms Build-up in Cuba, 22 October 1962."

249 **release the secret tapes**: The danger was far greater than Kennedy realized at the time. Neither he nor the members of ExComm knew that the Soviets had placed dozens of tactical nuclear weapons in Cuba and that Khrushchev had given commanders in the field the authority to use them against an invading American force. Also, the CIA had seriously underestimated the number of Soviet troops on the tiny island: a whopping forty-two thousand—not eight thousand to ten thousand. Had Kennedy pursued the military option of air strikes followed by a land invasion, the situation could easily have escalated into a nuclear war between the two nations.

249 **atmospheric and underwater nuclear testing**: Dallek, *Unfinished Life*, 819.

250 **the superiority of Western values**: The crowd was so enthusiastic that it overlooked that Kennedy, who struggled with foreign languages and who had practiced the phrase for days, should have said, "*Ich bin Berliner,*" instead of "*ein Berliner,*" which meant "jelly donut." See Dallek, *Unfinished Life*, 827, Kindle.

250 **"We will never have another"**: Reeves, *President Kennedy*, 537.

251 **"everybody was quite clear"**: Haas, *Kennedys in the World*, 123.

251 **"so that we could withdraw"**: Schlesinger, *Thousand Days*, 547; Roger Hilsman, "Mc-Namara's War—Against the Truth: A Review Essay," *Political Science Quarterly* 111, no. 1 (Spring 1996): 155.

251 **he even drew a parallel**: Miller, *Lyndon*, 283.

252 **"we'll use our beer bottles"**: LBJ Interview, Transcript, Lyndon Baines Johnson Oral History Special Interview, LBJPL, August 12, 1969.

252 **the vice president did not recommend**: Robert Dallek, *Flawed Giant: Lyndon B. Johnson and His Times, 1961–1973* (New York: Oxford University Press, 1998), 17.

252 **"be regarded as a coward"**: Strober and Strober, *Let Us Begin Anew*, 413.

254 **World War II had taught**: Smith, *Eisenhower in War and Peace*, 196–97.

254 **"all phases of the government"**: Spitz, *Reagan*, 303–4.

255 **For Reagan, withdrawal from Vietnam**: Reagan, Annual Meeting of the Phoenix Chamber of Commerce, March 30, 1961, Garment 1968 Political Campaign File, 87:9, RRPL, box 21.

255 **he would tone down**: Reagan, Annual Meeting of the Phoenix Chamber of Commerce, March 30, 1961, Garment 1968 Political Campaign File, 87:9, RRPL, box 21.

256 **"Let them burn"**: Marvin Kalb, *The Road to War: Presidential Commitments Honored and Betrayed* (Washington, DC: Brookings Institution Press, 2013), 67–68.

256 **unequivocal support for South Vietnam:** Transcript of phone conversation, JFK and Ball, August 21, 1963, George W. Ball Papers, JFKPL, box 9.

256 **army officers assassinated both men:** "The Diem Coup in Vietnam," Miller Center, University of Virginia, accessed November 10, 2023.

256 **"the bottom to the top":** Dallek, *Unfinished Life*, 907.

257 **By 1963, he was questioning:** For the best, most thoughtful discussion of the "What if Kennedy had lived?" question, see Marc J. Selverstone, *The Kennedy Withdrawal: Camelot and the American Commitment to Vietnam* (Cambridge, MA: Harvard University Press, 2022).

258 **causes of the Great Depression:** "The Economy: The Pragmatic Professor," *Time*, March 3, 1961, 6, https://time.com/archive/6832658/the-economy-the-pragmatic -professor/.

258 **put money in people's pockets:** Allen J. Matusow, *The Unraveling of America: A History of Liberalism in the 1960s* (New York: Harper & Row, 1984), 46.

259 **"you are a liberal":** Walter Heller, "Meeting with President Elect Kennedy, December 16, at the house in Georgetown," Heller Papers, Heller and JFK, 1960–1964, JFKPL, box 5, 2–5.

259 **the cover of *Time* magazine:** James Tobin, "Walter W. Heller (August 27, 1915–June 15, 1987)," *Proceedings of the American Philosophical Society* 135, no. 1 (March 1991): 100–107.

259 **weekends to Hyannis Port:** Tobin, "Walter W. Heller," 100–107.

260 **"Most Americans," he charged:** Galbraith to Kennedy, July 10, 1962, (POF), special correspondence, John Kenneth Galbraith; Galbraith to Kennedy, August 20, 1962, (POF), special correspondence, JFKPL, Galbraith.

260 **"Galbraith Early Warning System":** Kermit Gordon and Walter W. Heller Oral History, JFKPL, #2, September 14, 1972, 58.

260 **"Dr. Heller can avoid":** Heller to Kennedy, September 8, 1961, "The Political Economy of the Next Recession," JFKPL, JFKPOF-073-008.

261 **"Keynes fired the opening salvo":** Heller to the President, September 8, 1961, "The Political Economy of the Next Recession," "CEA %1"; CEA Report, June 5, 1962, "Economic Prospects: A New Look," "CEA 6/1-6/15/62," POF, JFKPL, box 43; Sorensen, *Kennedy*, 424.

261 **"automatic cliché":** Kennedy, "Commencement Address at Yale University, June 11, 1962."

262 **"technical answers, not political answers":** Kennedy, "Commencement Address."

262 **a deficit of $10.2 billion:** John F. Kennedy, "Special Message to Congress on Tax Reduction and Reform," January 24, 1963, Public Papers (Washington, DC: Government Printing Office, 1963), 73.

262 **"a bona fide reduction":** "Separating Tax Cut, Reform Urged by Two House Leaders," *Evening Star* (Washington, DC), February 4, 1963.

262 **"certain to damage our currency":** "Eisenhower Cites Kennedy Administration for Extravagant, 'Risky Fiscal Adventure,'" *Wall Street Journal*, May 14, 1963; Kermit Gordon and Walter W. Heller, oral history, interview 2, September 14, 1972, 60, John F. Kennedy Oral History Project, JFKPL; Dallek, *Unfinished Life*, 777. For an excellent discussion of Kennedy's economic program, see Amy Elizabeth Davis, "Politics of Prosperity: The Kennedy Presidency and Economic Policy" (dissertation, Columbia University, 1988).

263 **"The Kennedy civil rights strategy":** Strober and Strober, *Kennedy Presidency*, 272; Dallek, *Flawed Giant*, 31; Schlesinger, *RFK and His Times*, 317.

264 **"as old as the scriptures":** Gillon, *Politics and Vision*, 146–47.

264 **"justice for all people":** Dallek, *Unfinished Life*, 800–802.

265 **Jackie was aware of:** Dallek, *Unfinished Life*, 631; Parmet, *JFK*, 112.

265 **JFK grew more affectionate:** Steven M. Gillon, *America's Reluctant Prince: The Life of John F. Kennedy Jr.* (New York: Dutton, 2019), 38.

265 **he took a host of pills:** Reeves, *President Kennedy*, 146–47; Dallek, *Unfinished Life*, 529–30, 625.

CHAPTER 9

267 **The time was twelve thirty:** Gillon, *24 Hours After*, 43.

268 **"he became much less vital":** Gillon, *Kennedy Assassination*, 46–49.

268 **Johnson was on the floor:** Michael Beschloss, "Lyndon Johnson on the Record," *Texas Monthly*, December 2001, 107.

268 **"unreal, shocking, and incredible":** Lyndon Baines Johnson, *The Vantage Point: Perspectives of the Presidency, 1963–1969* (New York: Holt, Rinehart and Winston, 1972), 10.

269 **in her blood-stained suit:** Lady Bird Johnson, *A White House Diary* (Austin: University of Texas Press, 2007), 6.

269 **Associated Press and CBS Radio:** Gillon, *24 Hours After*, 96–98.

269 **The majority learned of the shooting:** Thomas J. Banta, "The Kennedy Assassination: Early Thoughts and Emotions," *Public Opinion Quarterly* 28, no. 2 (Summer 1964): 216–24.

269 **LBJ asked Ike to come:** Telephone conversation transcript, Lyndon Johnson to Dwight Eisenhower, November 22, 1963, Recordings and Transcripts of Telephone Conversations and Meetings, LBJPL.

270 **"He loves to phone":** Notes for the President, November 23, 1963, "Memorandum of Subjects Covered Verbally in Conference with President Johnson which were not made off the record," Augusta—Walter Reed Series, DDEPL, box 2. Eisenhower had prepared a memo recommending that Johnson deliver a speech before a joint session of Congress. He wanted the president to announce that he would cut expenditures to make up for the tax cut that JFK had sent to Congress. Eisenhower, "Notes for the President," November 23, 1963, White House Famous Names (referred to hereafter as WHFN), LBJPL, box 2.

270 **repeating the mistakes of the 1930s:** Manchester interview with Dwight Eisenhower, William Manchester Papers, Special Collections & Archive, Wesleyan University (WUL), August 27, 1964; Johnson, *Vantage Point*, 31–32.

271 **"No one could say":** George W. Ball, *The Past Has Another Pattern: Memoirs* (New York: W. W. Norton, 1982), 316.

272 **"a pretender to the throne":** Doris Kearns Goodwin, *Johnson and the American Dream* (New York: Thomas Dunne, 2019), 170, Kindle.

272 **"right from the federal government":** Horace W. Busby, *The Thirty-First of March: An Intimate Portrait of Lyndon Johnson* (New York: Farrar, Straus and Giroux, 2005), 154; Jack Valenti, "Lyndon Johnson: An Awesome Engine of a Man," in *Lyndon Johnson Remembered: An Intimate Portrait of a Presidency*, ed. Thomas W. Cowger and Sherwin Markman (Lanham, MD: Rowman & Littlefield, 2003), 37.

273 **U.S. News & World Report:** Steven M. Gillon, *American Paradox: The United States Since 1945* (Boston: Houghton Mifflin, 2003), 80–81.

274 **"Hell, we're the richest country":** "We Are All Keynesians Now," *Time*, December 31, 1965, https://time.com/archive/6889039/the-economy-we-are-all-keynesians-now/; Randall B. Woods, *LBJ: Architect of American Ambition* (New York: Free Press, 2007), 49–51; Dallek, *Flawed Giant*, 303.

274 **facing down Communist expansion worldwide:** Robert M. Collins, *More: The Politics of Economic Growth in Postwar America* (New York: Oxford University Press, 2000), 54, 59–60.

275 **"whatever Americans wish to make":** Collins, *More,* 53.

275 **As columnist Walter Lippmann observed:** Collins, *More,* 60.

275 **administration had gone "too far":** *Collins, More,* 60.

278 **"What do they want?":** Steven M. Gillon, *Separate and Unequal: The Kerner Commission and the Unraveling of American Liberalism* (New York: Basic Books, 2018), 20, Kindle; James T. Patterson, *Freedom Is Not Enough: The Moynihan Report and America's Struggle over Black Family Life from LBJ to Obama* (New York: Basic Books, 2012), 589; Eric F. Goldman, *The Tragedy of Lyndon Johnson* (New York: Knopf, 1969), 337; Randall B. Woods, *Prisoners of Hope: Lyndon B. Johnson, the Great Society, and the Limits of Liberalism* (New York: Basic Books, 2016), 189.

279 **"No more of this coup shit":** Larry Berman, *Lyndon Johnson's War: The Road to Stalemate in Vietnam* (New York: W. W. Norton, 1989), 31; Olson, Dionisopoulos, and Goldzwig, "Rhetorical Antecedents to Vietnam," 305–52.

279 **"navy was shooting at whales":** Berman, *Lyndon Johnson's War,* 32.

280 **He also rejected any plan:** Gillon, *Politics and Vision,* 178; George C. Herring, *America's Longest War: The United States and Vietnam, 1950–1975* (New York: McGraw-Hill, 2013), 108–44.

281 **"make them pay a cost":** General Andrew Goodpaster, "Memorandum of Meeting with the President," February 17, 1965, LBJ Papers, 1963–1969, LBJPL, Meeting Notes File, box 1.

281 **"we would remove the limits":** Goodpaster, "Memorandum of Meeting with the President."

282 **"enemy comes in large":** Goodpaster, "Memorandum of Meeting with the President."

283 **fighting a limited war in Vietnam:** I'm grateful to Will Hitchcock for helping me to understand the continuity of Eisenhower's thought. Hitchcock to author, May 26, 2024.

283 **this defeat would occur:** Berman, *Lyndon Johnson's War,* 72–73.

283 **LBJ was "employing a policy":** LBJ to Eisenhower, March 5, 1965, WHFN, LBJPL, box 2; Eisenhower to LBJ, March 12, 1965, WHFN, LBJPL, box 2; LBJ to Eisenhower, April 28, 1965, and Eisenhower to Johnson, April 30, 1965, WHFN, LBJPL, box 2; "Eisenhower Backs Johnson on Vietnam," April 25, 1965, WHFN, LBJPL, box 2.

284 **connection to the broader populace:** "Memorandum of telephone conversation," July 2, 1965, Eisenhower Papers, Augusta—Walter Reed Series, DDEPL, box 2.

284 **the war would be hard-fought:** "Memorandum for the Record," Meetings on Vietnam, July 21, 1965, LBJ Papers, 1963–1969, LBJPL, Meeting Notes File, box 1.

285 **He did not believe that:** "Memorandum for the Record."

285 **desires of the Vietnamese people:** "Memorandum for the Record."

286 **"crashing the plane or jumping":** Cabinet Room—ExComm (SVN), December 1, 1964, Meeting Notes File, LBJPL, box 1.

286 **How could America wage war?:** "Memorandum for the Record," Meetings on Vietnam, July 21, 1965, LBJ Papers, 1963–1969, LBJPL, Meeting Notes File, box 1.

286 **updated him on events:** Edward Cuddy, "Vietnam: Mr. Johnson's War. Or Mr. Eisenhower's?," *Review of Politics* 65, no. 4 (Autumn 2003): 351–74.

286 **"I would be seen as":** Goodwin, *Johnson and American Dream,* 323.

287 **"kicking off World War III":** Goodwin, *Johnson and American Dream,* 324.

288 **"very much in their minds":** Khong, "Analogies at War," 71–96.

288 **"even larger and crueler conflict":** Khong, *"Analogies at War,"* 71–96; Berman, *Lyndon Johnson's War,* 46.

289 **When Eisenhower was hospitalized:** Johnson to General, August 19, 1965, Augusta—Walter Reed Series, DDEPL, box 2; Mamie Eisenhower to President, December 3, 1965, Augusta—Walter Reed Series, DDEPL, box 2.

290 **"learned something from that lesson?":** Max Frankel, "Military Pledge to Saigon Is Denied by Eisenhower," *New York Times*, August 18, 1965, 1; David S. Broder, "Eisenhower Backs Stand on Vietnam," *New York Times*, August 20, 1965, 1.

290 **"do whatever is needed":** "Memorandum for the Record," August 20, 1965, post-presidential papers, Augusta—Walter Reed series, DDEPL, box 1.

290 **the assassination of President Kennedy:** Ford threw himself into his work, questioning witnesses, traveling to the crime scene, and examining evidence. The commission, headed by Chief Justice Earl Warren, drew the conclusion that Lee Harvey Oswald, a disgruntled Marxist who had once defected to the Soviet Union, was the lone assassin. Ford remained skeptical. Hard-liners in his party were pressuring him to find some nefarious foreign connection, either to Cuba or the Soviet Union. He was one of the last commissioners to accept the conclusion that Oswald had acted alone. Ford, *A Time to Heal*, 74.

291 **"not simply remain advisors":** Andrew L. Johns, *Vietnam's Second Front: Domestic Politics, the Republican Party, and the War* (Lexington: University Press of Kentucky, 2010), 61, Kindle; Smith, *Eisenhower in War and Peace*, 207–8; Ford, *A Time to Heal*, 82–83.

291 **convince the Vietcong to end:** "Statement by the Joint Senate-House Republican Leadership," February 17, 1965, Ford Congressional Papers, Press Secretary and Speech File, GRFPL, box D9; "Statement by Rep. Gerald R. Ford on Viet Nam War," June 26, 1965, Ford Congressional Papers, Press Secretary and Speech File, GRFPL, box D9.

292 **But Winston Churchill understood:** "District of Columbia Young Republicans," Washington, DC, June 28, 1965, Ford Congressional Papers, Press Secretary and Speech File, GRFPL, box D18.

292 **LBJ worried his decision:** "Memorandum of telephone conversation," July 2, 1965, Eisenhower Papers, Augusta—Walter Reed Series, DDEPL, box 2.

292 **"in a condition of crisis":** Transcript, telephone conversation, August 24, 1965, post-presidential papers, appointment book series, DDEPL, box 2.

293 **craft a new Nixon:** Johns, *Second Front*, 40, 48.

293 **"Nixon was always one step":** Farrell, *Nixon*, 318; Stephen Ambrose, *Nixon*, vol. 2, *The Triumph of a Politician, 1962–1972* (New York: Simon & Schuster, 2014), 64; Nixon, *Memoirs*, 39.

293 **"There can be no substitute":** Richard M. Nixon, "Why Not Negotiate in Vietnam?," *Reader's Digest*, December 1965, 50–54, https://www.nixonfoundation.org/artifact/why-not-negotiate-in-vietnam-readers-digest-12-1965/.

293 **"the Ho Chi Minh Trail":** Nixon, *Memoirs*, 304–6, 322.

294 **"The choice today is not":** Johns, *Second Front*, 49, 83; Cable, "Nixon-Vietnam," February 12, 1965, WHFN, LBJPL, box 2.

294 **He believed that American leaders:** Johns, *Second Front*, 64–65; Nixon, "Why Not Negotiate?"

294 **Nixon put a partisan gloss:** Jacobsen to Christian, November 4, 1966, WHFN, LBJPL, box 8; Jacobsen to Panzer, "Here Are Some of Nixon's Political Attacks," November 6, 1966, WHFN, LBJPL, box 8.

295 **"hesitation, indecision, and even timidity":** Telephone conversation, Johnson and Eisenhower, post-presidential papers, October 3, 1966, Augusta—Walter Reed Series, DDEPL, box 1; Eisenhower to Nixon, October 7 and 21, 1966, post-presidential papers, special names series, DDEPL, box 14.

295 **"couldn't fart and chew gum":** "Excerpts from Speech at GOP Fund-Raising Dinner, Peoria, Ill.," September 26, 1966, Ford Congressional Papers, Press Secretary and Speech File, GRFPL, box D21; "Excerpts from Speech by Rep. Gerald R. Ford at GOP Dinner, Ridgefield, Connecticut," September 30, 1966, Ford Congressional Papers, Press Secretary and Speech File, GRFPL, box D21; Smith, *Eisenhower in War and Peace*, 235–36.

295 **Proposition Fourteen:** Steven M. Gillon, *American Paradox: A History of the United States Since 1945,* 3rd ed. (Boston: Wadsworth, 2013), 179; Dallek, *Flawed Giant,* 322.

296 **domestic concerns shaped the outcome:** Thomas Byrne Edsall with Mary D. Edsall, *Chain Reaction: The Impact of Race, Rights, and Taxes on American Politics* (New York: W. W. Norton, 1992), 52.

296 **Nearly half (47 percent):** "LBJ Administration Polls and Statements," 100:10, Pre-presidential Papers; "GOP County Chairmen Voice Criticisms of United States Vietnam Policy," Gallup poll, June 15, 1966, in 100:10, Pre-presidential Papers, RNPL, County Chairmen.

297 **"Now we need to slow down":** Jonathan Darman, *Landslide: LBJ and Ronald Reagan at the Dawn of a New America* (New York: Random House, 2014), 405; Gillon, *Politics and Vision,* 190.

CHAPTER 10

298 **The problem with liberals:** Ronald Reagan, "Taped Announcement on Candidacy for Governor of California," January 4, 1966, American Rhetoric Speech Bank, last modified October 2, 2021, https://www.americanrhetoric.com/speeches/ronaldreagancalgov candidacy.htm; Seymour Korman, "Reagan Enters Governor Race," *Chicago Tribune,* January 5, 1966, 1.

299 **wartime duties and SAG presidency:** Reagan, "Taped Announcement on Candidacy."

299 **"hundreds of times before":** Spitz, *Reagan,* 313.

300 **"to save our own skins'":** Nicholas Lemann, "The Speech: Reagan's Break from the Past," *Washington Post,* February 22, 1981, A1.

300 **William Jennings Bryan electrified:** Spitz, *Reagan,* 314–15; Matthew Dallek, *The Right Moment: Ronald Reagan's First Victory and the Decisive Turning Point in American Politics* (New York: Free Press, 2000), 60, Kindle.

301 **"He exudes warmth and enthusiasm":** Julius Duscha, "Reagan Picked to Win Nomination," *Washington Post,* June 5, 1966, A8; Korman, "Reagan Enters Governor Race," 1.

301 **a "witty, deft, engaging performance":** Darman, *Landslide,* 375; Reagan to Eisenhower, July 6, 1966, Governor Papers, RRPL, Series I, 1966 Campaign correspondence, box C7; "Ronald Reagan Campaign Speech Remarks at the National Press Club in Washington, DC," June 16, 1966, RRPL, https://www.reaganlibrary.gov/archives/audio /ronald-reagan-campaign-speech-remarks-national-press-club-washington-dc.

302 **attacking Brown for coddling criminals:** "Reagan Campaign Speech Remarks," June 16, 1966.

302 **"how do you refute a mood?":** "Governor Brown Criticizes Opponent," *New Journal and Guide,* June 18, 1966, 1.

302 **"Reagan speaks with flawless":** Duscha, "Reagan Picked."

303 **negotiate with the Soviets:** Korman, "Reagan Enters Governor Race," 7.

303 **he resorted to generalities:** Ronald Reagan, January 4, 1966, Reagan Gubernatorial Campaign: Files, 1966, Series III, RRPL, box C30; Darman, *Landslide,* 351–53; H. W. Brands, *Reagan: The Life* (New York: Doubleday, 2015), 144.

304 **nuances that Reagan lacked:** Matthew Dallek, *Right Moment,* 27.

304 **compromise amounted to delusion:** Reagan to Franklin, October 19, 1966, Governor Papers, Series I, 1966 Campaign correspondence, RRPL, box C7.

305 **"short of a declaration of war":** Reagan to Green, November 17, 1965, Governor Papers, Series I, 1966 Campaign correspondence, RRPL, box C7.

305 **those fighting in a war zone:** Reagan to Ferrington, May 4, 1966, Governor Papers, Series I, 1966 Campaign correspondence, RRPL, box C7. "Ronald Reagan for Governor,"

October 25, 1966, Governor Papers, Series I, 1966 Campaign correspondence, RRPL, box C7.

305 **Reagan scored 72 percent:** Brands, *Reagan*, 152; Darman, *Landslide*, 400, 404.

306 **"he's not reckless":** Meacham, *Destiny and Power*, 120–27.

306 **scored 56.2 percent of the vote:** Michael Nelson, "George Bush: Texan, Conservative," in *41: Inside the Presidency of George H. W. Bush,* ed. Nelson and Barbara A. Perry (Ithaca, NY: Cornell University Press, 2014), 33–35.

306 **"Negro vote was almost 100%":** Nelson, "George Bush: Texan, Conservative," 35–36; George to Dick (Richard Nixon), November 10, 1964; Nixon to George, November 12, 1964, George Bush Personal Papers, GHWBPL, Congressional File, Personal, box 1, stack G.

307 **the traditional Republican message:** "Elect George Bush and watch the action!," Campaign Pamphlet, n.d., George H. W. Bush Personal Papers, Congressional File, GHWBPL, General, box 1, stack G.

308 **political force: the New Right:** Bush, *All the Best,* 106.

308 **first Republican to represent Houston:** Nelson, "George Bush: Texan, Conservative," 37.

308 **"he is not completely unacceptable":** Nixon, *Memoirs*, 277; Jacobsen to Christian, November 4, 1966, WHFN, LBJPL, box 8.

309 **"made dissent all the more legitimate":** Charles DeBenedetti, "Lyndon Johnson and the Antiwar Opposition," in *The Johnson Years,* vol 2., ed. Robert A. Divine (Lawrence: University Press of Kansas, 1987), 28.

309 **"Hitler was, thank heaven":** Khong, "Analogies at War," 3–18.

310 **"picture of the world's greatest superpower killing":** Mark Atwood Lawrence, *The Vietnam War: A Concise International History* (New York: Oxford, 2008), 117.

310 **Rostow reassured the president:** Jonathan Kirshner, "When the Wise Men Failed," *New York Times*, October 31, 2017, https://www.nytimes.com/2017/10/31/opinion/lyndon-johnson-vietnam-war.html; Dallek, *Flawed Giant*, 462–63.

310 **speechwriter and advisor Harry McPherson:** Joseph A. Califano Jr., *The Triumph and Tragedy of Lyndon Johnson: The White House Years* (New York: Touchstone, 2015), 169.

311 **preferred cuts in domestic spending:** Darman, *Landslide*, 37; Califano, *Triumph and Tragedy*, 177–78.

311 **"LBJ unzipped his fly":** Dallek, *Flawed Giant*, 490.

311 **Kintner and Krim were initially:** Vicky to Junita, May 13, 1966, LBJA, Subject File, LBJPL, box 74.

312 **helped transform JFK into a martyr:** Shesol, *Mutual Contempt*, 309; DeBenedetti, "Johnson and Antiwar Opposition," 34.

312 **RFK charged:** Shesol, *Mutual Contempt*, 288–89; Darman, *Landslide*, 332.

312 **Manchester's book was a national:** Darman, *Landslide*, 414; Andrew Glass, "LBJ Depicted as Fleeing Dallas," *Washington Post*, January 24, 1967, A1.

313 **achieved only modest success:** Jim Bishop, *The Day Kennedy Was Shot* (New York: Harper Perennial, 2013), 307; Gillon, *24 Hours After*, xv–xvii.

313 **"Mr. Average Citizen":** Gillon, *American Paradox* (2003), 237–38; Dallek, *Flawed Giant*, 505–6.

314 **Reluctantly, Johnson agreed:** Kirshner, "When the Wise Men Failed"; Dallek, *Flawed Giant*, 508.

314 **Hubert Humphrey threw his hat:** Dallek, *Flawed Giant*, 512.

315 **"peace for our time":** Johns, *Second Front*, 190.

315 **"a grab bag of phrases":** Johns, *Second Front*, 196–99.

315 **both Kennedy and Johnson expressed:** Farrell, *Nixon*, 321.

316 **improve its negotiating position:** "News Release," April 1, 1968, Ford Congressional Papers, Press Secretary and Speech File, GRFPL, box D9.

317 **"going better in Viet Nam"**: George Bush Speech on Vietnam, January 11, 1968, George Bush Personal Papers, Congressional File, Vietnam, GHWBPL, box 1, stack G; Bush to Mrs. McKean, January 12, 1968, GHWBPL, George Bush Personal Papers, Congressional File, General, box 1, stack G.

317 **"makes me ashamed as an"**: Mack to Bush, March 27, 1968, GHWBPL, George Bush Personal Papers, Congressional File, General, box 1, stack G.

317 **"doesn't care about human lives"**: George to Dick (Richard Mack), April 14, 1968, George Bush Personal Papers, Congressional File, General, GHWBPL, box 1, stack G.

318 **Would he support the outcome?**: George to Dick (Richard Mack).

318 **"must be fought through to victory"**: Johns, *Second Front*, 184–85.

318 **He promised to oppose:** Memorandum for the Record, January 22, 1968, post-presidential papers, Augusta—Walter Reed Series, DDEPL, box 1; Dwight D. Eisenhower, "Let's Close Ranks on the Home Front," *Reader's Digest*, April 1968, 50–52; Johns, *Second Front*, 186, 199–200.

319 **"see the president win"**: "Meeting with General Eisenhower, Palm Desert," January 18, 1968, WHFN, LBJPL, box 2.

319 **central to their presidencies:** Woods, *Prisoners of Hope*, 360.

320 **"has a right to do so"**: "Congress Enacts Open Housing Legislation," *CQ Almanac 1968*, 24th ed. (Washington, DC: Congressional Quarterly, 1969), 14–152; George to Dick (Richard Mack), April 14, 1968, George Bush Personal Papers, Congressional File, General, GHWBPL, box 1, stack G; Matthew Yglesias, "Reagan's Race Record," *Atlantic*, November 9, 2007, https://www.theatlantic.com/politics/archive/2007/11/reagans-race-record/46875/.

321 **Reagan hoped to re-create his magic:** Darman, *Landslide,* 420.

321 **Reagan made a motion:** Darman, *Landslide,* 429.

321 **"pretty darn sensible"**: Smith, *Eisenhower in War and Peace*, 247; Brands, *Reagan* (Anchor), 167–68, Kindle; Ford, *A Time to Heal*, 85–86; George H. W. Bush, *All the Best, George Bush: My Life in Letters and Other Writings* (New York: Scribner, 2014), 147.

322 **"do nothing to destroy that respect"**: Fleming to President, August 19, 1968, WHFN, LBJPL, box 2; Dallek, *Flawed Giant*, 577–78.

322 **Johnson's well-deserved place in history:** Graham notes, September 8, 1968, WHFN, LBJPL, box 8.

322 **"Nixon is following my policies"**: Graham notes; Dallek, *Flawed Giant*, 580.

323 **he did signal a willingness:** Richard Nixon, "To Keep the Peace," CBS Radio Network, October 19, 1968, Speech File, 978.14, RNPL, box PPS 208; Richard Nixon, Statement, October 23, 1968, Speech File, 9730, RNPL, box PPS 208.

323 **never "pull out of Vietnam"**: Reedy to Vice President, September 18, 1968, WHFN, LBJPL, box 2.

323 **"It has not been discussed"**: LBJ, Nixon, James R. "Jim" Jones, and Walt Rostow, September 30, 1968, Presidential Recordings Digital Edition, University of Virginia.

324 **"no statement that would undercut"**: Johnson, Nixon, Humphrey, Walt Rostow, and George Wallace, October 16, 1968, Presidential Recordings Digital Edition, University of Virginia.

324 **"something big was afoot"**: Johns, *Second Front*, 225; Dallek, *Flawed Giant*, 582.

324 **"a just peace in Vietnam"**: Richard Nixon, Statement, October 25, 1968, Speech File, RNPL, 97:40, PPS 208.

324 **"Johnson was making the one move"**: Nixon, *Memoirs*, 383, Kindle.

325 **They promised Thieu:** Farrell, *Nixon,* 342.

325 **"we are gonna win"**: Walt Rostow to Johnson, November 2, 1968, Anna Chennault File, LBJPL, Lyndon Johnson; and Dean Rusk, November 3, 1968; Presidential Recordings

Digital Edition, University of Virginia; Farrell, *Nixon*, 342. Not surprisingly, Nixon made no mention of the affair in his memoirs.

326 **Nixon collapsed with laughter:** Farrell, *Nixon*, 343; Dallek, *Flawed Giant*, 589–90; LBJ and Nixon, November 3, 1968, Presidential Recordings Digital Edition, University of Virginia.

326 **"Anything RN can do?":** Farrell, *Nixon*, 342–43.

326 **"this was the most reprehensible":** Farrell, *Nixon*, 344.

329 **"ask Pat Brown to name one":** Jacobsen to Panzer, "Here Are Some of Nixon's Political Attacks," November 6, 1966, WHFN, LBJPL, box 8.

CHAPTER II

330 **"I'm not going to end up":** Kalb, *Road to War*, 107–8; Evan Thomas, *Being Nixon: A Man Divided* (New York: Random House, 2015), 218; Melvin Small, *The Presidency of Richard Nixon* (Lawrence: University Press of Kansas, 1999), 32.

331 **"switching a television channel":** Farrell, *Nixon*, 361–62; Thomas, *Being Nixon*, 219; David Fromkin and James Chace, "What Are the Lessons of Vietnam?," *Foreign Affairs* 63, no. 4 (Spring 1985): 743.

331 **"We must convince":** Tim Weiner, *One Man Against the World: The Tragedy of Richard Nixon* (New York: St. Martin's Griffin, 2016), 48.

331 **"I refuse to believe":** Johns, *Second Front*, 247; Thomas, *Being Nixon*, 235.

332 **destroying the levee system:** Between March 1969 and August 1973, America dropped 2,756,727 tons of bombs on Cambodia. That figure was nearly five times greater than the tonnage of all Allied bombing during World War II, including Hiroshima and Nagasaki. Weiner, *One Man Against the World*, 42, 69; Small, *Presidency of Nixon*, 71–73; Thomas, *Being Nixon*, 224.

332 **"we are Vietnamizing the search":** Karlyn Kohrs Campbell, *The Great Silent Majority: Nixon's 1969 Speech on Vietnamization* (College Station: Texas A&M University Press, 2014), 54–55, Kindle.

332 **to achieve rapprochement with China:** Herring, *From Colony to Superpower*, 770–71.

333 **they nonetheless laid the foundation:** Richard Nixon, "Inaugural Address, January 20, 1969," American Presidency Project, UC Santa Barbara, accessed January 6, 2023, https://www.presidency.ucsb.edu/documents/inaugural-address-1; Herring, *From Colony to Superpower*, 765, 773–75.

333 **Nixon's approach hearkened back to:** Herring, *From Colony to Superpower*, 785–86.

333 **The biggest obstacle was that:** Johns, *Second Front*, 251; Kalb, *Road to War*, 111–12.

334 **he spotted his own wife:** Weiner, *One Man Against the World*, 72.

334 **"If we are going to get":** Nancy Zaroulis and Gerald Sullivan, *Who Spoke Up? American Protest Against the War in Vietnam, 1963–1975* (New York: Holt, Rinehart and Winston, 1985), 269; Campbell, *The Great Silent Majority*, 7–48; Richard Reeves, *President Nixon: Alone in the White House* (New York: Simon & Schuster, 2001), 137–38; Small, *Presidency of Nixon*, 74; Kalb, *Road to War*, 116.

334 **Nixon remained secluded:** Reeves, *President Nixon*, 123, 139–41; Kalb, *Road to War*, 117; Small, *Presidency of Nixon*, 74–75.

335 **"a plan which will end the war":** Richard Nixon, "Address to the Nation on the War in Vietnam, November 3, 1969," American Presidency Project, UC Santa Barbara, accessed January 6, 2023, https://www.presidency.ucsb.edu/documents/address-the -nation-the-war-vietnam; Rick Perlstein, *Nixonland: The Rise of a President and the Fracturing of America* (New York: Scribner, 2008), 50; Kalb, *Road to War*, 118.

335 **"Only Americans can do that":** Nixon, "Address to the Nation on the War in Vietnam."

336 **"They talked as if":** Thomas, *Being Nixon,* 240–41; Reeves, *President Nixon,* 144.

337 **showed that nearly 75 percent:** "Nixon Declares 'Silent Majority' Backs His Speech," *New York Times,* November 5, 1969, 1; Russell Freeburg, "U.S. Reaction to Unity Plea Cheers Nixon," *Chicago Tribune,* November 5, 1969, 1.

338 **"[W]e've got those liberal bastards":** Small, *Presidency of Nixon,* 75.

338 **"He wants a massive bombing":** Kalb, *Road to War,* 122.

338 **"Richard Nixon was virtually alone":** Kalb, *Road to War,* 122–23.

339 **"The kids are going to retch":** Richard Nixon, "Cambodian Incursion Address, April 30, 1970," American Rhetoric Speech Bank, last modified January 4, 2022, https://www.americanrhetoric.com/speeches/richardnixoncambodia.html; Kalb, *Road to War,* 124; Thomas, *Being Nixon,* 265; Weiner, *One Man Against the World,* 87.

339 **ultimately lead to the Khmer:** Herring, *From Colony to Superpower,* 769.

339 **the 1964 Tonkin Gulf Resolution:** Small, *Presidency of Nixon,* 80–81; Kalb, *Road to War,* 126.

340 **"bums blowing up the campuses":** Small, *Presidency of Nixon,* 79.

340 ***Shell-shocked* was the word:** Kalb, *Road to War,* 125, 129.

340 **Nixon relished the cultural divide:** Thomas, *Being Nixon,* 277–78.

341 **"he was extremely unpopular":** Nixon, *Memoirs,* 669–70, Kindle.

342 **"trying to build a world":** Farrell, *Nixon,* 367–68, 405.

342 **"arrogantly kibitz in a game":** Donated Personal Paper Collection, Ronald Reagan 1980 Campaign Files, SERIES 01: Hannaford / California Headquarters, Subseries A: Ronald Reagan Files, RRPL, box 20.

343 **America would share the:** Donated Personal Paper Collection, Ronald Reagan 1980 Campaign Files.

343 **to keep a close eye:** Johns, *Second Front,* 261, 264, 288; UPI Report, May 19, 1970, Reagan Gubernatorial Papers, NGO153, RRPL.

343 **urging all Americans to support:** Gibbs and Duffy, *Presidents Club,* 268.

344 **"a most successful presidency":** Gibbs and Duffy, *Presidents Club,* 265–66; "Meanwhile, Back at the LBJ Ranch," *Time,* September 5, 1969, accessed January 12, 2023, https://time.com/archive/6637422/nation-meanwhile-back-at-the-lbj-ranch/; Weiner, *One Man Against the World,* 53.

345 **"loved by more people":** Thomas, *Being Nixon,* 226; Felix Belair Jr., "Eulogy by Nixon Calls Eisenhower Giant of His Time," *New York Times,* March 31, 1969, 1.

345 **"It would be goddamned easy":** Robert Dallek, *Nixon and Kissinger: Partners in Power* (New York: Harper, 2007), 96–99; Farrell, *Nixon,* 373.

345 **now appointed attorney general:** Weiner, *One Man Against the World,* 28; Small, *Presidency of Nixon,* 42–44; Dallek, *Flawed Giant,* 98–99.

346 **"He believed in nothing":** Dallek, *Flawed Giant,* 206; Weiner, *One Man Against the World,* 54–55.

346 **"'me against the world'":** Weiner, *One Man Against the World,* 10.

347 **"investigate some of the cocksuckers?":** George Lardner Jr. and Michael Dobbs, "New Tapes Reveal Depth of Nixon's Anti-Semitism," *Washington Post,* October 6, 1999, A31; Thomas, *Being Nixon,* 335; Reeves, *President Nixon,* 370.

347 **"You need a president for":** Thomas, *Being Nixon,* 206.

347 **bill died in the Senate:** Farrell, *Nixon,* 375.

348 **"Wants to hit pornography, dope":** Allen J. Matusow, *Nixon's Economy: Booms, Busts, Dollars, and Votes* (Lawrence: University Press of Kansas, 1998), 79–80.

348 **federal government had abandoned them:** Thomas Byrne Edsall with Mary D. Edsall, "Race," *Atlantic,* May 1991, 53–86, https://www.theatlantic.com/past/docs/politics/race/edsall.htm.

349 **Democrats received 4.1 million more:** Patterson, *Grand Expectations*, 737, Kindle.

349 **that vivid piece of advice:** Meacham, *Destiny and Power*, 126.

350 **the meeting never happened:** Bush to President, May 4, 1970, Donated Historical Materials, GHW Bush Personal Papers, GHWBPL, Congressional File, box 6.

350 **Bentsen prevailed:** Meacham, *Destiny and Power*, 126.

350 **"Wait a minute, Bob":** Reeves, *President Kennedy*, 281; Meacham, *Destiny and Power*, 151.

350 **"in ten days":** Meacham, *Destiny and Power*, 152; Engel, *When the World Seemed New*, 37, Kindle.

351 **index rose by 11 percent:** Nixon, Inaugural Address, January 20, 1969; Perlstein, *Nixonland*, 309; Matusow, *Nixon's Economy*, 15.

351 **"chances on screwing up 1972":** Collins, *More*, 122.

352 **"Richard Nixon's 'Vietnam'":** Farrell, *Nixon*, 445; Matusow, *Nixon's Economy*, 93.

352 **imports would become more expensive:** Small, *Presidency of Nixon*, 207; Herring, *From Colony to Superpower*, 781–82.

353 **lifting the excise tax:** Herring, *From Colony to Superpower*, 782–83.

353 **"'I think Mohammed was right!'":** William E. Leuchtenburg, *The American President: From Teddy Roosevelt to Bill Clinton* (New York: Oxford University Press, 2015), 495.

353 **the move sent shock waves:** Small, *Presidency of Nixon*, 209–10.

354 **"The piper must always be paid":** Collins, *More*, 127; Farrell, *Nixon*, 490.

354 **most Americans supported the president's:** Weiner, *One Man Against the World*, 173–74.

355 **his own secretary of state:** Thomas, *Being Nixon*, 410–11; Gibbs and Duffy, *Presidents Club*, 285.

356 **decision he would soon regret:** Engel, *When the World Seemed New*, 41.

356 **Congress had any appetite left:** Dallek, *Nixon and Kissinger*, 455.

357 **humiliating end of the war:** Farrell, *Nixon*, 486, 500, 539–40; Dallek, *Nixon and Kissinger*, 454.

357 **shortly before he died:** Thomas, *Being Nixon*, 424–25.

357 **overlooked his many flaws:** Farrell, *Nixon*, 426.

358 **to the South Vietnamese leader:** Thomas, *Being Nixon*, 332; Matthews, *Kennedy & Nixon*, 307. Kennedy was not the only Democratic president Nixon wanted to tear down. He also launched a "declassification project" to find evidence of Franklin D. Roosevelt's responsibility for Pearl Harbor.

358 **Ultimately, the Supreme Court ruled:** Farrell, *Nixon*, 426–27.

358 **Cape Cod island of Chappaquiddick:** Matthews, *Kennedy & Nixon*, 317.

358 **looking for dirt on O'Brien:** Thomas, *Being Nixon*, 292–93; Matthews, *Kennedy & Nixon*, 285–86.

359 **"the most serious constitutional crisis":** Laura Kalman, *Right Star Rising: A New Politics, 1974–1980* (New York: W. W. Norton, 2010), 4; Perlstein, *Nixonland*, 187.

359 **Texas Democrats for Nixon:** Weiner, *One Man Against the World*, 293–94.

360 **Nixon backed off:** Gibbs and Duffy, *Presidents Club*, 289.

360 **Vice President Spiro Agnew:** Weiner, *One Man Against the World*, 284.

360 **a prospect Kissinger deemed "inconceivable":** Kalman, *Right Star Rising*, 31; Spitz, *Reagan*, 379.

360 **"blood on the floor":** Pat Buchanan, oral history, October 4, 2010, Gerald R. Ford Presidential Foundation, https://geraldrfordfoundation.org/centennial/oralhistory/pat -buchanan; Nixon, *Memoirs*, 1331, Kindle.

361 **"Jerry would be confirmed":** James Cannon, *Honorable Life*, 126; Spitz, *Reagan*, 384; Gibbs and Duffy, *Presidents Club*, 301.

361 **Ford was quickly confirmed:** Kalman, *Right Star Rising*, 5.

362 **"If I did anything else":** Meacham, *Destiny and Power*, 167; Bush, *All the Best*, 186; Ford, *A Time to Heal*, 5.

362 **"do you join the haters":** Richard Nixon, "Remarks on Departure from the White House, August 9, 1974," American Presidency Project, UC Santa Barbara, accessed March 4, 2023, https://www.presidency.ucsb.edu/documents/remarks-departure-from -the-white-house; George H. W. Bush, "President Richard Nixon's Last Hours in Office, 1974," Diary Entry, August 9, 1974, 1, National Archives, accessed March 4, 2023, https://www.archives.gov/exhibits/eyewitness/html.php?section=12.

362 **"Ike without the heroics":** Bush, *All the Best*, 191–92.

363 **Bush noted in his diary:** Bush, *All the Best*, 191–92.

363 **"will have my total support":** Meacham, *Destiny and Power*, 174.

363 **it could help Ford attract:** Ford, *A Time to Heal*, 142–43; James Cannon, *Honorable Life*, 210–11.

364 **"Barbara and I craved change":** Meacham, *Destiny and Power*, 175; Bush, *All the Best*, 196–97; George H. W. Bush, *The China Diary of George H. W. Bush: The Making of a Global President*, ed. Jeffrey A. Engel (Princeton, NJ: Princeton University Press, 2008), xii, Kindle.

364 **serve as an endless distraction:** Gibbs and Duffy, *Presidents Club*, 303.

365 **"wrong in not dealing with Watergate":** Becker, "History and Background of Nixon Pardon," Nixon Pardon—Becker's Memorandum, Benton L. Becker Papers, GRFPL, box 2, https://www.fordlibrarymuseum.gov/library/document/0238/1126646.pdf.

365 **"The famous Nixon jowls":** Becker, "History and Background of Nixon Pardon."

365 **22 points in a Gallup poll:** Thomas, *Being Nixon*, 505; Spitz, *Reagan*, 387. Ronald Reagan, "To Restore America" (speech), March 31, 1976, RRPL, https://www.reaganlibrary .gov/archives/speech/restore-america.

366 **1972 election mandate was clear:** Rick Perlstein, *Reaganland: America's Right Turn 1976–1980* (New York: Simon & Schuster, 2020), Kindle, 311.

366 **Ford was out of his depth:** Kalman, *Right Star Rising*, 50; Perlstein, *Reaganland*, 310.

366 **"They like you":** Donald Rumsfeld and Richard Cheney to the President, memorandum, October 24, 1975, Rumsfeld Papers, https://library.rumsfeld.com/doclib/sp/174 /1975-10-24%20To%20Gerald%20Ford%20re%20Re-election%20and%20Rumsfeld %20and%20Cheney%20Resignations.pdf; Kalman, *Right Star Rising*, 20.

367 **humiliating symbol of American impotence:** Ford, *A Time to Heal*, 248–50.

368 **he clung to the illusion:** James Cannon, *Honorable Life*, 374.

368 **"I do not believe":** W. R. Smyser to Secretary Kissinger, memorandum, "Lessons of Vietnam," May 12, 1975, GRFPL, accessed February 10, 2022, https://www.fordlibrary museum.gov/library/exhibits/vietnam/032400091-002.pdf.

369 **"damned if I know":** Bush, *China Diary*, 254, 276–78; Engel, *When the World Seemed New*, 43–45.

369 **"ask young men to fight":** Chester Pach, "Ronald Reagan's Noble Causes," Ronald Reagan Institute, accessed February 2, 2024, https://www.reaganfoundation.org/media /360190/pach-essay-upload-1.pdf.

370 **a message that resonated:** Reagan to Nixon, April 25, 1975, 1:1 Post-Presidential Correspondence with Ronald Reagan, RNPL.

370 **only 33 percent in 1976:** Rick Perlstein, *The Invisible Bridge: The Fall of Nixon and the Rise of Reagan* (New York: Simon & Schuster, 2014), 56–57, Kindle; Kalman, *Right Star Rising*, 111; Steven M. Gillon, "The Tie Between the Kennedy Assassination and Trump's Conspiracy Mongering," *Washington Post* online, November 22, 2020, https://www .washingtonpost.com/outlook/2020/11/22/tie-between-kennedy-assassination-trumps -conspiracy-mongering/.

371 **But it also threatened jobs:** Gillon, *American Paradox* (2003), 315–16.

371 **"less heat, less electricity, less gasoline":** Perlstein, *Invisible Bridge*, 196.

372 **"détente in space":** Kalman, *Right Star Rising*, 89–90; Herring, *From Colony to Superpower*, 827.

372 **"a morbid fear of war":** Kalman, *Right Star Rising*, 122.

373 **"the bones of dead civilizations":** Reagan, "Restore America."

373 **lost its nerve to fight:** James Cannon, *Honorable Life*, 418.

374 **"continue to be a world power":** Minutes, National Security Council Meeting, May 12, 1975, GRFPL, National Security Council Meeting File, box 1.

374 **"It shows our spine":** Ford, *A Time to Heal*, 275–79; Perlstein, *Invisible Bridge*, 463; Kalman, *Right Star Rising*, 117; Engel and Bush, *China Diary*, 290.

374 **"41 American lives were lost":** Kalman, *Right Star Rising*, 181; Perlstein, *Invisible Bridge*, 464.

375 **"show of nerve and steel":** Kalman, *Right Star Rising*, 118; James Cannon, *Honorable Life*, 374–77; Perlstein, *Invisible Bridge*, 465.

375 **while secretly campaigning for president:** Reagan, *An American Life*, 196–99; Spitz, *Reagan*, 395.

376 **They resonated with the frustrations:** "'Welfare Queen' Becomes Issue in Reagan Campaign," *New York Times,* February 15, 1976, 51, accessed August 6, 2024, https://timesmachine.nytimes.com/timesmachine/1976/02/15/113445299.html?pageNumber=51.

376 **"never thought Reagan would run":** James Cannon, *Honorable Life*, 388; Ford, *A Time to Heal*, 363; Lou Cannon, *Governor Reagan: His Rise to Power* (New York: PublicAffairs, 2003), 398–402.

376 **"burned the hell out of me":** Perlstein, *Invisible Bridge*, 545; Gibbs and Duffy, *Presidents Club*, 320.

376 **Reagan biographer Lou Cannon wrote:** Lou Cannon, *Governor Reagan*, 396.

377 **a violent military coup:** Seymour M. Hersh, "Huge C.I.A. Operation Against Antiwar Forces, Other Dissidents in Nixon Years," *New York Times*, December 22, 1974, 1; Meacham, *Destiny and Power*, 186–87; "Memorandum of Conversation," March 29, 1976, GRFPL, accessed June 10, 2023, https://www.fordlibrarymuseum.gov/library/document/0314/1553410.pdf.

377 **"president wants me to do":** Meacham, *Destiny and Power*, 186–87; James Cannon, *Honorable Life*, 380–81; Engel, *When the World Seemed New*, 45.

377 **Bush won approval:** Richard D. Lyons, "Senate Confirms Bush as C.I.A. Director," *New York Times*, January 28, 1976, 10.

378 **"There is no place in America":** James Cannon, *Honorable Life*, 428–29.

378 **"'no substitute for victory'":** James Cannon, *Honorable Life*, 432; Kalman, *Right Star Rising*, 170; Ronald Reagan, "Republican National Convention Speech 1976," August 19, 1976, RRPL, accessed January 10, 2024, https://www.reaganlibrary.gov/archives/speech/republican-national-convention-speech-1976.

378 **"would have felt duty bound":** James A. Baker III with Steve Fiffer, *"Work Hard, Study . . . and Keep Out of Politics!": Adventures and Lessons from an Unexpected Public Life* (New York: G. P. Putnam's Sons, 2006), Kindle, 2; James Cannon, *Honorable Life*, 432.

379 **"party structure controlled the vote":** Nixon to Ron, August 20, 1976, Post-Presidential Correspondence with Ronald Reagan; Ron to Mr. President, August 27, 1976, Post-Presidential Correspondence with Ronald Reagan, RNPL, 1:1.

379 **cultural resentment and nostalgia:** Craig Shirley, *Reagan's Revolution: The Untold Story of the Campaign That Started It All* (Nashville: Thomas Nelson, 2010), Kindle, 336.

CHAPTER 12

381 **His powerful words brought tears:** Ronald Reagan, "June 6, 1984, at Pointe du Hoc on Normandy Beach in France" (speech), Ronald Reagan Presidential Foundation and Institute, https://www.reaganfoundation.org/ronald-reagan/the-presidency/d -day/.

382 **"Can we honestly look back?":** Lou Cannon, *Governor Reagan*, 8; Richard Reeves, *President Reagan: The Triumph of Imagination* (New York: Simon & Schuster, 2005), xiv; Brands, *Reagan* (Anchor), 281, Kindle; "The Reagan D-Day Speech That Moved a Nation," *Washington Post*, June 7, 1984. Reagan was actually referring to Roosevelt's 1937 quarantine speech, accessed May 3, 2022, https://sites.temple.edu/immerman/franklin -d-roosevelts-quarantine-speech/.

382 **a Manichean struggle against America:** Engel, *When the World Seemed New*, Kindle, 1–14; Herring, *From Colony to Superpower*, 866. For the best discussion of Reagan's speech, see Douglas Brinkley, *The Boys of Pointe du Hoc: Ronald Reagan, D-Day, and the U.S. Army 2nd Ranger Battalion* (New York: Harper Perennial, 2006).

382 **For Reagan, uncompromising opposition:** Reagan, *An American Life*, 265; Herring, *From Colony to Superpower*, 863.

383 **Washington "has declared a 'crusade' ":** Engel, *When the World Seemed New*, 14–15.

384 **dangerously low approval ratings:** Andrew E. Busch, *Reagan's Victory: The Presidential Election of 1980 and the Rise of the Right* (Lawrence: University Press of Kansas, 2017), Kindle, 240; "My Opinion of the Russians Has Changed Most Drastically . . . ," *Time*, January 14, 1980, 10–16.

385 **traveled an astonishing 246,000 miles:** Busch, *Reagan's Victory*, 902, 922.

385 **"a résumé instead of a rationale":** Timothy Naftali, *George H. W. Bush* (New York: Times Books, 2007), 35, Kindle; Meacham, *Destiny and Power*, 209, 211.

385 **"angel of our better natures":** John Kenneth White, *The New Politics of Old Values* (Hanover, NH: University Press of New England, 1988), 5, 39; Garry Wills, "What Happened?," *Time*, March 9, 1987, https://content.time.com/time/subscriber/article /0,33009,963714,00.html.

386 **"It's a revolution against government":** Steven M. Gillon, *The Democrats' Dilemma: Walter F. Mondale and the Liberal Legacy* (New York: Columbia University Press, 1992), 282; Steven M. Gillon, "Reagan Tied Republicans to White Christians and Now the Party Is Trapped," *Washington Post*, March 22, 2021, https://www.washingtonpost.com /outlook/2021/03/22/reagan-tied-republicans-white-christians-now-party-is-trapped/.

387 **conservatism of Dwight Eisenhower:** Leuchtenburg, *American President*, 595; Reeves, *President Reagan*, 7, 22–23; Reagan, *An American Life*, 219.

387 **"I may have won the debate":** Louise Dufresne, "Ronald Reagan's Testy Moment in the 1980 GOP Debate," CBS News online, last modified February 11, 2016, https://www .cbsnews.com/news/reagans-testy-moment-in-the-1980-gop-debate/; Brands, *Reagan*, 217; Reagan, *An American Life*, 213.

388 **South Carolina, Alabama, Florida, Georgia:** Brands, *Reagan*, 221; Meacham, *Destiny and Power*, 229.

388 **Reluctantly, he dropped out:** By the end of the primary season, Bush had managed to secure 3 million votes (compared to Reagan's 7.7 million) and to win four of the thirty-three primaries.

388 **"I can't take him":** Perlstein, *Reaganland*, 798–99; Dufresne, "Reagan's Testy Moment"; Peter Baker and Susan Glasser, *The Man Who Ran Washington: The Life and Times of James A. Baker III* (New York: Doubleday, 2020), 187; Naftali, *Bush*, 36–37; Reagan, *American Life*, 213.

389 **"Ford will be president before"**: James Cannon, *Honorable Life*, 454–56; Karen Tumulty, *The Triumph of Nancy Reagan* (New York: Simon & Schuster, 2021), 224; Reeves, *President Reagan*, 3–4.

389 **"As far as Ronnie was"**: Richard V. Allen, "George Herbert Walker Bush; The Accidental Vice President," *New York Times*, July 30, 2000, sec. 6, 36; Perlstein, *Reaganland*, 803; Meacham, *Destiny and Power*, 249; Reagan, *American Life*, 215.

389 **Bush effortlessly switched his position**: Meacham, *Destiny and Power*, 243; Allen, "Accidental Vice President."

390 **use television to inspire voters**: Everett Carll Ladd, "Bush and Reagan: Differences, Similarities," *Christian Science Monitor*, December 16, 1988, https://www.csmonitor.com /1988/1216/eladd.html; Perlstein, *Reaganland*, 803; Meacham, *Destiny and Power*, 249; Allen "Accidental Vice President."

390 **"make America great again"**: Busch, *Reagan's Victory*, Kindle, 1636; Ronald Reagan, "Ronald Reagan Republican National Convention Acceptance Speech, 1980," July 17, 1980, RRPL, accessed April 3, 2024, https://www.reaganlibrary.gov/archives/speech/re publican-national-convention-acceptance-speech-1980.

390 **conservatives perceived as broken**: Hendrick Smith, "Reagan Is Promising 'A Crusade to Make Nation Great Again,'" *New York Times*, July 15, 1980, A1.

391 **a white-haired fiscal conservative**: Jimmy Carter, "Remarks Accepting the Presidential Nomination in 1980, August 14, 1980," American Presidency Project, UC Santa Barbara, accessed April 3, 2024, https://www.presidency.ucsb.edu/documents/remarks -accepting-the-presidential-nomination-the-1980-democratic-national-convention-new.

391 **"privileges their whiteness once afforded"**: Jeff Stein, "Trump and the Racist Ghost of George Wallace," *Newsweek* online, last modified May 25, 2015, https://www.news week.com/donald-trump-george-wallace-racist-ghost-432164; Bob Herbert, "Righting Reagan's Wrongs?," *New York Times*, November 13, 2007, accessed April 8, 2024, https://www.nytimes.com/2007/11/13/opinion/13herbert.html; Perlstein, *Reaganland*, 674.

392 **Culver City, California**: Perlstein, *Reaganland*, 875.

392 **"will certainly win the audience"**: Nixon Letter to Reagan, September 12, 1980, RR 1980 Campaign Papers, Series I, Hannaford/ California Headquarters, Subseries A, Ronald Reagan Files, box 6.

392 **His lead widened considerably**: The Reagan team had worried earlier that Carter might pull off an "October surprise" by winning the freedom of the Americans held hostage in Iran. According to Ben Barnes, a prominent figure in Texas politics, he and John Connally traveled to the Middle East in the weeks before the election to deliver the message that Iran should wait until after the election to release the hostages. There were also rumors that William Casey, Reagan's campaign manager and future head of the CIA, had met with representatives of Iran and promised to deliver weapons to Iran if it held the hostages until after the election. In fact, the Iranians released the American hostages as Reagan was being inaugurated on January 20, 1981. There was no evidence that Reagan himself was involved in the proposed deal, but Iran did hold the hostages until after the election, and the administration did later sell weapons to Iran. According to the historian H. W. Brands, "it would not have been out of character for him [Casey] to seek to stall the release of the hostages until after the election so that Carter would be retired to Georgia." If so, the Reagan campaign, like the Nixon campaign in 1968, would have violated the Logan Act that barred private citizens from engaging in diplomacy. Separate Senate and House committees investigated the allegations, but the Reagan administration stonewalled, denying the investigators access to key witnesses and relevant documents. Neither investigation found evidence of a deal, but they also acknowledged

that many pieces of evidence remained missing. Brands, *Reagan*, 232–37; Peter Baker, "A Four-Decade Secret: One Man's Story of Sabotaging Carter's Re-election," *New York Times*, March 18, 2023, 1.

393 **pent up for decades:** Ian Haney-Lopez, "The Racism at the Heart of the Reagan Presidency," *Salon*, last modified January 11, 2014, https://www.salon.com/2014/01/11/the _racism_at_the_heart_of_the_reagan_presidency/#:~:text=Reagan%20was%20 different.,racial%20resentment%20were%20inextricably%20fused; Perlstein, *Reaganland*, 907–9.

393 **"government is not the solution":** Ronald Reagan, "Inaugural Address 1981," January 20, 1981, RRPL, accessed April 11, 2024, https://www.reaganlibrary.gov/archives/speech /inaugural-address-1981.

394 **Americans being held hostage:** William Safire, "Silent Majority's Roar," *New York Times*, November 6, 1980, A35.

394 **guiding the nation boldly:** Leonard Silk, "Trying to Repeal Keynes: President's Plans Considered as Revolutionary as Those Espoused by the New Deal in the '30s," *New York Times*, February 20, 1981, A1.

394 **"Can't find a wound":** Gillon, *American Paradox* (2003), 341.

395 **president was out of danger:** Brands, *Reagan*, 273–74; Baker and Glasser, *Man Who Ran Washington*, 240; Leuchtenburg, *American President*, 588, 596. Earlier that afternoon, an excited Secretary of State Alexander Haig had marched into the White House press room and, misinterpreting the Constitution, informed a stunned nation that he was "in control." Naftali, *Bush*, 40.

395 **unemployment rate of 9.5 percent:** Gillon, *American Paradox* (2003), 341.

396 **"I intend to wait and see":** Brands, *Reagan*, 313–15, 344–45; Leuchtenburg, *American President*, 605–6.

396 **"example of the drunk preaching":** Leuchtenburg, *American President*, 615.

396 **Nearly 60 percent of voters:** Joshua Green, "Reagan's Liberal Legacy: What the New Literature on the Gipper Won't Tell You," *Washington Monthly* online, last modified January 1, 2003, https://washingtonmonthly.com/2003/01/01/reagans-liberal-legacy/.

397 **a first-strike capability:** Daniel Deudney and G. John Ikenberry, "Who Won the Cold War?," *Foreign Policy* 87 (Summer 1992): 123–28; Herring, *From Colony to Superpower*, 870.

398 **shrilled an Italian newspaper:** Brands, *Reagan*, 421.

398 **"uphold the global position":** Logevall and Osgood, "Ghost of Munich," 13–26.

398 **"possibly die in a war":** John T. Correll, "The Weinberger Doctrine," *Air & Space Forces* online, March 2014, https://www.airandspaceforces.com/article/0314weinberger.

399 **"equivalent of our Founding Fathers":** Herring, *From Colony to Superpower*, 887–88, 892–94; Kyle Longley, "An Obsession: The Central American Policy of the Reagan Administration," in *Reagan and the World: Leadership and National Security, 1981–1989*, ed. Bradley Lynn Coleman and Kyle Longley (Lexington: University Press of Kentucky, 2017), 211–38.

399 **"at each other's throats":** Herring, *From Colony to Superpower*, 865; Leuchtenburg, *American President*, 610.

400 **"distilling the post-Vietnam consensus":** Correll, "Weinberger Doctrine"; Marvin Kalb and Deborah Kalb, *Haunting Legacy: Vietnam and the American Presidency from Ford to Obama* (Washington, DC: Brookings Institution Press, 2011), 83–238.

400 **"complete abdication of the duties":** Correll, "Weinberger Doctrine."

401 **Muammar al-Qaddafi:** Michael Schaller, *Reckoning with Reagan: America and Its President in the 1980s* (New York: Oxford University Press, 1992) 13–39; Reagan, *An American Life*, 437. Political scientists have speculated that those men who witnessed combat were

the most restrained in their use of force as president, while those who served but remained far from the fighting were the most likely to flex America's military power. This claim seems especially true in the cases of Eisenhower and Kennedy, but Reagan appears to be the exception. He wore the uniform but never came close to combat, and despite his bombastic rhetoric, he was fairly restrained in the use of force as president. See Michael C. Horowitz and Allan C. Stam, "How Prior Military Experience Influences the Future Militarized Behavior of Leaders," *International Organization* 68, no. 3 (Summer 2014): 527–59. The authors, along with Cali M. Ellis, expanded on their ideas in *Why Leaders Fight* (New York: Cambridge University Press, 2015). See also Samuel P. Huntington, *The Soldier and the State: The Theory and Politics of Civil-Military Relations* (Cambridge, MA: Belknap Press of Harvard University Press, 1957), 69–70.

401 **"to start an unnecessary war":** Leuchtenburg, *American President*, 615; Strobe Talbott, "Buildup and Breakdown," *Foreign Affairs* online, February 1, 1984, https://www.foreignaffairs.com/articles/russian-federation/1984-02-01/buildup-and-breakdown.

402 **six minutes "to unleash Armageddon!":** Reagan, *An American Life*, 585–86.

402 **"Gov Reagan could hardly speak":** Julie to Daddy, October 30, 1974, Nixon post-presidential papers, RNPL, Reagan, 1.1.

403 **"the preeminent post–World War II":** Reeves, *President Reagan*, 236–37.

403 **"she became a force":** Spitz, *Reagan*, 588–89.

403 **from seventy-one to fifty-eight:** Reeves, *President Reagan*, 481; Melvyn P. Leffler, "Ronald Reagan and the Cold War," in *The Reagan Moment: America and the World in the 1980s*, ed. Jonathan R. Hunt and Simon Miles (Ithaca, NY: Cornell University Press, 2021), 25–43; Peter Baker, "How Reagan and Bush Overcame Skepticism to Collaborate with Gorbachev," *New York Times*, August 30, 2022.

404 **giving the Soviets fewer reasons:** Logevall and Osgood, "Ghost of Munich," 13–26; Herring, *From Colony to Superpower*, 895; Reagan, *An American Life*, 588–89.

404 **The entire episode reminded Reagan:** Leuchtenburg, *American President*, 633–34.

404 **the two men left disappointed:** Leuchtenburg, *American President*, 635–37.

405 **he sensed Reagan's genuine desire:** Brands, *Reagan*, 578–87; Engel, *When the World Seemed New*, 16–17; Leffler, "Reagan and the Cold War," 25–42; Leuchtenburg, *American President*, 35.

405 **Reagan later deemed the event:** Herring, *From Colony to Superpower*, 897.

405 **"entire position toward Adolf Hitler":** Leuchtenburg, *American President*, 640; Logevall and Osgood, "Ghost of Munich," 6.

405 **a series of public broadsides:** Jack Nelson, "Nixon, Kissinger Warn Reagan on Arms Control," *Los Angeles Times* online, April 26, 1987, https://www.latimes.com/archives/la-xpm-1987-04-26-mn-1552-story.html; Gibbs and Duffy, *Presidents Club*, 362.

406 **"different kind of Russian leader":** "Conversation with President Reagan on December 14, 1987, notes," December 14, 1987, RNPL, 1.8.

406 **"There is no way":** Memorandum to the file, "Meeting with President Reagan at the White House, 5 P.M. April 28, 1987," RNPL, 1.7.

406 **"Da! Da!" Gorbachev said:** Engel, *When the World Seemed New*, 17; Lesley Kennedy, "How Gorbachev and Reagan's Friendship Helped Thaw the Cold War," *History*, last modified October 24, 2019, https://www.history.com/news/gorbachev-reagan-cold-war; Schaller, *Reckoning*, 176.

407 **the details to his aides:** Brands, *Reagan*, 439, 551; Reeves, *President Reagan*, 225; Longley, "An Obsession," 211–38.

407 **turn over key documents:** Leuchtenburg, *American President*, 614–15.

407 **"President Reagan created the conditions":** Brands, *Reagan*, 726; Longley, "An Obsession," 211–38.

408 **an astounding 68 percent:** Lou Cannon, *President Reagan: The Role of a Lifetime* (New York: PublicAffairs, 2000), xi.

408 **"the Soviet Union gave up":** Engel, *When the World Seemed New*, 22.

408 **debt rose from $908.5 billion:** Herring, *From Colony to Superpower*, 916.

409 **He would leave it:** Gillon, *American Paradox* (2003), 361.

409 **James Baker coined the slogan:** Reeves, *President Reagan*, 477; Meacham, *Destiny and Power*, 263–65; Brands, *Reagan*, 464; Herring, *From Colony to Superpower*, 900.

409 **and never to Camp David:** Meacham, *Destiny and Power*, 263–67; Tumulty, *Nancy Reagan*, 225, 310–13; Leuchtenburg, *American President*, 9.

410 **Shultz and Weinberger expressed concerns:** Meacham, *Destiny and Power*, 299–300; Naftali, *Bush*, 45, 50.

410 **"obligations to the full truth":** Meacham, *Destiny and Power*, 302–33.

410 **winning sixteen of seventeen states:** Naftali, *Bush*, 55; Robert L. Fleegler, *Brutal Campaign: How the 1988 Election Set the Stage for Twenty-First-Century American Politics* (Chapel Hill: University of North Carolina Press, 2023), 126.

411 **"I trust George Bush":** Fleegler, *Brutal Campaign*, 181.

411 **"He picked a young senator":** Meacham, *Destiny and Power*, 338; Steven M. Gillon, "1988–2000," in *A Companion to Twentieth Century America*, ed. Stephen Whitfield (Malden, MA: Blackwell, 2004), Kindle, 123–40. I relied heavily on my previous writings to reconstruct the events described in this section.

412 **"Michael Dukakis on crime":** Leuchtenburg, *American President*, 661; Fleegler, *Brutal Campaign*, 134–35; James Davison Hunter, "America at War with Itself," *Washington Post*, September 13, 1992, https://www.washingtonpost.com/archive/opinions/1992/09/13/america-at-war-with-itself/e477b828-951c-46d7-86a5-94609bbe9142/.

412 **detailed proposals for student aid:** Leuchtenburg, *American President*, 661–62; Naftali, *Bush*, 61–62; Meacham, *Destiny and Power*, 331. The Bush campaign aired its own attack on the furlough program that raised the Horton case more subtly, showing darkened images of prisoners entering a turnstile but without highlighting Horton. However, the media, and most of the public, saw little difference between the two ads.

412 **less than one hundred days:** Reeves, *President Reagan*, 478; Fleegler, *Brutal Campaign*, 239.

412 **Democrats added two seats:** Gillon, "1988–2000," Kindle, 2301.

413 **Bush was in the Oval Office:** Reeves, *President Reagan*, 479; Leuchtenburg, *American President*, 676; Owen Ullmann, "Aides Boost Bush at Reagan's Expense," Knight-Ridder News Service, March 24, 1989, found in Nixon, Post-Presidential Correspondence, Reagan, 1.9.

414 **stare down a line of tanks:** Herring, *From Colony to Superpower*, 902; Gillon, "1988–2000," Kindle, 2318.

415 **"look at the long run":** Naftali, *Bush*, 80–81; Meacham, *Destiny and Power*, 374; Herring, *From Colony to Superpower*, 902–3; Leuchtenburg, *American President*, 685.

415 **"poke a stick in the eyes":** Naftali, *Bush*, 81–82; Herring, *From Colony to Superpower*, 906.

416 **"I don't think we can be":** Herring, *From Colony to Superpower*, 906; Naftali, *Bush*, 85–86; Meacham, *Destiny and Power*, 400–401.

416 **"and enters another epoch":** Leuchtenburg, *American President*, 688.

416 **and reduce chemical weapons:** Gillon, "1988–2000," Kindle, 2313–14.

417 **"take precedence over START":** Nixon to Bush, November 16, 1989, Post-Presidential Correspondence with George Bush, RNPL, 1.6.

417 **On Christmas Day 1991:** Herring, *From Colony to Superpower*, 912–23; Leuchtenburg, *American President*, 383–86.

417 **"Russian nationalism will take power":** Richard Nixon, "How to Lose the Cold War," Richard Nixon Foundation, accessed May 3, 2024, https://www.nixonfoundation.org

/artifact/how-to-lose-the-cold-war/?gad_source=1&gclid=CjwKCAiA_tuuBhAUEi
wAvxkgTtqWizecFtoT7kXdGoNb1mmAWy9HU8ZvpbcaMGTnpKGB7YRj_9kGY
hoC3mUQAvD_BwE.

417 **a $24 billion aid package:** Leuchtenburg, *American President*, 390, 393.

418 **an invasion of Saudi Arabia:** Meacham, *Destiny and Power*, 421–22.

418 **"It has to be withdrawal":** H. W. Brands, "Neither Munich nor Vietnam: The Gulf
War of 1991," in Brands and Suri, *The Power of the Past*, 73–98.

419 **troops to lead a multinational:** Gillon, "1988–2000," Kindle, 2318.

419 **"I look at today's crisis":** Bush, *All the Best*, 497; Bush to George, Jeb, Neil, Marvin,
Doro, December 31, 1990, https://bush41library.tamu.edu/files/select-documents/letter
_to_family12-31-90.pdf; "Text of President Bush's Address on the Middle East," August
8, 1999, White House Office of Records Management, Subject Files, CO, Countries,
Iraq, stack G; Brands, "Neither Munich nor Vietnam," 73–98; Meacham, *Destiny and
Power*, 455.

420 **"agree to a halfway effort":** George H. W. Bush, "The President's News Conference,"
November 30, 1990, American Presidency Project, UC Santa Barbara, accessed January
8, 2024, https://www.presidency.ucsb.edu/documents/the-presidents-news-conference
-19; Meacham, *Destiny and Power*, 513.

420 **the Iraqis out of Kuwait:** Philip Smith, *Why War?: The Cultural Logic of Iraq, the Gulf
War, and Suez* (Chicago: University of Chicago Press, 2010), Kindle, 2298–774.

421 **his own children to battle:** Helen Dewar and Tom Kenworthy, "Congress Opens Debate on Using Force in Gulf," *Washington Post*, January 11, 1991, https://www.washing
tonpost.com/archive/politics/1991/01/11/congress-opens-debate-on-using-force-in-gulf
/3ad9df28-5172-4bcb-b888-8af183b3b3b5/; "War and Peace: A Sampling from the Debate
on Capitol Hill," *New York Times*, January 11, 1991, A8.

421 **"Either we stop him now":** Dewar and Kenworthy, "Congress Opens Debate"; "War
and Peace," A8; Gillon, "Competing Voices: America After the Cold War, 1988–2000,"
in *American Experiment* online, https://college.cengage.com/history/us/gillon/am_exp
/2e/instructors/voices/ch32.html.

422 **"held to an absolute minimum":** George H. W. Bush, "Address to the Nation Announcing Allied Military Action in the Persian Gulf," January 16, 1991, GHWBPL,
accessed June 1, 2024, https://bush41library.tamu.edu/archives/public-papers/2625.

422 **"Such was the lingering impact":** "Address to the Nation Announcing Operation
Desert Storm, 1991: A Spotlight on a Primary Source by George H. W. Bush," Gilder
Lehrman Institute of American History, accessed June 1, 2024, https://www.gilderlehr
man.org/history-resources/spotlight-primary-source/address-nation-announcing
-operation-desert-storm-1991.

423 **"trampled on the public's right":** George C. Herring, "Reflecting the Last War: The
Persian Gulf and the 'Vietnam Syndrome,'" *Journal of Third World Studies* 10, no. 1
(Spring 1993): 37–51.

423 **the long-term consequences:** Engel, *When the World Seemed New*, 437–38; Meacham,
Destiny and Power, 467; Herring, *From Colony to Superpower*, 910–12.

423 **"we've kicked the Vietnam syndrome":** Alexander M. Haig Jr., "Gulf Analogy: Munich or Vietnam?," opinion, *New York Times*, December 10, 1990, A19.

424 **But he never established:** Naftali, *Bush*, 96.

424 **"and they're enormous":** Meacham, *Destiny and Power*, 361–62.

424 **"financial mess left by Reagan":** Leuchtenburg, *American President*, 683; Brands, *Reagan*, 719; Naftali, *Bush*, 132.

425 **less than 20 percent:** Leuchtenburg, *American President*, 703.

425 **"the economy, stupid!":** Gillon, "1988–2000," Kindle, 2355.

426 **burnish his political image:** Leuchtenburg, *American President*, 704–5.

426 **found avoiding service "offensive":** Meacham, *Destiny and Power*, 513.

427 **It was a blunt indictment:** Ford to Editor, September 9, 1992, White House Office of Records Management (WHORM), GHWBPL, Subject File—Federal Government, stack G.

427 **"would reaffirm with some voters":** Gillon, "1988–2000," Kindle, 2342–55.

428 **but scored especially well:** Gillon, "1988–2000," Kindle, 2342–55; Dan Balz and Ann Devroy, "Clinton Sweeps In," *Washington Post*, November 4, 1992, A1.

EPILOGUE

429 **"Gosh, I miss the Cold War":** Gillon, "1988–2000," 2393, Kindle.

430 **"Just imagine if leaders":** "Transcript: Clinton Addresses Nation on Yugoslavia Strike," CNN online, last modified March 25, 1999, https://edition.cnn.com/ALLPOLITICS /stories/1999/03/25/clinton.transcript/.

430 **"bunch of fucking bond traders?":** Steven M. Gillon, *The Pact: Bill Clinton, Newt Gingrich, and the Rivalry That Defined a Generation* (New York: Oxford University Press, 2008), 114.

431 **United States could reconstruct Iraq:** Gillon, *American Paradox*, 3rd ed., 407; "Rhetoric Starts Here," opinion, *Washington Post* online, November 2, 2002, https://www .washingtonpost.com/archive/opinions/2002/11/03/rhetoric-starts-here/82adce7e-ee01 -4bc4-a76c-21182dde62e0/.

432 **all presidents become Keynesians:** Gillon, *Paradox*, 3rd ed., 409.

433 **American economy on the rebound:** Gillon, *Paradox*, 3rd ed., 425.

434 **"in terms of changing their behavior":** Dan Murphy, "Is the Iran Nuclear Deal Like Munich 1938? Not Really," *Christian Science Monitor* online, last modified July 22, 2015, https://www.csmonitor.com/World/Security-Watch/Backchannels/2015/0722/Is-the -Iran-nuclear-deal-like-Munich-1938-Not-really,

434 **Trump told audiences in 2016:** Nicholas Fandos, "Trump Defiantly Rallies a New 'Silent Majority' in a Visit to a Border State," *New York Times*, July 12, 2015, 20; Steven M. Gillon, "The Revolution That Was 1968," History, last modified January 31, 2009, https://www.history.com/news/the-revolution-that-was-1968.

434 **referencing the discredited isolationist movement:** Jeff Stein, "Trump's Quest to Shatter GOP Economics Reached Its Culmination in 2019," *Washington Post* online, December 27, 2019, https://www.washingtonpost.com/business/2019/12/27/trumps -quest-shatter-gop-economics-reached-its-culmination/; Paul Krugman, "The Economics of Donald J. Keynes," *New York Times*, May 7, 2019, A23.

436 **without long-standing repercussions:** Steven M. Gillon, "Convicting Trump Would Have Required Accepting a Half-Century of Republican Guilt," *Washington Post* online, February 16, 2021, https://www.washingtonpost.com/outlook/2021/02/16/convicting -trump-wouldve-required-accepting-half-century-republican-guilt/.

437 **"I assure you: He will not":** Joseph Biden, "Remarks of President Joe Biden—State of the Union Address as Prepared for Delivery," March 7, 2024, The White House, accessed June 2, 2024, https://www.whitehouse.gov/briefing-room/speeches-remarks /2024/03/07/remarks-of-president-joe-biden-state-of-the-union-address-as-prepared-for -delivery-2/.

437 **"It's the people from within":** Holly Otterbein, Elena Schneider, and Jonathan Lemire, "Why Biden's Campaign Keeps Linking Trump to Hitler," *Politico*, last modified December 19, 2023, https://www.politico.com/news/2023/12/19/biden-trump-hitler -00132367; Isaac Arnsdorf, "Trump Equates His Domestic Political Opposition to WWII Enemies Abroad," *Washington Post*, February 22, 2024, https://www.washing tonpost.com/politics/2024/02/22/trump-threats-world-war-ii/.

437 **"four hundred thousand American GIs":** Alessio Atria, "Former Trump Chief-of-Staff John Kelly Says Former President Praised Adolf Hitler in the White House," uInterview, last modified March 17, 2024, https://uinterview.com/news/former-trump-chief-of-staff-john-kelly-says-former-president-praised-adolf-hitler-in-the-white-house/.

439 **"what America stands for":** Brett Samuels and Alex Gangitano, "Biden Invokes Memory of Pointe du Hoc to Make Case for Democracy," *The Hill* online, last modified June 7, 2024, https://thehill.com/homenews/administration/4709958-biden-pointe-du-hoc-democracy/mlite/.

INDEX

Acheson, Dean, 244, 246
Ackley, Gardner, 274
Adams, Sherman, 203
The Affluent Society (Galbraith), 259
Afghanistan, 384, 431
African Americans. *See also* civil rights
    elections and, 204, 224, 306, 308
    JFK and, 263–264
    Reagan and, 393
    rioting by, 278, 296, 319
    World War II and, 196, 199–200
Agnew, Spiro, 321, 337, 360, 465n211
Albert, Carl, 297, 361
Albert, Raymond, 72, 74
Albright, Madeleine, 430
Allen, Richard, 389
Alsop, Joe, 265
Amagiri, "Heavenly Mist" (Japanese
    destroyer), 74–75
Ambrose, Stephen
    on Battle of the Bulge, 108
    on contrasting approaches to crises
        of Nixon and Eisenhower, 345
    on Eisenhower and *Brown,* 196
    on Eisenhower and national
        defense, 209
    on Eisenhower and Overlord,
        101, 104

on Eisenhower at Cairo
    Conference, 95
on Eisenhower's leadership
    ability, 62
on Nixon's attacks on Voorhis, 147
on Nixon's background, 26
on Nixon's criticism of Johnson's
    Vietnam policy, 293
Anderson, John, 391, 393
Anderson, Marian, 8
Anderson, Samuel E., 44, 45
Angelou, Maya, 122
anti-Semitism, 124, 346–347
Army Times, 134
Arvad, Inga, 24–25, 53–54

B-17 bombers "Flying Fortresses," 93–94
Baker, Howard, 405
Baker, James, 399–400, 409, 426
Baker, Russell, 222
Ball, George
    Bay of Pigs and, 237
    Cuban missile crisis and, 245
    on JFK and Americans in
        Vietnam, 252
    on Johnson's temperament, 271
    Vietnam and, 179, 285, 286, 310
Bao Dai, 191

493

ABOUT THE AUTHOR

Steven M. Gillon is professor emeritus at the University of Oklahoma and a senior fellow at the Miller Center for the study of the presidency at the University of Virginia. He spent more than two decades as the scholar in residence at the History Channel, where he hosted a number of shows, consulted on projects, and produced prime-time documentaries. He has written or edited more than a dozen books about modern American political and cultural history, including the *New York Times* bestsellers *America's Reluctant Prince: The Life of John F. Kennedy Jr.* and *The Pact: Bill Clinton, Newt Gingrich, and the Rivalry That Defined a Generation.*